W9-CGN-526

PRICE
THEORY
AND
APPLICATIONS

FOURTH EDITION

JACK HIRSHLEIFER

UNIVERSITY OF CALIFORNIA
LOS ANGELES

With the assistance of
MICHAEL SPROUL

Prentice Hall, Englewood Cliffs, N.J. 07632

Library of Congress Cataloging-in-Publication Data

Hirshleifer, Jack.
  Price theory and applications.

  Includes index.
  1. Microeconomics.   I. Title.
HB172.H55   1988   338.5   87-25735
ISBN 0-13-699752-X

Editorial/production supervision: Madelaine Cooke
Interior design: Anne Bonanno and Suzanne Bennett
Cover design: Peggy Finnerty
Manufacturing buyer: Barbara Kittle

 ©1988 by Prentice-Hall, Inc.
A Division of Simon and Schuster
Englewood Cliffs, New Jersey 07632

Printed in the United States of America

10   9   8   7   6   5   4   3   2   1

ISBN 0-13-699752-X 01

Prentice-Hall International (UK) Limited, *London*
Prentice-Hall of Australia Pty. Limited, *Sydney*
Prentice-Hall Canada Inc., *Toronto*
Prentice-Hall Hispanoamericana, S.A., *Mexico*
Prentice-Hall of India Private Limited, *New Delhi*
Prentice-Hall of Japan, Inc., *Tokyo*
Simon & Schuster Asia Pte. Ltd., *Singapore*
Editora Prentice-Hall do Brasil, Ltda., *Rio de Janeiro*

CONTENTS

PREFACE

Theory is useless unless it leads to applications. The opposite side of the coin is that actual real-world problems remain a buzzing, blooming confusion in the absence of systematic theory to put them in some intellectual order. The various editions of this book have pioneered, I believe, in weaving theory and applications together, in showing how microeconomic analysis casts light upon intellectual and policy issues. The dozens of brief boxed examples scattered throughout the book direct attention to a host of specific applications. These discussions, based as they usually are upon recent research reported in scholarly articles and books, also help the student gain some idea as to the scientific work that professional economists actually do. (In view of the standard media picture of the profession as a squabbling band of rival soothsayers—some of them saying business will be good, others always predicting doom—students may be surprised to find that there are actual scientific results in economics.) In addition, at appropriate places in the text there are more extensive discussions of many other applied topics such as the negative income tax, rationing in wartime, internal pricing when products are transferred between divisions of a corporation, alleged monopolistic suppression of inventions, and minimum wage laws.

I would like to mention two other methodological points. First, economics is not a body of facts or propositions to be memorized but *a way of thinking*. There are diligent students who say, "Prof, just tell me what pages you want me to learn and I guarantee I'll know every word." But to understand economics, memorization is not enough; insight and intuition must also be cultivated. Once again, only breadth of exposure to a wide variety of applications makes it possible to gain some idea as to what propositions are relevant in any specific context. On the other hand, not everything can be left to inspiration. Insight and intuition must be earned by hard intellectual labor.

Second, traditional economic theory has been guilty of tunnel vision in limiting attention almost exclusively to rationalistic individual behavior and to market interactions. But economics is really a universal science. There is an economic problem whenever the constraint of resource scarcity impinges upon life. Human decisions that are subject to the law of scarcity, and therefore amenable to economic analysis, include not only market choices but also social choices (how many children to have, whether to live in the city or the suburbs, whom to seek out as friends) and political ones (our nation must strike a balance, for example, between affluence and defense, between relief for persons unable or unwilling to work versus incentives to those who are productive, between regulation of improper behavior and greater freedom of the individual). I have therefore made use of materials from scientific work in anthropology, psychology, political science, social biology, and so forth, wherever convenient for illustrating economic principles. To cite one instance, students may possibly resist the idea that businessmen ever engage in anything as subtle or complex as marginal analysis. But biologists have discovered that marginal analysis explains many aspects of the behavior of birds and bees, or of animals generally (see "Birds Do It! Bees Do It" in Chapter 2), and businessmen are surely more clever than birds and bees.

On the side of technique, only recently has the classical scientific method of *experiment* begun to play an important role in economic research. This is a very exciting development. Accordingly, I have devoted quite a few of the examples to reports of experimental studies. One important instance: while the conditions of perfect competition are never fully satisfied in the real world, experiments have shown that even highly imperfect markets may lead to results very close to the competitive ideal (see Chapter 13).

As to coverage and level of difficulty, this is not a minimal "thin-gruel" book. I have wanted to meet the needs of a range of users, and especially to build in growth potential so that the text can serve as reference and guide for readers going on to additional self-study or coursework. (And there is the additional plus, from a commercial point of view, of making the book less likely to be dumped immediately on the second-hand market.) But perhaps the main reason for the breadth of coverage is simply that there are so many fascinating applications and extensions of the basic theory. In consequence there is more here than can usually be handled in a brief (one-term) microeconomics course. To meet the needs of instructors and students in such briefer courses, a shorter book-within-the-book exists in the series of *Core Chapters* (Chapters 1 through 8 and 11 through 13). Also, if time pressures so dictate, a number of more advanced or tangential discussions (set apart in sections marked by asterisks within the chapters) can be omitted with little or no loss of continuity. With a two-term undergraduate price theory course, all or almost all the material in the text can be covered.

A special effort has been made to provide expository aids, which now include the following: (1) Detailed descriptive legends accompany the diagrams. The analytical high points of a chapter can often be efficiently reviewed by rereading these legends in sequence. (2) Each chapter is followed by a summary and by two groups of questions—a first group for straightforward testing of recollection and recall, and a second group providing challenges for further thought and discussion. (3) A large number of numerical exercises have been introduced, with worked answers, right into the main text.

Users of the preceding edition will find that the organization of chapters remains substantially as before. However, the text has been completely rewritten in the interests of improving clarity. In addition, since this book is increasingly used in schools of business administration and management as well as departments of economics, I have introduced or expanded a number of topics of significance for business policy, such as the discussion of on-peak versus off-peak operations in Chapter 6 and of internal pricing within the firm in Chapter 8. Among the many other new topics and applications covered in this edition are land rent and urban location (Chapter 12), the economics of exhaustible resources (Chapter 14), "envy-free" allocations of income (Chapter 15), and the median-voter theorem for decisions made by majority voting (Chapter 16).

In addition to the preceding, a number of features of this book represent improvements upon conventional textbook coverage. Among them I will mention the following:

1. Traditional intermediate texts offer no price-theoretic explanation for *money*. In Part Five the analysis of exchange as a costly economic activity provides the foundation for understanding how a monetary commodity works. And even earlier, in Part Three, it will have been indicated that the existence of business firms is also a consequence of the costliness of exchange.

2. "Monopolistic competition" is covered in Part Three under a more general heading—variation of product. The topics under this heading also include equilibrium of product *quality* and of product *assortment*.

3. Saving and investment are tied to the underlying theory of intertemporal choice and equilibrium in Part Six. The coverage here provides a bridge to macroeconomics and to the business-finance literature.

4. In Part Seven, "Political Economy," after a treatment of the traditional normative issues of welfare economics in Chapter 15, the final Chapter 16 moves on to a *positive* analysis of government. Two views of the state, a voluntarist or public-choice model versus an exploitative or conflict model, are contrasted. The novel theory of *conflict interactions* offered here represents, I believe, the first time this overwhelmingly important topic has been addressed in an intermediate economics text.

As in previous editions, calculus techniques are employed only in marked mathematical footnotes. But the delta (Δ) notation used in defining marginal concepts will be naturally translated into derivative or differential terms by the student equipped with calculus. The instructor should of course warn students that further command of college math is needed for study of economics beyond the intermediate level.

Whether a proper balance has been struck between coverage and simplicity, between theory and application, between technical accuracy and intuitive suggestion, only the reader can judge. I will be grateful for guidance on this point from instructors and students, as well as for specific corrections where errors appear.

As in past editions, a Teacher's Manual for this fourth edition of *Price Theory and Applications* is available to instructors, upon request, from the publisher. A Study Guide to accompany the text will be available for purchase by students. The Study Guide has been prepared by Michael Sproul.

Acknowledgments

In its several editions this book has had the advantage of helpful reviews by many colleagues, by now too numerous to be individually named here. I am particularly grateful to the teachers, students, and other readers who have independently taken the trouble to send me valuable corrections and comments. Thanks are also due to my research assistants over the years, who have worked mainly on the boxed examples and on the questions and answers for the various chapters. Once again the number has grown too large for a complete listing, but I would like to name especially Charles Knoeber for assistance on the initial edition, and for this fourth edition, Michael Sproul, Nancy Burnett, and Joel Lander. Since Michael Sproul's aid throughout all phases of the preparation of this edition was so extensive, his assistance is acknowledged on the title page as well. Typing services of an exceptional order were provided for this edition by Lorraine Grams.

THE NATURE AND SCOPE OF ECONOMICS

Economics concerns decisions—choosing among actions. The first thing to appreciate about decisions is that every possible course of action has its pros and cons, pluses and minuses, benefits and costs. Tennis may trim your figure and improve your disposition, but take time from your studies and damage your joints. If you drop out of college you can start earning an income right away, but completing your degree might lead to a more rewarding lifetime career. And similarly in business and government: every conceivable decision—whether it be the corner grocer putting a price-tag on potatoes or the Congress of the United States voting on a declaration of war—will encounter arguments for and against. How then can we ever decide? Economics develops methods for determining the *best* action through a systematic assessment of all the relevant pros and cons.

Economics also studies what happens when different people's decisions *interact*, as they usually will. If the grocer raises the price of potatoes, customers may decide to buy less—so that the higher price may not, after all, yield the grocer any bigger profit. And similarly when it comes to plans for solving social problems. Once the likely responses of all the people affected are taken into account, the outcome often turns out to be much less attractive than first appears. Take a scheme that might seem at first glance to alleviate suffering, for example a law requiring all grocers to cut food prices in half so that the poor can afford to buy more to eat. Before concluding that this is a good idea we would surely have to allow for the reactions of the grocers and of their suppliers—will they be able and willing to provide grocery products at the lower prices? (A law forcing sellers to cut prices in half may seem like something unlikely ever to happen. But when, for example, a price-control law freezes apartment rents during a generally inflationary period, in *real* terms the price of housing services is being sharply cut.)

Economics has been called the dismal science. The reason is that economists are so often the ones who have to bring the bad news: that a superficially appealing project or scheme may turn out not to be such a great idea once the responses of *all* the affected individuals are considered.

Let's look at some other examples. The following table lists a number of social problems with possible solutions. (Notice that sometimes the same problem has diametrically opposed "solutions.") Take a moment yourself to think of possible objections to each solution listed. Then note the "hidden" adverse consequences mentioned for each.

How many of these "hidden" consequences did you think of yourself? Are there others that should be added? Finally, why is it that such consequences are so often overlooked? [*Probable answer*: Because they involve something not directly

Social Problems	"Solutions"
1. Our country's steel producers are threatened by competition from imports.	Impose a tariff on imported steel.

Possible "hidden" consequences: (a) Our country's steel consumers will have to pay more for steel and so will consume less. (b) Foreigners, once they sell fewer goods to us, will buy less of our country's exports.

2. Apartment rentals have gotten very high.	Freeze apartment rents.

Possible "hidden" consequences: (a) Landlords will skimp on upkeep and repair of apartments. (b) In the longer run, fewer rental units will be constructed.

3. Women's wages are less than men's.	Adopt "comparable-worth" laws requiring equal pay for men and women doing comparable jobs.

Possible "hidden" consequences: (a) Employers will hire fewer women at the higher wage. (b) Wages will be set by bureaucrats instead of by market forces.

4. Commercial fishing for tuna kills large numbers of dolphins.	Require our nation's fishermen to use special nets that permit dolphins to escape.

Possible "hidden" consequences: (a) Consumers will have to pay more for tuna. (b) Foreign fishermen will take over more of the tuna trade.

5. Medical costs are very high.	Have government pay a share of medical bills, especially for the poor.

Possible "hidden" consequences: (a) Doctors' bills and hospital charges will rise even more than they have previously. (b) Taxes will have to go up.

6. Huge numbers of people are becoming addicted to drugs.	Toughen enforcement of narcotics laws.

Possible "hidden" consequences: (a) Street prices of narcotics will rise, forcing addicts to engage in more antisocial behavior to feed the habit. (b) Huge financial stakes in the narcotics trade will lead to more corruption of the police and judiciary.

7. Same as number 6.	Abandon enforcement of narcotics laws.

Possible "hidden" consequences: Increased availability and lower prices of narcotics will widen usage and addiction.

visible here and now, *changes* in people's behavior as they react to the imposed "solution."]

Economic reasoning requires that *all* the consequences, favorable and unfavorable, be considered and weighed. But when people become committed to one side of the question they generally don't want to listen to contrary arguments. So learning to think like an economist may not make you very popular, although it will make your private decisions more effective and your views on social issues more balanced.

The economist is the opposite of the *advocate*, someone who looks only for arguments favoring his or her side of the question. There is a time and a place for advocacy. If you were on trial for murder you'd probably not want your lawyer to present the evidence for your guilt with the same enthusiasm as the evidence for your innocence. And we all know of people who can never stop saying "But on the other hand..." who are incapable of needed action. ("The native hue of resolution is sicklied o'er by the pale cast of thought"—*Hamlet*.) Nor can the economist replace the *prophet* and *poet* who inspire us to aim at ideal goals. Prophets and poets, men and women of action, and even advocates are needed elements in society. But so are economists.

1.A
ECONOMICS AS A SOCIAL SCIENCE

It may have struck you that the outlook attributed to the economist is essentially the same as that of the *scientist*. And indeed this book is an introduction to economics as a science: as a body of models (theories) that explain the real world. More specifically, economics is a *social* science; it aims to explain how human beings interact with one another in the world of affairs.

1.A.1 □ Is Economics a Science?

Is economics really a science? Let's first hear from a cynic: "Anyone who reads the papers knows that economists are always disagreeing with one another—that doesn't give me much confidence that economics has arrived at scientific truth. Furthermore, if economists can scientifically predict financial and commercial events, why aren't they all rich?"

Differences among economists do not necessarily mean that economics is unscientific. All sciences advance through disagreement. In astronomy the geocentric model of Ptolemy was opposed by the new heliocentric model of Copernicus; in chemistry Priestley supported the phlogiston theory of combustion while Lavoisier propounded the oxidation theory; and in biology the creationism of earlier naturalists was countered by Darwin's theory of evolution. It is not universal agreement but rather the willingness to consider evidence that signals the scientific approach. For Galileo's opponents to disagree with him about Jupiter's moons was not unscientific of itself; what was unscientific was their refusal to look through his telescope and see. The important issues of economics, for example the monetarist versus fiscalist hypotheses in macroeconomics and the effectiveness of centralized planning for achieving economic growth, are under continuous scientific evaluation. The lack of a general scientific consensus[1] may be due to the complexity of the problem or to the incompetence of the investigators, but there will always be unresolved issues in any living science.

Are there, however, any *resolved* issues in economics? This book will highlight a great many, in the area of price theory or microeconomics. (For some comments on *macro*economics, see Section 1.D below.) Economists today rarely disagree on the essentials of such topics as the impact of taxes or subsidies upon prices and outputs, the implications for consumers of competitive versus monopolistic market structures, or the effects of reducing tariffs.

Observers often exaggerate not only the extent of disagreement among economists but also the degree to which the natural sciences (sometimes miscalled the "exact" sciences) have been mastered. Few topics have been so well studied as strength of materials in applied physics. Yet engineers, after going through their

---

[1] *Scientific* consensus need not imply general agreement as to *policy*, however. See Section 1.A.3, "Positive versus Normative Analysis."

calculations, commonly add on a huge safety factor (50 percent or even 100 percent) before undertaking construction of a bridge or a dam. And even so, bridges still collapse and dams wash away. If economists predicting the rate of inflation were permitted as wide a safety factor as engineers, they would rarely go astray.

EXAMPLE 1.1
Hydrology versus Economics

In 1955 the Board of Water Supply of New York City projected that the city's future rate of water use would reach 1320 MGD (million gallons per day) as of 1960, rising further to 1500 MGD by 1970. The "safe yield" from existing water sources was confidently estimated by the city's hydrologists to be 1550 MGD. With only a thin safety margin (1550 − 1500 = 50 MGD) anticipated as remaining by 1970, the Board of Water Supply decided to acquire a new water source to come into service before that date.

A team of economists reviewed this decision in 1960. They concluded that the Board's projections of water use were much too high; the economists' prediction was that actual water use in New York City would surely not reach 1500 MGD by 1970, if ever. Since the "safe yield" supposedly guaranteed by hydrologic science already equaled 1550 MGD, the economists concluded that an enormously expensive new supply was not warranted.

After 1960, the economists' prediction about actual use was borne out. Water consumption in New York City stabilized well below 1300 MGD, far under the Board's projected rate of 1500 MGD, and never came anywhere near the supposed "safe yield" of 1550 MGD. So all should have been well. Instead, the city was hit by a catastrophic water shortage. What had happened? Throughout the early 1960s the *actual* yield of water sources was far, far below the hydrologists' "safe yield." In the four successive years 1962 through 1965, the *highest* actual water yield was only 1204 MGD. Economics, one of the social sciences, thus proved to be immensely more reliable than one of the vaunted natural sciences.[a]

COMMENT: In making policy recommendations, the economist may be in a position of having to evaluate the reliability of other sciences as well as his own.

[a] See J. Hirshleifer and J. W. Milliman, "Urban Water Supply: A Second Look," *American Economic Review*, v. 47 (May 1967), pp. 169–78.

What about the charge that if economics were truly a science, economists would all be rich? Several answers are commonly offered. It is sometimes argued that a scientific knowledge of economics ought *not* to be expected to lead to financial success. If Henry Aaron had studied the aerodynamic equations governing the motion of spheroidal missiles, would that have helped him beat Babe Ruth's home-run record? This argument should not be pressed too far, however. After all, what is the use of economics (or of aerodynamic knowledge, for that matter) if it does not lead to *some* practical result? In the case of economics this usefulness is surely in understanding market phenomena, which ought to lead to higher cash income. While the general run of people can hardly be expected to match the achievements of geniuses like Henry Aaron in his field or J. Paul Getty in his, there ought to be some observable effect of economics training upon income. And indeed, it seems, to some degree there is.

EXAMPLE 1.2
Salaries

The table shows salaries for college instructors in a number of selected fields.

Salaries of University or College Instructors with Ph.D.'s (1975)

Field	Median Salary
Engineers	$18,900
Medical scientists	18,700
Economists	18,400
Agricultural scientists	18,200
Oceanographers	18,100
Computer specialists	18,000
Statisticians	17,800
Physicists	17,700
Earth scientists	16,900
Psychologists	16,900
Mathematicians	16,800
Sociologists/anthropologists	16,800
Social scientists, other than economists or sociologists	16,800
Chemists	16,600
Biological scientists	16,200

Source: National Science Foundation, *Characteristics of Doctoral Scientists and Engineers in the United States.* 1975 Surveys of Science Resources Series, pp. 112–13.

COMMENT: Economists rank near the top of teaching salaries in the United States, third in this table. The only academic fields with more earning power are engineering and medicine. Both of these other fields (and, to a lesser extent, economics as well) are characterized by excellent opportunities outside of college teaching, in business employment or independent professional practice. (As we shall see in Chapter 12, employers of teachers must compete against all other possible employers of trained professionals, so that salaries in teaching are influenced by these outside opportunities.)

Nevertheless, the data in Example 1.2 do not prove that it is *the economics training* that leads to the higher incomes reported. There are other possible explanations. It might be that economics is so unpleasant that its practitioners must be paid more—rather like sewage workers or hangmen. Or perhaps the higher salaries that economists earn are only normal rewards for those exceptional talents necessary to understand economics in the first place.

The following quotation from Aristotle (384–322 B.C.) is also of some relevance. Aristotle is discussing his predecessor Thales (approx. 636–546 B.C.), considered to be the first Greek philosopher and scientist.

Thales...was reproached for his poverty, which was supposed to show the uselessness of philosophy; but observing from his knowledge of meteorology (so the story goes) that there was likely to be a heavy crop of olives, and having a small sum at his command, he paid down earnest-money, early in the year, for the hire of all the olive presses in Miletus and Chios; and he managed, in the absence of any higher offer, to secure them at a lower rate. When the season came, and there was a sudden and simultaneous demand for a number of presses, he let out the stock he had collected at any rate he chose to fix, and making a considerable fortune he succeeded in proving that it is easy for philosophers to become rich if they so desire, though it is not the business which they are really about. (Aristotle, *Politics*, I.)

Thales was renowned not only as a meteorologist but as an astronomer, mathematician, and statesman. Still, we may doubt Aristotle's assertion that "it is easy for philosophers to become rich if they so desire"—unless, like Thales, a philosopher happens to be a pretty good economist as well.

1.A.2 □ The Scope of Economics

Economics is not the only social science. Sociology, anthropology, political science, social psychology, and social biology have much to contribute to our understanding of how human beings behave. No absolute boundaries can be drawn between the topics covered by economics and those addressed by her sister social sciences. That the boundaries are indistinct is actually a healthy intellectual situation, since the modes of attack of different disciplines can then compete over the bordering territories. But the nucleus of economics covers a limited range of human activity: *rational behavior* and *market exchange*.

What is "rational behavior"? At least two meanings are in common use (and are often confused). The first meaning refers to *method*, the second to *result*. In terms of method, rational behavior is action selected on the basis of considered thought rather than habit, prejudice, or emotion. In terms of result, rational behavior is action that does in fact achieve your goals. The two are not the same. In the first place, good method can lead to bad result: "The best laid schemes o' mice and men/Gang aft a-gley" (Robert Burns). Actually, the seemingly inferior methods available to creatures with very limited capacity for thought often work very well. Anyone who has chased a fly with a swatter knows that the insect, despite its tiny brain, may defeat us and achieve its goal of survival. But in general, on the human level we expect that considered thought will (at least on average) lead to better action.

Everyone behaves irrationally to some extent—out of passion, thoughtlessness, mental defect, or just plain perverseness. Some do so to such a degree that they are institutionalized for their own or others' protection. In view of the prevalence of human irrationality, how can rationality be assumed in economics? Clearly, only to the extent that the assumption provides valid predictions of how people will behave. Economists have found that theories that assume rationality work better than those that do not. And yet economics as a science is not irrevocably wedded to the rationality postulate. When an alternative that proves more useful comes along, it will be adopted instead.

EXAMPLE 1.3
Rational Psychotics?[a]

With 44 female psychotics (primarily schizophrenics) as experimental subjects, the psychologists T. Ayllon and N. H. Azrin studied responsiveness of patients in a mental institution to changes in systems of reward for services. Prior to the beginning of the experiment patients were allowed to choose among a variety of tasks (laundry service, dietary service, etc.) The reward took the form of tokens convertible into commissary articles (clothing, toiletries, cigarettes, etc.) or into hospital privileges (e.g., privacy, leave from the ward).

During the first 20 days patients were given tokens only upon completion of their tasks—a system the psychologists term "contingent reinforcement." After 20 days it was announced that the same number of tokens as before would henceforth be paid each patient automatically, *whether or not the tasks were performed*—in psychological jargon, a shift to a system of "noncontingent reinforcement." On an average day in the first period of "contingent reinforcement" (that is, where wages were paid for services rendered), the 44 patients worked 45 hours in total, just a bit over one hour per patient per day. After the shift to "noncontingent reinforcement" (i.e., to the free gift of tokens) the total number of hours worked by the 44 patients declined to 35 on the first day and to 20 hours on the third. Shortly afterward the bottom dropped out, and close to zero hours were worked thereafter.

Then, at the end of the second period of 20 days, the earlier system of "contingent reinforcement" was reinstated. The total number of hours worked jumped immediately to 45 hours per day, and remained near that level to the end of the experiment 20 days later.

> CONCLUSION: The experimental subjects may have been psychotic, but they were not stupid. They showed an ability to adapt to systems of rewards in their society. When working was necessary to earn these rewards, they worked; if the rewards came without working, they chose not to work.

[a] Discussion based upon T. Ayllon and N. H. Azrin, "The Measurement and Reinforcement of Behavior of Psychotics," *Journal of Experimental Analysis of Behavior*, v.8 (Nov. 1965).

So psychotics can be pretty rational, at least at times. How do they compare with college students?

EXAMPLE 1.4
Rational Economics Students?

In recent years economists have been making increasing use of the technique of *experimentation* that has proved so valuable in the natural sciences. Such experiments usually test how well individuals do in arriving at economically sound decisions. But making rational decisions can involve hard thinking. Not everyone is inclined to work hard, physically or mentally, purely in the interests of advancing economic science.

David M. Grether conducted a number of experiments with UCLA economics students. Half the students were given $7 for participating in the experiment, regardless of their performance. (This was like "noncontingent reinforcement" in the experiments on psychotics.) The other subjects were paid either $5 or $25, depending upon their success rate (equivalent to "contingent reinforcement"). The students were offered a selection of possible gambles, the object being to choose the one that had the greatest win probability. Figuring out the best gamble required some complex mathematical calculations. It was up to the students to determine for themselves the correct way of evaluating the gambles offered. The table indicates some of the results obtained. The first row shows, for example, that 33 of the 48 students receiving rewards committed no errors, but only 17 of the 49 students not receiving rewards succeeded in avoiding errors.

Error Frequencies Per Student

Errors	With Rewards	Without Rewards
0	33	17
1	5	6
2	3	10
3	3	3
4	1	4
5	1	1
6	1	2
7	1	1
8 or more	0	5
Totals	48	49

Source: Calculated from charts in David M. Grether, "Financial Incentive Effects and Individual Decisionmaking," California Institute of Technology Social Science Working Paper 401 (Sept. 1981), p. 11.

Evidently, the UCLA students behaved rationally—in being more willing to be careful and correct in their decisions when they derived some financial benefit from doing so.

Rationality is an instrumental concept. It requires the prior existence of goals. Economics does not examine the process of goal formation. Only the net results of this process, the patterns called *tastes* or *wants* or *preferences*, are relevant for economics. From the economist's point of view, goals are arbitrary. In one society individuals may protect children but eat cattle; another society may protect cattle but permit infanticide. Either way, the scientific economist is prepared to make predictions about the social consequences of the given preferences.

Of course, goals and preferences are not determined randomly. Psychologists explain them in terms of primitive instincts, as reinforced or suppressed by socialization processes. Anthropologists analyze the relevance of culture for goal formation, and sociologists the role of class or other group identification. Social biologists argue that human tastes and preferences are the result of evolutionary pressures, since otherwise the process of natural selection would have eliminated them in the long period of development of the human species. While economists are now beginning to study the sources of preferences, for the most part they have left the explanation of the formation of tastes and goals as a task for other social sciences.

The economist treats preferences as *stable*, rarely changing factors underlying human choices. If a tax on liquor is imposed, economic analysts will usually assume that the desire to drink is just as great—only that the tax makes it more expensive to indulge that desire. This represents a possible blind spot. Take liquor: the remarkable temperance campaign of Father Mathew around 1850 in Ireland aimed at reducing the desire to drink, and in fact Irish consumption of spirits fell drastically from 12,000,000 to 5,000,000 gallons per annum. (But only temporarily.) And if a higher tax has been placed on liquor, that may itself reflect increased revulsion against drinking. Nor is the assumption of unchanging tastes very helpful for analyzing the element of fashion and style in consumption. Far more important, many of the really great social changes in human history have clearly stemmed from shifts in people's goals for living. Indeed, the economist is in danger of trivializing these fundamental values and goals by suggesting that they are merely arbitrary "tastes." From the prophets of ancient Israel to the ministry of Jesus to the recent decline of belief in God, the changes in the kinds of rewards that people seek from life have had an enormous effect upon the shape of the social system of the West. The ethical messages of Buddha and Confucius have perhaps had similar impacts upon the civilization of the East. The aspects of human behavior that the economist fails to explain are therefore at least as important as those subjected to economic analysis.

Critics sometimes say that economics assumes everyone is completely selfish. This is an uninformed accusation. It is true that, observing facts as they really are, the economist ordinarily operates on the premise that individuals seek their own advantage. "It is not from the benevolence of the butcher, the brewer, or the baker, that we expect our dinner, but from their regard to their own interest."[2] Nevertheless, charity is an important feature of economic life; people have, in a sense, a taste for benevolence. Even so, the economist is likely to say, if benevolence were made less costly (for example, if the Internal Revenue Service permitted more ample tax deductions for charitable giving) we would surely see more of it. As another example, the aid that parents give children can hardly be explained in terms of complete selfishness. But again, to elicit a higher degree of love and care on the part of parents, a financial inducement would help.

Economics focuses on rational behavior in a market setting. If a consumer wants bread from the baker, it may seem like rational behavior to get a job and earn the price of a loaf. But it may also be rational, in certain circumstances, to simply steal the bread. Alternatively, the consumer might organize a political party with the object of passing laws that would force bakers to give away their bread. Or he might attempt to persuade the bakers that it is their charitable duty to do so. Economics concentrates upon the first of these forms of interaction: voluntary exchange *through the market.* For the most part crime has been left to sociology, the uses of state power to political science, and techniques of persuasion to psychology. But the vigor and rigor of economic science are proving increasingly useful in these related areas. Economics has tended, therefore, to overflow these boundaries, as the following example shows.

[2] Adam Smith, *The Wealth of Nations*, Book I, Chap. 2.

EXAMPLE 1.5
Rational Criminals?

Crime sometimes does pay. It is perfectly rational for a criminal to steal rather than work if he feels the gains are worth the risks. However, the dominant opinion in modern criminology (a field of study which, until quite recently, made no use of economic analysis) has been that criminals are best thought of as individuals with "deviant" motivations. The solution to crime, it has therefore been inferred, should be sought on the psychological level—for example, by improving the mental health of potential criminals, or providing them with better role models to follow. Economic analysis, without necessarily denying that criminals are psychologically "deviant" in some ways, suggests nevertheless that they may still respond to incentives in a way that could be regarded as rational.

A study by Isaac Ehrlich asked whether commission of major felonies was affected by the punishments and rewards for crime in the different states of the United States.[a] As economists would expect, the crime rate tended to be lower the more effective the punishment. The rate of commission of robberies, for example, decreased about 1.3 percent in response to each 1 percent increase in the proportionate *probability* of punishment and also decreased about 0.4 percent for each 1 percent increase in the *severity* of punishment (length of imprisonment). Another seemingly rational response was that the property crime rate in a state tended to be higher where average income and inequality of income were both high. Presumably, in those states criminals were relatively poor individuals living in an environment containing many attractive targets.

The most controversial of Ehrlich's results concerned the effect of capital punishment in deterring murder. The standard view in criminology, emphasizing the abnormal psychology of murderers, had been that murderers are surely too "deviant" to be deterred by the threat of execution. Yet Ehrlich's investigation indicated very big deterrent effects: according to one set of data each execution was associated with 7 to 8 fewer murders, according to another set 20 to 24 fewer murders.[b]

These inferences were, however, based upon complex statistical analyses possibly subject to more or less serious reservations or objections. A panel of the National Academy of Sciences, mainly consisting of noneconomists, was set up to review the conclusions of Ehrlich and the broadly similar results reached by other economists studying crime. The panel, while conceding that the evidence tended to support the deterrence hypothesis, nevertheless regarded it as still unproven.[c] As more data are accumulated and more accurate analytical techniques are devised, we can expect this scientific disagreement ultimately to be resolved.

[a] I. Ehrlich, "Participation in Illegitimate Activities: A Theoretical and Empirical Investigation," *Journal of Political Economy*, v. 81 (May/June 1973).

[b] I. Ehrlich, "The Deterrent Effect of Capital Punishment: A Question of Life and Death," *American Economic Review*, v. 65 (June 1975), p. 414; "Capital Punishment and Deterrence: Some Further Thoughts and Additional Evidence," *Journal of Political Economy*, v. 85 (Aug. 1977), p. 779.

[c] Panel on Research in Deterrent and Incapacitative Effects, *Deterrence and Incapacitation: Estimating the Effects of Criminal Sanctions on Crime Rates* (Washington, D.C.: National Academy of Sciences, 1978).

These results suggest that economic analysis is applicable also to nonmarket interactions. And indeed, even animal behavior is beginning to be analyzed by biologists in economic terms.[3] One important human nonmarket form of interaction is *politics*, a topic that will be examined from the economic point of view in Part Seven of this book.

Returning to market interactions, these have distinctive characteristics that set them apart from other forms of human transactions. *The market relation is mutual and voluntary.* Theft, a nonmarket interaction, is clearly *involuntary* on one side. The gift relation, another nonmarket interaction, is voluntary but not *mutual*. Two different objections can immediately be raised on this score. First, if A is hungry and B has bread, can their relation really be voluntary? Must not the A's of this world be "wage slaves" of the B's? Then how does the market differ from coercive dominance? Second, suppose some highwayman declares to his victim, "Your money or your life!" Isn't he offering a voluntary deal? Then how can criminal extortion be distinguished from market exchange?

The explanation of these puzzles turns on the legal concept of *property*. Taking the highwayman first, he is indeed proposing a market deal: to "sell" the victim back his or her own life, in exchange for money. But under our legal system each person has property in his or her own life. The seemingly voluntary transaction proposed by the highwayman is premised upon his seizing power over something he has no right to—his victim's life. As for the "wage slave" contention, it is of course true that those endowed with more valuable property will be better off in the market than those possessing little in the way of resources. But there is a vast difference between laborers possessing property rights in their own labor power, who are in a position to bargain with alternative employers for the best available terms, and slaves. The latter have no property; indeed, they are property. They cannot market or trade their labor, for it is not legally theirs to sell.

1.A.3 □ Positive versus Normative Analysis: "Is" versus "Ought"

In its scientific aspect economics is strictly *positive*. It answers the question "What is reality like?" But *normative* issues in public policy, turning upon the question "What ought to be done?", also require economic analysis. Given a social objective, scientific economists can use their knowledge of "what is" to analyze the problem and suggest ways of achieving "what ought to be."

When economists disagree on policy issues, it may be because they are seeking different goals: one may be more concerned with achieving social equality, another with promoting individual freedom. Where the difference is on such a philosophical plane even the most complete scientific understanding of economic reality will not resolve the conflict. But it is often the case that disagreement among economists is over *means* rather than *goals*: over how to do it rather than over what to do. Further scientific progress in positive economics will, over time, tend to eliminate this source of disagreement.

---

[3] Martin L. Cody, "Optimization in Ecology," *Science*, v. 183 (Mar. 22, 1974); David J. Rapport and James E. Turner, "Economic Models in Ecology," *Science*, v. 195 (Jan. 18, 1977).

EXAMPLE 1.6
When Do Economists Disagree?

In a recent study, questionnaires were sent to a random sample of 600 members of the American Economic Association asking their opinions on a variety of important issues. The sample was stratified to assure representation of economists employed by universities, by government, and by the private nonacademic sector.

A total of thirty questions were asked, representing a mixture of microeconomic and macroeconomic, and of positive and normative issues. The table here summarizes results for six of the questions, divided equally between positive and normative, but all falling more or less under the microeconomics heading.

Q.	Proposition	Generally Agree (%)	Agree with Provisions (%)	Generally Disagree (%)	Index of Consensus*
Positive issues					
7.	A minimum wage increases unemployment among young and unskilled workers	68	22	10	58
16.	A ceiling on rents reduces the quantity and quality of housing available	78	20	2	76
24.	The fundamental cause of the rise in oil prices of the past three years is the monopoly power of the large oil companies	11	14	75	64
Normative issues					
10.	The distribution of income in the United States should be more equal	40	31	29	11
12.	Antitrust laws should be used vigorously to reduce monopoly power from its current level	49	36	15	34
30.	The economic power of labor unions should be significantly curtailed	32	38	30	2

*For explanation, see text.

Source: Adapted from J. R. Kearl, Clayne L. Pope, Gordon C. Whiting, and Larry T. Wimmer, "A Confusion of Economists," *American Economic Review*, Papers and Proceedings, v. 69 (May 1979), p. 28.

The column labeled "Index of Consensus" has been constructed from the original data by comparing "Generally Agree" with "Generally Disagree," subtracting the smaller of these from the larger. ("Agree with Provisions," the middle position, was omitted.) As can be seen, the amount of scientific consensus on the *positive* issues is impressive; note the much larger range of opinion on the *normative* issues.

THE INVISIBLE HAND

As astronomy has Newton's principle of universal gravitation, and biology has Darwin's principle of evolution through natural selection, economics also has a great unifying theme. Its discovery was, like Newton's and Darwin's, one of the important intellectual achievements of humanity.

Adam Smith's *The Wealth of Nations* appeared in 1776. The key idea is suggested by the following quotation:

> But it is only for the sake of profit that any man employs [his] capital...he will always, therefore, endeavour to employ it in the support of that industry of which the produce is likely to be of the greatest value, or to exchange for the greatest quantity either of money or of other goods...he is in this, as in many other cases, led by an invisible hand to promote an end which was no part of his intention. Nor is it always the worse for the society that it was no part of it. By pursuing his own interest he frequently promotes that of the society more effectually than when he really intends to promote it.[4]

In more modern language we might say: A person will be led by self-interest to put his or her resources to use wherever they earn the most. But to earn, you must produce something that people want to buy. Consequently, seeking your own advantage automatically leads you to produce goods or services that suit consumers' desires.

Does this seem obvious? Two centuries ago people commonly believed (and a great many today still do believe) that the only way to help others is by benevolent assistance—by "doing good." More sophisticated individuals know, with Adam Smith, that you often help others more by trade than by direct aid. Nevertheless, it is not so easy to understand just why an economic system of untrammeled selfishness does not lead to mutual harm, or even to total chaos. How is it that the city of New York can be regularly fed by converging food shipments from all corners of the earth—without any governing plan to make sure that the Kansas farmer, the New England fisherman, and the Florida orange-grower actually deliver to the hungry city? Yet the city is fed, although none of its suppliers need be motivated by any particular love and concern for New Yorkers. Kansas farmers simply find it more profitable to ship to New York than to eat their own wheat, and similarly for the others.

To quote *The Wealth of Nations* still once more: "In civilized society [man] stands at all times in need of the cooperation and assistance of great multitudes, while his whole life is scarce sufficient to gain the friendship of a few persons."[5] The "Invisible Hand" is what leads an individual to work for the good of other persons, practically all unknown to him, in an orderly economy that has arisen without anyone having planned it that way.

Adam Smith's object in composing *The Wealth of Nations* was largely policy-oriented or *normative*; he opposed the then politically dominant "mercantilists,"[6]

---

[4] Book IV, Chap. 2.

[5] Book I, Chap. 2.

[6] The mercantilists believed that a nation's well-being required the accumulation of gold and silver, and that to achieve this aim government policies should encourage exports and restrain imports.

arguing instead in favor of a policy of "natural liberty."[7] But it is not his policy recommendations that will mainly concern us. His key conception is that *the economy follows scientifically determinable laws*. In early times, some people thought the planets were pushed in their courses by angels. The development of astronomy eventually led to the scientific idea of gravitation to explain planetary motions. Similarly today, many people find it utterly incomprehensible that (for example) water is cheap and diamonds are expensive, a strange situation that they are all too likely to attribute to the actions of angels or devils. We owe to Adam Smith the scientific idea of the market economy as a mechanism, driven by the self-interest of participants, yet so integrating their activities that *each is led to serve the desires of others*. How this leads to water being cheap and diamonds expensive we shall see in the pages to come.

1.C
ELEMENTS OF THE ECONOMIC SYSTEM, AND THE CIRCULAR FLOW OF ECONOMIC ACTIVITY

That *there is an economic system*—that there are laws of economics—is the first message to learn. We can now survey some of the basic elements of the economic system.

1.C.1 □Decision-making Agents in the Economy

This book deals with three main types of decision-making units: individuals, firms, and governments.

Individuals are the basic units of social systems, the only agents said to have goals or *preferences* and to engage in the process of *consumption* (to be discussed in Part Two). Actually, recognizing the mutual support and cohesiveness of the family, some economists prefer to consider the "household" to be the effective consumption unit. Except where otherwise specified, the individual here will be understood as making decisions for his or her family or household.

The business firm is an artificial unit; it is ultimately owned by or operated for the benefit of one or more individuals. Surprisingly, this fact is often not appreciated. It is sometimes argued, for example, that corporations can be taxed without cost to the people. But of course taxing a corporation will hurt some people: the company's owners will suffer reduced profits, its workers may find it harder to get wage increases, its customers are likely to find that prices of its products have been increased. (At the same time, the taxes paid by corporations allow government to provide assistance to other people—as usual, every choice of policy involves both costs and benefits.) The economist finds it convenient to think of firms as distinct agents specializing in the process of *production*, the conversion of resource inputs into desired goods as outputs. Firms will be the center of attention in Part Three of the text. In point of fact, however, much production actually

[7] Smith recommended free trade among nations and *laissez-faire* within.

takes place within the household: cooking, gardening, and home maintenance are examples.

Individuals and firms are not the only economic decision-making agents. A third category, government, is of great and growing importance. Governments, like firms, are artificial groupings. They differ from firms in not being owned by individuals, and also by having the legal right to take property without consent (as by taxation). From the economic point of view governments are agencies engaging in a number of productive activities, the scope of which is determined by a political rather than a market process. Perhaps even more important, governments establish the legal framework within which the entire economy works. (The role of government is examined in Part Seven.)

In complex modern economies there are still other "collective" decision-making units. Trade unions and cartels, to be discussed in Chapters 11 and 8, respectively, are organizations of sellers in markets. Also of economic importance are voluntary associations like clubs, foundations, and religious institutions, through which individuals combine for certain collective consumption choices.

1.C.2 □ Scarcity, Objects of Choice, and Economic Activities

The source of all economic problems is *scarcity*. People will always want more than they can have. Even if all desired goods were present in unlimited quantities, we would not have enough *time* to enjoy them all. And, in addition, we all desire things other than material commodities: power, love, prestige. There can never be enough of these. It is the fact of scarcity that forces us to make economic decisions—that is, to produce and/or trade with a view to obtaining desired goods.

The objects of economic choice are called *commodities*, or *goods and services*. (The term "goods" is usually understood to include services as well as physical wares or merchandise.) Services represent a flow of benefits over a period of time, derived either from physical goods (like the shelter service provided by a house) or from human activities (like the entertainment provided by concert performers).

Consumption is one of the main economic activities. In their consumption decisions, individuals pick the goods they like best, given their incomes. We shall say that goods are the *objects of choice* for the consumption decision.

Production by individuals and firms is another main economic activity. We usually think of production as changing inputs into outputs, converting resources into consumable goods. More fundamentally, production is any activity adding to the social totals of some goods (which necessarily means giving up the opportunity to produce other goods with the same resources). Production might be a change *of physical form*, as in the conversion of leather and human labor into shoes, but not necessarily so. Transformations would still be regarded as productive if they took place *over space* (shipment of oranges from Florida to Maine) or *over time* (storing potatoes after harvest so as to distribute consumption over the year).

Of course, to be economically rational, production should represent a conversion from a less desired to a more desired form. To burn an antique Chippendale chair for heat is a kind of production, but ill-advised under ordinary conditions. (On the other hand, a person on the point of freezing to death might find the conversion from chair to warmth exceedingly advantageous.)

The third main economic activity is *exchange* (to be discussed in Part Five). For the individual, exchange is also a kind of conversion—he or she trades away some objects for others. But from the social point of view, exchange is distinguished from production in that the totals of commodities are unaffected; goods and services are reshuffled in trade, but wherever one person has less someone else must have more. Thus, exchange is a kind of transfer. But it is a mutual and voluntary transfer; *all* parties involved must be satisfied or they would not have traded in the first place.

1.C.3 □ The Circular Flow

In a simplified world with only two types of economic agents, individuals and business firms, the relations between them can be pictured as in Figure 1.1. Individuals and firms have dual aspects, and thus transact with one another in two distinct ways. Individuals are in one aspect *consumers of goods*, while firms are *producers of goods*. Thus, the diagram shows a "real" flow of consumption goods (solid upper channel) from firms to individuals. But the goods must be produced. To permit this there must be a "real" flow of productive services (solid lower

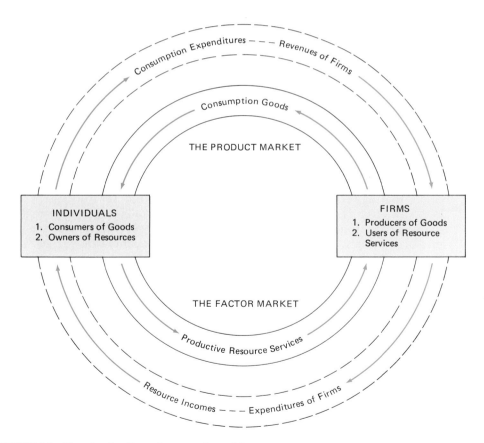

FIGURE 1.1 The circular flow of economic activity.

channel), from the individuals in their second aspect as *owners of resources* to the firms as *employers of resource services.*

In a socialist command economy these flows of goods and resources might be directly ordered by a dictator. But in a private-enterprise economy the relations are based on exchange and so must be mutual and voluntary. Hence, offsetting the "real" flows are reverse "financial" flows of claims that in a modern economy normally take the form of money payments. The consumers' financial expenditures on goods (dashed upper channel) become the receipts or revenues of the firms. The exchange of consumption goods between individuals and producing firms in return for financial payments take place in what economists call "the product market." (Actually, there will of course be a host of separate product markets, one for each distinct consumption good.)

The revenues received from sales to consumers provide firms with the wherewithal to buy productive services from resource-owners (dashed lower channel). This closes the circle; the firms' payments for productive services become income to the individuals, available once more for spending on consumer goods. Purchase and sale of productive services take place in what economists call "the factor market," again, really a number of distinct markets for the various types of productive services.

Looking within the box representing the firms as economic agents, what takes place there is the process of *production*, the physical transformation of resources into products. Within the box representing individuals, *consumption* of the produced goods takes place. Here again, the circle is closed by the fact that consumption is necessary to recreate the main productive resource—labor power—for the next cycle.

1.D
MICROECONOMICS AND MACROECONOMICS

A distinguished professor of logic, deploring the division of his subject between deductive reasoning and inductive reasoning, once declared: "In our textbooks on deduction we explain all about logical fallacies; in our textbooks on induction, we then commit them." Economic theory has a similar split between microeconomics and macroeconomics. In microeconomics we see how and why the Invisible Hand operates (how and why people's self-interest leads them to serve one another in a spontaneous system of productive cooperation); in macroeconomics we examine why the Invisible Hand sometimes fails to work satisfactorily.

Microeconomics concentrates mainly upon equilibrium states of particular markets, presuming an equilibrium of the market system as a whole. But it seems to be the case that the equilibrium of the market system as a whole is not as robust as might be hoped. The *overall* circular flow of economic activity may become disrupted, leading perhaps to inflation or to large-scale unemployment. It is these malfunctions of the system as a whole that macroeconomics studies.

For some period of time, starting in the 1930s, macroeconomists attempted to develop modes of reasoning largely independent of any microeconomic foundation. Some theorists went so far as to dismiss classical microeconomics as obsolete or irrelevant. It is now generally recognized that this attempt has failed.

Significant recent progress in macroeconomics has been made precisely by improving the logical connection of the subject with the microeconomic theories of production, consumption, and exchange. So the study of microeconomics is needed even for a proper understanding of macroeconomics.

□ SUMMARY OF CHAPTER 1

Economics is a social science, whose nucleus is the study of the *rational behavior* of individuals and firms as they interact with one another through *market exchange*. Rational behavior is the appropriate choice of means for achieving given ends—always involving comparison of benefits and costs, of the advantages and disadvantages of alternative courses of action. Economists do not ordinarily ask why people have certain tastes or wants or desires, but take these as facts which are to be explained (if at all) by the other social sciences. Individuals can try to satisfy their desires in human society in a number of ways, for example by persuasion, by force, by theft, or by calling upon government power. But economics mainly studies market relations, in which people seek to achieve their aims through voluntary exchange.

Adam Smith's principle of the Invisible Hand shows how persons who are only interested in their own welfare are led to cooperate with one another through market exchange. The Invisible Hand is what makes the economy a system of spontaneous order, an integrated arrangement whose behavior follows scientifically determinable laws.

The main agents in the economic system are individuals (possibly acting on behalf of their families or households), firms, and governments. Individuals are the only agents who consume. Individuals may also produce goods and services. But, in modern economies, production takes place primarily through business firms—artificial agents created by individuals for that purpose. The activity of production must be distinguished from exchange: *production* transforms the physical shape or location or time-availability of commodities, whereas *exchange* merely reshuffles the existing goods and services among the economic agents.

The circular flow of economic activity summarizes the market interactions among economic agents. In *the product market*, individuals as consumers purchase consumption goods from firms; in *the factor market*, individuals as resource-owners provide productive services to firms. The "real" circular flow has resources moving from individual owners to firms, being converted by firms into consumption goods, whereupon they return to the individuals so as to complete the circle. In the "financial" circuit, funds are paid out by firms as they hire resources, thus providing individuals with an income for purchase of consumption goods; these purchases circulate the funds back once again to the firms, allowing the next cycle to begin.

□ QUESTIONS FOR CHAPTER 1

MAINLY FOR REVIEW

*R1. In what respects can it be said that economics is a science? Give an example of a prediction that modern economic science can confidently make. Are there predictions that economic science has not yet shown itself competent to make?

*R2. What is rational behavior? Give examples of rational and of irrational behavior. Can the economist's postulate of rationality be useful even when irrational elements strongly influence behavior?

R3. Does the economist assume stable preferences? Give an example of a change in preferences that has had important economic effects.

R4. Does the economist assume that everyone is selfish? Give an example of an area where unselfish behavior has important economic consequences.

R5. Market transactions are said to be both *mutual* and *voluntary*. Give an example of a nonmarket interpersonal transaction that is not voluntary. Of one that is voluntary but not mutual.

R6. What are positive issues in economics? Normative issues? Give an example of each.

*R7. How does the Invisible Hand lead individuals in a market economy to cooperate for mutual advantage even without any definite intention on their part to do so? Would self-interested behavior lead to mutual advantage in a monastic economy where all income is equally divided? In a dictatorship where the political authorities confiscate the lion's share? In an economy with no property, so that any person could take what he or she needs from any other persons?

R8. What are the most important classes of decision-making units in a modern economy? In what types of activity do they engage? In what sense are firms and governments "artificial" units?

*R9. In the circular flow of economic activity, distinguish between the real and financial circuits of flow. What is the relation between the two? Distinguish between the "product market" and the "factor market." How are these connected?

R10. "The principle of the Invisible Hand asserts that self-interested behavior on the part of resource-owners leads inevitably to chaos." True or false, and why?

R11. What is the difference between production and exchange?

FOR FURTHER THOUGHT AND DISCUSSION

*T1. Other things being equal, would you expect the murder rate to be lower in jurisdictions applying capital punishment? If the income-tax exemption granted for each child were increased, would you expect the birth rate to rise?

*T2. The psychiatrist T. S. Szasz argues that what is called mental illness is the result of rewarding people for disability. Not only is the patient motivated to become "ill," but there is a financial advantage to the healing professions in declaring personal problems to be "illnesses." How could mental illness be made less "rewarding"? Would doing this reduce mental illness?

T3. If government were to increase relief payments to the unemployed, would you expect unemployment to rise?

T4. In terms of the circular flow of economic activity, explain why some individuals are wealthy (in a position to consume a great deal in the product market) and others are poor.

*T5. If the Invisible Hand leads individuals to serve their own interests by serving others, why are some people led to a life of crime? Why do some corrupt politicians find it advantageous to serve themselves at the expense of their constituents? Why are dictators motivated to seize power? [*Hint*: Does the principle of the Invisible

---

* Answers to starred questions appear at the end of the book.

Hand apply to all kinds of social interactions, or does it hold only when individuals interact in a particular way?]

*T6. Would an effectively enforced law requiring drivers to wear seat belts tend to reduce driver deaths? Pedestrian deaths?

*T7. Dr. Samuel Johnson: "There are few ways in which a man can be more innocently employed than in getting money." Charles Baudelaire: "Commerce is satanic, because it is the basest and vilest form of egoism." What do you think each had in mind?

T8. Classify each of the following statements or propositions as either *positive* or *normative*. (Does the classification "positive versus normative" have any bearing upon truth or falsity?)
   a. Smoking in enclosed public spaces should be banned.
   b. Prohibiting smoking in public places would reduce the demand for cigarettes.
   c. Proposed legislation to limit the places in which smokers may indulge in their habit would elicit opposition from the tobacco industry.
   d. Nonsmokers' rights to breathe clean air are more important than smokers' rights to pollute the air.
   e. Antismoking laws will have no effect on sales of cigarettes because smokers will light up just as much as before but confine their puffing to legal areas.

T9. It may soon become possible to predict the place and time of earthquakes, weeks or even months before their occurrence. Some influential writers have argued that such predictions should be kept secret, or even that investigations leading to such predictions should be banned. Allegedly, the panic caused by predicting an earthquake would be more damaging than the earthquake itself. What does this view imply as to individual rationality? Would you be for or against banning earthquake prediction?

2

CORE CHAPTER

WORKING TOOLS

Let's start with some good news. It is a remarkable fact that practically all the analysis in this book, and even throughout economics generally, makes use of only two analytical techniques: (1) *finding an optimum* and (2) *finding an equilibrium*. Facing any question, the student who asks himself or herself, "Is this an optimization problem or an equilibrium problem?" will seldom go astray.

What's the difference between the two sorts of problems? Each row of the table below lists an optimization problem and a related equilibrium problem.

Optimization Problems	*Equilibrium Problems*
1. Would I do better to buy a new car, or stick a while longer with my old one?	1. Are new-car prices likely to be lower next year?
2. Will I be happier working, or should I drop out of the rat-race and be supported by "welfare" on a commune?	2. Would generous "welfare" provision for the unemployed raise the unemployment rate?
3. Is it more profitable to buy or lease?	3. What determines the ratio between the annual rental of a building and its purchase price?
4. To counter drug abuse, should narcotics laws be made stricter or more lenient?	4. If all narcotics laws were abolished, would drug usage increase?
5. Is now the time to go out on strike, or had we better accept management's offer?	5. Do strikes raise the wage of workers?

This is not the place for presenting answers. The main point is to grasp the essential difference between the two types of problems. The first type, the optimization problems, are always of the form: "Is it better for me (or for my business, or my nation, or even humanity as a whole) to take this action or that action?" The second type, the equilibrium problems, are of the form: "What explains the observed prices and/or quantities in markets?"

Each of these two techniques employs a characteristic working tool. To solve optimization problems, to find the best choice, the student must have an understanding of the relations among total, average, and marginal magnitudes. To solve equilibrium problems, to find the condition of balance in the market, the student must be able to use supply-demand analysis. Almost all readers of this book will already have some command of these working tools. What this chapter provides is therefore mainly a review, plus illustrative applications.

2.A
EQUILIBRIUM: SUPPLY-DEMAND ANALYSIS

2.A.1 □ Equilibrium of Supply and Demand

The supply-demand diagram of Figure 2.1 should be familiar, but let's go over some of the details. The horizontal axis represents the quantity Q of some particular good—to be specific, let's say grain (in tons).[1] The vertical axis of the diagram represents price P per ton of grain. *A price is a ratio of quantities*: it signifies the amount of some other commodity that must be given up to obtain a unit of the desired good. Thus, we might speak of the price in cigarettes of a hat, or the price in labor-hours of a loaf of bread. In modern societies prices are normally quoted in terms of *money*. While money is a very peculiar "good" whose nature and role will not be examined until much later in the book, for the present let us think in terms of money prices. Consequently, the vertical axis (price axis) of Figure 2.1 is labeled $\$/Q$—dollars per ton of grain.

The demand curve DD shows, for each price P, the quantity that consumers are able and willing to buy. The negative slope of the demand curve reflects the fact that buyers are willing to purchase more, the lower the price. [*Verification*: Stores often try to win more customers by claiming to be offering unusually low

[1] In accordance with the idea that the economy represents a continuing *circular flow* of activity, it is sometimes important to think of quantity as a rate per unit time: for instance, tons per month or per week. That quantities represent flows over time will be taken as understood throughout this book.

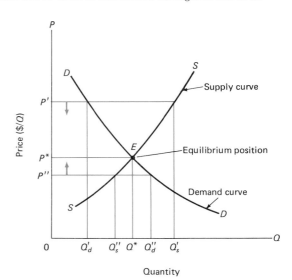

FIGURE 2.1 **Demand and supply.** The equilibrium at point *E* determines the price *P** and quantity *Q** where supply and demand are in balance.

prices. Do sellers ever try to attract customers by asserting that their prices are exceptionally high?] Similarly, the positive slope of the supply curve SS indicates that sellers will normally offer more of the good, the higher the price.

In Figure 2.1 market equilibrium is represented by the intersection point E, at quantity Q^* and price P^*.[2] Suppose the market price were, momentarily, at a price higher than P^*—for example, at P' in the diagram. At that price, sellers are offering the quantity Q'_s while buyers only want Q'_d. Not all the suppliers can find customers. What will then happen? Some suppliers will quote lower prices rather than be left holding unsold stocks of goods. So there is *downward* pressure on price, indicated in the diagram by the arrow pointing downward from the horizontal line representing the price P'.

What if market price were momentarily at some level lower than P^*, such as P'' in Figure 2.1? Then the quantity demanded would be Q''_d, which exceeds the supply quantity Q''_s offered on the market. Not all demanders would be able to buy as much as they want, and hence some of them will start to bid up the price. Here there is *upward* pressure on price, indicated in the diagram by the arrow pointing upward from the horizontal line representing the price P''.

Clearly, one or the other process will always be at work so long as price is not at the equilibrium P^*. Only at P^* are the demand-quantity Q_d and the supply-quantity Q_s equal to each other. When Q_d equals Q_s, we have the market equilibrium quantity Q^*.

How realistic is this picture? What we are dealing with here is a *model* of reality, not reality itself. It is a model (as will be explained later) of perfect competition among individuals interacting in a perfect market. The question of scientific interest is not the literal truth of the model but rather its usefulness. This is the subject of the next section.

> *CONCLUSION:*   The intersection of the demand curve and the supply curve determines the equilibrium values of price and quantity.

2.A.2 □ Comparative Statics of Supply and Demand: Shift of Equilibrium

Equilibrium was determined, in the picture of Figure 2.1, by the intersection of *given* supply and demand curves. But what about *changes* in supply and demand? Such changes can be interpreted as shifts of the supply curve, of the demand curve, or of both at once.

Suppose that, perhaps as a result of altered preferences, buyers suddenly want to consume more of some good at each possible price. This is called an *increase of demand*. As shown in Figure 2.2, the demand curve shifts *to the right* (from a position like $D_1 D_1$ to $D_2 D_2$). Where the old equilibrium price was P_1^* and quantity Q_1^*, the new equilibrium price and quantity are P_2^* and Q_2^*.

How does the revision of the equilibrium position actually come about? Suppose the price remained unchanged at P_1^* after the demand curve shifted to $D_2 D_2$ in Figure 2.2. Then consumers would want to buy Q'_d, but at price P_1^* suppliers would still be offering only the quantity Q_1^*. So there would be upward pressure

---

[2] Asterisks will generally be used in this text to designate *solution values* (values of the variables associated with equilibrium or optimum positions, as the case may be).

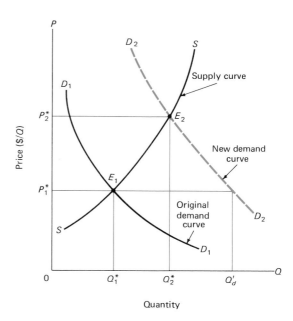

FIGURE 2.2 Increase in Demand. When consumers' preferences change, so that they desire to purchase more at each price, the demand curve shifts to the right from D_1D_1 to D_2D_2. Equilibrium price and equilibrium quantity both increase.

Price ($/Q)

Quantity

on price. In a free market, price will respond to this pressure and continue to move upward until Q_d equals Q_s, at the new equilibrium price P_2^*.

This description of price-quantity adjustment is not entirely free of problems. For example, some transactions might actually take place at "wrong" prices (before P_2^* is reached), and these "wrong" transactions might in turn affect the supply or demand curves. That is, the final equilibrium reached might conceivably depend upon the path for getting there. Such issues are topics in *economic dynamics*. We will not be able to consider dynamics in this text. Instead, we will be comparing only the initial and final equilibrium situations. This is called *the method of comparative statics*. While some aspects of reality cannot be successfully modeled without use of dynamics, comparative statics can still tell us a great deal.

Our basic technique, then, in analyzing some economic change will be to ask: Is the change reflected in a shift of supply, or a shift of demand (or, possibly, of both)? It will be immediately evident from Figure 2.2 that *an increase in demand alone leads to an increase in both equilibrium price and equilibrium quantity*. What of an increase in supply? In Figure 2.3 an increase in supply is shown as a rightward shift of the supply curve (from S_1S_1 to S_2S_2), since at each price a larger quantity is offered. (*Warning*: A common slip is to think of an "increase" of demand or supply as an *upward* shift of the corresponding curve; this is correct for the demand curve but incorrect for the supply curve. To avoid error, interpret an "increase" always as a rightward shift of the curve.) *An increase in supply thus leads to an increase in equilibrium quantity, but to a decrease in equilibrium price.* [*Question*: What can be said if both supply and demand increase together?]

> PROPOSITION: If demand increases, equilibrium price and quantity *both* rise. If supply increases, equilibrium quantity rises but equilibrium price falls.

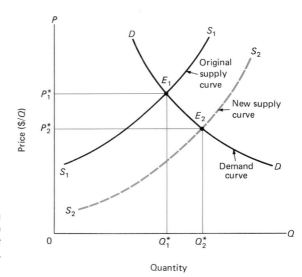

Price ($/Q)

Quantity

FIGURE 2.3 Increase of Supply. When a change in conditions induces sellers to offer more at each price, the supply curve shifts to the right from $S_1 S_1$ to $S_2 S_2$. Equilibrium quantity increases, but equilibrium price falls.

What causes supply and demand curves to shift? It is sometimes useful to distinguish between those sources of change originating "outside" and those originating "inside" the economic system. The "outside" sources of variation include: (1) *Changes in tastes* (a temperance campaign may alter people's willingness to consume hard liquor); (2) *changes in technology* (Eli Whitney's invention of the cotton gin vastly increased the market availability of cotton); (3) *changes in resources* (an important oil discovery will enlarge the world's supply of petroleum); and (4) *changes in the political-legal system* (decriminalization of marijuana can be expected to increase both the market supply and the market demand for that substance). All these changes can be regarded, in some degree at least, as originating autonomously rather than in response to economic factors.

Shifts of supply and demand curves may also stem from movements "inside" the economic system. Such "inside" variations might include: (1) *Changes in prices (or quantities) of goods related in demand* (an increase in the price of butter will tend to raise the demand for margarine); (2) *changes in prices (or quantities) of goods related in supply* (a rise in the production of beef will almost necessarily increase the supply of hides on the market); and (3) *changes in levels of income* (the higher incomes recently received by petroleum-exporting countries raised their demands for consumption goods).[3]

The following examples should help develop your intuition as to how equilibrium prices and quantities are likely to respond to "outside" or "inside" sources of economic change.

[3] There is no hard-and-fast rule as to what elements lie "outside" and what "inside" the economic system. While the text speaks of changes in resources as an "outside" source of variation, prospecting for mineral resources would surely be affected by mineral prices, by tax policies, and so forth. Even population, regarded as a resource, is likely to respond to economic incentives—for example, if governments subsidize large families. The pace and direction of technological change also vary with the financial inducements offered to inventors. (When the British government in the eighteenth century announced a prize for an accurate chronometer, significant advances in time-keeping were made by inventors.)

EXAMPLE 2.1
Catholics and Fish

For over a thousand years the Roman Catholic Church required believers to abstain from consuming meat on Fridays. But a liberalization of the regulations of the Church abolished this requirement for American Catholics as of December 1966 (except for Fridays falling within Lent).

Frederick W. Bell studied the impact of the liberalization upon the price of fish in New England (population approximately 45 percent Catholic). The study compared a ten-year period before the liberalization with the nine-month period just after (excluding Lenten months). In estimating the shift of the demand curve for fish landed by New England fishermen, it was necessary to adjust for a number of factors such as imports of fish, prices of closely competitive foods (poultry and meat), and personal income. Having made these adjustments, the effect of the liberalization on fish prices can be seen in the table.

Prices of Fish, Monthly Data, 1957–1967

Species	Change Due to Liberalization (%)
Sea scallops	-17
Yellowtail flounder	-14
Large haddock	-21
Small haddock (scrod)	-2
Cod	-10
Ocean perch	-10
Whiting	-20

Source: F. W. Bell, "The Pope and the Price of Fish," *American Economic Review,* v. 58 (Dec. 1968), p. 1348.

The results show that the prices received for fish of all seven species were lower after the liberalization than before.

The "Catholics and Fish" example clearly represents a decrease in the demand for fish. (The demand curve for fish shifted leftward, rather than rightward as in Figure 2.2.) The source of the variation would seem to lie clearly "outside" the economic system, since the modification in Church regulations was not in any evident way a response to market factors.

EXAMPLE 2.2
Potatoes

That vegetables are cheap at harvest time may well have been the first law of economics observed in primitive society. In the case of potatoes there is some production throughout the year, but the major crop is harvested in the fall.

The table shows the average U.S. prices and production of potatoes in the various seasons of the year during the period from 1968 to 1970.

Prices and Production of Potatoes, 1968–1970

Season	Average Production (CWT)	Average Price Received By Farmers ($/CWT)
Fall	237,391	1.90
Winter	3,765	2.09
Early spring	5,154	2.48
Late spring	20,977	2.71
Early summer	13,483	2.73
Late summer	29,790	2.07

Source: Data from U.S. Dept. of Agriculture, *Agricultural Prices, 1970 Annual Summary,* p. 22; *Crop Production,* July 9, 1971, p. A2, July 10, 1969, p. 2.

What we see here is obviously an *increase in supply* (rightward shift of the supply curve) in the main fall harvest season. Quantity is biggest, and price is lowest, in that season. Are you perhaps surprised that the price variation is so small, given the enormous production swings over the year? The main reason is that potatoes are *stored* from harvest on. Therefore, price is still relatively low in the winter season just after the fall harvest, even though production is at a minimum in the winter. As stored holdings are gradually consumed, price rises steadily over the year until the new crop begins to arrive in the late summer season.

The original source of agricultural supply variation over the year is the "outside" element of God-given seasonal climate. But note that the "inside" element of storage activity greatly modifies the force of the external factors. Other economic activities like improvements in transportation, changes in agricultural practices, and development of new seed varieties may also be at work to stabilize price despite seasonal variation of supply.

EXAMPLE 2.3
Heating Oil

The supply of petroleum is relatively constant over the year, but there is substantial seasonal variation on the demand side. Gasoline purchases tend to be highest in the summer months, and of course heating oil is most required during the winter.

The first column of the table is an index of monthly consumption of distillate fuel oil, which is largely used for heating purposes, during the period 1984 to 1985. (The index figure of 100 represents average consumption over the entire year.) A slight adjustment has been made in the data to account for the differing numbers of days in the months. The second column is a similar index of the monthly prices per gallon of heating oil at retail. Here an adjustment has been made in the data to eliminate the effect of continuing inflation, which tends to make all end-of-year prices higher than beginning-of-year prices.

Indexes of Retail Sales and Prices, Distillate Fuel Oil, in the United States, 1984–1985

Month	Index of Average Consumption (Adjusted for Number of Days in Month)	Index of Average Price (per Gallon, Retail, Adjusted for Inflation)
January	119	102.7
February	114	107.0
March	109	107.2
April	101	100.3
May	92	98.6
June	91	95.3
July	85	93.5
August	90	93.5
September	93	96.7
October	97	100.1
November	99	102.2
December	106	102.9

Source: Indexes calculated from data in American Petroleum Institute, *Petroleum Facts and Figures, 1986 ed.,* p.486, and U.S. Dept. of Commerce, *Survey of Current Business,* Jan. 1984 through Dec. 1985.

Consumption of fuel oil varies widely over the year, with December through March by far the highest months. Evidently, demand is greatest (the demand curve is farthest to the right) in those months. Increased demand is also accompanied by higher prices. As before, it may seem surprising that the price swings are so small. Here once again, the explanation is that *storage* over the year permits a buildup of stocks to meet the peak winter demand. As another factor in the situation, refineries in winter months can adjust their operations to produce larger fractions of heating oil from their petroleum input. So a rightward shift of heating oil *supply* partially offsets the larger winter demand. The storage feature is also reflected by the way the price index lags slightly behind the quantity index. In early winter, December is a high-consumption month but price is still moderate because stocks are ample. By February, consumption has begun to decline; nevertheless, prices are high in February since inventories have been drawn down to their lowest levels.

EXAMPLE 2.4
Brides

Among the Sebei in Uganda, husbands obtain wives by purchase. The anthropologist Walter Goldschmidt secured data on bride-prices paid by husbands in two communities: the cattle-herding district of Kapsirika and the farming district of Sasur.

The Kapsirika herders pay higher prices for brides than the Sasur farmers, even though the herders are not generally wealthier. The rate of polygyny (plural wives) is also higher among the Kapsirika; their wife/husband ratio is 1.52, whereas among the Sasur farmers it is only 1.17.[a] There is a substantial intermarriage rate, but it takes entirely the form of herder husbands buying farmers' daughters. Thus, the herders' demand curve for brides seems to be higher; they pay more, and so they get more.

[a] Walter Goldschmidt, "The Brideprice of the Sebei," *Scientific American*, v. 229 (July 1973), pp. 74–85.

In the "Potatoes" and "Heating Oil" examples, supply and demand changed over time. The "Brides" example shows how demand can vary across communities at a single point in time. The herders' demand curve for brides can be regarded as greater than (lying to the right of) the farmers' demand curve. The *source* of the difference might be the "outside" factor of different preferences for brides on the part of the males in the two communities. An alternative "inside" explanation is that wives are better productive assets for herders than for farmers. One interesting question is why any bride-price difference persists: if Kapsirika herders and Sasur farmers compete to buy wives, why don't they end up paying about the same price? The answer appears to be that intermarriage takes only the form of the Kapsirika "importing" wives; it seems that the "importers" must pay some kind of premium in order to overcome unwillingness of brides to move from one community to the other.

EXAMPLE 2.5
Electricity[a]

Throughout most of the nineteenth century, steam power was the dominant energy source in manufacturing. This era came to an abrupt end when Thomas Edison introduced the first commercial electric generating plant in 1882. At first used primarily for lighting, electricity gradually came to be the standard source of power in factories. In 1902 electricity accounted for only 4 percent of all power used in manufacturing, but by 1920 this figure had risen to over 50 percent.

The quantity of electricity in use rose steadily as technology improved. In 1902, 7.3 pounds of coal were needed to produce one kwh of electricity; by 1932 only 1.5 pounds were required. Thus, at any given price for electricity, it was becoming possible for the generating companies to profitably provide larger and larger quantities. As the supply curve shifted to the right, the price of electricity fell—by more than 50 percent between 1900 and 1929. At the same time wholesale prices in general approximately doubled, so that in real terms electricity could be bought in 1929 for around one-fourth of the price paid in 1900.

[a] This discussion is based upon Arthur G. Woolf, "Energy and Technology in American Manufacturing: 1900–1929," *Journal of Economic History*, v. 42 (Mar. 1982).

In the "Electricity" example, technological advances brought about an increase in supply—a rightward shift of the supply curve—leading to an increase in quantity and a fall in price. At the same time, business firms were in the process of learning how to use electricity, and so the demand curve was surely also shifting to the right. This makes the drastic reduction in price all the more remarkable, since the demand shift considered separately was placing *upward* pressure upon the electricity price.

2.A.3 □ Algebra of Supply-Demand Analysis

We have seen that the price-quantity equilibrium is found geometrically where the supply curve and the demand curve intersect. The student should also be able to solve for the equilibrium algebraically. This is easy to do if the demand and supply curves are straight lines, as pictured in Figure 2.4. Panel (a) shows a demand curve with the equation $P = 10 - Q$. The supply curve has the equation $P = 1 + 1/2Q$. To find equilibrium, we can set either the prices or the quantities equal. Here it is more convenient to equate the prices: $10 - Q = 1 + 1/2Q$. Solving, we get $Q = 6$. Now insert $Q = 6$ into the demand equation to find the equilibrium price: $P = 10 - 6 = 4$.

Panel (b) is a more general picture, one that gets away from the specific numbers of Panel (a). The general demand equation (assuming it is a straight line) can be written $P = A - BQ_d$, where Q_d is the quantity demanded and A and B are positive constants. Geometrically, A is the intercept of the demand curve with the vertical price axis (the price so high that purchases are zero); $-B$ is the negative demand-curve slope (as suggested by the little right triangle, with base 1 and altitude B, drawn along the demand curve). The supply curve has the equation $P = C + DQ_s$, where Q_s is the quantity supplied. Here the positive constant C is the intercept of the supply curve on the vertical axis (the price so low that none of the good will be supplied), and the positive constant D represents the supply-curve slope. Think of the intercept A as the "choke price for demand," while C is the "choke price for supply."

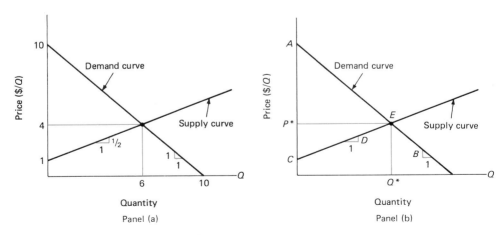

FIGURE 2.4 **Linear Supply and Demand Curves.** In Panel (a) the straight-line demand curve $P = 10 - Q$ and supply curve $P = 1 + 1/2Q$ intersect to determine the equilibrium quantity 6 and price 4. Panel (b) corresponds to the more general equations $P = A - BQ_d$ and $P = C + DQ_s$. At the equilibrium point E, the quantities demanded and supplied are equal: $Q_d = Q_s$.

The condition of equilibrium can be written:

(2.1)
$$Q_d = Q_s$$

Since $Q_d = Q_s$, we can drop the subscripts and just use Q. So we have two simultaneous equations:

(2.2)
$$\begin{cases} P = A - BQ \\ P = C + DQ \end{cases}$$

Exercise 2.1 Suppose that in a certain market the demand schedule is given by the linear equation $P = 300 - Q_d$ and the supply schedule by $P = 60 + 2Q_s$. Find the solution values for price and quantity.

Answer: Setting the right-hand sides of Equations (2.2) equal, after substituting the numerical values for A, B, C, and D, we have $300 - Q = 60 + 2Q$. The solution is $Q^* = 80$, $P^* = 220$.

More generally, Equations (2.2) can be solved algebraically to yield the solution values:

(2.3)
$$Q^* = \frac{A - C}{B + D} \quad \text{and} \quad P^* = \frac{AD + BC}{B + D}$$

Substituting the numbers in the exercise above for A, B, C, and D in these equations provides a check on the answers obtained for P and Q.

What about the comparative-statics analysis of *changes* in equilibrium? If an increase in demand takes place (rightward shift of the demand curve), it is easy to show that the numerical value of A must rise in the demand-curve equation $P = A - BQ_d$. Equations (2.3) then tell us that equilibrium quantity Q^* and price P^* both increase (compare Figure 2.2). On the other hand, if an increase in supply takes place (rightward shift of the supply curve), the numerical value of C in the supply-curve equation $P = C + DQ_s$ falls! (You should satisfy yourself that this is the case, if necessary by drawing a sketch.) Equations (2.3) then tell us that Q^* rises but P^* is lower (compare Figure 2.3).

Exercise 2.2 Starting from the data of Exercise 2.1, suppose the supply-curve slope D rises from $D = 2$ to $D = 3$. (That is, with the same vertical intercept the supply curve has become steeper.) Find the new solution.

Answer: The demand-curve equation remains $P = 300 - Q_d$, but the supply-curve equation becomes $P = 60 + 3Q_s$. Setting the right-hand sides equal we have $300 - Q = 60 + 3Q$. The numerical solution is $P^* = 240$ and $Q^* = 60$; price has risen, but quantity has fallen.

2.A.4 □ An Application: Introduction of a New Supply Source

Let's now take up a more challenging problem. Suppose that a certain country, having previously barred imports of grain, now permits imports. Figure 2.5 pictures the situation. The demand curve is D, the "home" supply curve is S^h, and

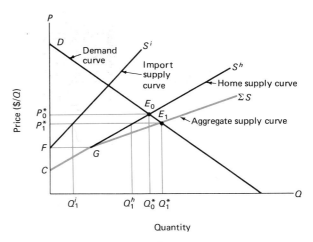

FIGURE 2.5 **Introduction of an Import Supply.** In the absence of imports, the equilibrium E_0 is at the intersection of the demand curve D and the home supply curve S^h. When the import supply S^i also becomes available, the new equilibrium is E_1. The aggregate supply curve ΣS represents the horizontal summation of S^h and S^i, within the positive range for each supply curve.

the "import" supply curve is S^i. Initially, with no imports the equilibrium E_0 is at the intersection of the D and S^h curves. When imports are allowed to enter, the new equilibrium E_1 must represent the intersection of the demand curve with the aggregate or *summed* supply curve. In the diagram, the curve labeled ΣS (read this as "sigma-S") is the *horizontal* summation of the S^h and S^i curves. [*Note the slightly tricky feature:* Below the import choke price F, the ΣS curve is identical with S^h; only for prices high enough for imports to enter does ΣS diverge to the right of S^h.] In the situation pictured in the diagram, allowing imports to enter will clearly reduce the equilibrium price ($P_1^* < P_0^*$) and raise the equilibrium quantity ($Q_1^* > Q_0^*$). [*Question*: What would happen if the initial equilibrium price P_0^* were less than the import choke price F?]

Exercise 2.3 Assume that the demand curve $P = 300 - Q_d$ of Exercise 2.1 is still applicable. Assume also that the "home" supply curve is numerically the same as the supply curve of Exercise 2.1, so that $P = 60 + 2Q_s^h$. Then the initial equilibrium E_0 has $P_0^* = 220$ and $Q_0^* = 80$ as before. Let the new "import" supply curve be $P = 80 + 4Q_s^i$. Find the new equilibrium, E_1.

Answer: Note first that the import choke price, 80, is below the original equilibrium price, $P_0^* = 220$. So imports will surely enter, and we must calculate the aggregate supply curve ΣS. This is done by summing the quantities at each price, so we will have to put Q on the left side of the equations. (Warning: Do not put P on the left side of the equations and then sum. This would be adding the prices, where we want to sum quantities.) Rewriting the home supply curve, we have $Q^h = (P - 60)/2$. Doing the same for imports, we have $Q^i = (P - 80)/4$. Then the summation supply equation is $Q = Q^h + Q^i = 3P/4 - 50$. Solving this simultaneously with the demand equation leads to the numerical solution $P_1^* = 200$ and $Q_1^* = 100$, of which $Q^h = 70$ and $Q^i = 30$.

2.A.5 ☐ An Application: Effects of a Tax on Transactions

Suppose a seller faces the demand curve DD shown in Panel (a) of Figure 2.6. The government now imposes a tax of $2 on every unit sold. Before the tax, suppose the seller could have received $7 apiece when he sold three units. He can

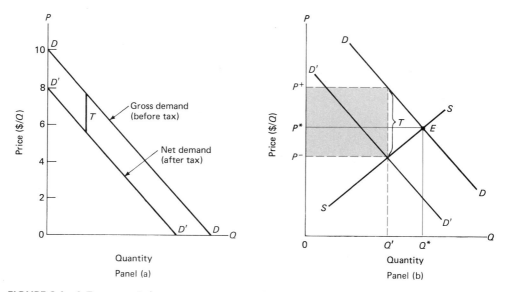

FIGURE 2.6 A Tax upon Sales. Imposing a tax of $\$T$ per unit shifts the demand curve (*net* of tax) downward to $D'D'$. The original DD is the *gross* demand curve. The equilibrium quantity Q' is less than the untaxed equilibrium quantity Q^*. The equilibrium gross price P^+ paid by consumers (inclusive of tax) is higher, but the net price P^- received by sellers is lower, than the original untaxed price P^*.

still sell three units after the tax is imposed, at a *gross* price of $7, but the *net* (after-tax) price he receives will now be only $5. To the seller, therefore, the demand curve has shifted down by the amount of the tax—in this case by $2. (As an exercise, calculate the gross and net prices for quantities of 4, 6, and 9 units.) If the tax is T we can write:

$$P^+ = P^- + T$$

where P^+ is the gross price and P^- the net price.

It is important to note that the tax only changes the demand curve *as seen by the seller*. The tax does not change consumers' desires or incomes, so the true demand curve is still DD. The seller, however, sees after-tax demand as $D'D'$.

To find the after-tax equilibrium, notice where the after-tax demand curve $D'D'$ intersects the supply curve in Panel (b). You can see that quantity falls from Q^* to Q'. Be careful here. To find the new *gross* price P^+ (what the consumer pays), go from Q' up to the gross demand curve DD. To find the new *net* price P^- (what the seller gets), go from Q' up to the net demand curve $D'D'$.

> PROPOSITION: A tax on transactions reduces the equilibrium quantity sold, raises the *gross* price paid by consumers, but lowers the *net* (after-tax) price received by sellers.

It may seem arbitrary that our analysis here took the form of shifting the demand curve down rather than supply curve up. This would seem logical if the tax were, legally, levied upon buyers. What if it were levied on sellers instead? It is left for the student to determine, as an exercise, that a shift of the supply curve upward by the vertical distance T would lead to exactly the same solution as before. So supply–demand analysis leads to a possibly surprising conclusion: *It makes no difference whether a tax on transactions is legally levied upon buyers or upon sellers.*

For the algebra, let us start again with Equations (2.2), but now we distinguish between the price *gross of tax* (P^+) and the price *net of tax* (P^-), using the relation $P^+ = P^- + T$. The consumers must of course pay the gross price, while the suppliers receive only the net price. So there are three simultaneous equations:

$$\begin{cases} P^+ = A - BQ & \text{(demand equation)} \\ P^- = C + DQ & \text{(supply equation)} \\ P^+ = P^- + T & \text{(tax equation)} \end{cases}$$

The solution is found by solving the above three equations simultaneously. Skipping over the algebraic details, the solution values are:

$$Q' = \frac{A - (C + T)}{B + D} \qquad P^+ = \frac{AD + B(C + T)}{B + D} \qquad P^- = \frac{(A - T)D + BC}{B + D}$$

Since T is necessarily positive, Q' here is surely less than Q^* in the solution in Equation (2.3)—the tax has reduced the volume of transactions. The new gross price P^+ is greater than and the new net price P^- is less than the old solution price P^*, thus confirming the geometrical result.

Exercise 2.4 Starting from the supply curve and demand curve of Exercise 2.1, suppose an excise tax $T = 15$ is imposed. Find the new equilibrium.

Answer: The three simultaneous equations of the text become, numerically: $P^+ = 300 - Q$, $P^- = 60 + 2Q$ and $P^+ = P^- + 15$. Substituting from the third equation, the second equation can be rewritten as $P^+ - 15 = 60 + 2Q$. We now have the first and second equations in terms of two variables P^+ and Q, and so can easily solve to obtain the solution values $Q' = 75$ and $P^+ = 225$, from which it follows that $P^- = 210$. As expected, imposition of the tax has reduced quantity exchanged (from 80 to 75), and raised the *gross* price to 225 but lowered the *net* price to 210 (in comparison with the previous no-tax price of 220).

2.A.6 ☐ Interferences with Equilibrium

Government action may sometimes help the market process work. For example, the judicial system enforces private contracts, making it easier for people to trade (as compared with a system where it's up to each person to enforce any agreement he or she makes with others).

Government interventions, however, sometimes may *prevent* markets from reaching equilibrium. Supply-demand analysis helps the economist to understand the consequences of such interventions.

We are all familiar with attempts to hold down inflation by "freezes" or other forms of maximum wage-price controls. During the deflationary period of the 1930s in the United States, in contrast, *minimum* wage-price controls were imposed

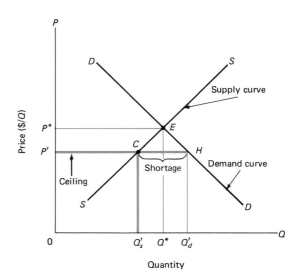

FIGURE 2.7 A Price Ceiling. An effective price ceiling $P' < P^*$ reduces the quantity traded from Q^* to Q'_s.

under the NRA (National Recovery Administration). The extent to which "price ceilings" or "price floors" can actually cure a general inflation or a general deflation is a question in macroeconomics that does not concern us here. Instead, our interest is in the effects of price controls upon particular markets.

Figure 2.7 pictures a "meaningful" ceiling price P'. (To be meaningful, the ceiling must be *below* the equilibrium price P^*.) At the ceiling price the quantity demanded Q'_d exceeds the quantity supplied Q'_s, so there is upward pressure on price, indicated by the upward-pointing arrow. However, the arrow is blocked by the fixed ceiling at P'. (We do not consider here the possibility of illegal trading at higher prices—black markets.)

What about the actual quantity traded? There is a fundamental maxim of markets, "It takes two to tango." That is, exchange requires willing buyers *and* willing sellers. At the fixed ceiling price P' the buyers want Q'_d, but the sellers are willing to offer only Q'_s, so Q'_s is the amount that will actually be traded. (Notice that the actual quantity traded is not some compromise between the two quantities. It is always the *smaller* of the two.) So the final outcome is at point C in the diagram. The distance CH represents the "shortage"—the excess of the demand quantity over the supply quantity at the legal ceiling price.

EXAMPLE 2.6
Repressed Inflation and Trekking

During and after World War II all the major belligerent powers were troubled by severe inflationary pressures. Heavy government expenditures led to enormous budget deficits, covered largely by printing new money. And yet consumer prices were frozen at low ceiling levels. Since the necessities of life were scarce, there was strong upward pressure on prices. Indeed, often the absolutely minimal needs of life were not legitimately available. In postwar Germany, for example, the official daily ration at one point was down to the incredibly low figure of 1180 calories.

In these circumstances the curious institution of "trekking" developed in a number of different countries. City-dwellers would leave town for a day and scour the nearby countryside for food, making private black-market deals with farmers or, indeed, often simply stealing. The more the governments succeeded in controlling prices in the legitimate markets, the more the abnormal system of trekking flourished. On one single day, it was reported, over 900,000 persons trekked from Tokyo into the countryside.[a] In Germany, the "Erhard reforms" of 1948 abolished price freezes and thus eliminated trekking. But a curious and unexpected consequence was a financial crisis for the State railroads. Short-haul railroad passenger traffic dropped immediately to less than 40 percent of its pre-reform volume, evidencing the massive volume of trekking that had previously been going on.[b]

[a] Jerome B. Cohen, *Japan's Economy in War and Reconstruction* (Minneapolis: University of Minnesota Press, 1949), p. 378.
[b] Lucius D. Clay, *Decision in Germany* (Garden City, N.Y.: Doubleday, 1950), p. 191.

A meaningful price *floor* is pictured in Figure 2.8. At the legal floor P'', the quantity Q''_d offered by sellers exceeds the quantity Q''_d desired by buyers. There is downward pressure on price. Here the effective price is higher than the unregulated P^*, but the effective quantity is again *lower* than the equilibrium Q^*, as indicated by the bold vertical line drawn through the point F. Once more, "It takes two to tango." Although price ceilings and price floors have opposite effects on price, they have similar effects upon the quantity traded; *in either case, the quantity exchanged is less than in the unregulated market.* (Again, a kind of black market may come into existence, permitting the trading of somewhat larger quantities at illegally low prices.)

The picture changes when floors are *supported.* Support takes the form of a "buyer of last resort"—Uncle Sam in the case of agricultural price supports in the

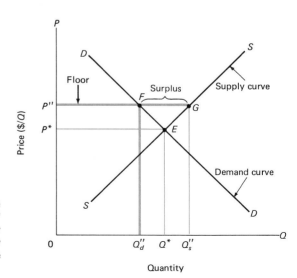

FIGURE 2.8 A Price Floor. An effective price floor $P'' > P^*$ reduces the quantity traded from Q^* to Q''_d. However, if the floor is "supported" by government purchases, the amount Q''_s will actually be supplied. The government must absorb the "surplus," the difference between Q''_s and Q''_d.

United States. Going back to Figure 2.8, private buyers are only willing to take Q''_d at the high floor price P''. But now suppose the government as buyer of last resort purchases the "surplus." Then suppliers will sell the quantity Q''_s; the actual situation is represented by the position G in the diagram. There is no black-market problem with a supported floor, because no supplier would sell for less than the floor price. Instead, there is a problem of surplus disposal, since the buyer of last resort must accumulate larger and larger unwanted stocks.

CONCLUSION: Meaningful ceilings hold down prices; meaningful floors keep them up. In either case, the quantity exchanged is *less* than in unregulated equilibrium. If, however, the floor is *supported*, quantity will be greater than equilibrium, but the "buyer of last resort" must accumulate inventories.

EXAMPLE 2.7
Agricultural Parity Prices

The U.S. government has attempted since the 1930s to maintain parity prices for agricultural products. "Parity" is interpreted to mean the relationship between agricultural and nonagricultural prices that obtained during the years 1910 to 1914, a period of farm prosperity. Throughout the 1950s and 1960s the primary method employed to achieve parity was price support of farm products: a federal agency called the Commodity Credit Corporation (CCC) stood always ready to buy any unsold fractions of supported crops at the support level—usually 90 percent of the parity price.

The "surpluses" purchased by the CCC were for the most part kept in storage, the intention being to release them to the market in years of deficient crops. But as parity corresponded to an unusually favorable price relationship

Yearly Acquisitions of Three Supported Crops by the Commodity Credit Corporation, Selected Years

	MILLIONS OF BUSHELS		
	Grain Sorghum	Corn	Wheat
1953	40.9	422.3	486.1
54	110.1	250.6	391.6
55	92.6	408.9	276.7
56	32.5	477.4	148.4
57	279.5	268.1	193.5
58	258.0	266.6	511.0
1963	125.1	17.9	85.1
64	66.8	29.1	86.9
65	85.0	11.2	17.4
66	0.3	12.4	12.4
67	9.1	191.0	90.0
68	13.7	34.4	182.9

Source: Commodity Credit Corporation charts, Nov. 1972, pp. 49, 75, 115.

from the farmers' point of view, years of deficient crops rarely occurred. By 1960 the CCC held in storage as much wheat as the entire 1960 crop.

To reduce the burden of maintaining such huge stores, food stamps and school lunch programs were initiated to subsidize market demand. More important, under a system of acreage limitations farmers were paid *not* to produce. In addition, the price-support levels were adjusted downward. The table shows the resulting reduction of CCC purchases in the 1960s.

2.B
THE OPTIMIZATION PROCEDURE: TOTAL, AVERAGE, AND MARGINAL MAGNITUDES

The second major category of economic problems is *optimization*, finding the best achievable situation. Economists have devised a method for solving optimization problems that does the work of the mathematical calculus without requiring any formal knowledge of calculus techniques. The key to this process is understanding the relationships among total, average, and marginal magnitudes.

For concreteness let us start with Total, Average, and Marginal *Revenue*. (The principles remain the same for Total, Average, and Marginal *Cost* or for Total, Average, and Marginal *Utility*, and so on.)

Consider Figure 2.9, which pictures the market demand curve for some good. Numerical data for this demand curve are shown in the first two columns of Table 2.1.

If we multiply Price P times Quantity Q, we obtain Total Revenue (sometimes called simply Revenue) R. Thus:[4]

(2.4) $$R \equiv PQ$$

[4] The triple equality sign $\equiv$ represents *mathematical identity*. This symbol will be used in the text where it is desired to emphasize that both sides of the equality are definitionally equivalent.

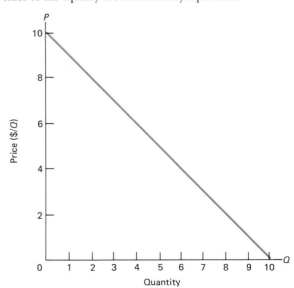

FIGURE 2.9 A Demand Curve. The demand curve, which shows price as a function of quantity, can also be regarded as an Average Revenue curve since $P \equiv R/Q \equiv AR$.

TABLE 2.1

Total, Average, and Marginal Revenue

Quantity (Q)	Price or Average Revenue (P ≡ AR)	Total Revenue (R ≡ PQ)	Marginal Revenue (MR)
0	10	0	
			9
1	9	9	
			7
2	8	16	
			5
3	7	21	
			3
4	6	24	
			1
5	5	25	
			−1
6	4	24	
			−3
7	3	21	
			−5
8	2	16	
			−7
9	1	9	
			−9
10	0	0	

Total Revenue is tabulated in the third column of Table 2.1, is shown graphically in the upper diagram of Figure 2.10.

Since Revenue R is a *total* magnitude, price P can be regarded as an *average* magnitude. In Table 2.1, for example, at quantity $Q = 2$ the Total Revenue R equals 16. If we ask what is the Average Revenue received when $Q = 2$, the answer is $16/2 = 8$, which is, of course, nothing but the price along the demand curve for that quantity. Formally, Equation (2.5) defining Average Revenue (AR) follows immediately from Equation (2.4):

$$(2.5) \qquad AR \equiv \frac{R}{Q} \equiv P$$

Dimensionally, price is measured in terms of *dollars per unit quantity* ($/Q), whereas Revenue is simply scaled in dollars.

Marginal Revenue MR is shown in the fourth column of Table 2.1. It is defined as the rate of change in Revenue per unit change in output. Like price, Marginal Revenue is measured as *dollars per unit quantity* ($/Q). [*Warning*: The vertical axis of the upper diagram of Figure 2.10 is scaled in dollars ($). The lower diagram is scaled in dollars per unit ($/Q). R should never be plotted in the same diagram as AR and MR, since the dimensions are different.] We can define MR in symbols as:

$$(2.6) \qquad MR \equiv \Delta R/\Delta Q$$

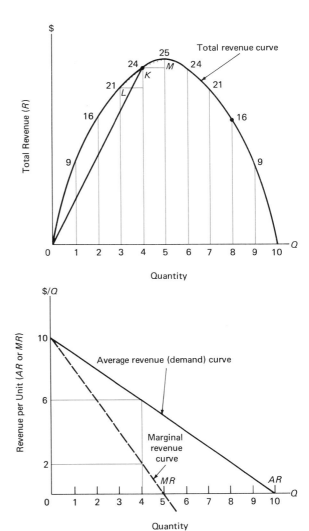

FIGURE 2.10 **Derivation of Average and Marginal Magnitudes from Total Function: Revenue.** The lower diagram illustrates the derivation of the magnitudes of *AR* and *MR* when *Q* = 4 and *R* = 24. The height of the *AR* curve in the upper diagram at *Q* = 4 corresponds to the slope of the bold line in the lower diagram, so that *AR* = 24/4 = 6. The height of the *MR* curve in the upper diagram equals the slope *along* the *R* function in the lower diagram. At *Q* = 4, it is found by averaging the slopes of the dotted lines *LK* and *KM*. Thus *MR* = (1/2)[(25 − 24) + (24 − 21)] = 2.

where ΔR stands for the change in Revenue and ΔQ stands for the change in quantity.[5] For example, as output changes from 1 to 2 in Table 2.1, Revenue R increases from 9 to 16, so over this interval $MR = 16 - 9 = 7$. If output were to increase again to 3 units, MR would be 5, and so on. Note that Marginal Revenue here is defined "between" two quantities of output. For example, MR equals 7 "between" $Q = 1$ and $Q = 2$, and $MR = 5$ "between" $Q = 2$ and $Q = 3$. To find Marginal Revenue "at" some output (say, at $Q = 2$), we can get a good approximation by interpolating. Since $MR = 7$ between $Q = 1$ and $Q = 2$, and $MR = 5$ between $Q = 2$ and $Q = 3$, we can average these to get an estimate of $MR = 6$ at

[5] *Mathematical Footnote*: For small changes, Marginal Revenue can be interpreted as the derivative dR/dQ:

$$MR \equiv dR/dQ \equiv \lim_{\Delta Q \to 0} \Delta R/\Delta Q$$

$Q = 2$. You should check that $MR = 2$ at $Q = 4$, that $MR = 0$ at $Q = 5$, and so on.

It is a common error, and often a numerically substantial one, to ignore this distinction and use the MR "between" two numbers for the MR "at" one of those numbers. In our example here, in trying to determine the MR "at" $Q = 2$ it would be poor practice to take it as simply the added revenue of 7 received when output increases from $Q = 1$ to $Q = 2$. We saw above that the correct answer obtained by interpolation is $MR = 6$. Finding the exact or true MR generally requires the use of calculus, but for a linear demand curve (like that shown here) the recommended method above will always lead to the exactly correct answer.[6] If the demand curve is not a straight line, the approximation error with the recommended method will almost always be substantially less than using the incorrect method described above.

Exercise 2.5: For the nonlinear demand curve $P = 100 - Q^2$, find MR at $Q = 4$.

Answer: Since $R = PQ$, the Total Revenue equation is $R = (100 - Q^2)Q = 100Q - Q^3$. At $Q = 3$, $R = 273$, and at $Q = 4$, $R = 336$, so MR "between" $Q = 3$ and $Q = 4$ is $336 - 273 = 63$. Since at $Q = 5$ we have $R = 375$, MR "between" $Q = 4$ and $Q = 5$ is $375 - 336 = 39$. To estimate MR "at" $Q = 4$, we interpolate by finding the number halfway between 39 and 63, which is $(39 + 63)/2 = 51$. (Using calculus, we would find MR by taking the derivative of R at $Q = 2$, getting the exact figure as $MR = 52$.) The incorrect method described above, taking the MR "between" $Q = 3$ and $Q = 4$ for the MR "at" $Q = 4$, would lead to the estimate $MR = 63$, which is quite far off.

To understand the geometrical relations between total, average, and marginal functions you should remember two main principles:

1. The marginal function is the slope of the total function.
2. The average function is the slope of a ray from the origin to the total function.

The first principle is demonstrated in the upper diagram of Figure 2.10. You can see that as Q rises from 3 to 4, R rises from 21 to 24, so Marginal Revenue MR is $24 - 21 = 3$ between $Q = 3$ and $Q = 4$. Now look at the dotted chord LK. The slope of LK is its "rise over run." It is approximately equal to the slope of the curve R on that interval. The rise is 3 and the run is 1, so the slope of LK is 3—the same as MR. This is no coincidence. The rise of LK is the change in Total Revenue (i.e., ΔR), and the run is the change in quantity (i.e., ΔQ). So when we find the slope of LK by dividing "rise over run" we are finding $\Delta R/\Delta Q$, which is the definition of MR. Try this again between $Q = 4$ and $Q = 5$. Over that interval MR equals $25 - 24 = 1$, and similarly, the slope of the chord KM is also 1.

To demonstrate the second rule, that Average Revenue AR is the slope of a ray from the origin to R, look again at the upper diagram in Figure 2.10. When $Q = 4$, it is easy to see that $R = 24$. Dividing R/Q we get $AR = 24/4 = 6$. Now look at the ray from the origin labeled OK. The slope of OK is its "rise over run." The rise is 24 and the run is 4, so when we divide "rise over run" we get $24/4 = 6$—the same as AR. Once again, this is not a coincidence. The rise is equal

[6] *Mathematical Footnote*: The demand-curve equation underlying Table 2.1 is $P = 10 - Q$. Then Total Revenue is $R = PQ = 10Q - Q^2$. Taking the derivative, Marginal Revenue is $MR = dR/dQ = 10 - 2Q$. At $Q = 2$, therefore, $MR = 6$. Thus, the recommended method is exactly correct.

to Total Revenue R, and the run is equal to Q. So dividing rise over run is the same as finding R/Q, which is the definition of AR.

In the lower panel of Figure 2.10 both AR and MR are falling throughout. Referring back to the upper panel, we can see that MR is falling because the slope of R declines as we move to the right. Note that the slope is initially positive, becomes zero at $Q = 5$ where the curve R reaches its maximum, and is negative thereafter. Similarly, AR must be falling throughout because the slope of the ray from the origin to points along the curve R falls steadily as we move to the right. Thus the slope of OR is less than the slope of OK. Note that at $Q = 10$ the line from the origin to R is flat. Its slope is zero, so AR is zero when the demand curve intersects the horizontal axis.

So long as Total Revenue R is rising as Q increases, it is obvious from Figure 2.10 that the slope along the R curve must be positive. Hence the Marginal Revenue MR, though declining as seen above, remains positive. When R is decreasing in the region past the hump in the upper diagram of Figure 2.10, however, the slope along the curve is negative, so in that region MR is not only declining but negative. Thus from the geometry we have the following propositions concerning the total and marginal functions:

PROPOSITION 2.1a: When a total magnitude is rising, the corresponding marginal magnitude is positive.

PROPOSITION 2.1b: When a total magnitude is falling, the corresponding marginal magnitude is negative.

But when R reaches a maximum (or a minimum), the function is neither increasing nor decreasing, that is, it is level. Drawing the obvious inference, we have:

PROPOSITION 2.1c: When a total magnitude reaches a maximum or a minimum, the corresponding marginal magnitude is zero.[7,8]

In the lower diagram in Figure 2.10 the geometry reveals several propositions concerning the average and marginal functions:

PROPOSITION 2.2a: When the average magnitude is falling, the marginal magnitude must lie below it.

Think of the average weight of people in a room. If someone walks in and the average weight falls, it must be that the *marginal* weight (the weight of the person who walked in) was less than the average weight. In Figure 2.10 each new unit lowers the Average Revenue (AR is always falling), hence the Marginal Revenue MR lies always below it.

[7] *Mathematical Footnote*: When $dR/dQ > 0$, the Total Revenue function R is increasing; when $dR/dQ < 0$, it is decreasing; when $dR/dQ = 0$, we have a stationary value of the function.

[8] Some technical qualifications should be made to these assertions. Not all minima or maxima are "flat." In the upper diagram of Figure 2.10, Total Revenue R has an interior maximum at $Q = 5$, where $MR = 0$. But it also has *minima* at $Q = 0$ and $Q = 10$ (where Revenue R is zero). But the curve is not flat at those points—that is, $MR \neq 0$. In this book we will be dealing almost always with flat minima or maxima, so that Proposition 2.1c holds.

What if the average magnitude is not falling but rising? Then we have the analogous proposition:

PROPOSITION 2.2b: When the average magnitude is rising, the marginal magnitude must lie above it.

And, of course, Propositions 2.2a and 2.2b together imply:

PROPOSITION 2.2c: When an average magnitude is neither rising nor falling (at a minimum or maximum), the marginal magnitude must be equal to it.[9]

[9] *Mathematical Footnote*: Let us verify Proposition 2.2a of the text, and specifically that *MR* is below *AR* when the latter is falling. For *AR* to be falling:

$$0 > \frac{d(AR)}{dQ} = \frac{d(R/Q)}{dQ} = \frac{Q(dR/dQ) - R}{Q^2}$$

This directly implies $dR/dQ < R/Q$, or $MR < AR$. Similar proofs for Proposition 2.2b and 2.2c can easily be shown.

EXAMPLE 2.8
Birds Do It! Bees Do It!

Critics of economic theory often argue that the reasoning required to solve optimization problems is too intricate for actual decision-making. It has been contended, for example, that business managers can hardly be expected to take account of anything as subtle as *marginal* concepts in deciding upon what price to charge or what output to produce.

Biologists, in contrast, have recently discovered that the decisions of animals can often be best interpreted in marginal terms. Consider a bird foraging for seeds or insects that are distributed in patches. The bird must decide when to leave its current patch and fly off to look for another. As it continues to exploit the current patch, food becomes sparser and sparser there—the marginal "revenue" (energy intake) the bird receives per unit of time spent in the patch is falling. But if the bird abandons its current patch, it must suffer an entire loss of energy intake in the dead time before it locates a fresh patch. Bioeconomic reasoning in this situation says that the bird should continue to exploit its current patch until the *marginal* "revenue" per unit of time spent there falls to equality with the *average* "revenue" it can attain elsewhere, allowing for the dead time between patches.[a]

Field studies have confirmed that foraging birds do indeed behave as if they can solve this economic problem. Under more controlled laboratory conditions, Richard Cowie[b] was able to study in more detail the foraging behavior of the great tit (*Parus major*). These birds were able to estimate quite precisely the marginal and average "revenue" (energy intake) of time spent in different patches of the environment.

And what the birds can do, the bees can too. C. M. Hodges and L. L. Wolfe[c] studied nectar consumption of bumblebees feeding on flowers containing, on average, 6.09 microliters of nectar. If the bees obeyed correct marginal principles, they calculated, a flower would be abandoned when its remaining nectar fell to 1.0 microliters. The actual measured amount of nectar left behind was 1.25 microliters, the difference of 0.24 being small enough to be attributed to sampling and measurement error.

[a] Eric L. Charnov, "Optimal Foraging, the Marginal Value Theorem," *Theoretical Population Biology*, v. 9 (April 1976).
[b] Richard J. Cowie, "Optimal Foraging in Great Tits (*Parus major*)," *Nature*, v. 268 (July 14, 1977).
[c] Clayton M. Hodges and Larry L. Wolfe, "Optimal Foraging in Bumblebees: Why Is Nectar Left Behind in Flowers?", *Behavioral Ecology and Sociobiology* (Spring 1981), p. 41.

The lower diagram of Figure 2.10, with its falling *AR* curve, illustrates Proposition 2.2a. To illustrate Propositions 2.2b and 2.2c, we need to look at average functions that have both rising and constant ranges. Such a function is shown in Figure 2.11. The upper diagram shows a firm's Total Cost curve *C*. The posi-

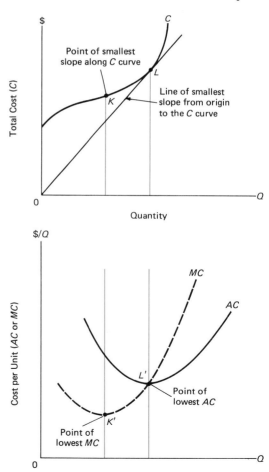

FIGURE 2.11 **Derivation of Average and Marginal Magnitudes from Total Function: Cost.** The lower diagram shows the average and marginal functions *AC* and *MC* derived from the Total Cost function *C* in the upper diagram. Where the slope along the Total Cost function is least, *MC* is at a minimum. Where the slope of the line drawn from the origin to the curve is least (tangent line in the upper diagram), *AC* is at a minimum. When *AC* is falling, *MC* lies below it; when *AC* is rising, *MC* lies above it.

tive vertical intercept of C reflects fixed costs (such as the rent on a building that must be paid even if nothing is produced).

To derive Marginal Cost MC from the Total Cost function shown, remember that MC is the slope of C. The slope along C in the upper diagram falls as we move to the right up to point K. After that C becomes steeper. Correspondingly, in the lower diagram MC falls until we reach K', then starts rising. Note that the minimum of MC is at K'.

To derive AC we use the rule that Average Cost at any output is given by the slope of a ray from the origin to the point on C at that output. As you move to the right along C, the slope of the ray out of the origin falls until you reach the point L. Then the slope rises as you move farther to the right. So, in the lower diagram, AC falls until we reach L', and rises after that. This means AC is minimized at L'. (Note that when $Q = 0$, the Average Cost $AC = C/Q$ must be infinite so long as there are any fixed costs.)

In the upper diagram, to the left of L a ray from the origin to C would be steeper than the slope along C itself. Since the slope of the ray is greater than the slope along C, Average Cost AC must be greater than MC in this range. This confirms Proposition 2.2a: When AC is falling, MC lies below it.

To the right of L, the ray from the origin to C is less steep than C itself, so AC is less than MC. This confirms Proposition 2.2b: When AC is rising, MC lies above it.

Finally, the ray from the origin to the point L along C has the same slope as C itself. This means that here $MC = AC$, and rule 2.2c is confirmed.

EXAMPLE 2.9
The Oil Entitlements Program

In the period 1973 to 1974 the Organization of Petroleum Exporting Countries (OPEC) was able to effect a startling increase in the world price of crude oil from about $2 to almost $12 per barrel (see "The OPEC," an example in Chapter 8). The U.S. government, concerned about its balance of payments, immediately tried to reduce oil imports. At the same time, United States policymakers wanted to eliminate "windfall" gains to domestic producers of crude oil. Unfortunately, the way chosen to achieve the second objective tended to defeat the first.[a]

To prevent domestic producers from reaping windfall gains, the U.S. government froze the price of domestic crude. This immediately caused a problem, because some refiners did and others did not have access to the limited supply of artificially cheap domestic crude. Again in the interests of "equity," the Entitlements Program was undertaken. The basic idea was that every refiner was entitled to buy, at the low frozen price, the nationwide average fraction of cheap domestic oil. This program forced those refiners having better access to cheap domestic crude to compensate those refiners who made more-than-average use of expensive imported crude. The unanticipated effect was to *encourage* rather than discourage imports.

From the point of view of the nation as a whole, the Marginal Cost of crude oil was a rising function, the highest-cost step being the imported crude at $12 per barrel. Had refiners been required to pay this full world price for imported crude, they would have had a strong incentive to reduce dependence upon OPEC supplies. But, under the Entitlements Program, each barrel imported entitled the importer to a great bargain: an equivalent amount of domestic crude at the artificially cheap frozen price. In effect, all refiners were "equitably" treated by being able to obtain crude at the nationwide *Average* Cost. But, as a result, no refiners were discouraged from using imported crude even though that source represented the highest *Marginal* Cost for the nation as a whole.[b]

[a] This is necessarily a very simplified discussion of the enormously complicated and ever-changing details of U.S. oil policy. In particular, the legal distinction between so-called "new domestic oil" and "old domestic oil" has been omitted here.

[b] Many discussions of the oil entitlements program are available. See, for example, C. E. Phelps and R. T. Smith, *Petroleum Regulation: The False Dilemma of Decontrol* (Santa Monica, Calif.: RAND Corporation, 1977).

The unintended effects of government policy illustrated in Example 2.9 stemmed from a failure to distinguish properly between average and marginal concepts. Confusion may sometimes exist between marginal and total concepts, as indicated below.

EXAMPLE 2.10
Taxes

The table here shows the personal income-tax schedule for single taxpayers in the tax year 1985. For any "Taxable Income"[a] bracket on the left-hand side of the table, the right-hand side shows the Total Tax at the bottom of the bracket and the Marginal Tax for increments of income within the bracket. In the $8,850 to $11,240 income bracket, for example, the Tax Due is stated as $870+16%. Therefore, $870 is the Total Tax for someone earning exactly $8,850, and $0.16 is the Marginal Tax per dollar of income thereafter (up to the top of the bracket).

The following fallacy is sometimes encountered. An employee is making an annual income of $8,850, at the top of the 15% Marginal Tax bracket, and paying a Total Tax of exactly $870. His employer offers him a raise of $100, which the worker refuses on the ground that it would put him in a higher tax bracket. The worker may think that in moving up to a higher *marginal* tax rate (16% instead of 15%) he will be taxed the extra 1% on his $8,850 in addition to the 16% he must pay on the $100 raise, ending up worse off. This is incorrect. The worker's additional tax would be only 16% of $100, or $16. Had he accepted the raise he would be better off by $100 − $16. His net loss of $84 is one of the costs of being unable to comprehend the marginal concept of economics.

TAXABLE INCOME		TAX DUE	
Over	But not over	Amount	Of excess over
$ 2,390	$ 3,540	$ 11%	$ 2,390
3,540	4,580	126.50 + 12%	3,540
4,580	6,760	251.30 + 14%	4,580
6,760	8,850	556.50 + 15%	6,760
8,850	11,240	870.00 + 16%	8,850
10,800	12,900	1,252.40 + 18%	11,240
13,430	15,610	1,646.60 + 20%	13,430
15,610	18,940	2,082.60 + 23%	15,610
18,940	24,460	2,848.50 + 26%	18,940
24,460	29,970	4,283.70 + 30%	24,460
29,970	35,490	5,936.70 + 34%	29,970
35,490	43,190	7,813.50 + 38%	35,490
43,190	57,550	10,739.50 + 42%	43,190
57,550	85,130	16,770.70 + 48%	57,550
85,130		30,009.10 + 50%	85,130

Source: Internal Revenue Service, Department of the Treasury, 1985 Federal Income Tax Forms, p. 40.

"Taxable Income" is earned income minus the exemptions, deductions, etc., provided in the tax law.

Marginal reasoning can even be applied to driving, as the following example shows.

EXAMPLE 2.11
Traffic Congestion

Each additional car on a freeway causes others to slow down. On uncongested freeways, an additional car will not slow traffic much, so the Total Flow (defined as the number of cars in a single lane passing a given point in one hour) increases. This means that the Marginal Flow (i.e., the change in traffic flow resulting from one more car per one-mile stretch of lane) is positive. Beyond a certain point, however, as additional cars enter the freeway the Marginal Flow may become negative owing to the slowing of traffic.

The table below represents a typical speed-density relationship for a single lane of U.S. four-lane freeways. Density is measured as the number of cars per one-mile section of one lane. You can see that as density rises from 38 to 39, traffic flow increases by 11. Thus Marginal Flow is 11. However, when density rises from 43 to 44, the additional congestion causes so much slowing that traffic flow actually falls by 3. This congestion phenomenon—the bane of traffic engineers—means that as more people try to use a freeway, fewer drivers will actually be able to use it.

Traffic Density, Speed, and Flow (one lane of a four-lane freeway)

Density (cars/mile)	Speed (miles/hour)	Total Flow (cars/hour)	Marginal Flow (cars/hour/car)
38	45.8	1,740	
			11
39	44.9	1,751	
			9
40	44.0	1,760	
			13
41	43.2	1,773	
			9
42	42.4	1,782	
			3
43	41.5	1,785	
			−3
44	40.5	1,782	
			−4
45	39.5	1,778	
			−2
46	38.5	1,776	
			−4
47	37.7	1,772	

Source: California Highway Research Board, *Highway Capacity Manual* (1965), pp. 49–50.

An implication of this marginal analysis is that it may be advisable to reduce access to the freeway at rush hours, for example, by a blinking traffic signal that feeds cars onto the road at a limited rate. Such a control will delay cars at the point of entry, but this may be warranted by the higher speed achieved once on the freeway.

□ SUMMARY OF CHAPTER 2

This chapter covers two main topics: (1) supply-demand analysis, and (2) the relations among total, average, and marginal magnitudes.

Supply-demand analysis is the main working tool for solving problems of *equilibrium*. Equilibrium price and quantity are determined by the intersection of a supply curve and a demand curve. Changes in demand or in supply are represented by shifts in the positions or shapes of one or both of these curves. An increase in demand (rightward shift of the demand curve) raises both equilibrium price and equilibrium quantity in the market; an increase in supply (rightward shift of the supply curve) raises equilibrium quantity but lowers equilibrium price. A tax on transactions will reduce the quantity exchanged; it raises the *gross price* (the price paid by buyers) but lowers the *net price* (price received by sellers).

Price ceilings or floors, if effective, prevent markets from reaching equilibrium. In such cases the quantity exchanged is always the *smaller* of the amounts demanded and supplied. (An exception: When government intervenes to *support* a price floor by buying up unsold quantities.)

The relations among total, average, and marginal magnitudes are essential for understanding problems of *optimization*. Regardless of the variable involved (whether revenue, or cost, or utility, or other), the marginal magnitude is positive, zero, or negative depending on whether the total magnitude is rising, level, or falling. And the marginal magnitude is below, equal to, or above the average magnitude depending on whether the latter is falling, level, or rising.

☐ QUESTIONS FOR CHAPTER 2

Mainly for Review

*R1. Which of the following are optimization problems? Which are equilibrium problems? [*Note:* You're not asked for the answers, but you might think about them.]
  a. As owner of a business, should I offer occasional special sales at reduced prices, or would I do better to stick with moderate prices year-round?
  b. If gold were discovered in Hawaii, would apartment rents rise on the island?
  c. If the punishment for murder were made more severe, would there be fewer murders?
  d. As a general, should I attack now when the enemy doesn't expect it—or wait for my reinforcements, even though the enemy will then be alerted?
  e. Over the year, why is the price of strawberries more variable than the price of potatoes?
  f. If my spouse and I have had three girl babies in a row, should we give up or try again for a boy?

R2. Supply-demand analysis is the key tool for which of the two main analytical techniques of economics? For what class of problem is the relation among total, average, and marginal quantities the key tool?

*R3. In what sense is price a "ratio of quantities"?

R4. Explain why market equilibrium is determined by the *intersection* of the supply curve and the demand curve.

R5. How does an "increase in demand" shift the demand curve? How does an "increase in supply" shift the supply curve? Do the effects upon equilibrium price and equilibrium quantity go in the same direction in the case of an increase in demand? In the case of an increase in supply?

*R6. In the analysis of a $T per unit tax described in the text, the demand curve was shifted downward by $T to find the new equilibrium. Would the same result have been achieved if instead the supply curve were shifted upward by $T? Explain.

*R7. In each of the following cases, state whether an excise tax will raise the (gross) price *paid* by consumers, or lower the (net) price *received* by sellers, or both.
  a. Supply curve upward-sloping, demand curve downward-sloping.
  b. Supply curve horizontal, demand curve downward-sloping.
  c. Supply curve vertical, demand curve downward-sloping.
  d. Supply curve vertical, demand curve horizontal.

R8. Suppose that an $S unit per *subsidy* upon sales of a particular commodity is put into effect. What would the implications be for the quantity exchanged? For the gross and the net price?

*The answers to starred questions appear at the end of the book.

*R9. What is a "meaningful" price ceiling or price floor? Why is it that meaningful floors and meaningful ceilings both *decrease* the quantity traded? What happens, however, if a price floor is "supported"?

R10. Starting from a given Total Revenue function R, show how the Average Revenue function AR is derived. Show how the Marginal Revenue function MR is derived.

R11. Starting from a given Total Cost function C, show how the Average Cost function AC and the Marginal Cost function MC are derived.

*R12. In terms of the general relations among total, average, and marginal quantities, which of the following statements are *necessarily* true, and which are not?
   a. When the total function is rising, the marginal function is rising.
   b. When the total function is rising, the marginal function is positive.
   c. When the total function is rising, the marginal function lies above it.
   d. When the marginal function is rising, the average function is also rising.
   e. When the average function is falling, the marginal function lies below it.
   f. When the marginal function is neither rising nor falling, the average function is constant.

FOR FURTHER THOUGHT AND DISCUSSION

*T1. For a particular commodity, suppose the supply curve is very steep (positively sloped, but almost vertical). Would a $T tax tend to have a relatively large or a relatively small effect upon the quantity exchanged in the market? Would there tend to be a relatively large or a relatively small effect upon the gross price paid by buyers? Upon the net price received by sellers? Explain in terms of the underlying economic meaning.

T2. Analyze correspondingly the case where the demand curve is very steep (negatively sloped, but almost vertical).

*T3. If the price of gasoline rises as a result of a reduction in petroleum supplies, what effect would you anticipate upon the price of automobiles? Upon the relative price of small, light cars versus large, heavy cars?

*T4. What assumptions underlie "the method of comparative statics"? Will these assumptions ever be met in the real world?

T5. During World War II in Great Britain, a ceiling was imposed to hold down the market price of bread. Explain why there was upward pressure upon the price of bread. What consequences of the upward pressure would you anticipate, given continuing enforcement of the ceiling? To help reduce this upward pressure, the British government took fresh bread off the market—all bread sold had to be at least one day old. Would you expect this regulation to achieve the desired effect?

*T6. In the year 302, the Roman emperor Diocletian "commanded that there should be cheapness." His edict declared:

> Unprincipled greed appears wherever our armies, following the command of the public weal, march, not only in villages and cities but also upon all highways, with the result that prices of foodstuffs mount not only fourfold and eightfold, but transcend all measure. Our law shall fix a measure and a limit to this greed.

Why do you think Diocletian found food prices higher wherever he marched with his armies? What result would you anticipate from the command that "there should be cheapness"?

*T7. Suppose that you were given a partial tabulation of a demand function, as indicated here. Estimate Marginal Revenue at $Q = 3$.

Quantity	Price
0	30
3	20
6	12

T8. The following is part of a price schedule, showing the quantity discounts offered by a printing shop. Does something peculiar happen as the size of your order approaches the upper limit in a given price range? Explain in terms of Marginal Revenue to the printing shop. Can you think of a more sensible way for the printing shop to offer quantity discounts?

Size of Your Order	Your Price ($)
1–10 units	.50 each
11–20 units	.40 each
21–50 units	.35 each
Over 50 units	.30 each

3

CORE CHAPTER

UTILITY AND PREFERENCE

In the previous chapter we emphasized the surprising fact that economists employ only two basic methods of analysis: *finding an optimum* and *finding an equilibrium*. Here in Part Two of the book we will apply the first of these methods to analyze the "optimum of the consumer"—finding the best combination of consumer goods.

3.A
THE DECISION PROBLEM OF THE INDIVIDUAL

People in a market economy face two main types of optimizing choices: (1) how to earn an income and (2) how to spend it. Part Two of this book considers how income is spent, taking the earning decision as given.

The economist describes the process of choosing the best decision as the *maximization of utility*. Utility as an index for preference will be the central topic of this chapter.

3.B
LAWS OF PREFERENCE

Scientific analysis always uses *theories* and *models* as simplified pictures of reality. Irrelevant details are stripped away to permit us to concentrate upon essentials.

The economist's simplified picture or *theory* of preference is based upon two axioms:

1. *Axiom of Comparison*: Any two distinct baskets *A* and *B* of commodities can be compared in preference by the individual. Each such comparison must lead to one of the three following results: (1) Basket *A* is preferred to basket *B*, or (2) *B* is preferred to *A*, or (3) *A* and *B* are indifferent.

The Axiom of Comparison is an idealization of reality, in that we suppose that the individual never says, "I simply can't compare *A* and *B*." Nor is he or she supposed ever to say, "Two-thirds of the time I prefer *A*, but the other one-third of the time I prefer *B*."[1]

2. *Axiom of Transitivity*: Consider any three baskets *A*, *B*, and *C*. If *A* is preferred to *B*, and *B* is preferred to *C*, then *A* must be preferred to *C*. Similarly, if *A* is indifferent to *B*, and *B* to *C*, then *A* is indifferent to *C*.

The Axiom of Transitivity is also an idealization, since violations of it no doubt take place. But if someone were to tell you, "I prefer apples to bananas and bananas to cherries," and were then to add, "but I'll always take cherries over apples!" you'd regard that person as rather odd.

[1] A number of economists have developed models of behavior that attempt to allow for limited ability to make comparisons. But as yet there is no general agreement as to how to deal with this complex problem.

EXAMPLE 3.1
Transitivity and Age

Arnold A. Weinstein administered a questionnaire asking people for preference rankings over ten commodity bundles, offered as pairs in random order. Among the bundles, all having a market value of about $3 at the time, were items such as: (1) $3 in cash; (2) the three latest Beatles 45-rpm phonograph records; (3) three men's clip-on bow ties, all with red polka dots, one brown, one blue, one gray; (4) a brush-stroke print of El Greco's "View of Toledo"; (5) a vanilla malted milk (two glasses) per day for ten days; and so forth.

The intent of the experiment was to detect possible intransitivities of preference over *triads* of offerings. An intransitivity would occur if, for example, a particular person chose cash over malted milk, malted milk over bow ties, but bow ties over cash. The great majority of the triads showed consistent transitive preferences. An interesting result obtained was that transitivity tended to increase with age, as indicated in the table.

Transitivity Experiment Results

Group	Transitive Responses (%)
52 children aged 9–12	79.2
36 teenagers aged 14–16	83.3
46 high-school seniors aged 17–18	88.0
18 mature adults (mostly teachers)	93.5

Source: Table compiled from data reported in Arnold A. Weinstein, "Transitivity of Preference: A Comparison among Age Groups," *Journal of Political Economy*, v. 76 (Mar./Apr. 1968), p. 310.

The experimenter's interpretation was that consistency (transitivity) in preference ordering is an acquired skill, hence more difficult for younger people to achieve. More arguably, he concluded that his results lent some support for placing legal restrictions upon the choices of young people.

As an alternative explanation, younger persons are more likely to engage in choices that seem inconsistent only because they are really *exploratory* in nature. "Don't knock it until you've tried it" is a dangerous maxim, but one with some appeal. If *all* possibilities are to be tried by actual consumption, some seeming intransitivities of choice are inevitable. Consider the three possibilities: cash, malted milk, and bow ties. If cash is chosen over malted milk and malted milk over bow ties, the only way to try out the bow ties is to choose them when offered next—even over cash. Since the Laws of Preference presume an already well-settled pattern of consumer desires, it is not surprising to find more violations of them among younger persons who are still exploring their own needs and desires.

The Axiom of Comparison and the Axiom of Transitivity taken together lead to the:

PROPOSITION OF RANK ORDERING OF PREFERENCES: *All conceivable baskets of commodities can be consistently ranked in order of preference by the individual.* This ranking is called "the preference function."

Exercise 3.1: John prefers the basket one beer + one taco to either two beers alone or two tacos alone—but as between the last two baskets, he would rather have the two beers. Do the facts just stated indicate that the Axiom of Comparison and the Axiom of Transitivity apply for John—at least among the three combinations described? If they do apply, what is his rank ordering of preferences?

Answer: As to the Axiom of Comparison, yes, the stated facts show that John can compare all three consumption baskets. As to the Axiom of Transitivity, the answer again is yes. Transitivity would tell us that if John prefers the mixed basket over two beers, and two beers over two tacos, he should prefer the mixed basket over two tacos—and, we are told, in fact he does. His rank ordering is, clearly: first the mixture, then the two beers, then the two tacos.

Suppose you are choosing between two commodities, X and Y. The amounts x and y are scaled[2] along the axes in Figure 3.1. Four possible baskets are represented by the points A, B, C, and D. The Laws of Preference tell us only two things about this situation: (1) that you are capable of ranking all four baskets; and (2) that if, for example, A is preferred to B and B to D, then A is preferred to D.

X and Y are called *goods* (as opposed to *bads* such as garbage and pollution) when more of each is preferred to less. Knowing that X and Y are goods, in the diagram A is the most preferred of the four points and D the least preferred, while B and C are intermediate.

DEFINITION: A *good* is a commodity for which more is preferred to less.

---

[2] Capital letters X and Y here designate the commodities; lowercase letters x and y indicate particular quantities of each.

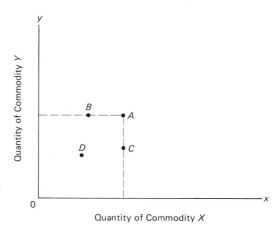

FIGURE 3.1 Alternative Consumption Baskets. Points *A*, *B*, *C*, and *D* represent different combinations or baskets of commodity *X* and commodity *Y*. If *X* and *Y* are both *goods*, then basket *A* is preferred to any of the other marked points.

3.C
UTILITY, PREFERENCE, AND RATIONAL CHOICE

The term "utility" was introduced by the British philosopher Jeremy Bentham. Bentham declared:

> Nature has placed mankind under the governance of two sovereign masters, *pain* and *pleasure*. . . . The *principle of utility* recognizes this subjection. . . . By the principle of utility is meant that principle which approves or disapproves of every action whatsoever, according to the tendency which it appears to have to augment or diminish the happiness of the party whose interest is in question.[3]

For Bentham, then, the maximization of utility simply means that human beings avoid pain and seek pleasure or happiness.

The modern economic theory of choice is not based upon the arguable premise that human goals are nothing but seeking pleasure and avoiding pain. Economists today simply say that individuals tend to make consistent choices: that the Laws of Preference of the preceding section, while undoubtedly idealized, are a good approximation of actual behavior. Since the Laws of Preference are really rules of rational choice, this reduces to the postulate of rationality discussed in Chapter 1.

What modern economists call "utility" reflects nothing more than rank ordering of preference. The statement "Basket *A* is preferred to basket *B*" and the statement "Basket *A* has higher utility than basket *B*" mean the same thing. They both lead to the empirical prediction: "Basket *A* will be chosen over basket *B*."

CONCLUSION: Utility is the variable whose relative magnitude indicates direction of preference. In finding the most preferred position, the individual maximizes utility.

---

[3] J. Bentham, *An Introduction to the Principles of Morals and Legislation* (1823 edition), Chap. 1.

UTILITY: CARDINAL OR ORDINAL MAGNITUDE?

Early economists had no doubt that utility could be measured like length or temperature. They would have regarded it as perfectly reasonable to employ a construction like the upper diagram of Figure 3.2 in which any individual's utility (scaled in "utils" according to the vertical column of numbers U in the diagram) is shown as a function of the quantity of a consumption good C. Some even believed it possible to add up these "util" numbers interpersonally: that 5 of John Doe's utils could be added to 7 of Richard Roe's so as to make a total of 12 utils for the pair. On this basis, it was thought that public policies—for example, how severely

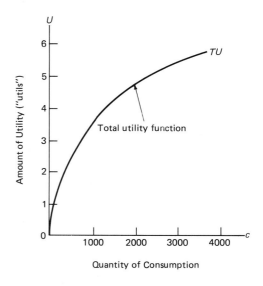

FIGURE 3.2 Cardinal Utility: Total and Marginal. The Total Utility curve *TU* in the upper diagram is a "cardinally measurable" utility function. Marginal Utility in the lower diagram can be derived from Total Utility, as explained in Chapter 2. As consumption rises, Total Utility increases but at a decreasing rate, and so Marginal Utility is positive but declining.

the state should punish crime, whether the rich should be taxed more or less heavily than the poor—could be determined by summing the utils of everyone involved. (This seems to be what Bentham meant in recommending public policies designed to achieve "the greatest good of the greatest number," a mystifying though noble-sounding expression.) Economists today generally believe that comparing or summing the utilities of different people is meaningless, and cannot be used as a basis for economic policy.

3.D.1 ☐ Cardinal versus Ordinal

What do we mean when we say that a variable is "quantitatively measurable"? We do not necessarily mean that there is only a *single* way of measuring or scaling it. Temperature is certainly quantitatively measurable, but there are alternative ways of doing so. For example, 32° Fahrenheit is 0° Celsius, and each degree up or down of Celsius corresponds to 1.8 degrees up or down of Fahrenheit. The two scales differ, but only in *zero point* and *unit interval*. Similarly, altitude could be measured from sea level or from the center of the earth (shift of zero-point) and in feet or meters (shift of unit interval). Both temperature and altitude are more technically called *cardinal* magnitudes, variables which have the following property: that, regardless of shift of zero-point and unit interval, the relative magnitudes of *differences* remain the same. In the case of altitude, for example, there's a bigger difference between the heights of the base and crest of Mount Everest than between the ground floor and roof of even the tallest building. This remains true whether we scale altitude in feet or in meters or whether we measure it from sea level or from the center of the earth.

In Figure 3.2 we are assuming that utility is cardinally measurable. As just indicated, it does not matter where we place the zero-point and what the unit interval is for U. What is really being asserted is that it is possible to compare the *relative magnitudes of utility differences*. For example, regardless of how we might shift the zero-point and the unit interval of the U scale along the vertical axis in the diagram, it remains true that moving from 1000 to 2000 consumption units yields a bigger utility improvement than moving from 2000 to 3000 units.[4]

Exercise 3.2: In the upper panel of Figure 3.2, verify that the utility difference between $c = 2000$ and $c = 1000$ remains greater than the utility difference between $c = 3000$ and $c = 2000$—even if an alternative "new-util" scale were adopted such that the "old-util" zero-point shown in the diagram is assigned the "new-util" value 10, and each unit up or down on the old scale would be 2 units on the new. (Thus the "new-util" measure U' is related to the "old-util" measure U by the formula $U' = 10 + 2U$.)

Answer: A visual estimate indicates that the "old-util" difference between $c = 2000$ and $c = 1000$ is around $4.8 - 3.6 = 1.2$, while the corresponding difference between $c = 3000$

---

[4] *Mathematical Footnote:* Two utility scales U and U' are cardinally equivalent if measurements along the two scales are related by the linear equation:

$$U' = a + bU \quad (\text{for } b > 0)$$

The constant a here represents the shift of zero-point, and the constant b the change in unit interval. Consider three quantities U_1, U_2, and U_3 along the U scale, where the difference $U_3 - U_2$ exceeds the difference $U_2 - U_1$. Then $U'_3 - U'_2$ also exceeds $U'_2 - U'_1$, as can be verified by direct substitutions. So the *ranking of differences* is unchanged for all cardinally equivalent scales.

and $c = 2000$ is about $5.4 - 4.8 = 0.6$. So the first utility difference is the larger, in fact about twice as big. On the "new-util" scale the first difference would be around $19.6 - 17.2 = 2.4$, while the second difference would be about $20.8 - 19.6 = 1.2$. Evidently, the first difference remains the larger, in fact still remains approximately twice as big.

Utility in the upper diagram of Figure 3.2 is a *total* function of consumption C. The corresponding *Marginal Utility* function, defined (as described in Chapter 2) as the slope or rate of change of the Total Utility function, is shown in the lower diagram of Figure 3.2. Since the slope of Total Utility is positive, Marginal Utility MU is positive. But since Total Utility in the upper diagram is increasing *at a decreasing rate*, the MU curve in the lower diagram declines as consumption increases. This property is called *diminishing Marginal Utility*.[5] In commonsense terms, we usually get more of a thrill from our first million than from our tenth.

[5] *Mathematical Footnote*: Since $U' = a + bU$, and b is positive, positive Marginal Utility according to the U scale ($dU/dc > 0$) implies positive Marginal Utility according to the U' scale ($dU'/dc = bdU/dc > 0$). Note that a change in zero-point a does not affect MU at all, and a change in unit interval b changes it only by the same positive multiplicative constant everywhere. *Diminishing* Marginal Utility according to the U scale ($d^2 U/dc^2 < 0$) similarly implies diminishing Marginal Utility according to the U' scale ($d^2 U'/dc^2 < 0$).

EXAMPLE 3.2
Does Money Buy Happiness?

While most economists do not believe that there is a valid cardinal scale for utilities, the economist Julian Simon disagrees. He has proposed to measure utility, among other ways, by asking people, "Are you happy?"[a] Psychologists have carried out questionnaire surveys asking people to classify themselves as very happy, pretty happy, or not too happy. The results in the table were obtained from a survey of residents in four small Illinois towns reported in 1965.

In interpreting these data, we still need a numerical utility (happiness) scale. Let us count "very happy" as $+1$, "pretty happy" as 0, and "not too happy" as

Income and Happiness

| | RESPONDENTS (%) | | | |
INCOME	Very Happy	Pretty Happy	Not Too Happy	Score*
Less than $3,000	14	55	31	−0.17
$ 3,000–3,999	21	63	16	+0.05
$ 4,000–4,999	27	61	12	+0.15
$ 5,000–5,999	26	64	10	+0.16
$ 6,000–6,999	24	65	10	+0.14
$ 7,000–7,999	30	60	10	+0.20
$ 8,000–9,999	29	63	7	+0.22
$10,000 or more	38	54	8	+0.30

*Method for computing score is described in text.
Source: N. M. Bradburn and D. Caplovitz, *Reports on Happiness* (Chicago: Aldine, 1965), p. 9.

−1. The average for each income group is then shown by the column headed "Score." If plotted, the score data would show (despite some irregularities) a picture not too different from Figure 3.2.

ª One of the other ways he suggests is to look at the suicide rate. See Julian L. Simon, "Interpersonal Welfare Comparison Can Be Made—And Used for Redistribution Decisions," *Kyklos*, v. 27 (1974).

EXAMPLE 3.3
The Weber-Fechner Law

The psychologists E. H. Weber (1846) and G. T. Fechner (1860) theorized that subjective ability to discriminate is a function of *proportionate* change in the magnitude of stimulus.

Applying this to utility, an individual's subjective satisfaction can be regarded as sensitive to *proportionate* changes of his or her income regarded as stimulus. For example, if an increase in income from $10,000 to $12,000 (i.e., by 20 percent) is valued as a "one-util" improvement, then a further 20 percent increase from $12,000 to $14,400 would add a second util and still another 20 percent increase from $14,400 to $17,280 would provide a third util. If this is the case, utility would be a *logarithmic* function of income. Such a function would accord with the general picture of Figure 3.2, and in particular would imply diminishing Marginal Utility.

Despite the discussions in the preceding examples, most modern economists do not believe that utility can be given a "cardinal" measure like length or temperature. If people can state that they prefer two million to one million—*but not by how much*—their utility is said to be an "ordinal" magnitude. Put another way, if Total Utility is an ordinal magnitude we cannot say anything about the *size* of Marginal Utility but we can still say whether MU is positive or negative. As will be seen in the next section, the concept of ordinal utility is all that is needed for the analysis of consumption decisions.

3.D.2 □ Utility of Commodity Baskets

Let us now consider the utility of *combinations* of goods. With just two goods X and Y, the utility function would be written $U(x,y)$.

Figure 3.3 pictures a possible cardinal $U(x,y)$. The quantities x and y are scaled along the horizontal axes. Utility in "utils" is measured in the upward direction, as the height above the base plane. When $x = x_1$ and $y = y_2$, for example, utility is the height TT'. If the quantity of Y is held constant at $y = y_1$, we can see how utility varies with x. This is shown by the curve PQR lying on the utility surface; note that Total Utility rises as x increases. If Y is held constant at $y = y_2$ instead, we get a similar curve STU; or if Y is held constant at $y = y_3$, we see the curve BVG. In each case the curves are rising (Total Utility is increasing) as x increases, and so Marginal Utility of X is positive. Similarly, the Marginal Utility of the other commodity Y remains positive as y increases.

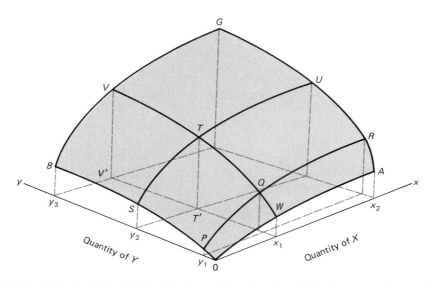

FIGURE 3.3   A Cardinal Total-Utility Function of Two Goods.   Utility is measured vertically, and the horizontal axes x and y represent quantities consumed of commodities X and Y. The curves OA, PR, SU, and BG along the surface show how Total Utility changes as x increases, holding y constant (at a different level for each curve). Similarly, the curves OB, WV, and AG show how Total Utility changes as y increases, holding x constant.

In terms of the satisfaction obtained, there is likely to be some interdependence between the goods. The Marginal Utility a consumer derives from another pound of butter normally depends also upon the current rate of consumption of other commodities like margarine (a "substitute") or bread (a "complement").[6] In the illustration here, the Marginal Utility of X at the point T (i.e., when $x = x_1$ and $y = y_2$), shown by the slope at point T along the curve STU, is not necessarily the same as the Marginal Utility of X at the point V (where $x = x_1$ but $y = y_3$), given by the slope at V along BVG. So we see that Marginal Utility of X may depend upon the quantity of Y, and vice versa.

Figure 3.4 is a different representation of the same utility function as Figure 3.3. The curves drawn here on the surface (CC, DD, and EE) are level curves or *contours* connecting points of equal altitude on the "utility hill"; in effect, they show slices into the hill at fixed heights. These contours therefore are *curves of constant utility*. They were first employed by Edgeworth (1881),[7] who called them *indifference curves*.

Suppose we looked at the contours of Figure 3.4 from above. We would see a picture like Figure 3.5. The contours remain visible, but we no longer see the hill itself. Geometrically, the vertical axis has been deleted so that we see the indifference curves in two dimensions. This step was taken by Pareto (1906).[8] Since X

[6] *Mathematical Footnote*: Where Utility $U(x, y)$ is a function of amounts consumed of both X and Y, the Marginal Utilities are defined as *partial derivatives*: $MU_x \equiv \partial U/\partial x$ and $MU_y \equiv \partial U/\partial y$. In general, each Marginal Utility will be a function of both x and y—that is, the cross-derivative $\partial^2 U/\partial x \partial y$ will not ordinarily be zero.

[7] Francis Y. Edgeworth, British economist, 1845–1926.

[8] Vilfredo Pareto, Italian economist and sociologist, 1848–1923.

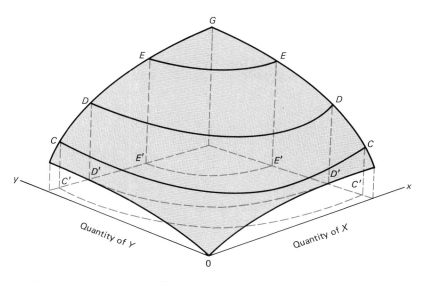

FIGURE 3.4 Cardinal Utility and Indifference Curves. The surface here is the same as in the preceding diagram, but the curves *along* the surface (*CC, DD, EE*) are contours connecting equal heights (levels of utility). The projections of these curves onto the base plane (*C'C', D'D', E'E'*) are the indifference curves.

and *Y* are both goods, "More is preferred to less." Hence the *preference directions* are north and east as indicated by the arrows on the diagram. Therefore, any indifference curve that can be reached moving up or to the right from another is "higher up" on the invisible utility hill. Apart from the indifference curves, the preference directions are all we need to know for evaluating how a consumer ranks baskets of goods. So long as we know which of two baskets is on the higher indifference curve, we know he or she will choose that one over the other.

The geometrical step of deleting the vertical dimension of Figure 3.4 corresponds to the shift from a *cardinal* to an *ordinal* utility concept. On an ordinal scale

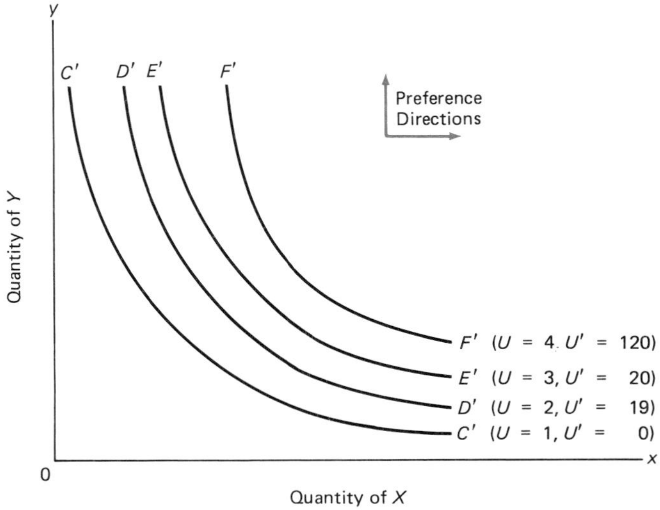

FIGURE 3.5 Indifference Curves and Preference Directions: Ordinal Utility. Here the cardinal scaling of utility has been stripped away, and we are left with the indifference curves. These indifference curves, together with the preference directions, give us all the information needed to rank alternative consumption baskets in terms of *ordinal* utility.

the only meaningful comparisons are whether two magnitudes are equal or, if not equal, how they are ranked (*direction* of difference.)[9] The two different cardinal preference scales U and U' attached to the indifference curves of Figure 3.5 are equivalent in the ordinal sense, since *they give the same answers as to which baskets are equal in utility* (lie along the same indifference curve) *and as to how baskets that are unequal in utility should be ranked* (preference directions).

3.E
CHARACTERISTICS OF INDIFFERENCE CURVES FOR GOODS

Assuming we are dealing only with *goods*, so that more is preferred to less, indifference curves have four crucial properties: (1) Indifference curves are negatively sloped; (2) indifference curves cannot intersect; (3) there is an indifference curve through each point in the graph; (4) indifference curves are "convex" (i.e., they bulge toward the origin).

1. *Negative slope*: For simplicity, assume there are only two goods X and Y. We plot their quantities as before in the x, y-plane (the *commodity space*). Since more is preferred to less, in Figure 3.6 all points northeast of any point like A are preferred to A, while A is preferred over all points to its southwest. It follows that all points *indifferent* to A must lie either to the southeast like points R or Q or to the northwest like points S or T. Thus an indifference curve passing through A cannot be within either the $+$ or $-$ region (relative to point A) shown in Figure 3.6. So any indifference curve must have a negative slope more or less like U_1 or U_2 in the diagram.[10]

2. *Nonintersection of indifference curves*: Employing Figure 3.6 again, suppose we were to tentatively assume that two indifference curves like U_1 and U_2 can actually intersect at point A as in the diagram. According to indifference curve U_1, points A and Q are indifferent. According to indifference curve U_2, points A and R are indifferent. By transitivity, Q and R must be indifferent. But R represents more of *both* goods than Q, so R and Q cannot be indifferent. Since the assumption that indifference curves intersect led to a contradiction, the assumption must be false. Indifference curves therefore cannot intersect.

[9] *Mathematical Footnote*: If the two utility scales are only ordinally equivalent, all we can say is that $U' = F(U)$ and $dU'/dU = F'(U)$, where $F'(U) > 0$. The positive derivative dU'/dU always preserves rankings of *magnitudes*: If $U_1 > U_2$, the associated $U_1' > U_2'$. Since the second derivative $d^2U'/dU^2 = F''(U)$ has indeterminate sign, however, the ranking of *differences* according to the U' scale need no longer correspond with their ranking on the U scale.

[10] *Mathematical Footnote*: In terms of calculus, along any indifference curve utility $U(x, y)$ is constant. So:

$$0 = dU \equiv \partial U/\partial x \, dx + \partial U/\partial y \, dy$$

Then the slope along the indifference curve is:

$$\left. \frac{dy}{dx} \right|_U = \frac{-\partial U/\partial x}{\partial U/\partial y}$$

Since $\partial U/\partial x$ and $\partial U/\partial y$ are both positive (X and Y are both *goods* with positive Marginal Utilities), the slope is negative.

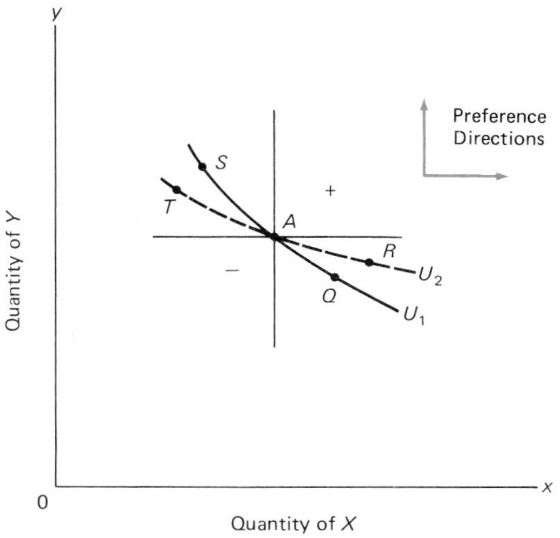

FIGURE 3.6 **Properties of Indifference Curves.** The preference directions indicate that every point in the + region is preferred to *A*, while *A* is preferred over every point in the − region. So any indifference curves through *A* must have negative slope. There can be only one indifference curve through *A*, since intersecting indifference curves violate transitivity of preference.

3. *Coverage of indifference curves*: The proposition that an indifference curve passes through each point in commodity space is called the coverage property. It follows that between any two indifference curves another can always be drawn. A corresponding property is possessed by the real number system. For example, between any two numbers like 17.4398 and 17.4399 we can always find another number like 17.43987 larger than the first and smaller than the second. The coverage property is equivalent to the Axiom of Comparison, which said that it is *always possible to compare* any baskets of commodities whatsoever. Hence, any basket must lie on some indifference curve. (Empirically, however, this is an idealization rather than a literal description of reality.[11])

4. *Indifference curves convex to origin*: In the two panels of Figure 3.7 we see the curvatures defined as "convex" and "concave" to the origin. The convex curve of Panel (a) represents the standard shape. In contrast with the previous three properties (negative slope, nonintersection, and coverage), *convexity cannot be proved from the postulates of rational choice*. Rather, it is based upon the well-established empirical principle of "diversity in consumption" (to be discussed in Chapter 4).

A commonsense justification for convexity is illustrated in Panel (a) of Figure 3.7. Suppose *X* stands for food and *Y* for entertainment.[12] At point *A* the person has plenty of entertainment but very little food. We would reasonably expect him to be willing to give up a lot of entertainment for only a little food. The diagram shows him as just willing to move from *A* to *B*, giving up (say) 3 units of entertain-

[11] Psychological experiments indicate that there is a minimum threshold below which sensations cannot be distinguished from one another. This suggests that indifference curves have some "width" in actuality, which would not fit very conveniently into our picture. But this is no more disturbing than the fact that Euclid's "lines" (straight curves with no breadth) cannot actually be observed in the world, since the best we can do in drawing a line leaves some crookedness and some breadth. In the interests of a more powerfully predictive theory, some economists have constructed models of choice that incorporate perception thresholds, but as yet there is no general agreement on this subject.

[12] Food and entertainment are aggregations, rather than simple commodities, but this does not affect the point at issue.

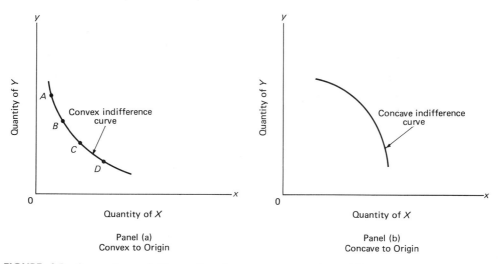

FIGURE 3.7 Convexity and Concavity. Between two goods, indifference curves must have negative slope. Curvature may be "convex to origin" as in Panel (a), or "concave to origin" as in Panel (b). The convex case is the normally observed situation, even though concavity would not necessarily violate the axioms of rational choice.

ment Y for just one unit of food X. Once he is at B his consumption is more diversified. Therefore he would not be quite as willing as before to give up entertainment for more food. In fact, he is barely willing to move from B to C, this time giving up only (say) 2 units of Y for 1 unit of X. Finally, from C to D, he is willing to give up only (say) 1 unit of his now scarce entertainment Y for 1 unit of food X. Convexity means, therefore, that the less you have of good X relative to good Y, the less you are willing to give up additional units of X for more of Y. Thus the picture of Panel (a) of Figure 3.7, and not of Panel (b), seems to fit our normal patterns of preference.

Exercise 3.3: (a) Someone claims that the two equations $xy = 100$ and $x + y = 20$ can both be valid indifference curves for an individual. Is this correct? (b) What about the curves corresponding to the equations $xy = 100$ and $xy = 200$?

Answer: (a) No, algebraically it may be determined that the curves corresponding to these two equations *intersect* at $x = 10$, $y = 10$. This violates indifference-curve property 2 of the text. (b) Because these curves never intersect, property 2 is satisfied. But we should also check the other properties. By algebra or by plotting, readers should be able to satisfy themselves that the curves are negatively sloped (property 1) and are convex toward the origin (property 4). So these two curves could both be valid indifference curves for some person.

Example 3.4 suggests something about the shape of parents' indifference curves between numbers of sons and daughters, regarded as "goods." (These goods happen to be of a kind ordinarily produced at home rather than purchased in the market, but how goods are acquired is quite apart from the preferences individuals might have.)

EXAMPLE 3.4
Preferences for Children: Number and Sex

In the table below, the two "goods" are girl children and boy children. As is typical for baskets of goods, parents seem to prefer diversity. The table shows that parents who had either all boys or all girls were more likely to have another child than parents with a mixture of boys and girls. For example, among two-child families with all boys or all girls, 56 percent of the parents had another child. But for the two-child families with one boy and one girl, only 51 percent had another. The difference means that the parents with one boy and one girl were relatively more satisfied and therefore less likely to try again.

This pattern of preferences means that parents' indifference curves—apart from the fact that fractional children are not possible!—are convex. With two children, for example, the combination $(1, 1)$ is preferred to (on a higher indifference curve than) either $(2, 0)$ or $(0, 2)$. This implies that parents' indifference curves bulge toward the origin, as in Panel (a) of Figure 3.7.

Families Who Had Another Child—By Number and Sex of Children

Number of Children	Number of Boys	Number of Families	Families Who Had Another Child (%)
2	2	35,674	0.56
	1	64,585	0.51
	0	31,607	0.56
3	3	10,431	0.47
	2	26,497	0.44
	1	24,897	0.45
	0	8,948	0.48
4	4	2,619	0.40
	3	8,260	0.40
	2	11,489	0.38
	1	7,527	0.40
	0	2,241	0.41

*Source:*1970 Census data reported in Yoram Ben-Porath and Finis Welch, *Do Sex Preferences Really Matter?* The RAND Corporation Paper Series, P-5560 (Dec. 1975), p. 7.

3.F
GOODS, BADS, AND NEUTERS

Not all commodities are *goods*. Consider pollution. Our society has to choose a combination of industrial production (a *good*) along with undesired by-products in the form of contamination of the environment (a *bad*).

One very important application of utility theory in recent years has been to the problem of *portfolio selection*, the balancing of an individual's wealth over assets like stocks, bonds, real estate, and so forth. Portfolio analysts construct utility functions that treat M, the *mean* asset return (average percent yield of the portfo-

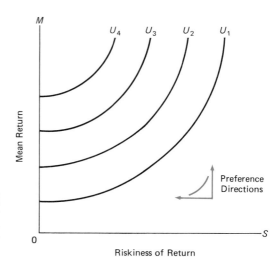

FIGURE 3.8 **Indifference Curves between a Good and a Bad.** Mean return M on assets is a good, but riskiness of return S is a "bad." The preference directions are therefore north and west, implying that the indifference curves have *positive* slopes.

lio) as a desired feature or good, while the *riskiness S* of the return enters as an undesired feature or bad. Figure 3.8 illustrates the indifference map of a typical investor. Note that the preference directions here are north and *west*. For the "good" M, more is preferred to less. But for the "bad" S, less is preferred to more. These preference directions imply that the indifference curves have *positive* slopes as shown in the diagram.

Our everyday experience also tells us that a commodity can be a good up to a point of satiation, and then become a bad beyond that point.

EXAMPLE 3.5
Ballpoint Pens and French Pastries

K. R. MacCrimmon and M. Toda[a] conducted an experimental study of indifference-curve patterns. The first choice offered was between money (which we may interpret here as the equivalent of a generalized consumption commodity) and ballpoint pens. The subjects' indifference-curve patterns all showed negative slope. The next choice offered was between money and French pastries, with the proviso that the pastries had to be actually eaten on the spot. Not surprisingly, French pastries became a bad after the first one or two; the subjects would eat more only if paid more money for doing so. Consequently, these indifference curves had normal negative slope only in the region marked as Zone 1 in Figure 3.9, west of the curve drawn through the lowest points of the successive indifference curves. In Zone 1 the preference directions are north and east as usual. In Zone 2, to the right of the dividing curve, French pastries have become a bad; the preference directions are north and west and the indifference curves take on a positive slope.

[a] Kenneth R. MacCrimmon and Maseo Toda, "The Experimental Determination of Indifference Curves," *Review of Economic Studies*, v. 37 (Oct. 1969).

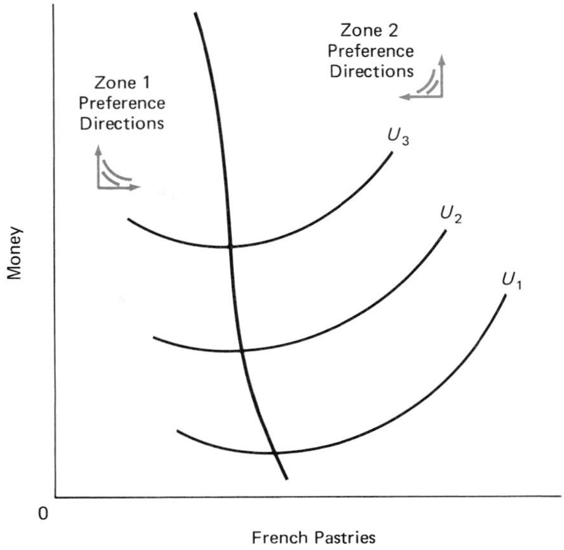

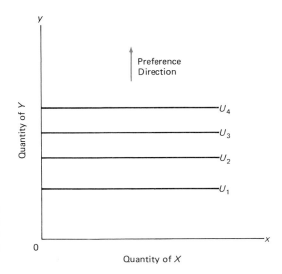

FIGURE 3.9 Satiation. In Zone 1 both commodities, money and French pastries, are goods, so that the indifference curves have negative slope. Zone 2 is the region of satiation for French pastries; in this region the preference directions are north and *west*, and the indifference curves have positive slope. In this region an individual would have to be paid to eat another pastry.

Sometimes the quantity of a commodity can leave a person entirely unaffected—he simply doesn't care whether he has more or less. We all perhaps know someone who feels that way about soap. (The quantity makes no difference, as he doesn't intend to wash anyway.) Such a commodity is called a neuter, neither adding to nor detracting from utility. Then the indifference-curve picture will be as in Figure 3.10.

Exercise 3.4: For each of the following algebraic utility functions, and assuming that x and y are always positive, indicate whether each commodity is a good, a bad, or a neuter: (a) $U = xy$. (b) $U = x/y$. (c) $U = 2xy/y$.

FIGURE 3.10 A Neuter Commodity. Here Y is a good, but X is a neuter commodity. The consumer does not care whether he has more or less of X. The only preference direction is north, and so the indifference curves are horizontal.

Answer: (a) Since utility U rises as x and y grow, both X and Y are goods. (b) Here U rises with x but falls as y increases, so X is a good while Y is a bad. (c) Note here that y cancels out, to leave the function simply $U = 2x$. So X is a good, but Y is a neuter (since utility does not depend at all upon y).

3.F.1 ☐ An Application: The Economics of Charity

The following observations, among others, can be made about charity: (1) Not everyone makes charitable contributions. (2) But some people do. (3) Those who give charity almost always give to persons poorer than themselves. The problem is to construct an indifference-curve picture or pictures consistent with these observations.

One approach is as follows. Figure 3.11 has axes "My Income" and "His Income." We are thinking solely of "my" preferences, so the feelings of the other individual are in no way involved in the picture. Imagine first that I am completely uninterested in whether he has any income or not. Then "His Income" is a neuter commodity for me; I do not care at all about movements north or south. This is the situation pictured in Panel (a) of Figure 3.11. Since "My Income" is surely a good for me, the only preference direction shown is *east*, and my indifference curves are vertical.

If my preferences were as pictured in Panel (a), would I give charity to the other person? If the initial situation were at E in Panel (a), I have 1000 units of income and he has zero. Suppose I could transfer income to him, on a one-for-one basis. In the diagram, this means that I could attain any point along the line EF. But any such movement from point E puts me on a lower indifference curve.

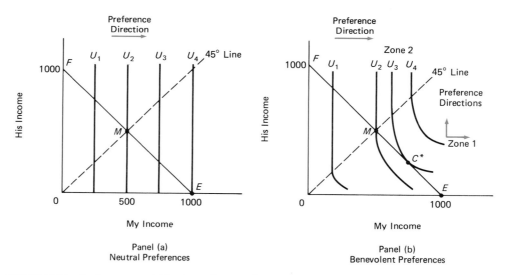

FIGURE 3.11 **Preference and Charity.** If my preferences are as pictured in Panel (a), "His Income" is a neuter commodity for me. Then I would never give charity. But if Panel (b) pictures my preferences, I may give charity, but only to people poorer than myself. ("His Income" is a good for me below the 45° line, but is a neuter commodity for me above the 45° line.)

So I would not give charity. Notice that I am in no way *malevolent* to the other individual here, but I am not *benevolent* either.

Panel (b) of Figure 3.11 is a more interesting case, because it pictures a degree of benevolence. But suppose that observation (3) above applies, that I am benevolent only to people poorer than myself. The positions where he is poorer than me are those lying *below the 45° line* (Zone 1 in the diagram). Only in Zone 1 am I benevolent, so that the indifference curves have their usual negative slopes. If my initial situation were at E, I would transfer just enough income to attain point C^*. (Why? Because C^* is a point on indifference curve U_3, my highest attainable level of utility.) If, on the other hand, my initial situation were at a point like M, any charity on my part *would make him richer than me* (would put me in Zone 2, above the 45° line. But I do not give charity under these circumstances, according to observation (3). Therefore, my indifference curves in this range must be vertical.

3.G
THE SOURCES AND CONTENT OF PREFERENCES

Why do people want some things and not others? Why are our desires for some goods easily satiated, for others not? Can anything be said about how preferences vary among people of different ages, with different ethnic origins, in different circumstances?

As indicated in Chapter 1, individuals' goals and preferences are taken as given in economics; their nature and formation are regarded as falling within the province of our sister social sciences. Yet in some cases the forces involved are clear enough. It is not hard to predict that iced drinks will be more popular in Georgia than in Alaska; that diapers are not a big merchandising item in retirement communities; that bagels sell better in Jewish neighborhoods, and soul food in Harlem. But what are the bases for these commonsense judgments? The economist who intends to apply his or her discipline should have some knowledge of the deeper forces determining preferences.

On a very primitive level, human beings as organisms normally favor (and so can be said to have preferences for) survival and comfort. We like to keep our skins intact, our body parts connected up nicely, and our blood temperatures not very far from 98.6° Fahrenheit. Physical considerations like these broadly explain the desires for food, for shelter, for protection against injury. But cultural and personal elements are clearly involved in whether these very general desires are translated, more specifically, into preferences for commodities like three-piece suits or Levi's, pizza pies or *pâté de foie gras*, split-level houses or mobile homes.

As people grow richer they can go beyond physiological needs and indulge their tastes for esthetics, for social distinction, for novelty. These nonmaterial "goods" therefore are more significant for the affluent than for the poor. If economics is to retain its validity for explaining behavior as overall wealth increases, it will increasingly have to address the question of these nonmaterial tastes and drives.

A very essential element in human society is the extent of help that individuals are willing to give one another, as in the charity behavior discussed above. One observation has already been made as to the nature of the "taste" for providing this kind of help: that people often give charity to those poorer than themselves, but only rarely to those richer than themselves. Another fact about the taste for helping others is even more obvious: that people are inclined to help their own children in preference to almost anyone else. This last fact suggests a biological evolutionary explanation. Organisms that choose to help their own offspring rather than others' offspring have tended to leave more descendants over the generations.[13]

The degree to which biology, or ethnic culture, or idiosyncracies of individual psychology determine the preferences of individuals remains an important topic that is only beginning to receive attention from economists.

□ SUMMARY OF CHAPTER 3

In finding his or her preferred consumption basket, the individual is said to maximize utility. We postulate that preferences follow two laws: (1) The Axiom of Comparison (a person can compare all possible pairs of consumption baskets) and (2) The Axiom of Transitivity (if someone prefers basket A to B, and B to C, then he or she will prefer A to C). These two laws together imply that the individual can *rank* all conceivable consumption baskets in order of preference.

If utility is quantifiable in the sense of being "cardinally" measurable, statements can be made about the shape of the Marginal Utility curve. But for most purposes in modern economics it suffices if utility is only "ordinally" measurable. If one basket is preferred to another we need only say that the utility of the former is greater—how much greater does not matter.

In choosing baskets of two (or more) commodities, cardinal utility would be represented by a quantifiable "utility hill." The ordinal utility interpretation lets us suppress the utility dimension and portray preferences in terms of *indifference curves*—contours connecting consumption baskets yielding equal utility—together with an indication of the *preference directions* (which way is up on the invisible utility hill). For a *good*, utility increases as the amount consumed increases. For a *bad*, utility decreases with the amount consumed. For a *neuter*, utility is unaffected by the amount consumed.

Indifference curves have three properties that follow from the laws of rational choice: negative slope, nonintersection, and coverage. There is also a fourth property, convexity to the origin, that is based upon the observation that individuals tend to diversify the commodities they consume.

□ QUESTIONS FOR CHAPTER 3

MAINLY FOR REVIEW

*R1. An individual is offered a choice between a ski trip to Aspen and four cases of Cutty Sark whiskey. Which of the following possible responses violate the laws of preference?

---

[13] W. D. Hamilton, "The Genetical Evolution of Social Behavior," *Journal of Theoretical Biology*, v. 7 (1964).

a. "They're so different, I can't choose."
b. "I don't care, you choose for me."
c. "Whichever I choose, I know I'll be sorry."

R2. Name a commodity that is a good for many people, but is a bad for you. Name a commodity which is a good for you, but only up to a point; after that it becomes a bad.

R3. Draw possible indifference maps between:
a. Two goods.
b. A good and a bad.
c. A good and a neuter.
d. A good and a commodity that is a good up to a point, but then becomes a bad.

*R4. What do modern economists mean by the term "utility"?

R5. Given a "cardinal" (quantitatively measurable) Total Utility function, show how a corresponding Marginal Utility function is derived.

*R6. What can be said about the Marginal Utility function if Total Utility is given only in "ordinal" terms?

R7. What are the four essential properties of indifference curves between two goods? Explain the justification for each of the four properties.

*R8. Which of the following requires only *ordinal* utility, which requires *cardinal* utility, and which requires *interpersonal comparability* of cardinal utilities?
a. Indifference curves can be drawn.
b. A Marginal Utility function can be drawn showing numerically how Total Utility changes as consumption of a good increases.
c. It can be determined which person is most desirous of receiving a particular prize.

FOR FURTHER THOUGHT AND DISCUSSION

*T1. Is it possible to give an exact meaning in utility terms to the expression "greatest good of the greatest number"?

T2. In suppressing the "cardinal" dimension of the utility hill so as to picture preferences only in terms of indifference curves, why is it necessary also to indicate the preference directions?

*T3. An example of an ordinal measure is the military rank system. A sergeant has more authority than a private, a lieutenant more than a sergeant, and so on. Give another example of an ordinal scale of magnitude.

T4. Since you probably would not want to eat pickles and ice cream together, does it follow that your indifference curves between these two goods are concave rather than convex?

*T5. For "His Income" and "My Income" regarded as goods, what shape for the indifference curves would correspond to the Golden Rule ("Love thy neighbor as thyself")?

*T6. In surveys of income and happiness, a puzzling discrepancy has been noted. While there is higher reported happiness with higher income *at a moment in time*, this conclusion does not seem to hold for comparisons *over time*. Even though wealth has risen over the years in the United States all across the scale so that both rich and poor have higher incomes than before, reports on happiness do not

---

* The answers to starred questions appear at the end of the book.

average higher than before.[14] The most natural explanation of this paradox is that happiness is more powerfully affected by *relative* income status than by absolute income. The poor are richer than before, but are still on the bottom of the heap and so still feel just as unhappy as before. How would you draw the preference map to picture this situation?

[14] See R. A. Easterlin, "Does Economic Growth Improve the Human Lot? Some Empirical Evidence," in P. David and M. Reder, eds., *Nations and Households in Economic Growth; Essays in Honor of M. Abramovitz* (New York: Academic Press, 1974).

4

CORE CHAPTER

CONSUMPTION AND DEMAND

In this chapter we get down to the specifics of the optimizing decision of the consumer. We will see how the individual's choices among consumption goods depend upon (1) his or her *preferences* (as discussed in the preceding chapter) together with (2) his or her *market opportunities*. Opportunities depend, in turn, upon the amount of income available and, of course, upon market prices. We will also learn how these considerations enable the economist to predict what will happen to consumption plans in the event of changes in people's tastes, in their incomes, or in the prices they face.

4.A
THE OPTIMUM OF THE CONSUMER[1]

4.A.1 □ The Geometry of Consumer Choice

The opportunities of a particular individual are pictured in Figure 4.1. The shaded triangle in the diagram shows all baskets of two goods, X and Y, that a consumer with given income can afford. This is called the *opportunity set*, or more specifically the *market opportunity set*.[2] The upper boundary of the opportunity set, the *budget line KL*, shows the baskets the person could purchase if he were to spend all his income on X and Y. (In this chapter we will usually assume that all income is spent, and none saved. This is not as unrealistic as it seems since saving is, in effect, spending for future consumption.)

As an illustrative example, suppose someone has income $I = \$100$ and faces the prices $P_x = \$2$ and $P_y = \$1$. Spending all his income on X, he could buy 50 units. This would put him at a point like L in the diagram. If he spent all his in-

---

[1] The optimum of the consumer is sometimes carelessly called, by textbook authors and others, the "equilibrium" of the consumer. Such wording blurs the distinction between the two key analytical concepts—equilibrium and optimum—that the student must learn to handle, each in its proper place. An *optimum* is the best possible choice for a decision-maker. An *equilibrium* represents simply a balance of forces as different individuals interact. Here we are dealing with an optimizing decision of a single consumer.

[2] Other types of consumption opportunity sets can also exist. Robinson Crusoe, for example, could be regarded as having an opportunity set in terms of the fish and bananas available on his island. Crusoe's consumption opportunity set would depend entirely upon his own isolated efforts, and in no way upon the possibility of transactions in markets.

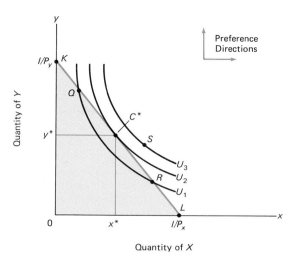

FIGURE 4.1 Optimum of the Consumer. The shaded region *OKL* represents the consumer's market opportunity set, bounded by the horizontal and vertical axes and by the budget line *KL*. The position of the budget line is determined by the individual's income *I* and the market prices P_x and P_y. The optimum is the point where *KL* touches the highest attainable indifference curve (point *C** on indifference curve U_2); this is the consumption basket yielding the greatest achievable utility.

come on Y he could afford 100 units, putting him at a point like K. He could also afford any combination of goods lying on the straight line between K and L. This line is his budget line or (as it is sometimes called) his "budget constraint."

Let us now look more systematically at the opportunity set and budget constraint.

The position of a person's budget line is determined by his or her income I and the market prices P_x and P_y. In a modern economy prices are generally quoted in money terms, but here we want to "pierce the veil" of money and deal only with the underlying *real* magnitudes. Consequently, we will think of prices and income as measured in terms of some standard real good called a "*numéraire*." Then P_x, the price of X, is the amount of the standard good that must be paid for a unit of X; P_y is the amount that must be paid for a unit of good Y; and income I is the amount available for spending, all three defined in units of the standard *numéraire* good.

Suppose that expenditures on commodities X and Y exactly exhaust income. Then we have the equation:

(4.1) $$P_x x + P_y y = I$$

This equation corresponds to the budget line KL in Figure 4.1, the northeast boundary of the shaded opportunity set. The horizontal intercept of the line equals I/P_x, which is the number of units of X bought if the individual were to spend all his income on commodity X. Similarly, the vertical intercept of the line is I/P_y, representing the number of units of Y obtained by spending all income on Y. Any mixed basket containing positive quantities of both X and Y will lie somewhere along the line between the two intercepts. The shaded opportunity set in Figure 4.1 is also bounded by the horizontal and vertical axes, since quantities purchased of X and of Y can never be negative.

Suppose we wanted to allow for the possibility of not spending all of one's income on the two goods X and Y. This would be expressed algebraically by the condition:

$$(4.1') \qquad\qquad P_x x + P_y y \leq I$$

The more general expression (4.1'), together with the non-negativity assumptions, describe the entire shaded opportunity region of Figure 4.1.

Since the preference directions are north and east, in a market situation only the budget line (the upper boundary of the opportunity set) is of concern to the consumer. (He can get to any position in the *interior* of the shaded region, starting from a point on the budget line, simply by throwing away some X or some Y or both. But since X and Y are goods, he would never want to do so.)[3]

We will frequently be referring to the *slope* of curves or lines drawn on x,y axes. The slope will be symbolized as $\Delta y/\Delta x$, the change in y per unit change in x along the curve. In the case of a line, the slope is constant throughout its length. The slope of the budget line specifically, symbolized $\Delta y/\Delta x|_I$, can be expressed as the ratio of the vertical intercept I/P_y to the horizontal intercept I/P_x.

$$(4.2) \qquad\qquad \left.\frac{\Delta y}{\Delta x}\right|_I = \frac{-I/P_y}{I/P_x} = -\frac{P_x}{P_y}$$

Along the budget line the slope is negative, since an *increase* in x is associated with a *decrease* of y.[4]

Algebraically, Equation (4.2) tells us that the slope of the budget line is equal to the negative of the price ratio P_x/P_y. If P_x were 10 and P_y were 2, giving up one unit of X would permit purchase of $10/2 = 5$ units of Y, so that -5 would be the slope of the budget line.

Exercise 4.1: Suppose prices are $P_x = 10$ and $P_y = 2$, while income is $I = 100$. (a) What is the equation of the budget line, and what are the intercepts on the two axes? What is the slope? (b) Describe what happens if, with I unchanged, the price P_x were to be cut in half. (c) Describe what happens if, with the original prices unchanged, income I were to double.

Answer: (a) The equation of the budget line $P_x x + P_y y = I$ becomes, after substituting the given numerical prices, $10x + 2y = 100$. The x-intercept is $100/10 = 10$ while the y-intercept is $100/2 = 50$. The slope is $-50/10 = -5$. (b) If P_x were cut in half, the new equation would be $5x + 2y = 100$. The x-intercept becomes 20 instead of 10, while the y-intercept is unchanged. So the budget line, after swinging around to the right, has a new, flatter slope equal to $-50/20 = -2\ 1/2$. (c) If, with the original prices, I were to double, then the equation becomes $10x + 2y = 200$. Both intercepts double. So the budget line retains the same slope as before: $-100/20 = -5$. In this case the line has moved outward, parallel to itself, doubling its distance from the origin in both the x-direction and the y-direction.

We have seen how the market opportunity set depends upon the commodity prices P_x and P_y (whose ratio determines the *slope* of the budget line), and upon in-

---

[3] Later on in the book we will be looking at *other* imposed constraints upon the consumption decision, such as rationing, which may force the individual into the interior of his market opportunity set.

[4] *Mathematical Footnote*: With the equation of the budget line as $P_x x + P_y y = I$, the slope is found as the derivative:

$$dy/dx|_I = -P_x/P_y$$

Since this derivative is a constant, it equals the ratio of finite increments $\Delta y/\Delta x|_I$ in Equation (4.2).

come I (whose magnitude determines the distances of the intercepts I/P_x and I/P_y from the origin and therefore the *position* of the budget line). With the data both as to preferences and opportunities in hand, we can proceed to the optimum of the consumer.

From inspection of Figure 4.1, it is evident that the consumer's most preferred position along the budget line KL (and, therefore, the best position attainable within the shaded market opportunity set) is the point C^*—the consumption combination containing x^* of commodity X and y^* of commodity Y. The highest indifference curve attainable, U_2, is the one just *tangent* to the budget line at C^*. The optimum must be at a tangency (if a tangency position exists, as discussed below). Nontangency points like Q and R in the diagram, both lying on indifference curve U_1 at the points where U_1 cuts the budget line, must necessarily be inferior in terms of preference to the tangency point C^* on indifference curve U_2. In terms of the invisible "utility hill" of Chapter 3, Q and R lie along a lower contour than C^*; the highest contour attainable is the one that can just barely be reached at the single tangency point C^*. It is true that a point like S on indifference curve U_3 would be even superior to C^*—but the combination S is not attainable since indifference curve U_3 never lies within the opportunity set.

> CONCLUSION: The optimum of the consumer is found at the tangency between the budget line and a convex indifference curve (if such a tangency exists).

In Chapter 3, we found that convexity of indifference curves did not follow from the pure logic of the Laws of Preference. We assume convexity because of the observed fact of "diversity in consumption." Imagine indifference curves that are concave instead of convex, as in Figure 4.2. The preference directions, shaded opportunity set, and budget line KL remain as in the previous diagram. Here there is again a tangency, the point T. But T is not the optimum. Indeed, T is the *least* preferred point on the budget line, lying as it does on U_2, the *lowest* indifference curve reached along KL. With the concave indifference curves shown here, the optimum is at C^{**}, where the consumer is spending all his income on Y. This

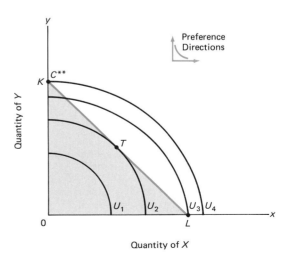

FIGURE 4.2 **Concave Indifference Curves and Corner Solution.** If the indifference curves are negatively sloped but concave to the origin, the best attainable position along the budget line KL must be a *corner solution*, along one or the other axis. In this case the optimum of the consumer is C^{**} on the y-axis, where indifference curve U_4 is reached.

is called a *corner solution*, as opposed to the *interior solution* C^* in Figure 4.1. But in the actual world people *diversify* their consumption, purchasing a mixture of many different commodities. Since concave indifference curves are inconsistent with diversified consumption, we can rule them out and always assume that indifference curves are convex.

It is true, however, that among the vast numbers of commodities that consumers recognize as goods, many are not actually purchased. The price is too high. You may enjoy the flavor of Beluga caviar, be able to afford at least a small quantity of it, and yet not be willing to pay the steep price required. Thus, you are at a corner solution with regard to the "caviar axis" of your utility function.

However, the fact that we see corner solutions for some goods is still consistent with convex indifference curves, as illustrated in Figure 4.3. Here, no tangency exists. The consumer's best position is the corner optimum C^{**} at point K. Convexity can thus explain both corner solutions and interior solutions.

> *GEOMETRICAL OPTIMUM PRINCIPLE:* The optimum of the consumer is the point on the budget line touching the highest attainable indifference curve. With convex indifference curves, the optimum may be an *interior solution* at a tangency between the budget line and the best attainable indifference curve. Or it may be a *corner solution* where the budget line reaches the highest attainable indifference curve along an axis.

4.A.2 ☐ Optimum of the Consumer: Analysis

This section moves beyond geometry to develop certain basic formulas that describe the optimum of the consumer.

If we were allowed to think in terms of "cardinal" preference, measured in utils, it would be meaningful to speak of the magnitude of Marginal Utility. Then

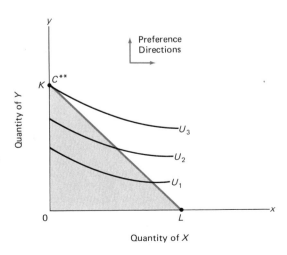

FIGURE 4.3 Convex Indifference Curves and Corner Solution. If indifference curves are convex to the origin, the optimum of the consumer may be either in the interior or at a corner. Here the optimum along the budget line *KL* is the corner solution *C*** on the *y*-axis.

the consumer will be at an (interior) optimum when the following Consumption Balance Equation is satisfied:[5]

(4.3) $$\frac{\text{Marginal Utility of } X}{\text{Price of } X} = \frac{\text{Marginal Utility of } Y}{\text{Price of } Y}$$

Consumption Balance Equation (Interior Solution)

The explanation is immediate: For any good, Marginal Utility divided by price is *Marginal Utility per dollar* spent on that commodity. At the optimum, the last dollar must yield equivalent satisfaction, whether spent on X or spent on Y. If this were not the case, the consumer would buy more of the commodity for which Marginal Utility per dollar was high, and less of the one whose Marginal Utility per dollar was low. He or she would continue this process until Marginal Utilities per dollar become equal over all commodities purchased.

What about the possibility of a corner solution? Suppose that, for some commodity like Beluga caviar, the Marginal Utility per dollar remains lower than that of the other commodity even when zero units of caviar are purchased. Then we would have a corner optimum, which can be expressed (letting X represent caviar) as the inequality:[6,7]

---

[5] *Mathematical Footnote*: In optimization problems in economics, a very neat technique called "the method of Lagrangian multipliers" is generally used. Specifically, in the present case we seek to maximize a cardinal utility function $U(x,y)$ subject to the constraint $P_x x + P_y y = I$ (where P_x, P_y, and I are constants). The technique involves setting up an artificial maximand in the following form:

$$\max_{(x,y,\lambda)} L = U(x,y) + \lambda(P_x x + P_y y - I)$$

The first-order conditions for a maximum are:

$$\partial L / \partial x = \partial U / \partial x + \lambda P_x = 0$$
$$\partial L / \partial y = \partial U / \partial y + \lambda P_y = 0$$
$$\partial L / \partial \lambda = P_x x + P_y y - I = 0$$

The first two conditions imply:

$$\frac{\partial U / \partial x}{P_x} = \frac{\partial U / \partial y}{P_y}$$

This is, of course, the Consumption Balance Equation (4.3). The technique works because in taking the partial derivative with respect to λ we obtain $P_x x + P_y y - I = 0$. This guarantees that the constraint condition (the budget equation) is always met, and also assures that the maximum of the artificial variable L is the same as the desired maximum of U. (The second-order conditions for a maximum are omitted here.)

[6] If there were many commodities, there might be corner solutions as between some pairs of goods and interior solutions for others. In the case of just three goods, the solution might take the form:

$$\frac{MU_x(x = 0)}{P_x} < \frac{MU_y(y > 0)}{P_y} = \frac{MU_z(z > 0)}{P_z}$$

Here positive amounts of commodities Y and Z, but not of commodity X, are being purchased.

[7] *Mathematical Footnote*: Since a corner solution is generally not at a tangency, calculus techniques involving equality of derivatives are not applicable; the optimum is not at a point where the indifference-curve slope equals the budget-line slope.

$$(4.3') \qquad \frac{MU_x \text{ (when } x = 0)}{P_x} < \frac{MU_y \text{ (when } y > 0)}{P_y}$$

So, at the optimum of the consumer either the Consumption Balance Equation (for an interior solution) or the Consumption Balance Inequality (for a corner solution) will be applicable. In addition, the consumer will also have to meet the budget-line condition (4.1) that constrains expenditure to equal income.

Exercise 4.2: Suppose that commodity X is bread, and commodity Y is wine. Imagine that the Marginal Utility of bread, MU_x, is given algebraically by the expression $MU_x = 40 - 5x$. Similarly, let $MU_y = 30 - y$. [Note the special assumption that MU_x depends only on the quantity x, and MU on the quantity y. This property, called "absence of complementarity," will be discussed shortly below.] (a) Let the prices be $P_x = 5$ and $P_y = 1$, and the consumer's income be $I = 40$. Find the optimum of the consumer. (b) What if $I = 10$?

Answer: (a) The budget equation (4.1) is $5x + y = 40$. Trying first for an interior solution, the Consumption Balance Equation is:

$$\frac{40 - 5x}{5} = \frac{30 - y}{1}$$

Solving the two equations simultaneously, we obtain $x^* = 3$, $y^* = 25$ (verifying that there is indeed an interior solution). (b) The budget equation here is $5x + y = 10$. Solving simultaneously with the Consumption Balance Equation we obtain $x^* = -2$, $y^* = 20$, which is impossible. So there is no interior solution. The correct corner solution is $x^{**} = 0$, $y^{**} = 10$.

This is very direct and simple. But, as we saw in Chapter 3, it is only with "cardinal" utility that quantitative measurement of Marginal Utility is possible. (With "ordinal" utility, we can do no more than determine when Marginal Utility is positive, zero, or negative.) The next step is to rework the solution without using measurable Marginal Utility.

Think now of the ratio at which the individual is *just willing to substitute* a small amount of Y for a small amount of X in his consumption basket. This ratio is called the Marginal Rate of Substitution in Consumption, denoted MRS_C. The expression "just willing to substitute Y for X" means the same as "a substitution of Y for X that leaves the consumer indifferent." So MRS_C corresponds geometrically to the slope of the indifference curve (in absolute value). Mathematically, we can write:

$$MRS_C \equiv - \left. \frac{\Delta y}{\Delta x} \right|_U$$

(Since the indifference-curve slope is negative, it has to be preceded by a minus sign to have a positive value for MRS_C.)[8]

---

[8] *Mathematical Footnote*: In terms of derivatives:

$$MRS_C \equiv -dy/dx \,|_U$$

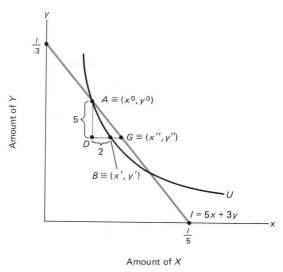

FIGURE 4.4 **Marginal Rate of Substitution in Consumption (MRS_C) and Marginal Rate of Substitution in Exchange (MRS_E).** MRS_C at point A is the absolute value of the slope of indifference curve U at that point. It is approximated by the ratio $AD/DB = 5/2$ in the diagram. MRS_E, which is also the price ratio P_x/P_y, is the constant absolute slope along the budget line. In the diagram it is given by the ratio $AD/DG = 5/3$. The inequality of MRS_C and MRS_E shows that A cannot be an optimum for the consumer.

Consider Figure 4.4. At position A the individual is holding the basket $(3, 15)$. He is contemplating a small move to position B representing the basket $(5, 10)$. Evidently, baskets A and B are indifferent for him, both being on indifference curve U. As the triangle ADB indicates, the ratio at which he is just willing to substitute small amounts of good X for good Y is 5:2, and this is approximately the numerical slope of his indifference curve U in this range. (The smaller the move considered, the better will the approximation be.)

We now know the ratio at which the consumer is *willing* to substitute Y for X in his consumption basket. The next question is, at what ratio is he *able to trade* in the market? This second ratio is called the Marginal Rate of Substitution in Exchange, denoted MRS_E, and is simply the price ratio: $MRS_E \equiv P_x/P_y$. In Figure 4.4, the assumed prices are $P_x = 5$ and $P_y = 3$. In other words, the individual is *able* to exchange 5 units of Y in the market for 3 units of X. This consumer is in a happy position. He is willing to give up 5 units of Y for just 2 units of X, but the market will give him 3 units of X for 5 units of Y. Geometrically, he is willing to move from A to B but his market opportunities permit a move to G, on a higher indifference curve. He will obviously make the trade.

EXAMPLE 4.1
Prisoners of War: Tea versus Coffee

The economist R.A. Radford had the unfortunate opportunity of studying, from the inside, social behavior in prisoner-of-war camps in Germany and Italy during World War II. He found that highly active economies functioned in these camps, particularly under the relatively "favorable" conditions that prevailed in the earlier war years.

Cigarettes served generally as the *numéraire* (or standard good) in terms of which prices were quoted. Coffee might go for about 2 cigarettes per cup, a shirt might cost 80 cigarettes, washing service 2 cigarettes per garment, and so on.

In the camp section holding English prisoners, tea was definitely preferred to coffee—and the reverse in the French section. A regular smuggling trade permitted prisoners in each section to adjust their consumption choices to the price ratio reflecting the overall supply-demand balance in the camp as a whole.[a]

> COMMENT: The two panels of Figure 4.5 illustrate the situations of typical English and French prisoners. In both camp sections prices were quoted, in cigarettes, for coffee (P_c) and for tea (P_t). The efficient smuggling trade between sections ruled out disparities between the prices in the two sections. Therefore, the Marginal Rate of Substitution in Exchange, $MRS_E = P_c/P_t$, was the same for both groups of prisoners. But for the English prisoners, the tangency point C^*, where $MRS_C = MRS_E$, was well over toward the tea axis, while for the French prisoners the optimum lay in the opposite direction, toward the coffee axis.

[a] R. A. Radford, "The Economic Organisation of a P.O.W. Camp," *Economica*, v. 12 (1945). In his enforced period of stay Radford made many other striking observations, some of which will be mentioned later in the text.

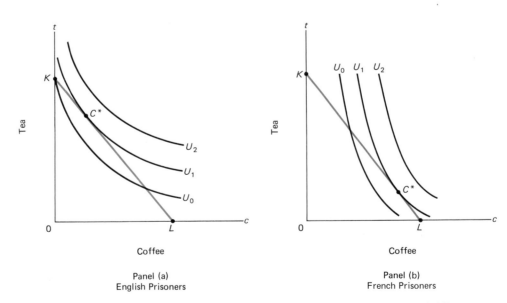

Panel (a)
English Prisoners

Panel (b)
French Prisoners

FIGURE 4.5 Coffee versus Tea in a P.O.W. Camp.   English and French P.O.W.s had different tastes for tea relative to coffee. An efficient smuggling system equalized the price ratio P_c/P_t, so both groups of prisoners faced the same MRS_E. For the French prisoners, the optimum C^* lay toward the coffee axis; for the English prisoners, toward the tea axis.

PART 2   PREFERENCE, CONSUMPTION, AND DEMAND

Summarizing the above discussion, in the case of an interior solution (positive consumption of both commodities), the consumer cannot be at an optimum position unless the rate at which he is *willing* to make small substitutions in his consumption bundle (MRS_C) equals the rate at which he *can* make trades in the market (MRS_E).

Mathematically, we can express this as the Substitution Equivalence Equation, which must hold for the consumer to be at an interior optimum:

$$(4.4) \qquad MRS_C = MRS_E \quad \text{or} \quad -\left.\frac{\Delta y}{\Delta x}\right|_U = \frac{P_x}{P_y} \qquad \begin{array}{c}\text{Substitution}\\ \text{Equivalence}\\ \text{Equation}\\ \text{(Interior Solution)}\end{array}$$

What about corner solutions? The corresponding condition is the Substitution Equivalence *Inequality*, which must take one or the other of the two following forms:

$$(4.4') \qquad \begin{array}{cc} MRS_C > MRS_E & \text{when} \quad y = 0\\ & \text{or}\\ MRS_C < MRS_E & \text{when} \quad x = 0 \end{array} \qquad \begin{array}{c}\text{Substitution}\\ \text{Equivalence}\\ \text{Inequality}\\ \text{(Corner Solutions)}\end{array}$$

[*Question*: Which of the inequalities holds for the corner solution in Figure 4.3?]

We can sum up as follows:

ANALYTICAL OPTIMUM PRINCIPLE: If the optimum of the consumer is at an interior solution, with positive amounts of both commodities being purchased, then: (1) the consumer must be spending all his income (i.e., he must be on his budget line) and (2) his Marginal Rate of Substitution in Consumption (MRS_C) must equal the Marginal Rate of Substitution in Exchange (MRS_E, or the price ratio P_x/P_y). These conditions correspond to the geometrical tangency of the budget line and indifference curve. If no tangency exists, then MRS_C and MRS_E cannot be set equal. They are brought as near to equality as possible by going to a corner solution, reducing consumption of one or the other commodity to zero.

One important implication of this analysis is that, despite differences of tastes, *on the margin* at an interior solution everyone places the same relative values upon the two goods (has the same MRS_C). In our prisoner-of-war example, French prisoners preferred coffee and English prisoners preferred tea. Nevertheless, once each group had adapted to the ruling prices, a French prisoner was no more willing than an English prisoner to give up a unit of tea for coffee. Thus, even though utility is "subjective," as a result of trade the "objective" price ratio between two goods in the market measures the *marginal* preference ratio for all the individuals actually consuming both goods.

We will digress here to examine the following question: How is it that the Substitution Equivalence Equation (4.4), while in effect doing the same work as the Consumption Balance Equation (4.3), allows us to dispense with any notion of cardinal utility?

First, by transposing we can rewrite (4.3) as:

(4.3a)
$$\frac{MU_x}{MU_y} = \frac{P_x}{P_y}$$

But (for small changes Δx and Δy) the Marginal Utility of X can be written $\Delta U/\Delta x$ and, similarly, MU_y is $\Delta U/\Delta y$. Substituting in the equation above, ΔU cancels out, proving that we do not need any cardinal measure of utility to find the optimum of the consumer.

If we like, however, we can think of MRS_C as a ratio of Marginal Utilities:

(4.5)
$$MRS_C \equiv \left| \frac{\Delta y}{\Delta x} \right| \equiv \frac{\Delta U/\Delta x}{\Delta U/\Delta y} \equiv \frac{MU_x}{MU_y}$$

Suppose, for example, that $MU_x/MU_y = 2$. This says that, in cardinal utility units, the individual gets twice as many utils from an extra unit of X as from an extra unit of Y. So the person would be *just willing* to make a small substitution of 2 units of Y for 1 unit of X. Thus the ratio of Marginal Utilities, 2, is numerically equal to MRS_C, the Marginal Rate of Substitution in Consumption.)[9]

Exercise 4.3: An individual has $MU_x = 40 - 5x$, and $MU_y = 20 - 3y$. If $I = 20$, $P_x = 5$, and $P_y = 1$, find the optimum of the consumer using the concept of the Marginal Rate of Substitution in Consumption (MRS_C).

Answer: Interpreting MRS_C as a ratio of marginal utilities, we can write:

$$MRS_C = \frac{40 - 5x}{20 - 3y}$$

The two equations that hold at an interior optimum are: $P_x x + P_y y = I$ and $MRS_C = P_x/P_y$. Inserting the given values, these become $5x + y = 20$ and $(40 - 5x)/(20 - 3y) = 5$. Solving simultaneously we get $x^* = 3$, $y^* = 5$. [Note that the answer here merely reinterprets the solution of Exercise 4.2.]

The fact that the indifference curve must be convex as in Figure 4.1 rather than concave as in Figure 4.2 means that the absolute value of the indifference-curve slope, or MRS_C, must be numerically decreasing moving along the indiffer-

---

[9] *Mathematical Footnote*: Along an indifference curve,

$$0 = dU \equiv \partial U/\partial x \, dx + \partial U/\partial y \, dy$$

Then:

$$-dy/dx \,|_U \equiv \frac{\partial U/\partial x}{\partial U/\partial y}$$

That is, MRS_C equals the ratio of the Marginal Utilities of X and Y.

ence curve to the right. That is, *decreasing Marginal Rate of Substitution in Consumption* is needed to guarantee that the Substitution Equivalence Equation (4.4) really determines the consumer's optimum.[10]

4.B
COMPLEMENTS AND SUBSTITUTES

Certain commodities like bread and butter, shoes and socks, tennis racquets and tennis balls, go well together and tend to be consumed jointly. Having more of one raises the desirability of the other. Such pairs of goods are called *complements*, and are said to exhibit positive complementarity. Other commodity pairs, like butter and margarine, brown shoes and black shoes, tennis racquets and badminton racquets, go poorly together and tend to be used to the exclusion of one another. Such pairs are called *substitutes* or *anticomplements*, and are said to exhibit strong substitutability or negative complementarity. Pairs of goods that are unrelated in people's preference patterns are said to be *independent* in consumption, or to exhibit zero complementarity.

Consider two commodities that consumers regard as *perfect substitutes*. A person might be completely indifferent between 2 nickels and 1 dime, 200 nickels and 100 dimes, or 2000 nickels and 1000 dimes. Then the typical preference map will have the appearance of Panel (a) of Figure 4.6: all the indifference curves will be parallel straight lines. For two goods that are close but not perfect substitutes, the indifference curves would be nearly linear but would show a slight degree of normally convex curvature, as in Panel (b) of Figure 4.6. For close substitutes, we can predict that a small change in relative prices will cause large changes in relative consumption. For two varieties of apples, the steep budget line SS' (high ratio of Macintosh price P_M to Jonathan price P_J) leads to an optimum solution S^* well over toward the northwest (mostly Jonathans are purchased). But the only slightly flatter budget line FF' (lower ratio P_M/P_J) is associated with a drastically different solution F^* toward the southeast (mostly Macintoshes are consumed). [*Query*: Will it be the case that, for perfect substitutes, the individual will almost always be at a *corner* solution—buying one good to the absolute exclusion of the other?]

The extreme opposite case is *perfect complementarity*. Here some fixed ratio of quantities (such as one left shoe for each right shoe) is of interest to the consumer. If this ratio is departed from, the additional units of whichever commodity is in excess are completely useless. Panel (a) of Figure 4.7 shows the right-angled indifference curves implied by perfect complementarity; the slope of the dashed line through the "elbows" represents the desired ratio of the two commodities. For two goods that are close complements (but not perfect), the indifference map would be as in Panel (b) of Figure 4.7. Other examples of highly complementary pairs are bacon and eggs, electricity and appliances, highways and automobiles. For complements, large changes in price ratios will lead to only small shifts in relative quantities purchased. As can be seen in Panel (b) of Figure 4.7, along the steeper budget line SS' (representing a high ratio of electricity price to price of

---

[10] *Mathematical Footnote*: We are dealing here with the *second-order* conditions for a maximum. The condition for indifference-curve convexity is $d(MRS_C)/dx < 0$.

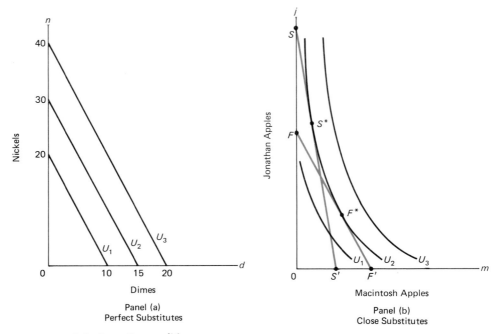

FIGURE 4.6 Substitute Commodities. The parallel straight-line indifference curves of Panel (a) indicate that the two commodities (nickels and dimes) are perfect substitutes. If the price ratio in the market, represented by the budget-line slope $-P_d/P_n$, diverges from the indifference-curve slope, the consumer will go to a corner solution. If $P_d/P_n > 2$, the consumer will purchase only nickels (corner solution along n-axis); if $P_d/P_n < 2$, only dimes (corner solution along d-axis). In Panel (b) the indifference curves have a slight degree of normal convex curvature, indicating that the two commodities (Macintosh apples and Jonathan apples) are good though not perfect substitutes. A relatively small change in the price ratio (from slope SS' to FF') would then tend to generate a relatively large change in the quantity ratio (from S^* to F^*), but not a total switch from one to the other.

appliances, P_e/P_a) the tangency solution S^* diverges very little from the optimum F^* along the flatter budget line FF' (low price ratio).[11]

[11] *Mathematical Footnote*: The most commonly used measure of substitutability is called the *elasticity of substitution* (symbolized as σ). The rationale underlying this measure can be indicated as follows. Along any indifference curve, the degree of curvature can be expressed as the rate of change of the absolute indifference-curve slope (of the Marginal Rate of Substitution in Consumption, MRS_C) as y/x varies. Thus, curvature can be represented as $d(MRS_C)/d(y/x)$, remembering that $MRS_C \equiv -dy/dx\rceil_U$. But as the degree of substitutability is inversely related to the curvature of the indifference curves (substitutability being greater the closer these curves approach linearity), we are interested in the reciprocal derivative $d(y/x)/d(MRS_C)$. The final step is, as in all elasticity measures, to deal with *proportionate* rather than absolute changes, in both numerator and denominator. The result becomes:

$$\sigma \equiv \frac{d(y/x)}{(y/x)} \bigg/ \frac{d(MRS_C)}{MRS_C}$$

Using the condition that at the consumer's optimum $MRS_C = P_x/P_y$, it can be verified that, if σ is large, then a small change in P_x/P_y will be associated with a large change in y/x along a given indifference curve.

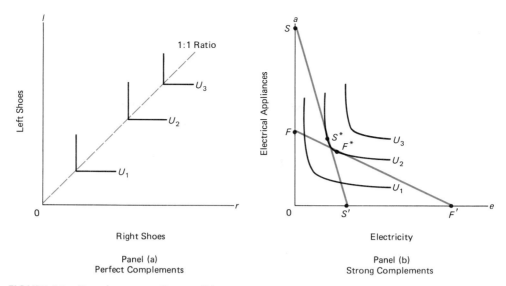

| Panel (a) | Panel (b) |
| Perfect Complements | Strong Complements |

FIGURE 4.7 Complementary Commodities. The right-angled indifference curves of Panel (a) indicate that the two commodities (right shoes and left shoes) are perfect complements. A change in price ratio will have no effect upon the quantity ratio chosen, which will always be 1:1 at the best attainable "elbow" point. In Panel (b) the indifference curves are nearly but not quite right-angled: the commodities (electricity and electrical appliances) are strong though not perfect complements. Here a relatively large change in the price ratio (from slope SS' to FF') will bring about only a relatively small change in the quantity ratio (from S^* to F^*).

Exercise 4.4: Suppose that for two commodities X and Y (as usual, think of Y as plotted on the vertical axis), the Marginal Rate of Substitution in Consumption is $MRS_C = y/x$. For another commodity pair F and G (think of G as on the vertical axis), $MRS_C = (g/f)^2$. Which pair are better complements (poorer substitutes)?

Answer: Plotting a few points, we can determine easily that the F, G indifference curves are more tightly "curled" than the X, Y indifference curves. Thus, the F, G pair are better complements.

EXAMPLE 4.2
Rats

A team of psychologists and economists investigated the consumption choices of rats in response to changes in "price ratios" of desired goods.[a]

In the first experiment, unlimited amounts of water and rat chow were provided, but there were two other commodities—root beer and Collins mix—that each animal could obtain only by pressing one of two levers. The total number of allowed lever presses per day was held fixed as the rat's "income." The number of presses needed per milliliter of fluid received was the "price." The price

[a] J. H. Kagel, H. Rachlin, L. Green, R. C. Battalio, R. L. Basmann, and W. R. Klemm, "Experimental Studies of Consumer Demand Behavior Using Laboratory Animals," *Economic Inquiry*, v. 13 (Mar. 1975).

ratio was varied by increasing one price and simultaneously reducing the other, so as to hold "real income" approximately constant. Root beer and Collins mix proved to be rather good substitutes for these experimental rats; the consumption ratio changed markedly, in the expected direction, when the price ratio changed even by a small amount.

In a second experiment, "free" food and water were no longer provided. Instead, these became the two commodities available only by paying a price (pressing the appropriate lever). When the price ratio was varied, again holding "real income" approximately constant, there was relatively little change in the ratio of quantities consumed. Food and water, it appears, were strong complements for these rats.

> COMMENT: In the second experiment, very drastic changes in the prices of food and water led to what the authors termed "disruptive" behavior. The rats sometimes failed to spend all their "income," and began to lose weight. This kind of irrational response to change may be found among humans as well, though not allowed for in standard economic theory.

4.C
HOW THE CONSUMER'S OPTIMUM VARIES IN RESPONSE TO CHANGING OPPORTUNITIES

With *preferences* assumed unchanging, the optimum of the consumer can vary only in response to changes in *opportunities*. The consumer's market opportunities, we have seen, depend upon two elements: (1) income, and (2) commodity prices. In this section we shall see how the consumer adjusts his or her consumption in reaction to changes in income and prices.

4.C.1 □ Income Expansion Path and Engel Curve

Suppose, to begin with, that income I increases while all prices remain unchanged. Then, in a simplified world of only two commodities X and Y, we can picture the situation as in Figure 4.8. The original optimum is at point Q, the tangency of the budget line KL with the indifference curve U_0. (This position corresponds to point C^* in Figure 4.1.) Now let income rise from I to I'. This will cause a parallel outward shift of the budget line from KL to $K'L'$. The slope of the budget line depends only upon the price ratio P_x/P_y and so the shift must leave the *slope* of the budget line the same as before. The new optimum position is shown as point R, where the budget line $K'L'$ is tangent to the higher indifference curve U_1.

A further increase in income from I' to I'' leads to a further expansion of the market opportunity set, as the budget line shifts outward to $K''L''$. Here the optimum is the tangency position S on the indifference curve U_2.

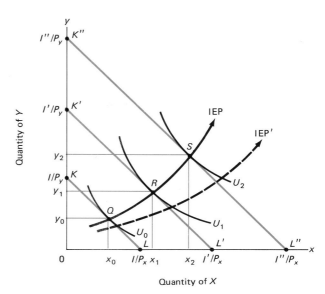

FIGURE 4.8 **Derivation of the Income Expansion Path (IEP).** As income increases from I to I' to I'', with prices P_x and P_y held constant, the budget line shifts outward parallel to itself from KL to $K'L'$ to $K''L''$. The tangency defining the consumer optimum correspondingly shifts from Q to R to S. The Income Expansion Path (IEP) shows all the consumer optimum positions attained as I varies, prices remaining the same. If the price ratio P_x/P_y were to become smaller (so that the budget lines become less steep), the IEP would shift to the southeast, as indicated by the dashed IEP' curve.

More generally, if I varies while prices and tastes remain unchanged, an entire curve—the Income Expansion Path (IEP)—will be traced out that connects all the different optimum positions like Q, R, and S in Figure 4.8. The Income Expansion Path indicates the response of the rational consumer to changes in income alone, prices held constant.

Since the IEP curve reflects the effect of changing income I given some particular price ratio P_x/P_y, it follows that each different *price ratio* would dictate a different IEP *curve*. In particular, Figure 4.8 shows how a smaller ratio P_x/P_y (implying flatter budget lines KL, $K'L'$, etc.) will have the effect of displacing the entire IEP to the southeast. [*Query*: Can two IEP curves drawn for the same individual ever cross?]

Exercise 4.5: Suppose an individual's Marginal Rate of Substitution in Consumption is given by the equation $MRS_C = y/x$. Let the market prices be $P_x = 5$ and $P_y = 1$. (a) What is the equation of the Income Expansion Path, and what does it look like? (b) How would the IEP change if P_x fell to $P_x = 4$?

Answer: (a) The Substitution Equivalence Equation (4.4) tells us that $y/x = P_x/P_y = 5/1 = 5$. So the equation for the IEP can be written $y = 5x$. It is a ray out of the origin with positive slope 5. (b) If P_x were to fall to $P_x = 4$, the IEP would rotate to the southeast, the new equation being $y = 4x$ (a flatter ray out of the origin, with slope 4).

What shapes are possible for the Income Expansion Path? Consider the three panels of Figure 4.9. In all three cases the original situation is at point Q, a tangency with indifference curve U_0 along the budget line KL. Now let income increase, so that the budget line shifts out to the position $K'L'$. In Panel (a) the new tangency R lies northeast of Q, and so the IEP has positive slope. This means that the quantities purchased of X and of Y have both increased with the rise in income; in this case X and Y are called *normal* goods.

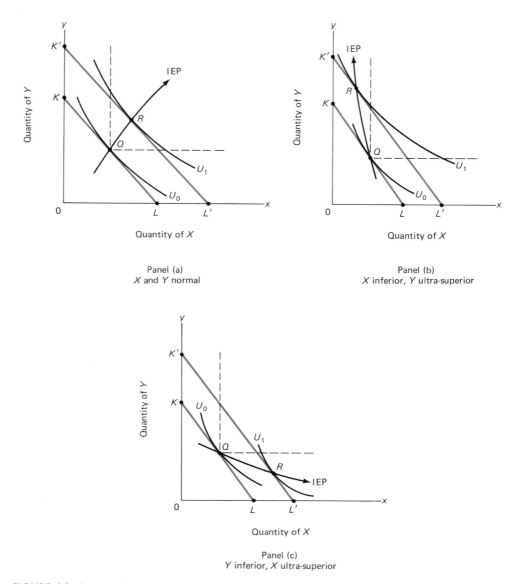

Panel (a)
X and Y normal

Panel (b)
X inferior, Y ultra-superior

Panel (c)
Y inferior, X ultra-superior

FIGURE 4.9 Income Expansion Paths, Three Cases. In all three diagrams the outward shift of the budget line (from KL to $K'L'$) represents an increase in income I, with prices P_x and P_y held constant. In Panel (a) the upward direction of the Income Expansion Path (IEP) is northeast. Here both X and Y are normal superior goods. In Panel (b) the upward direction of the IEP is northwest; X here is an inferior good, and Y an ultra-superior good. Panel (c) is the opposite case, where the upward direction of the IEP is southeast. Here Y is inferior, X ultra-superior.

In Panel (b) the new tangency R lies to the northwest of Q. The consumer is buying more Y but less X; the IEP has negative slope. A commodity like X here, whose consumption falls when income rises, is called an *inferior* good.

Economists have no standard term for the other commodity Y in this case. The expression "superior good" refers to any good that is not inferior—that is, whose consumption rises with income. Hence Y would be called superior in the situation of either Panel (a) or Panel (b), leaving us still in need of a way to express the distinction between the two cases. Let us adopt the term *ultra-superior* for the good that is a "partner" of an inferior good. Then Y is ultra-superior in Panel (b). The defining characteristic of an ultra-superior good may be expressed as follows: Since less of an inferior good is purchased when income increases, it follows that *more than* 100 percent of the increase in income has been devoted to additional purchases of the associated ultra-superior good.

Finally, Panel (c) shows the opposite situation, where Y is inferior and X ultra-superior. The IEP is again negatively sloped, but the new consumptive optimum position lies to the southeast (rather than northwest) as income rises.

In all three cases, the IEP curve has been drawn with an arrowhead pointing in the direction of rising utility (upward on the invisible utility hill). The arrow is convenient in permitting an immediate distinction, by inspection, between the X-inferior [Panel (b)] case and the Y-inferior [Panel (c)] case.

CONCLUSION: A positively sloped Income Expansion Path, for two goods X and Y, means that consumption of each rises as income grows. Then X and Y are both normal superior goods. If the IEP has negative slope, one of the goods must be inferior. The other good must of course be superior, but more specifically may be called ultra-superior because it accounts for more than 100 percent of the increment of income.

Exercise 4.6: (a) Suppose, for some individual, that $MRS_C = y/x$. Are goods X and Y both normal for him, or is one of them inferior? (b) What if $MRS_C = y$?

Answer: (a) When $MRS_C = y/x$ the Substitution Equivalence Equation (4.4) is $y/x = P_x/P_y$—so that, solving for y, the Income Expansion Path equation can be written $y = P_x x/P_y$. Since P_x and P_y are both positive constants, the IEP has positive slope, implying that X and Y are both normal goods. (b) If instead $MRS_C = y$, the equation for the IEP by a similar development becomes simply $y = P_x/P_y$. This implies that the IEP would be a horizontal line—meaning that any increase of income is spent *entirely* on good X. So Y, while not quite inferior, is just on the borderline of being so.

EXAMPLE 4.3
Luxuries versus Necessities in a P.O.W. Camp

Goods that are predominantly purchased by relatively wealthy people are commonly called luxuries. Correspondingly, a good that accounts for a large portion of the consumption budget of poorer people is sometimes termed a "necessity." Standard items of food like bread are generally considered necessities. For, while richer people can afford to and generally do buy more loaves of bread per person than poorer people (i.e., bread is not an inferior good), the *proportion* of the budget spent on bread falls as income rises.

In the prisoner-of-war economy already mentioned in Example 4.1, R. A. Radford[a] also made interesting observations about necessities and luxuries. Toward the end of the war, prisoners were living in severe privation as a result of the steady deterioration of the German economy. In August 1944 a further halving of rations, the two main items being food and cigarettes, took place. Unexpectedly, cigarettes proved to be more of a "necessity" than food (by the standard definition above). Despite the presence of many nonsmokers, in the market as a whole there was a net attempt to trade food for cigarettes. As a result, the price of food (in terms of cigarettes) became actually lower than before.

> COMMENT: The implied shape of indifference curves between cigarettes C and food F at the higher income level (point $Q°$) and the lower income level (point Q'), for a typical prisoner, is indicated in Figure 4.10. The Marginal Rate of Substitution in Consumption, $MRS_C \equiv -\Delta c/\Delta f\,|_U$ is less (the indifference curve has flatter slope) at the lower real-income point.

[a] R. A. Radford, "The Economic Organisation of a P.O.W. Camp," *Economica*, v. 12 (1945).

The IEP shows the effect of income on consumption of all goods. For any single good, the relation between income and consumption can be summarized in convenient form as the *Engel Curve*.[12] A portion of a typical Engel Curve is shown

[12] Ernst Engel (1821–1896), German statistician.

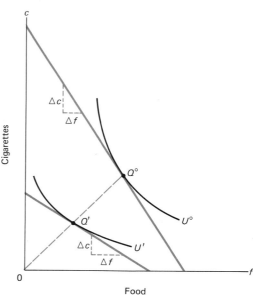

FIGURE 4.10 **Food versus Cigarettes in a P.O.W. Camp.** After a halving of cigarette and food rations, the typical P.O.W. was forced from an initial position like $Q°$ to a less preferred outcome Q'. Under these circumstances it was observed that P_f/P_c, the price of food in terms of cigarettes as *numéraire*, fell. Since $P_f/P_c = MRS_C$ at the consumer optimum, we know that MRS_C (the absolute value $\Delta c/\Delta f$ of the indifference-curve slope) must have been less at lower incomes. That is, cigarettes became relatively more preferred as income fell.

PART 2   PREFERENCE, CONSUMPTION, AND DEMAND

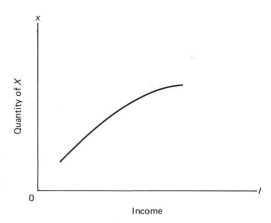

FIGURE 4.11 **Engel Curve.** For any good X, the Engel Curve shows the quantity purchased as a function of income I. For a superior good, the Engel Curve rises with income as shown here.

in Figure 4.11. In the case illustrated, the quantity of X consumed rises as income rises—that is, X is a superior good.

EXAMPLE 4.4
Polygyny in Maiduguri

The economist Amyra Grossbard studied how number of wives varied with male incomes in Maiduguri,[a] a region in Nigeria with an Islamic population. Under the primitive market conditions in that area, income and wealth could not be adequately measured in cash terms. One estimate was provided by an interviewer, who ranked the male subjects on a wealth scale from 1 to 4. It was found that each upward step was associated on average with a 0.16 increase in number of wives. Several indirect or "proxy" estimates of wealth also were used. For example, it was found that males owning houses had on average 0.23 more wives than nonowners. And males whose residences had piped water had on average 0.32 more wives.

> *COMMENT:* No single available measure of income was fully satisfactory, but the different estimates reinforced one another to indicate that wives are a normal "good" for Maiduguri males. The Engel Curves would therefore be somewhat as pictured in Figure 4.11.

[a] Amyra Grossbard, "An Economic Analysis of Polygyny: The Case of Maiduguri," *Current Anthropology*, v. 17 (Dec. 1976).

In practice we are not so interested in specific single commodities but rather in broader categories like food, clothing, vacation travel, and so forth. There is, however, no natural quantity unit for a broad commodity grouping like food or clothing. To handle this, we can replace the quantity of X on the vertical axis of the Engel Curve diagram of Figure 4.11 with consumer *expenditures* on X. If X is a single good, expenditures on it would of course be price times quantity purchased, or $P_x x$. And if X represents an entire grouping of consumption goods

$X_1, \ldots, X_G$, expenditure is $P_1x_1 + P_2x_2 + \ldots + P_Gx_G$. The income-consumption relation in terms of expenditures may be called the *Engel Expenditure Curve*. Both the simple Engel Curve and the Engel Expenditure Curve represent the same data as the Income Expansion Paths of Figures 4.8 and 4.9, but translated onto different axes. For the simple Engel Curve, x is plotted as a function of I; for the Engel Expenditure Curve, P_xx is plotted as a function of I.

DEFINITIONS: The *Engel Curve* relates consumption quantity x to income I. The *Engel Expenditure Curve* relates expenditure P_xx to income I.

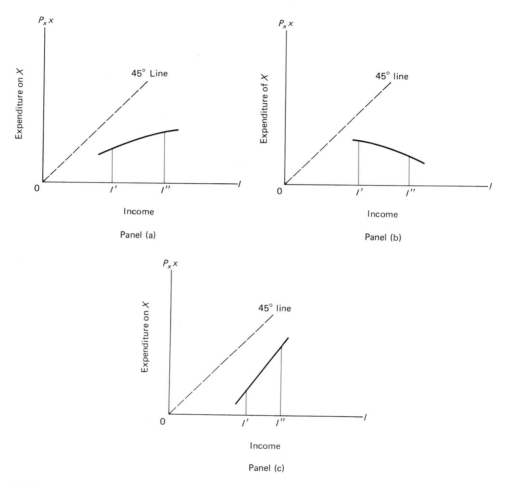

FIGURE 4.12 **Engel Expenditure Curves.** An Engel Expenditure Curve shows P_xx, the amount expended on good X, as a function of income I (price P_x held constant). If the curve were to touch the 45° line, at that point *all* of income would be spent on X. In Panel (a), P_xx rises with income but diverges from the 45° line, indicating that as I rises more is spent on *other* goods as well. In Panel (b) less is spent on X as income rises, so X must be inferior. In Panel (c), as income rises the curve approaches the 45° line; this means that less is being spent on other goods, so these other goods must therefore (in aggregate) be inferior.

The Engel Expenditure Curve has the additional advantage (over the simple Engel Curve) of directly displaying the difference between a normal superior good and an ultra-superior good. The Engel Expenditure Curves in the three panels of Figure 4.12 correspond to the three cases of Figure 4.9. To interpret Figure 4.12, first note the dashed 45° line from the origin. If for any commodity (or commodity grouping) the Engel Expenditure Curve were to lie along this 45° line, the consumer's entire income would be devoted to purchase of that commodity or grouping. Hence the 45° line constitutes an upper limit for the Engel Expenditure Curve.

In the situation pictured in Panel (a), expenditures on X rise as income I increases. But the slope of the rising curve is less than 45°. This means that expenditures on X have risen by *less* than the rise in income—that is, some of the increment of income must have been spent on a good or goods other than X. Hence this corresponds to the "normal" case in Panel (a) of Figure 4.9.

Jumping to Panel (c) of Figure 4.12, in the range between I' and I'' the Engel Expenditure Curve is rising *more* sharply than the 45° line. It follows that more than the total increase in income is being devoted to added consumption of X. This means that X is ultra-superior, as in the Panel (c) situation of Figure 4.9. Finally, in the middle Panel (b) of Figure 4.12, expenditures on X actually decline as income rises. Since P_x is constant, the quantity of X taken must have fallen; hence X is inferior, as in the situation pictured in Panel (b) of Figure 4.9.

EXAMPLE 4.5
Engel's Laws after a Century

The nineteenth-century statistician Engel asserted that, as income increases: (1) The proportion of the budget spend on food will fall; (2) the proportions spent on lodging and clothing will remain about the same; and (3) the proportion spent on all other goods will increase.

The table shows the proportionate expenditures on certain categories of consumer goods for U.S. urban families in 1960 and 1961 classified by income.[a]

Distribution of Expenditures (%)

	FAMILY INCOME AFTER TAXES			
EXPENDITURE CATEGORY	Under $2000	$2000–2999	$3000–3999	$4000 and Over
Food	29.5	28.4	25.9	23.7
Shelter, fuel, light, refrigeration, water	29.4	24.3	20.6	17.4
Clothing	5.9	8.2	9.0	10.8
Medical care	8.2	8.1	7.3	6.4
Automobile	3.2	6.5	11.3	13.9
All other	23.8	24.5	25.9	27.8
Total	100.0	100.0	100.0	100.0

Source: Bureau of Labor Statistics, "Consumer Expenditures and Income, with Emphasis on Low Income Families," July 1964.

The data confirm Engel in showing a declining proportion spent on food as income rises. But where he predicted constant proportions spent on lodging and clothing, the twentieth-century data show a falling proportion in the former and a rising proportion in the latter category. The "All other" category also rises with income, as Engel predicted. One striking feature is the very sharp increase in the proportion spent on the automobile as income rises; automobile transportation is evidently a strongly superior good.

[a] For a more complete survey, see H. Houthakker, "An International Comparison of Household Expenditure Patterns, Commemorating the Centenary of Engel's Law," *Econometrica*, v. 25 (Oct. 1957).

4.C.2 ☐ Price Expansion Path and Demand Curve

In the previous section we dealt with changes in income. In this section emphasis shifts to the effects of changes in price. It will be convenient to let Y be the *numéraire* commodity, its price being held constant at $P_y = 1$. So only the price of X varies. Here again the change affects the shape of the market opportunity set, and specifically of the budget line. But whereas a rise in income led to a *parallel* outward displacement of the budget line, a change in price leads to a *tilting* of this boundary.

In Figure 4.13, the optimum is initially at Q where the budget line KL is tangent to indifference curve U_0. Now let the price of X *fall*. Since the intercept of the budget line with the vertical Y-axis is at I/P_y, nothing has changed there; the point K remains as before. But the intercept of the budget line with the horizontal X-axis is at I/P_x, so the fall in P_x is associated with an expansion of the opportunity set taking the form of a flattening of the budget line to a new position like KL'. This tilting represents the fact that as X becomes cheaper, the consumer is able to buy more X. The new optimum of the consumer is at the point R where the new

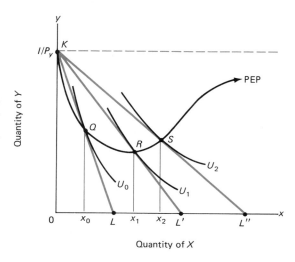

FIGURE 4.13 Derivation of the Price Expansion Path (PEP). As P_x falls, with income I and the price of the other good P_y held constant, the budget line tilts outward (from KL to KL' to KL''). The consumptive optimum position changes correspondingly from Q to R to S. The Price Expansion Path (PEP) connects all such consumptive optimum positions as P_x varies, the arrowhead on the PEP curve indicating the direction of utility improvement. Normally, the PEP curve moves eastward, and it can never cross above the horizontal drawn through point K. (K is the "corner solution" where, for sufficiently high P_x, none of commodity X would be purchased.)

budget line KL' is tangent to a higher indifference curve U_1. And a still further decline in P_x leads to a further outward tilting of the budget line, to the position KL''; here the optimum is at S on the still higher indifference curve U_2.

A curve can now be passed through all the possible optimum positions like Q, R, and S that are generated by changes in P_x. We call this curve the Price Expansion Path (PEP). The PEP curve indicates the response of the rational consumer to changes in P_x alone, income I and the price P_y being held fixed.

However, just as the entire IEP curve is shifted when prices change, the entire Price Expansion Path will be shifted if income I changes. Specifically, if goods X and Y are normal, an increase in income will tend to shift the Price Expansion Path upward and to the right. [Students should check this point to verify their understanding of the PEP curve.]

Exercise 4.7: Suppose some individual has $MRS_C = y$, income $I = 120$, and assume that $P_y = 1$. (a) What is the equation for the Price Expansion Path (PEP) and what is its shape? (b) How would it change if income increased to $I = 150$?

Answer: (a) Here the Substitution Equivalence Equation (4.1) becomes $y = P_x/P_y$ or, even more simply (since $P_y = 1$), just $y = P_x$. The budget line equation remains $P_x x + P_y y = I$ or numerically $P_x x + y = 120$. Thus we have two simultaneous equations: $y = P_x$ and $P_x x + y = 120$. The PEP is drawn on (x, y) axes, so we can eliminate P_x as a variable and simplify to obtain the single equation $yx + y = 120$. Or, in more convenient form, $y(x + 1) = 120$. This PEP curve has a y-intercept of 120. Like the PEP curve of Figure 4.13, it slopes down from the y-intercept—but unlike that curve, it never curls up again but approaches (without ever intersecting) the horizontal axis. (b) If income increased to $I = 150$, the equation would become $y(x + 1) = 150$. The intercept on the y-axis is higher and the curve shifts generally upward and to the right.

The following additional geometrical characteristics of the Price Expansion Path (PEP) are also of considerable economic interest.

1. As the price P_x falls, the PEP curve enters regions of higher and higher utility. Again, an arrowhead shows the direction of rising utility along the PEP in Figure 4.13. The level of satisfaction increases since, with income I held constant, a fall in P_x is equivalent to a rise in *real* income—increased ability to purchase desired commodities.

2. When the PEP curve has negative slope, as in the range between Q and R along the curve in Figure 4.13, at lower prices P_x the consumer purchases more of X but takes less of Y. If the PEP bends upward into a positive slope, as in the range between R and S in the diagram, as price P_x falls the consumer is willing and able to obtain more X while consuming more Y as well.

3. If there is some "choke price" P_x so high that no X at all is purchased, at that price (or any higher price) the optimum of the consumer is a *corner solution* on the Y-axis, as in Figure 4.3. If this condition holds, the Price Expansion Path will have a terminating point on the Y-axis (point K in Figure 4.13). On the other hand, no matter how low the price P_x falls (so long as it does not become negative), the budget line must lie below the dashed horizontal line drawn through K in the diagram and so the Price Expansion Path must also lie everywhere below this line.

4. Astonishing as it may seem, the PEP curve may conceivably curl back in a *northwesterly* direction, as in the circled region in Figure 4.14. In this region, as price P_x falls the quantity of X consumed also falls! When this condition applies, the commodity is

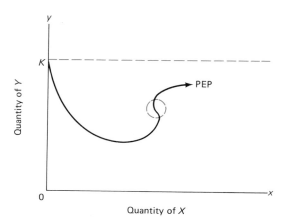

FIGURE 4.14 Price Expansion Path: Giffen Case. The Price Expansion Path (PEP) might conceivably curl back northwest over a limited range (circled region), where *less* of X is purchased as P_x falls. In this range X would be called a "Giffen good."

called a "Giffen good"[13] for this consumer. But the Giffen property can only hold over a limited range. With negatively sloped indifference curves and positive preference directions, the PEP cannot move northwesterly very long and still be entering regions of higher utility. (Giffen goods will be discussed further in Chapter 5.)

Finally, we can replot the data summarized by the Price Expansion Path as a relation between the quantity consumed of commodity X and the price of X, as in the curve *d* in Panel (a) of Figure 4.15. This is of course the individual's *demand curve* for the good X.

[13] Sir Robert Giffen, British statistician and economist (1837–1910).

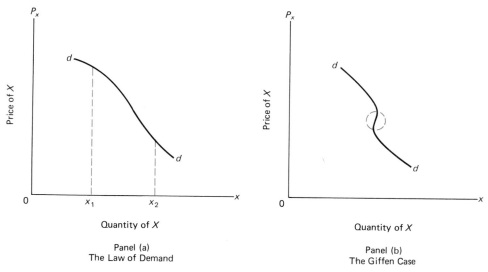

Panel (a)
The Law of Demand

Panel (b)
The Giffen Case

FIGURE 4.15 Demand Curves: The Law of Demand versus the Giffen Case. Panel (a) pictures a negatively sloped individual demand curve, satisfying the Law of Demand: as the price falls, more of X is purchased. In Panel (b) the demand curve has the exceptional "Giffen" property. In the small circled region (corresponding to the circled region in the previous diagram), more of X is purchased as P_x *rises*. The Giffen property can hold, if at all, only over a limited range of prices.

Exercise 4.8:   In Exercise 4.7, the Price Expansion Path $y(x + 1) = 120$ was obtained for an individual with $MRS_C = y$, income $I = 120$, and assuming that $P_y = 1$. What is the individual demand curve associated with this PEP curve?

Answer: The Substitution Equivalence Equation here, we saw in Exercise 4.7, is simply $y = P_x$. The demand curve is drawn on (x, P_x) axes, so we need to rewrite the PEP equation in terms of x and P_x. Using the fact that $y = P_x$ to eliminate y as a variable, the PEP equation $y(x+1) = 120$ becomes $P_x(x + 1) = 120$, or $x = 120/P_x - 1$. This is the equation for the demand curve. [*Query:* What happens at $P_x = 120$, or any higher price? *Hint:* $P_x = 120$ is the "choke price" for good X.]

If there is a Giffen range in which the PEP curls northwesterly (the circled region in Figure 4.14), then there will be a corresponding positively sloped range along the demand curve (the circled region in Panel (b) of Figure 4.15). In this range the demand curve has the "Giffen property" that at lower prices a smaller quantity is demanded. That demand curves always (or almost always) have negative slope (i.e., that the Giffen case rarely if ever occurs) is a principle called the *Law of Demand*. This principle, like convexity of indifference curves, does *not* follow from the pure logic of choice. Its justification is empirical observation of the world.

EXAMPLE 4.6
The Law of Demand: Animals and Humans

In 1978 the psychologist S.E.G. Lea[a] reviewed a wide variety of demand studies including animal experiments, retailing experiments, and econometric investigations. The following is a summary showing, for each class of study, the number of instances that either support or contradict the Law of Demand, or represent mixed or uncertain results.

	Law of Demand Supported	Law of Demand Contradicted	Mixed or Uncertain
Animal experiments* (18)	15	1	2
Retailing experiments† (9)	7	1	1
Selection of econometric studies‡ (25)	25	0	0

*Estimated visually from Lea, Fig. 1 (p. 447).
†Estimated visually from Lea, Fig. 2 (p. 448).
‡Estimated visually from Lea, Fig. 3 (p. 449).

[a] S.E.G. Lea, "The Psychology and Economics of Demand," *Psychological Bulletin*, v. 85 (1978).

Common sense tells us that the Law of Demand is consistent with the great majority of ordinary consumption decisions. But what about exceptional situations, like addicts' demand for narcotics or alcoholics' demand for liquor? Even then, income is limited. Suppose an addict were to spend literally all of his income upon drugs, regardless of price. Then he *must* buy less as price rises. It is true that, in order to support his habit as price increases, he might try to acquire more income—by stealing, begging, or even working. But the more income needed, the harder the effort involved, and the Law of Demand still tends to hold. So we are not surprised to read, for example, that when the effective street price of liquor in the United States rose during Prohibition, there was a decline in liquor consumption. (Indirect evidence: the incidence of cirrhosis of the liver fell.)[14]

[14] H. Kalant and O. J. Kalant, *Drugs, Society, and Personal Choice* (Don Mills, Ontario, Canada: Paperjacks, 1971), p. 117.

EXAMPLE 4.7
Shocking Alcoholics

As a portion of an experiment conducted by M. B. Sobell and L. C. Sobell,[a] forty alcoholics who had voluntarily admitted themselves to Patton State Hospital in California were randomly assigned to an experimental or a control group. The twenty patients assigned to the experimental group received a special sequence of sessions. In these sessions liquor was freely available, except that "inappropriate" drinking behavior was punished by an electric shock. Shocks were administered if the patient ordered a drink straight, took too large a sip, ordered drinks less than 20 minutes apart, or ordered more than three drinks in a session. During three of the thirteen sessions, however, no shocks were administered. The overall results were as follows:

Sessions	Average Inappropriate Behaviors*
With shocks	2.2
Without shocks	18.7

* Calculated from Sobell and Sobell, p. 39.

Note that this was a case *without* a fixed constraint on purchasing power. A patient could always "earn" the right to take another drink by undergoing an electric shock. Nevertheless, when the price of drinking was high, less of it occurred.

COMMENT: An interesting point, touching upon the nature and stability of "tastes" (as discussed in Chapter 3), was observed in follow-up studies. The experimental group seemed to have better success than the control group in remaining sober afterward. This suggests that life experiences can indeed change attitudes, not a very astonishing conclusion but one at odds with the standard economic assumption of unchanging preferences. A possible explanation is the

[a] Mark B. Sobell and Linda C. Sobell, *Individualized Behavior Therapy for Alcoholics: Rationale, Procedures, Preliminary Results, and Appendix*, California Mental Health Research Monograph No. 13 (1972).

following. It seems likely that admission to the hospital, which was voluntary, indicated a willingness on the part of these alcoholics to engage in *exploratory* behavior (like the children of Example 3.1), suggesting that they did not feel confident about their true preferences for being or not being an alcoholic. Seemingly, the shock treatment somehow induced more effective exploration of nonalcoholic lifestyles.

Figure 4.16 shows the effect of a change in income upon the demand curve. If X is normal or ultra-superior, then a rise in income will increase demand (rightward shift). If X is an inferior good (economy cars, for example) then a rise in income will decrease demand for X (leftward shift).

Exercise 4.9: For the individual of Exercise 4.8, what would happen to the demand curve if income rose from $I = 120$ to $I = 150$? Is X a superior good?

Answer: With $I = 120$ the demand equation was $P_x(x + 1) = 120$, or equivalently $x = 120/P_x - 1$. With $I = 150$, following the same technique we obtain $P_x(x + 1) = 150$ or equivalently $x = 150/P_x - 1$. The demand curve for X has shifted to the right at each price. Thus, commodity X must be a superior good.

4.D
INCOME AND SUBSTITUTION EFFECTS OF A PRICE CHANGE

Suppose the price of X falls. Economists have found it useful to distinguish two distinct effects upon the consumer's demand for X:

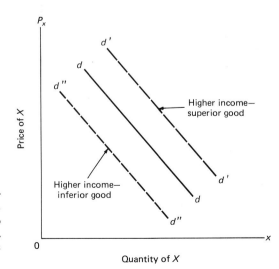

FIGURE 4.16 The Demand Curve: Effect of Income Changes. If X is a superior good (whether normal or ultra-superior), a rise in income implies larger purchases of X at any price P_x; the demand curve shifts to the right (from dd to $d'd'$). But if X is an inferior good, as income increases, *less* is purchased at any price P_x; the demand curve shifts to the left (from dd to $d''d''$).

1. Because of the fall in price, the consumer has higher *real* income. Being richer will generally affect his or her purchases of X. This is called the *income effect* of the price change.
2. At a lower P_x, the consumer would have bought more X even at the same level of real income. This is called the pure *substitution effect* of the price change.

Figure 4.17 pictures what is known as the Hicks[15] decomposition of the income and substitution effects. (Figure 4.17 shows the effect of a *fall* in the price of X, but a similar analysis can be employed for an increase in P_x.)

Suppose a consumer is at an initial optimum point Q on indifference curve U_0. When P_x falls he moves to a new optimum at S on indifference curve U_1. Since he is on a higher indifference curve than before, the price reduction has effectively raised his real income. Now, keeping the lower price P_x, imagine taking away just enough income to leave the consumer on his old indifference curve U_0. This leads to a kind of artificial budget line (the dashed line MN) parallel to KL' but just touching indifference U_0 at point R. The movement from point Q to point R eliminates the change in real income and therefore isolates the *pure substitution effect* of the price change. In terms of the quantity of X, the substitution effect is the distance $x_R - x_Q$.

The *income effect* of the price change is the remainder, the movement from R to the new optimum at S. In terms of quantities of X, the income effect is $x_S - x_R$. Thus the overall change from Q to S has been decomposed into two movements: from Q to R (the substitution effect) and then from R to S (the income effect).

A key point is that the substitution effect is always negative. Quantity and price change in opposite directions. This must be the case since the pure substitution effect involves movement along an indifference curve, and all indifference curves have negative slope.

The income effect is more ambiguous. A fall in P_x will always raise real in-

[15] Sir John R. Hicks, contemporary British economist.

FIGURE 4.17 Income and Substitution Effects: Hicks Decomposition. A fall in price P_x, with I and P_y held constant, shifts the budget line from KL to KL' so that the consumptive optimum changes from Q to S. Since S lies on a higher indifference curve, there has been an increase in *real* income. The "income effect" of the price change can be separated from the pure "substitution effect" by constructing an artificial budget line MN that is parallel to KL' and tangent to the original indifference curve U_0 (at the position R). There is no utility improvement between Q and R, only between R and S. The income effect of the price change is therefore $x_S - x_R$; the pure substitution effect of the price change is $x_R - x_Q$.

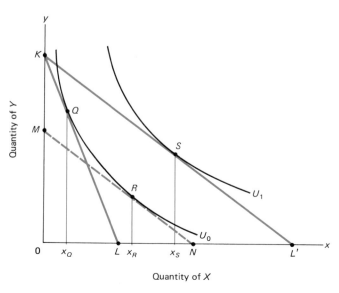

come, but the higher income could lead to greater consumption if X is a superior good or to less consumption if X is inferior. Figure 4.17 shows the case where X is superior. If X had been inferior, the new optimum S would lie above but *to the left* of R instead of to the right. An abnormal (negative) income effect might even outweigh the normal substitution effect. If this occurs a *fall* in price would lead to a net *fall* in quantity purchased; this is the "Giffen case" to be discussed further in Chapter 5.

4.E
FROM INDIVIDUAL DEMAND TO MARKET DEMAND

The *market demand curve* shows the aggregate quantity demanded by all consumers together, as a function of the price. Geometrically, the market demand curve is obtained simply by *horizontal summation* of the individual demand curves, as illustrated in Figure 4.18.

Suppose the market has only two consumers, with demand curves d_1 and d_2. At the price P_x the first consumer will buy x_1 units and the second x_2 units. The quantity demanded in the market is thus $x_1 + x_2$, which corresponds to the point A along the market demand curve. Repeating this process for every possible price traces out the entire market demand curve D. More generally, for any number of consumers:

(4.6) $$X = \sum_{i=1}^{N} x_i$$

This says that the market demand X is the sum of the demands of all N individuals in the market, where i indexes the individuals from 1 to N. (The aggregate

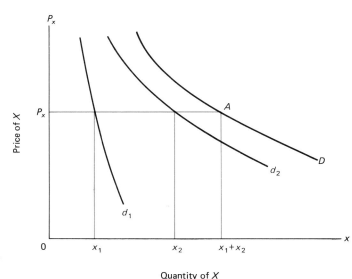

FIGURE 4.18 Individual and Aggregate Demand. Here d_1 and d_2 are the demand curves for two individuals. If these are the only two potential purchasers of the good, the overall market-demand curve D is the *horizontal* sum of d_1 and d_2.

market quantity here is symbolized by an uppercase letter, a convention we will usually follow throughout the text.)

Note that the market demand curve in Figure 4.18 has a much flatter *slope* than the individual demand curves. This tells us that, if price falls, the increase in the market quantity will ordinarily be much greater than the increase in quantity consumed by any single individual. However, the *percent* increase in X along the aggregate demand curve D need not be any greater than the *percent* increase along the individual demand curves. This point will be considered further when we take up the concept of "elasticity" in the next chapter.

An implicit assumption of the foregoing analysis is that the same price P_x is being charged to every individual in the market. Where this assumption is not appropriate, a market demand curve in the ordinary sense cannot be constructed.

CONCLUSION: The market demand curve is the *horizontal* sum of the individual demand curves.

Exercise 4.10: If individual j has demand curve $x_j = 10 - 2P_x$ for commodity X, while individual k has demand curve $x_k = 10 - 3P_x$, and if these are the only two consumers in the market, what is the market demand curve? Compare the individual demand slopes and the market demand slope.

Answer: Remember that we must sum the quantities demanded (*not* the prices). So the market demand equation is $X = x_j + x_k = 20 - 5P_x$. Price is on the vertical axis, so that the slopes are given by $\Delta P_x / \Delta x$. The slope of j's demand curve is $-1/2$, the slope of k's demand curve is $-1/3$, while the market demand slope is $-1/5$. Thus, as in the diagram of Figure 4.18, the market demand curve has notably flatter slope than any of the individual demand curves. [This market demand equation is invalid if $P_x > 10/3$. Why? (*Hint*: What is the "choke price" for individual k?)]

4.F
AN APPLICATION: SUBSIDY VERSUS VOUCHER

Governments often try to encourage people to consume more of a particular good—education, let us say. One possibility might be a general *subsidy* to producers or consumers of education. (Free public education is of course an extreme kind of subsidy.) *Voucher* schemes represent a somewhat different technique.

In Figure 4.19, E represents education and A "all other goods." Panel (a) shows the effect of a *subsidy*. The original (unsubsidized) tangency optimum is at Q on indifference curve U_0. A subsidy acts like a reduction in price; it rotates the budget line from KL outward to a new position KL'. The new optimum is at R, on indifference curve U_1. Apart from the unlikely possibility that E is a Giffen good in this range, there will be an increase in the consumer's purchases of education. In the diagram, the increase is the distance $e_1 - e_0$ on the horizontal axis.

Panel (b) of Figure 4.19 shows the effect of a *voucher*. The initial position Q on indifference curve U_0 is the same as before. The "voucher" is a *gift of income spendable only on the specified commodity E*. The distance KK' on the vertical axis represents the amount of the gift, so that the consumer's budget line shifts outward from KL to K'L'. But the gift can only be spent on E. This means the consumer cannot reach the dashed part of his budget line between K' and K". Therefore his

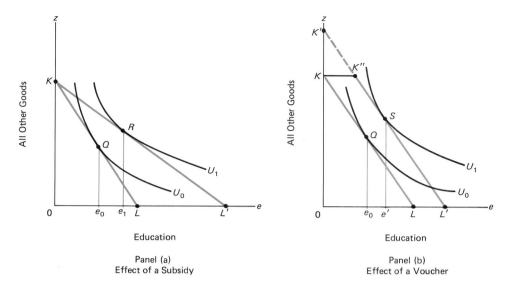

Panel (a)
Effect of a Subsidy

Panel (b)
Effect of a Voucher

FIGURE 4.19 Subsidy versus Voucher. In Panel (a) a subsidy to consumption of education (E) acts like a reduction in price P_e; the budget line shifts from KL to KL'. At the new consumptive optimum, the quantity purchased of E will be greater (unless E is a Giffen good in this range, which is highly unlikely). In Panel (b), the "voucher" amount KK' is a gift of income that is spendable only on good E. The budget line shifts to the right, from KL to $K'L'$, except that the consumer is not allowed to choose an optimum in the range between K' and K'' (since the full amount of the voucher would not then be spent on purchases of E). The new optimum at S will involve increased purchases of E, so long as E is not an inferior good.

effective new budget line is the kinked line $KK''L'$. In Panel (b) of Figure 4.19 the new optimum is at S on indifference curve U_1. The voucher will increase purchases of commodity E ($e' > e_0$) whenever E is a superior good (positive income effect). But it will decrease purchases if E is inferior.

So far it might appear that there is no great difference between the subsidy and voucher. The subsidy works through a price change, the voucher through an income change. But the voucher does have a certain special power in the case of a consumer who would *otherwise take very little or none* of the commodity E.

Consider Figure 4.20. Here the individual is initially at a *corner solution.* The optimum is the point K on indifference curve U_0, where he or she is consuming a zero quantity of commodity E. Even a fairly substantial subsidy, rotating the budget line outward to KL'', might have little or no effect upon his or her consumption of E. But the voucher displaces the entire budget line outward to $K'L'$ (of which only the solid range $K''L'$ is effective). The new optimum will be at K'' (not at K' which is outside the opportunity set). At K'' the individual has spent the entire voucher amount on purchases of E, and is spending the same amount on other goods as before. So, we see that a voucher will almost always be effective in increasing consumption of E *for someone previously not consuming it at all, or consuming an amount less than the voucher equivalent.* The only exception would be if E is a bad rather than a good for the individual. (If so, a voucher spendable only on E would simply remain unused.)

There are however at least two flaws in this analysis. First, an implicit assumption was that the market price of the good E remained unchanged through-

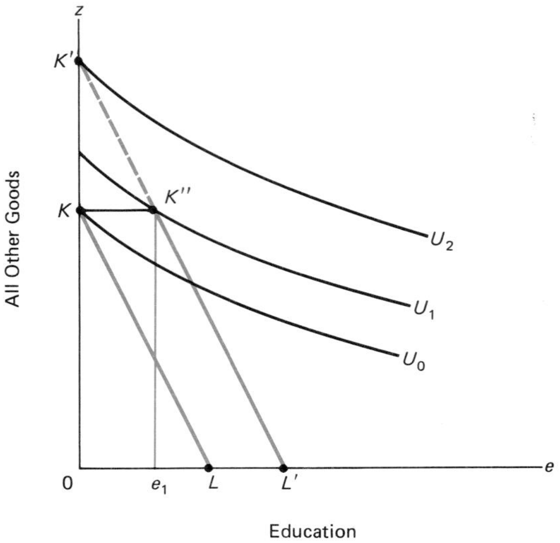

FIGURE 4.20 Corner Solution and Voucher. The initial consumptive optimum is the corner solution at K; none of commodity E is being purchased. A voucher gift of income in the amount KK' leads to a new consumptive optimum at K''. (The consumer would still prefer a corner solution at point K', but this is unattainable.) The voucher leads to increased consumption of E, provided only that E is a good for this individual.

out. This would be a reasonable assumption if a subsidy or voucher were granted only to a single individual, whose own increased consumption would almost surely not significantly affect market price. But if, as is normally the case, the benefit is granted to a large class of consumers, the increase in demand due to a subsidy or voucher would tend to force the price of good E upward, which we have not allowed for. Second, the analysis failed to indicate the *source of the funds* needed to finance the subsidy or voucher. Collection of these funds via taxes would reduce the spendable income of some or all consumers. So our discussion does not tell the whole story.

☐ SUMMARY OF CHAPTER 4

The optimum of the consumer involves the interaction of his or her *preferences* (indifference curves) and *market opportunities* (budget line). The optimum position is where the budget line bounding the opportunity set touches the highest attainable indifference curve. There are two types of optimum positions: (1) For an interior solution, the optimum occurs at a tangency point. (2) But if no interior tangency exists, the highest indifference curve attainable is found at zero quantity for one of the commodities (corner solution). In the real world both situations are observed: we consume mixtures of commodities, but do not purchase positive amounts of every possible good. Convex indifference curves are consistent with the possibility of both corner and interior solutions.

Analytically, the budget equation for an individual whose income is I, with goods X and Y available at prices P_x and P_y, is:

$$P_x x + P_y y = I$$

The optimum condition (for an interior solution) can be expressed, if utility is cardinal, as the Consumption Balance Equation:

$$\frac{MU_x}{P_x} = \frac{MU_y}{P_y}$$

That is, Marginal Utility per dollar (the utility of the last dollar) spent on either commodity is the same. This implies the Substitution Equivalence Equation:

$$MRS_C = MRS_E$$

This latter form is more general, because it does not require that utility be cardinally measurable. MRS_C corresponds to the indifference-curve slope, and MRS_E to the budget-line slope. The equality of the two, together with the equation for the budget line, determine the (interior solution) optimum of the consumer.

It is useful to distinguish between pairs of goods that have positive complementarity (are poor substitutes) versus those that have negative complementarity (are good substitutes). Strong complements like bread and butter, or electricity and electrical appliances, tend to be consumed together; consequently, even a large change in the price ratio between them is likely to have only a small effect upon the ratio in which they are consumed. Close substitutes like Fords and Toyotas, or movie theaters and cable TV entertainment, tend to be consumed to the exclusion of one another. Hence, even a small price shift may lead to a big change in the ratio in which they are purchased.

As income I increases, with prices held constant, the budget line shifts parallel to itself and outward from the origin. The optimum positions attained, for given prices P_x and P_y, are shown by the Income Expansion Path (IEP). If both X and Y are normal superior goods, the IEP has positive slope (the upward direction in utility terms is northeast). If either good is inferior (in which case the other good can be called ultra-superior), the IEP has a negative slope; the upward direction is northwest or southeast, depending upon which good is inferior. The data in the IEP can also be plotted on I, x axes as an Engel Curve showing how the quantity of X purchased varies as income increases, or on $I, P_x x$ axes as an Engel Expenditure Curve showing how the amount $P_x x$ spent on good X varies as income increases.

As price P_x falls, with I and P_y held constant, the budget line tilts outward while retaining the same intercept on the y-axis. The optimum positions attained are represented by the Price Expansion Path (PEP). The upward direction along the PEP is (almost always) eastward. When the data represented by the PEP are plotted on x, P_x axes as a demand curve, we normally find that more of X is purchased as P_x falls (the Law of Demand). But the Law of Demand may conceivably be violated over a limited range of prices (the Giffen case).

A fall in P_x, with I and P_y held constant, implies an increase in *real* income (higher level of satisfaction in utility terms). It is possible to separate the "income effect of the price change" from the "pure substitution effect of the price change." The substitution effect is always in the normal direction; when P_x falls more of X will be purchased. But the direction of the income effect depends upon whether X is superior or inferior. The Giffen case results when the substitution effect (which always enlarges consumption of X as P_x falls) is overbalanced by an inferior-good income effect which is not only negative in direction (tending to reduce purchases of X at higher levels of real income) but unusually large in magnitude.

Market demand is aggregated from individual demands simply by adding up, at each price, the quantities purchased by all the consumers (horizontal summation).

Subsidies and vouchers can change an individual's consumption. A subsidy works like a change in price, while a voucher works like a change in income. A voucher is especially effective in the case of someone who would otherwise have consumed very little of the good or none at all.

□ QUESTIONS FOR CHAPTER 4

MAINLY FOR REVIEW

R1. What is the meaning of the expression "the optimum of the consumer"?

R2. In a situation with just two goods X and Y, how does the amount of income I affect the shape of an individual's market opportunity set? How do the prices of the two goods affect the shape?

*R3. What is the "budget line"? What is its equation? What determines the slope of the budget line?

*R4. What is the geometrical condition for the optimum of the consumer? (Distinguish between a corner solution and an interior solution.)

R5. If indifference curves were concave, why would the consumer's optimum never be in the interior?

*R6. What is the Consumption Balance Equation that expresses the optimum of the consumer? Relate this to the Substitution Equivalence Equation. Do the equations hold for an interior solution, a corner solution, or both?

R7. Give examples of pairs of goods that are strong complements, versus pairs that are close substitutes. What is the observable market characteristic that distinguishes them?

R8. Characterize a normal good, an inferior good, and an ultra-superior good. Give examples of each. For two goods X and Y, which of the above must they be if the Income Expansion Path has positive slope? What can you say if the IEP has negative slope?

R9. Prove that if X and Y are goods, the IEP never points southwest.

*R10. A positively sloped Income Expansion Path implies what shape for the Engel Curve? For the Engel Expenditure Curve? If good X is inferior, what can you say about its Engel Curve?

R11. Show how an individual's demand curve can be derived from his or her Price Expansion Path.

R12. Is there a utility-increasing direction along the IEP? Along the PEP?

*R13. What does the Law of Demand say about the shape of the PEP?

R14. How does the Hicks decomposition separate the "income effect" and the "substitution effect" of a price change?

R15. Using the Hicks decomposition, show that the Giffen condition (violation of the Law of Demand) can hold only for an inferior good.

R16. How is the market demand curve derived from knowledge of individuals' separate

*Answers to starred questions appear at the end of the book.

demand curves? Can individual demand curves be determined from knowledge of the market demand curve?

*R17. "As compared with a simple subsidy, the voucher scheme is particularly effective for consumers who would otherwise have chosen little or none of the commodity." Illustrate and explain.

FOR FURTHER THOUGHT AND DISCUSSION

*T1. Could you imagine an experiment that might reveal an individual's Marginal Rate of Substitution in Consumption (MRS_C) between two goods? His Marginal Utility for either good?

T2. Is diminishing Marginal Utility actually necessary if the Consumption Balance Equation is to express an optimum? Why is decreasing Marginal Rate of Substitution in Consumption necessary if the Substitution Equivalence Equation is to express an optimum?

*T3. Why can the Giffen condition hold only over a limited range of the PEP? Could the PEP ever circle around and rejoin itself at its starting-point on the y-axis?

*T4. Would a change in P_x tend to shift the position of the IEP? Would a change in income I tend to shift the position of the PEP?

T5. If an individual's demand curve cuts the vertical price axis at some finite "choke price" P_x^o, show the equivalent situation in terms of the individual's indifference curves and budget line. Must the consumer's optimum then be a corner solution at price P_x^o?

T6. "I think I could be a good woman if I had five thousand a year"—Becky Sharp, in Thackeray's *Vanity Fair*. Here are two possible interpretations:
   a. "Being a good woman" is a good for Becky, but one she can't afford until her income gets up to five thousand a year.
   b. Becky regards "being a good woman" as unpleasant (a bad, like hard labor). But for a fee (like wages for hard labor) of five thousand a year she would be a good woman.

   Which interpretation is correct? Can you imagine a test that would distinguish which of the two Becky meant?

*T7. Consider a pair of commodities like bread and butter, which are strong complements, versus another pair like butter and margarine, which are close substitutes. Which pair is more likely to have a member that is an inferior good? Explain.

*T8. Why is the income effect of a price change usually small compared to the substitution effect?

T9. "Since 1900, real income has increased tremendously, yet the average number of children per family has decreased." Consider the following possible explanations, and illustrate in terms of market opportunity sets and family indifference curves between number of children x and "all other goods" y.
   a. Children are an inferior good; since we're richer now, we want fewer of them.
   b. Children are not an inferior good; however, it has become more expensive to bear and raise children.
   c. Children are not an inferior good, nor have they become relatively more expensive. What has happened is that tastes have changed; couples today want smaller families than couples did in 1900.

*T10. In the comparison of subsidy versus voucher in the text, it was assumed that the price of the good remained unchanged. Would it be correct to anticipate some change of price? In which direction is this likely to go? Show the effect upon the market opportunity set.

T11.   Still another consideration is that government expenditures on subsidies or vouchers must ordinarily be financed by taxes. Suppose that the mode of financing works out as a reduction in the typical individual's income I. Show the effect upon his or her market opportunity set of a tax-financed subsidy. Of a tax-financed voucher.

*T12.   The following is sometimes given as an example of a Giffen-good situation. A person must make a 1000-mile train trip and has only $100 in funds available. He prefers first-class travel to coach travel, but his first priority is to complete his trip. Suppose first-class travel costs 20 cents per mile and coach costs 5 cents per mile. Then it can be verified that he will travel 333 1/3 miles in first class and 666 2/3 miles in coach. Now let the price of coach travel rise to 10 cents per mile. Then the traveler cannot afford any first-class miles at all if he is to complete his trip, so the amount of coach travel will rise from 666 2/3 to 1000 even though its price has doubled! Question: Is coach travel an inferior good here? (What would happen if the travel budget were to rise above $100?) Under what circumstances will the traveler choose a corner solution with only coach travel? With only first-class travel?

*T13.   If two commodities are perfect substitutes, is it true that the consumer's optimum will almost always be a corner solution? Will it ever not be?

*T14.   At a given price ratio, variations in income I generate an Income Expansion Path IEP. If the price ratio were different, we know that a different IEP curve would be generated. For the same individual, could these two IEP curves ever cross?

*T15.   In one of the exercises above, for a certain individual with $MRS_C = y$, income $I = 120$, and assuming that $P_y = 1$, the demand-curve equation $x = 120/P_x - 1$ was derived. What happens when $P_x = 120$? Is the equation above valid for prices $P_x > 120$, and if not, what is the correct equation in that price range?

T16.   Suppose a gasoline tax is imposed, taking the form of a fixed number of cents per gallon (the same for regular and for premium gas). Consider the following arguments. (1) While we'd expect the quantity demanded of both premium and regular gasoline to fall after the tax is imposed, there should be a *relatively smaller* effect for the premium quality—since a fixed number of cents is a smaller *proportionate* tax for the premium gas. (2) On the contrary, we'd expect a *relatively bigger* effect for the premium quality—because premium gasoline is more of a "luxury" good, and regular gasoline more of a "necessity" good. Is one or the other of these arguments totally wrong, or is it a matter of which of two valid arguments is the stronger? Analyze each argument separately, and explain.

5

CORE CHAPTER

APPLICATIONS AND EXTENSIONS OF DEMAND THEORY

EXAMPLES

We know that a gasoline tax will raise prices to consumers. And so, by the Law of Demand, it will reduce consumption—but by how much? Similarly, a business recession will depress consumer incomes, but to what extent would that discourage gasoline usage? This chapter describes the concepts used by economists to *quantify* the effects upon the demand for a commodity of changes in income, of changes in the commodity's own price, and of changes in prices of related goods. The chapter also covers a number of important applications and extensions of demand theory.

5.A
THE ENGEL CURVE AND THE INCOME ELASTICITY OF DEMAND

How do changes in income I affect consumption of some good X? The most direct measure is the ratio $\Delta x/\Delta I$. For small changes Δx and ΔI, this ratio is the slope of the Engel Curve.[1] Figure 5.1 shows portions of a number of alternative Engel Curves, assumed for simplicity to be straight lines. The slopes of these curves indicate differing possible ways in which consumption of X might respond to changes in income.

There is one serious difficulty with the simple ratio $\Delta x/\Delta I$, however: it is affected by the *units of measurement*. If commodity X were butter, the numerical value of the ratio would vary depending upon whether we measured butter in ounces or pounds or income I in cents or dollars. This type of problem arises in many different branches of economics. To eliminate the difficulty, we make use of the concept of *elasticity*. Elasticity is a measure of relationship in which the changes in both numerator and denominator are expressed in proportionate (percentage) terms. Specifically here, the proportionate response of quantity purchased to a proportionate change in income is called "the income elasticity of demand."

> *DEFINITION:* The income elasticity of demand is the proportional change in the quantity purchased divided by the proportional change in income.

---

[1] *Mathematical Footnote:* We can write this slope as $\partial x/\partial I$. A partial derivative symbol is used since other independent variables, such as the price P_x, are being held constant.

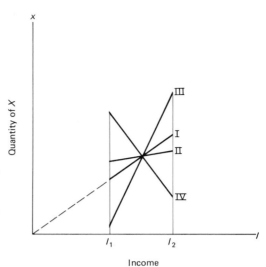

FIGURE 5.1 Engel Curves and Income Elasticity of Demand. Four possible Engel Curves relating consumption of X to income I are shown. Income elasticity is the ratio of the slope *along* a curve to the slope of a ray drawn from the origin *to* the curve. So curve I has income elasticity equal to unity, II less than unity, and III greater than unity. Curve IV has negative income elasticity.

Symbolizing the income elasticity of commodity X as ϵ_x, this definition is represented by the first ratio in Equation (5.1).[2] The other two algebraic forms are also useful to remember and work with.

$$(5.1) \qquad \epsilon_x \equiv \frac{\Delta x/x}{\Delta I/I} \equiv \frac{\Delta x/\Delta I}{x/I} \equiv \frac{\Delta x}{\Delta I}\frac{I}{x}$$

Exercise 5.1 The following table shows a consumer's income and his purchases of butter B and apples A over two successive years. Compute the income elasticities.

	Year 1	Year 2
Income	$10,000	$11,000
Apples purchased	100	116
Butter purchased	20 oz.	22 oz.

Answer: The change in income is $\Delta I = \$1000$. The income elasticity formula also requires a value for I, and immediately the question arises: Which do we use, $10,000 or $11,000? The simplest good approximation is to use the value halfway between: $I = \$10,500$. Similarly for apples $\Delta a = 16$ and $a = 108$ while for butter $\Delta b = 2$ and $b = 21$. Substituting into Equation (5.1) yields the income elasticities:

$$\text{Apples:} \quad \epsilon_a = \frac{16}{1000}\frac{10,500}{108} = 1.56$$

$$\text{Butter:} \quad \epsilon_b = \frac{2}{1000}\frac{10,500}{21} = 1$$

[2] *Mathematical Footnote:* In terms of derivatives,

$$\epsilon_x \equiv \frac{\partial x}{\partial I}\, I/x$$

So a 1 percent rise in income would increase purchases of apples by about 1.56 percent and purchases of butter by about 1 percent.

Elasticity is illustrated geometrically in Figure 5.2. On the positively sloped Engel Curve ADB the two points A and B lie on a straight line through the origin. Then between A and B the variables x and I have increased in the same proportion, so that by the definition [the first ratio in Equation (5.1)] income elasticity along ADB equals one. Or, using the middle ratio of Equation (5.1), the numerator fraction in this ratio, $\Delta x/\Delta I$, corresponds to the slope *along* the curve ADB. The denominator fraction, x/I, corresponds to the slope of a line drawn from the origin *to* a point on the curve. In the diagram these slopes are evidently the same and so $\epsilon_x = 1$ for the Engel Curve ADB.

Now consider the curve CDE lying above the line-segment AB but just tangent to it at the single point D. This is an Engel Curve along which the income elasticity of demand is changing. But at the specific tangency point D, we can think of *very small* changes Δx and ΔI along CDE as approximated by movement along the line ADB. Thus, the Engel Curve CDE has $\epsilon_x = 1$ in the neighborhood of point D.

Returning to Figure 5.1, we can see that Engel Curve I is like ADB in Figure 5.2: it lies on a line through the origin and so has income elasticity equal to 1. Engel Curve II has positive slope, but it is flatter than curve I. This means that x increases in a lesser proportion than I as the latter rises, i.e., $\epsilon_x < 1$. Geometrically, notice that such an Engel Curve has a positive intercept on the vertical axis. By reversing the argument, we see that the steeper Engel Curve III, with a positive intercept on the I axis, represents an income elasticity $\epsilon_x > 1$. What of Engel Curve IV? This one differs from the others in being negatively sloped. Here x *decreases* as I rises, so X must be an inferior good. Its income elasticity is negative, i.e., $\epsilon_x < 0$.

PROPOSITION: Income elasticity is positive and greater than, equal to, or less than 1 depending upon whether the slope *along* the Engel Curve is greater than, equal to, or less than the slope of a ray drawn from the origin *to* the curve. If the Engel Curve has negative slope, income elasticity is negative.

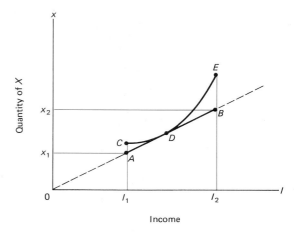

FIGURE 5.2 Engel Curve and Unitary Income Elasticity. The straight-line Engel Curve ADB has income elasticity of unity, since the slope *along* the curve is the same as the slope of a ray from the origin *to* any point on the curve. The nonlinear Engel Curve CDE, tangent at point D to ADB, therefore also has unitary income elasticity for small changes in the neighborhood of point D. In the range CD the slope *along* the curve CDE is less than the slope of rays from the origin *to* the curve, so income elasticity ϵ_x is less than unity. Correspondingly, $\epsilon_x > 1$ in the range of CDE between D and E.

Notice that *any* positively sloped straight-line Engel Curve through the origin has income elasticity of unity, but such lines can be drawn from very nearly vertical (steep slope) to very nearly horizontal (small slope). It is not the steepness alone of an Engel Curve at a particular point that indicates elasticity, but rather the steepness *as compared with a line through the origin*.

Exercise 5.2   The following four linear equations correspond to possible Engel Curves. Determine the slope and the income elasticity for each at the point $(I, x) = (200, 25)$: (a) $x = I/8$; (b) $x = 5 + I/10$; (c) $x = -75 + I/2$; (d) $x = 30 - I/40$. In which of these cases is the commodity an inferior good? (e) What if the Engel Curve were $x = 5 + I/8$?

Answer: (a) The slope $\Delta x/\Delta I$ all along the curve is evidently 1/8. The income elasticity is the ratio of this slope to $x/I = 25/200 = 1/8$. So the income elasticity is $\epsilon_x = (1/8)/(1/8) = 1$. (b) The slope is 1/10, and so $\epsilon_x = (1/10)/(1/8) = 0.8$. (c) Slope is 1/2, $\epsilon_x = (1/2)/(1/8) = 4$. (d) Slope is $-1/40$, $\epsilon_x = (-1/40)/(1/8) = -0.2$. [Note that the four curves correspond generally to those pictured in Figure 5.1.] Commodity X is inferior only in case (d), where the income elasticity is negative. (e) We tried to trick you here. The equation given is perfectly possible for an Engel Curve, but the specific point $(I, x) = (200, 25)$ does not lie on the curve so the question cannot be answered.

It is sometimes important to distinguish between elasticity at a *point* along a curve and elasticity over some finite range or *arc*. The definition in Equation (5.1) can cover both cases. In Exercise 5.1 the income elasticities for apples and butter were arc elasticities; in Exercise 5.2 they were point elasticities. Arc elasticity is a kind of average of the point elasticities within the range considered. As the intervals Δx and ΔI shrink down toward zero, the arc elasticity approaches the point elasticity along the curve.

There is an important general proposition that states a relation which must hold among the income elasticities for a given consumer:

> PROPOSITION: The weighted-average income elasticity, calculated over all consumption goods, must be equal to one.

If there is, say, a 10 percent increase in income with all prices held constant, then consumption of some goods may rise by more than 10 percent and of others by less than 10 percent. But since all of the increase in income must somehow be spent, those goods for which consumption rises by less than 10 percent must be offset by others for which consumption rises by even more than 10 percent. On the average, therefore, consumption must rise by the same proportion as income. If there were just two commodities X and Y, the weighted average of the income elasticities is:

(5.2) $$k_x \epsilon_x + k_y \epsilon_y = 1$$

Here the weight $k_x \equiv P_x x/I$ is the proportion of the consumer's budget spent on commodity X, and similarly $k_y \equiv P_y y/I$.

Exercise 5.3   Suppose there are just two goods, bread X and wine Y. If bread accounts for 95 percent of the budget and has income elasticity $\epsilon_x = 0.9$, what can you say about the income elasticity ϵ_y of wine?

Answer: Equation (5.2) here has the form $0.95(0.9) + 0.05\epsilon_y = 1$, and so $\epsilon_y = 2.9$. [Note that a good which accounts for a very large fraction of the budget must have income elasticity near one. If a good has rather high income elasticity, like wine in this example, you can be pretty sure that it accounts for only a small portion of the budget.]

EXAMPLE 5.1
The Declining Public-Transit Industry

Table 5.1 illustrates the declining trend of rapid-transit ridership in the United States during the early postwar years. Generally speaking, ridership declined sharply between 1946 and 1956, and then more slowly between 1956 and 1962. (For some cities, such as Cleveland, the trend is distorted by the opening of new transit lines.) The declining trend in riders has continued since 1962.

TABLE 5.1

Rapid Transit System Ridership (1956 = 100.0)

Year	New York	Chicago	Philadelphia	Boston	Toronto	Cleveland
1946	151.8	136.8	177.8	185.1		
1950	121.9	95.2	137.3	140.2		
1951	117.5	97.1	126.3	132.3		
1952	114.1	97.0	123.0	127.0		
1953	114.0	96.1	114.8	122.8		
1954	103.9	95.8	109.2	112.1		
1055	101.0	97.2	102.8	103.6	97.0	
1956	100.0	100.0	100.0	100.0	100.0	100.0
1957	99.5	97.2	95.6	96.6	101.0	107.0
1958	96.7	92.8	92.0	94.1	99.1	105.7
1959	97.2	98.1	89.5	92.4	99.1	121.0
1960	98.7	97.6	90.1	91.2	95.7	124.7
1961	100.0	95.2	92.9	-	91.0	120.9
1962	100.5	98.9	89.4	-	91.0	117.5

Source: J. R. Meyer, J. F. Kain, and M. Wohl, *The Urban Transportation Problem* (Cambridge, Mass.: Harvard University Press, 1965), p. 96.

The declining trend of ridership is mainly due to the low income elasticity of transit in a period of rising incomes, especially in comparison with the private automobile. Example 4.5, "Engel's Law after a Century," revealed a strong positive relationship between income and automobile expenditures. In the $2000 to $2999 income bracket, for example, 6.5 percent of total expenditure was devoted to the automobile; in the $3000 to $3999 bracket, it was 11.3 percent. Using midpoints of the brackets, the income elasticity of automobile expenditures[a] over the arc can be computed as:

$$\epsilon_x = \frac{0.113(3500) - 0.065(2500)}{3500 - 2500} \cdot \frac{3000}{0.5[0.113(3500) + 0.065(2500)]}$$

$$= \frac{233}{1000} \cdot \frac{3000}{279} = 2.5 \text{ (approximately)}$$

In contrast, the income elasticity of public transit appears to be very low, or even negative.

COMMENT: Repeated attempts have been made to encourage use of public transit in place of the private automobile—in order to reduce road congestion, to counter "urban sprawl," to minimize air pollution, to save energy, and so forth. Despite substantial public subsidies to transit, these efforts seem always to fail. The higher income elasticity of auto transportation, given the historical trend of rising levels of income and wealth, has defeated efforts to promote public transit.

[a] We can use auto *expenditures* $P_x x$ in the income elasticity formula since:

$$\frac{\Delta(P_x x)}{\Delta I} \cdot \frac{I}{P_x x} \equiv \frac{\Delta x}{\Delta I} \cdot \frac{I}{x}$$

5.B
THE DEMAND CURVE AND THE PRICE ELASTICITY OF DEMAND

Income elasticity measures the response of consumption to changes in *income*. Now consider the response of consumption to changes in *price*. Again the most obvious measure would be the ratio of differences $\Delta x / \Delta P_x$.[3] For small changes Δx and ΔP_x, the ratio $\Delta x / \Delta P_x$ corresponds to the *reciprocal* of the slope[4] of the demand curve. The alternative demand curves labeled I, II, III, IV in Figure 5.3 illustrate more and less steep slopes. The steeper the curve, the smaller the absolute magnitude of $\Delta x / \Delta P_x$.

As in the case of income, a slope measure like $\Delta x / \Delta P_x$ would be affected by changes in units of measurement in the numerator (e.g., changes from pounds to tons) or in the denominator (e.g., changes from dollars to cents). To avoid this difficulty, once again we can use an elasticity measure, the ratio of *proportionate* changes. This concept is formally known as "the price elasticity of demand." (The expression "elasticity of demand" standing alone is understood to refer to the price elasticity.)

Since *slope* depends on units of measurement, it would be meaningless to assert, for example, that the demand curve for wheat is steeper than, say, the demand curve for haircuts, and therefore to conclude that the demand for wheat is less responsive to price changes. The demand curve for wheat could be made to seem as steep or flat as desired by converting from tons to pounds to ounces as quantity units, or from dollars to cents as money units. But it would be meaningful to say that the demand for wheat is *less elastic* than the demand for haircuts; if

[3] *Mathematical Footnote:* In terms of derivatives, this is $\partial x / \partial P_x$.

[4] Since economists conventionally draw demand curves with price P_x on the vertical axis, the slope of the demand curve is $\Delta P_x / \Delta x$. To measure the effects of price changes upon quantity consumed, we need to take the reciprocal.

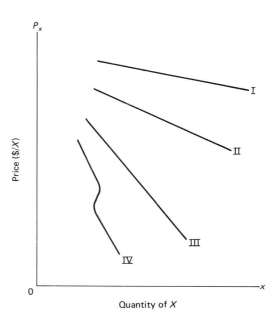

FIGURE 5.3 Alternative Demand-Curve Slopes. The four demand curves represent different responses of quantity purchased to changes in price. Since demand curves are conventionally drawn with price on the vertical axis, a greater response is represented by a flatter demand curve. Curve IV has a region that represents the exceptional Giffen case.

that were the case, we could validly conclude that the demand for wheat is less responsive to price changes than the demand for haircuts. More generally, the elasticity concept permits us to compare the price sensitivities of different goods.

> *DEFINITION:* The price elasticity of demand is the proportional change in the quantity purchased divided by the proportional change in price.

As in the case of income elasticity, there are several ways of expressing the formula for price elasticity of demand. Symbolizing price elasticity as η_x, the definition above is algebraically represented by the first ratio in Equation (5.3) below.[5]

$$(5.3) \qquad \eta_x \equiv \frac{\Delta x/x}{\Delta P_x/P_x} \equiv \frac{\Delta x/\Delta P_x}{x/P_x} \equiv \frac{\Delta x}{\Delta P_x} \cdot \frac{P_x}{x}$$

The other ratios, all identically equivalent, are also useful to remember.

When the demand curve is negatively sloped (the Law of Demand), Δx and ΔP_x have opposite signs. Thus, the price elasticity of demand η_x is normally negative. Conventionally, when we speak of elasticity being "high" we mean large in absolute value (a large negative number), and "low" elasticity means small in absolute value (a small negative number). Writing the absolute value of elasticity as $|\eta_x|$, "elastic demand" means $|\eta_x| > 1$ while "inelastic demand" means $|\eta_x| < 1$.

[5] *Mathematical Footnote:* In terms of derivatives,

$$\eta_x \equiv \frac{\partial x/x}{\partial P_x/P_x}$$

Exercise 5.4   The following are alternative linear equations representing an individual's possible demand for commodity X: (a) $x = 240 - 30P_x$; (b) $x = 320 - 50P_x$; (c) $x = 20 + 25P_x$. What are the associated price elasticities at the point $(x, P_x) = (120, 4)$? Which is a Giffen good? Of the others, which represents the more elastic demand?

Answer: We can use, from Equation (5.3), the algebraic form $\eta_x = (\Delta x/\Delta P_x)/(x/P_x)$. In each case, the denominator ratio is $x/P_x = 120/4 = 30$. Inserting the appropriate numerator ratio we have: (a) $\eta_x = -30/30 = -1$; (b) $\eta_x = -50/30 = -5/3$; (c) $\eta_x = 25/30 = 5/6$. Since the price elasticity is positive in the last case, the Law of Demand fails and (c) represents a Giffen good. [We saw in Chapter 4 that a good could have the Giffen property only over a limited range; therefore, an equation like (c) could not possibly be valid over the whole range of prices.] As between the other two cases, (b) is more elastic (i.e., shows greater responsiveness of quantity to changes in price).

For price elasticity as well as income elasticity, it is sometimes necessary to distinguish *arc elasticity* from *point elasticity*. Equation (5.3) covers both interpretations. For arc elasticity, we can compute the Δx and ΔP_x from the differences between the old and new values of the variables. (As usual, we can use the midpoints of the old and new values to find the x and P_x to insert in the elasticity formula.) For point elasticity, the slope of the demand curve at a particular point together with the x, P_x coordinates of the point provide the information needed.

Suppose the price elasticity is (minus) one ($|\eta_x| = 1$). What happens to expenditure on X if there is a small decrease in price? From the first ratio in Equation (5.3) we know that, with unitary elasticity, the proportionate *increase* in quantity $\Delta x/x$ must equal the proportionate *decrease* $\Delta P_x/P_x$ in price. But since the consumer's expenditure on good X is $P_x x$, the proportionate increase of x just offsets the proportionate decrease of P_x—so that total expenditure remains unchanged. If the price elasticity is greater than one ($|\eta_x|) > 1$, or "elastic demand", the proportionate increase in quantity is larger than the proportionate decrease in price so total expenditure $P_x x$ increases when price falls. Put another way, Marginal Revenue for this consumer is positive. By a similar argument, if demand is "inelastic," a decrease in P_x leads to a less-than-offsetting rise in x so total expenditure $P_x x$ decreases. (*MR* is negative.)[6]

> *PROPOSITION:*   A reduction in price P_x will increase a consumer's expenditures $P_x x$ on commodity X if the demand for X is elastic, will decrease $P_x x$ if demand is inelastic, and will leave $P_x x$ unchanged if demand elasticity is unitary (equal to -1).

[6]*Mathematical Footnote:*

$$\frac{\partial(P_x x)}{\partial x} = P_x + x\frac{\partial P_x}{\partial x} = P_x + \left(\frac{x}{P_x}\frac{\partial P_x}{\partial x}\right)P_x = P_x\left(1 + \frac{1}{\eta_x}\right)$$

Or,

$$MR = P_x\left(1 + \frac{1}{\eta_x}\right)$$

Recall that the sign of η_x is negative. Then the derivative on the left representing the change in expenditure (Marginal Revenue) is positive, zero, or negative depending upon whether η_x is greater than, equal to, or less than unity in absolute terms.

Exercise 5.5 A consumer's demand curve for good X is given by the equation $x = 100 - 2P_x$. (a) What is the elasticity of demand at the point $(x, P_x) = (20, 40)$? (b) If price were to fall from $P_x = 40$ to $P_x = 35$, what happens to total expenditure $P_x x$ and what does this imply about the elasticity of demand? (c) Verify by computing the arc elasticity of demand over the interval. (d) Compare this arc elasticity with the point elasticity obtained above.

Answer: (a) Along this linear demand curve, the ratio $\Delta x/\Delta P_x$ is a constant equal to -2. Using the second expression for η_x from Equation (5.3), we have

$$\frac{\Delta x/\Delta P_x}{x/P_x} = \frac{-2}{20/40} = -4$$

(b) At $P_x = 40$ we know that $x = 20$, and so total expenditure is 800. At $P_x = 35$, the demand equation tells us that $x = 100 - 2(35) = 30$, and so total expenditure is 1050. Since expenditure is greater at the lower price, demand is elastic. (c) Over the interval, $\Delta x/\Delta P_x = 10/-5 = -2$. Taking the midpoint values for x and P_x, the arc elasticity is $-2/(25/37.5) = -3$, confirming that the demand is elastic over this interval. (d) The point elasticity -4 previously calculated at the quantity $x = 20$ is larger in absolute value than the arc elasticity -3 over the interval between $x = 20$ and $x = 30$. The two numbers would be much closer if the point elasticity were calculated at the midpoint of the interval. In fact, the point elasticity at the midpoint $(x, P_x) = (25, 37.5)$ is *exactly* equal to the arc elasticity over the interval—a result that always holds for linear demand curves.

5.C
THE CROSS-ELASTICITY OF DEMAND

The amount of butter demanded will depend not only upon its own price but also to some extent upon the prices of related goods like bread or margarine. Once again, it is convenient to use a unit-free elasticity measure—called the *cross-elasticity of demand*. The definition is:[7]

$$\eta_{xy} \equiv \frac{\Delta x/x}{\Delta P_y/P_y} \equiv \frac{\Delta x}{\Delta P_y} \cdot \frac{P_y}{x}$$

Bread and butter, we know, are complements: having more of either makes the other more desirable. For complements the cross-elasticity of demand is negative. A higher butter price tends to reduce consumption of butter (the Law of Demand), thus lowering the desirability of and therefore also reducing the consumption of bread. In contrast, as the price of butter rises margarine will be more in demand; thus, between substitutes like butter and margarine the cross-elasticity of demand is surely positive.

[7] *Mathematical Footnote:* In terms of derivatives:

$$\eta_{xy} \equiv \frac{\partial x/x}{\partial P_y/P_y}$$

EXAMPLE 5.2
Elasticities of Electricity Demand

A study of electricity demand over the period 1946 to 1972 took as the determining variables: (1) electricity price, (2) income, and (3) the price of a competing commodity—gas. It was found convenient to classify the data according to residential, commercial, and industrial use.

Elasticities of Electricity Use

With respect to:	Electricity Price	Income	Gas Price
Residential	−1.3	+0.3	+0.15
Commercial	−1.5	+0.9	+0.15
Industrial	−1.7	+1.1	+0.15

Source: D. Chapman, T. Tyrrell, and T. Mount, "Electricity Demand Growth and the Energy Crisis," *Science,* v. 178 (Nov. 17, 1972), p. 705.

The elasticities of electricity demand with respect to its own price were found to be negative and in the elastic range ($|\eta_x| > 1$), showing a more than proportionate response of consumption to price change. This was the most important result of the study, running counter to the common but uninformed opinion that people have some kind of absolute "requirement" for electricity independent of price. The positive elasticities with respect to income show that electricity is a normal superior good. And the positive cross-elasticities with respect to gas price show that gas and electricity are substitutes.

> *COMMENT:* The results here refute the crude techniques for projecting future electricity demands often employed in "energy crisis" debates. Government planners, industry insiders, and outside critics sometimes argue as if purely mathematical extrapolations, which simply extend historically observed rates of demand growth into the indefinite future, represent valid estimates of what will happen. This is surely mistaken; the rate of growth of electricity demand is *strongly* responsive to price. And the price of electricity is bound to increase as fuels become more expensive and as requirements for environmental protection add to cost. (Indeed, since the period of the study electricity prices *have* gone up sharply, with the anticipated discouraging effect upon electricity use.)

5.D
AN APPLICATION: FITTING A DEMAND CURVE

The economic statistician or econometrician, starting with historical data, sometimes attempts to "fit" a demand curve that best explains the underlying observations of prices and quantities. Any such fitted curve is more or less artificial; a statistician can do no more than approximate the true demand function.

5.D.1 □ Constant-Slope versus Constant-Elasticity Functions

To keep the statistical problems manageable, the econometrician usually assumes that the demand curve has either *constant slope* or *constant elasticity*. Figure 5.4 compares two such curves. While the constant-slope demand curve is a straight line on X, P_x-axes,[8] the constant-elasticity demand curve is "convex" (bowed toward the origin).

Consider the straight-line demand curve DD' illustrated in Figure 5.5. First of all, recall the definition of price elasticity:

$$\eta_x \equiv \frac{\Delta X / X}{\Delta P_x / P_x} \equiv \frac{\Delta X}{\Delta P_x} \frac{P_x}{X}$$

From this we see that elasticity of demand must be zero at the intersection with the horizontal axis—since at that intersection P_x is zero. Similarly, elasticity is infinite at the intersection with the vertical axis where X is zero. So evidently, elasticity rises (in absolute value) as we move upward along a straight-line demand curve.

There are several geometrical ways of finding the point elasticity of demand at any point like T along the linear demand curve DD'. Perhaps the simplest is to divide the slope of a ray from the origin *to* the curve by the slope of the curve itself. Mathematically, we are using the definition of elasticity in the form:

---

[8] The uppercase symbol X indicates that we are now dealing with *aggregate* consumption or demand in the market.

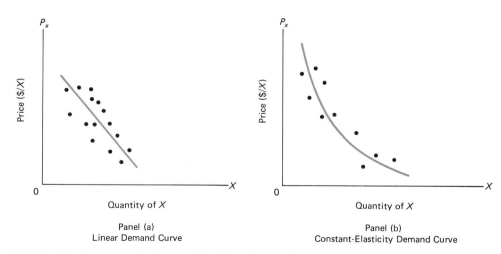

Panel (a)
Linear Demand Curve

Panel (b)
Constant-Elasticity Demand Curve

FIGURE 5.4 Linear and Constant-Elasticity Demand Curves. Simple functional forms are ordinarily assumed in attempting to estimate (to "fit") demand curves, given observed data shown as clusters of points in the diagrams. The functional forms most commonly used are linear demand as in Panel (a) and constant-elasticity demand as in Panel (b).

$$\eta_x \equiv \frac{P_x/X}{\Delta P_x/\Delta X}$$

The denominator here represents the (ordinarily negative) slope *along* the curve—the constant slope of DD' in Figure 5.5. The numerator P_x/X is the (necessarily positive) slope of the ray from the origin *to* the curve *(OT)*. To find the elasticity at the point T, divide the slope of OT by the slope of DD'. In the diagram, OT is steeper (in absolute value terms) than DD', so at T the elasticity of demand is greater than one.

A direct corollary of this result is: elasticity is always unitary ($\eta_x = -1$) at the *midpoint* of a linear demand curve. In Figure 5.5, at the midpoint M along DD' the positive slope of OM is equal in absolute value to the negative slope along DD'. That is, OMD' is an isosceles triangle.

Exercise 5.6 Consider the demand curve $P_x = 30 - X/4$. What is the elasticity of demand when $X = 60$? When $X = 120$? When $X = 0$?

Answer: The slope of this linear demand curve is $-1/4$, so elasticity at any point is equal to $(P_x/X)/(-1/4)$ or $-4P_x/X$. At $X = 60$, $P_x = 15$, so elasticity is -1. At $X = 120$, $P_x = 0$ and so elasticity is zero. At $X = 0$, finally, elasticity is negative infinite.

We can use the same technique on any demand curve, not just linear ones. Suppose we want to find the elasticity of the *nonlinear* demand curve FF' at point T. Since FF' has the same slope as DD' at point T, and since the location of point T is the same as before, the numerator and denominator ratios in the expression above for η_x both remain unchanged. So the ratio of the slope of OT to the slope

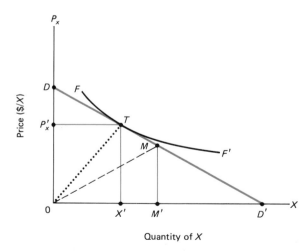

Quantity of X

FIGURE 5.5 Graphical Measure of Elasticity. Elasticity at a point T along a linear demand curve DD' is given numerically by the ratio of the positive slope of OT (the slope of the ray from the origin to the curve) to the negative slope of DD' (the slope along the curve). In the situation pictured, OT is steeper (slope is larger in absolute value) than DD', so the demand elasticity at T is greater than one. Elasticity always equals one at the midpoint M along a linear demand curve like DD' (since OMD' is an isosceles triangle). For a nonlinear demand curve like FTF', the demand elasticity at point T is identical with the elasticity at T along the tangent straight-line demand curve DD.

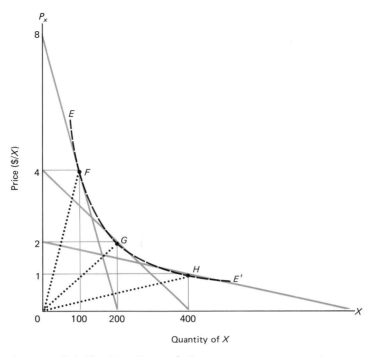

FIGURE 5.6 Constant-Unit-Elasticity Demand Curve. *EE'* is a demand curve with constant elasticity $\eta_x = -1$. At all points like *F, G, H* along *EE'*, consumer expenditures $P_x X$ equal 400.

of *DD'* measures the point elasticity of demand at *T* for both the straight line demand curve *DD'* and the nonlinear demand curve *FF'*.

In Figure 5.6 the demand curve *EE'* has constant elasticity. This means that the slope of the ray *OF* divided by the slope of the demand curve at *F* will be the same as the slope of the ray *OG* divided by the slope of the demand curve at *G*, and similarly for every other point on the demand curve. As we have seen before, when elasticity is equal to − 1 the Marginal Revenue is zero. So, for a constant-elasticity demand curve with $\eta_x = -1$, like *EE'* in the diagram, the consumers will spend the same amount of dollars on *X* no matter what the price. [*Query*: What is the fixed dollar expenditure associated with demand curve *EE'*?] This constant-expenditure property holds only for demand curves with constant elasticity equal to − 1. If the elasticity were constant but equal to − 2 instead, every 1 percent fall in price would cause a 2 percent increase in quantity. Then expenditure would steadily rise moving downward along the demand curve.

*5.D.2 ☐ Demand as a Function of Several Variables

A demand curve of constant slope is of course a straight line. We can write it as a linear equation:

*Marked sections, beginning with a single asterisk and ending with a double asterisk, may contain somewhat more difficult or advanced material and can be omitted without appreciable loss of continuity.

$$(5.4) \qquad X = A + BP_x$$

Here A and B are constants; B is normally *negative* according to the Law of Demand. When we take into account other variables that affect demand, such as income I and the price of a related good Y, we obtain a *generalized demand function in linear form*:

$$(5.5) \qquad X = A + BP_x + CI + DP_y$$

Here, $A, B, C,$ and D are all constants. B is again normally negative. C is the slope of the Engel Curve, and is only negative when X is inferior. The sign of D is positive if X and Y are substitutes, negative if they are complements.

When an econometrician statistically fits a linear demand function to the data, the equation can be valid only within a limited range. Taken to extremes, it will give absurd results. For example, interpreted literally, Equation (5.5) says that people may buy some X even if they have zero income I. This is of course impossible.[9]

---

[9] It is true, however, that allowing for borrowing and lending would make it possible for consumption expenditures in any single time period to diverge from income *of that period*. This topic will be taken up in Chapter 14.

EXAMPLE 5.3
Demand for Distilled Spirits

To estimate the demand for distilled spirits, T. J. Wales employed sales data from different states of the United States,[a] leading to the estimated linear equation:

$$X_j = 0.5084 + 0.0004079I_j - 0.1771P_j$$

Here X_j represents the number of cases of spirits per adult resident sold in state j; I_j is the disposable income per adult resident of state j; and P_j is the average liquor price, in dollars, within the state. This equation indicates that, for example, a \$1000 increase in average income leads to a consumption increase of about 0.4 case per adult resident per year. (A case consists of 12 fifths, so the increase is about 5 bottles per year.) A one-dollar increase in price leads to a decrease of around 0.18 case, or around 2 bottles per year.

But Wales suspected that the data were distorted by failure to allow for liquor sales to *non*residents crossing state lines to take advantage of lower prices. Correcting for the estimated effect of this factor led to the revised linear equation:

$$X_{jj} = -0.4615 + 0.0004379I_j - 0.00375P_j$$

Here X_{jj} represents the cases sold in state j to *residents* of that state.

As may be seen, the effect of income differences remains about the same. But the effect of price is much less; demand is now highly price-inelastic. Indeed, these data suggest that the impact of price differences between states is almost entirely limited to the effect upon out-of-state purchasers.

> COMMENT: The differences in prices of distilled spirits between states are mainly due to differences in liquor *taxation*. (In some states liquor is a state monopoly, in which case a high monopoly price is substantially equivalent to a high tax.) A very inelastic demand for liquor is convenient if the purpose of the tax is simply to generate tax revenues. But if the purpose is to discourage consumption, liquor taxation does not seem very effective.

> [a] T. J. Wales, "Distilled Spirits and Interstate Consumption Effects," *American Economic Review*, v. 58 (Sept. 1968), esp. p. 858.

Often, a better statistical fit is achieved with a demand curve of constant *elasticity* rather than constant slope. The algebra of such curves involves logarithms. For our purposes, using the common logarithms to the base 10, there are three rules to know:

(5.6a) $$\log(XY) = \log X + \log Y$$

(5.6b) $$\log(X^a) = a \log X$$

(5.6c) $$\text{If } \log Y - \log X = k, \text{ then } Y/X = 10^k$$

The third rule says that equal *arithmetic* steps of the logarithm represent equal *proportionate* steps of the variable. For example, if $k = 1$ so that $\log_{10}X$ (the logarithm of X to the common base 10) goes from 1 to 2 to 3, the variable X goes from 10 to 100 to 1000.

When an economist fits a linear demand curve as in Panel (a) of Figure 5.4, he finds the best straight line answering the question, "How do arithmetic (numerical) changes of quantity depend upon numerical changes of price?" When he fits a constant-elasticity demand curve as in Panel (b), this is equivalent to finding the best straight line answering the question, "How does the *logarithm* of quantity depend on the *logarithm* of price?" Or, equivalently, "How do proportionate changes of quantity depend upon proportionate changes of price?" Mathematically, he is fitting an equation of the form:

(5.7) $$\log X = \log a + b \log P_x$$

where $\log a$ is the horizontal intercept of the line on ($\log X$, $\log P_x$) axes.

Using the rules of logarithms above, Equation (5.7) can be rewritten:

$$\log X = \log(aP_x^b)$$

Taking the anti-logs,[10] this becomes:

[10] The anti-log is the natural number corresponding to any given logarithm.

(5.8)
$$X = aP_x^b$$

This is the form of the constant-elasticity demand equation when the logarithms are converted into ordinary units. The parameters a and b are estimated from the data. A handy feature of the logarithmic function is that the coefficient b is the elasticity of demand.[11] (So that b will be normally negative.)

We can also use logarithms to estimate more general demand equations that allow for changes in income and in the prices of related goods. These equations have the form:

(5.9)
$$\log X = \log a + b \log P_x + c \log I + d \log P_y$$

Taking the anti-logs:

(5.10)
$$X = aP_x^b I^c P_y^d$$

Here the coefficient b is the price elasticity η_x once again, c is the income elasticity ϵ_x, and d is the cross-elasticity η_{xy}.[12]

---

[11] *Mathematical Footnote:* If $X = aP_x^b$, then:

$$\eta_x \equiv \frac{dX/dP_x}{X/P_x} = \frac{baP_x^{b-1}}{X/P_x} = \frac{bX/P_x}{X/P_x} = b$$

[12] *Mathematical Footnote:* If $X = aP_x^b I^c P_y^d$, we can use the method of the preceding footnote with *partial* derivatives to verify that $\eta_x = b$, $\epsilon_x = c$, and $\eta_{xy} = d$.

EXAMPLE 5.4
Demand for Coffee

Coffee demand is relatively stable over time, whereas the supply can shift drastically owing to crop fluctuations in the major producing countries—especially Brazil. These changes in supply produce a "scatter" of price-quantity combinations over the years that provide a good basis for estimating the demand function.

Cliff J. Huang, John J. Siegfried, and Farangis Zardoshty estimated the U.S. demand for coffee over the period 1963 to 1977.[a] For regular coffee (but not soluble coffee), they found that the elasticity of demand was practically the same at high prices as at low. This justified their employing a logarithmic equation form. The equation that best fit the data for regular coffee was:

$$\log X = -.1647 \log P + .5115 \log I + .1483 \log P_t - .0089T + \text{constant}$$

Here X represents the quantity of coffee demanded, P is its price, I is income, P_t is the price of tea, and T is time. (There were also some seasonal factors, omitted here.) Since in logarithmic form the coefficients of the variables are elasticities, we see that the price elasticity for coffee is $-.1647$, which means that the demand is quite inelastic. The income elasticity is .5115, so coffee is a normal good, though not a very strongly superior one. Since the cross-elasticity of .1483 is positive, tea, as expected, is a substitute for coffee. Finally, the time coefficient is negative, indicating that consumption of regular coffee was subject to a declining trend.

For soluble (instant) coffee, the researchers obtained rather different results. First of all, the logarithmic form of equation was not employed since the elasticity of demand proved not to be constant. Elasticity was high at high prices and low at low prices (which is what occurs with a linear demand curve). The price elasticities for soluble coffee ranged from − .89 at the highest prices down to − .02 at the lowest prices during the period. There was no time trend, suggesting that the increasing convenience value of instant coffee (due, among other things, to the rising fraction of married women working away from home) just about offset the negative overall decline in coffee consumption.

COMMENT: One rather surprising result obtained was that substitution between regular and soluble coffee did not appear as a significant factor in the demand for either. This seems hard to believe, but the explanation remains a problem for future research.

[a] Cliff J. Huang, John J. Siegfried, and Farangis Zardoshty, "The Demand for Coffee in the United States, 1963–77," *Quarterly Review of Economics and Business*, v. 20 (Summer 1980).[**]

5.E
DETERMINANTS OF RESPONSIVENESS OF DEMAND TO PRICE

Why is it that some commodity demands are highly sensitive to price, while others are not? Economists have discussed a number of possible explanations.

1. *Closeness of substitutes*: Demand for a commodity will be more elastic, the more numerous and the closer are the substitutes available. This argument is based upon the "substitution effect" of the price change (see Chapter 4). Panel (a) of Figure 5.7 pictures two goods that are close substitutes, like butter and margarine. Here a fall in P_x, tilting the budget line from KL to KL', leads to a relatively large change in the quantity of X demanded (x_1 is considerably greater than x_0). For close substitutes like butter and margarine, as the price ratio changes people will shift their purchases substantially to buy more of the cheaper commodity. Panel (b) pictures two goods that are strong complements, like tennis balls and tennis racquets. Here we see that at the lower price the new quantity x_1 is only a little larger than x_0. For strong complements like balls and racquets, people will still want to buy both goods in about the same proportions, regardless of the price ratio.

2. *Luxuries versus necessities*: Demand for a "luxury" will tend to be more elastic than demand for a "necessity." (Recall that a luxury is a strongly superior good, so that a great deal more is purchased as income rises. A necessity is a good with low income elasticity so that an increase in income causes only a small increase in consumption.) Thus the argument runs in terms of the "income effect" of a price change. A fall in

[**]End of marked section.

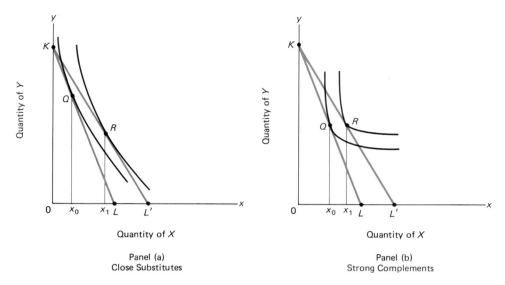

FIGURE 5.7 Closeness of Substitutes and Demand Elasticity. In Panel (a) the two goods are close substitutes. Then a fall in P_x, with consequent shift in the budget line from KL to KL', leads to a relatively large change (from x_0 to x_1) in consumption of X. In Panel (b) the two goods are poor substitutes (strong complements), and a reduction in P_x leads to only a small change in the amount of X purchased.

the price P_x will tend to enrich the consumer, and this enrichment will lead to a larger consumption increase of a luxury good as compared with a necessity good.

3. *Importance of the commodity*: It is sometimes said that a commodity that is "unimportant" for the consumer—that is, one accounting for only a small fraction $k_x \equiv P_x x / I$ of his or her budget—tends to have inelastic demand. For example, if the price of salt were to fall, you'd be unlikely to buy much more salt. It would follow, of course, that a commodity that is "important" must then tend to have elastic demand. The argument here once again is based upon the income effect: if the price of an "important" commodity falls, the consumer is in effect a lot richer, and so can buy considerably more of it. But this argument contains a fallacy. It is indeed true that if, for some consumer, X is an "important" commodity and its price P_x falls, we can expect the *absolute* increase in his or her consumption, Δx, to be large. But elasticity concerns *proportionate* changes, not absolute changes. Since for an "important" commodity the individual's consumption x was large to begin with, the *percentage* change $\Delta x / x$ need not be particularly big.[13] In the case of salt, its inelastic demand is not due to its "unimportance" in consumers' budgets but probably to the fact that salt is a *necessity* with *no close substitutes*.

4. *High-priced versus low-priced goods*: High-priced goods tend to have elastic demands, and low-priced goods inelastic demands. What is a "high" price? The natural interpretation is that a high price for a given consumer is one near the choke price, the vertical intercept of his or her demand curve. In fact, if the demand curve actually intercepts the vertical axis, elasticity is indeed infinite at that point. And at an inter-

[13] Consider the special case of an "all-important" commodity, accounting for 100 percent of the consumer's budget ($k = 1$). For such a commodity the price elasticity of demand is not extraordinarily large. Indeed, the elasticity must be exactly -1.

cept with the horizontal axis, elasticity must be zero. But it is also perfectly possible to have a constant-elasticity demand curve, for which elasticity remains constant however closely the axes are approached. (Of course, such a demand curve cannot actually *intersect* either axis.) So the logic of the argument here is not fully compelling.

5.F
AN APPLICATION: GIFFEN GOOD

An interesting application of these concepts is to the Giffen case, for which the Law of Demand is violated—a lower price P_x is associated with a *smaller* quantity demanded. It follows that the elasticity η_x has reversed (positive rather than the normal negative) sign.

Here is an example commonly given. Suppose you are so poor that you live mainly on potatoes (the cheapest source of calories), and can only afford a small amount of bread (a more desired but more expensive food). Since you spend most of your income on potatoes, if the potato price falls you will be richer as a result. But when you are richer you buy more bread, and your consumption of potatoes might actually fall.

A Giffen good must have two properties:

1. It must be inferior, so that the *income effect* of a price change is negative.
2. It must account for a large fraction of the budget. This makes the negative income effect a big one, large enough to overcome the normal substitution effect of a price change.

These properties are illustrated in Figure 5.8. The consumer starts at Q. The price of potatoes falls and the "pure" substitution effect moves him to S along the artificial dashed budget line $\hat{K}\hat{L}$ (as in Figure 4.17). But the inferior income effect (compare Figure 4.9) leads him to consume so many fewer potatoes as to overwhelm the substitution effect. At the new optimum R, he is consuming fewer potatoes at the lower price.

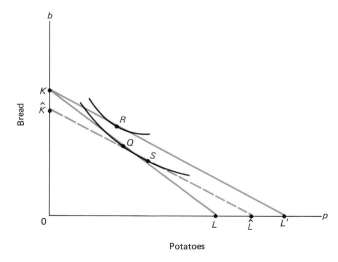

FIGURE 5.8 Conditions for Giffen Good.
This diagram shows how potatoes might have been a Giffen good for impoverished consumers in Ireland. At the initial high potato price the consumptive optimum is at Q along budget line KL. When the potato price falls, shifting the budget line to KL', the consumer is sufficiently enriched to prefer buying fewer potatoes and more wheat bread at position R. The movement from Q to R consists of a small substitution effect (Q to S) and a large negative income effect (S to R). For this Giffen result to occur, potatoes must be strongly inferior.

EXAMPLE 5.5
Was Bread a Giffen Good?

Economists today usually cite *potatoes* in nineteenth-century Ireland as a possible example of a Giffen good. A fall in the price of potatoes supposedly permitted the Irish poor to buy more wheat bread instead of potatoes. Actually, the idea of a Giffen good was first suggested by historians to describe the behavior of rural laborers in England at the end of the eighteenth century. Here it was *wheat bread* that was, supposedly, a Giffen good in comparison with cheese and meat as superior substitutes.

A study by Roger Koenker[a] casts doubt upon this British example. In the late eighteenth century, the very limited transportation network in Britain permitted considerable local price differences to develop from community to community. These differences, as well as changes over time, provided data for estimating typical demands for bread as price varied.

Using a linear (constant-slope) assumption, a demand function for English rural laborer households was estimated as:

$$Bread = .401 + .413 \; Family \; size + .0245 \; Weekly \; expenditures$$
$$- .355 \; Bread \; price + .570 \; Meat \; price$$

Here bread is measured in loaves per week, the bread price in pence per loaf, and the meat price in pence per pound. Weekly expenditures in pence per week (for all food items) were the best available measure of overall income.

The negative coefficient for bread price refutes the contention that bread was a Giffen good for these consumers. In fact, the positive coefficient for weekly expenditures (income) shows that bread was a normal and not an inferior good. (Recall that while an inferior good *may* be a Giffen good, a normal or superior good cannot be.) The positive coefficient for meat price does however support the historians' contention that bread and meat were substitutes. And, as would be expected, it turned out that meat was a high-income-elasticity or "luxury" good in comparison with bread.

[a] Roger Koenker, "Was Bread Giffen? The Demand for Food in England circa 1790," *Review of Economics and Statistics*, v. 59 (1977), pp. 225–29.

5.G
MULTIPLE CONSTRAINTS

In Section 4.A the *budget line* was introduced as the upper (northeast) boundary of the market opportunity set. The familiar equation of the budget line, for two commodities X and Y, is:

(5.11)
$$P_x x + P_y y = I$$

The market opportunity set as a whole is the shaded region of Figure 5.9. Mathematically, it is the set of points satisfying the inequalities:

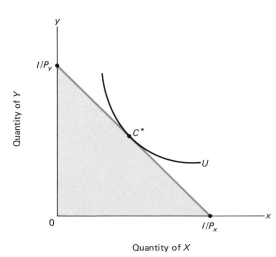

FIGURE 5.9 **Market Opportunity Set.** The normal market opportunity set is the shaded area bounded by the budget line $P_x x + P_y y = I$ and the vertical and horizontal axes.

$$
(5.12) \qquad
\begin{cases}
P_x x + P_y y \leq I \\
\qquad\quad x \geq 0 \\
\qquad\quad y \geq 0
\end{cases}
$$

The last two conditions specify that you cannot consume a negative quantity of either good.

5.G.1 ☐ Rationing as an Additional Constraint on Consumption

Governments sometimes ration goods—in wartime, for example. Even though a consumer may have enough income to buy more of the good, he or she may not be legally allowed to do so.

Three cases are illustrated in Figure 5.10. In Panel (a) the ration limit is indicated by the vertical dashed line at the quantity $x = R_x$. Here the ration limit is so large that it is ineffective for this consumer. In Panel (b) the ration limit R_x is *potentially binding*; it does bite into (truncate) the market opportunity set (it reduces the size of the shaded area). However, given the individual's preferences, the ration limit is not *actually* binding, since he does not even want to consume as much of X as the ration permits. Only in Panel (c) is the ration limit R_x actually binding. In the absence of rationing the consumer would have reached the preferred tangency position T. With the ration constraint, the best achievable point is C^*. Notice that a *binding* ration will always reduce utility.

Exercise 5.7 Suppose an individual's preferences are represented by a Marginal Rate of Substitution $MRS_C = 2y/x$, that prices are $P_x = 3$ and $P_y = 1$, and that income is $I = 180$. (a) What is the optimal consumption basket? (b) What happens if a ration limit $R_x = 50$ is applied to commodity X? (c) What if the ration is tightened to $R_x = 20$? (d) Returning to the original ration limit $R_x = 50$, what would happen if income had doubled to $I = 360$?

Answer: (a) Setting $MRS_C = P_x/P_y$ as usual, and letting Y be the *numéraire* so that $P_y = 1$,

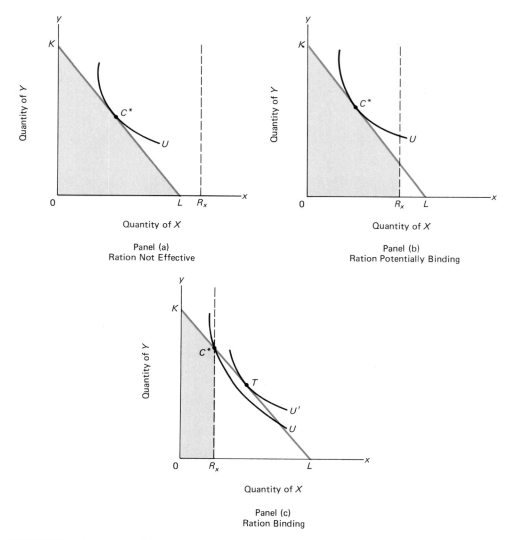

FIGURE 5.10 Rationing of One Commodity. The ration limit R_x upon purchases of commodity X is shown by the vertical dashed lines. In Panel (a) the ration limit is so large that it does not constrain the consumer's choices at all. In Panel (b) the ration limit truncates the market opportunity set, but the consumer's preferences are such that the limit is not actually binding. In Panel (c) the ration limit is binding; it forces the consumer to choose less of X (and more of Y) than he or she would have otherwise preferred.

we have $2y/x = P_x$ or $2y = P_x x$. Then the budget equation $P_x x + P_y y = I$ can be written $2y + y = 3y = 180$. The solution is $y = 60$, $x = 40$. (b) If $R_x = 50$ the X-ration is *potentially* binding (since the individual might have purchased as many as $I/P_x = 180/3 = 60$ units of X). But, since he preferred to buy only $x = 40$, the ration is not actually binding and the optimum is unchanged. (c) If $R_x = 20$ the ration limit is binding: he will obviously want to purchase his full allowed ration, so $x = 20$. With the remaining income $I - P_x x = 180 - 60$ he will buy $120/P_y = 120$ units of commodity Y. (d) It is easy to verify that when $I = 360$ the unconstrained optimum would become $x = 80$, $y = 120$. Then the ration limit $R_x = 50$ would be binding, and he would have to choose $x = 50$, $y = 210$.

What if commodities X and Y were *both* rationed? In Figure 5.11 we see only the more interesting situations where both of the ration limits R_x and R_y are at least *potentially* binding—that is, where the market opportunity set is truncated at both ends. Panel (a) shows that even when both ration limits are potentially binding, neither may *actually* be effective at the consumptive optimum position C^*. In Panel (b), only the ration limit R_y for commodity Y is actually binding; it forces the

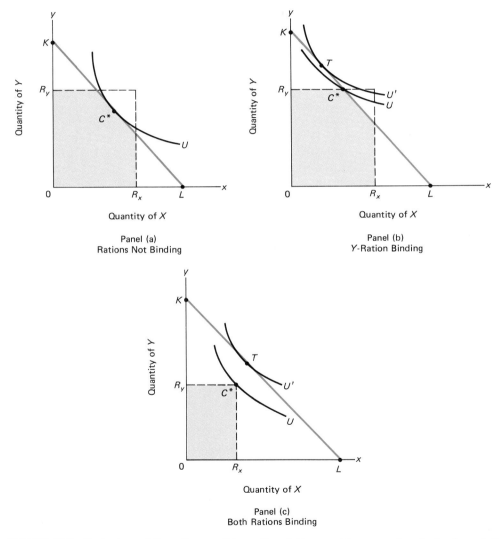

FIGURE 5.11 Rationing of Two Commodities. X and Y are subject to ration limits R_x and R_y (vertical and horizontal dashed lines). In Panel (a) neither ration limit is binding. In Panel (b) R_y is binding, forcing the consumer to choose less of Y (and more of X) than would otherwise be the case. In Panel (c) both ration limits are binding, so that the income constraint on consumption is ineffective.

individual to a position C^* inferior to the tangency optimum T that would otherwise be chosen. (There would of course be an opposite case, not diagrammed here, in which only the ration limit R_x is binding.) Panel (c) shows the case in which *both* ration limits are actually effective. Here it is the budget constraint that is not binding. This would correspond to the situation of a rich person, well endowed with income, but unable to legally spend it all because of severe rationing.

Mathematically, the constraints defining the consumption opportunity set under rationing can be written as:

(5.13)
$$\begin{cases} P_x x + P_y y \leqq 1 & \text{Income Constraint} \\ 0 \leqq x \leqq R_x & \\ 0 \leqq y \leqq R_y & \end{cases} \text{Ration Constraints}$$

Rationing is usually imposed under conditions of special scarcity, as in wartime. The reason is ordinarily to assure that poor people can buy at least minimal quantities of essential goods.[14] But simple quantity rationing is a crude technique. It does not guarantee that poor people will receive goods; it only limits the consumption of the rich in the hope there will be more left over for the poor. But since rationing a good reduces the profitability of producing it, overall supply is likely to fall. Another problem is that goods do not go where they are wanted most. Someone who doesn't like tea would have no use for a tea ration, while a tea-lover will probably get a tea ration that is too small.

In the later years of World War II, several countries adopted more sophisticated "point-rationing" schemes aimed at giving consumers a wider choice. Instead of an absolute ration limit, people were granted a "ration-point income" N to be spent as they chose. Rationed goods were assigned "point prices" p_x and p_y in addition to money prices P_x and P_y. To buy an item, the consumer had to pay the money price and also the point price.

Three possible shapes of the opportunity set under point rationing are shown in Figure 5.12. In Panel (a) "point income" is so large relative to ordinary income that only the income constraint is binding. This might be the situation of a poor person. Panel (b) represents the opposite case, a rich person for whom ordinary income is so ample that only the point constraint is binding. And finally, Panel (c) pictures a situation in which over a certain range ordinary income is binding, but elsewhere point income is binding.

Formally, the opportunity set under point rationing is determined by the inequalities:

(5.14)
$$\begin{cases} P_x x + P_y y \leqq I & \text{Income Constraint} \\ p_x x + p_y y \leqq N & \text{Point Constraint} \\ x \geqq 0, \quad y \geqq 0 & \text{Non-negativity Conditions} \end{cases}$$

---

[14] This may not be the only purpose of rationing. In Nazi Germany, for example, smaller rations were assigned to Jews than to Aryans. Similarly, during the "war communism" period 1917 to 1921 in revolutionary Russia, members of the former upper and middle classes were allowed smaller rations than individuals of proletarian origin.

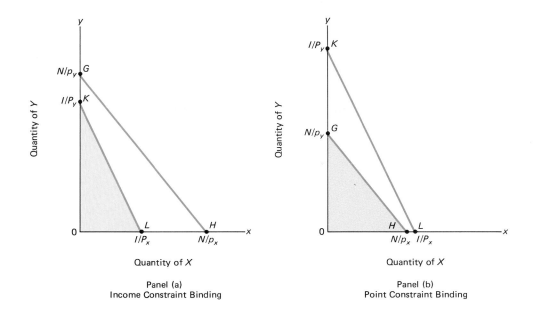

Panel (a)
Income Constraint Binding

Panel (b)
Point Constraint Binding

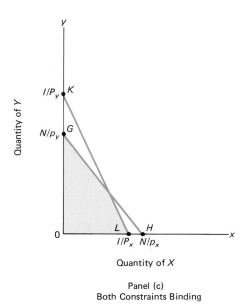

Panel (c)
Both Constraints Binding

FIGURE 5.12 Point Rationing. Consumption is subject to an income constraint I and also to a ration-point constraint N. Commodity X is more expensive in terms of income, and commmodity Y in terms of points, so the income budget line KL is steeper than the point budget line GH. In Panel (a) "point income" is so large that only money income is binding; Panel (b) represents the opposite case. In Panel (c) each constraint is binding over a certain range.

In the cases illustrated in Figure 5.12, the income budget line KL is always steeper than the point budget line GH. That is, $P_x/P_y > p_x/p_y$. Commodity X is therefore comparatively more expensive in terms of ordinary income, and commodity Y is more expensive in terms of points. It follows that consumers who like commodity X would tend to find the income constraint binding; those more interested in Y would tend to find the point constraint binding.

EXAMPLE 5.6
Wartime Point Rationing

Among the commodities rationed by points during World War II in the United States were cheese and canned fish. The table compares the 1942 (pre-rationing) purchases of different income groups with the quantities purchased during 1944 when rationing was effective.

Average Weekly Purchases by Housekeeping Families in Cities (lb)

Income	$1000 or less	$1000–2000	$2000–3000	$3000–4000	Over $4000
1942					
Cheese	0.26	0.57	0.64	0.81	1.03
Canned fish	0.21	0.36	0.56	0.44	0.37
1944					
Cheese	0.24	0.33	0.44	0.49	0.52
Canned fish	0.06	0.12	0.17	0.22	0.18

Source: L. A. Epstein, "Wartime Food Purchases," *Monthly Labor Review,* v. 60 (June 1945), p. 1148.

This table compares the binding power of income versus points at different income levels. Looking only at the three highest income groups (last three columns), we see that their consumption patterns in 1944 were almost identical. Consumers in this income range were in the situation pictured in Panel (b) of Figure 5.12—consumption of cheese and canned fish was almost entirely limited by points, and higher income made little difference. An important fact about this period is that the money price of canned fish relative to cheese approximately doubled between 1942 and 1944. The fish/cheese consumption ratio for the lowest income group consequently fell from $0.21/0.26 = 0.808$ in 1942 to $0.06/0.24 = 0.25$ in 1944, showing strong sensitivity to the price change (fish and cheese were evidently close substitutes). But for the highest income group the 1942 fish/cheese consumption ratio ($0.37/1.03 = 0.359$) remained almost unchanged ($0.18/0.52 = 0.346$) in 1944. The reason was that, owing to the rationing, the dollar prices were simply not binding for them.

*5.G.2 □ Time as a Constraint

Time as well as *income* may constrain consumption. Activities like playing a round of golf, watching a movie, or eating a meal take time as well as cash. As society becomes more affluent the importance of the time constraint grows. People become more wealthy, but increasingly harried for time to do all the things they can financially afford.

Let t_x and t_y be the time inputs ("time prices")—assumed constant for simplicity—required to consume X and Y, respectively. The consumer has to satisfy both an income constraint $P_x x + P_y y = I$ and a time constraint $t_x x + t_y y = T_c$, where T_c is the total time devoted to consumption. However, time and income can be converted into each other to some extent. Someone who engages in income-earning activities outside the home is reducing his or her available consumption time T_c but raising consumable income I. The same can be said of household activities like home repairs that reduce the need to earn outside income. Since time can be sold to obtain income, the two form a single constraint upon consumption.[15] Let us suppose that the individual could work any number of hours at a given wage w.[16] Then, in effect, the total "time endowment" T is worth wT in income units. If the person has in addition an ordinary income endowment of I_0, his or her overall constraint upon consumption choices is given by:

$$(5.15) \qquad (P_x + wt_x)x + (P_y + wt_y)y \leqq I_0 + wT$$

The effective price π_x for commodity X is not the money price P_x alone but the expression $P_x + wt_x$, the money price plus the income value of the required time input. And similarly, of course, for commodity Y the effective price is $\pi_t = P_x + wt_y$.

Suppose we wanted to compare the elasticity of demand with respect to the cash element of the effective price, $\eta_{x \cdot P}$, as against the elasticity with respect to the time element $\eta_{x \cdot wt}$. This second measure indicates the responsiveness of quantity consumed to changes in the time input required in order to consume. The definitions are:

$$(5.16) \qquad \eta_{x \cdot P} \equiv \frac{\Delta x / x}{\Delta P_x / P_x}$$

$$(5.17) \qquad \eta_{x \cdot wt} \equiv \frac{\Delta x / x}{\Delta wt_x / wt_x}$$

Since the wage w is assumed constant, it cancels out in (5.17) so that:

---

[15] In contrast, "points" could not legally be converted into cash under wartime rationing systems.

[16] This is of course a simplification. Shifting an additional hour from consumption to work might actually yield more than the normal wage w (if, for example, overtime work at time-and-a-half is available). Alternatively, the individual might only be able to earn a lower rate of pay for additional hours because of fatigue, or because his or her second "moonlighting" job pays less. The optimum balance between time and income will be considered further in Part Five.

*Marked sections, beginning with a single asterisk and ending with a double asterisk, may contain somewhat more difficult or advanced material and can be omitted without appreciable loss of continuity.

$$(5.17') \qquad \eta_{x \cdot wt} = \frac{\Delta x}{w\, \Delta t_x} \frac{wt_x}{x} = \frac{\Delta x}{\Delta t_x} \frac{t_x}{x} = \eta_{x \cdot t}$$

This gives us the elasticity of demand with respect to the "time-price" t_x.

EXAMPLE 5.7
Time-Price of Gasoline

In the spring of 1980 a quirk of government regulation required certain Chevron gasoline stations in California to charge from 16 to 21 cents per gallon less than competing stations. As expected, long lines formed at the low-priced Chevron pumps. Motorists could then choose whether to wait in line for the cheap gasoline or to buy more expensive gasoline elsewhere without delay.

Robert Deacon and Jon Sonstelie surveyed customers at a low-priced Chevron station and at two neighboring stations, a Mobil and a Union, where prices were uncontrolled. The table shows a number of average statistics for the 109 Chevron customers and the 61 non-Chevron customers.

Average Values of Variables

	Chevron	Non-Chevron
Gallons purchased	11.6	8.8
% weekend customers	31.2	26.2
% with passengers	7.3	18.0
% employed full-time	67.9	83.6
% employed part-time	5.5	1.6
% students	4.6	4.9
% housewives	5.5	3.3

Source: Adapted from Robert T. Deacon and Jon Sonstelie, "Rationing by Waiting and the Value of Time: Results from a Natural Experiment," *Journal of Political Economy*, v. 93 (Aug. 1985), p. 636.

As can be seen, where waiting in line was required the average purchase made was substantially larger. The Chevron customers, the ones willing to wait in line, were also more likely to be purchasing on weekends (where time pressures are normally less severe) and to be employed part-time. Customers choosing not to wait in line were more likely to be carrying passengers (where passengers are involved, at least two people must suffer the loss of time) and to be employed full-time. The data also suggest, surprisingly perhaps, that students do not fall into the more "leisured" category of those more willing to wait in line.

Calculating in terms of the size of purchase and the minutes spent in line waiting, the authors were also able to provide some estimates of customers' value of time. The average Chevron customer saved $1.94 by waiting 14.6 minutes, implying a time value of $7.97 per hour. But this value differed by type of customer, ranging from $3.52 to $5.39 per hour for part-time workers to $11.26 to $17.26 per hour for those fully employed and reporting income over $40,000. **

** End of marked section.

5.H
THE "NEW THEORY OF CONSUMPTION"

What explains people's desire for market goods? According to a novel and somewhat richer theory of consumption recently developed by economists, goods are desired only because of their utility-relevant qualities or *attributes*. We want bread not for its own sake but because bread has satisfying attributes: tastiness, calories, proteins, and so on. Similarly, an automobile is desired only insofar as it can be the source of transportation, comfort, prestige, and the like.

The new theory has a number of interesting implications:

1. Why some market goods are close substitutes, and others are not, becomes much easier to understand. Bread and potatoes are substitutes because they have generally similar attributes; bread and haircuts do not. So we have a basis for predicting when goods will be substitutes, and for which consumers. For example, we expect that bread and pastry are closer substitutes for poor consumers interested only in calories than for rich ones who can afford to buy tastiness as well as calories.

2. The process whereby market commodities are combined with consumers' time and efforts can be regarded as *production within the household*. Production within the household often competes directly with market production, as in home washing versus commercial laundries. An interesting empirical question concerns how much of the historical advance in standards of living has been due to improved methods of business production (such as interchangeability of parts, more powerful energy sources, newer and better-yielding crops) and how much to improvements that have facilitated home production (such as electric light, home appliances, and the automobile).

*5.I
AN APPLICATION: INDEX NUMBERS

Suppose we want to know whether consumers are better off in one situation or another. That is, in which situation does the individual get, on the average, a larger quantity of desired goods to consume? The average measure designed to answer such a question is called an *index number of quantity*. A closely related question is: In which situation does the consumer, on the average, have to pay a higher price for the goods he or she consumes? An average measure constructed to answer this question is called an *index number of price*.

Index numbers are used to make international or interregional comparisons, or to measure inflation and economic growth (comparisons over time). For example, a worker may want to know if his rising money income in an inflationary period has kept up with the rising money prices of the commodities in his consumption basket.

---

*Marked sections, beginning with a single asterisk and ending with a double asterisk, may contain somewhat more difficult or advanced material and can be omitted without appreciable loss of continuity.

5.1.1 □ Index Numbers of Quantity

Index numbers of quantity provide a way to compare a consumer's well-being in two different time periods *without* knowing the shape of his or her indifference curves. Panel (a) of Figure 5.13 shows a person's "base-year" (period 0) consumptive optimum as Q_0 on the initial budget line $K_0 L_0$. Note that the indifference curves are not drawn in. Suppose that in the next period (the "given year"), prices and income change so that the optimum moves to Q_1 on the new budget constraint $K_1 L_1$. In this case we can tell at once that the individual is better off in the given year, since Q_1 involves larger amounts of both goods. We say that Q_1 *dominates* Q_0. Panel (b), on the other hand, is not clearcut: neither optimum dominates the other. Let us leave open for the moment the question of whether we can tell here in which period the consumer is better off.

Figure 5.14 shows that there are circumstances in which comparisons can be made even where there is no dominance. In Panel (a) the bundle Q_0 does not dominate Q_1: Q_1 has less Y but more X. Nevertheless, if you look carefully you can see that Q_0 must be preferred. When the consumer was at Q_0, the bundle Q_1 was within his opportunity set. In other words, he had the choice of Q_0 or Q_1, and he chose Q_0. Therefore Q_0 must be the more desirable combination. An observer would thus have to conclude that the consumer's standard of living fell between the base year (year 0) and the given year (year 1).

Panel (b) is the reverse case. In the base year the consumer was at Q_0, and in the given year he is at Q_1. This time we can determine that Q_1 is preferred. Now

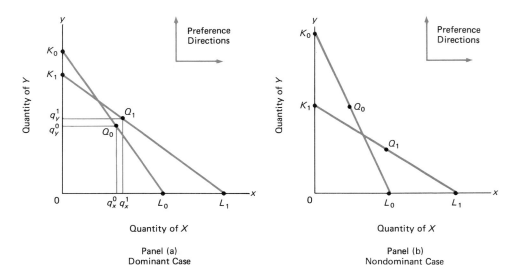

Panel (a)
Dominant Case

Panel (b)
Nondominant Case

FIGURE 5.13 Standard of Living Comparisons. Here $K_0 L_0$ represents the base-year budget line, $K_1 L_1$ the given-year budget line. In Panel (a) an observer, without knowing the consumer's preferences except that X and Y are both goods, would realize that the standard of living has been improved—since the consumer at Q_1 purchases more of both goods than at Q_0 (Dominant Case). In the Nondominant Case of Panel (b), however, preference maps might be constructed for which Q_1 is preferred to Q_0 or vice versa.

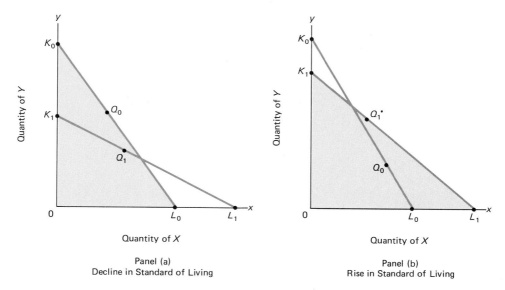

Panel (a)	Panel (b)
Decline in Standard of Living	Rise in Standard of Living

FIGURE 5.14 Unambiguous Changes in Standard of Living. Here the consumption basket Q_1 does not dominate Q_0, nor does Q_0 dominate Q_1. Nevertheless, in Panel (a) an observer could detect that Q_0 is preferred to Q_1. Since Q_1 lies within the $K_0 L_0$ budget line it *could* have been purchased in period 0, but was not. Hence Q_0 must have been preferable. In Panel (b) we see that Q_0 lies within the $K_1 L_1$ budget line and so could have been purchased in period 1, but was not. So here Q_1 must be preferable.

that he is at Q_1 the bundle Q_0 is affordable, but is not the one chosen. Therefore Q_1 is preferred and the standard of living has risen from year 0 to year 1.

Looking back at Panel (b) of Figure 5.13, we see that the situation pictured there is not consistent with the diagrams in either panel of Figure 5.14. This shows that in some cases we simply cannot tell, without knowing the preference function, whether the consumer is better off in period 0 or in period 1.

Panel (a) of Figure 5.15 amplifies Panel (a) of the previous diagram and illustrates in another way why Q_0 must be preferred over Q_1. An artificial budget constraint (dashed line) has now been drawn through Q_1 parallel to the old budget line $K_0 L_0$. The old budget line $K_0 L_0$ lies everywhere above this new dashed budget line. In terms of the common slope of these two lines, we can see that the old budget line through Q_0 represents a higher income than this new line through Q_1. So the standard of living has fallen between year 0 and year 1.

We now want an algebraic measure or index that will correspond to the geometrical interpretation just provided. The equation of the budget line always takes the form $I = P_x x + P_y y$. Let us write q_x^0 for the quantity of X consumed in the base year. In this notation the equation of the original base-year budget constraint becomes:

$$I_0^0 = P_x^0 q_x^0 + P_y^0 q_y^0 = \Sigma P^0 q^0$$

Here the Σ sign represents summation. Income I_0^0, which corresponds to the $K_0 L_0$ budget line, is associated with the base-year quantities (subscript 0) and the base-

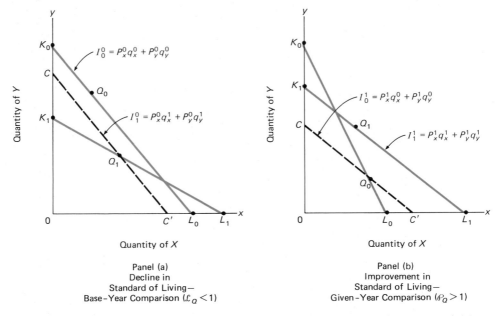

FIGURE 5.15 Unambiguous Changes in Standard of Living: Quantity Indexes. Panel (a) represents the same situation as Panel (a) in Figure 5.14. The artificial budget line CC' has the same slope (represents the same price ratio) as $K_0 L_0$, but passes through the given-year consumption basket Q_1. CC' corresponds to an expenditure or income $\Sigma P^0 q^1$ while $K_0 L_0$ corresponds to $\Sigma P^0 q^0$. So Q_0 must be preferred to Q_1 if the Laspeyres condition $\mathcal{L}_Q < 1$ holds. By a similar argument, the comparison in terms of given-year prices P^1 in Panel (b) shows a situation in which Q_1 must be preferred to Q_0. This is represented algebraically by the Paasche condition $\mathcal{P}_{Q} > 1$.

year prices (superscript 0). For the artificial (dashed) budget line, prices remain unchanged (since the budget lines have the same slope). But we know that the dashed line goes through Q_1 instead of Q_0. The equation of the dashed line is therefore:

$$I_1^0 = P_x^0 q_x^1 + P_y^0 q_y^1 = \Sigma P^0 q^1$$

Here the income I_1^0 is associated with the given-year quantities (subscript 1) and the base-year prices (superscript 0).

From the geometrical interpretation we know that the standard of living has fallen if the old budget line $K_0 L_0$ is above the dashed line. This is equivalent to $I_1^0 < I_0^0$ (or a ratio I_1^0/I_0^0 less than 1). Substituting from the above equations, this becomes:

(5.18)
$$\mathcal{L}_Q \equiv \frac{I_1^0}{I_0^0} = \frac{P_x^0 q_x^1 + P_y^0 q_y^1}{P_x^0 q_x^0 + P_y^0 q_y^0} = \frac{\Sigma P^0 q^1}{\Sigma P^0 q^0}$$

The ratio $\mathcal{L}_Q$ is known as the *Laspeyres index of quantity*. In words, it is the sum of given-year quantities valued at base-year prices, divided by base-year quantities valued at base-year prices. If the Laspeyres index is less than one, as in Panel (a) of Figure 5.15, then the standard of living has surely fallen. If the Laspeyres index were greater than one, then we would have a situation like that in Panel (b) of Figure 5.13, where we cannot tell for sure whether the standard of living has risen or fallen.

An alternative way of comparing real income at different dates is the *Paasche index* $\mathcal{P}_Q$. In Panel (b) of Figure 5.15, the consumer prefers Q_1 to Q_0—since he chose Q_1 when he could afford either. This means the standard of living has risen from the base year to the given year. The equation of the new budget line K_1L_1 is:

$$I_1^1 = P_x^1 q_x^1 + P_y^1 q_y^1 = \Sigma P^1 q^1$$

The artificial (dashed) budget line in Panel (b) is determined by the base-year quantities, since it goes through Q_0, and by the new prices, since it has the same slope as the new budget line. Thus the equation of the artificial budget line is:

$$I_0^1 = P_x^1 q_x^0 + P_y^1 q_y^0 = \Sigma P^1 q^0$$

Dividing I_1^1 by I_0^1 gives the Paasche quantity index:

$$\mathcal{P}_Q \equiv \frac{I_1^1}{I_0^1} = \frac{P_x^1 q_x^1 + P_y^1 q_y^1}{P_x^1 q_x^0 + P_y^1 q_y^0} = \frac{\Sigma P^1 q^1}{\Sigma P^1 q^0}$$

If the Paasche index is greater than one, it means the new budget line K_1L_1 is above the dashed line and the standard of living has risen. If it is less than one, then we once again have a situation like that in Panel (b) of Figure 5.13, where we cannot tell whether the standard of living is higher or lower.

> CONCLUSION: Comparing a given year with a base year, the standard of living has surely fallen if the Laspeyres index is less than one. The standard of living has surely risen if the Paasche index is greater than one. If the Laspeyres index is greater than one and the Paasche index is less than one, then the change in the standard of living is uncertain.

5.1.2 □ Index Numbers of Price

We now turn to index numbers of *prices*. Laspeyres and Paasche indexes of prices may be defined algebraically in the same way as for quantities. But here, because it is the prices which are being averaged, the quantities serve as weights. The definitions are:

(5.20)
$$\mathcal{L}_P \equiv \frac{\Sigma P^1 q^0}{\Sigma P^0 q^0}$$

(5.21)
$$\mathcal{P}_P \equiv \frac{\Sigma P^1 q^1}{\Sigma P^0 q^1}$$

It is useful also to define an index of income change as:

$$(5.22) \qquad \mathcal{E} \equiv \frac{\Sigma P^1 q^1}{\Sigma P^0 q^0} \equiv \frac{I_1^1}{I_0^0}$$

This is, of course, simply the ratio of total expenditures in the two periods.

It is clear that there must be a close connection between the quantity and the price indexes. This connection turns out to involve the index of income change ϵ as well.

We know from the discussion above that the consumer is surely better off in the given year if $\Sigma P^1 q^1 > \Sigma P^1 q^0$ so that the Paasche quantity index is greater than one. Dividing both sides of the inequality by $\Sigma P^0 q^0$, we have:

$$\frac{\Sigma P^1 q^1}{\Sigma P^0 q^0} > \frac{\Sigma P^1 q^0}{\Sigma P^0 q^0} \quad \text{or} \quad \mathcal{E} > \mathcal{L}_P$$

Thus, if the income index $\mathcal{E}$ exceeds the Laspeyres index of prices, the consumer is better off in the given year then in the base year. (This result is equivalent to a Paasche index of quantity exceeding one.)

Correspondingly, of course, the consumer is worse off in the given year when the index of income change is less than the Paasche index of prices, or $\mathcal{E} < \mathcal{P}_P$. (This is equivalent to a Laspeyres index of quantity $\mathcal{L}_Q$ that is less than unity.)

The economic interpretation is quite direct. If the income index has risen more than in proportion to prices, using the Laspeyres price index, then the average quantity consumed must have increased and the consumer is better off. If income has risen less than in proportion to prices, using the Paasche price index, the average quantity consumed must have decreased and real income has fallen.

Grasping the logic underlying Laspeyres versus Paasche indexes is helpful for understanding the relations among price and income changes. In practice, however, the really important issues are much simpler ones. The Laspeyres and Paasche indexes almost never differ very much, unless we are comparing situations so different as to invalidate the *assumption of constant preferences* that underlies the entire analysis. In terms of common sense, the main message is that a person whose income index has risen, but less than in proportion to the index of money prices (Laspeyres or Paasche makes little difference), is *not* really better off. For such a person, *real* income (index of quantity consumed) has fallen rather than risen.

But a further warning is also very much in order. Official price indexes may be misleading. An important instance is where price floors or ceilings are in force (see the discussion in Chapter 2). With price ceilings, for example, consumers may be worse off even though no price increases are registered in the official price indexes. Reasons might include: (1) degradation of quality (including range of varieties offered); (2) elimination of customary discounts or special sales; (3) provision of some portion of goods through illegal black-market or unofficial channels at unreported high prices; (4) forcing consumers to less-preferred combinations, at existing money prices, by devices like coupon rationing, queue rationing, or simple unavailability. Another practice that governments often resort to in order to disguise price increases is to subsidize those particular commodities appearing in the officially quoted index. This is like lowering the recorded temperature in a room by pressing an ice cube against the thermometer.

EXAMPLE 5.8
Cost of Living in Wartime Britain

During World War II Great Britain, like most of the nations on both sides of that conflict, engaged in inflationary war finance and yet used price ceilings to hold down the prices of consumer goods. Superficially, the latter policy seems to have been successful. The official Ministry of Labor index (based on 1938 prices = 100) of the cost of living for a working-class family rose only from 127 in 1941 to 130 in 1945.

A closer look casts some doubt on this performance, however. To hold the official index down, the British government subsidized just those goods whose prices were counted in the statistical averaging process. This led to a divergence between the index as calculated and what it was supposed to measure: the actual cost of maintaining the prewar standard of living. Estimates based upon an alternative index were reported by Dudley Seers. Some of his data are summarized in the table here.

Cost-of-Living Indexes

	1940	1945
Official (working class)	127	130
Alternative (working class)	130.5	149
Alternative (lower middle class)	133	154
Alternative (upper middle class)	139	170

Source: Dudley Seers, "The Cost of Living 1938–48," *Oxford Institute of Statistics Bulletin*, v. 11 (May 1949), pp. 129, 131.

According to the alternative index, prices rose much faster than indicated by the official index. Still, even the alternative index shows an increase of only about 14 percent for the working class over the four years. (The working class fared relatively well because the goods entering into the official index and therefore chosen for subsidy were predominantly those commodities entering into the consumption baskets of less affluent families.) However, even the alternative index fails to allow for the effects of rationing, the necessity to wait in line for goods, or simple unavailability. As shown in the discussion of multiple constraints above, such limitations on consumption force individuals onto lower indifference curves representing reduced real standards of living—without showing up in any cost-of-living index at all.**

** End of marked section.

THE INCOME-COMPENSATED DEMAND CURVE

In Chapter 4 we saw that the results of a change in price could be separated into an income effect and a substitution effect. The *income-compensated* demand curve (or *compensated* demand curve for short) shows, for any change in price, the resulting change in quantity demanded due to the substitution effect alone.

Figure 5.16 compares the compensated demand curve with the ordinary demand curve, using the Hicks decomposition discussed in Chapter 4. In the upper panel, as usual we set $P_y \equiv 1$ so that the absolute slope of the budget line P_x/P_y reduces simply to P_x. At the initial position Q along budget line KL, the individual is consuming x_Q units of X. This corresponds to the point T in the lower panel, whose coordinates are the price P_x^o and quantity x_Q. Suppose the price of X now falls to P_x', as shown by the outward rotation of the budget line from KL to KL'. The new optimum is at S. In the lower panel this corresponds to point V, where

*Marked sections, beginning with a single asterisk and ending with a double asterisk, may contain somewhat more difficult or advanced material and can be omitted without appreciable loss of continuity.

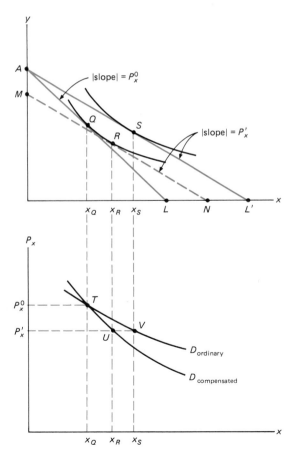

FIGURE 5.16 Income-Compensated versus Ordinary Demand Curve. The initial optimum position at Q in the upper panel corresponds to the price-quantity point T in the lower panel. When price falls from P_x^o to $P_{x'}$, the individual's new optimum is at S in the upper panel, corresponding to the price-quantity point V in the lower panel. Points T and V lie along the individual's "ordinary" demand curve. When the price change is combined with an income change so as to leave the individual along his initial indifference curve, the new optimum is at R in the upper panel, corresponding to the price-quantity point U in the lower panel. Points T and U lie along the individual's "income-compensated" demand curve.

price is P_x' and quantity x_S. T and V are thus two points on the ordinary demand curve.

The *compensated* demand curve shows what the consumer would have bought if there had been no income effect. Conceivably, this could occur if the government lets the price of X fall as before, but then taxes away enough income so as to return the individual to his or her old indifference curve. So the new optimum is at R, where the artificial (dashed) budget line MN is tangent to the original indifference curve U_0. In the lower panel, this corresponds to moving from T to U. Thus T and U are two points on the consumer's *compensated* demand curve.

There are several points of interest concerning the income-compensated demand curve:

1. For a normal or superior good, in the upper panel S will always lie to the right of R. Thus V will lie to the right of U in the lower panel. It follows that the compensated demand curve for a normal good will be steeper than the ordinary demand curve. For an inferior good, however, S will lie to the left of R and so the compensated demand curve will be flatter than the ordinary demand curve.

2. The great importance of the income-compensated demand curve stems from the fact that this is the relation actually obtained from statistical studies of price and quantity observations. In such studies it is almost always necessary to allow for *income differences*. For example, it would hardly be possible to simply fit a demand curve to price-quantity data from both California and Mississippi without allowing for the real-income differences between those states. And in time-series analysis, it will similarly be necessary to allow for historical growth of real income over time. But the statistician, by fitting a demand function (as in Section 5.D.2 above) that makes a separate allowance for differences in real income, is thereby *eliminating the income effect* from the price-quantity data. This necessarily makes the statistical result—for example, the coefficient B in Equation (5.5)—an approximation of the "pure substitution effect" of price changes.

3. It is sometimes thought that the essential distinction between the ordinary and the compensated demand curves is due to money. Some authors say that the ordinary demand curve holds *money income constant* while the compensated demand curve holds *real income constant*. This is incorrect; the existence of money is not the essential here. Suppose money had not been invented so that prices were quoted in terms of some real *numéraire* commodity. It would still be possible logically to distinguish the "ordinary" demand curve from the "compensated" demand-curve relation (which employs the Hicks adjustment technique to eliminate the real-income effect of price changes).

4. Nor is it true that the income-compensated demand curve is a more sound or a more valid concept than the ordinary demand curve. Each has its uses. The ordinary demand curve, for example, is the function that is relevant when a business makes decisions concerning what price to charge.[**]

□ SUMMARY OF CHAPTER 5

The *income elasticity* of demand for commodity X, denoted ϵ_X, represents the *proportionate* change of purchases in response to a proportionate change in in-

[**] End of marked section.

come. The first ratio below represents the definition; the others are useful alternative algebraic forms.

$$\epsilon_x \equiv \frac{\Delta x/x}{\Delta I/I} \equiv \frac{\Delta x/\Delta I}{x/I} \equiv \frac{\Delta x}{\Delta I}\frac{I}{x}$$

Income elasticity is positive for superior goods, negative for inferior goods. On the average over all goods, income elasticity must be one (weighting each elasticity by the proportion of consumer expenditures represented by that good).

The price elasticity of demand for X, denoted η_x, represents the proportionate change of purchases in response to a proportionate change in the price P_x. The first ratio below represents this definition, and again the others are useful alternative algebraic forms:

$$\eta_x \equiv \frac{\Delta x/x}{\Delta P_x/P_x} \equiv \frac{\Delta x/\Delta P_x}{x/P_x} \equiv \frac{\Delta x}{\Delta P_x} \cdot \frac{P_x}{x}$$

If the Law of Demand holds, price elasticity is negative. Demand is called "elastic" or "inelastic" depending on whether the absolute value of η_x is greater or less than one. If demand is elastic, a reduction in price leads to an increase in consumer expenditures $P_x x$; if inelastic, a reduction in price leads to a fall in $P_x x$.

The *cross-elasticity* of demand η_{xy} is the proportionate change in purchases of X in response to a proportionate change in the price of *another* commodity P_y. The definition and an alternative algebraic form are:

$$\eta_{xy} \equiv \frac{\Delta x/x}{\Delta P_y/P_y} \equiv \frac{\Delta x}{\Delta P_y} \cdot \frac{P_y}{x}$$

If the cross-elasticity is positive the two goods are called *substitutes*, since a rise in the price of Y increases the purchases of X. If η_{xy} is negative the two goods are called *complements*.

Demand functions are commonly estimated from the data ("fitted") by using either linear or constant-elasticity functional forms. The price elasticity of demand increases (in absolute value) moving upward from the horizontal intercept along a linear demand curve. A constant-elasticity demand curve, correspondingly, cannot be a straight line; it must be convex to the origin.

The following are often mentioned as causes of high price elasticities of demand: (1) If a commodity has *close substitutes*, the large substitution effect of the price change will lead to a large increase in consumption as its price falls. (2) If a commodity is a "*luxury*" (a strongly superior good), the large income effect of the price change will again cause a big increase in consumption as its price falls. These two contentions are valid. (3) If a commodity is *important* (accounts for a large proportion of the consumer's budget), it is sometimes thought that this tends to make the demand relatively elastic. However, the argument is fallacious, since the large response of an important commodity to a price change need not be large in *percentage* terms. (4) At *high prices*, elasticity tends to be large if the demand curve is approximately linear. But since demand curves need not have a linear form, this generalization is not very strongly grounded.

The consumer may be subject to constraints apart from income. *Rationing* of one or more commodities, if effective, truncates the consumption opportunity set.

More sophisticated schemes of "point rationing" impose a dual price scheme—money prices and point prices—upon consumers. *Time* is also often an important additional constraint upon consumption.

Economists have devoted a great deal of attention to the theory of index numbers of prices and quantities, although this question is more of technical than of practical significance. The issue is to determine conditions such that an observer can detect when consumers are better or worse off, *without* knowing their preference functions. In some cases this can be done. In particular, the consumer's situation has surely improved if the Paasche quantity index (which averages consumption quantities using the new prices as weights, and therefore measures ability to buy the old consumption basket at the new prices) is greater than one. This is equivalent to a Laspeyres price index (which averages prices using the old consumption quantities as weights) having risen by less than the index of income (ratio of new income to old income). However, in some cases the result remains indeterminate. As a matter of much greater practical importance, if (as often occurs under inflationary conditions) rationing by coupon or by points is imposed upon consumers, conventional price indexes will very seriously understate the true rise in cost of living.

In order to separate the effects of income changes and price changes upon consumption decisions, it is sometimes convenient to use an *income-compensated* demand curve—that is, a demand curve from which the "income effect" has been eliminated, leaving only the pure "substitution effect." In statistical work it is standard to fit a demand curve while allowing separately for the influence of income changes. When this is done, it is the income-compensated demand curve that is being estimated. But the income-compensated demand curve is no more valid than the ordinary demand curve; it simply answers a different type of question.

☐ QUESTIONS FOR CHAPTER 5

Mainly For Review

R1. What is the general definition of all elasticity measures? Why is the income elasticity of demand considered a more useful measure than the simple slope along an Engel Curve? Why is the price elasticity of demand considered a more useful measure than the simple slope along a demand curve? Are elasticity measures always better than the simple measures? (See the question following.)

*R2. Consider this paradox: Income elasticity is supposed to measure the responsiveness of consumption to changes in income. But income elasticity is unity along *any* Engel Curve that is a straight line though the origin, whether very steep or very flat. Since Engel Curves of different steepness surely show different responses of consumption to income, how can they all be characterized as having the same income elasticity?

R3. True or false: "Income elasticity is unity at any point along an Engel Curve such that the tangent at that point extends through the origin." Explain.

R4. True or false: "Since income elasticities must average out to unity, any commodity accounting for a very large fraction of income expenditure cannot have an income elasticity very far from unity." Explain.

*Answers to starred questions appear at the end of the book.

*R5. What is meant by "elastic demand" and "inelastic demand"? How can elasticity at a point along a linear demand curve be determined by inspection? Along a nonlinear demand curve?

*R6. If the demand curve is $P = A - BX$, where A and B are positive constants, what is the elasticity at $X = 0$? At $X = A/B$? At $X = A/2B$?

R7. If the demand curve is $PX = 100$, what is the elasticity at $X = 10$? At $X = 50$? At $X = 100$?

R8. What is the analytical form of a demand function that is linear in both income and price? What is the analytical form of a demand function that has *constant elasticities* with respect to both income and price? Explain the economic meaning of each form.

*R9. If there is a single "all-important" commodity that absorbs all of the individual's income, what is its price elasticity? Income elasticity?

*R10. Gasoline rationing was proposed in 1973 and again in 1979 as a possible remedy for the "energy crisis." If rations are distributed on an egalitarian basis, compare the opportunity sets of a wealthy and a poor consumer for gasoline consumption versus "all other goods." Show typical indifference maps if automobile usage is a luxury. Would permitting sale of coupons be a good idea?

R11. Show the geometrical meaning of a Laspeyres quantity index that is less than unity. Show the geometrical meaning of a Paasche quantity index that exceeds unity. Can we draw conclusions as to relative well-being in these two cases? If not, why not?

*R12. "If the ratio of new income to old income is greater than the ratio of the new cost to the old cost of the old commodity bundle, the consumer is surely better off." To what statement about indexes does this correspond? Is the statement true?

R13. What is an income-compensated demand curve? How does it differ from the ordinary demand curve? For a normal good (positive income elasticity), which of the two curves is the more elastic?

For Further Thought and Discussion

*T1. Prove the proposition that on average over all goods, income elasticity must be unity.

*T2. a. Consider the demand curve $PX = 100$. What happens to the elasticity of demand as price falls? What happens to "importance" (share of the consumer budget spent on X) as price falls?
b. Same questions, for the demand curve $P^2 X = 100$.
c. Ditto, tor the demand curve $P^{1/2} X = 100$.
d. What can you infer about the relation between elasticity and "importance"?

*T3. The American economist Irving Fisher argued in 1891 that a poor community will hardly distinguish quality grades of a commodity like beef, while a rich community would.

> In the country districts of "the west" all cuts of beef sell for the same price (about 10 cts. per lb.). In the cities of the west two or three qualities are commonly distinguished, while in New York a grocer will enumerate over a dozen prices in the same beef varying from 10 to 25 cts. per lb.[17]

[17] Irving Fisher, *Mathematical Investigations in the Theory of Value and Prices* (New Haven, Conn.: Yale University Press, 1925), p. 74.

Construct the implied indifference curves, at low and high levels of income, between "low-quality beef" and "high-quality beef." Why should different beef qualities be better substitutes at low incomes than at high incomes? What would you anticipate about the price elasticity of demand for low-quality beef? For high-quality beef?

T4. Name some goods you expect to have elastic demand. Inelastic demand. Justify your choices.

*T5. Tickets to the King Tut exhibition are available only on a black-market basis. Professor X, calling from out of town, gives purchasing instructions to his secretary: "If the price is $30 each, buy one ticket for me; at $20 each, buy two; if it is $10, buy three." The secretary says: "Prof, there must be something wrong here. You're saying you'd be willing to pay more in total for two tickets than for three!" Is the secretary correct? Explain.

*T6. For a commodity with snob appeal, consumers might be willing to buy more at a higher price than at a lower price (violation of the Law of Demand). Is this possible or likely? Explain.

*T7. If uninformed consumers judge quality by price, they may also be willing to buy more at a higher than at a lower price. Is this possible or likely? Explain.

*T8. In wartime rationing situations it is generally illegal to buy another person's ration allowances for cash, or to exchange ration coupons. Is there any justification for this? Are there adverse consequences of forbidding such exchanges?

*T9. It is often thought that the wealthy must have a great deal of leisure. On the other hand, members of present-day richer societies tend to be more harried and pressed for time than were their own grandparents who lacked modern time-saving devices. Interpret in terms of the time constraint on consumption.

T10. Since nomadic tribes have a serious portability problem, they are somewhat reluctant to acquire heavy material possessions. Analyze in terms of nomads' income and "carrying capacity" as multiple constraints. What types of goods have high "prices" in terms of carrying capacity?

T11. In the spring of 1979, gasoline sales in the United States were subject to a price ceiling. It became necessary in many areas to wait in long lines for gasoline. The U.S. Department of Energy had, evidently, set gasoline prices too low to clear the market in those areas. If the money price of gasoline was 90 cents per gallon, if the typical consumer had to wait 30 minutes to obtain a refill of ten gallons, and if his or her time was worth $5 per hour, estimate what the market-clearing money price would have been. Comparing higher money prices versus long waits in line, which system is *relatively* more advantageous for rich people versus poor? For working people versus the retired and unemployed? For owners of cars with large gas tanks versus small?

T12. What would be wrong with an economic system in which everything was allocated by waiting in line rather than by charging money prices? [*Hint*: Would the Invisible Hand be able to serve its function?]

*T13. Supermarkets A and B are in close competition. Market A advertises: "A scientific study took the typical market basket of our shoppers, and found that buying that basket costs less in our store than in our competitor's store. This proves that our prices are lower." Simultaneously, Market B makes exactly the same statement. Both are telling the truth about the scientific studies. Explain, and indicate why you would expect both to be able to make such a claim. What would be needed to really prove that one market's prices are lower than another's?

6
CORE CHAPTER

THE BUSINESS FIRM

Part Two of this book focused on the consuming *individual*. In Part Three we will be concentrating upon the *business firm*, and upon the collection of firms in a given market that we call the *industry*. This chapter is devoted specifically to the business firm. The following chapter will develop the relationships between the firm and the industry in perfect competition; later chapters will be devoted to imperfect competition and its consequences.

6.A

FIRMS AND THE CIRCULAR FLOW OF ECONOMIC ACTIVITY

In Chapter 1, Figure 1.1 pictured the circular flow of economic activity. Two classes of economic agents were shown: individuals or households, and business firms. Economic analysis usually takes the nature and number of the people in a society as a given fact determined "outside" the economic system. (But actually, the size of the human population does respond to economic incentives, as has been recognized since the time of Malthus.[1] Good or bad harvests, or business conditions more generally, affect birth rates and death rates together with immigration and emigration.) Individuals or households constitute the *demand side* of the "product market," the market for consumption goods and services discussed in previous chapters.

Business firms, on the other hand, are clearly created in response to economic incentives. Firms are the crucial *productive* agents of society, engaged in the conversion of resources into final goods. Of course, households also engage in production, but in modern economies production mainly takes place through business firms. For our purposes, then, as pictured in Figure 1.1 firms constitute the supply side of the product market and individuals the demand side.

[1] T. R. Malthus (1766–1834), English clergyman and economist. Malthus maintained that population would always tend to expand to the limits of subsistence. His views had an important influence upon Charles Darwin's thinking that culminated in the theory of biological evolution.

Why do firms exist? There are two interrelated reasons: (1) To take advantage of team production, and (2) to reduce contracting costs.

Team production is a fact of economic life. Many goods simply cannot be produced without a team of workers, each trained for a specific task (clerk, assembly-line worker, inspector, foreman, etc.). But the mere fact of team production is not enough to explain why the business firm exists. Without forming a firm, it would in principle be possible to combine resources by means of a *multilateral contract* among all the individuals concerned. In creating a motion picture the producer, director, writer, stars, supporting actors, stagehands, camera operators, electricians, and so forth—plus the suppliers of costumes, film, sets, utilities, and the like—might all get together and agree upon a contract indicating what types and quantities of resources each party would contribute, at stated times, to the productive process. The contract would also specify, of course, each party's financial obligations and rewards. Multilateral contractual arrangements are relatively rare because of the high costs of negotiating and (what is of extreme importance) the high costs of enforcing them. The business firm provides a way of reaping the advantages of team production without going beyond *bilateral* contracting. Each resource-owner need not deal separately with every other participant but instead only with the firm itself.

In actuality, however, the "firm" is an abstraction. People can really deal only with other human beings. Therefore some person or group, called the "management," must be authorized to deal in the name of the abstract firm. The management may simply be the *owner or owners* of the firm, who are those receiving the residual return after making all contractual payments. But here again, especially with large firms, a division of labor tends to arise. Management itself becomes a specialized kind of employed resource whose purpose is to direct the resources of the firm—that is, to make and enforce contracts with other resource-suppliers.

EXAMPLE 6.1
Effectiveness of Management

Using "predelinquent" boys in a youth home as experimental subjects, the psychologist E. L. Phillips[a] conducted experiments to evaluate the effectiveness of payment systems for the performance of various tasks. Task completion was "reinforced" by points awarded, which could be converted into desired commodities or privileges. One of the experiments involved bathroom cleaning chores.

The youths were assigned sixteen specific tasks to do in cleaning the bathroom. Among the experimental setups examined were the "group" condition and the "manager" condition. In the "group" condition, responsibility was collective. All boys received the same reward or fine, depending upon the overall group performance. In the "manager" condition, there was a weekly auction for the right to be responsible for the collective performance. The auction winner as manager could assign every boy to tasks, and then distribute rewards or fines based upon his judgment of the work performed. The manager himself was rewarded or fined in accordance with the overall level of achievement.

Results under the "group" condition typically showed completion of about six of the sixteen tasks. Under the "manager" condition, in contrast, about fourteen of the sixteen tasks were usually completed.

> COMMENT: Under the "group" condition each boy failing to complete any task suffered only a portion of the overall penalty (which was assessed upon *every* boy in the group). So the incentive to work rather than shirk was weak. The manager, in contrast, was paid *solely* in terms of the group achievement, so he had a strong incentive to make the others toe the mark. (The question of how to arrange for efficient *collective action* will be discussed in more detail in Part Five, as a problem of "political economy.")

[a] E. L. Phillips, "Achievement Place: Token Reinforcement Procedures in a Home-Style Rehabilitation Setting for 'Pre-delinquent' Boys," *Journal of Applied Behavior Analysis*, v. 1 (Fall 1968).

If a manager is not personally the owner of the firm, who will monitor him or her? Ultimately, it is up to the owner or owners to perform this task themselves. This inescapable decision-making aspect of firm ownership is called entrepreneurship. Firms are created, we have seen, in order to achieve certain economies in transacting among resource-suppliers. But unavoidably, there must be a contract among the owners (if there is more than one) that sets up the firm, and a contract between the owners and the manager of the firm (if those two functions are not combined). The execution and enforcement of these contracts pose considerable difficulties.

With regard to the contract among owners that establishes the firm, the invention of the *corporate form* has greatly eased matters. By doing business as a corporation, large groups of people can combine their resources in order to exploit even very big and very risky multiperson projects. The key features of the corporation are *limited liability* and *transferable shares*. Legal and contractual obligations of the corporation cannot be brought home to the individual owner's personal account. Ownership shares may become valueless (at worst), but the rest of the stockholder's assets are safe. And an individual who is dissatisfied with the policies of the other owners, or with the manager, has the option of selling out his or her shares. In consequence, the corporation can acquire and commit large amounts of resources to projects far beyond what would be achievable by a partnership without the advantages of limited liability and transferability of ownership interests. With regard to the contract between owners and management, devices like profit-sharing and stock options aim at linking managers' interests more closely with those of the shareholders, thus reducing the need for the owners to monitor the managers.

One interesting question is: Which people tend to become the *entrepreneurs* or owners of the firm, whose income comes from residual profit rather than fixed contractual payments? In farming, the landowner may be the entrepreneur, hiring labor at a fixed wage. Or the working farmer (supplier of labor input) may be the entrepreneur instead, using land leased for a fixed rental payment. There are also mixed "share cropping" cases, where the supplier of land and the supplier of labor share the uncertainty of profit and loss. In general, we would expect those individuals more able and willing to bear risks to become entrepreneurs. Another consideration is the need for monitoring. Resource inputs that are more easily monitored will tend to be purchased or rented, while inputs for which monitoring of performance is more difficult tend to be provided by owners. An example: in a small restaurant the cashier or even the chef is more likely to own the business than the landlord of the building or the supplier of the silverware.

6.C
THE GOAL OF THE FIRM

Individuals maximize utility, but what do firms maximize? Economists usually assume that the firm maximizes *profit*—the difference between *revenue* and *cost*.

Revenue consists of the receipts from sales—that is, price times quantity sold. *Cost* is a more complicated concept. The economic cost of any activity is the value of the *best forsaken alternative*. The firm, in order to attract the resources or "factors" necessary to engage in production, must pay resource-owners amounts sufficient to induce them to sacrifice their best alternatives, whether these alternatives be employment elsewhere or leisure. For hired resources, the firm must of course pay the going market prices. So *cost can be regarded as the sum, taken over all resources employed, of factor prices times factor quantities.*

There is a tricky feature, however, when some of the resource services are provided by the owner. Part of what accountants call profit may really be a payment for the owners' self-supplied services. Consider a butcher who owns his own shop. His accountant tells him that his profit for the year was $33,000. However, suppose a local supermarket would have paid the butcher $20,000 per year for his services, and that he could have rented the shop to another merchant for $10,000 net of all expenses. The true "economic profit" is therefore only $3000. If his accounting profit had instead been $5000, then his business would have been suffering an economic loss of $25,000. (We are setting aside here any possible extra satisfaction he may enjoy from having his own business.) And even for large corporations, "profit" as reported to the IRS includes a normal interest return on the stockholders' investment.

So in calculating economic cost we must allow also for the alternative uses of inputs provided by the owner. Specifically, economic profit is derived by subtracting the achievable alternative return on all inputs contributed by the owner or owners from the accounting profit. Put another way, economic profit is revenue minus economic cost, not revenue minus accounting cost.

The idea that the aim of the firm is to maximize (economic) profit has not gone unchallenged. Some observers maintain that the behavior of large modern corporations cannot be described as profit maximization. These critics point especially to the *separation of ownership and control*. For very large firms, where no single stockholder-owner accounts for more than a tiny fraction of the shares outstanding, management may (it is contended) be in a position to run things without significant monitoring by owners.

Of course, there are limits. If the shareholders were literally powerless, management could do whatever it wished, even dissipate the value of the firm by enormous executive salaries and expense accounts. But no management is ever given a license to steal. Shareholders as owners can sue for damages if they believe that management has violated the contract with the owners. Such lawsuits frequently do take place, indicating that at least some owners are actually monitoring the management. Perhaps a more important check is the presence of competing groups eager to take over the managerial function. Suppose a self-serving or inefficient management is in control of a corporation. Then the reduced earnings now and in prospect make the market value of the corporate shares lower than they could be. An alternative management group is likely to buy up shares, at their current low prices, with the hope of obtaining enough for control. Or the new group may instead try to win the votes of existing shareholders to defeat the current management in a proxy contest.

The challenge to the profit-maximizing model need not, however, be so extreme. The critics might concede that management aims to do just well enough for the shareholders to avoid lawsuits. But beyond this level, the contention is, management pursues its own goals rather than those of owners. Managers may seek power ("empire-building"), publicity in the form of a "corporate image" (really a management image), amenities like luxurious offices and attractive secretaries, and a stable environment without risk of unpleasant surprises.

There is no doubt that managers sometimes serve their own interests at the expense of the owners. But is this problem significant enough to make the profit-maximization hypothesis unworkable? That is a question for empirical investigation. So far at least, for purposes of economic analysis no alternative description of the goals of the business firm has proved to be more useful than the standard concept of the profit-maximizing firm.

EXAMPLE 6.2
The Separation of Ownership and Control

Harold Demsetz and Kenneth Lehn studied the concentration of ownership in a sample of 511 very large U.S. corporations.[a] Their view was that higher concentration of ownership, as measured by the proportion of stock in each company controlled by the five largest ownership interests, should lead to more effective *monitoring* of management by owners.

On average in these corporations, the five largest ownership interests controlled over 25 percent of the shares in 1980. Furthermore, individuals and families owning large fractions of a particular firm typically did not own significant numbers of shares in *other* firms. This makes sense in terms of achieving effective monitoring. Since overseeing management is costly and difficult, other things equal wealthy individuals and families will not want to diffuse their monitoring efforts over many separate companies, but will instead prefer to specialize their holdings in a single firm that they can supervise closely. On the other hand, there is a big risk in concentrating wealth in a single company, since individuals and families that do so lose the advantages of diversification.

Monitoring will be the more needed, Demsetz and Lehn believed, the more unstable the environment in which the corporation finds itself. Their study used several different measures of instability, such as (1) the variation in monthly rates of return on corporate shares and (2) the variability from year to year of accounting profit rates. For all the measures of instability, it was found that the greater the instability, the larger the concentration of ownership. This is strong evidence in favor of the thesis that large holdings are associated with monitoring, since otherwise an individual would want to hold a *smaller* proportion of his or her wealth in a very risky stock.

Demsetz and Lehn also found that, other things equal, in percentage terms larger corporations had less concentration of ownership. This is logical in view of the greater cost of acquiring any given fraction of the shares, but also because a smaller percent is more effective as a controlling interest in larger corporations where the bulk of the shares tend to be widely diffused. Regulated industries also tended to have smaller concentration of ownership, presumably because regulation provides some *outside* monitoring that makes *inside* monitoring of management by owners less vital. As a final interesting point, Demsetz and Lehn found significantly greater concentration of ownership in media firms and sports firms. The reason offered is that in each of these industries there are significant "amenities" attached to being an owner. Owners of sports firms may enjoy being in the public eye and associating with celebrities, while owners of newspapers and magazines may derive utility from being able to influence public opinion. Thus, ownership and supervision of management may be desired for "nonprofit goals" as well as for higher profit.

[a] Harold Demsetz and Kenneth Lehn, "The Structure of Corporate Ownership: Causes and Consequences," *Journal of Political Economy*, v. 93 (Dec. 1985).

How effective are monitoring and takeover threats at keeping managers' activities in line with shareholders' interests? The following example brings some illustrative evidence to bear.

EXAMPLE 6.3
Owners versus Managers

When managers of a corporation are not performing as well as they might in terms of profit achieved, this fact will be reflected in a lower stock price. Outsiders who believe they can run the company more profitably are then in a better position to take over—by buying a controlling number of shares in the market, by winning shareholder support in a proxy fight, or by negotiation with the existing management.

If in fact the new management will be running the company more profitably, or at least if that is the general market opinion, then a successful takeover will lead to a jump in the stock price. An article by Michael C. Jensen and Richard S. Ruback reviewed a considerable number of studies of this question. Adjusting for other forces such as general movement of the stock market, they calculated the "abnormal" effects attributable to the takeover itself. The table here represents their summary of the available evidence, averaged over a large number of successful and unsuccessful takeover attempts.

Abnormal Stock Price Changes

Takeover Technique	Price Change (%)
SUCCESSFUL TAKEOVERS	
Tender offers	30
Mergers	20
Proxy contests	8
UNSUCCESSFUL TAKEOVERS	
Tender offers	−3
Mergers	−3
Proxy contests	8

Source: Michael C. Jensen and Richard S. Ruback, "The Market for Corporate Control: The Scientific Evidence," *Journal of Financial Economics*, v. 11 (1983).

The tender offer and the proxy contest represent ways of taking over a corporation against the will of existing management. Merger, by contrast, is a voluntary arrangement. (However, such agreement may have been achieved by threat of an involuntary takeover.) In either case, stockholders evidently profited substantially on average from successful takeovers, suggesting that previous management was not in fact maximizing profit for the shareholders. Shareholders did not do particularly well after unsuccessful takeovers. This might have been due to market disappointment that a potentially more effective management had failed to gain control. On the other hand, possibly the takeover attempts failed because existing management was really, in the opinion of the stockholders, doing as well as possible.

While the data summarized here might be taken as evidence that American corporate managements are quite commonly failing to maximize profits for corporate shareholders, this conclusion is really not warranted. After all, the great majority of American companies have *not* been the targets of takeover attempts.

COMMENT: An interesting sidelight is the fact that *bidder* companies, as opposed to the target corporations, have gained very little on average from the takeover efforts—whether successful or unsuccessful. This suggests either that there might have been "nonprofit amenities" such as empire-building or power-seeking involved in motivating takeover efforts, or alternatively that the takeover business is so competitive that there are no large profits to be earned, at least on average.

The following example casts some additional light upon possible conflicts of interest between owners and managers.

EXAMPLE 6.4 _____
Savings and Loan Associations: Stock versus Mutual

Some savings and loan associations are organized as corporations owned by stockholders ("stock associations") while others are cooperatively owned by depositors ("mutual associations"). Corporate managers, we have seen, may be tempted to pursue their own interests rather than those of the stockholders, but this tendency is controlled to some degree by the threat of takeover through a tender offer or a proxy battle. In the case of mutual associations, a variety of legal provisions make it practically impossible for the owners (the depositors) to replace management. So we might expect that managers of mutuals, largely free of owner-depositor control, would feel under less pressure to achieve efficiency and might even find ways of diverting association income to their own advantage.

Alfred Nicols[a] compared the performance of stock versus mutual savings and loan associations. At the time of his study most states barred stock associations, thus shielding the mutuals from competition by the alternative corporate mode of organization. But in California both mutual and stock associations were permitted. Using a variety of measures, Nicols found that in California the stock associations significantly outperformed the mutuals. The operating costs of the mutuals were from 63 to 73 percent higher. There were also a number of possibly suspicious indicators of self-serving behavior. For example, he found that the proportion of association officers with the same family name as the chief executive officer was 18 percent for the stock associations but 33 percent for the mutuals. In consequence, while the mutuals participated in the booming expansion of the California economy, growing by 327 percent between 1953 and 1963, in the same period the stock associations grew by 649 percent.

COMMENT: Consistent with our preceding analysis, it therefore appears that the takeover threat is an important spur to managerial efficiency.

[a] Alfred Nicols, "Stock versus Mutual Savings and Loan Associations: Some Evidence of Differences in Behavior," *American Economic Review*, Papers and Proceedings, v. 57 (May 1967).

6.D
THE OPTIMUM OF THE COMPETITIVE FIRM

We are assuming that the firm aims to maximize profit, the difference between *revenue* received and (economic) *costs* incurred.

This chapter deals with the *competitive* or "price-taking" firm. The market price P is assumed to be constant, regardless of the firm's level of output. (While never literally true, this may be a usable approximation of reality.) Then Total

Revenue R, which is by definition price P times quantity q (that is, $R \equiv Pq$), can be plotted in the upper panel of Figure 6.1 as a ray through the origin with slope P. Price being constant, Total Revenue is zero when output q is zero, and thereafter increases proportionately with q. The vertical axis in the upper panel of Figure 6.1 is scaled simply in dollars, since dollars are the units in which revenue is measured.[2]

Total Cost is usually shown as a curve like C in the upper panel of the diagram. The following are three main features of typical Total Cost curves:

1. The vertical intercept represents the Fixed Cost, such as the rent on a building which must be paid even if nothing is produced. Thus even when $q = 0$, Total Cost C may be positive.

2. At low outputs, C rises but only at a decreasing rate, owing to the advantages of large-scale production.

[2] Why money is used as a medium of exchange will be covered in Chapter 13.

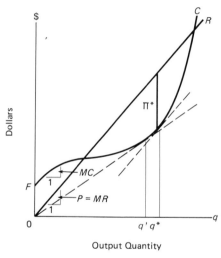

FIGURE 6.1 **Optimum of the Competitive Firm.** At the optimal output q^*, in the upper panel the vertical difference between the Total Revenue curve R and the Total Cost curve C is maximized. The maximized profit is Π^*. At q^* the slopes along the R and C curves are equal, so in the lower panel the Marginal Revenue curve MR and the Marginal Cost curve MC intersect. At output q', a ray from the origin in the upper panel is just tangent to the Total Cost curve, and so in the lower panel q' is the output where Average Cost AC is at a minimum.

3. At high outputs, however, C rises at an increasing rate, reflecting the Law of Diminishing Returns.

Profit is Revenue minus Cost. In symbols, $\Pi \equiv R - C$. In the upper panel, profit is maximized at output q^* where the positive vertical difference between the R and the C curves is greatest. This maximum level of profit, Π^*, is shown as the vertical bold line-segment. As is geometrically evident, the profit maximum occurs where the Total Cost curve C is parallel to (has the same slope as) the Total Revenue curve R. (The parallelism is suggested by the dashed tangent drawn along the C curve at $q = q^*$.) This fact provides the key to the connection between the solution in "total" units as shown in the upper panel of Figure 6.1 and the solution in "average-marginal" units portrayed in the lower panel.

The relations among total, average, and marginal magnitudes were explained in Chapter 2. We saw there that (1) a *marginal* function corresponds to the rate of increase along a total function and (2) an *average* function is simply the total function divided by the underlying variable (which here is quantity of output, q).

First look at revenue. Marginal Revenue MR was formally defined in Chapter 2 as:[3]

$$(6.1) \qquad MR \equiv \frac{\Delta R}{\Delta q}$$

As with all marginal concepts, the Δ notation in $\Delta R/\Delta q$ indicates that we are dealing with small changes in each case. Geometrically, in the upper panel of Figure 6.1, MR is the *slope* of the Total Revenue curve. This slope is a constant equal to the market price P. (Note the small triangle drawn along the R curve in the diagram.) Since Marginal Revenue, the addition to receipts from producing one more unit of output, is constant and equal to P, it is plotted in the lower panel as a horizontal line of height P. Note that the vertical axis of the lower panel is scaled in units of $\$/q$, the dimensions of price.

Average Revenue AR is defined as R/q. But since $R \equiv Pq$, it is always definitionally true that $AR \equiv P \equiv R/q$. In this case, since price P is constant, the Average Revenue curve AR in Panel (b) must also be a horizontal line at the level of P. Thus, for a price-taking firm the AR and MR curves coincide as a horizontal line at height P. (This is an example of Proposition 2.2c in the text: When the average function is constant, the marginal function is equal to it.)

Exercise 6.1: If a firm faces market price $P = 25$, independent of its own level of output q, what is the equation for its Total Revenue R? Marginal Revenue MR? Average Revenue AR?

Answer: The equation for Total Revenue is $R = 25q$. Since $\Delta R/\Delta q$—the increase in R per unit increase in q—is always 25, we know that Marginal Revenue is a constant, with equation $MR = 25$. And, since $R/q = 25$, Average Revenue is also constant with equation $AR = 25$.

---

[3] *Mathematical Footnote:* The calculus definition would be: $MR \equiv \lim_{\Delta q \to 0} \Delta R/\Delta q$. This is of course the derivative dR/dq.

For Marginal Cost MC, the definition is:[4]

(6.2)
$$MC \equiv \frac{\Delta C}{\Delta q}$$

Again, the notation $\Delta C/\Delta q$ will be used on the understanding that we are dealing with small increments Δ. Geometrically, in the upper panel MC is the (changing) slope along the Total Cost curve. (Note the small triangle drawn along the C curve.) This slope is first positive but decreasing (corresponding to the region where Total Cost is rising at a decreasing rate) and then positive and increasing (corresponding to the region where Total Cost rises at an increasing rate).

Average Cost AC is C/q. In the upper panel it is represented by the slope of a ray drawn from the origin to the Total Cost curve. At $q = 0$, this ray would be vertical, so AC is infinite at the vertical axis. As output increases, the slope of the ray falls until output reaches q', which is where the minimum of the Average Cost curve occurs. Thereafter, the slope of the ray rises as q increases further.

The lower panel shows the Average Cost curve AC and Marginal Cost curve MC. From Propositions 2.2a–c we know that when AC is falling, MC lies below it; when AC is rising, MC lies above it; and when AC is constant (at a minimum), $MC = AC$. So we see in the lower panel of Figure 6.1 that MC lies below AC up to output q', then MC cuts AC at its minimum at q', and finally MC rises above AC for outputs larger than q'. In the upper panel we saw that profits are maximized at q^*, where Total Revenue R and Total Cost C have the same slope. Since MR is the slope of R and MC is the slope of C, it follows that in the lower panel Marginal Revenue and Marginal Cost are equal at q^* (i.e., the MR and MC curves intersect).

In terms of economic logic, if a one-unit increase in output will add more to revenue than it does to cost ($MR > MC$), then the additional unit of output should be produced. If $MR < MC$, on the other hand, the last unit produced increased cost more than revenue, and so output should be reduced. For profit to be a maximum, then, the condition $MC = MR$ must hold. And since we are dealing with competitive (price-taking) firms for which $MR \equiv P \equiv AR$, this condition takes on the specific form:

(6.3) $MC = MR \equiv P$ Maximum-Profit Condition, Competitive Firm

One complication is worth noting. $MC = MR$ is an optimum *only if the* MC *curve cuts the* MR *curve from below.* In the lower panel of Figure 6.1 there are two places where $MC = MR$ (two intersections of the MC curve with the horizontal MR curve). But at the left-hand intersection, MC cuts MR *from above.* This means that just to the right of that intersection, we have $MR > MC$. And so economic logic tells us that it pays to produce more units until the right-hand intersection is reached[5] where MC cuts MR *from below.*[6]

---

[4] *Mathematical Footnote:* The calculus definition $MC \equiv \lim_{\Delta q \to 0} \Delta C/\Delta q$ corresponds to the derivative dC/dq.

[5] The left-hand intersection of MC and MR in the lower panel corresponds to a *minimum*-profit (or maximum-loss) output.

[6] *Mathematical Footnote:* We are maximizing $\Pi = R - C$ with respect to q. Differentiating and setting equal to zero, we have as the *first-order* condition for a maximum: $dR/dq = dC/dq$, or $MR = MC$. The *second-order* condition for a maximum is $d^2\Pi/dq^2 < 0$, or $d^2R/dq^2 < d^2C/dq^2$. This says that MR must be falling relative to MC—i.e., that MC must be cutting MR from below.

PROPOSITION: The profit-maximizing output for the firm occurs where Marginal Cost equals Marginal Revenue, provided that the *MC* curve cuts the *MR* curve from below.

Exercise 6.2: A firm faces a price $P = 38$ that is independent of its own output q. Marginal Cost is given by $MC = 2 + (q - 10)^2$. (a) At what output level or levels does $MC = MR$? (b) Where does the *MC* curve cut the *MR* curve *from below*? (c) What is the most profitable level of output?

Answer: (a) Marginal Revenue here is $MR = P = 38$. Solving the equation $2 + (q - 10)^2 = 38$ leads to two solutions: $q = 16$ or $q = 4$. The *MC* and *MR* curves intersect at both of these output levels. (b) By plotting some points we can verify that *MC* cuts *MR* from below only at the larger output, $q = 16$. (c) The most profitable level of output is $q = 16$.

The *size* of the economic profit, at the profit-maximizing output $q*$, was represented in the upper panel of Figure 6.1 as the bold vertical line-segment $\Pi*$ between the Total Revenue and the Total Cost curves. In the lower graph, we see that profit *per unit* is the vertical distance $AR - AC$. Then total profit is $(AR - AC)q$. That is, profit equals the difference between Average Revenue and Average Cost, multiplied by the number of units of output. So in the lower panel maximum profit is shown as the shaded rectangle whose area is $(P - AC)q*$.

Table 6.1 illustrates a hypothetical set of revenue and cost data for a competitive profit-maximizing firm. Price is constant at $P = 60$, so the Total Revenue column (R) is simply $R = 60q$. The assumed cost function is $C = 128 + 69q - 14q^2 + q^3$. This formula was used to compute the Total Cost column C. If plotted, the Total Revenue and Total Cost functions would have the general shapes pictured in the upper panel of Figure 6.1, and the average and marginal functions would resemble those in the lower panel.

TABLE 6.1

Hypothetical Revenue and Cost Functions: Competitive Firm

$P = 60$, or $R = 60q$
$C = q^3 - 14q^2 + 69q + 128$

q	P	R	C	MC$_1$ (poorer approximation)	MC$_2$ (better approximation)	MC (exact)	AC	VC	AVC
0	60	0	128	–	–	69	∞	0	–
1	60	60	184	56	45	44	184	56	56
2	60	120	218	34	26	25	109	90	45
3	60	180	236	18	13	12	78.8	108	36
4	60	240	244	8	6	5	61	116	29
5	60	300	248	4	5	4	49.6	120	24
6	60	360	254	6	10	9	42.3	126	21
7	60	420	268	14	21	20	38.3	140	20
8	60	480	296	28	38	37	37	168	21
9	60	540	344	48	61	60	38.2	216	24
10	60	600	418	74	–	89	41.8	290	29

Three different Marginal Cost concepts are shown by separate columns in the table. Suppose we wanted to estimate the Marginal Cost at $q = 7$. The "poorer approximation," MC_1, is based upon the additional cost incurred by increasing output from $q = 6$ to $q = 7$—i.e., it is the *cost of the last unit produced*. Using this approximation, $MC_1 = 268 - 254 = 14$ is taken as the Marginal Cost at $q = 7$. The "better approximation" takes this same cost increment, 14, but regards it as providing an estimate of the Marginal Cost not at $q = 7$, but halfway between $q = 6$ and $q = 7$—specifically, $MC_2 = 14$ at $q = 6\ 1/2$. To obtain the better approximation MC_2 at $q = 7$, we would have to average the estimate of 14 just obtained for the Marginal Cost at $q = 6\ 1/2$ with a similar estimate of the Marginal Cost at $q = 7\ 1/2$. The latter is the cost difference $296 - 268 = 28$ incurred by increasing output from $q = 7$ to $q = 8$. Thus, the "better approximation" MC_2 at $q = 7$ is the average of 14 and 28, or 21. The averaged or interpolated "better approximation" estimates, for integer values of q, are shown in the MC_2 column.

Finally, the *true* Marginal Cost at integer values of q is shown by the column labeled "MC (exact)." These numbers were computed using the equation $MC = 69 - 28q + 3q^2$, which was derived by calculus techniques.[7]

With $P = 60$, setting the true $MC = P$ leads to the profit-maximizing solution $q* = 9$. (Using MC_2 and interpolating would yield a close approximation, while using MC_1 would lead to a substantial error.) At $q* = 9$, Total Revenue is $R = 540$ and Total Cost is $C = 344$; hence the maximized profit is $\Pi P* = 196$.[8]

Exercise 6.3: Suppose Total Revenue remains $R = 60q$ as in Table 6.1, but the Total Cost function is $C = 10 + 5q^2$. (a) How does this Total Cost function differ from that pictured in the upper panel of Figure 6.1? (b) How does Marginal Cost differ from that pictured in the lower panel of Figure 6.1? (c) What is the profit-maximizing output, and the amount of the maximized profit?

Answer: (a) Plotting several points and sketching, we can see that the C curve here is always rising at an increasing rate, whereas in Figure 6.1 there was an initial range where the C curve was rising at a decreasing rate. (b) Using the "better approximation" method of the text, the points obtained fit the equation $MC = 10q$. (This is also the exact Marginal Cost that can be obtained by calculus techniques.) Unlike the MC curve in the diagram, here MC is a straight line of positive slope through the origin. (c) Since $MC = 10q$ and $MR = P = 60$, setting $MC = MR$ leads to a profit-maximizing solution at output $q* = 6$. (There is only a single intersection of the MC and MR curves.) At this output, $R = 6(60) = 360$ and $C = 10 + 5(6^2) = 190$, so profit is $\Pi* = 360 - 190 = 170$.

The last two columns of Table 6.1 show *Total Variable Cost VC* and *Average Variable Cost AVC*. Total Variable Cost is simply Total Cost less Fixed Cost: $VC \equiv C - F$. Average Variable Cost is, correspondingly, $AVC \equiv VC/q \equiv (C - F)/q$. The relations between Total Cost and Total Variable Cost are shown geometrically in the upper panel of Figure 6.2. Note that Variable Cost VC is everywhere lower than Total Cost C by a constant vertical distance equal to the amount of the Fixed Cost F.

The relations among MC, AC, and AVC are pictured in the lower panel of Figure 6.2. Average Cost AC and Average Variable Cost AVC are vertically far-

---

[7] *Mathematical Footnote:* $C = 128 + 69q - 14q^2 + q^3$. Then $MC \equiv dC/dq = 69 - 28q + 3q^2$.

[8] There is also a false solution (where MC cuts MR *from above*) at $q = 1/3$. At this point $R \equiv Pq = 60(1/3) = 20$, while the fixed cost alone is 128, so profit is negative.

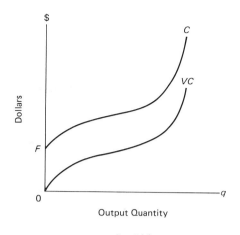

Panel (a)
Total Magnitudes

Panel (b)
Average–Marginal Magnitudes

FIGURE 6.2 The Cost Function. In the upper panel, Total Cost C rises with output, first possibly at a decreasing rate but ultimately at an increasing rate. The curve VC showing Total Variable Cost lies below the curve C by the amount of the fixed cost F. In the lower panel the MC curve cuts first through the low point of AVC and then through the low point of AC. P_C is the long-run shutdown price, below which the firm will not permanently stay in business. P_V is the short-run shutdown price, below which the firm will not produce positive output even temporarily.

thest apart at the vertical axis since, at $q = 0$, AC is infinite. As q rises, AC and AVC converge. The reason is that Fixed Cost becomes a smaller fraction of Total Cost as q rises. Mathematically, $AC = (F + VC)/q = F/q + AVC$. As q rises, the F/q term gets smaller, so AC and AVC approach each other. Marginal Cost was originally defined as the slope of the Total Cost curve C, but at any given output q the Variable Cost curve VC will have the same slope as the Total Cost curve. In other words, the level of fixed costs does not affect the magnitude of the Marginal Cost.

Some other important features of Figure 6.2 are:

1. At $q = 0$, $MC = AVC$. This can be seen in Table 6.1. Note that for the first unit produced $MC = AVC = 56$.[9]

[9] *Mathematical Footnote:* At $q = 0$, $AVC = 0/0$ is indeterminate. But applying L'Hôpital's Rule, it can be seen that AVC approaches a finite limit as q approaches zero. This limit is the Marginal Cost MC at $q = 0$. So MC and AVC coincide at $q = 0$.

2. *MC* is related to *AVC* in the same way as to *AC*. That is, when *AVC* is falling, *MC* < *AVC*; when *AVC* is rising, *MC* > *AVC*; and when *AVC* is constant (minimized), *MC* = *AVC*.

3. *AVC* is minimized to the left of the minimum of *AC*. This results from the fact that *MC* is positively sloped and cuts the minimum points of both *AC* and *AVC*.

In the table, the true *MC* = *AVC* = 20 when $q = 7$; hence this is the minimum of *AVC*. The table indicates that *MC* = *AC* = 37 at $q = 8$; this is the minimum of the Average Cost *AC*.[10]

The maximum-profit condition for the competitive firm is $MC = MR \equiv P$. This is valid even if the firm is losing money (in which case it becomes a "minimum-loss" condition)—*provided* that the firm does not shut down instead. When should the firm choose to shut down? There are two different shutdown conditions, one for the short run and one for the long run. In the short run a firm will continue to operate as long as Total Revenue exceeds Total Variable Cost:

(6.4a) *R* > *VC* or equivalently *P* > *AVC*   No-Shutdown Condition (short-run)

The minimum price meeting the short-run No-Shutdown Condition is symbolized as P_v in Figure 6.2.

In the long run, a firm can only continue to operate if *all* its costs are covered, so the long-run No-Shutdown Condition is:

(6.4b) *R* > *C* or equivalently *P* > *AC*   No-Shutdown Condition (long-run)

The minimum price meeting the long-run No-shutdown Condition is symbolized as P_c in Figure 6.2.

These conditions are illustrated further in Figure 6.3. Suppose a firm is selling 10 shirts per day at a price of $15. Suppose Average Variable Cost *AVC* at this output is $10 per shirt, while Average Cost *AC* (which includes fixed costs) is $17 per shirt. This means the firm is losing $20 ($2 per shirt), which is the area *ABCF*

---

[10] *Mathematical Footnote:* To find the minimum of *AVC*, differentiate $AVC = q^2 - 14q + 69$ and set equal to zero. The solution is $q = 7$. To find the minimum of *AC*, differentiate $AC = q^2 - 14q + 69 + (128/q)$. A cubic equation is obtained, but the only root in the relevant range is $q = 8$.

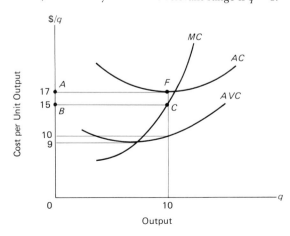

FIGURE 6.3 **Short-run versus Long-run Shutdown.** At price *P* = $15, the short-run optimal output (where *MC* = *P*) is 10 shirts per day. Since Average Cost *AC* equals $17 at that output, an aggregate loss of $20 (area *ABCF*) is being suffered. In the long run the firm would shut down unless conditions improved. But since *P* = $15 exceeds Average Variable Cost *AVC* = $10, the firm would continue operating in the short run.

in the diagram. What if the firm were to shut down? It would then be receiving no revenue, while in the short run the fixed costs continue to run on; for example, the building rent must be paid even if nothing is produced. In this case these fixed costs equal $(17-10)10 or $70 in total. So the firm might as well produce as long as it can cover its variable costs. But if price fell below $9, the minimum of the AVC curve, the firm would be better off shutting down.

In the long run, any price below $17 is unacceptable. The firm cannot lose money indefinitely, so it will dispose of its fixed plant and shut down if price remains permanently below AC.

> PROPOSITION: A competitive (price-taking) firm will maximize profit where $MC = MR = P$, provided that $P > AVC$ in the short run and $P > AC$ in the long run.

6.D.1 □ An Application: Division of Output among Plants

Sometimes a firm must divide output between two or more plants. Suppose there are just two plants, a and b. Then, by an obvious extension of Equation (6.3), the firm's optimizing rule becomes:

(6.5) $$MC_a = MC_b = MR \equiv P$$

That is, the firm should so divide its production as to make the Marginal Costs of output the same in both plants; furthermore, the total output should be such that this level of Marginal Cost equals Marginal Revenue MR. (For a price-taking firm, of course, MR is identical with price P.)

Figure 6.4 is a geometrical representation of the division of output between two plants. The given total of output, $q_a + q_b = q$, is indicated by the horizontal distance between the two vertical axes. The output q_a of plant a is measured in the usual way, as the distance to the right of the left-hand axis. But q_b is, as indicated by the arrow, measured in the reversed direction as the distance to the left of the

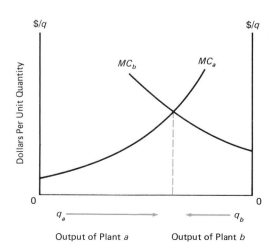

FIGURE 6.4 Division of Output between Plants. A firm with two plants a and b will divide any given output q in such a way that the two Marginal Costs MC_a and MC_b are equal.

right-hand axis. This construction is convenient since the optimal division of output, where $MC_a = MC_b$, is then at the intersection of the two Marginal Cost curves (both assumed rising throughout).[11] The *total* output of the firm will be correct if the $MC_a = MC_b$ so determined is also equal to Marginal Revenue.

What if the MC_a and MC_b curves, each an increasing function of its own plant output, do not intersect at all? This means that for the specified total output q, one plant *always* produces less cheaply than the other. Then the higher MC plant should not be operated at all.

Exercise 6.4: (a) Suppose the Marginal Cost functions for the two plants are $MC_a = 5 + 2q_a$ and $MC_b = 40 + q_b$. If the total output is $q = 25$, how should the outputs be divided? (b) What if the total output were $q = 15$?

Answer: (a) Setting the Marginal Costs equal, we have $5 + 2q_a = 40 + q_b$. Making use of $q_a + q_b \equiv q = 25$ and substituting, the solution obtained is $q_a = 20$, $q_b = 5$. (b) For $q = 15$, if we try to set the Marginal Costs equal as before, a negative output would be indicated for plant b. This is impossible. The explanation, which can be verified by sketching, is that the MC_a and MC_b curves do not intersect if the total output q is only 15. The best solution is to assign all output to plant a—that is, to set $q_a = 15$ and $q_b = 0$. When we do so, at $q_a = 15$ the first plant's Marginal Cost is still only 35—while, for plant b, Marginal Cost is *never* less than 40.

[11] There are interesting complications if one or both of the plant MC curves are falling rather than rising functions of output, but these topics cannot be pursued here.

EXAMPLE 6.5
Load Dispatching: Electrical Engineers as Economists

Electric power is typically generated by firms that operate a number of separate producing plants. Electricity suppliers are normally required to meet all demands placed upon them by consumers, so the operating problem at any moment of time is to divide output most economically among the generating plants. Since the required output varies from moment to moment within the day, a method for providing quick solutions is needed.

Fred M. Westfield[a] investigated the operating practices of a leading American electric utility company. He discovered that the company employs a dispatcher to actually "assign the load" from moment to moment among the different plants. The dispatcher is guided by a Station-Loading Sliderule that shows the Marginal Cost function of each plant. By mechanically manipulating this sliderule, the dispatcher automatically equates Marginal Cost for all plants in operation, satisfying Equation (6.5) and also meeting the total generation requirement. For some older plants, Marginal Cost is quite high throughout. These plants are operated only in peak-demand periods.

The company's method of dividing output, and the sliderule itself, were developed by engineers with no knowledge of economic theory! The company's engineers thus independently "discovered" Marginal Cost analysis.

[a] F. M. Westfield, "Marginal Analysis, Multi-plant Firms, and Business Practice: An Example," *Quarterly Journal of Economics*, v. 69 (May 1955).

"In the short run some costs are fixed; in the long run they become variable." This is the fundamental difference between long run and short run. The distinction is a matter of degree. The longer the run contemplated, the greater the range of costs regarded as variable rather than fixed.

Consider a manufacturing firm. Toward the variable cost end are the expenses of inputs like electric power, supplies of materials, and ordinary labor services; toward the fixed end are costs associated with ownership or leasing of real estate and machinery. Suppose an interruption of supplies or breakdown of machinery calls for a very short, say an hour's, reduction of output. Some electric power would be saved in the slowdown, and there would be reduced usage of materials, but little else could or would be changed. If output were to be cut back over a period as long as a day, some labor might also be laid off. Over a period like a month a large fraction of the labor force might be furloughed (their wages would become a variable cost), and perhaps some leased equipment like trucks would be dispensed with. Finally, for a permanent reduction in output the firm will sell off machinery and scale down its real-estate commitments.

For simplicity, in the discussion that follows we shall treat the long-short distinction as if it were more clearcut: The "long run" will mean that *all* costs are variable; the "short run," that some costs are fixed. The relations between *total* short-run and long-run costs, under this assumption, are shown in Figure 6.5. The single Long-Run Total Cost curve $LRTC$ goes through the origin, since there are no long-run fixed costs. So, when $q = 0$ then $LRTC = 0$. The $LRTC$ function shows the *lowest cost* of producing any given level of output. Why the lowest cost? Because, when *all* costs are variable, at any output q the firm is free to choose the best (most economical) mix of all resources employed.

Three different Short-Run Total Cost functions are shown in the upper panel. First, $SRTC_1$ is associated with a low level of fixed cost F_1. This is optimal for the relatively small rate of output q_1 at which $SRTC_1$ is tangent to $LRTC$. The reason is that at q_1, as we can see in the diagram, $SRTC_1 = LRTC$. Since $LRTC$ represents the *lowest* possible cost of producing output q_1, we cannot do better than $SRTC_1$, which is tangent to $LRTC$ at that output.

Operating along $SRTC_1$ is fine for small outputs. On the other hand, at larger outputs the curve $SRTC_1$ rises steeply—increments of production beyond q_1 are becoming very costly. The next curve, $SRTC_2$, is most suitable for a middling rate of output, q_2 in the diagram. The fixed cost F_2 is at a sufficiently high level to make moderately large levels of production cheaper along $SRTC_2$ than along $SRTC_1$; on the other hand, should it turn out that only small output is desired, then it would have been better to be operating along $SRTC_1$. Finally, $SRTC_3$ represents a level of fixed cost F_3 that is optimal for the large output rate q_3. It represents the best of the three situations for high production amounts, but the worst if only a small output is wanted.

A common confusion runs somewhat as follows: "Suppose the firm desires to increase its output. It knows that certain factors are fixed in the short run but are variable in the long run. Since short-run adjustments are made by increasing only *some* of the factors, while long-run adjustments may involve increases in *all* factors, short-run costs must be less than long-run costs. Isn't it cheaper to in-

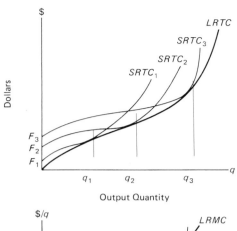

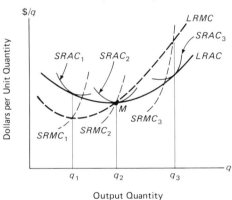

FIGURE 6.5 **Short-Run and Long-Run Cost Functions.** In the upper panel, *LRTC* is the Long-Run Total Cost function showing the cost of producing any output q when all factors are allowed to vary. The Short-Run Total Cost curve $SRTC_1$ applies when the fixed factor is held constant at a level appropriate for small-scale production (q_1); similarly, $SRTC_2$ and $SRTC_3$ are associated with the higher levels of fixed cost appropriate for medium-scale production (q_2) and large-scale production (q_3). The corresponding average and marginal curves are shown in the lower panel. At output q_1, $SRAC_1 = LRAC$ (a tangency) and $SRMC_1 = LRMC$ (an intersection), and similarly for output levels q_2 and q_3. At any output, the Total Cost curves and the Average Cost curves are *never* higher in the long run than in the short run. (Note that no such statement can be made for the Marginal Cost curves.)

crease output by expanding only variable costs than by expanding both variable and fixed cost?" Expressed this way, the fallacy is evident. The firm would accept an increase in its fixed cost precisely because doing so is *less costly* (involves a more economical mix of the various factors) than trying to expand output by increasing variable cost alone.

Let us now translate from the total units in the upper panel of Figure 6.5 to average-marginal units in the lower panel. Since $SRTC_1$ lies always above $LRTC$ except at the tangency point q_1, it follows that the corresponding Short-Run Average Cost curve $SRAC_1$ will lie always above the Long-Run Average Cost curve $LRAC$ except at q_1.[12] A similar argument applies for the relation between $SRTC_2$ and $SRAC_2$, between $SRTC_3$ and $SRAC_3$, and so forth. The upshot is that the Long-Run Average Cost curve $LRAC$ is a "lower envelope" of the Short-Run Average Cost curves just as $LRTC$ is a "lower envelope" of the Short-Run Total Cost curves.

There is a famous puzzle about the shapes of the $SRAC$ curves relative to the $LRAC$ curve. For $SRAC_1$, the point of contact with $LRAC$ is along the downward slope, and so the minimum of the $SRAC_1$ curve lies to the right of (at a greater

[12] $SRTC_1 > LRTC$ implies $SRTC_1/q > LRTC/q$. But $SRTC_1/q$ is simply $SRAC_1$ and $LRTC/q$ is simply $LRAC$, so $SRTC_1 > LRTC$ evidently implies $SRAC_1 > LRAC$. At the point of contact itself, at output q_1, the equality $SRTC_1 = LRTC$ implies the equality $SRAC_1 = LRAC$.

output than) the tangency point q_1. For $SRAC_3$ the situation is reversed, and the minimum of $SRAC_3$ is to the left of q_3. This seems strange; the student may wonder why the points of tangency with $LRAC$ do not all occur at the minimum points of the $SRAC$ curves.

Experimenting with the curves will show that it is geometrically impossible to draw an $LRAC$ curve through the minimum points of the $SRAC$ curves and still have it lie everywhere *below* these curves. For $LRAC$, what we·really want to know is the lowest unit cost of producing any given level of output—that is, the "lower envelope" of the $SRAC$ curves. A point on this envelope is *not generally the lowest-cost output for any given level of fixed cost*—that is, a minimum along any specific $SRAC$ curve.

Consider now the short-run and long-run *Marginal* Costs. At the tangencies of the $SRTC$ and $LRTC$ curves in the upper panel of Figure 6.5, not only the *levels* but also the *slopes* of the curves in contact are equal. But the marginal function is always the slope of the corresponding total function. It follows that at output q_1, the short-run $SRMC_1$ equals the long-run $LRMC$; at q_2, $SRMC_2 = LRMC$; and at q_3, $SRMC_3 = LRMC$. This leads to the relation among the various short-run and the long-run marginal curves shown in the lower panel. Note that $LRMC$ has a generally flatter slope than the Short-Run Marginal Cost curves. This feature will play a role in the distinction between the short-run and long-run *supply functions of the firm*, to be discussed in the next chapter.

Exercise 6.5:   A firm has a Long-Run Total Cost curve given by $LRTC = q^2$. Its Short-Run Total Cost curve is $SRTC = 2B + q^4/8B$, where B represents the level of the factor that is "fixed" in the short run, for example the number of machines. Suppose $B = 4$, so that $SRTC = 8 + q^4/32$. Then it can be shown by calculus (or approximated by tabulating) that the associated Marginal Costs are $LRMC = 2q$ and $SRMC = q^3/8$. (a) At what output are $LRTC$ and $SRTC$ tangent? (b) Are the Average Cost functions, $LRAC$ and $SRAC$, also tangent at this output? [The answer here requires use of calculus.] (c) What can you say about the Marginal Cost functions, $LRMC$ and $SRMC$, at this output? (d) Does the overall picture here differ from the cost function diagrammed in Figure 6.5, and, if so, how?

Answer: (a) At a point of tangency, the curves must touch and have equal slopes. If $LRTC$ and $SRTC$ touch, it must be that $LRTC = SRTC$. So we can set $q^2 = 8 + q^4/32$. The solution is $q = 4$. We now must verify whether the slopes are equal at that output. Since the marginal functions correspond to the slopes of the total functions, we need to know whether $LRMC = SRMC$ at $q = 4$. Direct substitution in the $LRMC$ and $SRMC$ equations given above proves that this equality holds. So $LRTC$ and the $SRTC$ curve associated with $B = 4$ are indeed tangent at $q = 4$. (b) Since $LRTC = SRTC$ at $q = 4$, it is obvious that $LRTC/q \equiv LRAC$ must equal $SRAC \equiv SRTC/q$ at $q = 4$. But to show that the *slopes* are equal, we must use calculus. Comparing the derivatives of the curves will show that both curves have slope equal to 1 at $q = 4$, and so they are indeed tangent. (c) We have already seen, in (a) above, that $LRMC = SRMC$ at $q = 4$. By calculus or by plotting we can show that $SRMC$ is steeper; $LRMC$ and $SRMC$ intersect at $q = 4$, but are not tangent to one another. (d) The main difference is that the $LRTC$ curve here rises throughout at an increasing rate. This implies that both $LRAC$ and $LRMC$ are positively sloped throughout, rather than U-shaped as in the diagram. The *short-run SRAC* curves all have the usual U-shape, however.

There is one difficulty with the concept of fixed costs that now ought to be faced. Common sense tells us that, for an hour's shutdown of output, a firm will not sell off its buildings and machinery with the intention of buying them back when output picks up again. But is this consistent with our analytical models? Why should a firm continue to incur any needless "fixed" costs? Why not sell off the buildings if not needed today? It is sometimes said that "fixity" is the result of previous contractual arrangements—for example, a mortgage on an owned building or a long-term lease on a rented one. But mortgages and leases can always be renegotiated; any losses incurred in the process are attributable to past errors of judgment, and are in no way costs of current production.

"Fixity" is in part due to the *costs of exchange transactions* discussed earlier in the chapter. The difficulty of negotiating and executing complex contracts is what makes absurd the idea of sale and repurchase of factory buildings for an hour's production shutdown. But a second element may also be involved: the specialization of resources to the firm.

Many different types of resources may be specialized to the firm. Machinery can be made to order, and buildings partitioned or remodeled. Workers may be given specific training useful only within the firm. Highly specialized assets owned by the firm will be of little use to other firms and thus have little or no resale value. Hence, the firm cannot profitably sell off such assets to meet a temporary reduction of output. Also, knowing that the resale value will be low, the firm is less ready to acquire more of such a resource merely to achieve a temporary increase in production. Even if such specialized resources are *leased* rather than *owned* (specialized labor may be placed in this category), the cost of cancellation of the lease will tend to be high. The owner of a building to be remodeled for a particular tenant, for example, will surely protect himself by insisting upon steep cancellation penalties. And a specialized worker must be paid a higher wage or else given long-term job protection.

In the absence of transaction costs, and if only unspecialized resources were employed in production, *there would be only a single cost function*—the distinction between "long run" and "short run" would be meaningless. But with specialized resources there are two ways of responding to a decline in demand: (1) The "short-run" response, appropriate for a *temporary* reduction of output, holds the firm's specialized resources fixed and continues to count their cost as a cost of doing business. Thus, "a loss may be incurred in the short run" (*AC* may exceed *P*), meaning that it is rational for the firm to accept a temporary loss rather than dispose of a specialized factor that would shortly have to be repurchased or rehired. (2) The "long-run" response, appropriate for a *permanent* decline in output, is to dispose of the specialized resources. Hence their cost is no longer "fixed." (Any accounting loss suffered in the disposition of specialized factors is a "sunk" cost, the result of a past error of judgment which is not a relevant cost for any current decision.)

Corresponding considerations apply to an *increase* in demand. If the increase is regarded as temporary, the firm will not want to incur the cost of specializing additional resources, since the expense of doing so will not be fully recovered when the time comes to dispose of them. To the extent that the demand change is regarded as permanent, however, it will become increasingly attractive for the firm to incur additional "fixed" costs that make it possible to produce large rates of output cheaply.

CONCLUSION: Factors may be held fixed in the face of a temporary demand fluctuation, in order to avoid round-trip transaction costs associated with purchase and resale (or sale and repurchase), and also to save the costs of specializing factors to the firm. When this occurs, the firm is making a *short-run* response to the fluctuation in demand. A *long-run* response, in which all factors are varied in amount, will be made if the demand change is regarded as permanent.

6.F
RISING COSTS AND DIMINISHING RETURNS

Throughout this chapter both Marginal Cost and Average cost have been pictured as eventually rising functions of output q. These characteristics must apply if the firm is actually operating under competitive price-taking conditions.

What if Marginal Cost were instead falling throughout? Recall that Equation (6.3), $MC = MR = P$, is valid as the condition for optimal output only if the MC curve cuts the MR curve *from below*. Since competitive conditions dictate a horizontal Marginal Revenue curve MR, the Marginal Cost curve MC cannot cut MR from below when MC is falling. So if MC is falling throughout, a competitive optimum cannot be found.

Exercise 6.6: What would actually happen if the firm's MC curve were falling throughout—for example, if $MC = 20 + 8/(1 + q)$? Let the fixed cost be F, and suppose the market price is $P = 22$.

Answer: Setting $MC = MR \equiv P$, the algebraic solution is $q = 3$. But clearly MC exceeds $P = 22$ for all $q < 3$, so at $q = 3$ the firm is incurring a loss—even without allowing for the fixed cost F. On the other hand, as output exceeds $q = 3$ a profit is earned on each unit, and this profit increases with output forever! The firm would then try to produce an infinite output, which is obviously impossible. (If it were to try to expand output indefinitely, eventually the market price P would have to decline, which means that competitive conditions would no longer apply.)

What if *Average* Cost were falling throughout? Then a firm with large output could always produce more cheaply than any number of smaller firms adding up to the same output, and so the smaller competitors would be driven out of business. A falling Average Cost curve is one of the possible sources of what is called "natural monopoly," a topic to be discussed in Chapter 8. [*Question*: Was it necessary to discuss falling MC and falling AC separately? If Marginal Cost is falling everywhere, does it follow that AC must be falling? If AC is falling everywhere, must MC be falling? *Answer*: The student should verify that everywhere-falling AC does *not* dictate falling MC. On the other hand, everywhere-falling MC does dictate falling AC.]

Eventually-rising Marginal and Average Cost are associated with the famous Law of Diminishing Returns, a topic to be covered in more detail when the theory of production is discussed in Chapter 11. The "law" is actually a technological principle, intended to explain, for example, why all the world's food could not be grown in a flowerpot. More formally, the principle can be stated as follows: If one or more productive factors are held fixed, in order to produce additional amounts of output the other (variable) factors will have to be increased at an increasing rate. Thus, holding constant the amount of earth in the flowerpot, the attempt to generate increasing amounts of output—if successful at all—will require ever-rising additions of labor, fertilizer, and so forth. Of course, rising amounts of inputs imply rising levels of cost. Thus, diminishing returns (marginal and average) translate into rising costs (marginal and average).

The Law of Diminishing Returns clearly applies to the *short run*, which (we have just seen) is defined by the condition that one or more factors are being held fixed by the firm. But in Figure 6.5 not only the *SRMC* and *SRAC* curves but also the long-run *LRMC* and *LRAC* curves are shown as eventually rising. Can this be justified? If it were literally the case that in the long run *all* factors of production were variable, the Law of Diminishing Returns would not apply. It would be possible to choose the best combination of factors, and then increase or decrease all factors together in proportion. The Long-Run Average Cost curve *LRAC* would be horizontal, in which case the Long-Run Marginal Cost curve *LRMC* would be also horizontal and equal to *LRAC* (Proposition 2.2c). But it is not really possible to vary literally all factors together. One or more factors, and in particular *entrepreneurship*, may not be readily expandable by the firm. Also, the very nature of the firm may be associated with some unique productive opportunity. A mining company, for example, may be exploiting some particular body of ore. It could try to obtain more output by increasing the use of labor and machines and other variable factors, but there is no way for the firm to duplicate the ore body itself. The existence of fixed factors thus explains why, in any economically possible long run, the Law of Diminishing Returns ultimately applies—so that the *LRMC* and *LRAC* curves must be eventually rising.

EXAMPLE 6.6
Diminishing Returns in Emissions Control

In 1970 the U.S. Congress enacted that a 95 percent reduction in certain harmful emissions from auto exhausts be achieved by 1976. Critics, especially from the automobile industry, questioned the economic rationality of such an extreme goal. They contended that it is disproportionately more costly to go to higher and higher levels of emissions control, just as it is harder and harder to squeeze the last few drops from an orange.

A later government study tended to support this objection. In the table, note how sharply the increments of cost begin to rise after 80 percent emissions reduction has been achieved.

Costs of Emissions Reductions

Reduction in Emissions (%)	Cost Per Car
50	$45
55	55
60	62
65	70
70	80

Reduction in Emissions (%)	Cost Per Car
75	90
80	100
85	200
90	375
95	600

Source: *Cumulative Regulation Effect upon the Cost of Automotive Transportation*, Office of Science and Technology RECAT Report, Feb. 28, 1972.

The fact that rising levels of emissions control are increasingly expensive does not tell us just how far society should or should not go in this direction. So the data above do not tell us that the Congress was wrong, although it might raise a question in our minds. We shall consider the principles that might guide such social decisions in Chapter 15, under the heading "Welfare Economics."

EXAMPLE 6.7
Electricity: Short-Run and Long-Run Costs

There have been many studies of the *long-run* costs of electricity production. The general conclusion has been that economies of scale exist—that is, that the Long-Run Average Cost curve *LRAC* is a declining function of output.[a] Thus, electric power firms appear to characteristically choose levels of capacity (i.e., of "fixed" plant) so as to operate to the left of the minimum of the *LRAC* curve in the diagram of Figure 6.5. This means, in particular, that Long-Run Marginal Cost *LRMC* is less than *LRAC*.

The main technological source of economies of scale is in power *generation*; almost without exception, the larger the generating-plant capacity, the cheaper the power output. The main counterbalancing force is the cost of power *transmission*. The greater the concentration of power generation in a single plant of huge capacity, the higher are the transmission losses when power is carried to geographically dispersed customers.

With regard to *short-run* costs, the picture is quite different. A power system must provide for enormous variation in usage even within short periods like a single day; since electricity is nonstorable, in peak hours far more power must be produced and delivered than in off-peak quiet hours. Of course, it would be absurd to expect electricity generating firms to respond by adjusting "fixed" capacity up and down within the day. And in any case, since these demand fluctuations are obviously temporary, the firm would not want to do so. So the Marginal and Average curves appropriate for contractions and expansions of short-run output will look like $SRAC_1$ and $SRMC_1$ in Figure 6.5. In particular, with capacity held fixed, *rising* average and marginal costs should be encountered, at least at the high outputs required for meeting peak demands.

Technologically, there are two main reasons for rising short-run costs: (1) Pieces of electrical equipment generally have a rated "capacity." This is not an absolute limit; capacity can be temporarily exceeded. But doing so will lead to losses from overheating, risk of breakdowns, etc. (2) Any power system has various plants, and generating units within plants, of differing "technical efficiency" (output/fuel ratio). Rationality dictates that the most efficient equipment will typically be run continuously to carry the "base load." As demand grows, somewhat less efficient units will be started up, so that average costs rise. (The less efficient units may be obsolescent equipment close to replacement, but not necessarily. It can pay an electrical system to invest in units with relatively poor fuel efficiency, provided that such units possess other desirable properties such as low capital costs, rapid startup, etc.)

The "Load Dispatching" example showed that integrated power systems do take account of the rising $SRMC$ curves of generating plants. If plant $SRMC$ curves were not rising, there would be no need for dispatching; all the load would always be assigned to the single most efficient plant!

[a] A review of recent studies is contained in D. Huettner, *Plant Size, Technological Change, and Investment Requirements* (New York: Praeger, 1974), especially pp. 29–39.

*6.G
AN APPLICATION: PEAK VERSUS OFF-PEAK OPERATION

An important practical problem in many industries is how to deal with sharp variations between peak and off-peak demands. Telephones are more heavily used during business hours than during evenings or weekends; local transit demands are greatest in the morning and afternoon commuting hours; in the arid West of the United States, water is more intensely demanded in summer than in winter months; restaurants are busiest at regular mealtimes, and so on. For a firm facing both peak and off-peak demands for its product, the optimization problem is how to divide its efforts between the two.

Assume for simplicity that the peak and off-peak periods are of equal duration. Under pure competition the firm would be a price-taker in both the peak and off-peak markets. In the peak market it would face a higher price P_p and in the off-peak market a lower price P_o—but, in either market, the price will be independent of the firm's own level of output (see Figure 6.6). An example might be a city served by a number of competing taxicab suppliers, daytime hours being the peak demand period and evening hours the off-peak demand period. (It might at first appear that the picture of Figure 6.6 is inapplicable, since quoted taxicab fares do not usually vary with time of day. However, the *effective* price of taxicab service does vary. In peak periods taxis earn a higher effective price, since there is less "dead time" waiting for a customer. And similarly, the customers have to pay

*Marked sections, beginning with a single asterisk and ending with a double asterisk, may contain somewhat more difficult or advanced material and can be omitted without appreciable loss of continuity.

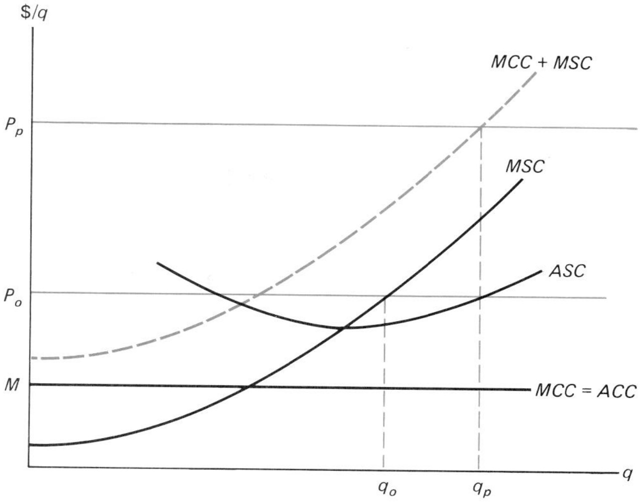

FIGURE 6.6 Peak versus Off-peak Operation, I. In the peak-demand period, the price-taking firm will set the sum of the Marginal Common Cost and the Marginal Separable Cost (MCC + MSC) equal to the peak-period price P_p. In the off-peak period only the separable costs are incurred, so the firm should set MSC equal to the off-peak price P_o. Peak-period output is q_p and off-peak output is $q_o < q_p$.

a higher effective price in peak periods, since on average they have to wait longer for a taxi to become available.)

In analyzing the peak/off-peak situation it is essential to distinguish between "common costs" and "separable costs." *Common* costs are those that apply to both peak and off-peak service. In the case of taxicabs they would include the costs of providing the cabs themselves, of running the central dispatching system, and so on. *Separable* costs are those incurred in serving each specific market. For taxicabs they might include gasoline and drivers' wages. The distinction between common and separable costs is quite apart from the distinction discussed above between fixed and variable costs. Common costs can be fixed or variable, and the same holds for separable costs.

For concreteness the following additional assumptions are employed for the situation pictured in Figure 6.6: (1) There are no common *fixed* costs at all, and furthermore the Marginal Common Cost MCC is a constant magnitude M. In the diagram, therefore, MCC is shown as a horizontal line with height M, which means that the Average Common Cost ACC also equals M. (2) The separable costs include both fixed and variable elements, but the cost *function*—represented by the curve of Marginal Separable Cost MSC—is the same in either market. (It is assumed to cost exactly the same to put any given number of cabs on the road during daytime hours or evening hours.) However, the firm may want to operate at different points along the cost curves in serving the two markets. A taxicab firm, for example, may choose to put a larger number of cabs on the road during the peak period.

Figure 6.6 pictures a possible solution. The rationale goes as follows: As far as the *off-peak* trade is considered, the Marginal Common Cost MCC may be regarded as already having been incurred on behalf of the larger peak business. (The off-peak trade is therefore like a "by-product.") In accordance with this reasoning, only the separable costs need be considered for the off-peak decision. Setting $MSC = P_o$, the taxicab firm will produce just q_o trips off-peak. For the peak period, in contrast, both the common and the separable costs are incurred in serving the larger demand. So the relevant overall Marginal Cost is the *vertical summation* $MC_P = MCC + MSC$ (the dotted curve). This summation curve intersects the horizontal P_p line at the output q_p—where MC_p equals the peak-period price. At this solution notice that $q_p > q_o$. More taxicab service is indeed produced in the peak period.

Surprisingly, however, this is not the only possible case. Figure 6.7 pictures another possibility, the key difference being that now the Marginal Common Cost MCC is larger than the *price difference* $P_p - P_o$. Here, blindly following the procedure outlined above—setting the peak output by the condition $MCC + MSC = P_p$ and the off-peak output by the condition $MSC = P_o$—leads to a paradoxical result. To wit, that peak output q_p' is *less* than off-peak output q_o'! This is of course absurd. What has gone wrong? The mistake was in assuming that the Marginal Common Cost MCC should always be charged to the peak demand *exclusively*. Doing so was valid in the case pictured in Figure 6.6, because there the *price difference* $P_p - P_o$ was sufficiently large that it was profitable to incur the MCC for each unit of additional output going to the peak market exclusively. But when $P_p - P_o < MCC$, as in Figure 6.7, incurring the Marginal Common Cost cannot be warranted by service to the peak trade alone. In this situation, incurring the MCC must be jointly justified by the outputs of both periods in combination.

It follows that, where $P_p - P_o < MCC$, the peak and off-peak outputs q_p and q_o must be equal. But equal at what level? The answer is that the relevant Marginal Cost here, of serving the two markets together, is the vertical summation $MCC + 2MSC$ (the dashed curve in the diagram). At each level of joint output, the common costs must be incurred as well as the separable costs in *both* markets. (Had the two periods not been equal in length, a weighted rather than a simple sum would have been required.) As for the demand side, the relevant Marginal Revenue MR in this case is the vertical sum $P_p + P_o$ (the dashed horizontal line).

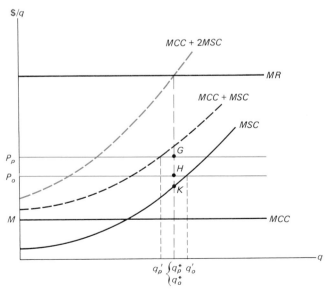

FIGURE 6.7 Peak versus Off-peak Operation, II. Here, if the common costs are charged solely to the peak-period demand (by setting $MCC + MSC = P_p$ for the peak period and $MSC = P_o$ for the off-peak period as in the previous diagram), a paradoxical result is obtained. The off-peak quantity supplied (q_o') would be larger than the peak-period quantity (q_p'), which cannot be correct. This paradox occurs when $P_p - P_o < MCC$—when the price difference between periods is less than the Marginal Common Cost. In this case the profit-maximizing solution is to produce the same in each period, setting $q_p = q_o$ at the level of output where $MCC + 2MSC = P_p + P_o$. At this output the *combined* prices are just sufficient to cover the Marginal Separable Costs and the Marginal Common Cost.

The correct q_p^* and q_o^* are determined by the intersection of the dashed curve and line, as shown in Figure 6.7.

We can summarize as follows:

PROPOSITION: For the price-taking firm facing peak and off-peak markets of equal duration, and assuming that Marginal Common Cost MCC is constant, there are two classes of solution: (a) If $MCC < P_p - P_o$, then peak output is determined by the condition $MC_p = MSC + MCC = P_p$ and off-peak output by the condition $MC_o = MSC = P_o$. The result is that $q_p > q_o$—more is produced on-peak. (b) If $MCC > P_p - P_o$, then the profit-maximizing peak and off-peak outputs are equal. The solution is determined by the condition $MC_p + MC_o = MCC + 2MSC = P_p + P_o$.

Another way of interpreting the solution for the $MCC > P_p - P_o$ of Figure 6.7 case is as follows. Notice that, at the correct joint output $q_p^* = q_o^*$, each period's price yields some excess over the Marginal Separable Cost. In the diagram, the distance GK is equal to $P_p - MSC$, which can be regarded as the "contribution" of the marginal on-peak sale toward covering the Marginal Common Cost. Similarly, the smaller distance HK equals $P_o - MSC$, which is the "contribution" of the marginal peak-period sale toward covering the MCC. By construction in the diagram, the sum of the distances GK and HK is exactly equal to MCC—so that, at the optimal joint output, the combination of the two "contributions" exactly covers the Marginal Common Cost.

When will the firm find it advantageous to abandon the off-peak market entirely? Many restaurants are open only for the dinner trade, and (except for fast-food and short-order places) most restaurants remain closed outside regular mealtimes. Similarly, in the wee hours of the night a taxicab company may take all its cars off the road. Clearly, the decision here is related to the "No-Shutdown Conditions" described earlier in the chapter.

We will consider here only the situation pictured in the earlier diagram, Figure 6.6. Notice that the graph there shows not only the Marginal Separable Cost MSC but also the Average Separable Cost ASC. Since ASC is initially declining, there must be some separable *fixed* costs as well as separable variable costs. In the taxicab case, the separable fixed costs might represent the expense of manning a centralized dispatching system, which can be avoided during periods when the business is shut down entirely. For the situation pictured in Figure 6.6, it does pay to continue operating during the off-peak period—because the price P_o is sufficiently high to cover the Average Separable Cost. Had the separable fixed costs been somewhat greater, the ASC curve would have shifted upward and it might have become more profitable for the firm to abandon the off-peak market entirely. **

** End of marked section.

In the circular flow of economic activity, business firms constitute the main *productive* agents of society, converting resource services into consumption goods. Firms face consumers as suppliers of goods in the product markets, and face resource-owners as demanders of resource services in the factor markets.

Firms are not absolutely required for production to take place. In principle all production could be arranged through multilateral contracts among all the resource-owners involved. But the costs of negotiating and enforcing multilateral contracts may make it advantageous to set up a firm as an artificial entity which can contract *bilaterally* with each separate resource-supplier. The owners of firms (entrepreneurs) are those who take ultimate responsibility, by agreeing to receive only those residual rewards that remain after making contractually agreed payments to other resource-suppliers. In their own self-interest, the owners must monitor performance, either directly or indirectly through a hired manager.

Standard economic theory postulates that the business firm attempts to maximize economic *profit*—the difference between revenue and economic cost. Economic costs include not only contractual payments made to hire resources but also implicit charges that represent the best alternative employments of resources self-supplied to the firm by owners. To maximize profit, the firm chooses that output at which the excess of revenue over economic cost is greatest.

For a competitive ("price-taking") firm in the product market, Total Revenue $R \equiv Pq$ is simply proportionate to output q. The constant price P is equal both to Average Revenue AR and to Marginal Revenue MR.

The Total Cost function C of the competitive firm is rising throughout, starting possibly from some positive level of fixed cost F. It is usually assumed to rise first at a decreasing rate (falling Marginal Cost MC) but eventually at an increasing rate (rising MC). Economic profit is the difference between Total Revenue and Total Cost ($\Pi \equiv R - C$), or equivalently it is the output quantity q multiplied by the difference between price P and Average Cost AC—that is, $\Pi \equiv q(P - AC)$.

The output level that maximizes profit (or minimizes loss) for the competitive firm is given by the condition:

$$MC = MR \equiv P$$

provided that the MC curve cuts the MR curve from below. (Or equivalently here, since the MR curve is horizontal, provided that MC is rising.) However, the firm will instead shut down entirely: (1) In the short run, if market price is less than the minimum of the Average Variable Cost—that is, if the Total Revenue at the best positive level of output fails even to cover the Variable Costs, or (2) in the long run, if market price is less than the minimum of Average Cost—that is, if, at the best positive level of output, Total Revenue fails to cover Total Cost.

The short-run and long-run cost functions differ; in the short run, certain factors are held fixed that are allowed to vary in the long run. At any level of output, Long-Run Total Cost can never exceed Short-Run Total Cost (and, similarly, Long-Run Average Cost is never greater than Short-Run Average Cost). This raises the problem of how it can be rational to respond to a demand change by moving along a short-run cost function. The answer is that short-run responses, which hold some factors fixed, are appropriate for demand changes expected to be only *temporary*. The amount of a fixed factor is not continually varied up or down in response to temporary price changes because of transaction costs, together with the fact that such a factor may have been specialized to the firm so as to have comparatively little value in alternative uses.

The eventually-rising Average Cost and Marginal Cost functions that characterize the price-taking firm have their source in the Law of Diminishing Returns. If one or more factors are held constant, eventually it must be the case that increasing increments of the variable factors are needed to produce additional units of output. Since the short run is defined by the fact that one or more factors are being held fixed, rising Short-Run Marginal and Average Costs are directly explained by this technological law. But even in the long run, not all relevant factors of production can be varied: the very nature of the firm dictates that entrepreneurship, and/or the unique production opportunity exploited by the firm, cannot be expandable without limit. Therefore, even the Long-Run Average Cost and Marginal Cost curves are eventually rising.

Firms often deal in markets with fluctuating demands. For a competitive firm, the fluctuation may take the form of a peak period with high price (P_p) and off-peak period with low price (P_o). The firm will incur some costs that are *common* to both markets and other costs that are *separable* to whichever is served. There are two types of solution: (1) If the Marginal Common Cost MCC is less than the price difference $P_p - P_o$, then the condition for the best peak output is $MCC + MSC = P_p$ and for off-peak output is $MSC \equiv P_o$, where MSC symbolizes the Marginal Separable Cost. In this case, more output will be produced for the peak market. (2) But if $MCC > P_p - P_o$, higher peak output alone cannot justify incurring the extra common costs. Here the same output will be produced for both markets, meeting the condition $MCC + 2MSC = P_p + P_o$.

☐ QUESTIONS FOR CHAPTER 6

MAINLY FOR REVIEW

R1. Why is most productive activity carried out by firms rather than simply by individuals who contract mutually with one another?

R2. Partnership firms are generally small and are generally managed directly by their owners. Why? How does the corporate form facilitate the organization of larger enterprises?

*R3. What is meant by economic profit? Is profit maximization an appropriate goal for owners? For managers? What tends to happen if owners are not themselves managers?

R4. What would be the effect upon the firm's decisions of a 50 percent tax upon economic profit?

*R5. If Marginal Cost MC is falling throughout, will the Average Cost curve AC necessarily be falling? If AC is falling throughout, is MC necessarily falling?

R6. If Marginal Cost MC is rising throughout, will the Average Cost curve AC necessarily be rising? If AC is rising throughout, is MC necessarily rising?

*R7. When will a firm respond to changes in economic conditions by a "short-run" adjustment? When by a "long-run" adjustment?

R8. Why is it that a Long-Run Average Cost curve $LRAC$ cannot be drawn with both of the following properties?

* The answers to starred questions appear at the end of the book.

a. It shows the lowest cost at which any given output can be produced (i.e., it is a "lower envelope" of the Short-Run Average Cost curves).

b. It shows the lowest-cost output at any given level of the fixed factor (i.e., it goes through the minimum points of all the *SRAC* curves).

Which of the two conditions is the correct one?

FOR FURTHER THOUGHT AND DISCUSSION

*T1. In railroading, about two-thirds of costs are said to be "fixed" and only one-third "variable." If so, *AVC* is approximately one-third of *AC*. It would therefore always be financially advantageous for railroads, it has been argued, to take on *additional* traffic even at rates lower than Average Cost. Is this argument valid? Explain.

*T2. Why will a firm ever keep *any* factors fixed in the face of changing economic conditions? What determines which classes of factors are held fixed, and which varied?

T3. Compare the effect upon the firm's decisions of (a) a tax of $1 per unit upon output versus (b) a license fee of $200 payable each year regardless of output.

T4. Is the firm's Total Cost curve necessarily rising, or can it have a falling range? Is the firm's Average Cost curve necessarily U-shaped, or can it be rising throughout (or falling throughout)? What of the Average Variable Cost curve? For each allowable shape of the *AC* and *AVC* curves, show the implied shape of the Marginal Cost curve *MC*.

T5. Consider the problem of dividing output most economically between two plants (as in electricity load dispatching). If the Marginal Cost curves are rising, when will one of the plants not be operated? What can be said if one or both of the Marginal Cost curves are falling?

*T6. What is wrong with the following reasoning on the part of a factory manager:

> My plant is working steadily at its most efficient output. Nevertheless, I could always meet a short-run surge in demand simply by running the machines a little faster and deferring maintenance. So in the short run my Marginal Cost is practically zero.

T7. Electric utilities commonly keep their most modern and efficient generating equipment, characterized by low ratio of fuel input to power output, working around the clock. Older equipment still on hand is used only to meet periods of higher load. What does this imply about the shape of the Short-Run Marginal Cost curve for generation of electricity? Why doesn't the firm *always* use only the most modern equipment?

*T8. An urban rapid-transit line runs crowded trains (200 passengers per car) at rush hours, but nearly empty trains (ten passengers per car) at off hours. A management consultant makes the following argument:

> The cost of running a car for one trip on this line is about $50 regardless of the number of passengers. So the per-passenger cost is about 25 cents at rush hour but rises to $5 per passenger in off hours. Consequently, we had better discourage off-hour business.

Is there a fallacy in the consultant's argument? "Commutation tickets" (reduced-price, multiple-ride tickets) sold by some transit systems are predominantly used in rush hours. Are such tickets a good idea?

7
CORE CHAPTER

EQUILIBRIUM IN THE PRODUCT MARKET— COMPETITIVE INDUSTRY

The preceding chapter was devoted to an *optimization* problem: How do firms go about maximizing profit? In this chapter the emphasis shifts to an *equilibrium* problem: How are price, and the quantity produced and consumed, determined in the market for a particular good? Equilibrium depends of course upon supply and demand. We will see in this chapter how the supply function of a competitive industry is derived from the supply decisions of the separate firms. Equilibrium is attained by putting the industry supply function together with the consumers' demand function (as already analyzed in Chapter 4). The chapter goes on to cover Consumer Surplus and Producer Surplus, measures of the benefits of market exchange to the consumers and to the suppliers of a commodity.

7.A
FROM FIRM SUPPLY TO MARKET SUPPLY: THE SHORT RUN

The competitive firm, by definition, takes market price P as beyond its control. By following the maximum-profit condition, $MC = MR \equiv P$, the firm chooses its best output q in response to the given market price. At each different possible price P the firm's q would also differ; the relation between P and q is the firm's *supply curve* pictured in Figure 7.1. In the diagram, point A (price P^o and quantity q^o) and point B (price P' and quantity q') are two points on the firm's supply curve.

Consider more specifically now the *short-run* supply curve. Recall the qualification expressed in Equation (6.4a): When market price is less than P_V, which is the minimum level of Average Variable Cost AVC, the optimal short-run output for the firm is simply zero. Thus, the competitive firm's short-run supply function s_f may have a discontinuity, as illustrated in Figure 7.1. First, s_f runs along the vertical axis from the origin up to the price P_V, indicating that at any price lower than P_V the output supplied will be zero. The supply curve then skips to the right (dotted line) and thereafter follows the rising branch of MC above the point K. [*Query*: Why do we say that the supply function "may" have such a discontinuity? *Hint*: Is it logically necessary for the curve of Average Variable Cost, AVC, to have an initial falling range?]

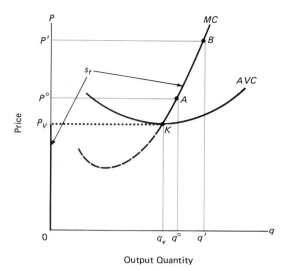

Price

P'

P°

P_V

MC

B

s_f

AVC

A

K

0

q_v q° q'

q

Output Quantity

FIGURE 7.1 Competitive Firm's Supply Function: Short Run. At product prices less than P_V, the minimum level of Average Variable Cost AVC, the quantity supplied is zero (the firm's supply curve s_f runs along the vertical axis). Above this price, s_f runs along the Marginal Cost curve MC.

Exercise 7.1:   Consider the firm's cost function of Table 6.1: $C = q^3 - 14q^2 + 69q + 128$. Find the supply function of the firm, using the exact formula for Marginal Cost: $MC = 69 - 28q + 3q^2$.

Answer: The firm's supply curve is based upon the rule $MC = P$, which implies $P = 69 - 28q + 3q^2$. However, this equation is valid only for $P \geqq P_V$, where P_V is the minimum of the Average Variable Cost curve AVC. From the equation for C it follows that $AVC \equiv (C - F)/q = q^2 - 14q + 69$. The minimum of this expression could be found by calculus. Or else, making use of the rule that MC and AVC intersect at the minimum of AVC, we can set $MC = AC$ or $69 - 28q + 3q^2 = 69 - 14q + q^2$. Solving algebraically, MC and AVC intersect at $q = 7$, where $MC = AVC = 20$. So the supply function can be written:

$$\begin{cases} P = 69 - 28q + 3q^2, & \text{for } P \geqq 20 \\ q = 0, & \text{for } P < 20 \end{cases}$$

Adding up outputs of all the firms producing a particular good (horizontal summation of the firm supply curves), the economywide supply curve is obtained. (Note the similarity with the *demand* aggregation in Chapter 4, where the separate demands of the individual consumers were horizontally summed to obtain the overall market demand curve.) Since firms tend to be somewhat specialized in production, any given good is typically produced only by a limited group of producers; this group of firms is called the *industry* associated with that good. So the economywide aggregate of the firm supply curves for a particular product is the *industry supply curve.*

Exercise 7.2:   Suppose an industry consists of 100 identical firms, each having the cost function of Exercise 7.1. What is the industry supply curve?

Answer: The industry output is $Q \equiv 100q$, where q is the output of each firm. Going directly to the supply function of Exercise 7.1 and substituting from the above, we have:

$$\begin{cases} P = 69 - 28\left(\dfrac{Q}{100}\right) + 3\left(\dfrac{Q}{100}\right)^2, & \text{for} \quad P \geqq 20 \\[4mm] Q = 0, & \text{for} \quad P < 20 \end{cases}$$

There is one complication, however. In Chapter 6 the competitive firm was defined as a price-taker with regard to *product price P*. However, it was also implicitly assumed that the competitive firm is a price-taker with regard to *factor prices* as well. The individual firm is so small that expansion of its output would not significantly drive up the prices of the factors it hires. But when *the industry as a whole* expands or contracts output, the aggregate effect may be big enough to have an impact upon hire-prices.

This effect is shown in Figure 7.2. Let us suppose that the initial product price is P' and industry aggregate output is Q'; this price and quantity therefore determine one point on the industry supply curve S. Initially each firm has a Marginal Cost curve, like MC in Figure 7.1, which (for prices $P > P_V$) is the supply curve of the firm. It might then be thought that the effect of a product price increase from P' to P'' can simply be found by moving along the curve $\Sigma s_f'$ in Figure 7.2—which is the simple horizontal summation of the firm's supply curves—to the output level $\hat{Q}$. But, if the collective expansion of industry output affects factor prices, *the industry as a whole* cannot expand output along $\Sigma s_f'$. Increased industry output would tend to raise the prices of factors used by the industry. But, with higher factor prices, at any level of output there would be an *upward shift* of all the firms' Marginal Cost curves and, therefore, of their supply functions. The consequence is that when product price rises from P' to P'', the new quantity supplied by the industry will not be $\hat{Q}$ along $\Sigma s_f'$ in Figure 7.2. The correct quantity Q'' lies along a somewhat higher summation curve $\Sigma s_f''$, which reflects the *firms'* upward-shifted MC curves at the higher level of *industry* output. The effect is to make the true supply curve, the dashed curve S in Figure 7.2, steeper. Put another way, an observer who failed to take this "factor-price effect" into account would predict too big a supply response of the industry to variations in price P.

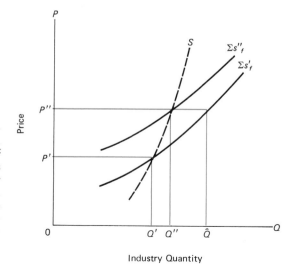

FIGURE 7.2 **Industry Supply Function: Factor-Price Effect.** At price P' the industry produces the quantity Q', as one point on the industry supply curve S. When actual industry output is Q', the aggregate of the supply curves *visualized by the separate firms* is $\Sigma s_f'$. But if product price increases to P'', as industry output expands factor prices tend to be driven up. This raises costs to the firms, forcing their separate supply curves upward so that the aggregate is represented by a curve like $\Sigma s_f''$. Thus, the effective industry supply curve tends to be steeper (less elastic) than the aggregate of the firms' supply curves.

CONCLUSION: The short-run supply curve of a competitive *firm* is identical to its *MC* curve (above the minimum of its *AVC* curve). The short-run supply curve of a competitive *industry* is the horizontal sum of the firms' supply curves, after allowing for the factor-price effect that raises or lowers the *MC* curves as industry output expands or contracts. The factor-price effect reduces the magnitude of the supply response to changes in demand—that is, it makes the industry supply curve steeper.

Just as the *elasticity of demand* measures the responsiveness of the quantity demanded to changes in price, the *elasticity of supply* measures the responsiveness to price of the quantity supplied.

DEFINITION: The elasticity of supply, symbolized as κ, is the proportional change in the quantity supplied, $\Delta Q/Q$, divided by the proportional change in price, $\Delta P/P$.

$$\kappa \equiv \frac{\Delta Q/Q}{\Delta P/P} \equiv \frac{\Delta Q}{\Delta P} \cdot \frac{P}{Q}$$

In contrast with elasticity of demand, the elasticity of supply is normally positive. *Cross*-elasticity of supply (response of supply of commodity X to changes in the price of some other commodity Y) could be symbolized as κ_{xy}. *Income* elasticity of supply could be defined as well.[1] But attention will be limited here to the direct price elasticity κ. To distinguish different commodities, we will write κ_x or κ_y, and so on.

Since elasticity is defined in terms of *proportionate* changes, it is independent of units of measurement. As explained in Chapter 5, this fact makes it meaningful to compare elasticities for different goods. We can also say, for example, that some single firm has greater or smaller supply elasticity than the industry as a whole. The relation between the firm supply curves and the industry supply curves in Figure 7.2 can be expressed in elasticity terms as follows:

PROPOSITION: The short-run elasticity of supply of an industry is normally *less* than the separate short-run elasticities of supply of its firms (because of the factor-price effect described above).

7.B
LONG-RUN AND SHORT-RUN SUPPLY

Figure 7.1 pictures a *short-run* firm supply function. The *MC* curve in the diagram represents the Short-Run Marginal Cost *SRMC* associated with some given quantity of a "fixed" factor. As explained in the previous chapter, a short-run response in which one or more factors remains fixed is appropriate when the firm is responding to temporary changes in product price. What if a price change takes

---

[1] The *cross-elasticity* of supply would be relevant for two goods related in production—for example, wool and mutton. The *income elasticity* of supply might be significant if, for example, higher individual incomes led to a withdrawal of labor from the industry. (In this case, the income elasticity would be *negative*.)

place that is regarded as *permanent*? Specifically, suppose P has permanently fallen. Then the firm will want to hire less of its fixed factors and move to the left along its Long-Run Marginal Cost curve *LRMC* until $P = LRMC$ once again.[2] In the opposite case, of course, the firm would react to an *increase* in price that is regarded as permanent by moving to the right along *LRMC*—increasing its employment of the fixed factors.

The competitive firm's long-run supply function Ls_f is shown as the broken bold curve in Figure 7.3. It is identical to *LRMC*, except that below the minimum of *LRAC* (point M) the supply curve lies along the vertical axis. This means that if price were to fall *permanently* below P_C the firm would shut down. Suppose price is initially P^o, so that the firm is producing q^o (setting *SRMC* and *LRMC* both equal to P^o). Now imagine that price suddenly jumps to P'. If the price change is regarded as *temporary*, the correct reaction will be to set $SRMC = P'$ at output level q'_s; if regarded as *permanent*, the correct reaction is to set $LRMC = P'$ at output level q'_L. Of course, there will be various degrees of "temporary" and "permanent" price changes. In addition, firms may differ in their estimates as to the permanence of the price changes. So we would typically expect to observe within any industry some *mixture* of "short-run" and "long-run" responses.

Exercise 7.3: Using the information in Exercise 6.6 of the preceding chapter, suppose $LRTC = q^2$ and $SRTC = 2B + q^4/(8B)$, where B is the amount of the "fixed" factor. It can be shown by calculus that $LRMC = 2q$ and $SRMC = q^3/(2B)$. (a) If $B = 4$, find the short-run supply curve. (b) Find the long-run supply curve. (c) At what price and output do these supply curves intersect, and what is the significance of this intersection? (d) What

---

[2] How *rapidly* it pays to move from the overexpanded to the correct level of the fixed factor depends upon the durability and the resale value of the "excessive" fixed equipment specialized to the firm. If resale value is relatively high, the firm may sell off the excess equipment and move to the correct scale almost immediately. But if resale value is very low, it may pay the firm to retain the equipment until it wears out. Note that it may or may not take a long period of *calendar* time to make a "long-run" scale adjustment.

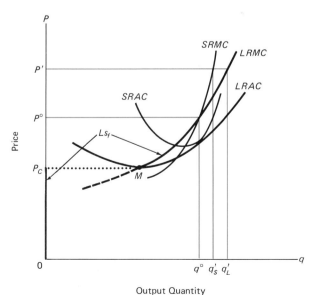

FIGURE 7.3 Firm's Long-Run Supply Function. The firm's long-run supply function Ls_f runs along the vertical axis (zero quantity supplied) up to P_C, the minimum level of the Long-Run Average Cost curve *LRAC*. Above this price, the supply function is represented by the curve of Long-Run Marginal Cost *LRMC*.

would happen if price rose to $P = 27$, and were interpreted as either (1) a temporary change, or (2) a permanent change?

Answer: (a) The *short-run* supply curve is given by the condition $SRMC = P$, or $P = q^3/8$. (b) The *long-run* supply curve is $P = 2q$. [*Note*: We did not have to allow here for any discontinuity in either the long-run or short-run supply curve. Why?] (c) The curves intersect at output $q = 4$, price $P = 8$. The significance of the intersection is that the scale of the fixed factor, $B = 4$, is optimal when $P = 8$—since the short-run supply curve and long-run supply curve dictate the same output $q = 4$. (d) If price rose to $P = 27$ and the change were regarded as temporary, the firm would respond along its short-run $SRMC$ curve, setting $q^3/8 = 27$. The short-run optimal output would be $q = 6$. If the price change were regarded as permanent, the firm would make a long-run response and set $LRMC = 2q = 27$ so that output would be 13 1/2. Evidently, the long-run output response is greater—that is, the long-run supply curve is more elastic.

EXAMPLE 7.1
Cotton Spindles[a]

Cotton spinning in the United States is generally regarded as a good approximation of a competitive industry. There are two main geographical concentrations of the industry, in New England and in the South. The table shows, for each region, the average variation (by calendar quarters over the period 1945 to 1959) in "spindle hours." Spindles as fixed equipment are of course an essential element of spinning, so that spindle hours can be regarded as measuring output. "Changes in Hours per Spindle" may be interpreted as an index of the firms' *short-run* adjustment to the price changes taking place quarter by quarter. "Changes in Active Spindles" represents a *long-run* adjustment—variation in the amount of fixed equipment.

Changes in Cotton Spinning, per Quarter, 1945–1959

Area	Changes in Hours Per Spindle	Changes in Number of Active Spindles (%)
Southern states	90.5	9.2
New England	76.5	21.8

Source: U.S. Census data cited in G. J. Stigler, *The Theory of Price*, 3rd ed. (New York: Macmillan, 1966), p. 144.

Evidently, the quarterly price changes in this period were predominantly interpreted by firms as temporary, since only to a small extent did they lead to changes in the quantities of "fixed" equipment.

The difference between the two regions appears to be due to the fact that the industry, while relatively static in the South, was definitely declining in New England. In periods of low prices, the higher-cost New England firms were more likely to make long-run adjustments, gradually disposing of their fixed spindle equipment.

[a] Discussion based upon G. J. Stigler, *The Theory of Price*, 3rd ed. (New York: Macmillan, 1966), pp. 143–44.

The *industry* long-run supply curve, like the industry short-run supply curve, is based upon the horizontal summation of the firm supply curves. As before, allowance must be made for the impact of industry-wide output changes upon factor prices, as shown in Figure 7.2. For both short-run and long-run supply, this factor-price effect makes the industry supply curve less elastic.

There is one additional element that operates in the long run: *entry and exit of firms.* In long-run equilibrium, for every firm that remains in the industry, price must cover Average Cost: $P \geqq LRAC$. Or, we may say, *economic profit* cannot be negative. Firms that cannot make a profit at any achievable level of output will eventually go out of business (the entrepreneur will shift to a new industry or take a non-entrepreneurial job). And if an outside firm—whether newly organized, or already in existence but operating in some other industry—can earn a profit within the industry, it will eventually enter.

Summarizing, a price change leads to a larger supply reaction when firms in the industry adjust along *LRMC* (i.e., when they interpret the price change as permanent) than when they adjust only along *SRMC* (i.e., when they interpret the price change as temporary). Entry and exit work in the same direction. A high price leads in the long run not only to a larger quantity response along existing firms' *LRMC* curves but also to an increase in the *number* of firms; a low price leads in the long run not only to output reductions along *LRMC* curves but also to a contraction in the *number* of firms.

The effect of "length of run" upon the supply-demand equilibrium is pictured in Figure 7.4. The initial equilibrium situation is represented by price P^o and Q^o along demand curve DD. Now suppose demand shifts upward to $D'D'$. The vertical curve labeled *IS* is what is sometimes called the "immediate-run" supply function. It is supposed to represent a period of time so momentary that production has no chance to respond. Quantity being fixed, price is determined by the intersection of supply curve *IS* with the demand curve $D'D'$ at the level P_I. If we allow the demand change to last long enough for firms to adjust their variable

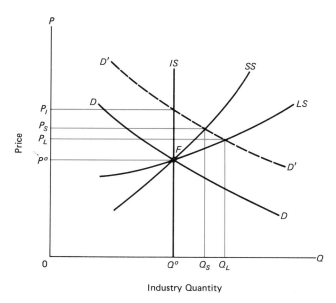

FIGURE 7.4 Market Response to Change in Demand. Starting from an equilibrium at point F (price P^o and output Q^o), the demand curve shifts upward from DD to $D'D'$. In the "immediate run," quantity Q^o cannot be changed at all (vertical supply curve *IS*); the entire impact is therefore upon price, which rises to P_I. In the "short run" (that is, if firms can vary output but evaluate the demand change as temporary), the sloping supply curve SS is relevant; aggregate quantity increases to Q_S and price comes back down to P_S. In the "long run" (if firms evaluate the demand change as permanent), LS becomes the relevant supply curve; the change in quantity is greatest (Q_L), and the change in price is least (P_L).

Industry Quantity

PART 3   THE FIRM AND THE INDUSTRY

factors, there will be some quantity response as indicated by the positive slope of the short-run supply curve SS. In the new *short-run* equilibrium, price P_S is higher than the initial P^o but lower than the immediate-run price P_I. Finally, the long run supply LS is still more elastic. So, in *long-run* equilibrium, price comes back down to P_L—which is still higher, however, than P^o.

> CONCLUSION: As the industry responds to changes in demand, in progressing from the immediate run to the short run to the long run the impact upon price is reduced while the change in the quantity produced becomes greater.

EXAMPLE 7.2
Preclusive Buying of Wolfram[a]

A striking example of the responsiveness of supply to price was provided by the Allied powers' "preclusive buying" program in World War II. In this program the United States and Great Britain attempted to buy up supplies of strategic materials to prevent their shipment to enemy Axis nations.

Wolfram is an ore of tungsten, a vital alloying metal for steel. It is produced in Spain and Portugal, neutral countries that were potential suppliers to the Axis. In August 1940, before the commencement of preclusive buying, the market price of wolfram in Portugal and Spain was $1144 per ton. Since the Allies were trying to buy up literally *all* the wolfram that would otherwise have gone to Germany and Italy, the price was rapidly driven to unprecedented levels. By October 1941 it had reached $20,000 per ton. Portugal reacted by controlling the price and allotting the wolfram supply between the Axis and the Allies. Spain, however, chose to let the market process operate unhindered (to the advantage of the Spanish wolfram miners).

The program "succeeded" in the sense that Germany eventually (in July 1943) quit bidding for Spanish wolfram, making do with substitutes for tungsten alloy. But before this occurred, wolfram production in Spain had increased to ten times its prewar level. In undertaking the program, the long-run supply elasticity of wolfram production had been seriously underestimated.

[a] Discussion based on D. I. Gordon and R. Dangerfield, *The Hidden Weapon* (New York: Harper & Brothers, 1947), pp. 105–16.

7.C
DETERMINANTS OF THE INDUSTRY'S SUPPLY FUNCTION

The determinants of industry supply can be classified into three categories: (1) elements that are *internal* to the separate firms of the industry; (2) elements that are *external* to the separate firms (but still "internal" to the industry as a whole); and (3) elements that are associated with entry of firms into, or exit of firms from, the industry.

The elements *internal* to the firms are reflected in the firms' short-run and long-run cost functions. What are called the *internal diseconomies* of scale dictate rising short-run supply curves for the firms in an industry. And, although supply is more elastic in the long run, the Law of Diminishing Returns nevertheless must eventually apply. So the competitive firm's Ls_f curve, while more elastic than its short-run supply curve s_f, will still be upward-sloping reflecting internal diseconomies of scale.

As for the second category, elements *external* to the separate firms but nevertheless internal to the industry, the "factor-price effect" pictured in Figure 7.2 is one example. When the industry *as a whole* expands, the prices of factors heavily used by that industry are driven up. The factor-price effect is thus normally an *external diseconomy* of scale. As shown in Figure 7.2, it makes the supply curve of the industry less elastic than the simple horizontal sum of the separate firms' supply functions.

External economies and diseconomies can be divided into two categories: "pecuniary" and "technological." In both cases, the externality exists because changes in the *output of the industry* affect the *cost function of its firms*. For a "pecuniary" economy or diseconomy, industry output affects the firm's cost function solely through changes in the market *prices* of inputs. The factor-price effect is an external *pecuniary diseconomy*.

For a "technological" economy or diseconomy, on the other hand, industry output directly affects firms' physical possibilities of production—the firms' production functions. As an example, consider first a favorable externality, an *external technological economy*. Take farming on marshy soil. In order for farmer A to produce, he must drain his land. But pumping water out of his marshy soil will help to drain the lands of his neighboring competitors $B, C, D, \ldots$. The neighboring farmers find that their lands, being less marshy than before, now produce better (Average Cost and Marginal Cost are lower). Similarly, any drainage efforts by neighbors $B, C, D, \ldots$ will help to shift AC and MC downward for farmer A. If all try to expand output together, all engaging in more drainage, the situation is as shown in Figure 7.5. The original industry price–quantity equilibrium is at point

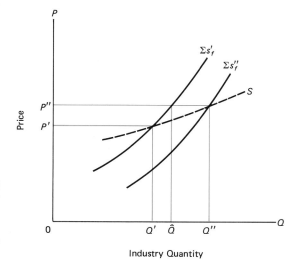

FIGURE 7.5 Industry Supply Function: External Economy. Owing to an "external economy," firms' costs of production fall as industry output expands. The effect is to flatten the industry supply curve. (Note that the picture here is the reverse of Figure 7.2.)

P', Q'. With a rise in price to P'', the $\Sigma s_f'$ curve (the simple horizontal sum of the firms' s_f' curves) would indicate industry output $\hat{Q}$. But since the "external economy" here shifts the firms' MC curves downward, the curve $\Sigma s_f'$ shifts down to $\Sigma s_f''$ so that the new equilibrium will be at Q''. The industry supply curve S is thus more elastic than the separate supply curves of its component firms. The direction of this external effect is the reverse of that pictured in Figure 7.2.

Now consider a *technological external diseconomy*. Suppose now that the farm lands are too dry rather than too wet. Each farmer must irrigate, pumping water up from underground wells. Doing so drains water away from neighbors' wells, thus *increasing* their Average Cost and Marginal Cost. Here the true industry supply curve S is steeper than the horizontal sum of the firms' supply curves, like the picture in Figure 7.2.

Is it possible for a favorable externality to be so powerful as to make the industry supply curve actually slope downward? That is, can the *external economies* be so great as to override the inevitable *internal diseconomies* of scale? The answer is yes. Such a possibility is illustrated in Figure 7.6. Starting from an initial equilibrium at F, demand increases from D' to D''. As firms begin to expand output, the resulting increase of industry output sharply reduces costs of production owing to a technological or pecuniary external economy. Point G shows the ultimate result: In response to an upward shift of demand, equilibrium quantity is larger and price lower. Thus, the industry supply curve has negative slope. Notice however that the *firm* supply curves must still be positively sloped; we know that, for an optimum, the firm's Marginal Cost curve MC must cut the horizontal $MR \equiv P$ from below (see Figure 7.1).

Exercise 7.4: An industry consists of 100 identical firms, each with Marginal Cost $MC = 10 + 8q - Q/10$, where q is the firm's own output and Q is the industry output. (a) Is this an external economy or diseconomy? (b) What is the equation for the industry supply curve? (c) Which diagram in the text pictures this situation?

Answer: (a) From the equation for MC, larger industry output Q reduces Marginal Cost. So this situation represents an external economy. (b) Since the firm sets $MC = P$, its supply

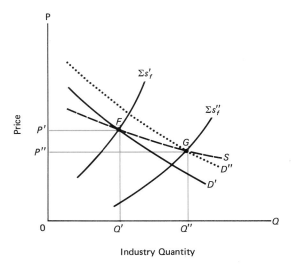

FIGURE 7.6 Negatively Sloped Supply Function Due to External Economies. As demand shifts upward from D' to D'', temporarily raising price, firms begin to respond along their individual supply curves whose summation is indicated by the Σs_f curve through the original price-quantity equilibrium point F. But the assumed external economy means that increased industry output sharply reduces firms' costs of production, shifting the summation of the firm's supply curves downward to $\Sigma s_f'$. If the external economy is sufficiently strong, as shown here, the new equilibrium point G represents larger quantity at lower price. Thus, the industry's supply curve S is negatively sloped.

function is given by $P = 10 + 8q - Q/10$. Using $Q \equiv 100q$ and substituting, the industry supply curve is $P = 10 + 8Q/100 - 0.1Q$, or simplifying: $P = 10 - 0.02Q$. (c) The situation is like the picture in Figure 7.6—that is, the supply curve is actually negatively sloped.

The third important determinant of the industry supply curve is entry and exit of firms. This is a long-run phenomenon. We have seen that exit and entry make the industry supply curve more elastic: the industry response to changes in price, upward or downward, will be greater than if output adjustments only on the part of existing firms were allowed for. Indeed, if there were an indefinitely large number of essentially identical firms standing ready to enter or leave, an industry's supply curve would be effectively horizontal (infinitely elastic).[3] But this is unlikely. Some firms will have a cost advantage in one industry, other firms will have a cost advantage in other industries. Those firms already in an industry will tend to be the ones with the lowest costs. New firms will typically have higher costs, ruling out a horizontal long-run supply curve. (This need not mean that the new firms are "inefficient"; it may be only that their alternatives elsewhere are relatively more attractive.)

CONCLUSION: In a competitive industry, the *internal* determinants (effects of a firm's own output upon its costs) are predominantly diseconomies—tending to make the industry supply curve upward-sloping. But this effect is less strong in the long run (long-run supply is more elastic). The *external pecuniary* effects, which are due to changes in factor hire-prices as the industry output changes, also are normally diseconomies (tending to make the industry supply curve more inelastic). But *external technological* effects, which work through changes in production functions, can be either economies or diseconomies, and in the former case may even lead to a downward-sloping industry supply curve. *Exit and entry* of firms always tend to make the industry supply curve more elastic.

7.D
FIRM SURVIVAL AND THE "ZERO-PROFIT THEOREM"

Competition always works to erode economic profit. Wherever profit exists, new firms enter and expand industry output, forcing product prices downward. Simultaneously, resource prices are forced upward. Profit is thus squeezed from above and from below.

Where does this process end? Entry stops (long-run equilibrium is attained) when no firm still outside the industry can see its way to earning a profit within. It follows that the "marginal firm," the one just on the borderline of entering or leaving the industry, can earn only negligibly more within the industry than outside. Thus, its *economic* profit (excess of revenues over the best alternative foregone) in the industry is essentially zero.

Does it follow that the established firms—which, as we have seen, typically have lower costs—are earning positive economic profits in long-run equilibrium?

[3] *Qualification:* For this to hold, external economies and diseconomies must also be absent.

No, because there would still be upward pressure on *factor* prices. The reasoning goes as follows. If an established firm is earning positive economic profit, it must be that its Average Costs are lower than those of the marginal firm. Some unusually productive resource must be responsible for its unusually low cost of production. *All firms in the industry will be bidding for the right to employ that special resource*, so in the long run its hire-price will be driven upward so as to eliminate the profit.

A clear case occurs in mining. Suppose the demand for copper rises, so that the long-run equilibrium price for copper is higher than before. New firms enter to develop copper-ore bodies previously too lean to work. If the marginal firm working a very thin ore just breaks even, it might be thought that an established firm exploiting a richer ore deposit should be making a handsome profit. And indeed it may, in the short run. But in the long run all firms in the industry will be bidding for the right to work the richer ore. Consequently, the owner of the resource, i.e., the owner of the richer body of ore, will be able to charge a higher price that will recapture any economic profit that might have existed. What if the mining firm itself owns the richer ore deposit? Here is where the distinction between *economic profit* and *accounting profit* (see Chapter 6) becomes essential. The accounting profit of a firm controlling a rich ore body may indeed be high. But that firm could always lease or sell the deposit to another firm. It should therefore charge itself, as an *economic cost* of its mining operations, the highest bid an outsider would make for the right to exploit its ore. In this way, its *economic profit* as a mining firm also becomes zero in long-run equilibrium.

> PROPOSITION: In the long run, economic profit for any firm in a competitive industry is zero.

Of course, in an ever-changing world the "long run" may never actually arrive. Something almost always happens to change the conditions of long-run equilibrium before that state is achieved. But the *tendency* toward zero economic profit, due to downward pressure on product price and upward pressure on factor prices, is an important aspect of competitive industries.

EXAMPLE 7.3
Economies of Scale and the Survivor Principle: Medical Practice

The continuing pressure upon firm survival provides a source of information about *efficient scale* of production. Those firms having chosen wrong levels of "fixed" factors will have high Average Costs of production. In the long run, if they are to survive in the industry, such firms must shift to a more appropriate scale. What is known as "the survivor principle" looks at changes in the proportions of industry output generated by large and small firms for evidence concerning typical cost functions in the industry.

The survivor principle was applied to medical practice by H. E. Frech, III, and P. Ginsberg, who compared the market shares of physicians engaged in solo versus joint practice for the years 1965 and 1969. A later study by William D. Marder and Stephan Zuckerman extended the results through 1980. As can be seen from the table, the share accounted for by solo or two-physician practices declined, whereas larger-sized groups gained steadily in market share between 1965 and 1980. But it seems that by 1980 the decline in one- or two-physician practices was tapering off and may have reached a limit.

Market Share by Group Size, Medical Practice (%)

Group Size	1965	1969	1975	1980
1–2	84.69	78.25	68.67	67.45
3–7	8.37	11.53	13.31	13.14
8–25	4.30	5.09	8.53	7.78
26–99	1.33	3.00	5.08	4.66
100+	1.31	2.12	4.42	6.97
Total	100.0	100.0	100.0	100.0

Sources: H. E. Frech, III, and P. Ginsberg, "Optimal Scale in Medical Practice: A Survivor Analysis," *Journal of Business*, v. 47 (Jan. 1974), p. 30; and William D. Marder and Stephan Zuckerman, "Competition and Medical Groups: A Survivor Analysis," *Journal of Health Economics*, v. 4 (June 1985), p. 167.

The data in the table can be interpreted quite differently depending upon whether a static or dynamic viewpoint is adopted. From the static point of view, even in 1980 the great bulk of the market was accounted for by single- or two-physician groups. This strongly suggests that small size must indeed be the most efficient in medical practice. On the other hand, it is precisely this size that is declining, relative to all others. So it appears that, *on the margin*, firms of moderate and large size have been more profitable. New entrants find it advantageous to form groups of moderate or large size, while exiting firms must have come disproportionately from the small one-to-two physician class.

A possible explanation is that at any point of time there is an efficient *mixture* of firm sizes. Even though the small one-to-two physician firm may on the whole be most efficient in medical practice, there may still at the present moment be relatively *too many* in this size class. So we observe the market shares shifting in favor of the larger groups.

7.E
THE BENEFITS OF EXCHANGE: CONSUMER SURPLUS AND PRODUCER SURPLUS

One of the most important principles of economics is the Fundamental Theorem of Exchange:

PROPOSITION: Trade is mutually beneficial.

Voluntary exchange increases utility for all parties involved. An alternative, mistaken view is the "exploitation theory," which claims that in exchange one side's gain is the other side's loss. The proof of the Fundamental Theorem of Exchange, and disproof of the exploitation theory, is quite elementary. Since exchange is a voluntary activity, a rational person will engage in trade *only* if he or she expects to gain.

In practical applications is it very helpful to have measures of the benefits of trade, scaled in objective units that do not depend upon individuals' subjective utilities. *Consumer Surplus* and *Producer Surplus* are such measures.[4]

In Figure 7.7 the market supply-demand equilibrium is at price P^* and quantity Q^*. Consumer Surplus is represented by the upper shaded area, lying beneath the demand curve D but above the horizontal line P^*B. The general intention is to *show the net advantage to consumer-buyers of being able to buy at the ruling price P^**, even though they would have been willing to pay higher prices (as shown by the height of the demand curve) for smaller numbers of units. The Producer Surplus is the corresponding lower shaded area, lying above the supply curve S but below the horizontal line P^*B. It shows the net gain to producer-sellers of receiving a price as high as P^* for *all* units sold even though they would have been willing to supply some units at lower prices.

The concepts of *demand price* (height of demand curve at any quantity Q) and *supply price* (corresponding height of supply curve) are useful here. For the very first unit purchased, the demand price in Figure 7.7 is OA. But the price charged is only OP^*—hence a Consumer Surplus of $OA - OP^* = AP^*$ is gained on the first unit bought. Now extend this argument to all successive units. Then, at the aggregate transaction quantity $Q = Q^*$, the sum of successive demand prices (which may be called the consumers' aggregate *willingness to pay* for quantity Q^*) is the roughly trapezoidal area $OABQ^*$ in Figure 7.7. But the aggregate amount ac-

---

[4] The names of these measures are, unfortunately, somewhat misleading. The benefits stem from *trading* (buying or selling), not from consuming or producing.

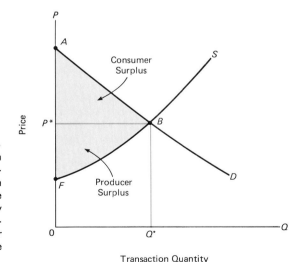

FIGURE 7.7 **Consumer Surplus and Producer Surplus: Traditional Measures.** At the transaction quantity Q^*, Consumer Surplus is the area lying below the demand curve D but above the equilibrium price P^*. It is the difference between the aggregate willingness to pay for the quantity Q^* (the roughly trapezoidal region $OABQ^*$) and the amount actually paid (the rectangle OP^*BQ^*). The Producer Surplus is similarly the area above the supply curve S but below the equilibrium price.

tually paid is only the rectangle OP^*BQ^*. The upper shaded (roughly triangular) area AP^*B—the difference between aggregate willingness to pay and aggregate actual payments—is the Consumer Surplus. A corresponding argument applies to Producer Surplus, which can be regarded as the difference between sellers' aggregate actual receipts OP^*BQ^* and the minimum aggregate payment $OFBQ^*$ they would accept—the difference being the area FBP^*.

7.E.1 □ An Application: The Water-Diamond Paradox

Many people cannot understand why a vital commodity like water is very cheap, while diamonds—satisfying relative insignificant human needs—are so dear. They conclude that there is something wrong with a market system that makes the frivolous commodity, diamonds, so much more expensive.

Elementary textbooks explain the supposed "paradox." We have to consider *supply* as well as demand. If water were as scarce as diamonds, it would be far more valuable. Using some common physical unit (e.g., gallons) as in Figure 7.8, *for equivalent quantities* the demand curve for water, D_w, is surely far higher than the demand curve for diamonds, D_d. But at the actual tremendously disparate quantities, the market price of water is lower. Municipal water typically costs about $100 per acre-foot, or 3 cents per hundred gallons. At this price water consumption is commonly about 150 gallons (five-eighths of a ton) per capita *per day*. Diamond quantities are measured in terms of the carat (one-fifth of a gram), and gem-quality prices run upward from $1000 per carat. At such prices (on the order of $20,000,000 per *gallon*) the number of gallons of diamonds demanded per day (or even per year or per lifetime) is small.

In terms of the benefits of trade, the Consumer Surplus derived from water purchases must then be enormous in comparison with the actual market value of water bought and sold. This market value, $P_w Q_w$, is represented in the diagram by the very low, flat rectangle lying just above the horizontal axis. The enormously greater shaded area, above this rectangle but below the demand curve D_w approximates the Consumer Surplus. Using the instructive terminology of Adam Smith,

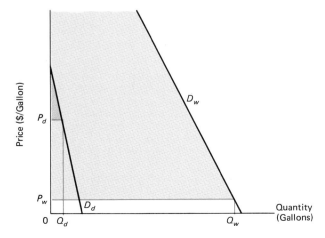

FIGURE 7.8 The Water-Diamond Paradox. For equivalent quantities (gallons), water is "more valuable" than diamonds, in the sense that consumers' aggregate willingness to pay (total area under the demand curve) is greater. But the quantity of water available is so enormous, in comparison to demand, that the *market value* of water (rectangle of width Q_w and height P_w) is small. Purchasers of water therefore derive a huge Consumer Surplus (shaded region). For diamonds the quantity on the market is tiny relative to the demand. Compared to the area under the demand curve, the market value of diamonds (rectangle of width Q_d and height P_d) is large and so Consumer Surplus is small.

the *value in use* of water (its total worth to consumers, or their total willingness to pay) is very, very large in comparison with its *value in exchange*—the difference between the two being the Consumer Surplus. For diamonds, on the other hand, Consumer Surplus is only the small dark area under the D_d curve. Thus, for diamonds the market value represents the great bulk of the value in use and so there is little Consumer Surplus.

7.E.2 □ Hindrances to Trade

In Chapter 2, taxes on transactions were analyzed. The conclusion was that, regardless of whether a tax is imposed upon buyers (shifting the demand curve down) or upon sellers (shifting the supply curve up), the effects are identical. As illustrated in Figure 7.9, the tax causes quantity traded to fall from Q^* to Q^o. As for price, after-tax, there are *two* prices to consider: a "gross price" P^+ inclusive of tax and a "net price" P^- exclusive of tax. Buyers would be paying the gross (demand) price, whereas sellers would be receiving only the net (supply) price; hence, it is P^+ that is relevant for transaction *demand* decisions and P^- that is relevant for transaction *supply* decisions. Figure 7.9 shows that the gross price is higher than, but the net price lower than, the pre-tax equilibrium price P^*. (While it is often said that taxes raise prices, this is only partially correct: a transaction tax does raise the price to the buyer but it lowers the price received by the seller.)

We can use Consumer and Producer Surplus to analyze how a tax affects the gains from trade. In Figure 7.9, when the price paid by buyers rises to P^+, Consumer Surplus falls by the upper shaded area *FHBL*. Since the price received by sellers has fallen to P^-, Producer Surplus is reduced by the lower shaded area *LBGK*. The combined loss of Consumer and Producer Surplus is therefore the entire shaded area *FHBGK*. This amount is not a total loss to society, though. Since the government has acquired the blue rectangle *FHGK* as tax revenue, this

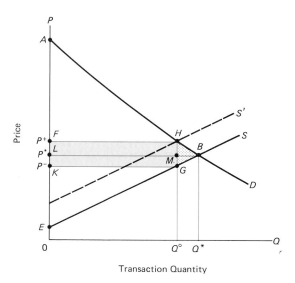

FIGURE 7.9 Effects upon Consumer Surplus and Producer Surplus of a Transactions Tax. A unit tax on transactions lowers the quantity exchanged from Q^* to Q^o. The gross price paid by consumers rises from P^* to P^+ while the net price received by sellers falls from P^* to P^-. The upper shaded area is a transfer from Consumer Surplus and the lower shaded area is a transfer from Producer Surplus, the two transfers together constituting the amount of tax collections. The small dotted areas represent losses of Consumer Surplus and Producer Surplus that are not balanced by tax collections.

area represents a *transfer* from buyers and sellers to the government. If we cancel out the amount of this transfer we are left with the dotted triangle *HBG*. This is the net loss to society from having imposed the tax, the loss being due to the reduced amount of mutually beneficial exchange.

This inevitable "deadweight loss" seems to imply that the costs of a tax are always greater than the benefits. However, conceivably the tax dollars may be spent on a project that is valuable enough to outweigh the loss of the triangle *HBG*. For example, the tax receipts may provide for essential national defense. From a cost-benefit standpoint, then, we cannot say whether or not a tax "should" be imposed without knowing the value of the projects to be financed with the tax revenue.

> PROPOSITION: Taxes imposed on transactions reduce both Consumer Surplus and Producer Surplus. Some of the loss takes the form of a transfer from consumers and producers to the beneficiaries of government expenditures. But there is also a deadweight or efficiency loss due to the reduction in the volume of trade.

Exercise 7.5: Suppose the market demand curve is given by $P = 300 - Q$ and the market supply curve by $P = 60 + 2Q$. The initial solution is $Q^* = 80$, $P^* = 220$. (a) If a per-unit tax of $T = 15$ is imposed, what is the new equilibrium? (b) What is the loss of Consumer Surplus? What is the loss of Producer Surplus? (c) What is the amount of the transfer (tax collections)? (d) How great is the efficiency loss?

Answer: (a) Using the method introduced in Chapter 2 for analyzing a tax on transactions, we can verify that the new equilibrium quantity is $Q^o = 75$, and that the gross price (paid by purchasers) rises to $P^+ = 225$ while the net price (received by sellers) falls to $P^- = 210$. (b) The original Consumer Surplus corresponds to the area *ABL* in Figure 7.9. Since the supply and demand curves here are linear, the area is an exact triangle with size $(300 - 220) \times (80) \times (1/2) = 3200$. The new Consumer Surplus is the smaller area *AHF* or $(300-225) \times (75) \times (1/2) = 2812.5$. So the loss of Consumer Surplus is 387.5. Similarly, the old Producer Surplus (the area *EBL*) was $(220-60) \times (80) \times (1/2) = 6400$; the new Producer Surplus (the area *EGK*) is $(210-60) \times (75) \times (1/2) = 5625$; and so the loss of Producer Surplus is $6400 - 5625 = 775$. (c) The transfers or tax collections (the rectangular area *FHGK*) equal $(225-210) \times (75) = 1125$. (d) The remainder of the summed losses of Consumer Surplus and Producer Surplus is the efficiency loss, corresponding to the small dotted triangle *HGB*. Numerically it is $387.5 + 775 - 1125 = 37.5$.

Taxes hamper trade through their effect on *prices*, by driving a "wedge" between the gross price P^+ effective for buyers and the net price P^- effective for sellers. *Quantitative* restrictions on trade—rations or quotas—may also be analyzed in terms of Consumer Surplus and Producer Surplus.

Using Figure 7.10, suppose government regulations dictate that only a fixed *quota* equal to Q' (less than the equilibrium quantity Q^*) of the good can be supplied to the market. (We leave open the question of just which suppliers are allowed portions of the overall supply quota.) The reduced quantity Q' would then be sold at "whatever price the market will bear," which is P' as determined along the demand curve D. We want to compare this outcome with the unregulated equilibrium at price P^* and quantity Q^*. The upper (shaded) rectangle *ABGF* is a loss of Consumer Surplus that now goes *to the suppliers* rather than to government. (And, of course, the suppliers retain the lower shaded area, *FGDE*.) It follows that

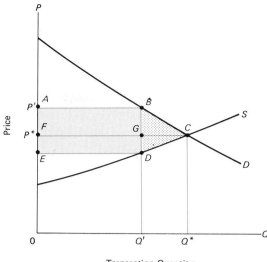

FIGURE 7.10 **Effects upon Consumer and Producer Surplus of a Quota Limit on Supply.** Market
supply is limited to the quota Q', so price rises from
P^* to P'. As before, Consumer Surplus is reduced by
the upper shaded area (a transfer) plus the upper
dotted area (an efficiency loss). But here the transfer
is received by the sellers. If the transfer they receive
(upper shaded area) exceeds the sellers' efficiency
loss (the lower dotted area), the sellers benefit from
imposition of the quota. But buyers and sellers, considered together, lose by the amount of the dotted
areas representing the combined efficiency losses.

suppliers *may* benefit from the quota: they will do so if their transfer gain (upper
shaded area *ABGF*) is larger than their deadweight loss from the reduced sales
(lower dotted area *GCD*). The buyers, on the other hand, suffer *both* a transfer
loss (*ABGF*) and a deadweight loss (*BCG*). Thus, the buyers are surely worse off.

Now consider a *demand* quota Q'' (less than Q^*), such as occurs when a commodity is rationed to consumers. If only those possessing ration tickets were allowed to buy, the demand curve would, as shown in Figure 7.11, in effect drop
down vertically from the point H representing the ration quantity Q''. The effective price would be P'' along the supply curve in Figure 7.11. A ration ticket would
be worth the difference $P' - P''$. An analysis of the areas of transfers versus

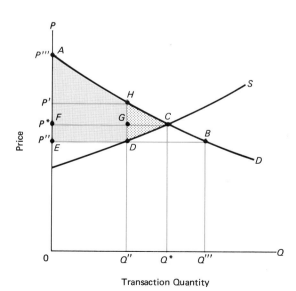

FIGURE 7.11 **Effects upon Consumer and Producer Surplus of a Ration Limit on Demand.** If a
ration limit in the amount Q'' is imposed upon demand, price falls to P''. The lower rectangle *FGDE* is
a transfer to consumers from suppliers. The shaded
area *AHDE* is the Consumer Surplus under rationing, which may be larger than at the original
Q^*, P^* equilibrium. However, the dotted areas *HCD*
still represent an efficiency loss to consumers and
producers taken together.

losses of Consumer and Producer Surplus will show that although the *buyers* in this case *may or may not gain* on balance, the *suppliers must lose.*

Unfortunately, the geometry of both Figure 7.10 and 7.11 pictures only a portion, sometimes a small portion, of the efficiency loss from supply or demand quotas. To take the rationing case, there will be an *additional* loss of Consumer Surplus resulting from the fact that ration tickets may not be assigned to the individuals willing to pay the most. In Figure 7.11 suppose a ration ticket is given to someone who is only willing to pay P'' while the person who values the good the most (who would have been willing to pay up to P''') does not receive any ration at all. If so, there will be an additional efficiency loss of $P''' - P''$ on that single unit. [*Query*: Is it possible for rations to be assigned so perversely as to block trade entirely (assuming the ration tickets themselves are nonsalable)?] A similar analysis applies also for *supply* quotas.

> PROPOSITION: Supply quotas lead to a transfer of surplus from consumers to producers; rationing of demand causes a transfer from producers to consumers. In either case there will be an efficiency loss due to the reduced volume of trade. An even larger efficiency loss may come about if rights to buy (ration tickets) are not assigned to those individuals with highest willingness to pay, or if rights to sell are not assigned to the lowest-cost suppliers.

EXAMPLE 7.4
Sugar Quotas

Under the Sugar Act of 1948 and its successors, supply quotas to the U.S. market were assigned to foreign countries and to domestic production areas. The U.S. market price for sugar is consequently at a substantial premium over the world price: for example, a 35 percent premium in 1960, 61 percent in 1968, and 40 percent in 1970. By December of 1985 the disparity had become much more extreme: the U.S. price of sugar was 19.6 cents per pound, while the world price was only 5.51 cents.

The effects of the quotas were studied by Ilse Mintz for the year 1970 when the premium was still relatively moderate; the figures here are based upon her "low" estimates.[a] The underlying situation is pictured in Figure 7.12. Panel (a) represents the hypothetical free-market equilibrium that would have occurred in the absence of quotas. The world price is 5.5 cents per pound, and the domestic price would have to equal this. United States domestic production along the supply curve S_{US} is 2.9 million tons at this price, and imports are 8.7 million, making up a total of 11.6 million tons along the curve S_w showing world supply (inclusive of domestic supply) to the United States. Since this is an equilibrium situation, the U.S. demand curve D intersects S_w at this price. Producer

[a] Ilse Mintz, *U.S. Import Quotas: Costs and Consequences* (Washington, D.C.: American Enterprise Institute for Public Policy Research, Feb. 1973).

Surplus of the *domestic* producers is the small lower shaded area in Panel (a), and the U.S. Consumer Surplus is the huge upper shaded area.

The effects of the quotas are shown in Panel (b). The quota assignments (6.0 million tons of domestic supply, 5.2 million tons of imports) aggregate to only a little less than the 11.6 million tons that would have been supplied annually under free markets. But because demand is highly inelastic (price elasticity of −0.1, according to the "low" estimate), the U.S. domestic price is sharply higher at the observed 8.07 cents per pound.

The deadweight loss of Consumer Surplus (the smaller dotted triangle in Panel [b]) is estimated by assuming that the demand curve D is linear between 11.2 million and 11.6 million tons. The area of the dotted triangle is 0.5 × (8.07 cents − 5.5 cents) × (.8 billion pounds) or $10,280,000 per year.

But the most obvious feature of the situation is the tremendous cost increase to consumers. This amounts to (22.4 billion pounds) × (8.07 − 5.5 cents) or $575,680,000 annually.

The increased cost to U.S. consumers, all at the expense of Consumer Surplus, is broken down into four numbered areas in Panel (b). Area 1 is the transfer from domestic consumers to foreign producers, calculated on the basis of the higher price received for the 5.2 million tons they continue to deliver to the U.S. market. This amounts to $267,280,000 per year. Area 2 is the transfer to domestic producers, calculated on the 2.9 million tons they would have delivered in either case. This amounts to $149,060,000 per year. Areas 3 and 4 are equal (assuming for simplicity that the domestic supply curve S_{US} is linear), and add up to the remaining $159,340,000. However, they are conceptually quite different. The upper area 3, like area 2, is a transfer from Consumer Surplus to domestic Producer Surplus. But the lower area 4 is a deadweight loss. It represents increased cost of production (higher supply price) on units produced domestically that could have been obtained more cheaply from foreigners. This is the type of deadweight loss, described in the text above, that is due to a *non-ideal distribution* of quantitative restrictions upon trading. Granting that only 11.2 million tons of sugar are to be sold in the United States, there is an additional loss to the extent that quotas are assigned to high-cost domestic rather than to low-cost foreign producers. This additional deadweight loss, the larger dotted triangle in Panel (b), amounts to one-half of $159,340,000—or $79,670,000.

If we regard the transfers as canceling out, the aggregate of the deadweight losses to the United States (the "efficiency loss" due to the sugar quotas) amounts to $89,950,000 per year.

A later study by Allen R. Ferguson[b] showed much greater losses, as would be expected from the more extreme gap in recent years between the world price and the domestic price. He calculated that in 1984 the program cost American consumers more than $3 billion (areas 1 through 5), while yielding a gain to U.S. producers of only $386,000,000 (areas 2 and 3).

[b] Allen R. Ferguson, "The Sugar Price Support Program," United States Cane Sugar Refiners' Association (May 1985).

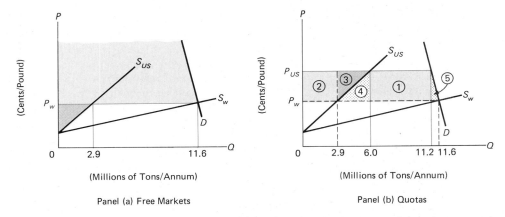

Panel (a) Free Markets   Panel (b) Quotas

FIGURE 7.12 Sugar Supply and Demand. In Panel (a), representing the unregulated situation, the small lower shaded triangle is the annual Producer Surplus of U.S. suppliers while the large upper shaded area is the annual Consumer Surplus of U.S. purchasers. In Panel (b), imposition of a quota smaller than the equilibrium market quantity raises price quite substantially (demand is extremely inelastic). U.S. Consumer Surplus *falls* by the amount of the five numbered areas. U.S. Producer Surplus *rises* by the amount of the numbered areas 2 and 3, both being transfers from domestic consumers. Area 1 is a transfer from domestic consumers to *foreign* producers. Area 4 is an efficiency loss due to displacement of low-cost foreign production by high-cost domestic production. Area 5 is an efficiency loss due to reduced exchange.

7.F

AN APPLICATION OF SUPPLY AND DEMAND: MANAGING A "SHORTAGE"

In the real world, equilibrium prices are always changing. A flood in Brazil may cause the price of coffee to rise; good farming weather in the Midwest will lead to a fall in the price of wheat; advancing technology steadily lowers the price of computers. If enough people are drastically affected by the price change the government may decide to do something about it—whether wisely or unwisely. Rising apartment rents will lead to pressure for rent control, falling wheat prices will lead to pressure for agricultural price supports, and so forth.

When the government controls the price of a good below the market-clearing level, there will be a "shortage"[5] A *shortage* is not the same as *scarcity*. Scarcity simply means that not all desires can be satisfied, and so scarcity is always present. Diamonds are scarce, but there is no shortage—anyone who can pay the price of a diamond can buy one. A shortage exists when goods are not just expensive but *unavailable* to some people—except perhaps by unlawful means. In a city with rent controls, newcomers may be unable to rent an apartment at all, regardless of their willingness to pay. Thus, faced with a supply shift or demand shift dictating a higher equilibrium price, consumers are bound to lose out one way or the other—either from the higher price if the market adjustment proceeds unim-

[5] In the opposite case, where government enforces a price *above* the equilibrium level, commodity "surpluses" are generated.

peded, or from the "shortages" that follow when government interventions keep the price low.

EXAMPLE 7.5
Two San Francisco Housing Crises[a]

In the 1906 earthquake and fire, the city of San Francisco lost more than half its housing facilities in three days. Nevertheless, the first post-disaster issue of the *San Francisco Chronicle* had no report of a "housing shortage"! Indeed, the newspaper's classified advertisements carried 64 offers of houses or apartments for rent and only 5 ads for apartments or houses wanted. Of course, prices of accommodations rose sharply.

In contrast, in 1947 San Francisco was gripped by the national postwar "housing shortage." In the first five days of 1946 newspapers carried only 4 ads offering houses or apartments for rent, but around 150 ads by persons wanting to rent houses or apartments. The explanation is that in 1906 the catastrophic reduction in the housing stock led to a price adjustment in the form of a sharp rise in rents. But in 1946, rents "frozen" below the market-clearing price left an excess of quantity demanded over quantity supplied.

> COMMENT: In the physical sense, housing supply relative to population was clearly much more scarce after the 1906 earthquake and fire than in 1946. The 1946 "shortage" was an outgrowth of the general price freeze aimed at controlling inflation during and after World War II. Actually, housing supply had not decreased at all in the wartime period. But rising money incomes, the return of war veterans, and a high rate of family formation led to an upward shift in demand for housing. With rents frozen, a "shortage" ensued.

[a] Discussion based on M. Friedman and G. J. Stigler, *Roofs or Ceilings*? (Irvington-on-Hudson, N.Y.: The Foundation for Economic Education, Sept. 1946).

Using the concepts of short-run and long-run supply developed earlier in the chapter, let us trace out the consequences of coping with upward pressures on price by imposing a "ceiling." In Figure 7.13 the ceiling holds price at its old equilibrium P^o after demand has shifted upward from D to D'. At the price P^o, there is a perceived shortage equal to the distance H. If the price were free to rise, it would jump to P_I in the "immediate run" but would eventually come down to the long-run equilibrium at P_L. The market would eliminate the shortage: in the short run primarily by a high price choking off demand, but in the long run by inducing more supply. At the new long-run equilibrium price P_L in Figure 7.13, the interval ΔD is the long-run *reduction* in demand quantity while ΔS is the long-run *increment* of supply.

Exercise 7.6: Suppose the market demand is described by the equation $P = 300 - Q$. The long-run supply curve is $P = 60 + 2Q$, and the short-run supply curve is $P = -180 + 5Q$. Verify that the market is in long-run and short-run equilibrium at

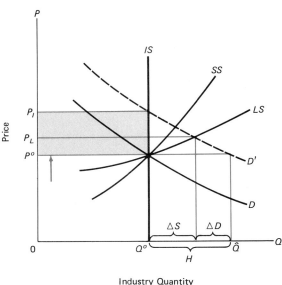

FIGURE 7.13 Effect of a Price Ceiling. An upward shift of demand in an uncontrolled market, from D to D', is met in the "immediate run" by an increase in price (from P^o to P_I). Producers benefit from a temporary windfall gain (shaded area). Ultimately, the higher price will induce a larger supply quantity, so that long-run equilibrium price comes back down part-way to P_L. But if a ceiling is enforced at the initial price P^o, the supply and demand adjustments are both blocked. H would be the perceived "shortage" at the ceiling price. If price were permitted to rise, ΔD of the shortage amount would be the demand quantity choked off by the higher price, while ΔS would be the supply increment provided.

quantity $Q^o = 80$, price $P^o = 220$. Now suppose the demand curve increases (shifts to the right), the new equation being $P = 360 - Q$. (a) What happens in the immediate run? (b) What is the new short-run price-quantity equilibrium (Q'_S, P'_S)? (c) The new long-run equilibrium (Q'_L, P'_L)? (d) What would be the perceived "shortage" if a price ceiling prevents price from rising?

Answer: (a) In the immediate run, quantity would be unchanged at $Q_I = 80$. The new equilibrium price would be found by using the new demand condition: $P_I = 360 - Q_I = 280$. (b) The new short-run equilibrium is $Q'_S = 90$, $P'_S = 270$. (c) The new long-run equilibrium is $Q'_L = 100$, $P'_L = 260$. Note that the long-run quantity increase is greater, and so price comes back down somewhat. (d) If price could not rise above $P = 220$, the quantity supplied would remain $Q = 80$ but the quantity demanded would be $Q = 360 - P = 140$. Then the perceived shortage would be $140 - 80 = 60$ units.

What about the effects of a price ceiling upon Consumer Surplus and Producer Surplus? It might be thought at first that, *in the immediate run*, what takes place is a mere transfer from buyers to sellers. Since the quantity supplied is unchanged, a ceiling price at P^o means only that producers fail to make a "windfall" gain at the expense of consumers. But this is a serious error. It fails to allow for the non-ideal assignment of ration tickets discussed above. Without the ceiling, the supply Q^o on hand would have gone to the consumers willing to pay the most. With the ceiling this may not be the case. It is quite possible that goods will go to people who are only willing to pay P^o or less instead of going to people willing to pay P_I or more. So even in the immediate run a price ceiling would not prevent some loss of Consumer Surplus.

Still another consequence of price ceilings is that they would encourage other forms of competition to acquire desired commodities. Ordinarily, people acquire goods by paying the market price. The limited supply goes to those willing to pay the most. But when a price ceiling prevents this, consumers may compete by waiting in line, by fighting, by using political influence, and so forth. These other forms of competition can be extremely wasteful, because what the consumer gives up (for example, time spent waiting in line) is not reflected in any benefit that the seller acquires in exchange.

Summarizing this discussion, price ceilings are responsible for two sources of loss in the immediate run: (1) the "wrong" (less highly valued) demands may be the ones satisfied, and (2) non-price competition to acquire the good may itself waste resources. And, of course, in the short run and increasingly in the longer run, the price ceiling reduces both Consumer Surplus and Producer Surplus by discouraging the development of additional supply to the market.

EXAMPLE 7.6
Gasoline Waiting Lines

Gasoline crises occurred in the United States in 1973, and again in 1979, when the cartel of oil-producing nations—the OPEC (Organization of Petroleum Exporting Countries)—reduced the supplies available to importing nations. Price ceilings on gasoline prevented the price from rising to a market-clearing level. Instead, long lines of cars had to wait at filling stations in the hope of getting some of the limited supplies available.

A study by H. E. Frech, III, and William C. Lee[a] examined the losses of Consumer Surplus during these crises. The authors employed statistical estimates of demand elasticities in the two periods in order to determine what the true equilibrium price would have been without the price ceilings. Even though the actual dollar price was frozen below the true price, consumers were paying the difference in the form of a *waiting-time price*—the value of time wasted standing in line. The authors found that rural users tended to pay higher waiting-time prices (i.e., they waited in line longer). It may have been that rural demand is more inelastic, since possible substitutes for auto travel (buses, subways, etc.) are less available. Or else, suppliers may have found it profitable to divert gasoline to the more accessible and concentrated urban markets. The table indicates the waiting-time prices in peak months of the earlier (1973 to 1974) and the later (1979) crises, in cents per gallon (adjusted to 1985 dollars).

Waiting-Time Prices in Two Gasoline Crises (Adjusted to 1985 Dollars)

	March 1974	May 1979
Urban users	57.0¢	40.3¢
(as percentage of money price)	(49.7)	(33.2)
Rural users	96.4¢	38.0¢
(as percentage of money price)	(84.0)	(31.3)

The authors estimated the losses in Consumer Surplus due to this waiting-time cost and also due to the reduced volume of transactions resulting from the discouragement of supply. Calculated by this method, the total losses in California alone were $506,000,000 for the December 1973 to March 1974 period, and $204,000,000 from May to June 1979.

There are some less visible consequences of price ceilings. Unable to raise price openly, firms may use subtler strategies. They may eliminate discounts or seasonal sales, reduce quality or variety or convenience of their offerings, or concentrate production in product lines that happen to have received a better break from the price-control authorities. Supplies may be sold abroad, leaving even less available for domestic consumers. And of course black markets may arise, providing a wider scope for people specializing in illegal activity. In extreme cases, there may be a breakdown of legitimate trade. In this connection, we can learn much from a previous great inflationary episode associated with World War II and its aftermath.

EXAMPLE 7.7
Repressed Inflation In Postwar Germany[a]

Germany, like most of the belligerent countries in World War II, had financed her war effort by inflationary expansion of money and credit—in effect, by printing money. Simultaneously, price freezes were employed to prevent the extra money in consumers' hands from driving up market prices. By the time the war ended in 1945 the German money supply had risen around tenfold, while prices were still largely at the levels frozen by the Nazi government back in 1936. And, of course, production was drastically below normal in the aftermath of a war in which Germany's cities and industry had been smashed by bombing. And Germany faced also the special problems of a defeated nation—divided, occupied, and subjected to punitive reparations.

In the early postwar years, the allied Occupation authorities directing the German economy maintained the wartime price freeze. (This was not a special attempt to punish Germany, but represented the "conventional wisdom" of the period; very much the same policies were pursued by the victorious nations in their own domestic economic programs.) But the levels of German prices were so drastically out of line with supply-demand reality that over most of the econ-

[a] Discussion based on J. Hirshleifer, *Disaster and Recovery: A Historical Survey*, The RAND Corporation, Memorandum RM-3079-PR (Apr. 1963), pp. 83–112.

omy production for legal sale could take place only at financial loss. Industrial production in the first half of 1948 was only 45 percent of the 1938 amount, despite a larger population.

Observers were puzzled, however, that the black market was estimated to account for only 10 percent of transactions. This figure was so low because in Germany the term "black market" was given a very narrow definition: to wit, outright trading of goods for cash at illegal prices (a practice professionally engaged in by a specialized class of disreputable individuals). In contrast, *everybody* engaged without moral taint in a form of transaction known as "bilateral exchange" or "compensation trade." Such trade took place at entirely legal prices in money, with one catch: No one could acquire goods or services for money alone. In addition to the money price, every buyer had to provide "compensation" in real goods and services. Estimates are that one-third to one-half of all transactions took this form. Even the Occupation authorities engaged in it; the noon meal provided to German employees of the Occupation administration was often a more important attraction than the nominal monetary salary. What was actually taking place was the *de facto* elimination of money as a medium of exchange—regression to the inefficiencies of barter (a topic to be taken up in Chapter 13).

While many relative prices were more or less seriously out of line, the overwhelming fact was that almost *all* money prices were too low. The Erhard policy of June 1948 was correspondingly double-barreled: (1) a drastic currency reform, exchanging new marks for old, cut down the money supply by a factor of about ten; and (2) price controls were removed. The effect was dramatic. According to one observer: "It was as if money and markets had been invented afresh as reliable media of the division of labor."[b] The German postwar economic miracle was under way.

[b] H. Mendershausen, "Prices, Money and the Distribution of Goods in Postwar Germany," *American Economic Review*, v. 39 (June 1949), p. 646.

☐ SUMMARY OF CHAPTER 7

The supply curve of the competitive firm is derived from the profit-maximizing condition $MC = P$, subject to a qualification about covering Total Variable Cost in the short run and Total Cost in the long run. As a result of these qualifications, the short-run and long-run supply curves of the firm may each have a discontinuity. For the short-run supply curve s_f, zero quantity will be offered at any price lower than P_V (the low point of the curve of Average Variable Cost AVC); above that price, s_f is identical with the Short-Run Marginal Cost curve. For the long-run supply curve Ls_f, the minimum price for non-zero output is P_C, the low point on the Average Cost curve AC; above that price, Ls_f is identical with the Long-Run Marginal Cost curve.

To find the industry supply curve, at each price the quantities offered by all firms are added (horizontal summation of the firms' supply curves). However, it is necessary to allow for the "external" effects upon firms' costs due to changes in industrywide output and also for entry into or exit from the industry.

External *economies* reduce firms' costs as industry output rises; external *diseconomies* do the opposite. The external effects may be "pecuniary" (changing industrywide output may affect the hire-prices of factors) or "technological" (changing industry output may affect firms' production functions). Pecuniary external effects are normally *diseconomies*, since increases in industry output generally drive up the hire-prices of factors used in that industry the result is to make the industry supply curve less elastic. But technological external effects can go either way. It is even possible for *external economies* to override the inevitable *internal diseconomies* of scale, so as to bring about a negatively-sloped industry supply curve.

In the "immediate run," quantity produced by the industry is constant (the *IS* supply curve is absolutely inelastic). The entire impact of any demand shift is therefore reflected by change in price. Allowing *short-run* adjustment of firms' outputs leads to the industry *SS* supply curve, along which elasticity is normally positive; the change in price will be less, since there is a positive quantity response. In the *long run*, the industry supply curve *LS* is still more elastic. This is due to the "internal" fact that *LRMC* curves slope less steeply upward than *SRMC* curves, and also to the entry of new firms in response to price increases (or the exit of old firms in response to price decreases).

Under competitive conditions there is always pressure on firms' profits. If profit exists, output expansion on the part of the industry tends to reduce product price (pressure from above) and to raise hire-prices of factors (pressure from below). In long-run equilibrium the *marginal* firm must be making zero economic profit. But even established firms also achieve only zero profit in the long run. Since different firms in the industry compete for any especially desirable input responsible for the low costs leading to positive profit, in the long run that factor will command a hire-price capturing the entire benefit for its owner.

Voluntary trade is mutually beneficial; this is the Fundamental Theorem of Exchange. Consumer Surplus is a measure of the benefit of trade to purchasers, and Producer Surplus a measure of the benefit to suppliers. Consumer Surplus is the difference between purchasers' aggregate *willingness to pay* and the aggregate total they must actually pay in the market for the good. Similarly, Producer Surplus is the difference between sellers' aggregate actual market receipts and the minimum terms at which they would have been willing to offer the good.

The burden of a hindrance of trade like a tax or a quota on supply can be measured in terms of losses of Consumer Surplus and Producer Surplus. Any such hindrance typically has two kinds of effects: redistributions between Consumer Surplus and Producer Surplus which are mere *transfers*, and uncompensated reductions of Consumer Surplus and/or Producer Surplus that represent *efficiency losses* to the economy.

If demand increases or supply decreases, the imposition of a price freeze creates a shortage—an excess of quantity demanded over quantity supplied. Consumers reap a transfer gain at the expense of suppliers by not having to pay a higher price. But the supply response that would have occurred in the long run is blocked, which is a source of efficiency loss to producers and consumers together. There are also losses of Consumer Surplus and Producer Surplus due to non-ideal distribution of the limited supplies available, and to the wasteful techniques (like standing in line, or using political influence) that consumers will employ in order to acquire the good at its artificially low price.

□ QUESTIONS FOR CHAPTER 7

MAINLY FOR REVIEW

*R1. At any rate of output, the industry *long-run* supply curve tends to be less steep than the *short-run* supply curve. Is it also necessarily more elastic? Explain.

*R2. "In the long run, a firm could always produce twice as much simply by doubling the amount of every factor employed. So in the long run there must be constant returns to scale." Evaluate.

R3. Does elasticity of supply for an industry tend to be great or small if the firms' Marginal Cost curves are sharply upward-sloping? What is the effect on elasticity of supply if higher industry output markedly drives up the hire-prices of factors employed in the industry?

*R4. If there are *N* identical firms and no "external" effects on factor hire-prices, is the *industry* supply curve more or less steep than the *firm* supply curve? More or less elastic?

R5. Explain the distinction between "internal" and "external" economies or diseconomies.

*R6. In long-run equilibrium, why does the marginal firm (the highest-cost firm in the industry) earn zero economic profit? Why do the other "infra-marginal" firms earn zero economic profit?

R7. Consider the exceptional case of an industry with a downward-sloping supply curve. Starting from an initial equilibrium, will a decline in demand lead to a rise or a fall in price? To a rise or a fall in output? Explain.

R8. If a tax is imposed upon some commodity, indicate the areas of: loss of Consumer Surplus, loss of Producer Surplus, tax collections (transfers of Consumer Surplus and Producer Surplus to government), and efficiency losses.

FOR FURTHER THOUGHT AND DISCUSSION

*T1. "In a competitive industry, for any firm there may be internal economies of scale over a certain range. But each firm must be actually operating in the region where internal *diseconomies* of scale dominate." True or false? Explain.

T2. Under what circumstances would you expect a rise in demand for an industry's product to be met primarily by a "short-run" output response on the part of existing firms? By a "long-run" response on the part of existing firms? By entry of new firms?

T3. Which of the following is a "pecuniary" effect, which a "technological" effect? Which is "internal" to the firm, which "external" to the firm (but internal to the industry)?
   a. As the number of films produced rises, actors' salaries go up.
   b. As fishing activity intensifies, each fisherman finds fish scarcer.
   c. As new retail shops open, existing shops find customers scarcer.
   d. Steel mills along a river use the water for cooling—but the greater the use, the warmer the water gets, so that the river becomes less effective for cooling.

*T4. If at a certain equilibrium price every firm in the industry is earning zero economic profit, doesn't that imply that a fall in market price would mean that no firms at all could continue to survive? Explain.

*The answers to starred questions appear at the end of the book.

T5. A number of techniques are available to cope with increased scarcity and higher world prices of petroleum. Analyze the following in terms of supply-demand responses in the short run and long run.
a. Price freeze and "rationing by queue" (waiting in line for gasoline).
b. Price freeze and rationing by coupon (nonsalable).
c. Rationing by coupon (nonsalable) without a price freeze.
d. A tax on all petroleum used.
e. A tariff on *imports* of petroleum.

*T6. In policy (c) above (rationing by coupon without a price freeze), suppose consumers were permitted instead to sell ration coupons to one another. Would this tend to elicit more supply? Would the limited supplies be reallocated to those with greater willingness to pay? Explain the consequences in terms of Consumer Surplus.

*T7. If a price ceiling is imposed on some good *X*, is it possible for assignment of (nonsalable) ration tickets to be such as to block all trade in *X* entirely? What if the tickets were made salable?

T8. Suppose that, after a decline in demand for a product, a *floor* is placed under its market price. Then the problem arises of managing a "surplus" instead of a "shortage." What are the disadvantages of a price floor? Would the disadvantages tend to increase over time, as in the case of managing a shortage? Would black markets tend to develop?

*T9. Under recent petroleum regulation in the United States, a price freeze was placed on "old oil"—defined, roughly speaking, as petroleum from existing wells. The justification was that producers had to be offered more to induce them to drill new wells, but the output from existing wells would be forthcoming even at low prices. Is this argument correct?

T10. In the longer run, the presence or even the threat of price freezes may induce firms to integrate vertically (to merge with "upstream" supplier firms or with "downstream" customer firms). Explain why.

*T11. Analyze the effects upon Consumer Surplus and Producer Surplus of a *subsidy*. If a tax as a hindrance to trade is associated with an efficiency loss, does it follow that a subsidy as an encouragement to trade will generate an efficiency gain?

8

CORE CHAPTER

MONOPOLY

A monopoly is said to exist when the industry contains only a single firm. If that firm is able to drive out competitors because its costs of production are lower, the situation is termed "natural monopoly." Not all monopolies are "natural," however. One other important source of monopoly is exclusive privilege granted by government, as in the case of a franchised public utility or a legal patent. At the other extreme from monopoly is the large-numbers or "competitive" case. Actually, the number of firms is economically significant only as a clue to behavior. In the large-numbers situation, what is essential is *price-taking behavior:* each firm has so negligible an effect upon price that it acts as if price were independent of its own output decision. (But as we shall see when cartels are examined later in this chapter, large numbers of firms can sometimes behave like a collective monopolist.) The output of a monopolist will certainly affect the price of the product; since the monopolist will surely know this, price-taking behavior cannot be expected. Geometrically, the competitive firm faces a horizontal demand curve, while a monopolist's demand curve is downward-sloping.

Where there are more than one but still only a very few firms in an industry, the market structure is called *oligopoly*—competition among the few. Under oligopoly each single firm's output decision noticeably affects the demand conditions faced by each of the other firms. When firms are aware that their decisions interact in this way, they may engage in "strategic" rather than price-taking behavior, as will be explored in Chapter 10. Another important market structure is *monopolistic competition*, which arises when different firms produce distinct products that nevertheless compete closely with one another—for instance, brands of toothpaste. Monopolistic competition will be covered in Chapter 9. This chapter takes up the cases of (1) a single-firm monopolist and (2) a cartel of firms acting collectively as a monopoly.

8.A
MONOPOLY AND NONPROFIT GOALS

One's first impression might be that monopolists, as compared with competitive firms, are exceptionally ruthless in their search for profit. But the opposite argument is more frequently heard: that a monopoly firm, sheltered from competition, would be inclined to give more weight to *nonprofit* goals (as discussed in Chapter 6). In pure competition, the ever-present problem of sheer survival does not leave a firm much leeway for pursuing nonprofit goals. A monopolist, in contrast, may have some freedom of choice. Among the possible nonprofit goals of a monopolistic firm might be empire-building for ambitious managers (or, alternatively, an easy life for unambitious ones), support of charitable institutions, granting favors to friends and relatives, and exercise of discrimination against unpopular demographic groups.

However, the argument that monopolies are especially inclined to pursue nonprofit goals is by no means clearcut. Owners of a monopolistic firm are likely to put as much pressure upon managers to maximize profit as would owners of a competitive firm. Consider a monopoly organized as a corporation. The value of the corporation's stock will depend upon the firm's present and future profits. If a monopoly earns less than it otherwise could, the loss will be borne by shareholders—who can be expected to complain, to sue in the courts, or to support an alternative management group threatening to take over the firm.[1] In this chapter we will assume that profit maximization remains the operative goal, even for monopolistic firms.

8.B
MONOPOLY PROFIT-MAXIMIZING OPTIMUM

8.B.1 □ Price-Quantity Solution

Figure 8.1 shows the basic price-quantity optimum for the monopolistic firm. As usual the upper panel here shows the solution in terms of the Total Cost function C and Total Revenue function R. And the lower panel shows the solution in terms of AC, AR, MC, and MR (the corresponding average and marginal functions of output Q).[2] The bold line-segment labeled Π^* in the upper panel is the maximized profit—the excess of Revenue over Cost at the optimal output Q^*. At this optimal output the R and C curves are farthest apart, so their slopes must be parallel, as suggested by the dashed tangent lines drawn at the points R^* and C^*. Consequently, in the lower panel the Marginal Revenue MR (representing the slope of the Total Revenue function) and the Marginal Cost MC (representing the slope of the Total Cost function) intersect at this same output Q^*. The maximized profit Π^* is represented in the lower panel by the shaded rectangle, whose base is the optimum quantity Q^* and whose height is $P^* - AC \equiv AR - AC$.

The difference between the competitive and monopoly solutions lies on the revenue side. For the competitive firm of Figure 6.1, price was constant so that the Total Revenue curve R was a ray out of the origin. But for the monopolistic firm, price P falls as output increases. In consequence, the Total Revenue curve R

---

[1] If *owners* are not willing to accept a reduction of profits, does that mean that empire-building, nepotism, group prejudice, and the like will in fact not occur? Such a conclusion is unwarranted. Even if the owners are uninterested, it may be that *suppliers of resource services* will accept a lower hire-price in order to achieve such goals. A manager might serve at lower pay if he or she is able to hire relatives, for example. Or males might work for less if female employees are (or, perhaps, are not) also employed, or vice versa.

[2] The capital letter Q has previously been used to signify *industry* output. Since the monopolist is a single-firm industry, Q can be used to denote the output of a monopolist firm.

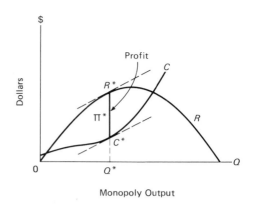

Monopoly Output

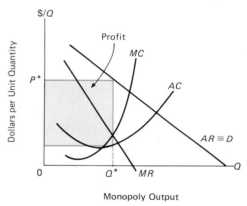

FIGURE 8.1 Monopoly Profit-maximizing Solution. Maximum profit Π^* occurs at output Q^*, where the vertical difference between the Total Revenue curve R and the Total Cost curve C in the upper panel is greatest. At this output the R and C curves are parallel (note the dashed tangent lines). In the lower panel, the curves of Marginal Revenue MR and Marginal Cost MC intersect at output Q^*. Profit in the lower panel is represented by the shaded area, equal to Q^* times the difference between price P^* and Average Cost AC^* at that output: $Q^*(P^* - AC)$.

Monopoly Output

in the upper panel of Figure 8.1 is concave downward, like the cross-section of a mountain.

Geometrically, we know that Marginal Revenue MR is the slope along the Total Revenue curve R. Along the concave-downward R function in the upper panel, slope decreases throughout—which means that MR is always falling. In the range where R is positively sloped, MR in the lower panel is positive. When R reaches its maximum, MR becomes equal to 0. And, where R is falling, MR is negative. Since the demand curve D is identical with the Average Revenue curve AR, AR is also falling throughout.

In the lower panel MR always lies below AR—that is, Marginal Revenue is less than Average Revenue. This is of course an instance of Proposition 2.2a: *When the average magnitude is falling, the marginal magnitude must lie below it.*

WARNING: It is important not to confuse the *price* charged for the last unit sold with the *Marginal Revenue MR*. Note the two shaded areas in Figure 8.2. As sales increase from Q to $Q + 1$ units, the demand curve D shows that price must fall slightly from P' to P''. We can think of P'' as the price received for the last unit, represented by the thin, tall rectangle of width $\Delta Q = 1$ and height P''. But we must remember that price has fallen from P' to P'' *on all the other units* sold. The effect of this price reduction is represented by the flat, thin rectangle of width Q

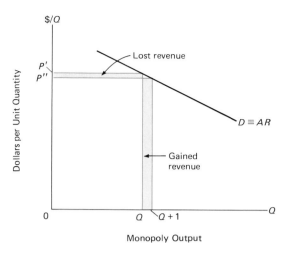

FIGURE 8.2 **Marginal Price versus Marginal Revenue.** Marginal *price*, the price of the last unit sold, corresponds in revenue terms to the area of the tall, shaded rectangle of unit base and height P''. To calculate *Marginal Revenue* we must deduct from this amount the thin, wide rectangle of height $P' - P'' \equiv \Delta P$ and width Q. This rectangle corresponds to the loss of receipts due to the reduced price on units that could have been sold at P'.

and height $\Delta P = P' - P''$. Marginal Revenue is equal to the area of the tall thin rectangle *minus* the area of the long thin rectangle.

So there are positive and negative elements entering into the Marginal Revenue of a monopolist. The positive element is the price P received for the last unit (the gained revenue). The negative element is the price reduction on all the other units (the lost revenue). Marginal Revenue can therefore be expressed as the algebraic sum:[3]

$$(8.1) \qquad MR \equiv P + Q\frac{\Delta P}{\Delta Q}$$

$\Delta P/\Delta Q$ is the slope along the demand curve. Since the slope is negative, it follows that the second term has negative sign. Then Marginal Revenue MR must be less than Average Revenue $AR \equiv P$.

The cost functions for the monopolistic firm (C, AC, and MC) have essentially the same appearance as for the competitive firm—apart from the fact that the monopolistic firm is likely to be producing at a relatively large scale.[4]

The monopolist's optimizing problem can be expressed as:

$$(8.2) \qquad \text{Maximize} \quad \Pi \equiv R - C \equiv PQ - C$$

where we must now remember that not only C but also P are functions of output

---

[3] This equation is strictly valid only if Marginal Revenue is defined as the *limit* of the ratio $\Delta R/\Delta Q$ for small changes in quantity. But if the "better approximation" MR_2 for Marginal Revenue (see Chapter 6) is used, Equation (8.1) will be found to hold almost exactly.

[4] There may be one underlying difference that is due to this larger scale of operation. The competitive firm was assumed in Chapter 6 to be a price-taker with respect not only to the product market but also to *factor prices*; in consequence, the competitive firm's cost function does not allow for any effects on factor prices. Only after turning to the supply function of the competitive industry in Chapter 7 was the factor-price effect encountered (as an "external" diseconomy). But the single monopolistic supplier is itself an entire industry. Hence, any factor-price effect would be displayed *within* the cost function of the monopolist firm. Since an increase in industry output will tend to push factor prices upward, the factor-price effect tends to make the monopolist firm's cost functions—total, average, and marginal—all rise more sharply as output increases.

Q. As usual, the condition of optimality (maximum of profit or minimum of loss) is the equality of Marginal Cost and Marginal Revenue.[5]

$$(8.3) \qquad MC = MR \equiv P + Q\frac{\Delta P}{\Delta Q} \qquad \text{Maximum-Profit Condition,} \\ \text{Monopolist Firm}$$

As in Chapter 6 for the competitive firm, there is again the technical qualification that the MC curve must cut the MR curve *from below* to have a profit maximum. If MC cuts MR *from above*, profit is a *minimum* (or loss a maximum) at that output.[6] Furthermore, the No-Shutdown Conditions of Chapter 6 also remain applicable: any firm will produce a positive output in the short run only if Total Revenue is at least equal to Total Variable Cost, and in the long run only if Total Revenue covers Total Cost.

The maximum-profit condition $MC = MR$ of Equation (8.3) is a generalized form that holds for competitive as well as monopolistic firms. For the competitive firm, which takes product price P as a constant, the ratio $\Delta P/\Delta Q$ would be zero in (8.3) so that $MC = MR$ reduces to $MC = P$.

The price elasticity of demand was defined in Chapter 5. In the notation of this chapter, elasticity of demand is:

$$(8.4) \qquad \eta \equiv \frac{\Delta Q/Q}{\Delta P/P} \equiv \frac{\Delta Q}{\Delta P} \cdot \frac{P}{Q}$$

(Recall that η ordinarily has a negative sign.) We can use (8.1) and (8.4) to obtain an important expression connecting Marginal Revenue MR and price elasticity η. First, dividing both sides of (8.1) by P leads to:

$$\frac{MR}{P} \equiv 1 + \frac{1}{\eta} \qquad \left(\text{since} \quad \frac{1}{\eta} \equiv \frac{Q}{P}\frac{\Delta P}{\Delta Q} \right)$$

The relation between MR and elasticity of demand is usually written in the form:

$$(8.5) \qquad MR \equiv P\left(1 + \frac{1}{\eta}\right) \qquad \text{or} \qquad MR \equiv P\left(1 - \frac{1}{|\eta|}\right)$$

Since elasticity η is ordinarily negative, we see again the MR is less than P.

It was noted in Chapter 5 that when demand is elastic (η greater than one in absolute value), a fall in price will increase consumer expenditure on the good. *Consumer expenditure* is, of course, *Revenue* to the firm. So when demand is elastic,

---

[5] *Mathematical Footnote*: Taking derivatives of profit Π as defined in Equation (8.2) and setting equal to zero:

$$\frac{d\Pi}{dQ} = \frac{dR}{dQ} - \frac{dC}{dQ} = 0$$

Marginal Revenue dR/dQ is $P + Q(dP/dQ)$, and Marginal Cost is of course dC/dQ, so $MC = MR$ follows directly.

[6] *Mathematical Footnote*: The second-order condition for a maximum of Π is $d^2R/dQ^2 < d^2C/dQ^2$. That is, MC must cut MR from below.

MR is positive. Similarly, when demand is inelastic, *MR* is negative. Since Marginal Cost *MC* is never negative, the condition $MC = MR$ dictates that the monopolist will produce where $MR > 0$—that is, in the range of *elastic* demand. (In the limiting case where $MC = 0$, the monopolist will set output so that $MR = 0$, which implies that demand is unit-elastic, or $\eta = -1$.)

> PROPOSITION: A profit-maximizing monopoly firm will always choose a price-quantity solution in the region of elastic demand along the market demand curve.

8.B.2 □ Monopolist versus Competitive Solution

Table 8.1 illustrates a hypothetical set of revenue and cost data for a monopolist firm. The cost data are exactly the same as those employed for a hypothetical competitive firm in Table 6.1. But on the revenue side, the monopolist's demand function is assumed here to be $P = 132 - 8Q$; price is a declining function of output.

In the table, the Marginal Cost column is the "exact" *MC* of Table 6.1. The Marginal Revenue column has been calculated according to the numerical method of Chapter 2 (Table 2.1). This corresponds to the "better approximation" technique for finding *MC* shown in Table 6.1. Thus, in the table here the revenue increment in moving from $Q = 1$ to $Q = 2$ is 108, so $MR = 108$ at $Q = 1\ 1/2$. Similarly, moving from $Q = 2$ to $Q = 3$ provides a revenue increment of 92, so $MR = 92$ at $Q = 2\ 1/2$. Interpolating, at $Q = 2$ the Marginal Revenue is $MR = 100$. *Note*: Since the demand curve here is linear, the "better approximation" for Marginal Revenue is identical to the "exact" *MR* that can be found by calculus.

TABLE 8.1

Revenue and Cost Functions: Monopolist Firm[7]
$P = 132 - 8Q$, or $R = 132Q - 8Q^2$, and $MR = 132 - 16Q$
$C = Q^3 - 14Q^2 + 69Q + 128$, and $MC = 3Q^2 - 28Q + 69$

Q	P	R	MR	C	MC	η
0	132	0	—	128	69	$-\infty$
1	124	124	116	184	44	−15.5
2	116	232	100	218	25	−7.25
3	108	324	84	236	12	−4.5
4	100	400	68	244	5	−3.125
5	92	460	52	248	4	−2.3
6	84	504	36	254	9	−1.75
7	76	532	20	268	20	−1.36
8	68	544	4	296	37	−1.06
9	60	540	−12	344	60	−0.83
10	52	520	—	418	89	−0.65

[7] *Mathematical Footnote*: If $P = 132 - 8Q$, then $R \equiv PQ = 132Q - 8Q^2$. Differentiating: $MR \equiv dR/dQ = 132 - 16Q$.

The monopolist has it in its power to behave like a competitive firm and set output Q where $MC = P$ (at $Q = 9$). But in the interests of profit maximization, the monopolist will set $MC = MR < P$ (Equation [8.3]). In this case the profit-maximizing output occurs at $Q = 7$ where MC and MR both equal 20. The corresponding price is $P = 76$. Total Revenue is $R = 532$ and Total Cost is $C = 268$, so the maximized profit is $\Pi^* = 264$.

It is easy to prove the following, without using calculus.

PROPOSITION: Given any *linear* demand curve $P = A - BQ$, the Marginal Revenue function is $MR = A - 2BQ$. Geometrically, starting at the same vertical intercept on the P-axis, the MR curve falls twice as fast as the AR curve. *Proof*: From Equation (8.3), $MR = P + Q(\Delta P / \Delta Q)$. Now $\Delta P / \Delta Q$ is by definition the slope of the demand curve, which is constant when the demand curve is a straight line. Given the demand equation $P = A - BQ$, this slope is equal to $- B$. Substituting on the right hand side of (8.3): $MR = (A - BQ) + Q(- B)$ or $MR = A - 2BQ$.

COROLLARY: The MR curve bisects the horizontal distance between the vertical axis and the demand curve, if the latter is a straight line.

It was stated above that the monopolist's solution must lie in the elastic range of demand—that is, where $|\eta| > 1$. The last column of Table 8.1 shows the demand elasticity at various levels of output. The computation is based on the relation $\eta \equiv P/(MR - P)$, derived by solving Equation (8.5) above for η. Note that had the monopolist been following the competitive rule ($MC = P$), in which case its output would have been $Q = 9$, the elasticity of demand would be less than one (in absolute value). We thus see that it is quite possible for a *competitive* industry's price-quantity equilibrium, but not for a monopolist's price-quantity optimum, to be in the inelastic range of demand.

PROPOSITION: The monopoly output solution occurs where $MC = MR < P$. Since competitive firms produce to where $MC = P$, a monopolized industry achieves higher price and produces smaller output than would a competitive industry.

One measure of "monopoly power" is the difference between Marginal Revenue MR and price P. From Equation (8.5) we see that the difference between MR and P is greater the *smaller* (in absolute value) is the price elasticity η. It is more convenient to measure monopoly power by the *ratio* P/MR (or P/MC). The more the ratio exceeds one, the greater the monopoly power. From Equation (8.5), and since $MC = MR$, it is algebraically easy to see that:

(8.5a)
$$\frac{P}{MR} = \frac{P}{MC} = \left(1 + \frac{1}{|\eta|}\right)$$

Notice that when elasticity is infinite, the ratio $P/MC = 1$—there is no monopoly power.

Exercise 8.1: Suppose the demand equation is $P = 10 - Q$. (a) What is the equation for Marginal Revenue? (b) If Marginal Cost is given by $MC = 1 + Q$, what is the profit-maximizing price-quantity solution? (c) What is the elasticity of demand at this solution?

Answer: (a) Since the demand curve is linear in the form $P = A - BQ$, we can use the Proposition that $MR = A - 2BQ$—specifically here, $MR = 10 - 2Q$. (b) Setting $MC = 1 + Q$ equal to $MR = 10 - 2Q$, the solution is $Q = 3$, $P = 7$. (c) Since the demand-curve slope is $\Delta P/\Delta Q = -1$, the elasticity of demand η is

$$\frac{P}{Q}\frac{\Delta Q}{\Delta P} = \frac{7}{3}\left(-1\right) = -\frac{7}{3}$$

which, as expected, is in the elastic range.

EXAMPLE 8.1
Specialists on the New York Stock Exchange

Each security listed for trading on the New York Stock Exchange (NYSE) is assigned to a member of the Exchange who becomes the specialist for that stock. The specialist's function is to "make a market" in the stock by always standing ready to buy or sell. On average, of course, if the specialist is to make money, his selling price must exceed his buying price. The difference between the two, or "bid-ask spread," reimburses the specialist for taking on the market-making function.

Only one specialist is assigned to a security listed on the New York Stock Exchange and so each such specialist has a monopoly position for dealings on the Exchange. But the Exchange may not have a monopoly of the trading process for a given security; some stocks are listed on other organized exchanges as well as on the NYSE. A study by S. M. Tinic showed that competition worked in the expected direction. The bid-ask spread on the New York Stock Exchange was lower, other things equal, *for those securities that were traded on other exchanges as well as on the NYSE.*[a] The Stock Exchange's specialist has a monopoly on that exchange, but competitors (firms offering similar services) on other organized exchanges reduce the specialist's monopoly power.

[a] S. M. Tinic, "The Economics of Liquidity Services," *Quarterly Journal of Economics*, v. 86 (Feb. 1972).

If consumers' demand for some good is highly elastic to begin with, even a single-firm monopolist will have little *monopoly power* as measured by P/MC in Equation (8.5a). We saw in Chapter 5 that elasticity tends to be high for luxury goods and for goods with close substitutes. Therefore, we would expect monopolists to have greater monopoly power for *necessity* goods and for goods *lacking close substitutes.*

EXAMPLE 8.2
Gas and Electric Utilities

Public utility corporations are generally granted exclusive (monopoly) rights to serve a particular locality. Among such public utilities are companies providing gas and electricity. In some areas these are provided by the same company, while in other communities the services are separately supplied. Since gas and electricity are close *substitutes* over a considerable range of uses, a company providing only one of them faces a more elastic demand (has less monopoly power). Such a company would always be seriously concerned about loss of business to the other energy source if it were to raise its price.

Bruce M. Owen made a comparative study of prices and outputs of combined versus separated gas and electricity services.[a] He found that private companies supplying combined gas and electric services charged, other things equal, on average about 6 percent more for electricity while providing about 15 percent less output in comparison with companies supplying only electricity. (On the other hand, there seemed to be no significant effect of combined versus separated service upon *gas* prices. Perhaps gas may have relatively elastic demand for reasons apart from availability of electricity as a substitute.)

> COMMENT: Privately owned public utility corporations are almost always *regulated* (as will be discussed below); the prices they charge must be approved by a government agency. The evidence above of seeming ability to exploit monopoly power suggests that regulation may have been of limited effectiveness.

[a] Bruce M. Owen, "Monopoly Pricing in Combined Gas and Electric Utilities," *The Antitrust Bulletin*, v. 15 (Winter 1970).

8.B.3 ☐ An Application: Author versus Publisher

In the publishing industry it is common practice for authors' royalties to take the form of a simple percentage of sales receipts. Is there any difference between the incentives of the author and the publisher as to what price should be set on a book?

Since there is only one seller of any single text, monopoly theory is applicable. Suppose that the author receives as royalty just 10 percent of Total Revenue R. Denote his or her royalty as $R_a = 0.1R$. Writing the net revenue to the publisher as R_p, it must be that $R_p = 0.9R$. In Figure 8.3 the Total Revenue R received from customers is divided between the dashed R_p (publisher's revenue) and the dotted R_a (author's revenue). The publisher would prefer the output Q_p^* such that the *slopes* along R_p and along the Total Cost curve C are equal; profit Π_p^* at that output is indicated by the height of the upper bold line-segment. The lower solid line-segment drawn along the same vertical is the royalty to the author.

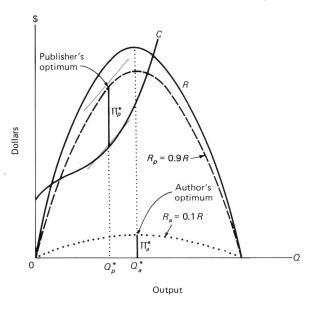

FIGURE 8.3 Author versus Publisher. Of the receipts from sales indicated by the Total Revenue curve R, 10 percent go to the author (R_a curve) and 90 percent to the publisher (P_p curve). Since the author bears no costs of production, from his or her point of view the optimal output is Q_a^* at the maximum of the R_a curve (at income Π_a^*). The publisher's maximum profit Π_p^* occurs at output Q_p^*, where the R_p curve has the greatest vertical divergence over the Total Cost curve C. The publisher will prefer a smaller output (will want to set a higher price) than the author.

The publisher's preferred output is not ideal for the author, however. *Since the author incurs no cost of production*, for him or her the optimum output Q_a^* occurs at the maximum of R_a. But $R_a = 0.1R$, and so the author prefers the price that will simply maximize Revenue R without regard to cost. The largest possible royalty for the author is shown by the bold line-segment Π_a^*, but then the corresponding profit to the publisher will be less. The upshot of the analysis is that *it is in the interest of the publisher to set a higher price (implying a smaller number of books sold) than the author would rationally prefer.*

In the publishing industry, authors do not normally have the power to fix price, which is the sole domain of the publisher. However, it might be advantageous for an author to make a deal accepting a smaller royalty percentage in return for the publisher setting a lower price.

Exercise 8.2: The demand function for a certain text is given by $P = 20 - 0.0002Q$ in dollars per copy, while the publisher's Marginal Cost is $MC = 6 + 0.00168Q$. The author's royalty is 20 percent of Total Revenue R. What is the publisher's preferred price-quantity solution? The author's?

Answer: The publisher wants to set Marginal Revenue $MR_p = 0.8MR$ equal to Marginal Cost. Since the combined Marginal Revenue from sales is $MR = 20 - 0.0004Q$, eight-tenths of this is $MR_p = 16 - 0.00032Q$. Equating MR_p to MC, the publisher's optimum is $Q = 5000$ copies, $P = 19$ dollars. The author simply wants to choose Q to maximize Revenue—that is, to set Marginal Revenue equal to zero. $MR = 20 - 0.0004Q = 0$ implies $Q = 50{,}000$ copies, $P = 10$ dollars. Note the big difference between the two solutions.

There is a possibly surprising similarity between the situation of an author seeking royalty income from a book and the situation of a state seeking tax income from racetrack betting.

EXAMPLE 8.3
Racetrack Betting

For a number of states in the United States, racetrack betting is an important source of tax income. Of the total amount wagered by bettors (the "handle"), a certain percentage (the "takeout") is withdrawn from the pari-mutuel pool and not paid out in winnings. From the point of view of the bettors, the takeout percentage is the price paid for the privilege of wagering. This takeout is divided, in varying proportions depending upon the specific regulations of each state, between taxes to the state and revenues for the racing industry (payments to the track management, horse owners, etc.) There is another source of receipts called "breakage," which is due to the usual practice of rounding down winnings to the next lower 10 cents. If the pari-mutuel odds would have paid off $5.18 on a winning $2 bet, for example, the state presumes that the bettor does not want to bother with the extra 8 cents. So the state kindly saves him or her the trouble and retains the odd amounts. For simplicity we can assume here that "breakage" is part of the "takeout."

The position of the state with regard to the takeout percentage is like an author with regard to the price of the book, in that neither the author nor the state *bears any part of the cost of production*. So, in accordance with the analysis above, the state, like the author, would prefer simply to maximize revenue (to set $MC = MR = 0$). But whereas the author is not usually in a position to set the price of his or her book, the state can and normally does fix the takeout percentage.

An implication is that the state, if it seeks to maximize its revenues, should fix the takeout percentage where the demand for wagering has elasticity $\eta = -1$. The evidence on this seems somewhat mixed. A study by Arthur Gruen[a] indicated that the takeout percentage could advantageously be lowered at New York racetracks (demand was in the elastic range). This was actually attempted for a 65-day trial period but without success—the overall handle did indeed increase but not by enough to offset the lower-percentage take. Possibly, the experiment did not last long enough for bettors to have become sufficiently informed about the more favorable takeout percentage.

A study by Donn R. Pescatrice,[b] using different methods of analysis, arrived at somewhat opposed results. He found the demand elasticity at New York tracks to be close to -1, suggesting that the takeout percentage was just about right. More typically around the country, demand appeared to be in the *inelastic* range, indicating that an increase in the takeout percentage would have been profitable. In fact, practically all changes in the takeout rate in recent years have been in the direction of increasing rather than decreasing the rate. Identifying 22 specific instances where rates had been increased, while other factors that might have affected the handle were more or less constant, Pescatrice found that revenues increased in 20 and fell in only 2 of these cases.

[a] Arthur Gruen, "An Inquiry into the Economics of Race-Track Gambling," *Journal of Political Economy*, v. 84 (Feb. 1976).

[b] Donn R. Pescatrice, "The Inelastic Demand for Wagering," *Applied Economics*, v. 12 (1980).

COMMENT: Since fixing the takeout percentage is a political decision, we cannot simply assume that profit maximization for the state (equivalent to revenue maximization) was the sole goal of the decision-makers. Bettors are a powerful interest group, and they are of course in favor of a low rather than a high takeout percentage. It seems reasonable to believe that political decision-makers would strike some balance between having more state revenue versus not angering the bettors excessively. The tendency toward higher takeout rates in recent years suggests that the need for more tax revenue has been growing politically more urgent than preserving the goodwill of bettors. (Political decision processes will be studied in detail in Chapter 16.)

This analysis of the monopolist's price-setting decision is subject to one very serious qualification. At the beginning of the chapter a distinction was made between two types of monopolies. One type of monopolist is protected from potential competitors by an exclusive privilege granted by law—as in the case of a patent awarded to an inventor, or a franchise granted a company to provide telephone or electric power within a particular service area. The other type, the so-called "natural monopoly," is a firm that remains the sole producer in its industry because it can produce at a lower cost than any potential competitor. The legally franchised monopolist need not fear entry of competitors, but may be subject to some type of governmental regulation (as will be discussed in Section 8.D). On the other hand, the natural monopolist, in attempting to exploit its position, cannot ignore the threat posed by potential competitors. In particular, if the monopolist does not want to attract a second firm into the industry, it cannot set a profit-maximizing price higher than the minimum AC of the lowest-cost potential entrant. (If the monopolist were willing to tolerate entry of a small number of additional firms, the situation would become one of *oligopoly*, which is to be covered in Chapter 10.)

CONCLUSION: A natural monopoly, if it is to prevent entry of competitors, cannot charge a price higher than the minimum Average Cost of the lowest-cost potential entrant into the industry.

8.C
MONOPOLY AND ECONOMIC EFFICIENCY

Monopoly, as compared to perfect competition, leads to higher price and lower output. Is this good or bad? Obviously, while a high price is bad for the customers it is good for the owners of the monopoly firm—who are, after all, also members of society. However, recall the Fundamental Theorem of Exchange—*trade is mutually beneficial*. We can use the concepts of Consumer Surplus and Producer Surplus to show that monopoly can be regarded as a *hindrance to trade*. As such, it leads to an "efficiency loss," apart from whatever transfer gain the monopolist might achieve at the expense of consumers.[8]

Figure 8.4 illustrates the monopoly profit-maximizing solution and compares it with the competitive solution. A competitive industry with supply curve S would produce where the supply and demand curves cross at (Q_c, P_c). Now, without introducing any changes in costs of production, suppose the industry is monopolized. The competitive supply curve S then becomes the Marginal Cost curve of the single large firm.[9] The monopolist sets $MC = MR$ and produces Q_m, selling at price P_m. (Notice that price is *not* the height of the point where MC and MR intersect. The price P_m is determined by the height of the *demand curve* at the quantity Q_m.)

The most obvious effect of monopoly is to raise price from P_c to P_m. The shaded area, which was part of Consumer Surplus under competition, is captured by the monopolist as Producer Surplus. It is thus a *transfer* from consumers to the monopolist. In addition, monopoly will bring about an efficiency loss owing to the reduced volume of production and exchange, measured by the Consumer Surplus and Producer Surplus from those units of the good no longer traded. The

---

[8] However, we cannot therefore conclude that monopoly should be abolished. (Any more than we could conclude in Chapter 7 that taxes, which also reduce Consumer Surplus and Producer Surplus, should be abolished.) There may be other considerations to be balanced against the efficiency loss.

[9] As explained in an earlier footnote, any "factor-price effect" is incorporated within the monopolist's MC curve.

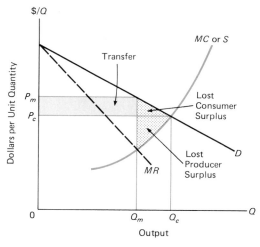

FIGURE 8.4 Monopoly and Efficiency Loss. If there are no *productive* losses or gains from organization of the industry into a single large firm versus competing small firms, the supply curve S of the competitive industry is identical with the Marginal Cost curve MC of the monopolist. The competitive equilibrium would occur at price P_c and quantity Q_c; the monopoly optimum is at the higher price P_m and smaller quantity Q_m. In comparison with the competitive outcome, the shaded area is a transfer from consumers to the monopolist supplier (equal to the price difference times the quantity still produced). The upper dotted area is the loss of Consumer Surplus due to the reduction in quantity traded (inability of consumers to buy the amount $Q_c - Q_m$ at the old price P_c). The lower dotted area is the analogous loss in Producer Surplus on the amount $Q_c - Q_m$, since Marginal Cost would have been less than price P_c in that range.

lost Consumer Surplus is the upper dotted triangle, and the lost Producer Surplus is the lower dotted triangle. Overall, consumers lose both the shaded rectangle (transfer) and the upper dotted triangle (efficiency loss). The monopolist, on the other hand, gains the shaded rectangle (transfer) but loses the lower dotted triangle (efficiency loss). Canceling out the transfer, the total efficiency loss is the dotted area in the diagram.

> CONCLUSION: In comparison with the competitive outcome, monopoly involves a transfer from consumers to suppliers. There is also an efficiency loss, which is the sum of the reductions in Consumer Surplus and Producer Surplus due to the lessened volume of trade.

EXAMPLE 8.4
Monopoly Efficiency Loss

A. C. Harberger[a] estimated the aggregate magnitude of the efficiency loss due to monopoly in the United States, for the period 1924 through 1928. He was able to do so only by making a number of heroic assumptions, in particular, that Marginal Cost was constant for all industries, and that the price elasticity of demand was equal to -1 everywhere. Identifying monopolized industries on the basis of high average profit rate on assets, he obtained a surprisingly low estimate of the loss: only around 0.1 percent of national income.

Harberger's results were criticized by G. J. Stigler[b] on several grounds, among them: (1) a rational monopolist will always produce in the range where elasticity is *greater* than one (as we have seen above); (2) reported profit rates for monopolists may omit monopoly returns in the form of disguised "cost" items such as patent royalties and executive salaries; and (3) for monopoly firms, "intangible" items may become counted among assets, so as to reduce the reported profit as a percentage of assets.

A number of later studies examined different sets of data, allowing in various ways for Stigler's objections. D. R. Kamerschen[c] studied the period 1956 through 1961, making rather strong assumptions toward the opposite extreme from Harberger. For example, he included royalties, intangibles, and advertising expenditures with the monopoly returns. He obtained demand-elasticity estimates by industry, averaging around (minus) 2 or 3. On this basis Kamerschen concluded that the annual welfare loss due to monopoly is around 6 percent of national income. Still later, D. A. Worcester, Jr.,[d] studied the period 1965 through 1969, using *firm* rather than *industry* data for added precision. Taking account of the Stigler objections in a variety of ways, and using an over-

[a] A. C. Harberger, "Monopoly and Resource Allocation," *American Economic Review*, v. 54 (May 1954).

[b] G. J. Stigler, "The Statistics of Monopoly and Merger," *Journal of Political Economy*, v. 64 (Feb. 1956).

[c] D. R. Kamerschen, "An Estimation of the 'Welfare Losses' from Monopoly in the American Economy," *Western Economic Journal*, v. 4 (Summer 1966).

[d] D. A. Worcester, Jr., "New Estimates of the Welfare Loss to Monopoly, United States: 1956-1969," *Southern Economic Journal*, v. 40 (Oct. 1973).

all elasticity figure of (minus) 2, he still obtained low "maximum defensible" estimates of the welfare loss due to monopoly, in the range of 0.5 percent of national income.

COMMENT: As this very condensed report suggests, we have here an as-yet-unresolved economic controversy, involving issues of both theory and statistical data. Even if the low estimates prove correct, it would be wrong to infer automatically that antimonopoly activities of government should be suspended. Perhaps the low monopoly losses are to be attributed to the success of those very activities.

There may be an additional efficiency loss not considered above: *the cost of getting or keeping the monopoly.* (This is an example of what is sometimes called "rent-seeking," to be discussed further in Chapter 15.) For example, if monopoly profits are $500 per day, then the monopolist would be willing to spend up to $500 per day to acquire or retain the monopoly position. Geometrically, in Figure 8.4 the monopolist would if necessary spend any amount up to the value of the monopoly gain (the excess of the shaded transfer rectangle over the lower dotted triangle of lost Producer Surplus). If there are several contenders for the monopoly position, we would still expect that all the contenders together would be willing to spend an amount about equal to the potential monopoly gain in order to acquire the privilege.[10]

The degree to which these costs of contending for the monopoly position are an *efficiency loss* depends on the way the contest takes place. Suppose the monopoly privilege is simply auctioned off by the government. Then the additional efficiency loss might be negligible, since an auction is not a very resource-consuming process. (Of course, the winning bidder will have to pay his bid, but this amount is a transfer to the government, not a net loss to society.) Cable TV franchises usually are awarded in this way; local governments offer an exclusive franchise to whichever cable company makes the most attractive bid. However, in some cases the struggle for a monopoly might itself be very costly. Chicago-style gang wars were attempts to gain monopoly over crime—evidently, a highly destructive process for all concerned. Less picturesque, entirely lawful, but still often quite expensive are contests in which prizes are awarded by a government authority at its discretion. The Federal Communications Commission awards broadcasting channels, the Patent Office grants patents, and so on. Here the proceedings typically involve extremely elaborate documentary submissions, hearings at which highly paid lawyers and consultants make their cases, and perhaps very large costs are secretly incurred in order to bring political or other pressures to bear.[11]

[10] Estimates of the expenses incurred to achieve monopoly positions in a number of industries are provided in R. A. Posner, "The Social Costs of Monopoly and Regulation," *Journal of Political Economy,* v. 83 (Aug. 1975).

[11] What if the prize were simply awarded to the contestant offering the highest bribe? This is like an auction, so that (to a first approximation, at least) there would be no efficiency loss! Only a transfer is involved, in this case going to the private purse of the corrupt official rather than to the government treasury. Note that illegal or immoral methods may involve an efficiency loss (gang war) or may not (bribery), just as legal and moral methods may or may not. (This fact may suggest that efficiency ought not be the *sole* criterion for social judgments.)

These *costs of achieving monopoly rights* are not essentially different from the costs involved in acquiring or defending any form of rights in our society. Rights to property, rights to sue in court, and even "civil" rights like freedom of speech can often only be gained or exercised at considerable cost.

8.D
REGULATION OF MONOPOLY

Monopoly is usually considered, we have seen, to lead to economic inefficiency. In addition, excessive monopoly profits are commonly regarded as unfair to consumers. Policies for dealing with monopoly range from *laissez faire* or toleration at one extreme to "trust-busting" at the other. Another possibility is to put monopolistic enterprises under government ownership, as is commonly done in Europe for railroads and telephone service. But the policy to be discussed here is *regulation* of the monopoly's price and quantity or quality of service by a government agency. In the United States regulation is standard practice for privately owned "public utilities" providing goods and services such as electric power, water and gas, telephone, and transportation—usually thought to be natural monopolies.

The standard philosophy of regulation aims at limiting the monopolist to a "normal profit." Normal profit is supposed to be just adequate to attract needed capital and other resources into the business, but not so high as to represent exploitation of consumers. As explained in Chapter 6, normal profit in the accounting sense corresponds to *zero economic profit*. And, we saw, zero economic profit did characterize long-run equilibrium in perfect competition. So, in a sense, regulation aims at achieving the result that would have occurred had competition been possible.

Figure 8.5 shows a monopoly firm with rising Average Cost and Marginal Cost, as in the preceding diagram. The picture repeats the monopoly solution (Q_m and P_m) and the competitive solution (Q_c and P_c) as before, and adds the zero-profit regulatory solution (Q_z and P_z). Zero economic profit is of course equivalent

FIGURE 8.5 Regulation of Monopoly: Increasing Cost. The regulatory solution, fixing price so that the monopolist receives zero economic profit, is the price–output combination P_z, Q_z where the AC and AR curves intersect. If this occurs in the range where Average Cost AC is rising, regulated output Q_z will be even greater than the competitive equilibrium output Q_c. In comparison with the competitive solution, the shaded rectangle is a transfer from suppliers to consumers. The dotted area ABC is an efficiency loss due to *excessive* output.

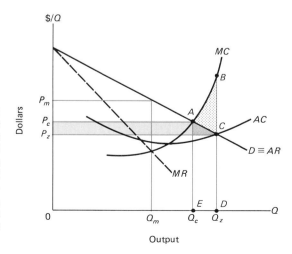

to setting a price and associated output (determined along the consumers' demand curve) such that $AC = AR$. In the situation pictured, whereas the unregulated monopoly solution had "too small" output and "too high" price in comparison with the efficient competitive outcome, here the regulatory correction overshoots the competitive solution. Output is "too high" and price "too low."

A striking feature of Figure 8.5 is that, in the range of output greater than Q_c, Marginal Cost MC exceeds the demand price (the consumers' "marginal willingness to pay"). In this range, therefore, the cost of producing additional units is greater than their value to buyers. The firm is employing resources that have more highly valued uses elsewhere. Geometrically, when output rises from Q_c to Q_z, the cost incurred on the additional units is $ABDE$—the area under MC. The benefit to consumers is only $ACDE$—the area under the demand curve. So the dotted area represents a net efficiency loss in comparison with the competitive ideal. (However, *in comparison with unregulated monopoly* the result is indeterminate. The unregulated monopoly here produces too little, the regulated monopoly produces too much, and we cannot say which is the more efficient.)

The usual argument offered for regulation does not apply to the picture of Figure 8.5 with its rising Average Cost curve, however. Proponents of regulation have in mind a special kind of "natural monopoly" that is characterized by an Average Cost curve AC that is falling throughout the relevant range,[12] as pictured in Figure 8.6.[13] If all the firms have this same cost function, then any single one able to achieve an output lead over the others would be able to produce more cheaply. The cost advantage grows as the output lead increases, and so the ultimate outcome is likely to be a single surviving firm.

Since in Figure 8.6 the Average Cost AC is falling throughout, Marginal Cost MC lies always below it (Proposition 2.2a). It follows that, as shown in the diagram, the regulatory solution where $AC = AR$ (at output Q_z and price P_z) lies *between* the monopoly solution (output Q_m and price P_m) and the competitive solution (output Q_c and price P_c). So, in this case, the regulatory solution is definitely an improvement over unregulated monopoly—it comes closer to the ideal. The dotted triangle shows the efficiency loss still remaining, owing to the fact that even the regulated output is still "too small."

There is a paradox here, however. At Q_c, the output representing the efficient ideal, notice that $MC = P$ and $MC < AC$. Thus Average Cost exceeds price, violating the long-run No-Shutdown Condition (the firm would be losing money). It does not seem reasonable to regard as an ideal a situation in which the firm would have to suffer a financial loss. The answer to the paradox is that, from the efficiency point of view, it would indeed be better to have the firm produce the larger output despite the financial loss.[14] In principle, the loss could be cov-

---

[12] Any firm that can produce at lower Average Cost AC than its competitors, as its scale grows large, has a natural monopoly. This *may* be due to a falling AC curve, where operating at a larger scale is what gives the firm a cost advantage. But there may also be a natural monopoly with rising AC, if the firm's Average Costs remain lower than its competitors' even at large outputs.

[13] The Average Cost curve cannot fall forever, since that would violate the Law of Diminishing Returns. But it may continue to decline throughout the range of practical interest.

[14] The justification is as follows. At the regulatory solution, $AC = P$ and there is no financial loss. Now we ask, ideally speaking in efficiency terms, should output be expanded from Q_z to Q_c? The answer is yes, since in the region between Q_z and Q_c the demand price always exceeds Marginal Cost. What the consumers are willing to pay for the *additional* units exceeds what it costs to provide those units.

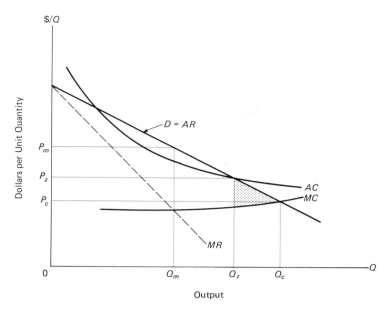

FIGURE 8.6 Regulation of Monopoly: Decreasing Cost.   Here the regulatory solution P_z, Q_z at the intersection of the AC and AR curves (zero economic profit) occurs in the range where Average Cost is falling. In this "natural monopoly" situation the regulated output Q_z, though greater than the profit-maximizing monopoly output Q_m, is still less than the ideally efficient output Q_c where $MC = P$. In comparison with the efficient outcome, the dotted areas represent losses of Consumer Surplus and Producer Surplus due to insufficient output.

ered by a lump-sum "transfer" of funds to the firm that would leave the amounts of Producer Surplus and Consumer Surplus unaffected.[15]

In the previous section, we saw that an unregulated natural monopolist with a rising Average Cost function (as in Figure 8.5) might not actually charge the supposed profit-maximizing monopoly price, to avoid attracting outsiders into the industry. The same holds when the natural monopoly is due solely to a falling Average Cost function (as in Figure 8.6). Even when it is always cheaper to produce at a larger than a smaller scale, so that only a single firm will survive in the industry, there may be *competition among different firms to be the single supplier*. Such situations are described as "competition for the field instead of competition in the field", or more concisely as "contestable markets."[16] An interesting current example is long-distance telephone service in the United States. Formerly, AT&T had a legally protected monopoly privilege, but owing to a change in the law there are now several competitors vying for the consumers' favor. If indeed the Average Cost function is declining, one of the contenders—very likely AT&T, because it is now the largest—will eventually be able to drive out the others. But the ever-

---

[15] Where would the funds come from? Conceivably, from a government subsidy. Or the consumers themselves might be willing to subsidize the firm in order to allow it to remain in business while still charging the efficient low prices.

[16] See Harold Demsetz, "Why Regulate Utilities?" *Journal of Law & Economics*, v. 11 (Apr. 1968) and William J. Baumol, "Contestable Markets: An Uprising in the Theory of Industry Structure," *American Economic Review*, v. 72 (Mar. 1982).

present threat of "competition for the field" is likely to prevent the winner from earning any great monopoly profit.

> CONCLUSION: With a rising AC curve, the regulatory zero-profit solution corrects the monopoly underproduction solution but goes too far—leading to "too-large" rather than "too-small" output. With a falling AC curve, the correction is again in the right direction but does not go far enough. However, the supposed problem of underproduction in the case of natural monopoly may not actually exist. The pressure of outsiders anxious to enter the industry may prevent the monopolist from actually by charging the profit-maximizing price. maximizing price.

There is a further problem with regulation, one that is not visible in Figures 8.5 and 8.6. Firms subject to regulation are relatively uninterested in reducing costs. Indeed, if regulation were perfectly effective in always maintaining the zero-profit condition $AC = P$, the firm would have no incentive at all to hold costs down. Any increase in cost of production would be immediately reflected in allowable higher prices, maintaining the "normal profit" of the firm. That this does not always happen is due to regulatory lag. When costs rise or fall, some time will pass before the regulatory commission gets around to adjusting prices. In addition, the regulatory authorities may punish a firm that too conspicuously fails to keep its costs of production under control. So the cost-reducing incentive is not totally absent for regulated firms, though it is indeed seriously weakened.

8.E
MONOPOLISTIC PRICE DISCRIMINATION

Until now we have assumed that the monopolist offers all customers a single price at which they are free to buy whatever quantity they want. Sometimes, however, a monopolist may be able to engage in more complex pricing practices that are called *price discrimination*. By offering different terms to different buyers, the monopolist may be able to divide the market (*market segmentation*). Or, for any given buyer, the monopolist might be able to charge different prices for different quantities (*multi-part pricing*). In the extreme a different price can be charged to each consumer for each unit he or she buys; this is called *perfect discrimination*. (Note that under pure competition there cannot be price discrimination. No consumer would pay more than the market-determined competitive price, and no firm would sell for less.)

8.E.1 ☐ Market Segmentation

Suppose the monopolist divides the customers into two or more separate portions and charges "whatever the market will bear" in each. Japanese auto manufacturers have been accused, for example, of charging more for their cars in Japan than abroad, since the overseas car market is more competitive than the highly protected Japanese market. Note that the two markets must be kept separate for the scheme to work. If cars are priced at \$10,000 in Japan and \$7,000 in the United States, and assuming shipping costs are less than \$3,000, Americans could simply ship their \$7,000 cars back to Japan and sell them for \$10,000. Any price difference in excess of the shipping cost would tend to disappear.[17]

We suggested above that sellers would charge a lower price in the more competitive market segment. More precisely, price will be lower in the segment with more *elastic demand*. ("Dumping abroad," as in the Japanese car example, occurs because demand is generally more elastic in the competitive world market than in a firm's protected home market.) Imagine a monopolist is selling in two markets. Denote the separate prices as P_1 and P_2, and the Marginal Revenues as mr_1 and mr_2. First of all, the firm will set $mr_1 = mr_2$. (If not, profit could be increased by withdrawing units from the market with low Marginal Revenue and selling them in the market with high Marginal Revenue.) Furthermore, the firm will set Marginal Cost MC equal to $mr_1 = mr_2$. In other words, it will operate where the extra cost of producing one more unit is equal to the extra revenue gained from selling in either market. Thus:[18]

(8.6) $MC = mr_1 = mr_2$ Market-Segmentation Optimality Condition

From Equation (8.5), and knowing that $mr_1 = mr_2$, we see that:

(8.7)
$$P_1\left(1 - \frac{1}{|\eta_1|}\right) = P_2\left(1 - \frac{1}{|\eta_2|}\right)$$

It follows that if, for example, $|\eta_1| > |\eta_2|$ (demand in market 1 is the more elastic), then $P_1 < P_2$. Thus, as asserted above, the *segment with more elastic demand receives the lower price*.

Figure 8.7 provides a geometrical illustration. The key device is the curve labeled Σmr, the horizontal sum of mr_1 and mr_2. The intersection of the firm's Marginal Cost curve MC with Σmr at the point W establishes the optimal total output $Q = q_1 + q_2$. Drawing a horizontal line from W will show the optimal quantities for the separate markets. The intersection T gives us q_1, and the intersection U gives us q_2. The associated prices P_1 and P_2 are found along the respective demand curves d_1 and d_2. [*Challenge to the reader*: Show that the lower price corresponds to the *more elastic* demand.]

In addition to dumping abroad, there are other possible examples of market segmentation. Movie theaters and buses may offer special discounts to the elderly or to children (markets segmented by age). There may also be price variation according to season at resorts, and by time of day at restaurants or places of entertainment. (But these price variations in some cases may be due to *differing costs* of serving the different types of customers, so we cannot always be sure they are instances of monopolistic price discrimination.) The discount coupons offered by supermarkets are another possible·example, since they represent a way of charg-

---

[17] However, the insulation of the two segments need not be *total*. The monopolist could accept some "leakage" and still remain ahead.

[18] The technical qualification earlier, that MC must cut MR from *below*, here takes the following form: MC must cut the horizontal sum of the *mr* curves (see Figure 8.7) from below.

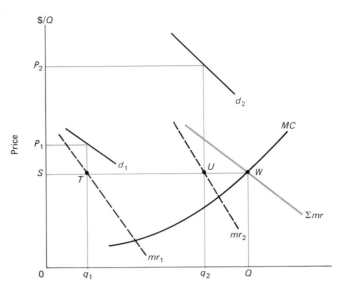

FIGURE 8.7 Market Segmentation. The market is divided into two segments whose independent demand curves are d_1 and d_2. The profit-maximizing solution for the firm is to produce where $MC = mr_1 = mr_2$. Geometrically, the optimal output Q is at the intersection of Marginal Cost MC with the Σmr curve representing the horizontal sum of the separate Marginal Revenue curves mr_1 and mr_2. Of this total output the amount q_1 (which equals ST) is sold to the first sector at price P_1 while q_2 (SU, which equals TW) is sold to the second sector at price P_2.

Firm Output and Segment Sales Quantities

ing lower prices to those people willing to take extra time and trouble. In most of these cases the discounts appear to be aimed at less affluent individuals, who presumably have *lower* demand prices (less "willingness to pay"). But we have to be careful here, since profit-maximizing market segmentation does not depend upon the *heights* of the demand curve but upon the demand *elasticities*. [*Challenge to the reader*: In each of the instances cited, can you show that the discounts are offered to the more elastic market?]

Exercise 8.3: A monopolist in a certain country has its domestic market protected by law from import competition. The domestic demand curve for its product is given by $P_d = 120 - q_d/10$. The firm can also sell in the more competitive world export market, where the price is $P_e = 80$ independent of the quantity q_e exported. (That is, this firm is a price-taker so far as the world market is concerned.) Marginal Cost is given by $MC = 50 + Q/10$, where $Q \equiv q_d + q_e$. (a) Find the best overall output Q and its division between the two markets. (b) Compare the prices and demand elasticities in the domestic market versus the world market.

Answer: (a) We know that the Marginal Revenues in the two markets, mr_d and mr_e, and also Marginal Cost MC, must all be equalized. Since the domestic demand curve is linear, we have: $mr_d = 120 - q_d/5$. And since the export demand curve is horizontal: $mr_e = P_e = 80$. Equating the Marginal Revenues: $120 - q_d/5 = 80$, which implies $q_d = 200$. Equating MC to mr_e leads to: $50 + Q/10 = 80$, which implies $Q = 300$. It follows that $q_e = 100$. (b) The export price remains $P_e = 80$, and demand elasticity in that market is minus infinity. In the domestic market, $q_d = 200$ implies $P_d = 100$. The demand elasticity is:

$$\eta_d = \frac{P_d}{q_d}\frac{\Delta q_d}{\Delta P_d} = \frac{100}{200}(-10) = -5$$

The price is of course higher in the less elastic domestic market.

8.E.2 □ Multi-Part Pricing

Whereas market segmentation involves charging different prices to different customers, *multi-part pricing* occurs when the seller charges different prices to a single customer. For example, a pound of detergent might sell for $1.00 while a two-pound package sells for $1.50. The seller is thus charging a customer $1.00 for the first pound bought, and $0.50 for the second.

Figure 8.8 shows the demand curve of a single consumer. Suppose that without price discrimination the monopolist would have charged $P*$ for all units sold. Consumer Surplus would have been equal to the entire shaded triangle. However, the monopolist could charge as much as P_1 for the first q_1 units sold and then sell an additional q_2 units at the lower price $P_2 = P*$. Doing this allows the monopolist to capture the darker rectangle as revenue, rather than leaving it as Consumer Surplus. The rectangle is thus a transfer from consumers to the monopolist.

A qualification is needed, however. The monopolist would not ordinarily be able to do quite this well. The reason is that the high initial price will tend to impoverish the consumer, reducing his or her demand for additional units (owing to the "income effect of a price change," as discussed in Chapter 4). Only if there is no income effect (if the income elasticity of demand is zero) will the demand curve be unaffected by multi-part pricing.[19] Multi-part pricing will therefore not be able to capture quite as much additional revenue as indicated in Figure 8.8.

Another limitation upon the profitability of multi-part pricing stems from differences among consumers. Ideally, the monopolist would like to use a different multi-part price schedule for each buyer. But this is usually impractical. If the same price schedule is used for all, some consumers may be charged too high a price and others too low a price for maximizing the firm's profit. Figure 8.9 illustrates this possibility. At the initial block price P_1, this consumer buys q_1 units. But

---

[19] It follows from this that the geometrical picture of Consumer Surplus we have been using, as an area under the ordinary demand curve (the demand curve applicable with simple pricing), is not quite correct either.

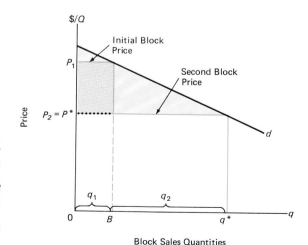

FIGURE 8.8 Two-Part Pricing. Here $P*$ is assumed to be the profit-maximizing simple price for a monopolist. If d is the demand curve of a typical consumer, the monopolist can do better by charging a higher price P_1 on an initial block quantity B and $P_2 = P*$ thereafter. This two-part pricing scheme allows the monopolist to capture the portion of Consumer Surplus represented by the rectangle lying within the shaded area.

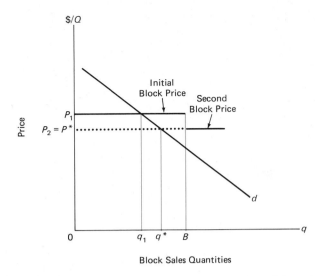

$/Q

Price

P_1
$P_2 = P^*$

Initial
Block Price
Second
Block Price

d

0   q_1 q^* B   q

Block Sales Quantities

FIGURE 8.9 Unsuccessful Two-Part Pricing. Here we see a two-part pricing scheme inappropriate for this particular consumer. No sales are actually made at the second block price, so in effect a simple price P_1 is being charged.

the second block price P_2 is too high; the consumer will not buy any additional units at all. Thus for this consumer the multi-part price schedule is inoperative; in effect, P_1 has become a simple price.

As another practical difficulty, multi-part pricing will also involve higher transaction costs for the seller. So it is not always evident that the monopolist will gain.

At first sight, it may appear that discrimination via multi-part pricing is very common. Electric and water utilities, for example, normally charge on a "declining-block" basis. There is an initial high price for the first block consumed in any period, and a lower price thereafter. The price schedules may often have four or five parts (blocks), and also, possibly, some market segmentation of different classes of customers as well. Printers and furniture-movers also commonly have declining-block pricing arrangements. Indeed, wherever "quantity discounts" are encountered, multi-part price discrimination may be suspected.

However, the suspicion is not conclusive; the pricing scheme may be due not to discrimination but to the costs incurred in serving different classes of customers. In the case of electric utilities, for example, there may be a lump-sum cost of providing the consumer's connection to the main cable, a cost that is essentially independent of the number of kilowatt hours consumed. Similarly, for printing jobs there is normally a lump-sum cost per transaction (such as the cost of setting up the type for a printing order) and a variable cost representing the actual run of the press. Ideally, then, charges to consumers should have a lump-sum and a variable component. For a variety of reasons, it may be more convenient to bill the consumer for the recurring lump-sum component by charging an extra-high price on the first few units taken. Thus, what appears to be discriminatory multi-part pricing may really represent a "cost-justified" quantity discount.

8.E.3 ☐ Perfect Discrimination

Under the logical extreme of *perfect price discrimination*, the monopolist employs a separate pricing schedule for each customer, the prices changing for each successive unit bought. If this were feasible the monopolist could extract the full amount the consumer is willing to pay, effectively capturing all of the Consumer Surplus.

In Figure 8.10 we see a four-part pricing schedule, an extension of the two-part schedule pictured in Figure 8.8. As in the previous analysis, we make the simplifying assumption of zero income effect (zero income elasticity of demand) for the commodity. Then the quantities taken at the lower prices are unaffected by the higher amounts paid out for earlier units. As can be seen, such a multi-part schedule can transfer large portions of the Consumer Surplus to the seller; in Figure 8.10, only the small shaded areas remain as Consumer Surplus.

When this process is carried to the limit, with different prices for each successive infinitesimal unit, *all* the Consumer Surplus will have been transferred from the buyer to the seller. By repeating this process with every separate consumer, the perfectly discriminating monopolist absorbs essentially all the achievable mutual advantage of trade.

Despite the seeming "inequity" of this totally unbalanced distribution of the benefits from trade, a remarkable thing about the perfect-discrimination solution is that it is *efficient*—there are no efficiency losses, only transfers! For the last infinitesimal unit purchased by each consumer, the monopolist will charge an amount equal to Marginal Cost. Notice that, under perfect price discrimination as under perfect competition, the condition $MC = P$ is satisfied for the *last* unit sold. Since each buyer's marginal willingness to pay (demand price) is thus equal to the

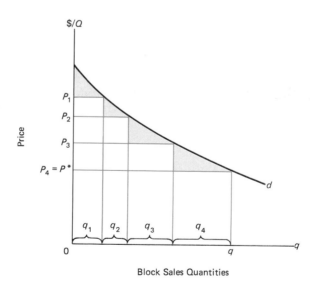

FIGURE 8.10 Four-Part Pricing. In the case illustrated, a four-part pricing scheme leaves only the shaded areas as Consumer Surplus.

seller's Marginal Cost of production, there can be no efficiency gain from either increasing or decreasing output. Therefore, even though the scale of the output under perfect price discrimination will not in general be *the same* as under perfect competition, we cannot say that the outcome is less efficient.

*8.F
AN APPLICATION: INTRA-COMPANY PRICING

In order to achieve the benefits of decentralization, many companies have split their operations into divisions that act as more or less autonomous "profit centers." These profit centers typically are allowed, within certain limits, to make their own price and output decisions. Their executives, furthermore, are judged on the basis of the divisional profits achieved.

Suppose a commodity or a service is to be exchanged between two profit centers of a single company. The firm may produce copper metal in one profit center and fabricate it into copper wire in a separate profit center. Or *production* may take place within one profit center and *marketing* of the company's product within another. The question then arises of how to price the internal transaction of, for example, supplying copper metal to the copper-wire division. The supplying division will of course be interested in having the intermediate product valued at a high price, the receiving division at a low price. Several practical issues arise, such as: What should be the basis of such "internal" pricing, in terms of maximizing the overall profit of the company as a whole? If the receiving division can acquire the intermediate product from an *external* supplier instead, should it be permitted to do so? Are the divisional profits measured using these internal prices a useful guide for judging managers' performance?

Let us assume that the company has monopoly power (faces a downward-sloping demand curve) in the *final product* market. With regard to the market for the *intermediate product* exchanged between the two divisions, three cases will be examined here: (1) no external market exists for the intermediate product; (2) an external market for the intermediate product exists, and is perfectly competitive; (3) an external market exists, and the firm has monopoly power there as well as in the market for the final product.

Let us start with case (1), where there is *no external market* for the intermediate product. We can think of the supplying division as the "manufacturing" profit center, with Marginal Manufacturing Cost *mmc* as illustrated by the dashed curve in Figure 8.11; the receiving division is the "retailing" profit center, with Marginal Distribution Cost *mdc* as pictured by the light, solid curve. Since there is no external "wholesale" market for the intermediate product (i.e., there are no independent distributors of the firm's manufactured product), the two divisions of the

---

* Marked sections, beginning with a single asterisk and ending with a double asterisk, may contain somewhat more difficult or advanced material and can be omitted without appreciable loss of continuity.

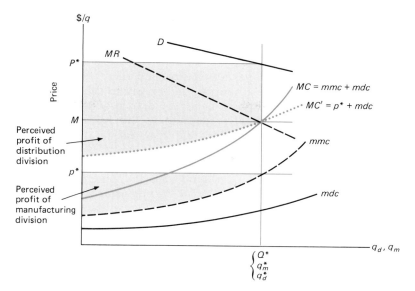

$/q

Price

Perceived
profit of
distribution
division

Perceived
profit of
manufacturing
division

D

MR

P^*

M

p^*

$MC = mmc + mdc$

$MC' = p^* + mdc$

mmc

mdc

q_d, q_m

$\begin{cases} Q^* \\ q_m^* \\ q_d^* \end{cases}$

Quantity Manufactured and Distributed

FIGURE 8.11   Internal Pricing, I: No External Market for Intermediate Product.   In the absence of
an external market for the intermediate product, the firm's profit-maximizing output Q^* occurs where
overall MC (the sum of the marginal manufacturing cost mmc and marginal distribution cost mdc)
equals Marginal Revenue MR in the final-product market. The correct internal price for the
intermediate product, p^*, is equal to mmc at output Q^*. When the manufacturing division maximizes
its profit by setting $mmc = p^*$ it will produce $q_m^* = Q^*$, while the distribution division in setting
$p^* + mdc = MR$ will sell the same amount: $q_d^* = Q^*$.

firm will have to coordinate their outputs. The "ideal" solution *for the firm as a
whole* is obvious. The firm's overall Marginal Cost is the bold MC curve, the vertical sum of mmc and mdc (since by definition $MC \equiv mmc + mdc$). The profit-maximizing output Q^* for the firm, which must be equal here to the coordinated divisional outputs q_m^* and q_d^*, will be such that $MC = MR$. The price P^* for the final
product is of course found along the demand curve. (We assume, without drawing the AC curve, that the profit-maximizing price P^* in the final-product market
will be high enough to meet the No-Shutdown Condition.)

Knowing the ideal solution, what can we say about the correct "internal pricing" arrangement? The answer here is that the *internal* price p^* must be set equal
to mmc at output $Q^* = q_m^*$. If so, it is evident in the diagram that the supplier division will indeed want to produce q_m^*, since that is where $mmc = p^*$. (Notice that we
are assuming "price-taking behavior.") What about the receiving division? Its *perceived* Marginal Cost, the bold dotted curve MC' in the diagram, is defined as the
vertical sum $MC' \equiv p^* + mdc$—its own Marginal Distribution Cost, plus the internal price it has to pay for the product. Setting its perceived $MC' = MR$, the re-

tailing division is also led to the correct output q_d^* and the associated final-product price P^*. [*Challenge to the reader*: Verify also that the shaded areas represent the perceived profits (apart from any fixed costs not shown in the diagram) of the two separate divisions.]

There remains the operational problem of who is to set the internal price p^*. One possibility would be a neutral umpire within the firm, or an outside consulting economist. The main point is that the decision ought not be left within the discretion of either the supplying division or the receiving division. The reason is that the supplier division can increase its divisional profit by *acting as a monopolist* at the expense of its internal customers, and would therefore want to set the internal price p^* too high; the receiving division would similarly be a "monopsonist" (sole buyer), and would want to set p^* too low. In effect, while the firm wants to use its monopoly power to hold back output so as to exploit *outside* customers, it does not want its internal divisions attempting to exploit one another!

Now let us take up case (2), where there is a *perfectly competitive external market* (with an established external price $\bar{p}$) for the intermediate product. If the supplying and the receiving divisions of the firm are allowed to deal on this external market, their outputs q_m and q_d will no longer necessarily be equal. The supplier division may be able to meet internal requirements and still have something left over to sell to independent wholesalers, or in the opposite case the receiving division may use the external market to supplement its internal supply.

Under these circumstances *the internal price p^* cannot differ from the external price $\bar{p}$*—else one or the other division would refuse to deal with its internal trading partner. The case illustrated in Figure 8.12 has $q_m^* > q_d^*$, meaning that the manufacturing division is able to offer some product on the external market even after meeting the internal requirements. It could equally well occur that $q_d^* > q_m^*$—the retailing division could be handling the entire internal output, plus additional amounts procured on the external wholesale market. [*Challenge to the reader*: Once again, verify that the shaded areas represent the respective perceived profits of the two divisions, apart from fixed costs.]

The third and last case is the most interesting and most difficult. Here we assume that the firm has monopoly power in *both* the intermediate-product market and the final-product market. For example, the firm might have a world monopoly of its manufactured product, which it supplies to independent foreign distributors in a world wholesale market, while still retaining a retail monopoly of the distributed final product in its home country. The firm's manufactured output q_m will now necessarily be greater than its domestic retail output q_d. The key question is: Should the manufacturing division, having established a profit-maximizing external monopoly price $\bar{p}$ for outside distributors on the intermediate wholesale market, charge *the same* internal price p^* to its internal trading partner? Or, alternatively, in the interests of the firm as a whole should it be required to provide the intermediate product on more favorable terms to its internal customer (that is, should it set $p^* < \bar{p}$)?

In Figure 8.13 notice the similarity of the lower panel to the "market segmentation" picture of Figure 8.7. From the point of view of the manufacturing division, one market segment is the *external demand* for the intermediate product (quantity q_e) and the other is the *internal demand* (quantity q_d)—where, of course, $q_m \equiv q_d + q_e$.

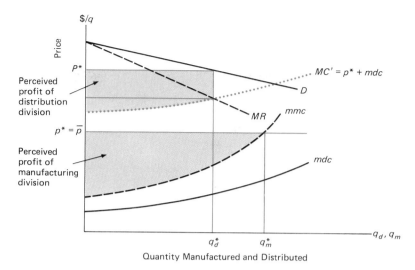

FIGURE 8.12 Internal Pricing, II: Competitive Market for Intermediate Product. With a ruling competitive price $\bar{p}$ for the intermediate product, the internal price p^* must equal $\bar{p}$, else one or the other division would refuse to engage in internal trading. As before, the manufacturing division would set output q_m^* where $mmc = p^*$, and the distribution division would choose q_d^* where $p^* + mdc = MR$ in the final-product market. But here the two divisions would generally have differing outputs, and either could be larger than the other.

The upper panel is an auxiliary diagram designed to derive the "net Marginal Revenue" curve nMR, which is by construction the vertical difference between the MR and the mdc curves—that is, $nMR \equiv MR - mdc$. This represents the net value to the distribution division of another unit sold before allowing for the internal price p^* it has to pay. The nMR curve is then reproduced in the lower panel to picture the *internal* demand segment. The *external* demand segment is shown by the sloping demand curve d and associated Marginal Revenue curve mr. As in the previous market-segmentation analysis, nMR and mr are now *summed horizontally* to arrive at the Σmr curve. The overall manufacturing output q_m is given by the intersection of mmc and Σmr at point M. Moving along the horizontal line we can pick off the associated external quantity q_e at point E and the internal quantity q_d at point D. The monopoly price in the external market, at which the quantity q_e is sold, is found at $\bar{p}$ along the external demand curve d. With $mmc = p^*$ then, as before, the firm's actual $MC \equiv mmc + mdc$ in the final-product market becomes equal to the *perceived* Marginal Cost $MC' \equiv p^* + mdc$ of the retail division. When the retail division maximizes its perceived profit by setting $MC' = MR$, for the firm as a whole the profit-maximizing condition $MC = MR$ is being met.

The conclusion, therefore, is that the internal price p^* should be set at Marginal Manufacturing Cost mmc, which is *less* than the external price $\bar{p}$. Once again the firm wants to exploit the external customers but not the internal customers for the intermediate product.

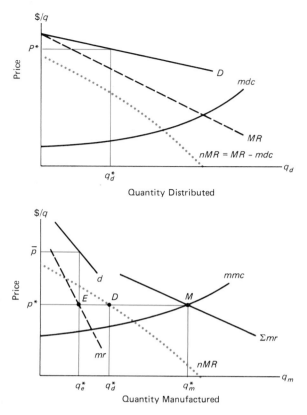

FIGURE 8.13 Internal Pricing, III: Monopoly Power in both Markets. In the upper panel, the distribution division's net Marginal Revenue curve *nMR* is derived as the vertical difference between final-product *MR* and Marginal Distribution Cost *mdc*. The internal price p^* should be set where the Marginal Manufacturing Cost curve *mmc* intersects the Σmr curve—the latter being the horizontal sum of *nMR* (net Marginal Revenue in the final market) and *mr* (Marginal Revenue to external sales in the intermediate market). The manufacturing division will then be motivated to produce q_m^*, of which q_e^* is sold externally in the intermediate market and q_d^* is taken by the distribution division for sale in the final market. The profit-maximizing final-product price P^* and external intermediate-market price $\bar{p}$ are pictured in the upper and lower panels, respectively. Note that $p^* < \bar{p}$—the internal price is lower than the price charged to outside purchasers of the intermediate good.

Finally, one important limitation of this analysis must be pointed out. Returning to Figure 8.11, notice again the shaded areas that represent the perceived profits of the respective divisions (apart from fixed costs) calculated in terms of the internal price p^*. Imagine that the supplier division finds a way of reducing cost which happens to leave its *Marginal* Manufacturing Cost *mmc* unchanged. Then p^* will remain the same, and the division responsible for the improvement will reap no benefit in terms of perceived profit. What is worse, a cost improvement will frequently reduce *mmc*, in which case the receiving division rather than the supplier division will receive the benefit. In short, while the analysis here leads to internal prices p^* that are correct in terms of the *marginal* conditions for the respective outputs, the profits calculated in terms of these internal prices may not be appropriate for such purposes as rewarding management or deciding whether to start up or to abandon a division.[20] **

8.G
CARTELS

A cartel is a group of firms combining to restrict output and raise price, the aim being to behave as a collective monopoly. Each firm in a cartel agrees to produce less than it would under unrestrained competition, in order to drive the price up so that all in the group will benefit.

Cartels have an Achilles heel. However desirable the arrangement is to the firms as a group, for any single one of them it pays to "chisel" on the agreement. Consider a firm in a cartelized industry that would otherwise have been perfectly competitive. Figure 8.14 illustrates such a situation. At the price P° that would rule in perfect competition, d° is the familiar horizontal demand curve *as viewed by* the competitive firm. Assuming that the No-Shutdown Condition is met, the firm would produce output q° where Marginal Cost $MC = P^\circ$. If a cartel is to raise price, industry output Q must somehow be cut back—for example by fixing pro-

---

[20] These issues are discussed further in Jack Hirshleifer, "Internal Pricing and Decentralized Decisions," in C. P. Bonini, R. K. Jaedicke, and H. M. Wagner, eds., *Management Controls: New Directions in Basic Research* (New York: McGraw-Hill, 1964).

**End of marked section.

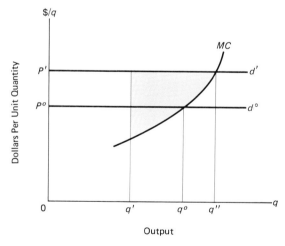

FIGURE 8.14   Incentive to Chisel under a Cartel.   If the competitive equilibrium price is P°, a price-taking firm would produce output q°. A cartel can drive price up only by forcing its members to cut back production. If this firm's assigned production quota were q', and the cartel succeeded in driving price up to P', the firm's potential gain from chiseling (potential increase in profit due to exceeding its quota) would be the shaded area. Note that, at the high price P', the firm would find it profitable to produce output q'', which is *greater* than its competitive output q°.

duction quotas for each firm. Suppose this firm is assigned an output quota q', and furthermore that the cartel is successful in pushing price up to P'. The incentive to chisel is evident. The new demand curve *as viewed by* the firm (a tiny slice of the industry demand curve) is d'—effectively horizontal, just like the $d°$ curve before cartelization. This means that by charging an infinitesimally lower amount, any single firm can get as much business as desired, taking away sales from others. Even at the old competitive price $P°$ the firm would have liked to produce $q°$, more than the quota q'. (Cartel production quotas must of course be smaller than what competitive firms would have produced, else the price could not rise from $P°$ to P'.) But once the cartel has raised price, the incentive to chisel is that much greater. At price P' the firm would want to sell output q'' in the diagram. The potential profit increase available to a chiseler, assuming all the other firms are faithfully abiding by the cartel agreement, is indicated by the shaded area in the diagram.

> CONCLUSION: Cartels can only raise prices by cutting firm outputs. But at the higher prices, member firms are motivated to produce even more than at competitive equilibrium. So the more successful the cartel, the greater the incentive to chisel.

Exercise 8.4: Suppose there are 100 identical firms in an initially competitive market. Market demand is given by $P = 10 - Q/200$ and market supply by $P = 1 + Q/200$. (a) Find the competitive equilibrium price $P°$, industry output $Q°$, and firm output $q°$. (b) If the 100 firms formed an effective cartel, what would be the price-quantity solution P', Q' for maximum aggregate profit? [Assume that the industry supply curve is simply the horizontal sum of the firm Marginal Cost curves.] (c) At this price, to what output quota q' would the typical firm have to be limited? How much would it like to produce?

Answer: (a) Equating supply and demand, we have: $10 - Q/200 = 1 + Q/200$. The solution is $Q° = 900$, $q° = 9$, and $P° = 5\ 1/2$. (b) Since the demand curve is linear, Marginal Revenue is $MR = 10 - Q/100$. Marginal Cost for industry output as a whole is, by assumption, $MC = 1 + Q/200$. The profit-maximizing solution for the cartel is $Q' = 600$, $P' = 7$. (c) At this price the typical firm would have to be limited to output $q' = 6$. But it would like to set its $MC = 1 + q/2$ equal to $P = 7$, implying desired output of $q = 12$.

Cartels, therefore, require enforcement devices to prevent chiseling. In a number of European countries, the law may treat a cartel agreement as a legally enforceable contract. Some jurisdictions take a neutral position: the cartel agreement is not unlawful, but the power of the state will not enforce it. Finally, as in the United States, the law may be actively hostile to cartels as "conspiracies in restraint of trade." In such a situation a cartel would require enforcement devices that are *both effective and secret*—an unlikely combination when any detected chiseler can complain to the authorities.

Illegal restraints of trade are prosecuted in the United States mainly by the Antitrust Division of the Department of Justice and by the Federal Trade Commission. (In addition, it is possible for individuals or firms to sue privately for damages suffered.) But it is a curious paradox that other branches of the United States government actively encourage cartel agreements. A number of agricultural products, for example, are sold subject to governmentally sponsored "marketing orders" designed to limit production and sales.

EXAMPLE 8.5
Agricultural Marketing Orders

On the basis of federal legislation, the growers of certain agricultural products may draw up an agreement to limit supply and assign marketing quotas. If two-thirds of the growers (by number or volume) vote for such an agreement the Secretary of Agriculture is authorized to make it binding upon *all* growers.

Quantities produced beyond the marketing quotas are "dumped" abroad, used in special government programs outside normal trade channels (e.g., school lunches), or simply destroyed. In effect, the cartel (representing the growers as an aggregate) buys up excess production in order to limit supplies and drive up price in the primary market. However, this means that each individual producer has an incentive to produce more and more. In addition, as the price rises, growers of *other* commodities tend to shift over to the cartelized product. Consequently, we would expect over time to see an increasing percentage of the cartelized crops having to be diverted away from primary markets. This trend is illustrated in the table.

Annual Supply Diverted from Primary Markets under Federal Marketing Orders (%)

Crop	1960–64 Avg.	1965–68 Avg.
California raisins	28.2	39.6
California-Arizona lemons	55.2	62.5
California almonds	15.0	21.2
California-Oregon-Washington walnuts	0.8	7.5
Oregon-Washington filberts	21.8	27.5
California dates (Deglet Noor)	21.4	28.2

Source: John A. Jamison, "Marketing Orders and Public Policy for the Fruit and Vegetable Industries," *Food Research Studies in Agricultural Economics, Trade, and Development*, v. 10, no. 3 (1971), p. 347.

Some cartel agreements, we have just seen, are supported or even promoted by branches of government. As for the anti-cartel activities of other branches of government, it is not always clear whether these are well-designed or effective.

EXAMPLE 8.6
Antitrust and Prices[a]

The Antitrust Division of the U.S. Department of Justice is responsible for prosecuting cartels engaged in illegal price-fixing. If this activity is effective, detection of a price-fixing conspiracy and indictment of its members should be followed by a decline in prices. The table shows, for the thirteen accused industry cartels for which U.S. Census data were available, what the average prices were before and after indictments were obtained.

[a] This analysis is based upon unpublished research of Michael Sproul.

Price Indexes Before and After Indictment

Industry	Average of 3 Prior Months	Month of Indictment	Average of 3 Following Months
1976 AND BEFORE			
Gypsum board	98.6	100.0	104.6
Diamond abrasives	100.2	100.0	100.9
Sugar	76.1	100.0	79.2
Folding cartons	98.5	100.0	100.9
Potash	105.1	100.0	86.0
Paper bags	102.1	100.0	99.5
AFTER 1976			
Wiring devices	99.7	100.0	100.9
Cardboard	100.2	100.0	100.1
Electric fuses	99.9	100.0	100.3
Titanium products	99.5	100.0	100.0
Water heaters	98.9	100.0	101.9
Welded steel tubing	98.5	100.0	101.7
Screws	104.4	100.0	100.0

Source: U.S. Bureau of the Census, *Producer Price Index: Detailed Report*, monthly issues from Jan. 1970 through Dec. 1980.

The table reveals that, for the most part, indictments had little or no effect upon prices. It is curious that in the case of potash—where the tabulated data do suggest that the indictment brought about a sharp drop in prices—all the defendants were actually acquitted of price-fixing.

There are two main possible explanations as to why, in most cases, prices did not fall after the indictment: (1) Even where a price-fixing agreement existed, the prices may not have actually been higher than the competitive level. Or, (2) the penalties may not have been severe enough to force a change in behavior. The data in the table provide a test of these competing theories. Under new legislation passed in 1976, price-fixing became a felony so that much more severe financial penalties and even jail terms could be imposed. However, if anything the effect of indictments upon prices was even smaller in the later period.

Of course, there can hardly be anyone in the world unfamiliar with the most successful cartel in history—the Organization of Petroleum Exporting Countries (OPEC).

EXAMPLE 8.7
The OPEC

In pre-OPEC days, before 1960, the international oil companies (especially the seven or eight "majors" such as Royal Dutch Shell and Standard Oil of New Jersey) were often accused of acting as a cartel. If their aim was to keep prices high they failed, as became evident later when the OPEC came into existence and *really* raised prices. In fact, it was the attempt of the majors to cut oil prices that led the exporting nations to establish the OPEC in 1960. (The U.S. State Department, in what must have been an all-time low point for intelligent foreign economic policy, actively encouraged formation of the OPEC!) The subsequent history of the world petroleum market may be divided into five phases.

Phase 1 (1960–1973): The OPEC nations, by requiring the private oil companies to reduce production levels, prevented prices from falling. Over most of this period the price for Arabian light crude was about $1.80 per barrel, rising to $2.59 by 1973.[a] Also during this period the exporting nations solidified their control over pricing and production, in effect expropriating the private oil concessions. (Thenceforth, the private oil companies in OPEC countries received only what amounted to fees for extraction and marketing services. For example, Saudi Arabia captured as government take all but about $.60 of the price in effect on January 1, 1973.)

Phase 2 (1973–1978): In solidarity with the attack of Egypt and Syria upon Israel in late 1973, the Arab countries dominating OPEC reduced output in order to use oil as an economic weapon. While the attempt to embargo shipments to Europe and America was unsuccessful, the cutback of production drove the price dramatically upward. By January 1, 1974, the price had more than quadrupled, to $11.65 per barrel. It says something about economic gullibility that the Shah of Iran, the King of Saudi Arabia, and other oil potentates succeeded in convincing a large part of the Western public that the high prices were due not to OPEC's production squeeze but to the machinations of the wicked private oil companies. (These companies were in fact typically receiving from their OPEC concessions little more than the same $.60 per barrel they had been earning before.)

The problem for the OPEC was and is to hold production down despite member countries' incentives to "chisel." Each separate exporting nation can gain by expanding output so long as the others are holding back. In fact, in the period from 1974 to late 1978 most of the member countries were probably not holding back but were instead producing all-out. The cartel was viable in that period only because a few major producers, notably Saudi Arabia and Kuwait, were willing to hold their production at a relatively low level. Nevertheless, OPEC's power was gradually weakening. While the official price rose from $11.65 per barrel at the beginning of 1974 to $13.00 five years later (an increase of about 12 percent), the U.S. dollar depreciated by around 38 percent over the same period. Thus, by January 1, 1979, the real price of OPEC crude oil was down substantially from its peak.

Phase 3 (1979–1982): The turmoil in Iran paralyzed production there and permitted OPEC to start another round of price increases. Even after the new government took over from the Shah, Iranian exports remained drastically less than before. The official OPEC price rose ultimately to $34 per barrel in late 1981. (And at the peak some OPEC suppliers were demanding and receiving a premium of as much as $5 above the official price.) However, especially toward the end of the period, maintaining these high prices necessitated increasingly

---

[a] Data on prices have been collected from several sources including *International Economic Report of the President*, Washington, D.C.: U.S. Government Printing Office, Feb. 1974, pp. 110-11, and *Los Angeles Times* (Mar. 15, 1983), p. 1.

severe production cutbacks by the major OPEC producers—in particular, by Saudi Arabia.

Among the adverse features from the OPEC point of view were: (1) *Elasticity of demand*: Demand elasticity proved greater in the long run than in the short run. The continuing high price impelled consuming nations to use oil more economically, and to shift toward substitute fuels. (2) *Inducement of new entry*: High prices encouraged non-OPEC nations like Britain and Mexico to develop and expand their capacity to extract crude oil. The combined effect of lesser demand and increased non-OPEC supply led to:

Phase 4 (beginning early 1982): In this phase, OPEC attempted to maintain its high quoted price while coping with the "oil glut" inevitably created thereby. The only possible way of doing so was for OPEC to cut back production. OPEC output fell from a 1979 peak of 32 million barrels per day (bgd) to less than half that amount by early 1983.[b] And within OPEC the brunt of the decline fell upon the largest producer, Saudi Arabia, which was forced to curtail its output from a peak of 10.2 bgd to less than 4 bgd. (Even so, the nominally fixed $34 per barrel price was slipping in real terms; the dollar depreciated about 5 percent between October 1981 and March 1983.) Bowing to economic reality, in March 1983 OPEC was finally forced to cut the dollar price to $29 per barrel.

Phase 5 (beginning late 1985): Saudi Arabia finally followed through on its longstanding threat to expand production in retaliation for the failure of other OPEC members to abide by their quotas. This meant that the Saudis were abandoning their role as the price stabilizer. In November 1985 the price of oil was $30 per barrel; by February 1986, the price had fallen to $15.[c] By August, the price had dropped further to $10. At this time, OPEC members agreed to a production-limiting strategy, and in fact there was a reduction in OPEC output from more than 20 million barrels per day to less than 15 million barrels per day. The price of oil, after having rebounded to $17, by October settled at $14 per barrel.[d] It remains doubtful how long OPEC will be able to maintain even its reduced effectiveness as a cartel.

[b] Production figures from S. Fred Singer, "What Do the Saudis Do Now?" *Wall Street Journal* (Mar. 18, 1983), p. 20.

[c] Terri Thompson, "The Perils of Cheap Oil," *Business Week* (Apr. 21, 1986).

[d] Sarah Miller, "OPEC Will Have to Run Hard Just to Stay in Place," *Business Week* (Oct. 6, 1986).

☐ SUMMARY OF CHAPTER 8

A monopoly exists when the industry consists of a single firm. This may be the result of a legally enforced government license or franchise. A second possibility, "natural monopoly," is said to occur whenever one firm can produce more cheaply than any larger number.

Monopolists, like ordinary firms, are assumed to be profit-maximizers. Profit is maximized by setting output (or price) such that:

$$MC = MR$$

For the monopoly firm, in contrast with the price-taking firm, Marginal Revenue MR is less than price P. The relation between these two variables involves the demand elasticity η:

$$MR \equiv P(1 + 1/\eta)$$

"Monopoly power" may be measured by the divergence between $MC = MR$ and price P; it tends to decrease with the number of firms in the industry, and with the consumers' elasticity of demand for the product. Thus, monopoly power tends to be greater for necessity goods and for goods without close substitutes. However, the extent to which a single firm in an industry can exploit its position and actually achieve a monopoly profit is limited by the competitive threat from outsiders. Unless the monopolist is protected by an exclusive legal franchise, it will not be able to charge a price higher than the Average Cost at which an outsider could enter and produce.

Assuming the firm can exploit its monopoly position, output will be less and price higher than under pure competition. There is an efficiency loss (reduction in Consumer Surplus and Producer Surplus) due to the smaller volume of production and exchange, and also a pure transfer from consumers to the monopolist seller. There may also be an additional efficiency loss if resources are expended in the struggle to gain and maintain a monopoly position.

Monopolies, and in particular franchised public utilities, are often subjected to regulation. The goal of regulation is commonly to ensure that the monopolist receives only enough revenue to attract and retain the resources employed in the industry—that is, receives only a "normal" profit and no *economic* profit. Then Average Revenue and Average Cost must be equal. If the monopolist's Average Cost curve is rising, the intersection of AC and AR "overshoots" the competitive equilibrium; there will be an efficiency loss due to *excessive* production in this industry. On the other hand, if AC is in its falling range, the regulated solution lies between the monopolist's profit-maximizing output and the competitive outcome.

By engaging in price discrimination, a monopolist can acquire still more revenue from given consumer demands (can capture more of what would have been Consumer Surplus). Under *market segmentation*, the monopolist would set overall Marginal Cost of production equal to the Marginal Revenue in each segment. It follows from the equation relating P, MR, and elasticity η that higher prices will be charged in segments with less elastic demands. *Multi-part pricing*—an alternative form of price discrimination—captures some of Consumer Surplus via a declining-block price schedule. This type of discrimination is most effective if an individualized schedule can be offered to each consumer. *Perfect* discrimination is a limiting case in which each consumer is charged the maximum he or she would be willing to pay for each unit—so that no Consumer Surplus at all remains. Surprisingly, there is no efficiency loss under perfect discrimination.

Cartels are associations of smaller firms that act collectively like a monopolist. Since a higher price can only be achieved if production is cut back, output quotas typically have to be imposed upon members of a cartel. Each member is therefore motivated to "chisel" (produce beyond quota). In addition, potential producers outside the cartel have an inducement to enter the industry. As a result, cartels have historically been fragile except where supported by government power.

□ QUESTIONS FOR CHAPTER 8

MAINLY FOR REVIEW

*R1. Why will a monopolist's profit-maximizing rate of output always be in the region of elastic demand?

R2. Why is monopoly power over price smaller as elasticity of demand increases?

*R3. "Monopoly is a bad thing for consumers, but a good thing for producers. So, on balance, we can't be sure that monopoly is responsible for any loss in economic efficiency." Analyze.

R4. A competitive industry may have its equilibrium in the range of inelastic demand. Then the industry would receive more revenue if its output were smaller. Does it follow that such a competitive industry is producing "too much" of the good in terms of efficient use of resources?

*R5. Monopoly firms are accused of pursuing "nonprofit goals" to a greater degree than competitive firms. Why might a monopolist be any less interested in profit than a competitor?

R6. Compare the profit-maximizing conditions for simple monopoly, for market-segmentation monopoly, and for perfect-discrimination monopoly. Why is only the last of these said to be *efficient*?

*R7. In making efficiency comparisons between a monopolized and a competitive industry, the Marginal Cost function of the monopolist was said to correspond to the supply function of the competitive industry. Explain why.

R8. When will zero-profit regulation of a monopoly lead to too high a price from an efficiency point of view? Too low a price?

R9. Show how behavior of its own members may threaten the survival of a cartel. Show how behavior of outsiders may threaten it.

FOR FURTHER THOUGHT AND DISCUSSION

*T1. Is there a contradiction between the assertions that: (1) the oil industry is an effective monopoly (cartel), and (2) higher prices for petroleum products will do little to discourage demand?

T2. Is it better (more efficient) to have a monopolized industry, or no industry at all?

*T3. In comparison with a simple monopolist, does a perfectly discriminating monopolist *possibly* or *necessarily* produce more output? Does a market-segmentation monopolist? A multi-part pricing monopolist?

*T4. Market segmentation tends to be more common in the sale of services (e.g., discrimination by income for medical services, by age for transportation services) than in the sale of manufactured goods. Explain.

* The answers to starred questions appear at the end of the book.

*T5.   Movie theaters often offer price discounts to the young. Is there likely to be a "leakage" problem in this form of market segmentation? Can the discount be explained in terms of differing elasticities of demand?

*T6.   Are supermarket discount coupons a form of market segmentation? If so, how is "leakage" controlled? Do the consumers who choose to use the coupons have a more elastic demand for grocery products? Explain.

T7.   Doctors often charge poorer customers lower fees for medical services. They usually explain this as a charitable gesture. Alternatively, is this possibly an example of market segmentation?

T8.   It has been alleged that sellers' cartels are more effective in dealing with *government* as a buyer because of the existence of public records of all transactions in which government engages. Explain. How might the contention be tested?

T9.   Historically, governments have sometimes auctioned off the right to monopolize a commodity. (The *gabelle*, or salt monopoly, of pre-Revolution France, was an example.) Show diagrammatically the maximum amount the government might expect to acquire by auctioning off a monopoly. Is this likely to generate more or less income for the government than the most lucrative excise tax the government might impose?

*T10. If an organization like the Mafia effectively monopolized illegal activity, would you expect to observe less crime than under competitive free entry into this "industry"?

9

SUPPLEMENTARY CHAPTER

PRODUCT AS A VARIABLE

So far we have discussed the firm's choice of what *quantity of output* to produce. In this chapter we turn to the *characteristics of the product* offered the consumers. Publishers can print romances or mysteries, farmers can grow different strains of wheat, barbers can offer haircuts in various styles. The "new theory of consumption" (Chapter 5) indicated that consumers are not ultimately interested in physical goods as such. Rather, consumers want the services provided by the goods. People don't "consume" calculators, for example; the calculator is bought for the services it provides. So, the question is, what kinds and amounts of services will producing firms package into a commodity like a calculator?

We will be distinguishing two types of questions: the problem of *variety*, and the problem of *quality*. *Variety* is a matter of taste. Some people like red roses, some pink, some white. Some people like conservative cars, others prefer flashy ones. *Quality*, on the other hand, is something everyone can agree on. Durability, strength, reliability, and the like, are things that everyone desires in a purchased commodity.

The firm will select the characteristics of product to offer consumers, whether it be a matter of variety or of quality, on the basis of whatever maximizes profit. Such *optimization* on the part of the firms will lead to an *equilibrium* level of variety or of quality in the industry as a whole.

9.A
OPTIMAL PRODUCT ASSORTMENT: MONOPOLY

Let us start by considering how a monopolist would solve the problem of variety—the profit-maximizing assortment of products to be offered to consumers whose tastes differ. Products may of course vary in many ways, but for simplicity we can consider a single dimension of variation. In the case of clothing, this might be the assortment of *sizes* or *colors*.

With regard to the *size* dimension, imagine that consumer preferences are distributed over a line-segment as in Figure 9.1. A consumer looking for a small-sized product can be regarded as located toward the left; one desiring a large size is toward the right. We would normally expect to find more customers toward the middle. As shown in Figure 9.1, desires for extreme sizes are usually less common than demand for medium sizes. However, for simplicity we will suppose instead that preferences are *uniformly* distributed over the range. One other change will

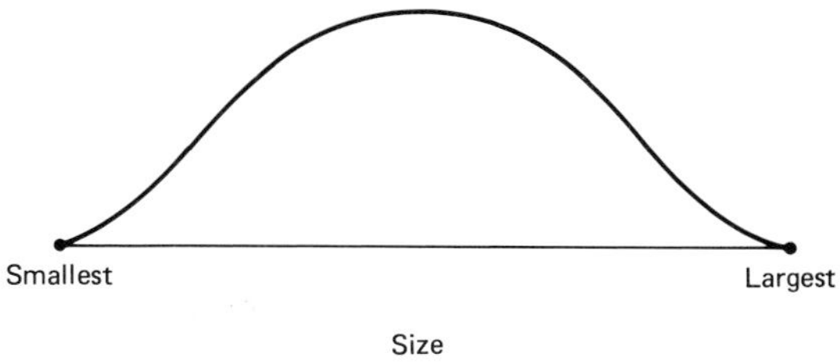

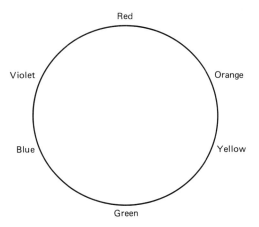

FIGURE 9.1 Distribution of Linear Preferences. For a characteristic like size, more consumers will be found toward the middle than toward the ends (intermediate sizes will be more popular than extreme sizes).

Smallest

Largest

Size

be made from the picture given by Figure 9.1: it is more convenient to assume that the product characteristic is not something like *size,* which has a lower limit and upper limit (smallest and largest), but instead can be described by a ring, as in Figure 9.2. *Color* might be such a characteristic. If as many people prefer red as yellow as green, and so on, consumers can be thought of as distributed·uniformly around the color circle of Figure 9.2.

The product characteristic (color) most desired by any consumer can be thought of as a point on the ring, which we will call his or her *consumption locale.* Similarly, any given variety actually produced and offered in the market can be regarded as a *production locale.* Since only a few consumers would be located exactly at production locales, the typical consumer would have to pay some cost of transporting the good from the point of production to the point of consumption. (We are using geographical distance here as a metaphor for the imperfect matching of consumer preferences with the available products.) For example, a consumer wearing size 9 dresses (consumption locale) might find that only sizes 8 and 10 (production locales) are available on the market. After making a purchase, she might make alterations or simply tolerate the imperfect fit. Whichever she chooses, the loss she suffers is the economic equivalent of having to pay the cost of "transporting" the good from point of sale to point of consumption.

Returning to the ring of Figure 9.2, the first problem for the monopolist is *how many* varieties to produce—that is, the number of distinct production locales or plants to establish around the ring. The next decision is *how much* to produce at each plant, and what *prices* to charge for the outputs. Increasing the number of

Red

Violet

Orange

Blue

Yellow

Green

FIGURE 9.2 Ring of Circular Preferences. An attribute like color may be described as a circle, rather than as a line-segment with end-points.

varieties is like increasing the number of production locales around the ring—which would reduce the average gap between what the consumer wants and what he or she can find in the market. The smaller the average gap, the larger the total amount consumers will be willing to pay. What prevents carrying this process to the limit (having a separate plant for each consumer) is *economies of scale*. Over some range, Average Cost per plant will ordinarily fall as plant output expands. So the monopolist must balance savings in production costs from having fewer plants against savings in transport costs from having more plants. Put another way, the monopolist must choose between returns to large-scale production versus the advantage of offering consumers a more varied assortment of products.

Suppose costs of production are the same regardless of location around the ring. Then, given a uniform distribution of consumers, the producing plants (whatever their number) should be spaced evenly around the circle in order to minimize the transport costs. The price at the factory (the "f.o.b. price") will also be identical at each producing plant. Each consumer must pay this f.o.b. price *plus* the transport cost from the nearest plant.

Looking first at the demand side, note in Figure 9.3 the limiting (highest) aggregate consumer demand function D_∞. This represents the ideal case in which every consumer is located next to a plant—or, we will say, there are an infinite number of production locales around the ring. Because consumers then incur no transport costs, their desires for product are wholly reflected in the effective demand curve. At the opposite extreme is the curve labeled D_1, which shows effective demand when there is just a single productive plant (placed at any arbitrary point on the ring). Here the most distant consumer must pay for shipment halfway around the ring; the *average* transport cost per consumer corresponds to a quarter-circle of circumference about the ring. The curve D_2 represents the effective demand faced by a monopolist with two plants, where the average consumer is separated by an eighth-circle from the nearest production locale. The D_{10} curve in the diagram shows the effective demand with ten plants. Note that the curve of effective demand shifts upward, *but at a decreasing rate*, as the number

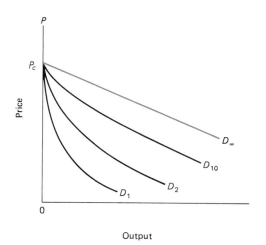

FIGURE 9.3 **Aggregate Demand as Related to Number of Producing Plants.** $D_1, D_2, \ldots, D_\infty$ show the rising aggregate effective demand, as viewed by a monopolist seller, achieved by increasing the number of plants (production locales) spaced evenly around the ring of Figure 9.2. Effective demand increases with the number of plants, since consumer preferences are better matched (there is less wastage in transport costs), but demand grows at a decreasing rate.

of plants is increased—that is, as the assortment offered more closely approximates the distribution of consumer preferences.[1]

To arrive at the solution we also need the cost function for output. Let us assume for convenience that production costs are linear. Thus for the nth plant, $C_n = A + Bq_n$. Here A is the Fixed Cost of each plant, and B is the constant Marginal Cost. Then if there are N identical plants, the overall Total Cost is $TC_N = NC_n$. So $TC_N = N(A + Bq_n) = NA + BQ$, where $Q \equiv Nq_n$ is the monopolist's overall output. For a range of possible numbers of plants N, the overall Total Cost functions TC_N are shown by the dashed lines $TC_1, TC_2, \ldots$ in Figure 9.4. Because of the existence of the Fixed Cost A *per plant*, the Total Cost of producing any aggregate output Q rises as the *number* of plants N increases.

The Total Revenue functions for different numbers of plants are also shown in Figure 9.4. TR_1 is the Total Revenue curve with one plant (corresponding to the effective demand curve D_1 of the previous diagram). TR_2 similarly is the Total Revenue curve with two plants (corresponding to D_2), and so forth.

For any given number of plants N, the monopolist chooses the f.o.b. price P_m and the associated quantity Q by using the familiar condition $MC = MR$ so as to maximize profit—which is the vertical distance between the appropriate pair of TR_N and TC_N curves (compare the upper panel of Figure 8.1). For different numbers of plants N, some of the various possible profits are indicated by the vertical bold line segments in Figure 9.4. As may be seen, there will normally be a range

---

[1] The detailed shapes of the curves in Figure 9.3 involve some tricky points. First, a "choke price" P_c high enough to cut off all demand at *any* producing location will do the same at *every* location. Therefore, all the curves intersect at P_c on the vertical axis. But away from the vertical axis the D_N curves (where N is the number of producing locales) must lie in such a way that the larger is N, the higher up is the curve. We leave it as a challenge to the reader to explain why the various D_N curves eventually become parallel to the D_∞ curve. [*HINT:* Transport costs can be regarded as a *tax* upon consumption, but the tax is effective only for consumers who are not "choked out" of the market.]

FIGURE 9.4 **Monopoly Total Revenue and Total Costs, as Related to Number of Plants.** The aggregate Total Revenue curves $TR_1, TR_2, \ldots$ represent the same data as shown by the aggregate demand curves (curves of Average Revenue) $D_1, D_2, \ldots$ of the previous diagram. As number of plants N rises, Total Revenue TR_N also rises *but at a decreasing rate*. The Total Cost curves $TC_1, TC_2, \ldots$ show the aggregate cost of producing any output Q with $1, 2, \ldots$ plants. Under the assumption of an identical linear cost function for each plant, TC_N shifts upward by a constant amount as N rises (since an additional Fixed Cost is incurred each time a new plant is brought into production). The bold vertical segments show the highest achievable profit for each N; the greatest of these is the profit maximum Π^*, which occurs here at $N = 4$.

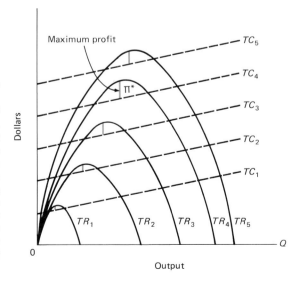

in which profit increases as N rises. In this range the gain in revenue from better matching of products to consumer desires (i.e., from the fact that consumers are willing to pay more when they avoid the "transport costs") is greater than the increased cost due to the larger number of production locales. But the gains from increasing N tend to taper off. Meanwhile costs rise steadily as N grows, because of the necessity of incurring another fixed-cost element A each time a new plant is added. There will, consequently, be an optimum number of plants. In Figure 9.4, the largest profit Π^* is achieved at $N = 4$; having exactly four production locales represents the best compromise between production costs and transport costs.

9.B
MONOPOLISTIC COMPETITION

We now turn from the variety decision under simple monopoly to the market structure known as *monopolistic competition*. It is assumed that—as in pure competition—firms do not collude on price or quantity, and also that free entry into the industry (or exit from it) is possible. The monopolistic element in monopolistic competition is *product differentiation*: each firm has its own unique variety of product. This gives the firm some monopoly power, since each enterprise will have a "clientele" of customers closest to it on the ring of preference. In a particular city, for example, there may be a dozen supermarkets. They may be closely competing in some respects, but each has some monopoly power due to geographical location or other special features that make it the favorite of a fraction of the customers. We will see that a group of monopolistically competitive firms will produce more and charge less than would a monopolist operating several plants.

Returning to the monopolist firm, if there are N identical plants distributed evenly around the ring of preference, the industry demand faced by the monopolist is shown as D_N in Figure 9.5. Marginal Revenue is MR_N. Each of the plants serves the fraction $1/N$ of the total demand, so that each plant's pro-rata share of the overall demand is $D_n = D_N/N$. Marginal Revenue for each plant is $MR_n = MR_N/N$. If $N = 4$, the D_n and MR_n curves would then represent one-fourth of the output quantities along the corresponding overall D_N and MR_N curves. With the assumed constant Marginal Cost $MC = B$, the profit-maximizing solutions are Q_N^* for the entire monopolist firm and q_n^* for each of its separate plants. The same price P_m is of course arrived at either way.

Now suppose the industrial structure changes from simple monopoly to monopolistic competition. This means that each *plant* now becomes a separate *firm*. Intuition suggests, correctly, that output will be higher and price lower once the competitive element is introduced. But it is important to understand just how this works out.

The key point is that each independent firm would produce more output than a monopolist would allow its plant to produce. The reason is that, as shown in Figure 9.6, the independent firm's *perceived* demand curve d_n is more elastic (flatter) than the monopolist's per-plant demand curve D_n. The curve d_n is more elastic than D_n because, by lowering price relative to its neighbors, each firm figures that it can win customers away from them. (The monopolist, of course,

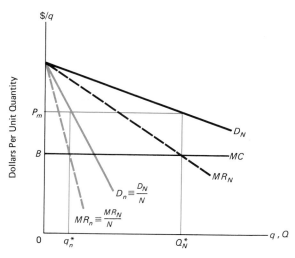

FIGURE 9.5 Monopoly Solutions, Aggregate and Plant. For a given number of plants N, the monopolist's effective *aggregate* demand curve is D_N. And $D_n \equiv D_N/N$ is the pro-rata *plant* demand curve. MR_N and $MR_n \equiv MR_N/N$ are the associated Marginal Revenue curves. Under the linear cost assumption, the constant Marginal Cost is shown by a horizontal MC curve at the level B. The profit-maximizing *aggregate* output is Q_N^* (where $MC = MR_N$), and plant output is q_n^* (where $MC = MR_n$). Of course, $Q_N^* = Nq_n^*$. For either the plant or the firm solution, the same profit-maximizing price P_m is found along the associated demand curve.

would not permit its separate plants to cut price at one another's expense.) Corresponding to the *more elastic* firm demand curve d_n is a *higher* perceived Marginal Revenue curve mr_n.[2] The firm in Figure 9.6 will therefore want to produce output q_n' where $mr_n = MC$ (point H in the diagram). Since output q_n' is greater than the monopoly output q_n^*, price P' will be less than the monopoly price P_m.

Figure 9.6 suggests that the output of a firm under monopolistic competition will surely be larger than the per-plant output of an ordinary monopolist. But there is a flaw in the argument so far. The solution in Figure 9.6, with output q_n' sold at the price P' along demand curve d_n, is not possible as an *overall equilibrium*

---

[2] Since $MR \equiv P(1 - 1/|\eta|)$, when the demand elasticity η is greater (in absolute value) the Marginal Revenue is higher.

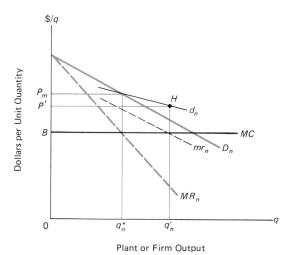

FIGURE 9.6 Monopoly Plant versus Monopolistic-Competition Firm, at Monopoly Solution. The solution for the monopoly plant, where $MC = MR_n$ at output q_n^* and associated monopoly price P_m, is the same as in the preceding diagram. But once the monopoly plant becomes an independent firm, at price P_m the *perceived* demand curve would be d_n. This is more elastic than the pro-rata demand curve D_n, since the firm can win customers from its neighbors if it lowers its price. The firm will therefore attempt to achieve the solution H at output q_n' where Marginal Cost MC cuts the curve mr_n.

of the industry. With a fixed number N of firms, at any price each firm can sell no more than its pro-rata share of demand $D_n \equiv D_N/N$. The flatter demand curve d_n in the diagram is therefore *an illusion* (like the illusion of the seemingly horizontal demand curve faced by the firm in pure competition). Any single firm can hope to cut price so as to expand output along d_n. But N identical firms *must all end up choosing the same price*. In trying to sell output q'_n at price P', they will each find that sales expand less than expected, along the steeper pro-rata demand curve D_n in the diagram rather than the "illusory" d_n curve.

When all the independent firms cut price, therefore, the new equilibrium must lie at a point on the pro-rata demand curve D_n, like S in Figure 9.7. Each firm produces quantity q''_n, and the price is P''. Once again the firm *perceives* a flatter demand curve d_n, but the d_n pictured in Figure 9.7 is such that the firm's perceived optimum (determined by the intersection of MC with mr_n) lies along the pro-rata demand curve. Thus, the solution on the firm level is now consistent with its pro-rata share of the overall consumer demand. At this solution each firm's output is still clearly greater than what the monopoly plant would produce ($q''_n > q^*_n$). And the price to consumers will of course be lower ($P'' < P_m$).

We are not yet at the full or *long-run* equilibrium for monopolistic competition, however. Since there is free entry or exit, changes in the *number* of firms in the market must also be taken into account. Depending upon the fixed costs, the short-run equilibrium shown in Figure 9.7 might either be a profitable one for firms in the industry (inducing entry) or an unprofitable one (dictating exit). Let us assume that the short-run equilibrium is profitable. Then new firms will enter. As a result, the true pro-rata demand curve $D_n \equiv D_N/N$ and the illusory d_n as viewed by an existing firm will both *shift inward* toward the vertical axis.[3]

The long-run solution is shown in Figure 9.8 for the representative firm. Here, in addition to the conditions satisfied in the preceding diagram, that $MC = mr_n$ and that the firm's price-output combination be consistent with the pro-rata demand curve D_n, we have a *zero-profit solution*. This is represented in the diagram by the tangency at point L of the firm's demand curve d_n with its Average Cost curve AC_n, the output being q''_n and price P''.

This analysis bears upon an important question: whether, under monopolistic competition as compared with multi-plant monopoly, there will or will not be *more variety* offered consumers. It turns out that the result can go either way. We have just seen that when the plants operated by a monopolist become independent competing firms, the per-plant profit will be less than before. But, if the profits are still positive, new firms will enter—so there will indeed be increased variety in the market (i.e., a better matching of products to the range of consumer desires). On the other hand, it could be the case that what was a positive per-plant

---

[3] This shift is due to dividing the aggregate demand curve D_N horizontally by a larger N. There is a countervailing factor, however, since a larger N is associated with a more perfect matching of consumer desires (as shown in Figure 9.3). So both the numerator and the denominator of the ratio D_N/N (which defines the pro-rata demand curve D_n) rise as N increases. However, the numerator tends not to rise as fast as the denominator. When the number of firms increases from two to three, there is a 50 percent increase in N but not in general such an enormous improvement in the matching of production locales to consumer preferences. So, despite this countervailing factor, the D_n curve (and therefore also the d_n curve) must, at least eventually, shift inward as N rises.

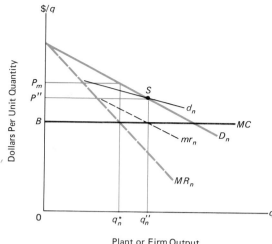

FIGURE 9.7 **Monopoly Plant versus Monopolistic-Competition Firm, at Monopolistic-Competition Equilibrium.** With N firms, point S in the diagram represents a monopolistic-competition equilibrium. Each firm is maximizing profit since $MC = mr_n$, where mr_n is the Marginal Revenue associated with the *perceived* (flatter) firm demand curve d_n. And this outcome is consistent with overall equilibrium of the industry as a whole, since the combination of output q_n'' and price P'' constitutes a point on the pro-rata demand curve D_n. Price is lower and output greater than in the monopoly case.

monopoly profit turns into a loss when the separate plants become independent firms which compete by cutting price. Then there will be exit from the industry and so less variety.

> CONCLUSION: In comparison with multi-plant monopoly, under monopolistic competition aggregate output will be greater and product price lower. And, in long-run equilibrium, zero economic profit will be earned. But there may or may not be a larger number of producing locales. Thus, while consumers benefit from a lower price, they may or may not find a better assortment of varieties available.

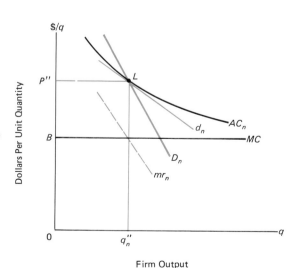

FIGURE 9.8 **Long-Run Equilibrium, Representative Firm in Monopolistic Competition.** The short-run equilibrium conditions of the preceding diagram continue to hold: $MC = mr_n$, and the representative firm's price–output combination constitutes an achievable point on the true pro-rata demand curve D_n. The additional long-run condition is that entry or exit takes place until the representative firm is earning zero profit (price equals Average Cost AC_n). All these conditions are met at point L in the diagram.

EQUILIBRIUM QUALITY LEVEL: COMPETITION AND MONOPOLY

We now turn from the question of *variety* to the question of *quality*. Suppose there is some single service characteristic that all consumers want from the product. In the case of light bulbs, buyers might simply be seeking light output. For gasoline, transportation mileage might be the desired feature. It is no longer a matter of some customers preferring white shirts and others blue, or big men wanting big sizes and small men small sizes, but instead of everyone agreeing on what makes a product desirable. (Of course, there may be more than one factor involved. Gasoline may be valued for rapid acceleration and easy starting as well as for mileage. The color or shape or size of light bulbs might be important to customers, aside from light output in lumens. In the interests of simplicity, however, we will think in terms of a single measurable characteristic.)

There is one key idea to be kept in mind. While producers and consumers are dealing in quantities of *product* Q (e.g., gasoline), more fundamentally they are really interested in amounts of the *service* S (e.g., mileage). The price and quantity of the product (gasoline) will depend ultimately upon the price and quantity of the service (mileage) produced and consumed. *Quality* of a product is simply the amount of service provided per unit. Put another way, service is quantity times quality.

To begin with, let us assume a fixed number N of competitive firms. Each firm produces quantity q_n of its physical product, each unit of which contains z_n units of the quality characteristic. So the firm's *output of the service* is defined by:

$$(9.1) \qquad s_n \equiv z_n q_n$$

For example, a refinery producing $q_n = 1{,}000{,}000$ gallons of gasoline per day, with quality $z_n = 20$ miles per gallon, is effectively providing $s_n = 20{,}000{,}000$ units per day of "mileage" service for sale to consumers.

Since it is the service that consumers are really concerned with, the price P_n of the nth firm's physical product will (assuming that consumers are fully informed) directly reflect the going market price P_s for the service (P_s).

$$(9.2) \qquad P_n \equiv z_n P_s$$

For example, if one firm's gasoline is known to yield 10 percent greater mileage per gallon than another's, its price must be 10 percent higher.

What determines P_s? As usual there will be an overall balance of supply and demand. Each separate firm will want to set MC_s, its Marginal Cost of producing the service, equal to P_n. But MC_s will generally depend upon both the *quantity* q_n and the *quality* z_n produced by the firm. Panel (a) of Figure 9.9 pictures an initial situation where the firm is providing quantity $q_n = q_n^o$ and quality $z_n = z_n^o$, determining a service output $s_n^o = q_n^o z_n^o$. Two different Marginal Cost MC curves are shown. The dotted curve shows the cost of providing increments of service by varying only *quantity* (i.e., holding *quality* constant at z_n^o), while the dashed curve represents the

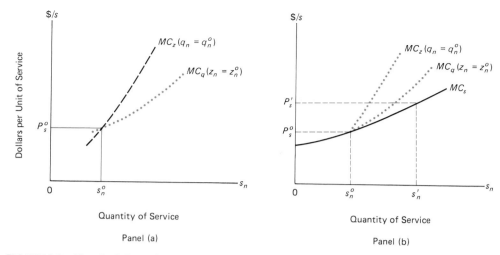

FIGURE 9.9 Marginal Cost of Quantity versus Quality. In Panel (a) the dashed and dotted curves MC_z and MC_q show the Marginal Cost of producing more service output by increasing *quality* of product or *quantity* of product, respectively. Panel (b) shows that the true Marginal Cost of service is ordinarily lower than either of the dotted and dashed curves. So, as price rises from P_s^o to P_s', the firm will normally expand output of the service by producing *both* more quantity and higher quality.

cost of increasing service output by varying only quality (holding *quantity* constant at z_n^o). The two Marginal Costs are equal at service output s_n^o, which means that the firm's choices of z_n and q_n are in balance. Generalizing this point, we can say:

> *PROPOSITION:* At any level of service output, the firm's quality and quantity choices are in balance when the Marginal Cost of expanding service by increasing quantity *(MC_q)* and the Marginal Cost of expanding service by increasing quality *(MC_z)* are equal. Furthermore, the true Marginal Cost MC_s of the service must be the same as MC_q and MC_z *when these are equal*. So, in the diagram, s_n^o is the firm's profit-maximizing output of service at price P_s^o.

Balancing quality and quantity at *each* output of service permits us to construct the overall MC_s curve, the solid curve in Panel (b) of the diagram. Notice that the MC_s curve is lower than either of the MC_q and MC_z curves separately. This means that it is generally cheaper to provide additional service output by *a balanced increase of both quality and quantity* rather than by increasing quantity alone or quality alone. The upward-sloping branch of the firm's MC_s curve is its supply curve of service. Specifically, in Panel (b) we see that an increase of the service price from P_s^o to P_s' will raise the firm's service output from s_n^o to s_n'. And the *industry's* supply of the service would as usual be the horizontal sum of the firms' separate MC_s curves (adjusted for any factor-price and exit-entry effects, as discussed in Chapter 7). The overall equilibrium would be at the price P_s and quantity S where the industry's supply curve and the consumers' demand curve for the service come into equality.

Would all competitive firms produce the *same* quality z_n? The answer is no, since there is no reason for the different firms to have identical cost functions with respect to quantity and quality. Some mining firms might be working richer and others leaner deposits, and so selling different grades of ore. In each case what the purchaser is really buying is the valuable mineral—gold or silver or iron—contained in the ore. So the different prices of ores (P_n) will really reflect the single underlying price of the mineral (P_s) in accordance with Equation (9.2).

EXAMPLE 9.1
Price and Quality: Movie Theaters

R. D. Lamson studied the relation between quality characteristics and the prices charged for movie admissions in a large metropolitan area during the period 1961 to 1964.[a] The adult evening admission price P (in cents) was estimated from the data by the equation:

$$P = 4.13 + 31.46 \log_{10} U + 5.77L + 8.21T - 7.68D - 1.13F + 27.09S + 0.81R$$

The symbols used on the right-hand side represent several different quality variables:
  U: average percentage of unused seating capacity per showing
  L: theater location (1 if suburban, 0 if city center)
  T: theater age (1 if less than 10 years since construction or major renovation, 0 otherwise)
  D: type of theater (1 of outdoor, 0 if indoor)
  F: parking (1 if provided, 0 otherwise)
  S: screening policy (1 if first-run, 0 otherwise)
  R: average film rental (cents per ticket charged by distributor)

The results were generally in the directions anticipated. For example, other things equal, newer (or renovated) theaters charged on the average 8.21 cents more per admission; first-run houses charged 27.09 cents more; each penny per ticket paid for film rental (a measure of *film* quality or, at least, film popularity) was associated with a 0.81-cent increment to admission price; and so forth. The one paradoxical component of the equation is parking provision, associated with a 1.13-cent *reduction* in price. This is very likely due to an intercorrelation of parking availability (a positive quality element) with remote or low rental location (an unfavorable element) not captured in the crude index L.

One interesting point concerns U, unused capacity. This can be regarded as a quality measure of movie seating—*uncrowdedness*. The equation shows that a 10 percent increase in unused seating capacity (e.g., from 20 percent to 22 percent) is associated with a 1.3-cent increase in admission price. Notice that *quality* in the form of uncrowdedness U automatically rises when *quantity* of sales falls off in response to a rise in admission price. So the true (quality-constant) elasticity of demand for movie admissions must be greater than that implicit in these data.

[a] R. D. Lamson, "Measured Productivity and Price Change: Some Empirical Evidence on Service Industry Bias, Motion Picture Theaters," *Journal of Political Economy*, v. 78 (Mar./Apr. 1970).

We saw in Chapter 8 that monopoly provides a smaller *quantity* of product, in comparison with a competitive industry, but our analysis there did not take quality variations into account. The question here is, would a monopolist tend to offer consumers a lower *quality* of product? Two separate issues should be distinguished: (1) At a *given* industry output of service S, would the monopolist produce a lower quality grade? (2) Since the monopolist will surely be producing a *smaller* output of service, would this be associated necessarily or normally with *both* lower quality z and smaller quantity q?

With regard to the first question, recall that the monopolist's MC curve is essentially equivalent to the supply curve of the competitive industry—which is, in turn, based upon the horizontal sum of the competitive firms' MC curves. It follows that in producing any given industry service output S, *the monopolist would make use of the same quality-quantity combination as the competitive industry* (since that represents the least-cost way of producing). At any given output, a monopolized mining industry would operate the same mines to produce the same mixture of ores as a competitive industry. Were this principle violated, the monopolist would be operating some of its mines at higher Marginal Cost than others, which would evidently be inefficient.

However, turning now to the second question, we know that the monopolist would not choose the same but instead would produce a smaller service output S than the competitive industry. Since increases of service output tend to be provided by balanced increments of both quantity and quality, the smaller service output of the monopolized industry would normally involve some combination of reduced quantity and reduced quality.

CONCLUSION: A monopolist, producing a smaller service output S than a competitive industry, will generally do so by some combination of lesser quantity q and reduced quality z.[4]

[4] Previous editions of this text had an erroneous treatment of this topic. I thank S. J. Liebowitz for the correction.

EXAMPLE 9.2
Cartels and Quality

While a monopoly tends to produce a somewhat lower quality of product than a competitive industry, the situation of a cartel is quite different. As shown in Chapter 8, when a cartel assigns production quotas each firm has a motive to "chisel"—to produce beyond quota. It is generally harder for a cartel to police the *quality* than the *quantity* of product. So the members of a cartel, unable to expand quantity of output, are likely to attempt to compete by quality improvement.

In 1981, Japan and the United States negotiated an agreement whereby Japanese auto firms engaged in "voluntary export restraints" limiting their shipments of cars to the United States. The American motive was protectionist, since Japanese cars were winning out over U.S.-built cars in the American market. But from the Japanese point of view, the effect of the agreement was to convert their auto industry into a highly profitable cartel. The production quotas required to make the cartel effective were administered by Japan's Ministry for International Trade and Industry. How profitable this was is evidenced by the fact that shares in Japanese auto companies jumped by an average of around 24 percent in the month when the arrangement was announced. In the following two months a further 16 percent increase in share values occurred.[a]

Naturally, with reduced imports the prices of Japanese cars rose substantially in comparison with American-made cars. But apart from the obvious scarcity effect, the decreased numbers of Japanese cars available on the U.S. market, there was also a quality effect. The cartelized Japanese exporters competed with one another to offer American consumers a higher-quality product. (While this quality improvement raised prices, it was worthwhile to buyers, as evidenced by their willingness to pay.) According to a study by Robert C. Feenstra, the price index of Japanese cars in the United States rose by 48.3 percent in the period 1980-1985, whereas the quality index rose 25.4 percent. Thus, the quality improvement offset around half of the observed price increase.[b]

[a] Arthur T. Denzau, "Made in America: The 1981 Japanese Automobile Cartel," Center for the Study of American Business, Washington University (Aug. 1986).

[b] Robert C. Feenstra, "Quality Change Under Trade Restraints: Theory and Evidence from Japanese Autos," Dept. of Economics, University of California, Davis (May 1986).

9.D
AN APPLICATION: SUPPRESSION OF INVENTIONS

Monopolists are sometimes accused of suppressing inventions. Let us define an "invention" as a discovery permitting production of a higher-quality product at given cost, or a given quality of product at lower cost.[5] Then it can be shown, under the key assumption that buyers are fully informed as to the quality improvement, that suppression is *never* rational.

Suppose there is a monopolist of gasoline, and that consumers are interested only in the service produced (mileage). The monopolist discovers a way, let us say, of costlessly doubling the mileage per gallon of its gasoline. The crucial point is that this *quality-improving* invention is also, from the firm's point of view, a *cost-reducing* invention, which it would surely be absurd to suppress.

Figure 9.10 shows how a cost-reducing invention affects a monopolist's *output of service S* (mileage) versus *output of product Q* (gasoline). Suppose the invention doubles the quality (mileage) of the product with no effect on production cost. This shifts the Total Cost curve from $C°$ to C'—a horizontal doubling (stretching) to the right. The key assumption, that consumers are fully informed, means that the *Total Revenue curve in terms of service S remains unchanged*. Consumers have no interest in gasoline as such; whether quality is high or low, they only pay for what concerns them—mileage.

In Figure 9.10 the profit-maximizing levels of service output are $S°$ before the invention and S' after the invention. The maximized pre-invention profit is

[5] Obviously, there is no problem in explaining the "suppression" of discoveries that lead to production of a *lower*-quality product at the same cost, or a constant-quality product at *higher* cost.

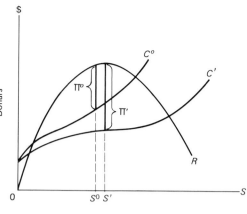

FIGURE 9.10 A **Quality-Improving** (Cost-Reducing) **Invention.** A monopolist is considering adoption of an innovation that costlessly doubles quality of its product. Since the horizontal axis represents amount of service S, the original Total Cost curve C^o shifts to C'—service output is doubled at each level of cost. Fully informed consumers are interested only in amount of service, and so the Total Revenue function R is unchanged. The monopolist will necessarily achieve a higher profit by adopting rather than suppressing the invention. In the situation pictured, the increased profit is Π'. Consumers also benefit, since more service is produced to be sold at a lower price.

Quantity of Service (Mileage)

Π^o. The necessarily larger post-invention profit is Π'. The diagram illustrates a "normal" case in which the monopolist's output of service increases as a result of the invention ($S' > S^o$) but by less than a doubling ($S' < 2S^o$). This means that consumers benefit from having more service S (mileage) while the firm saves some cost by having to produce less physical quantity q (gallons).

If the Total Revenue curve were rising almost linearly, however (i.e., if Marginal Revenue MR were almost constant), it might conceivably happen that output of service S *more* than doubles. The stretching of the Total Cost curve from C^o to C' would tend to reduce Marginal Cost MC in the relevant range. If throughout the doubling interval MC remains lower, while MR is nearly unchanged, the profit-maximizing output of service S will be *more than* twice the pre-invention amount. Here the consumers would be reaping a very big benefit, while of course the firm gains as well.

Paradoxically, it is logically possible for the output of service at the post-invention solution to fall ($S' < S^o$). In this case, while the invention will not have been suppressed, consumers are nevertheless worse off! How this might happen is visible in Figure 9.11 which is in Average-Marginal rather than Total units. The demand curve D and Marginal Revenue curve MR, defined here in terms of units of service, are unchanged by the invention. The quality-improving invention reduces the Average Cost of producing any amount of service—the new AC' curve (dashed) is therefore everywhere lower than the original AC^o curve (solid). Nevertheless, as the diagram shows, there may be a range in which the Marginal Cost MC' associated with the new technology is *higher* than the original MC^o. If, as occurs here, the intersection of Marginal Cost with Marginal Revenue occurs in this range, the firm's profit-maximizing output of attribute will be smaller ($S' < S^o$). This implies that monopoly price will be higher, and so consumers must be worse off!

The assumption of *full knowledge* on the part of consumers is essential to this analysis. If the invention really improves product quality but the consumers do not believe it, they would not (at least initially) be willing to pay any more for the higher-mileage gasoline. This would of course impair the monopolist's incentive to introduce the innovation. In this case, however, we should really consider the *cost of informing consumers* as a part of the economic cost of invention. It is not

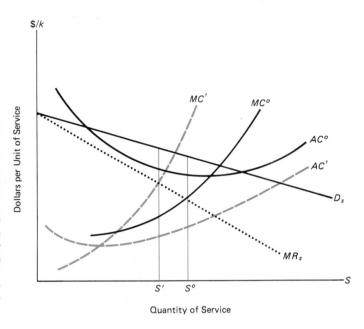

FIGURE 9.11 A Quality-Improving (Cost-Reducing) Invention Adverse to Consumers. A quality-improving invention is equivalent to a reduction in the Average Cost of producing the service, and so the new AC' curve lies everywhere below the original $AC°$ curve. Nevertheless, as shown here, there may be a range in which the new Marginal Cost MC' is *higher* than the original $MC°$. As a result, the new $MC' = MR$ intersection may determine a profit-maximizing level of service S' that is *smaller* than before. If so, consumers will be worse off for the invention.

really "suppression" when an invention, even though a genuine improvement of quality, cannot be put on the market except at a cost that is too great (including the cost of spreading the information) in comparison with the benefit received.

Another possible motivation for suppression emerges in a case where the invention *would destroy the monopoly*. Suppose one firm had a monopoly of the only currently exploitable aluminum ore—bauxite. Imagine that this monopolist finds a cheap process for extracting aluminum from alumina instead. Since alumina is too abundant a mineral to be monopolized, the firm could lose its monopoly. Even here, the monopolist can in principle do better by not suppressing the invention. The monopoly *of the information* as to how to reduce alumina to aluminum is more valuable than the previous monopoly of bauxite. The monopolist could patent and license the new process, or alternatively use it while keeping the key steps a trade secret.[6]

CONCLUSION: Monopoly cannot validly be accused of *suppressing* inventions (assuming buyers are fully informed). But a monopolist might possibly use inventions in such a way that consumers may derive no benefit therefrom, or may even be made worse off.

□ SUMMARY OF CHAPTER 9

In previous chapters a firm could vary only the *amount* of output produced, and possibly (if it has monopoly power) also the *price*. In this chapter it is assumed that a firm can also change the characteristics of its own product. Under this gen-

[6] In practice, however, there might be difficulties either with patenting or with maintaining secrecy.

eral heading, two main topics are the problem of *variety* and the problem of *quality*.

The problem of *variety* arises when consumer desires are distributed, as a matter of personal taste, over a range of some characteristic (size, color, weight) of the commodity. Then the greater the number of different varieties produced, the less the average consumer's dissatisfaction from having to choose a good with characteristics less close to what he or she desires. The diagram of the ring of preference permits us to think of "closeness" in geographical terms.

The solutions for the profit-maximizing number of varieties offered consumers (and for the associated price and quantity decisions) were compared for two market structures: *monopoly* and *monopolistic competition*. Under monopoly, the separate producing locations (plants) are operated for the profit of the firm as a whole. Under monopolistic competition, each producing location becomes an independent firm working for its own profit. Each separate firm has some monopoly power over those consumers closest to its production locale; the competitive element is the presence of neighboring firms to whom customers can transfer their business. In comparison with ordinary monopoly, under monopolistic competition there will be greater aggregate output and lower price, but consumers may or may not have more variety to choose from.

The problem of *quality* applies when all consumers prefer larger amounts of some underlying service generated by the physical goods produced. Demand and supply ultimately determine an equilibrium price and quantity of the service. Each firm will produce that physical output and quality (amount of service per unit of commodity) which maximizes its profit. In general, because of differing production conditions, firms' outputs will be of differing qualities. If consumers are fully informed, however, they will be paying only for the service contained in each firm's product. So the price of a firm's product must be simply proportional to its quality. In equilibrium, therefore, consumers are indifferent as to buying higher quality at a higher price or lower quality at a lower price.

A monopolist would tend to restrict service output, and would normally do so by a balanced reduction of both quantity and quality. But a rational monopolist would never suppress an invention that costlessly *increases quality*—since such an invention, when consumers are fully informed, is equivalent to one that *reduces cost* (of producing the service desired by consumers). By adopting the invention, the monopolist can always increase profit. The consumers usually gain as well, from increased output of the service. It is, however, logically possible for the monopolist's profit-maximizing output of service to fall, in which case the consumers would be worse off after adoption of the invention.

☐ QUESTIONS FOR CHAPTER 9

MAINLY FOR REVIEW

*R1. If consumers are distributed among different locations, is it true that the greater the number of distinct producing plants the larger will be aggregate demand for the product? How is this argument analogous to one concerning the number of distinct *varieties* offered consumers?

*The answers to starred questions appear at the end of the book.

*R2. What stops the monopolist from offering an infinite number of varieties? Under what circumstances will only a single variety be produced?

R3. How does monopolistic competition differ from pure competition? From pure monopoly?

R4. In monopolistic competition, why is the firm's "perceived" demand curve flatter than the "true" demand curve?

R5. Why is the firm's "perceived" demand curve in monopolistic competition analogous to the horizontal demand curve faced by the firm in pure competition?

*R6. If a monopolist normally produces less *quantity* of a product than a competitive industry would, is it correct to presume that the monopolist would normally also offer a product of lower *quality*?

*R7. Would a monopolist ever suppress an invention reducing the cost of producing its given product? Would it ever suppress an invention raising the quality of product at its given cost? Will consumers in either case be necessarily better off if the invention is adopted?

FOR FURTHER THOUGHT AND DISCUSSION

*T1. Is there a reason to expect monopolistic competition (rather than pure competition) to emerge when the desired commodity is really a single "quality" characteristic contained in the marketed good? Explain.

T2. Would the price-quantity equilibrium under monopolistic competition tend to lie between that achieved under pure monopoly on the one hand, and pure competition on the other? Explain.

T3. Can you explain the shapes of the demand curves in Figure 9.3, showing how consumers' aggregate demand increases with the number of varieties produced?

T4. Suppose the ring of preference of Figure 9.2 were replaced by linear preferences as in Figure 9.1, with some concentration of individual desires toward the middle. What considerations would determine how a *monopolist* firm would space its plants? What would happen under monopolistic competition?

*T5. Could a quality-improving invention in a *competitive* industry ever be adverse to the consumers' interests?

*T6. It is sometimes argued that only relatively high-quality products can "bear the cost" of shipment to distant locations. Thus, California oranges shipped to New York are (on average) of better quality than those consumed by Californians at home. Does this follow from the analysis in this chapter? [*Hint*: Does it cost much more to ship high-quality oranges than low-quality oranges?]

*T7. In seeming contradiction to the statement in the preceding question about California versus New York oranges, for lobsters it is said that one can never get top quality except at the New England shore. Can this be explained?

*T8. Would imposition of a fixed per-unit tax (e.g., 10 cents per gallon of gasoline) tend to increase or decrease the equilibrium *quality* of gasoline (miles per gallon) offered on the market?

T9. Mr. A says: "A monopolist will produce a product of higher quality, since cutthroat competition must lead to a decline in quality." Mr. B says: "A monopolist produces a smaller *quantity* of product than would a competitive industry, and by the same logic will also produce a product of lesser *quality*." Is either correct, or are they both wrong?

*T10. Poor people seem to purchase articles of lower quality than do rich people. Can this be explained in terms of the analysis in the text?

*T11. In an attempt to reduce tobacco production and thereby raise prices received by tobacco farmers, a government program introduced in 1933 allotted quotas to farmers that fixed the number of *acres that could be planted*. Over the years production expanded anyway, since the farmers responded by applying more fertilizer, irrigating more intensively, etc. In 1965 the program was reformed, replacing acreage limitations with quotas that fixed the number of *pounds that each farmer could sell*. Would you expect the original and the reformed programs to have different effects upon the *quality* of tobacco produced by American farmers? Explain.

10

SUPPLEMENTARY CHAPTER

OLIGOPOLY AND STRATEGIC BEHAVIOR

Oligopoly is competition among the few. It is thus an intermediate case between pure competition (many firms) and monopoly (one firm). Whether the outcome is more like competition or more like monopoly depends upon the degree to which the firms act either as *rivals* or as *cooperators.*

10.A
STRATEGIC BEHAVIOR: THE THEORY OF GAMES

A "strategic" situation exists when what is best for A to do depends upon B's choice, and B in turn must take into account the options open to A. So the concept of *optimizing*, choosing a "best" outcome, can become somewhat hazy. Behavior in strategic situations may involve promises, threats, or other types of communications among the parties. There is room for conscious *cooperation* or *conflict.* These topics are studied in the "theory of games," a new field of mathematics stimulated in large part by the economic problem of oligopoly.

In all market interactions there are both conflicting and common interests. The sellers have a common interest in keeping prices high, but a conflict of interest as to who gets more customers. The buyers have a common interest in keeping prices low, but a conflict of interest as to which ones will be able to buy the low-priced goods. Between sellers and buyers there is of course conflict of interest over the price to be set, but (owing to the mutual advantage of trade) there is a strong shared interest in having exchange take place.

The theory of games provides a systematic way of exploring mixtures of conflicting versus common interests. As an extreme case, Table 10.1 illustrates a "payoff matrix" representing a so-called "zero-sum" game. An Attacker can invade by land or by sea. The Defender, let us suppose, will win the battle *if* he guesses the attack route correctly, but if he guesses wrong Attacker will win. Along the left margin the rows are Attacker's strategy choices—attack by Land or by Sea—and across the top the columns are the corresponding Defender's choices. Within each of the four cells the payoff to the row player (Attacker) appears first, and then the payoff to the column player (Defender). The crucial point is that in each cell the payoffs add up to zero—the Attacker's gain is always the Defender's loss, and vice versa. This is therefore a situation of *pure conflict of interests.*

TABLE 10.1

Zero-Sum Game: Land or Sea?

		DEFENDER'S CHOICE OF STRATEGY	
		Land	Sea
ATTACKER'S CHOICE OF STRATEGY	Land	−10, +10	+10, −10
	Sea	+25, −25	−10, +10

But situations of pure conflict are uninteresting to the economist. Economics is concerned with situations where there is some prospect for mutual gain (recall the Fundamental Theorem of Exchange). Let us therefore pass on to the opposite case—*purely common interests*. Table 10.2 pictures a situation where two players will both win if they coordinate their strategies, but otherwise will both lose. Imagine that two drivers are traveling in opposite directions along a dark road, where the options are "Drive on the right" versus "Drive on the left." It might be, as assumed here, that the players do a little better both driving on the right rather than both driving on the left. But the main point, of course, is that failure to coordinate would be disastrous for both: if one drives on the right and the other on the left, the outcome for each is −100.

TABLE 10.2

Mutuality of Interests: Drive on Right or Left?

		B'S CHOICE OF STRATEGY	
		Right	Left
A'S CHOICE OF STRATEGY	Right	+10, +10	−100, −100
	Left	−100, −100	+8, +8

It might seem that the players in Table 10.2 should have no difficulty agreeing to drive on the right. (And notice that neither has any incentive to violate the agreement once made.) Even if they never meet to discuss it, two intelligent players equipped with the information in the table should be able to figure out that driving on the right is the better strategy for both. But pure-coordination games like that of Table 10.2 are also rather uninteresting to economists. We are almost always concerned with mixed cases, containing elements of conflict as well as elements of common interests.

How opposed and parallel interests can be mixed together is shown by an important type of situation studied in the theory of games: the Prisoners' Dilemma. Suppose the police have apprehended two men, accomplices in a crime, but the evidence against them is weak. Lacking a confession, the authorities will be able to convict the prisoners only of a minor infraction. With a confession from either, on the other hand, conviction on a major count is guaranteed. Keeping the prisoners out of communication with each other, the district attorney offers to let either of them off for turning state's evidence—provided that he confesses, while the other does not! (Should both confess, each will receive a reduced yet still substantial penalty.)

In Table 10.3, along the left margin the rows show the possible choices of prisoner A: *Confess* versus *Don't confess*. Across the top are the same choices for prisoner B. Within each cell the numbers represent the penalty in months of imprisonment. (Since imprisonment outcomes are bad, they have minus signs attached.)

TABLE 10.3

The Prisoners' Dilemma: Months of Imprisonment

		B'S CHOICE OF STRATEGY	
		Confess	Don't Confess
A'S CHOICE OF STRATEGY	Confess	−24, −24	0, −36
	Don't confess	−36, 0	−1, −1

The prisoners evidently have a common interest, since both do pretty well if neither confesses (only 1 month's imprisonment). But looking at the payoffs from A's point of view, note that *he is better off choosing "Confess" regardless of what B chooses!* Suppose B has chosen "Confess." Then, comparing the two cells in the left-hand column, if A selects "Confess" he gets −24; if he chooses "Don't confess" he gets −36. So, if B is a fink, A should also be a fink. But what if B were loyal and chose "Don't confess"? In the right-hand column of the table, A sees that selecting "Confess" yields him 0 (the best possibility of all), while if he selects "Don't confess" he gets −1. Even when his partner is loyal, therefore, it still pays A to be a fink. And B will reason in exactly the same way.

So, in the Prisoners' Dilemma situation, it appears that both will confess and both suffer 24 months' imprisonment. In the language of game theory, the strategy-pair "Confess, Confess" is called the *Nash*[1] *solution* for this game. It is an equilibrium since, once the choices are made, neither party has any motive to change his action. Each is doing the best he can for himself, given the decision of the other.

A more general representation of the Prisoners' Dilemma is shown in Table 10.4. The two strategies here are called "Be disloyal" versus "Be loyal" (to one's partner or partners), corresponding to "Confess" versus "Don't confess" in the original story. The numbers indicate, for each player, the *rank* ordering of the outcomes: 4 is best, 3 second best, 2 next, and 1 is worst. Any situation describable in the form of Table 10.4 corresponds logically to a Prisoners' Dilemma. The "Nash solution" is at the upper left where each party receives 2 (his or her next-to-worst outcome)—although by cooperation each could have achieved 3 (the next-to-best outcome).

The Prisoners' Dilemma is a picturesque story, but how does it apply to the real world? One situation that fits this picture is "chiseling" in cartels (Chapter 8). The strategy choices would be "Produce only assigned quota" (Be loyal) or

[1] J. F. Nash, contemporary American mathematician.

TABLE 10.4

The Prisoners' Dilemma: Rank-ordered Outcomes

		B'S CHOICE OF STRATEGY	
		Be disloyal	Be loyal
A'S CHOICE OF STRATEGY	Be disloyal	2, 2	4, 1
	Be loyal	1, 4	3, 3

"Produce beyond quota" (Be disloyal). Despite the mutual gain to all members of the cartel together if they can resist temptation, each firm separately is motivated to produce beyond quota regardless of what the others do. As another example, consider international armaments. All nations together might be better off if nuclear weapons were abolished. But if only one side has them, it will be at a great advantage. The upshot is that both sides have nuclear armaments.

Despite the temptation to chisel, cartels do sometimes persist (see the OPEC example of Chapter 8). There may be ways of escaping the Prisoners' Dilemma, particularly when the parties know one another's identity and are likely to have a continuing relationship. Under oligopoly—competition among the few—these conditions are often met. As a result, a number of different outcomes become possible, as will be discussed in the next section.

Up to now we have looked only at games that were completely *symmetrical* in structure. Each player's situation was the mirror image of the other. Game theory can also be used to analyze *asymmetrical* situations.

An important illustration of an asymmetrical game is the problem of *entry deterrence*. Suppose a monopoly presently exists, but a potential competitor is threatening to enter the industry. If entry occurs, the former monopolist might start a price war to drive out the newcomer, or else it can settle for a share of the former monopoly profit. Table 10.5 pictures the situation, which is asymmetrical in three different ways: (1) The payoff numbers no longer fall into the mirror-image pattern. (2) The strategy options of the players are no longer identical: Player A has the choices "Enter" and "Stay out" while player B's choices are "Resist" and "Tolerate." (3) There is now a definite *sequence* of moves: player A makes his entry decision first, and then player B chooses a response.

To find the equilibrium here, first think of the choices facing the responding player B. If A has chosen "Stay out," B receives his 100 profit; no decision on his part is required. But if A has chosen "Enter," B does better to select "Tolerate"—

TABLE 10.5

The Entry-Deterrence Game

		PLAYER B (MONOPOLIST)	
		Resist	Tolerate
PLAYER A (POTENTIAL ENTRANT)	Enter	−10, 30	20, 80
	Stay out	0, 100	0, 100

where he gets a remaining profit of 80—rather than "Resist," where he receives only 30. Knowing that B will reason in this way, A will therefore choose "Enter." So the outcome is at the upper-right corner of the table, where the newcomer has succeeded in capturing 20 of the monopolist's former 100 profit.

Now suppose instead that the monopolist threatens the potential competitor as follows: "If you choose 'Enter,' I will choose 'Resist' and you will end up with −10 rather than +20. So you had better stay out." If this threat were *credible*, the logical thing for player A to do is "Stay out." But in the situation assumed the threat is *not credible*. Once A has made his entry move, B can only lose by carrying out his threat. To make his threat credible, the monopolist somehow has to change the game. He might tell player A: "The numbers in Table 10.5 don't tell the full picture. Because, if I give in to you now I will have to do the same to lots of other potential entrants. In fact, I will end up losing all my monopoly profit. So, to achieve a tough reputation and thereby deter others, I will simply have to choose 'Resist' if you insist on entering." [*Query*: Can you think of other things the monopolist might do to make his threat credible?]

In the following sections of the chapter, we will distinguish two cases: *homogeneous* versus *heterogeneous* oligopoly. In the homogeneous case the products are identical. Then even a slightly lower price quoted by one seller will capture all sales, and so the firms will have to end up charging the same price. In heterogeneous oligopoly, consumers can distinguish the firms' outputs, some preferring one firm's product and some another firm's. Then each firm will have a "clientele"; up to a point, it can raise price without losing *all* of its customers.

10.B
HOMOGENEOUS PRODUCTS

Let us assume for simplicity that: (1) there are exactly *two* selling firms, so that oligopoly becomes the special case called "duopoly"; (2) the firms are identical; (3) production is carried on at zero cost (i.e., the Total Cost, Average Cost, and Marginal Cost functions are all zero throughout). For example, suppose each of two firms owns a mineral spring gushing forth costlessly and in unlimited volume forever. In the case of a *monopolist*, we saw above, it makes no difference whether we think of the profit-maximizing decision as choosing the most profitable price or the most profitable quantity. But in *oligopoly*, whether the decisions are in terms of price or in terms of quantity turns out to make a difference.

Suppose *quantity* is the decision variable. Table 10.6 lists several different oligopoly (duopoly) solutions.[2] The table is based on an *industry* demand curve expressed by the equation $P = 100 - Q$, where the industry output Q is the sum of the two firm outputs: $Q \equiv q_1 + q_2$. (Recall that zero production cost is assumed.)

The first solution shown in Table 10.6 is the Collusive outcome. Here the two firms act together as a collective monopolist or cartel, sharing the gain equally. A monopolist would want to set Marginal Revenue *MR* equal to Marginal Cost *MC*, both defined for the industry as a whole. Since production costs are assumed zero throughout, Marginal Cost must be zero. The industry demand equa-

---

[2] We are making use here of a somewhat similar discussion in M. Shubik, "Information, Duopoly and Competitive Markets: A Sensitivity Analysis," *Kyklos*, v. 26 (1973), p. 748.

TABLE 10.6

Duopoly Solutions, with Industry Demand Curve $P = 100 - (q_1 + q_2)$

	q_1	q_2	Q	P	Π_1	Π_2
SYMMETRICAL						
Collusive	25	25	50	50	1250	1250
Cournot	33 1/3	33 1/3	66 2/3	33 1/3	1111 1/9	1111 1/9
Competitive	50	50	100	0	0	0
ASYMMETRICAL						
Stackelberg	50	25	75	25	1250	625
Threat	50	0	50	50	2500	0

tion has the linear form $P = 100 - Q$, so industry Marginal Revenue is $MR = 100 - 2Q$.[3] Since $MC = 0$, the monopoly-optimum condition $MR = MC$ becomes $100 - 2Q = 0$. Then $Q = 50$ is the profit-maximizing industry output, and $P = 50$ is the associated price along the demand curve for the industry. Total Revenue $R \equiv PQ$ is 2500 which, in the absence of any costs, is also the total profit Π. With equal division, each firm's profit under the Collusive solution will be $\Pi_1 = \Pi_2 = 1250$.

This Collusive solution assumes that the problem of the Prisoners' Dilemma has somehow been solved by the two parties, who have reached the most profitable outcome in terms of mutual gain. But what if the problem cannot be solved? Skipping to the third line of the table, the opposite extreme is the Competitive solution. It is based upon two assumptions: (1) that cooperation is not achieved, so that each firm operates in its own short-run selfish interest; (2) and, in addition, that each firm acts as a price-taker. So the firms are each assumed to be adopting the decision rule $MC = P$. Since $MC = 0$, acting as price-takers the firms would each be willing to produce indefinitely large amounts for *any* price P greater than zero. The result is that the competitive equilibrium price ends up at $P = 0$. Combined output is 100, as dictated by the demand equation, but revenue and profits are zero for both firms.

On the second line of the table, lying between the Collusive and the Competitive outcomes, is the "Cournot[4] solution." Here the assumptions are: (1) As in the Competitive case, cooperation is not achieved. (2) Each firm knows that increasing its own output will reduce the market price. (3) Each firm assumes that *the other firm's output decision is fixed.* The Cournot solution corresponds therefore to the Nash equilibrium in game theory: each decision-maker is doing the best he can given the decision of the other. (This outcome is accordingly sometimes known as the Nash-Cournot solution.)

The analysis of the Cournot case goes as follows. For any output level q_1 that might be chosen by the first firm, there will be some profit-maximizing output choice q_2 for the second firm. In effect, firm 2 becomes a monopolist over the remaining demand not satisfied by the first firm's output q_1. Specifically, the demand equation for firm 2 becomes $P = (100 - q_1) - q_2$, with q_1 regarded as constant. This is still a linear demand equation, so for firm 2 the Marginal Revenue is $MR_2 = (100 - q_1) - 2q_2$. For example, if $q_1 = 10$ the condition $MR = MC$ for

---

[3] Recall that if $P = A - BQ$, then $MR = A - 2BQ$.

[4] Antoine Augustin Cournot (1801–1877), French mathematician and economist.

firm 2 leads to the equation $90 - 2q_2 = 0$, so that firm 2's output would be $q_2 = 45$. Plotting the q_2 chosen by firm 2 as a function of the given output of firm 1 leads to a "Reaction Curve" RC_2 like that shown in Figure 10.1. There will be a corresponding Reaction Curve RC_1 for firm 1. *The curves are mutually consistent only at the point of intersection*, which is therefore the equilibrium solution. At the equilibrium here the outputs are $q_1 = q_2 = 33\ 1/3$, intermediate between the Collusive and the Competitive solutions. Thus the Cournot solution is a kind of imperfect collusion technique.

The "dynamic" process whereby this equilibrium can be reached is also illustrated in Figure 10.1. Suppose firm 2 is initially producing q_2^o. The RC_1 curve then indicates that firm 1 will produce q_1' in response (point A in the diagram). But when firm 1 is producing q_1', firm 2 reacts by moving to point B on its Reaction Curve RC_2 where it produces q_2'. Firm 1 in turn responds by moving to point C; firm 2 then moves to point D, etc. The end result is that both firms produce at the intersection of the two Reaction Curves.[5]

Exercise 10.1: Find the equations for the Reaction Curves RC_1 and RC_2 in the numerical example above, and verify whether their intersection is indeed the Cournot solution of Table 10.6.

Answer: For firm 2, since it takes the output q_1 of firm 1 as given, Marginal Revenue is: $MR_2 = (100 - q_1) - 2q_2$. Marginal Cost MC_2 is zero, and so the firm sets $MR_2 = 0$, implying $q_2 = 50 - q_1/2$. This is the equation of RC_2. Similar reasoning yields the equation $q_1 = 50 - q_2/2$ for RC_1. Note that the curves are generally similar to those pictured in Figure 10.1—in particular, RC_1 will be steeper than RC_2—except that here the two Reaction Curves are actually straight lines. Solving RC_1 and RC_2 simultaneously, the solution is indeed $q_1 = q_2 = 33\ 1/3$.

---

[5] If the labels on the two RC's were interchanged, the "dynamic" process would lead *outward* rather than *inward* toward the intersection. Then one of the firms would necessarily drive out the other—that is, this would be a "natural monopoly" situation.

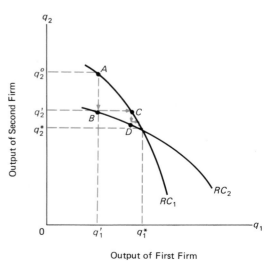

FIGURE 10.1 **Duopoly Reaction Curves.** Given any output q_2 of the second firm, the first firm can determine its profit-maximizing output q_1. Considering all possible levels of q_2, a Reaction Curve RC_1 for the first firm is thereby defined. Similar reasoning (based on taking q_1 as given) leads to the construction of RC_2, the Reaction Curve of the second firm. The intersection of the two Reaction Curves is a Nash equilibrium.

The Cournot solution represents rather shortsighted behavior on the part of the two firms. Each reacts to the other's decision *without* allowing for the fact that the other firm will react in turn. This is unreasonable. Unfortunately, more plausible assumptions about firm behavior make the analysis much more complicated, and it is difficult to arrive at any definite solution.

EXAMPLE 10.1
Pioneering Oligopoly Experiment

One of the very first scientifically controlled economic experiments was conducted by the economist Lawrence E. Fouraker and the psychologist Sidney Siegel.[a] The experimental trials set up a duopoly situation. Each subject, acting as a seller, was asked to choose an output, but the profit to be received depended upon the quantities offered by the two sellers together. In one case ("complete information") each subject was informed of the other player's output choice and profit schedule; in the second case ("incomplete information") each knew the quantity decision but not the profits of the other player.

There were 28 trials—14 for each of the two informational conditions. The results were as follows: (1) In the complete-information case, 5 trials most closely approximated the Collusive solution, 7 1/2 the Cournot solution, and 1 1/2 the Competitive solution. (The fraction was due to a tie.) (2) In the incomplete-information case, all 14 trials most closely approximated the Cournot solution.

> COMMENT: These results suggest that the Cournot solution, in which each player takes as given the quantity decision of the other, does successfully describe what actually tends to happen in oligopoly situations—especially under conditions of incomplete information. While the parties could have gained more by colluding, they were usually not able to achieve such an arrangement. On the other hand, each was sufficiently aware of his own impact upon price so as to avoid, almost always, the unprofitable price-taking behavior of the Competitive solution.
>
> The sensitivity of the experimental observations to the informational conditions was also an important finding. Later studies have shown that other actual details of the market process—for example, whether prices are secretly negotiated or openly posted—affect the extent to which the final outcome approaches the collusive or the competitive end of the spectrum of possibilities.[b]

[a] L. E. Fouraker and S. Siegel, *Bargaining Behavior* (New York: McGraw-Hill, 1963).
[b] See Charles R. Plott, "Industrial Organization Theory and Experimental Economics," *Journal of Economic Literature*, v. 20 (Dec. 1982).

Let us now allow for *asymmetrical* behavior. In the lower portion of Table 10.6, firm 1 is assumed to be aggressive (a "leader") while firm 2 is passive (a "follower"). The leader *acts* while the follower only *reacts*. An aggressive firm, if sufficiently knowledgeable, can make use of the other's Reaction Curve RC_2 to improve its situation.

The first solution in the lower part of Table 10.6 is called the *Stackelberg*[6] equilibrium. It involves "pre-emptive" behavior on the part of the player who moves first. Knowing the follower's Reaction Curve, the leader (firm 1) picks an output level and proclaims that it will not modify that decision. If the proclamation is believed (that is, if the threat is *credible*), the best that firm 2 can do is indeed to choose a point along its Reaction Curve RC_2. Of course, the leader will choose that output q_1 which, when combined with the follower's correctly predicted output q_2, leads to the most profitable outcome for itself. In this numerical example, firm 1 optimizes by setting $q_1 = 50$. Firm 2 then monopolizes the remainder of the market, setting $q_2 = 25$. The leader achieves as much profit for itself as under the symmetrical Collusive solution, while the follower reaps only half the profit of the leader firm.[7]

The *Threat* solution is a still stronger asymmetrical outcome. Suppose the leader proclaims that if the follower enters the market at all, it (the first firm) will produce enough to drive price P all the way down to zero. If this proclamation is believed, the second firm will see no way to make a profit in the market. Hence it might as well stay out entirely. In the Threat solution, the leader does as well as if it had the sole monopoly of the industry.

Finally, we may ask, what would happen if *both* firms attempted to act as leaders? Each would make its threat only to be defied by the other. Actual execution of the threats would push both firms toward the Competitive zero-profit outcome of the upper part of the table.

Table 10.6 was constructed upon the premise that the decision variable for both firms was *quantity* of output. What if *price* rather than quantity were the decision variable? Here the situation is entirely different. The key point to appreciate is that, since the products are identical in the homogeneous case, the firm quoting the lower price will (however small the price differential) attract *all* the customers. Then the Cournot solution of the table disappears, or rather it coincides with the Competitive solution.[8] Suppose the leader (firm 1) quotes any specific price P_1. Then firm 2 will quote a P_2 just barely undercutting it. But then firm 1 will want to barely undercut P_2, and so on. There is no stable outcome short of $P_1 = P_2 = 0$—the Competitive solution.

The asymmetrical Stackelberg solution also disappears if price is the decision variable. The reason is that no one will want to be the leader. If firm 2 announces that it will stick to some fixed price P_1 regardless of what firm 2 does, firm 2 will as above choose a P_2 that barely undercuts it. On the other hand, the asymmmetrical Threat solution is still valid. Here firm 2 as leader announces that, if firm 2 attempts to do *any business at all* by either matching or undercutting the leader's

---

[6] Heinrich von Stackelberg, twentieth-century German economist.

[7] This solution may be verified as follows. Firm 1, the leader, knows that firm 2 will behave as a Cournot reactor—that is, that firm 2 will choose output q_2 to satisfy the equation $MR_2 = (100 - q_1) - 2q_2 = 0$. So $q_2 = (100 - q_1)/2$, and this is known to firm 1. Substituting in the industry demand curve:

$$P = 100 - Q = 100 - q_2 - q_1 = 100 - \frac{100 - q_1}{2} - q_1 = 50 - \frac{q_1}{2}$$

This becomes the overall demand curve facing firm 1, and is again linear. Then $MR_1 = 50 - q_1$, and $MR_1 = MC_1 = 0$ imply $q_1 = 50$. For firm 2, the condition $MR_2 = MC_2 = 0$ becomes $MR_2 = 50 - 2q_2 = 0$, so that $q_2 = 25$. The total industry output is $Q = 50 + 25 = 75$, and market price is $P = 25$.

[8] This was the point of a famous attack upon the Cournot model by the French nineteenth-century mathematician Joseph Bertrand.

price, firm 1 will quote a price of zero and so drive its competitor out. If this threat is believed, firm 2 might as well stay out of business completely. Firm 1 gains all the profit—as on the bottom line of Table 10.6.[9]

EXAMPLE 10.2
Predatory Price-Cutting

The Threat solution of Table 10.6, but with price rather than output as the decision variable, corresponds to what is known as "predatory" price-cutting. A ruthless firm, if it has the resources to carry out its threat, might always stand ready to undertake a price war to drive out any competitors. Having achieved this reputation such a "predator" would not need to execute its threat often. Occasional punishment meted out to foolish interlopers would suffice to deter others.

John D. Rockefeller's old Standard Oil Company—dissolved in 1911 as a result of a landmark antitrust decision—is often described by historians as a predatory price-cutter firm. Standard Oil had achieved, before that date, a substantial degree of monopoly in oil refining through mergers and acquisitions. It is widely believed that these mergers and acquisitions were mainly secured under threat of predatory price-cutting.

A study by John S. McGee demonstrated, surprisingly, that the tale is a myth.[a] Standard Oil rarely if ever started costly price wars to achieve its monopoly. Rather, its practice was to buy out competitors on relatively handsome terms. A later study by Elizabeth Granitz[b] indicated that what made this possible was Rockefeller's ability to use his power as a large customer of the railroads. While the railroads had attempted repeatedly to form a cartel and raise shipping rates, these efforts had always collapsed. In return for specially favorable rates, Rockefeller agreed to act as an "evener"—which meant that he divided his shipments among the railroads so as to enforce the shipping quotas assigned by the railroad cartel. Independent refiners were therefore very much at a disadvantage, which made them willing to accept an offer from Rockefeller's company.

[a] J. S. McGee, "Predatory Price Cutting: The Standard Oil (N.J.) Case," *Journal of Law and Economics*, v. 1 (Oct. 1958).

[b] Elizabeth Granitz, unpublished UCLA Ph.D. dissertation in progress.

10.C
HETEROGENEOUS PRODUCTS

In the preceding section we saw that, depending upon the degree of rivalry among the sellers, there are a number of solutions for oligopolists selling a single or *homogeneous* product. All the different solutions had one thing in common: the firms' identical products sold in the market at the same price. But when oligopolists produce differing or *heterogeneous* products, prices will usually *not* be identi-

[9] The student will find it interesting to plot these solutions in terms of the firms' Reaction Curves, but with the *prices* charged by the two firms on the two axes.

cal. Nevertheless, the same underlying forces remain. On the one hand the sellers might like to cooperate to achieve a collusive monopoly outcome, but on the other hand there is a temptation for each to benefit at the expense of the others (as in the Prisoners' Dilemma) by aggressive or rivalrous behavior.

10.C.1 ☐ The "Kinked" Demand Curve: A Partial Solution?

In the early part of the twentieth century, prices in the American steel industry were remarkably stable. The industry had few firms and so fit the pattern of an oligopoly. The theory of the kinked demand curve was proposed in order to explain why oligopolies might have unusually stable prices. Given some initial equilibrium, it has been alleged, the demand curve for any single oligopolist has a kink at the point of equilibrium. Figure 10.2 pictures a single oligopolist firm after an initial price has been established at P^*. The argument goes as follows. Suppose this firm attempts to sell more by cutting price. Then all the other oligopolists will respond by *meeting* the price cut, so that the firm will be able to sell only a little more at the lower price. In other words, in the region below the initial equilibrium price P^* the firm's demand curve will be steep. What if firm 1 attempted to raise price? Then, assertedly, competing oligopolists would *not* meet the price increase, so that the firm loses a lot of sales. In other words, in the region above

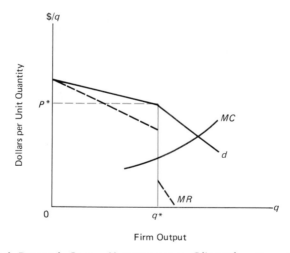

FIGURE 10.2 **Kinked Demand Curve: Heterogeneous Oligopoly.** For oligopolists producing heterogeneous (nonidentical) products, suppose an initial equilibrium exists where the firm produces output q^* at price P^*. If the firm were to cut its price, the other oligopolists meet the price reduction so that the price-cutter's sales gain is small; if the firm raises price, the others do not follow the increase and the sales loss is large. These assumptions define a *kink* in the firm's demand curve d which is associated with a *vertical gap* in the curve of Marginal Revenue MR. The profit-maximizing condition $MC = MR$ is therefore met at the initial equilibrium. The equilibrium price P^* will be relatively stable, since demand and cost conditions can shift somewhat without affecting the fact that the MC curve cuts through the vertical gap of the MR curve at output q^*.

$P*$ the firm's demand curve is relatively flat. Note that the argument makes sense only in the heterogeneous case, since only then can any price difference persist.[10]

This hypothesis is not a complete theory. It says nothing about how the original ruling price $P*$ was determined. But there is nevertheless an interesting implication: *Equilibrium prices arrived at by oligopolistic sellers will be relatively stable.*

In Figure 10.2 note that the kink in the firm's demand or Average Revenue curve becomes a *vertical* jump in the Marginal Revenue curve. It is simple to see this geometrically in the special case where the two branches of the demand curve are linear. For any linear demand curve, the Marginal Revenue curve must bisect the horizontal distance to the vertical axis. With two separate linear branches of the demand curve, there must then be a vertical break or jump in the *MR* curve as shown.

For the price-quantity pair $P*, q*$ to be a stable solution, Marginal Cost must equal Marginal Revenue at $q*$. Geometrically, the *MC* curve must *cut through* the vertical jump of *MR*. Now suppose some disturbance changes the shape of the *MC* curve. Nevertheless, as long as *MC* continues to intersect *MR* within the vertical gap in *MR*, the firm will still produce $q*$ at price $P*$. Alternatively, suppose that the disturbance changed the *demand* for the firm's output. Again we can see geometrically that shifts of *MR* to the right or left (if not too large) are likely to preserve the property that the Marginal Cost curve *MC* cuts through the vertical jump of *MR*. When this happens, price $P*$ will remain unchanged, but output $q*$ will change in the direction of shift of the Marginal Revenue function.

The competing oligopolists' behavior, on this hypothesis, is *strongly rivalrous*. How then did the initial equilibrium, which suggests a degree of collusion, come about? One possible explanation: the firms might have agreed on the initial price, and also agreed to punish any firm that violates the agreement—by meeting its price cuts and not meeting its price increases.

[10] *Query*: Assume, under *homogeneous* oligopoly, that a single firm finds that competitors meet its price cuts but do not meet its price increases. Would the firm's demand curve here also be "kinked"? What would the shape of the demand curve be above the initial price $P*$? Below $P*$?

EXAMPLE 10.3
Oligopoly and Price Rigidity

If oligopolists face kinked demand curves, demand and cost conditions can vary to some extent without affecting the prices charged by firms. For a simple monopolist, on the other hand, any shift of the Marginal Cost or Marginal Revenue curves should lead to a new optimizing price. Consequently, an implication of the kinked-demand hypothesis is that oligopoly prices should be relatively rigid.

This implication was tested by G. J. Stigler. The data in the table are typical of his findings. As can be seen, there is a strong indication that oligopoly prices are *less* rigid than monopoly prices. This is certainly true in terms of the number of monthly price changes, and tends to be confirmed by the quantitative measure of price change represented by the "coefficient of variation" (the standard deviation of monthly prices divided by their mean).

Price Flexibility (June 1929–May 1937)

	Number of Firms in Industry	Number of Monthly Price Changes	Coefficient of Variation of Prices
OLIGOPOLIES			
Bananas	2	46	16
Grain-binder	2	5	3
Plows	6	25	6
Tires	8	36	9
MONOPOLIES			
Aluminum	1	2	6
Nickel	1	0	0

Source: G. J. Stigler, "The Kinky Oligopoly Demand Curve and Rigid Prices," Journal of Political Economy, v. 55 (1947), p. 443.

One possible objection to Stigler's test is that *interindustry comparisons* of price changes cannot be made with very much confidence. Conditions of conducting business vary from one industry to another, and it may have just so happened that the "monopolized" sectors in the table would have had relatively rigid prices regardless of number of firms. Another objection is that what is statistically reported as a *single* industry is often mere convention. Had aluminum and nickel been placed together in a single "nonferrous metals" category, they would have been classed as an oligopoly with heterogeneous products rather than as two separate monopolies.

A study by Julian L. Simon[a] employed data that were less vulnerable to these objections. He studied prices quoted for business-magazine advertising, where the magazines had been classified into groups by the Standard Rate and Data Service (SRDS). Since all the groups fell into the business-magazine category, there was relative uniformity in conditions and methods of price quotation. And since the classification by SRDS was undertaken for the convenience of customers (advertisers), the grouping of magazines was presumably economically meaningful.

There were 148 groupings ranging in size from 1 to 29 magazines. A magazine without competitors in its grouping could then be considered a monopolist. The data for two different periods, 1955 to 1961 and 1961 to 1964, once again suggested that the monopoly groups had *more* rigid prices than the oligopoly groups. Simon's test thus confirmed Stigler's previous negative conclusion as to the kinked-demand hypothesis. (However, the *quantitative* differences found by Simon were by no means as great as those reported by Stigler.)

COMMENT: One possible explanation of the observations, consistent with assigning at least some degree of validity to the kinked-demand hypothesis, runs in terms of *nonprofit goals*. We saw in Chapter 8 that

[a] J. L. Simon, "A Further Test of the Kinky Oligopoly Demand Curve," *American Economic Review*, v. 59 (Dec. 1969).

monopoly firms, sheltered from competition, may be in a relatively better position to pursue goals other than economic profit. It might well be that an important nonprofit goal for monopoly firms is the easy life, avoidance of difficult decisions. Changing price, rather than just leaving things as they are, can be a difficult decision. Not only is sheer mental effort required, but "rocking the boat" is liable to attract unwanted attention and complaints. We might then expect monopoly and oligopoly prices *both* to be rigid, for different reasons: for oligopolists the kinked-demand hypothesis might be valid, while for monopolists the "easy life" goal might lead to even greater rigidity of prices.

10.C.2 □ Variation of Product

In the heterogeneous case, an oligopolist can compete by changing not only price and quantity but also the product itself. Two main types of product variation were considered in the previous chapter: (1) product *variety* (the range of products meeting diverse consumer preferences), and (2) product *quality* (the degree to which the market commodity provides a service desired by all consumers). We will concentrate here on the topic of variety.

One model of oligopolistic product *variety* has received considerable attention. In Figure 10.3 (compare Figure 9.1 of the previous chapter), consumer preferences are supposed to be *uniformly* distributed along a line-segment scaled from 0 to 1, with midpoint $M = 1/2$. Suppose there is a constant per-mile transport cost t from any producing location to the consumer. If P is the f.o.b. price at the producing location R, the solid V-shaped lines show what the delivered price $P + ts$ would be at any distance s in either direction from point R; the dashed lines show

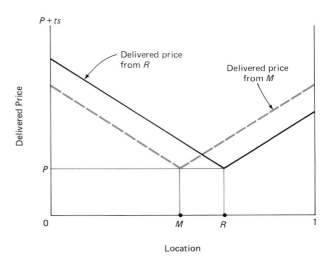

FIGURE 10.3 Delivered Price. If P is the f.o.b. price, t is the unit transportation cost, and s the distance from a production point, the delivered price from that point to any consumer location is $P + ts$. The solid lines in the diagram show the delivered prices from a production locale at R; the dashed lines show the delivered prices from a production locale at the midpoint M.

the delivered prices if the production locale is at the midpoint M. For example, M and R might represent two coal suppliers along a railroad. The price of coal at any point along the road, including transportation charges, is given by the height of the V-shaped line.

A curious solution to this problem has been proposed by H. Hotelling.[11] Assume that there are just two firms (duopoly), with identical costs of producing and delivering the commodity. Now suppose that consumers everywhere along the line-segment want exactly one unit of the commodity, and are willing to pay any price for it. (Each person's demand is absolutely inelastic, but only for a single unit of the good.) Suppose one firm is located at the midpoint M in Figure 10.3 and the second firm at some other point R. Comparing the dashed and solid lines, we see that the firm located at M has an advantage: it can sell at a lower delivered price for all consumers located to the left of M and also for some of the consumers located to the right. So the firm at R would have an incentive to move toward the midpoint M. The conclusion is that in equilibrium the duopolists would locate back to back, at either side of the midpoint M. In that way each is closer to half of the market that serves as its "clientele."

Interpreted in terms of product *variety*, the equilibrium here has both firms supplying nearly identical products of middling character. Essentially no variety is offered to consumers at all! This model explains (so it has been claimed) not only why different companies' toothpastes and refrigerators are very much alike but why the Republican and Democratic political platforms tend to converge toward a middle-of-the-road position, why Catholics and Protestants over time tend to minimize their theological differences, and so forth.

In the Hotelling equilibrium, *not enough* variety is offered by suppliers. Putting it in locational terms, resources are wasted in transporting the good to consumers. When both firms are located at M the average distance between consumers and the nearest production point is $1/4$. If the two firms were to spread apart and ideally locate at the quartile points, the average distance would be reduced to $1/8$ instead. Thus, by offering more variety the two firms could better satisfy the range of consumer preferences at no extra cost. In terms of Table 10.6 the Hotelling result is similar to a Cournot solution; each firm reacts (chooses a location) on the presumption that the other firm's decision will not change.

Absolutely inelastic individual demand is of course a highly unreasonable assumption. (If this were really the case, the duopolists could earn an infinite profit by colluding to set price indefinitely high.) Once we allow some elasticity of consumer demand, the duopolists would be pulled away from the midpoint locations. In Figure 10.3, suppose there were initially two firms located back-to-back at M— the firm just to the right having as "clientele" all those to the right, while the firm just to the left takes the rest. Suppose that the right-hand firm moved further to the right. Since delivered price would then be lower for most of its old clientele, it could sell more product to them—while losing to its competitor only a small fraction of its old clientele (those located in the immediate neighborhood of M). The other firm would behave similarly. So some variety would after all be offered to consumers. However, even if demand is quite elastic, the firms will not move as far as the ideal quartile locations.

[11] H. Hotelling, "Stability in Competition," *Economic Journal*, v. 39 (Mar. 1929).

Another oddity of the Hotelling model is that the whole argument collapses when there are more than two suppliers. A third firm would want to locate an infinitesimal distance on one or the other side of the initial pair. But then one of the original two would be boxed in, leaving it without any clientele at all. Such a firm would then surely "jump" to the outside, to be followed by the one now left in the middle, and so on in an unending musical-chairs situation. So with more than two firms there cannot be a Cournot-Hotelling equilibrium.

What if consumers are distributed uniformly *around a ring* (see Figure 9.2) rather than along a line-segment? With downward-sloping demand, Cournot behavior in the ring model would lead to an efficient result. The first firm can choose any arbitrary location, and then the second will locate 180° away at the opposite point around the circle. So transport cost is minimized. The ring model also generalizes easily to any number of firms, which are always motivated to spread themselves evenly around the circle. Whether the ring metaphor or the line-segment metaphor is more appropriate depends upon the actual situation.[12]

10.D
OLIGOPOLY AND COLLUSION

The oligopoly models discussed so far seem to give inconclusive results. Another approach[13] has been to treat oligopoly situations as *imperfect collusive arrangements* (i.e., imperfect cartels as described in Chapter 8). In any industry, we know, all firms can gain from collusion. But owing to the temptation to "chisel," collusion requires a policing mechanism. Since policing is costly, there will be some equilibrium amount of slippage from the Collusive solution. This is the best the sellers can realistically expect. Thus, the parties involved will agree upon forming a cartel with some kind of policing scheme, hoping that it will be tolerably (though imperfectly) effective.

What helps oligopolists to collude? First and most obviously, the fewer the firms involved, the easier it is for them to police one another—hence, the more effective the cartel. Second, secret price cuts are more likely to be offered to large than to small buyers. A chiseling deal with a single big customer might be kept quiet; to try to get the same increase of business from ten small customers is stretching secrecy too far. The presence of larger buyers tempts suppliers to chisel, making cartels less effective. Third, enforcement of collusion should be much easier where the product is homogeneous. Otherwise, price cuts can take the hard-to-penetrate guise of better quality. (Even where the physical commodity is homogeneous, a firm might still chisel by offering better credit terms or delivery.) Fourth, the more unstable the conditions of the industry, the harder it will be to negotiate and maintain agreements.

---

[12] In politics, for example, a ring may sometimes be a better picture than a line-segment. Supporters of extreme-left parties are often psychologically very similar to those on the extreme right—the extremes may have more in common with one another than either has with moderate positions.

[13] Proposed in G. Stigler, "A Theory of Oligopoly," *Journal of Political Economy*, v. 72 (Feb. 1964).

EXAMPLE 10.4
Industry Concentration and Monopoly Power

Collusion is easier when there are fewer firms. But at what point does a competitive industry or an oligopoly become effectively collusive? Frederick Geithman, Howard Marvel, and Leonard Weiss examined this question using the "four-firm concentration ratio"—the percentage of a market served by the largest four firms in the industry. They found that collusion is not a problem in industries with a concentration ratio of less than 40, that is, where the largest four firms serve less than 40 percent of the market. However, concentration ratios above this seemed to promote collusion, as evidenced by higher prices. Using data from gasoline retailing (1964–1971) and grocery supermarkets (October 1974), they found that average prices tended to rise with the concentration ratio.

Prices and Concentration Ratios

| Concentration Ratios (%) | PRICE | |
	Regular Gasoline*	Groceries†
0–40	28.2	89.6
40–44	29.5	92.8
45–49	29.5	93.7
50–55	32.0	93.0
55–60	—	94.1
60–65	—	95.5
75–95	—	98.9

*$/gallon

†Value of standard grocery basket.

Source: Frederick Geithman, Howard Marvel, and Leonard Weiss, "Concentration, Price, and Critical Concentration Ratios," *Review of Economics and Statistics,* v. 63 (Aug. 1981), pp. 349, 350.

10.D.1 □ An Application: "Most-Favored-Customer" Clauses[14]

Certain types of price guarantees to purchasers may facilitate collusion. Imagine two duopolists producing distinct products, and therefore able to set different prices P_1 and P_2. For simplicity, assume that firm 1 considers only two possible price quotations, high and low: P_1^H and P_1^L. Similarly, firm 2 chooses between P_2^H and P_2^L. Suppose the profit payoffs to each firm are summarized by the game matrix of Table 10.7. The duopolists here are once again caught in a Prisoners'

[14] This analysis is based largely upon Steven C. Salop, "Practices That (Credibly) Facilitate Oligopoly Coordination," in Joseph E. Stiglitz and G. Frank Mathewson, eds., *New Developments in the Analysis of Market Structures* (Cambridge, Mass.: MIT Press, 1986).

TABLE 10.7

The Prisoners' Dilemma: Oligopoly Profits

		FIRM 2	
		P_2^H	P_2^L
FIRM 1	P_1^H	100, 100	−10, 140
	P_1^L	140, −10	70, 70

Dilemma. If both choose the high-price strategy, each firm can attain its second-best outcome (numerically, a profit of 100). Yet for either firm the low-price strategy is superior *regardless* of what the other does. So the two are likely to end up at their next-to-worst outcome—the Prisoners' Dilemma equilibrium strategy-pair P_1^L, P_2^L yielding profit of 70 to each.

Each firm would surely agree to quote its high price provided that the other did the same. However, in the United States such an agreement would be a clear violation of the antitrust laws. But the same effect might be achieved by subtler means. Imagine that each duopolist "generously" guarantees its customers that no other customer will be offered a lower price. That is, should a later reduced price be offered to anyone else, earlier customers will get a rebate. (This is called a "Most-Favored-Customer" clause.)

It seems that buyers ought to be happy about the Most-Favored-Customer clause. But notice in Table 10.8 how this has changed the duopolists' payoffs. Now if the P_1^H, P_2^H strategy-pair yielding (100,100) is achieved, neither firm has any reason to change. If firm 1, for example, were to cut price its profit will now be 90 instead of 100—while it may gain new sales by cutting price, it will have to give rebates to its old customers.

TABLE 10.8

The "Most-Favored-Customer" Clause

		FIRM 2	
		P_2^H	P_2^L
FIRM 1	P_1^H	100, 100	−10, 90
	P_1^L	90, −10	70, 70

Table 10.8 has a payoff pattern somewhat similar to Table 10.2. It is not quite the same, however. Table 10.2 represented completely parallel interests, whereas here some conflict of interest does remain (in the off-diagonal cells). But in both tables the players can reasonably be expected to achieve their mutually best outcomes. We can imagine that one of the firms, let us say firm 1, has the first move. Then it will reason: "If I choose the high price P_1^H then the other firm's superior strategy is to follow me and choose its P_2^H, whereas if I choose P_1^L the other firm will choose P_2^L. Either way, I do better to start off with the high price P_1^H."

A seeming paradox here is often seen in the theory of games: it may pay to sacrifice an opportunity *once the effect upon other players' decisions is taken into account.* In this case, by making the "sacrifice" of arranging to lose rather than gain profit by cutting price, each firm guarantees to the other that it will not be a price-cutter.

A somewhat parallel arrangement is the Meet-or-Release clause. Here the seller guarantees a customer who has not yet taken delivery that any lower price on the market will be matched—or else the customer is released from his obligation to purchase. (The Most-Favored-Customer clause guarantees that buyers will get the advantage of the seller's *own* later price cuts, if any; Meet-or-Release guarantees that buyers will get the advantage of *other firms'* lower prices.) The Meet-or-Release clause has the side-effect of encouraging the customer to report when competitors are cutting prices, thus reducing the likelihood of secret discounts and chiseling. [*Challenge to the reader*: Construct a payoff table corresponding to both firms' offering a Meet-or-Release clause.]

We should not, however, jump to the conclusion that the Most-Favored-Customer clause or the Meet-or-Release clause or similar arrangements are used only to keep prices high. They have other functions as well, for example, providing buyers with insurance against being the targets of price discrimination. Therefore, such clauses are not conclusive evidence of anticompetitive collusion.

□ SUMMARY OF CHAPTER 10

Oligopoly is *competition among a small number* of firms in an industry. With small numbers, all the decision-makers are likely to be conscious of the interdependence of their choices: what is best for each depends upon what the others are doing. So the firms are required to make *strategic* decisions, a topic studied in the mathematical theory of games. Depending upon the degree of rivalry versus cooperation, there are a number of different equilibrium or solution concepts possible.

"The Prisoners' Dilemma" is a class of situations in which there are potential gains from cooperation, and yet it is in the private interest of each party to behave selfishly—so that, in what is called the *Nash solution*, all lose. But where the parties know one another's identity and may be engaging in repeated interactions or plays of the game, as is often the case under oligopoly, they may be able to achieve a more cooperative outcome.

Oligopoly may be *homogeneous* (all the firms produce exactly the same product) or *heterogeneous* (the firms produce distinct, though similar, commodities). In the former case, no price difference between the firms can persist.

Under homogeneous oligopoly, and assuming for simplicity just two firms (duopoly), either *quantity* of output or *price* may be the decision variable. When quantity is the decision variable, and if the two firms behave symmetrically, at one extreme they may *collude* to attain the monopoly outcome—while at the other extreme they may act as *competitive* price-takers. But if each firm simply reacts optimally to what is perceived as a fixed output decision of the other, the "Cournot equilibrium" (a special case of the Nash solution) is attained, intermediate between the Collusive and Competitive outcomes. The key idea is that each firm chooses the best monopoly output for the *remainder* of the market, after subtracting the other firm's given production. If *asymmetrical* behavior is allowed, on the other hand, the more aggressive firm may be able to gain more profit by forcing the other to an inferior position—in the limit, driving the other out of the market entirely.

Considering instead that *price* is the decision variable, and that the firms behave symmetrically, then given each firm's choice of price the optimal reaction for the other firm is to just barely undercut it. Here the Cournot outcome reduces to the Competitive one. Possibilities remain, however, for profitable symmetrical *collusion* on price, or for asymmetrical gain to a more aggressive firm.

In *heterogeneous* oligopoly, in contrast, a price difference between the firms may persist. Apart from this, the analysis of the symmetrical and asymmetrical outcomes is much the same. In particular, the Cournot solution remains intermediate between the Collusive and Competitive outcomes.

For oligopolists producing heterogeneous products, one particular type of assumed strategic interaction leads to a "kinked" demand curve for any single firm. If the other producers will meet any price cut, the firm's demand curve below the current price will be steep (inelastic); if the others will not meet any price increase, above the current price, the firm's demand curve will be flat (elastic). The effect is to discourage price changes. This theory does not explain how the equilibrium price was originally arrived at, but suggests that once equilibrium is attained price will be rather stable.

In heterogeneous oligopoly the firms also choose what product to offer consumers. The Hotelling model concludes that an oligopolistic industry would provide *too little* variety to consumers. This result depends, however, upon doubtful features of the model, among them that individual preferences fall along a line. And in any case, the Hotelling model breaks down if there are more than two firms.

Oligopolists find it difficult to enforce collusion—given the temptation of each to chisel (as in the Prisoners' Dilemma). Collusion is easier if the number of oligopolists is small, if there are no large buyers, if the product is homogeneous, and if market conditions are stable. Certain contractual arrangements which at first appear to favor the buyers, such as Most-Favored-Customer clauses, may actually facilitate collusion and thus lead to higher prices.

□ QUESTIONS FOR CHAPTER 10

MAINLY FOR REVIEW

R1. What is strategic behavior? Why are suppliers more likely to engage in strategic behavior when there are only a few of them in the market?

*R2. What is the "Prisoners' Dilemma"? Do the participants in this game have an unexploited mutual gain from trade, and if so, why?

*R3. Distinguish oligopoly from monopolistic competition.

*R4. Justify the statement in the text that the Cournot oligopoly outcome is a special case of the Nash solution in the theory of games.

R5. Explain the Cournot solution to the duopoly problem.

* The answers to starred questions appear at the end of the book.

R6. Diagram the Reaction Curves for the asymmetrical Stackelberg and Threat cases (letting output be the decision variable).

*R7. Why does a "kinked" demand curve tend to lead to rigid prices? How might a kinked demand curve for any single oligopolist result from the behavior of others designed to enforce a collusive agreement?

FOR FURTHER THOUGHT AND DISCUSSION

T1. It seems somewhat strange that different duopoly solutions are obtained depending upon whether price or quantity is the decision variable. Which outcomes are different, and why?

*T2. Under the Cournot model, in making its output decision each duopolist firm *incorrectly* assumes that the other's output is fixed. Over time, however, each would surely learn that this assumption about the other's behavior is not valid. What would then be likely to happen?

*T3. In deterring entry, a monopolist faces the problem of making his threat—that he will always produce enough to drive out the entrant—*credible*. The difficulty lies in the fact that, once a newcomer has entered, it may be more profitable to share the market than to engage in a costly price war. How might a monopolist make his threat more credible?

*T4. Can a kinked demand curve arise under *homogeneous* duopoly? If so, what would be its shape?

T5. In recent antitrust cases, the courts appear to believe that small numbers almost inevitably imply cartel-like collusion. Is this inference justified?

*T6. Some economists have argued that "predatory price-cutting" to enforce the Threat solution will almost never be observed. The reason given is that the symmetrical Collusive solution is typically better for both parties. Is this necessarily correct? Is it ever correct? Under what circumstances will predatory price-cutting be likely to emerge, if ever?

T7. Construct a payoff table in which two duopolist firms both offer consumers a Meet-or-Release clause. Show that this permits them to escape from the Prisoners' Dilemma so as to charge higher prices.

11
CORE CHAPTER

DEMAND FOR FACTORS OF PRODUCTION

Previous chapters have covered the *product market*—the market for finished goods. Now we turn to the *factor market*, to the supply of and demand for productive services. (In terms of the circular flow diagram in Chapter 1, attention is shifting from the upper portion to the lower portion of the picture.) This chapter surveys the demand side of the factor market—the decisions of firms as to how much land, labor, or other productive services to hire. The following chapter will take up the supply side, the offer decisions made by owners of resources.

In the equilibrium of the factor market, *market structure* (the degree of competition) continues to play an important role. Indeed, we have to take account of market structure not only in the factor market itself but also in the associated product market or markets. A company may be a monopolist in its product market and still be only one among many employers (and therefore be a competitive or "price-taking" buyer) of a productive service like secretarial help in a large city. Conversely, a textile firm may face a highly competitive world market for its product and still be a "price-making" or *monopsonist*[1] employer of labor in a small town.[2]

11.A
SINGLE VARIABLE FACTOR

11.A.1 □ The Production Function

Suppose a firm is producing a single output good Q by using resource inputs $A, B, C, \ldots$. Its production function can be written:

$$(11.1) \qquad q = F(a, b, c, \ldots)$$

This expression means simply that there is some relation determining quantity of output q given the input quantities a, b, c, and so forth. Suppose, to begin with, all inputs other than A are held *fixed*. (Accordingly, we are dealing here with "the short run.") Then the production function can be written more simply as:

---

[1] A monopolist is a sole *seller* in a market; a monopsonist is a sole *buyer*.

[2] Firms might also be *oligopolists* or *monopolistic competitors* in their respective product markets, as discussed in Chapters 9 and 10, but only pure competition and pure monopoly will be covered here.

(11.2)
$$q = f(a)$$

The quantities of the fixed factors $B, C, \ldots$ no longer appear in the equation. But of course they still have an effect; the amounts of the fixed factors help determine the *shape* of the $f(a)$ function, showing how much Q can be obtained from a given input of A.

NUMERICAL ILLUSTRATION: Suppose the underlying production function for output Q has two inputs A and B, specifically, $q = 6a^{1/2}b^{1/4}$. This corresponds to Equation (11.1). If the quantity of factor B is held fixed at $b = 1$, the equation corresponding to (11.2) would take the simpler form $q = 6a^{1/2}$. With $b = 16$, however, (11.2) would become $q = 12a^{1/2}$.

Economists frequently make use of the technological relation between factor input and product output quantity known as the *Law of Diminishing Returns*. We have already seen in Chapter 6 how the Law of Diminishing Returns explains why firms' Marginal Cost and Average Cost curves eventually take on rising form. That is, diminishing returns correspond to increasing costs.

THE LAW OF DIMINISHING RETURNS: If one factor (or group of factors) is increased while another factor (or group of factors) is held fixed, Total Product q will at first tend to rise. But, eventually at least, a point will be reached where the rate of increase, the Marginal Product[3] $mp_a \equiv \Delta q/\Delta a$ of the variable factor, begins to fall; this is the point of diminishing *marginal* returns. With further increases of the variable factor, the Average Product $ap_a \equiv q/a$ will also begin to fall; this is the point of diminishing *average* returns. As the amount of factor A employed rises still more, eventually the Total Product q may actually begin to fall (i.e., A can become counterproductive, reducing the Total Product q). This is the point of diminishing *total* returns.

The Law of Diminishing Returns is illustrated in Figure 11.1. The upper panel shows the Total Product curve tp_a relating output quantity q and factor input a. The lower diagram shows the corresponding average function (the Average Product curve ap_a representing q/a) and the marginal function (the Marginal Product curve mp_a showing $\Delta q/\Delta a$). The general relations among the total, average, and marginal magnitudes, as first explained in Chapter 2, still continue to hold. When Total Product tp_a is rising or horizontal or falling, Marginal Product mp_a must be correspondingly positive or zero or negative (Propositions 2.1a, 2.1b, 2.1c). And the Marginal Product curve mp_a lies above the Average Product curve ap_a when ap_a is rising, intersects it when ap_a is horizontal, and lies below it when ap_a is falling (Propositions 2.2a, 2.2b, 2.2c).

---

[3] *Mathematical Footnote*: The Marginal Product is (like all marginal concepts) defined as a limit:

$$mp_a \equiv \lim_{\Delta a \to 0} \frac{\Delta q}{\Delta a} \equiv \frac{dq}{da}$$

(From this point on in the text, mathematical footnotes that simply translate marginal concepts into derivative notation will be omitted. Special notes will be provided only where points of difficulty may arise.)

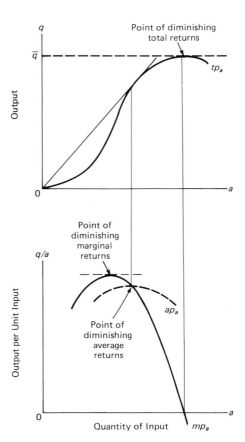

FIGURE 11.1 The Law of Diminishing Returns. The upper panel shows the Total Product function tp_a, and the lower panel shows the corresponding Average Product function ap_a and Marginal Product function mp_a of employing factor A. Diminishing *marginal* returns set in first (the mp_a curve reaches its peak), then diminishing *average* returns set in (the ap_a curve reaches its peak), and finally diminishing *total* returns set in (the tp_a curve reaches its peak, at the maximum producible output $\overline{q}$).

Exercise 11.1: A firm's Total Product function for factor A is given by the equation $tp_a \equiv q = 100a^2 - a^3$. The Average Product function is then, evidently, $ap_a \equiv q/a = 100a - a^2$. It can be shown by calculus that the exact Marginal Product function is given by $mp_a \equiv \Delta q/\Delta a = 200a - 3a^2$. (a) When do diminishing *marginal* returns set in? (b) Diminishing *average* returns? (c) Diminishing *total* returns? (d) Verify that when Total Product reaches a maximum, Marginal Product is zero. (e) Verify that when Average Product reaches a maximum, Marginal Product equals Average Product.

Answer: (a) It can be determined by calculus (or else by plotting the function) that Marginal Product reaches its maximum at $a = 33\ 1/3$. This is where diminishing *marginal* returns set in. (b) Average Product reaches a maximum (diminishing *average* returns set in) at $a = 50$. (c) Total Product reaches a maximum (diminishing *total* returns set in) at $a = 66\ 2/3$. (d) At $a = 66\ 2/3$, the formula for Marginal Product shows that $mp_a = 0$. (e) At $a = 50$, the formulas show that Average Product and Marginal Product are equal: $ap_a = 2500 = mp_a$.

The Law of Diminishing Returns is a physical law, taken as an "outside" fact by economists. At any output level there will be some most effective *proportion* among the several factors. When factor A rises from a very low level (say, from zero) with other factor quantities held fixed, we are likely to be moving rapidly toward the most effective factor proportion—and so Total Product tends to increase rapidly. This means that the Marginal Product of factor A will be high (and might even be increasing). As we approach the most effective factor proportions, additional units of factor A remain useful but decreasingly so. This means that the Marginal Product of A is positive but declining. Eventually, indeed, we may so swamp our productive process with factor A that Total Product falls (*negative* Marginal Product of factor A).

EXAMPLE 11.1
Corn Yields

In 1977 the University of Wisconsin Experimental Station at Arlington conducted an experiment in corn yields. Various combinations of potassium and nitrogen fertilizers were tried, with other factors being held constant. The table shows the resulting yields for increasing levels of nitrogen, with potassium held constant at 231 pounds per acre.

Available Nitrogen (lb/acre)	Total Yield (bu./acre)	Marginal Yield (bu./acre/lb N)
75	112	
		.679
131	150	
		.393
187	172	
		.250
243	186	
		−.089
299	181	
		−.268
355	176	

Source: Adapted from Ted F. Bay and Richard A. Schoney, "Data Analysis with Computer Graphics: Production Functions," *American Journal of Agricultural Economics*, v. 64, no. 2 (May 1982), p. 289.

The Marginal Yield column has been estimated here from the original source, by taking the difference between the Total Yields for successive rows and dividing by the nitrogen increment. Thus, the first Marginal Yield is calculated as $(150 - 112)/(131 - 75) = .679$. This number should be interpreted as an estimate of the Marginal Yield at the in-between nitrogen input of $1/2(131 - 75) = 103$ pounds per acre. Notice that in this experiment diminishing *marginal* returns applied throughout. Diminishing *total* returns set in somewhere around 250 pounds of nitrogen per acre.

11.A.2 □ From Production Function to Cost Function

This section shows how the properties of the production function, as just described, determine the shapes of the various cost functions (Total Cost, Average Cost, Marginal Cost) we have been using earlier in the book.

The firm is best thought of as *hiring* the factors of production. In other words, the firm buys the *services* of the factors rather than the factors themselves.[4] The "hire-prices" of factors $A, B, \ldots$ will be symbolized as $h_a, h_b, \ldots$. We assume in this chapter that the firm is a "price-taker" with regard to these factor-market prices of inputs. Therefore, all the hire-prices are constant.

The firm's Total Cost for any given combination of inputs is:

(11.3) $$C \equiv h_a a + h_b b + h_c c + \ldots$$

When all factors except A are held fixed, Total Cost can be divided into a fixed component F and a variable component V:

(11.3′) $$C \equiv F + V \equiv F + h_a a$$

Here $h_a a$, the expenditure on factor A, corresponds to the "variable cost" V while F corresponds to the "fixed cost" of all the other factors B, C, etc.

$C = F + h_a q^2$. More generally, the "inverted" production function can be expressed algebraically as:

(11.4) $$a = \phi(q)$$

Then:

(11.5) $$C \equiv F + h_a \phi(q)$$

With a single variable factor A, therefore, the Total Cost function depends upon the fixed cost F, the hire-price h_a, and the production function $q = f(a)$.

This transformation is shown geometrically in Figure 11.2. The shape of the Total Variable Cost curve V in the first panel suggests the shape of the tp_a curve of Figure 11.1, rotated 180° and flipped over. And in particular, the dashed *vertical* bound on the right here represents the same maximum output $\overline{q}$ as the dashed *horizontal* bound in Figure 11.1. (The dotted upper branch of the Total Variable Cost curve in Figure 11.2 is economically irrelevant—the firm would never produce a given output at greater cost if it can produce the same output at lower cost.) As for the Total Cost C, this curve always lies above V by the amount of the fixed cost F.

Comparing the lower panels of Figures 11.1 and 11.2, a kind of inverse rela-

---

[4] In some cases a firm may be able either to *hire* or to *buy*. A business can rent office space or buy a building. Later on we will find it useful to distinguish the hire-price h_a of a factor A from the price P_A of the factor itself—of the *source* of the productive services used by the firm. But in this chapter we will deal only with the hire-price h_a, the price of the factor's *services*.

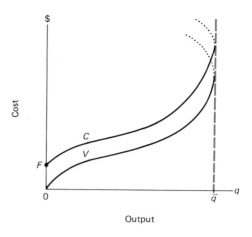

FIGURE 11.2 From Production Function to Cost Function: Geometry. If we multiply the horizontal axis of the previous diagram by the constant hire-price h_a, the dimensionality shifts from units of input (a) to units of Variable Cost $(h_a a)$. Rotated 180° and flipped over, the tp_a curve of the previous diagram becomes the Total Variable Cost V curve in the upper panel. The mp_a curve of the previous diagram becomes the Marginal Cost MC curve and the ap_a curve becomes the Average Variable Cost AVC curve in the lower panel.

tion is visible. Specifically, the MC and AC curves of Figure 11.2 look like upside-down versions of the mp and ap curves of Figure 11.1. Mathematically, the connection between Marginal Cost MC and Marginal Product mp_a is:

$$(11.6) \qquad MC \equiv \frac{\Delta C}{\Delta q} \equiv \frac{h_a \Delta a}{\Delta q} \equiv \frac{h_a}{\Delta q / \Delta a} \equiv \frac{h_a}{mp_a}$$

Since the hire-price h_a is assumed constant, this equation tells us that Marginal Cost moves inversely to Marginal Product. In particular, *rising* Marginal Cost corresponds to *diminishing* Marginal Product (diminishing marginal returns to employing factor A).

A corresponding inverse relationship holds between Average Product ap_a and Average Variable Cost $AVC \equiv V/q$:

$$(11.7) \qquad AVC \equiv \frac{V}{q} \equiv \frac{h_a a}{q} \equiv \frac{h_a}{q/a} \equiv \frac{h_a}{ap_a}$$

Because of the fixed cost term F, a slightly more complicated relation connects Average Cost AC and Average Product ap_a:

$$(11.8) \qquad AC \equiv \frac{C}{a} \equiv \frac{F + h_a a}{q} \equiv \frac{F}{q} + \frac{h_a}{ap_a}$$

Exercise 11.2: Suppose that the firm's short-run production function (Equation [11.2]) is $q = 2\sqrt{a}$. This of course is also the Total Product function tp_a. (a) For hire-price $h_a = 4$ and fixed cost $F = 50$, find the Total Variable Cost function V and the Total Cost function C. (b) Relate Average Variable Cost AVC to Average Product ap_a. (c) Relate Marginal Cost MC to Marginal Product mp_a.

Answer: (a) The "inverted" function (Equation [11.4]) is: $a = q^2/4$. Then $V \equiv h_a a = 4a = q^2$. And $C \equiv F + V = 50 + q^2$. (b) $AVC \equiv V/q = q^2/q = q$. And $ap_a \equiv tp_a/a = 2\sqrt{a}/a = 2/\sqrt{a}$. Equation (11.7) tells us that $AVC \equiv h_a/ap_a$, which can be verified as follows: $h_a/ap_a = 4/(2/\sqrt{a}) = 2\sqrt{a} = q = AVC$. (c) By calculus or tabulation, Marginal Cost can be found to be $MC = 2q$. Similarly, Marginal Product is $mp_a = 1/\sqrt{a}$. Equation (11.6) tells us that $MC \equiv h_a/mp_a$, which we can verify: $h_a/mp_a = 4\sqrt{a} = 2q = MC$.

Having seen how the shape assumed in Chapter 6 for the firm's cost function depends upon the underlying production function, we now return to the main business of this chapter—demand for the services of factors of production.

11.A.3 □ The Firm's Demand for Factor Services

For a price-taking firm in the factor market, the horizontal line in Figure 11.3 drawn at the level of the hire-price h_a can be regarded as the *factor supply curve* s_a. Denoting the cost of hiring factor A as $C_a \equiv h_a a$, where a is the quantity of factor A employed by the firm, this supply curve can be interpreted as a curve of *Average Factor Cost* ($afc_a \equiv C_a/a$). And, since the price per unit is constant, it is also a curve of *Marginal Factor Cost* ($mfc_a \equiv \Delta C_a/\Delta a$).

To determine its optimal (profit-maximizing) employment of factor A, the firm must balance the *returns* from hiring A against the hire-price h_a. Two elements are involved in calculating these returns: (1) the *physical productivity* of A as an input to production, and (2) the *revenue* gained from the units of commodity produced.

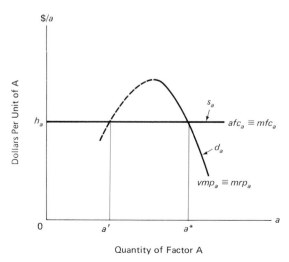

FIGURE 11.3 **Optimal Factor Employment, Price-Taking Firm in Both Factor Market and Product Market.** The horizontal line, showing the factor supply curve s_a to the price-taking firm at hire-price h_a, is the curve of Average Factor Cost (afc_a) and also of Marginal Factor Cost (mfc_a). If the firm is a price-taker in the product market as well, the Value of the Marginal Product (vmp_a) curve and the Marginal Revenue Product (mrp_a) curve coincide. The firm's demand curve d_a for factor A is then the downward-sloping branch of the $vmp_a \equiv mrp_a$ curve.

So far as physical productivity is concerned, only *Marginal* Product will be relevant to the firm's decision. However great the contribution to *Total* Product may have been for earlier units of factor, only the incremental yield from an additional unit will be considered in hiring that last unit. Thus, the Marginal Product mp_a curve, as in the lower panel of Figure 11.1, pictures the physical productivity element.

In dealing with the revenue element, by similar reasoning it is only the *Marginal* Revenue that matters. And in the competitive case where the firm is a price-taker in the product market, the increment to revenue from sale of one more unit of product is simply the given product price P. Valuing the factor's physical productivity at this price P leads to the concept called *Value of the Marginal Product* of factor A.

> DEFINITION: Value of the Marginal Product vmp_a equals product price P times physical Marginal Product mp_a.

(11.9)
$$vmp_a \equiv P(mp_a)$$

Since P is assumed constant, the curve showing vmp_a in Figure 11.3 will have the same graphical shape as the mp_a curve in the lower panel of Figure 11.1. The only difference is in the vertical scale, which was output per unit of input (q/a) in Figure 11.1 but becomes dollars per unit of input ($\$/a$) in Figure 11.3. Geometrically, the vertical scale of mp_a is "stretched" by the multiple P.

Turning to the employment decision, whenever vmp_a exceeds the price h_a it will surely pay the firm to employ an additional unit of A. And when $Vmp_a < h_a$, the firm would do better hiring less of A. Thus, the optimum condition for employment of factor A by a price-taking firm can be expressed as:

(11.10)
$$vmp_a = h_a$$

It so happens that this equality is satisfied at the two different employment levels a' and $a*$ in Figure 11.3. So something more is needed to specify the optimum employment. A secondary condition for an optimum is that the vmp_a curve be *falling* relative to the horizontal $afc_a \equiv mfc_a$ curve,[5] and this holds only at $a*$ in the diagram.[6] In terms of economic logic, to employ only a' units of A would be to

---

[5] This condition corresponds to the technical qualification (see Chapter 6) that the output optimum for the firm occurs at $MC = MR$ provided that the MC curve cuts MR *from below*. Here the optimum occurs when vmp_a cuts mfc_a *from above*.

[6] *Mathematical Footnote:* The firm chooses the amount of A to maximize profit $\Pi \equiv R - C \equiv Pq - h_a a - F$ (where F stands for fixed costs representing expenditures on factors other than A). Differentiating Π and setting the derivative equal to zero, we have a *first-order* condition:

$$P\frac{dq}{da} = h_a \quad \text{or} \quad P(mp_a) \equiv vmp_a = h_a$$

This corresponds to Equation (11.10). Taking the second derivative of Π, the *second-order* condition for a maximum is:

$$P\frac{d^2q}{da^2} < 0 \quad \text{or} \quad \text{(since } P \text{ is a positive constant)} \quad \frac{d^2q}{da^2} < 0$$

This means that Marginal Product mp_a (and so the curve vmp_a) must be *falling* to have a profit maximum.

forego the profitable range where the return from hiring an additional unit of the factor (vmp_a) exceeds the cost (h_a).

The conclusion, therefore, is that for a price-taking firm the demand curve for factor A is represented by the *downward-sloping range* along the vmp_a curve.

Exercise 11.3: Suppose the firm's Total Product function is $q = 2\sqrt{a}$ as in Exercise 11.2. Let the price of the product be $P = 60$, and the factor hire-price be $h_a = 4$. (a) Find the vmp_a curve, and the optimal factor employment a^*. (b) What is the associated output q^*? (c) What is the firm's demand curve for factor A?

Answer: (a) We saw above that, for this tp_a function, Marginal Product is $mp_a = 1/\sqrt{a}$. Thus, $vmp_a \equiv P(mp_a) = 60/\sqrt{a}$. To find the optimal factor employment set $vmp_a = h_a$, or $60/\sqrt{a} = 4$, which implies $a^* = 225$. (b) The associated output is $q^* = 2\sqrt{a^*} = 30$. (c) Since the vmp_a curve here is downward-sloping throughout, the demand curve is identical with the vmp_a curve. The demand-curve equation is $h_a = 60/\sqrt{a}$.

Now suppose the firm employing factor A, while still a price-taker in the *factor market*, is no longer a price-taker (now has monopoly power) in the *product market*. As a result, the firm's returns from increased factor employment will be adversely affected by the fact that product price P falls as more output is produced. This is pictured in Figure 11.4. For a monopolist firm, the return on the margin from the employment of an additional unit of factor A is not the *value* of the physical Marginal Product but the *revenue increment* achievable by sale of that Marginal Product. This leads to the concept known as *Marginal Revenue Product* of factor A, denoted mrp_a:

(11.11) $$mrp_a \equiv MR(mp_a)$$

DEFINITION: Marginal Revenue Product mrp_a equals Marginal Revenue MR times physical Marginal Product mp_a.

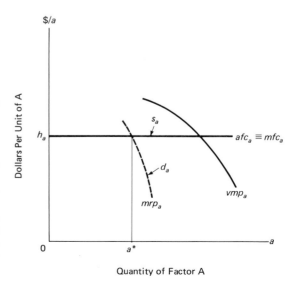

FIGURE 11.4 Optimal Factor Employment: Monopolist in Product Market. The firm is a price-taker or competitive purchaser in the factor market, as indicated by the horizontal supply curve s_a at the level of the going hire-price h_a. But here the firm has monopoly power in the product market. Since at any output the product price P exceeds Marginal Revenue MR, the curve of vmp_a (Value of the Marginal Product) will lie above the mrp_a (Marginal Revenue Product) curve. The firm's optimum is at the intersection of s_a and mrp_a, leading to employment a^* of factor A. The downward-sloping branch of the mrp_a curve is also the firm's demand curve for factor A.

Returning to the competitive (price-taker) firm in the product market (Figure 11.3), we know that for such a firm Marginal Revenue MR and price P are constant and equal to each other. It follows immediately that the vmp_a and the mrp_a curves are identical *for a competitive firm* in the product market. (This was indicated by the labeling $vmp_a \equiv mrp_a$ in Figure 11.3.) For a firm with monopoly power in the product market, on the other hand, Marginal Revenue MR and product price P both decrease as output increases and furthermore the MR curve falls faster than the demand or Average Revenue curve. So, for a monopoly firm, the mrp_a curve must lie below the vmp_a curve, as in Figure 11.4. The optimal factor employment $a*$ for the firm with monopoly power in the product market is determined in this diagram as the intersection of the mrp_a curve with the horizontal factor supply curve $s_a \equiv afc_a \equiv mfc_a$.[7] It follows that the monopoly firm's demand curve d_a for factor A is given by the mrp_a curve rather than by the vmp_a curve.

Exercise 11.4: Using the same Total Product function as before, $q = 2\sqrt{a}$, and recalling that Marginal Product is $mp_a = 1/\sqrt{a}$, assume now that the firm has monopoly power—and specifically, that it faces the downward-sloping demand curve $P = 90 - q$. Let the hire-price be $h_a = 4$ as before. (a) Find the vmp_a and mrp_a functions, and verify that mrp_a lies below vmp_a. (b) What is the optimal factor employment $a*$ and associated output $q*$? (c) What is the monopoly firm's demand curve for factor A? (d) Compare the solutions with those of Exercise 11.3.

Answer: (a) As before, $vmp_a \equiv P(mp_a)$, but now P is itself a function of output q and therefore of input a. Thus, $vmp_a = (90 - q)(1/\sqrt{a}) = (90 - 2\sqrt{a})(1/\sqrt{a}) = 90/\sqrt{a} - 2$. Since the product demand curve $P = 90 - q$ is linear, we know that Marginal Revenue falls twice as fast as price. So $MR = 90 - 2q$. Then $mrp_a = 90/\sqrt{a} - 4$, which tells us that mrp_a is always less than vmp_a. (b) Setting $mrp_a = h_a$ we have $90/\sqrt{a} - 4 = 4$, which implies $\sqrt{a} = 90/8 = 11.25$ or $a* = 126.56$. The associated output is $q* = 22.5$. (c) Since the mrp_a curve is everywhere downward-sloping, the demand curve coincides with it. The demand-curve equation is $90/\sqrt{a} - 4 = h_a$. (d) The firm here could produce 30 units of output and sell them at the market price $P = 60$, as did the price-taking firm of Exercise 11.3. But, because of its monopoly power, it produces only 22.5 units of output (and sells them at the higher price $P* = 90 - q* = 67.5$). Correspondingly, it employs fewer units of factor A (126.56 instead of 225).

The Factor Employment Condition that holds for *both* monopolist and pure competitor in the product market is:

		Factor Employment Condition,
(11.12)	$mrp_a = h_a$	Price-Taking Firm
		in Factor Market

---

[7] *Mathematical Footnote*: The firm is maximizing $\Pi = R - C = Pq - h_a a - F$ as before, but now recognizes that P is a decreasing function of output q—and so, indirectly, of input a. Differentiating and setting equal to zero, the first-order condition is:

$$P\frac{dq}{dq} + q\frac{dP}{dq}\frac{dq}{da} = h_a \quad \text{or} \quad \left(P + q\frac{dP}{dq}\right)\frac{dq}{da} = h_a$$

The element in parentheses is Marginal Revenue. So the condition can be expressed as:

$$MR(mp_a) \equiv mrp_a = h_a$$

This covers also the case of the competitive firm where vmp_a and mrp_a are identical, so that (11.12) reduces to Equation (11.10). Again, we have as a technical qualification that the mrp_a curve must cut the horizontal factor supply curve from *above*.

CONCLUSION: For a firm facing a given hire-price h_a, the optimal employment of factor A occurs when $mrp_a = h_a$ (in the downward-sloping range of the mrp_a curve). The curve of Marginal Revenue Product mrp_a is (in its downward-sloping range) therefore the firm's demand curve for A.[8] In Figure 11.3, picturing a competitive firm in the product market, the factor demand curve d_a coincides with the curve of $vmp_a \equiv mrp_a$. In Figure 11.4, for a monopolist in the product market, the factor demand curve d_a coincides with mrp_a (and *not* with vmp_a).

The separate treatments of the firm's *output* decision in Chapters 6 and 8 (for the competitive and monopolist firm, respectively) and of the *factor-employment* decision in this chapter might suggest that these are two distinct choices. But the two decisions are connected. Having made the factor-employment decision, the firm's output is determined by the production function. And, so long as we are dealing with a *single* variable factor, the converse is also true. Choosing output necessarily determines factor employment.[9]

That the output decision and the factor-employment decision imply each other can be shown by using the logical connection between Marginal Cost MC and Marginal Product mp_a derived above:

$$(11.13) \qquad\qquad MC \equiv \frac{h_a}{mp_a}$$

Dividing both sides by Marginal Revenue MR, we have:

$$(11.14) \qquad\qquad \frac{MC}{MR} \equiv \frac{h_a}{MR\,(mp_a)} \equiv \frac{h_a}{mrp_a}$$

So when the firm satisfies the Factor Employment Condition (11.12), $h_a = mrp_a$, it necessarily also satisfies $MC = MR$—which is the general Maximum-Profit condition of Chapter 8. The converse also holds, of course.

Exercise 11.5: For Exercises 11.3 and 11.4, verify that the condition for optimal input $(mrp_a = h_a)$ also implies optimal output $(MR = MC)$.

Answer: We saw in Exercise 11.2 that if $h_a = 4$ and Marginal Product is $mp_a = 1\sqrt{a}$, then Marginal Cost is $MC = 2q$. For a price-taking firm with $P = 60$, the Maximum-Profit Con-

---

[8] A technical qualification: Strictly speaking, this holds only for that portion of the downward-sloping range where the total expenditure $C_a \equiv h_a a$ on the variable factor A is less than Total Revenue R.

[9] With several variable factors, however, the determination of output still leaves a range of freedom for selection of the best resource combination to produce that output. This topic will be taken up in the next section.

dition $MC = MR \equiv P$ says that $2q = 60$, or $q^* = 30$—which confirms the result obtained in Exercise 11.3 using the Factor Employment Condition $vmp_a = mrp_a = h_a$. For a monopolist firm facing the demand curve $P = 90 - q$, the Maximum-Profit Condition $MC = MR$ becomes $2q = 90 - 2q$, or $q^* = 22.5$—which confirms the result in Exercise 11.4.

*11.B
SEVERAL VARIABLE FACTORS

When only one factor is variable, the firm is acting in the "short run"—whereas in the "long run," all factors become variable. Having more than one variable factor complicates the analysis of factor demand. To keep things as simple as possible let us assume here just two variable factors, A and B.

11.B.1 □ The Production Function

In some ways, a firm that is hiring factors is like an individual choosing consumption goods and services. Just as consumption goods can be regarded as generating *utility*, so factors generate *product*. If there are just two variable factors, the production function (11.1) can be written:

(11.15) $$q = F(a, b)$$

Diagrammatically, the production function is the three-dimensional "output hill" of Figure 11.5, which shows product quantity q as a function of the input amounts a and b. In contrast with the "utility hill" picture of Chapter 3, there is no "cardinal versus ordinal" problem here, since quantity has a natural cardinal (numerical) scale. This means that in using a two-dimensional "contour map" as in Figure 11.6, a definite numerical quantity q label can be attached to each contour or *isoquant*. We are not restricted, as we were in the case of utility, to merely "ordinal" comparisons of higher and lower.

It is important to distinguish between: (1) the effects of changing the employment of a *single* factor, versus (2) the effects of proportionate changes in *all* factors together (i.e., of a change in *scale*).

Figure 11.7 illustrates the effect of changing either factor A or factor B separately. The different curves drawn along the surface of the output hill show how output quantity q changes as one input increases while holding the other input constant. These can be regarded as *Total Product curves*, like the tp_a curve defined for a single variable factor A in the previous section. But there are now Total Product curves for each of the two factors—tp_a and tp_b. Indeed, for each factor there is a family of such curves, since in general both tp_a and tp_b will depend also upon the amount of the *other* factor. In the diagram the Total Product curves for factor A are given labels like tp_a $(b = b_0)$ and tp_a $(b = b_1)$. Each such curve shows Total Product q for varying inputs of factor A, factor B held constant—but for the

---

*Marked sections, beginning with a single asterisk and ending with a double asterisk, may contain somewhat more difficult or advanced material and can be omitted without appreciable loss of continuity.

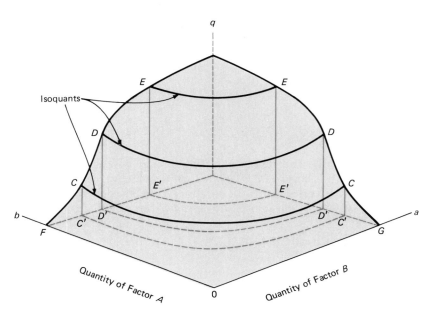

FIGURE 11.5 Output as a Function of Two Inputs. Output q, measured vertically, is shown as a function of input quantities a and b. CC, DD, and EE are contours of equal height (output) along the three-dimensional surface. The curves $C'C'$, $D'D'$, and $E'E'$ are the projections of these contours in the base plane.

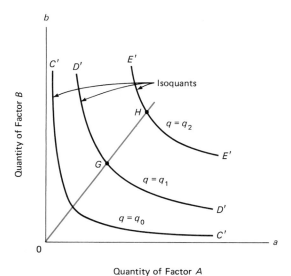

FIGURE 11.6 Isoquants of Output. The projections $C'C'$, $D'D'$, and $E'E'$ in the base plane of the previous diagram are shown here as isoquants (curves of equal output) in a contour map, without the overlying vertical dimension. Each isoquant is associated with a definite quantity of output (q_0, q_1, or q_2).

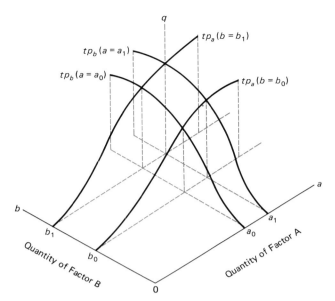

FIGURE 11.7 Total Product Functions. Here Total Product curves are drawn along an output hill. The Total Product curves for factor A, designated tp_a, hold constant the amount of the other factor B. However, the heights of the tp_a curves depend upon the specific constant values assumed for b in each case, and similarly the tp_b curves depend on the values assumed for a.

lower curve B is held constant at $b = b_0$ while for the upper curve B is constant at $b = b_1$. Similarly for the tp_b curves. Corresponding to each Total Product curve in Figure 11.7, it would be possible to construct an Average Product curve and Marginal Product[10] curve as in Figure 11.1.

In Figure 11.8 the two families of Total Product curves are shown in a different way. Here each single curve has a form similar to the tp_a curve of Figure 11.1, as dictated by the Law of Diminishing Returns. In Panel (a) the entire tp_a curve is shown as shifting upward as quantities on the other factor B rise from b_0 to b_1 to b_2, and similarly for the other factor in Panel (b). Such an upward shift must occur, if the "other" factor is productive.

Now let us consider changing all factors proportionately instead of just one at a time. In Figure 11.6 this would mean moving along a ray out of the origin from, say, point G to point H. In Figure 11.5 the same change would correspond to moving upward in a fixed direction along the surface of the output hill. Starting from the origin, the output hill may be growing steeper at first (increasing returns to scale). But, we will usually assume, the Law of Diminishing Returns eventually applies even when all factors are increased proportionately. Thus, the hill eventually flattens out.[11]

---

[10] *Mathematical Footnote*: With two or more variable factors, the Marginal Product of any single factor such as A becomes a *partial* derivative:

$$mp_a \equiv \lim_{\Delta a \to 0} \frac{F(a + \Delta a, b) - F(a, b)}{\Delta a} \equiv \frac{\partial q}{\partial a}$$

[11] *Mathematical Footnote*: It can be shown that; even with constant or increasing returns to scale, the separate tp_a and tp_b curves as in Figure 11.8 can have the normal diminishing-returns shape. An example is the production function $q = a^{.6}b^{.7}$. It can be verified here that doubling both a and b *more than doubles* q, so there are increasing returns to scale. But there are diminishing returns to factor A alone, since the Marginal Product $mp_a \equiv \partial q/\partial a = .6b^{.7}/a^{.4}$ decreases as a increases. (A similar analysis holds for factor B.)

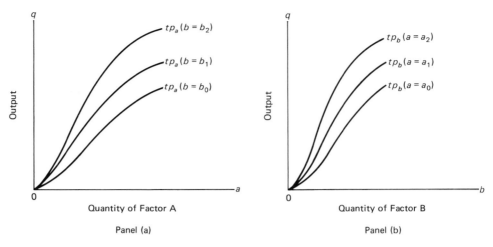

FIGURE 11.8 **Families of Total Product Curves.** Here tp_a curves like those drawn along the output hill of the previous diagram are shown on q, a axes in Panel (a); the tp_b curves are similarly shown on q, b axes in Panel (b).

EXAMPLE 11.2
Missouri Corn

An agricultural experiment in Missouri reported by J. Ambrosius studied how corn yield (bushels per acre) changed as two inputs (*number of plants* per acre and *pounds of nitrogen* per acre) were varied. Reading horizontally across any single row, the table shows selected points on the Total Product curve tp_a for plants per acre—with b, nitrogen input per acre, held constant along the row. Reading vertically down any column, points are shown on the tp_b curve for nitrogen input b—holding fixed the number of plants per acre, a. As expected, the entire tp_a curve tends to shift upward as b increases, and the tp_b curve tends to shift upward as a increases.

Bushels of Corn per Acre (Q)

NITROGEN PER ACRE (B)	NUMBER OF PLANTS PER ACRE (A)				
	9,000	12,000	15,000	18,000	21,000
0	50.6	54.2	53.5	48.5	39.2
50	78.7	85.9	88.8	87.5	81.9
100	94.4	105.3	111.9	114.2	112.2
150	97.8	112.4	122.6	128.6	130.3
200	88.9	107.1	121.0	130.6	135.9

Source: John Ambrosius, "The Effects of Experimental Size upon Optimum Rates of Nitrogen and Stand for Corn in Missouri," (1964), quoted in J. P. Doll, V. J. Rhodes, and J. G. West, *Economics of Agricultural Production, Markets, and Policy* (Homewood, Ill.: Richard D. Irwin, 1968), p. 89.

Diminishing returns apply here even to *proportionate variation* in both factors together. For example, a doubling of both inputs from the combination

$a_0 = 9000$, $b_0 = 50$ to the combination $a_1 = 18,000$, $b_1 = 100$ raises corn output from 78.7 only to 114.2.

The "Missouri Corn" example suggests a possible rationale for there being diminishing returns to scale (i.e., to proportionate variation of factors). Nitrogen and number of plants as inputs were varied in the experiment, but other factors—notably, the number of acres—were held constant. Something like this will always be the case. In the real world it will not generally be possible to vary literally *all* inputs. So the condition for the Law of Diminishing Returns to hold, that there be at least one fixed factor, will essentially always apply.

EXAMPLE 11.3
Pigs

The agricultural economist E. O. Heady[a] reported an experiment that involved varying the amounts of corn (high in carbohydrate content) and soybean oil meal (high in protein content) fed to young pigs. The experiment was conducted on 302 pigs, carried from a weaning weight of 34 pounds to a market weight of around 250 pounds. The output measure was weight gain.

It was found that rather different production functions were appropriate for different weight ranges, since the effects of inputs of carbohydrate versus protein upon weight gain tended to be different for younger (smaller) versus older (larger) pigs. The results obtained were as follows, where G indicates weight gain, P is input of soybean oilmeal (protein), and C is input of corn (carbohydrate)—all measured in pounds per pig.

$$G = 1.60 P^{.30} C^{.53}, \text{ for weights from 34 to 75 pounds}$$

$$G = 0.71 P^{.14} C^{.77}, \text{ for weights from 75 to 150 pounds}$$

$$G = 0.46 P^{.09} C^{.86}, \text{ for weights from 150 to 250 pounds}$$

The exponents of P and C in the different functions indicate, as is reasonable, that weight gain in young pigs responds relatively more to protein input while weight gain in older pigs responds more to carbohydrates.

COMMENT: It can be shown mathematically that, in functions of this form, there would be increasing returns to scale (more than proportionate effect upon output for proportionate variation of both inputs) if the *sum* of the exponents exceeds unity. Constant returns to scale hold if the sum of exponents exactly equals unity, and decreasing returns to scale if the sum falls short of unity. Evidently, all three production functions here show decreasing returns to scale.

[a] E. O. Heady, "An Econometric Investigation of the Technology of Agricultural Production Functions," *Econometrica*, v. 25 (Apr. 1957).

11.B.2 □ The Factor-Employment Decision: Geometry

Firms face two related production decisions: (1) how much to produce, and (2) how to produce it. The question of how much to produce was answered in Chapter 6: the profit-maximizing firm will set Marginal Cost equal to Marginal Revenue. In this part of the chapter we answer the question of how to produce—that is, how much of different factors to employ. Naturally, the answer to one question will affect the other.

Suppose the level of Total Cost is $100. Let the hire-price of factor A be h_a = $1 and of factor B be h_b = $2. If the firm were to employ only one factor it could afford 100 units of factor A or 50 units of factor B. The different combinations of factors A and B that $100 could buy are pictured by the *isocost* line labeled C' in Figure 11.9, with intercept C'/h_a on the horizontal axis and C'/h_b on the vertical axis.

> *DEFINITION:* An *isocost* is a curve showing all the combinations of two factors that can be hired at a given level of cost. When the hire-prices h_a and h_b are constant, the isocost will be a straight line.

In Figure 11.9 the isocost corresponds to a specific cost level $C' = h_a a + h_b b$. A family of output isoquants $q°, q', q'', \ldots$ are also shown in the diagram. Given the isocost C', the highest isoquant that can be reached is q'. The firm will maximize profit by hiring the input combination (a', b'). This analysis determines the best factor proportions at cost C' or output q'.

Figure 11.9 resembles the consumer's optimum diagrams of Chapter 4. Instead of indifference curves we have isoquants, and instead of a budget line we have an isocost. But there is one important difference. A consumer has only a single budget line, determined by his income. But a firm is not forced to operate along a single isocost. A firm *decides* how much cost to incur by setting $MC = MR$.

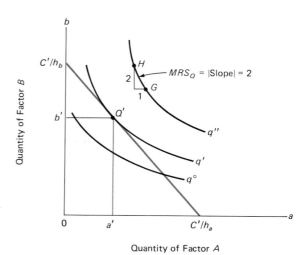

FIGURE 11.9 Optimal Factor Balance. At a given cost level $C' = h_a a + h_b b$, the best factor employments are a' and b' at point Q'—the tangency of the isocost line C' with the highest attainable output contour q'.

The production decision involves choosing the best isocost (the best scale of output) as well as the best factor proportions along that isocost.

Figure 11.10 pictures a family of isocosts $C^o, C', C'', \ldots$, as well as a family of production contours (isoquants) $q^o, q', q'', \ldots$. All the isocosts have the same slope. The curve drawn through the tangency points is called the Scale Expansion Path (SEP). It shows the best combination of inputs at each level of cost.

The firm will operate *somewhere* on the Scale Expansion Path—otherwise production would be inefficient. But exactly where? To answer this we need to know the cost and revenue functions. These can both be derived from the Scale Expansion Path, since we know also the numerical magnitudes associated with each isocost and each isoquant. In the diagram, for example, output q^o can be produced at a cost of C^o, output q' at a cost of C', and output q'' at a cost of C''. When these data are plotted on $(q, \$)$ axes the result is a Total Cost curve as in Figure 11.11. To construct the Total Revenue curve we need corresponding data for q and R. But since $R \equiv Pq$, the only additional information required is the demand function, which relates price to quantity. Multiplying each quantity by the demand price determines the Total Revenue R at each output q.[12] Putting Total Cost and Total Revenue together, we see in Figure 11.11 that profit is maximized at output q^*. Given this output, the Scale Expansion Path of Figure 11.10 tells us the best combination of inputs a^* and b^* to use in producing it.

11.B.3 □ The Factor-Employment Decision: Analysis

We will now derive some propositions about the firm's hiring decisions that are equivalent to the geometrical development above. Assuming diminishing mar-

---

[12] For a price-taking firm, of course, P is a constant and the revenue function $R \equiv Pq$ in Figure 11.11 would be a ray out of the origin.

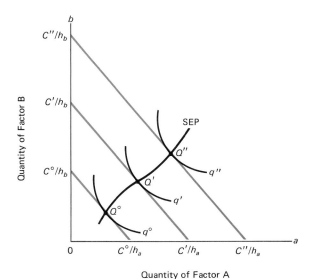

FIGURE 11.10 Scale Expansion Path. Along any isocost line, the tangency with an output isoquant represents the largest output attainable at that cost. Each such tangency shows the best factor proportions for that level of cost and output. The Scale Expansion Path (SEP) connects all these tangency positions.

Quantity of Factor A

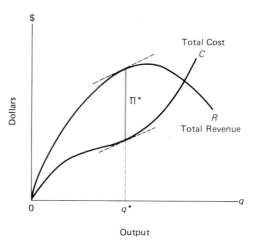

FIGURE 11.11 Total Revenue and Total Cost Functions.
Each point on the Scale Expansion Path of the previous diagram is associated with a particular level of cost C and output q. This information permits plotting the Total Cost curve C. Also, each level of output q is associated with a level of revenue $R \equiv Pq$, given the firm's demand function. This information permits plotting the Total Revenue curve R. The profit-maximizing output q* in this diagram also determines the firm's optimal factor employments a* and b* in the preceding diagram.

ginal productivity for each of the two factors, at any level of cost the firm will be at an (interior) optimum when the Factor Balance Equation holds.[13]

(11.16) $$\frac{mp_a}{h_a} = \frac{mp_b}{h_b}$$ Factor Balance Equation

That is, factor employments are properly balanced when the Marginal Products *per dollar* spent are equal for each factor employed.[14]

The Marginal Rate of Substitution in Production between factors A and B, MRS_Q, is defined as the amount of factor B which can be substituted for a small reduction of factor A without changing output q. Geometrically, this can be interpreted as the absolute slope along an isoquant. Thus:

---

[13] *Mathematical Footnote*: We can use again the "method of Lagrangian multipliers" to maximize output $q = F(a, b)$ subject to a given level of cost $C = h_a a + h_b b$.

$$\underset{(a, b, \lambda)}{\text{Max}}\, L = q + \lambda(h_a a + h_b b - C)$$

The first-order conditions are:

$$\frac{\partial q}{\partial a} + \lambda h_a = 0 \qquad \frac{\partial q}{\partial b} + \lambda h_b = 0, \quad \text{and} \quad h_a a + h_b b - C = 0$$

It follows that:

$$\frac{\partial q / \partial a}{h_a} = \frac{\partial q / \partial b}{h_b}$$

This is the Factor Balance Equation. (We omit discussion of the second-order conditions for a maximum.)

[14] If D is some third factor *not* actually being employed ($d = 0$) at current factor prices, its Marginal Product per dollar is related by an *inequality* condition to the others:

$$\frac{mp_a\,(a > 0)}{h_a} = \frac{mp_b\,(b > 0)}{h_b} > \frac{mp_d\,(d = 0)}{h_d}$$

For the optimal employment of D to be zero, its Marginal Product per dollar must be less than that of other factors, even for the very first unit of D.

$$(11.17) \qquad\qquad MRS_Q \equiv -\left.\frac{\Delta b}{\Delta a}\right|_q$$

In Chapter 4 we saw that (the absolute value of) the slope of an indifference curve could be regarded as the Marginal Rate of Substitution in Consumption MRS_C, where MRS_C is also equivalent to MU_x/MU_y (the ratio of Marginal Utilities). In production theory the corresponding idea is that the absolute slope of an *isoquant* is the Marginal Rate of Substitution in Production MRS_Q, which is equivalent to mp_a/mp_b (the ratio of Marginal Products).[15] Going back to Figure 11.9, suppose the firm is at point G and that $mp_a = 10$ and $mp_b = 5$. If we take away one unit of A, the firm will need 2 units of B to stay on the same isoquant at point H (since, on the margin, A is twice as productive as B). Thus the absolute slope of the chord connecting G and H is $2/1 = 2$. This equals the ratio of Marginal Products $mp_a/mp_b = 10/5 = 2$. For small changes, the absolute slope of the chord GH is approximately the same as the absolute slope of the isoquant, so we see that $mp_a/mp_b = MRS_Q$.

By similar reasoning, the Marginal Rate of Substitution in Exchange MRS_E is the absolute slope of the isocost, which is h_a/h_b. When the isocost and isoquant are tangent along the *SEP* in Figure 11.10, their slopes must be equal, so:

$$(11.18) \qquad\qquad MRS_Q = MRS_E$$

And this is also the same as saying:

$$mp_a/mp_b = h_a/h_b$$

So the tangency or equal-slopes condition (11.18) is equivalent to the Factor Balance Equation (11.16).

Exercise 11.6: A firm has the production function $q = a^{.5}b^{.5}$. It can be shown by calculus that the Marginal Product functions can then be written in the forms $mp_a = .5q/a$ and $mp_b = .5q/b$. The demand function is $P = 100 - q$. (Note that this firm has monopoly power in its market.) The factor prices are $h_a = 4$ and $h_b = 1$. (a) Find the equation of the Scale Expansion Path. (b) Derive the Total Cost and Total Revenue equations as functions of output q. (c) Find the profit-maximizing output q^*. (d) Find the associated factor employments a^* and b^*. (e) What is the magnitude of the maximized profit Π^*?

Answer: (a) The Factor Balance Equation can be written:

$$\frac{.5q/a}{4} = \frac{.5q/b}{1}$$

---

[15] *Mathematical Footnote:* Along any output isoquant, q is constant. Thus:

$$dq = \frac{\partial q}{\partial a}da + \frac{\partial q}{\partial b}db = 0$$

Then

$$-\frac{db}{da} = \frac{\partial q/\partial a}{\partial q/\partial b} \quad \text{or} \quad MRS_Q = \frac{mp_a}{mp_b}$$

From this it follows that $b = 4a$. This is the equation of the SEP. (b) Substituting into the production function equation, the latter can be written $q = a^{.5}(4a)^{.5} = 2a$. It follows that Total Cost $C = h_a a + h_b b = 4a + b = 8a = 4q$. (Notice that the cost function displays constant returns to scale.) As for Total Revenue, multiplying P in the demand equation times q leads to $R = 100q - q^2$. (c) The Marginal Cost associated with the cost function $C = 4q$ is of course $MC = 4$. The Marginal Revenue of the straight-line demand curve is $MR = 100 - 2q$. Setting $MC = MR$, the profit-maximizing output is $q^* = 48$. (d) Since $q = 2a$, then $a^* = 24$. And since $b = 4a$, then $b^* = 96$. (e) Total Cost is $4(48) = 192$. Total Revenue is $100(48) - 48^2 = 2496$. So profit is $\Pi^* = 2304$.

We now want to derive the firm's demand curves for factors A and B. First, note the following interpretation of the Factor Balance Equation:

$$(11.16') \qquad \frac{h_a}{mp_a} = \frac{h_b}{mp_b} = MC$$

That is, Marginal Cost $MC \equiv \Delta C / \Delta q$ equals the hire-price of factor A, $h_a \equiv \Delta C / \Delta a$, divided by its Marginal Product $mp_a \equiv \Delta q / \Delta a$. Similarly, of course, for factor B. When the firm is using the correct factor proportions as dictated by the Factor Balance Equation, it is equally costly to expand output by hiring a small extra amount of A, or of B, or any mixture of the two.[16]

Dividing through by Marginal Revenue MR, we have:

$$(11.19) \qquad \frac{MC}{MR} = \frac{h_a}{mrp_a} = \frac{h_b}{mrp_b}$$

So when a firm maximizes profit by setting $MC = MR$, it automatically satisfies the following Factor Employment Conditions:

$$(11.20) \qquad \begin{cases} mrp_a = h_a \\ \\ mrp_b = h_b \end{cases} \quad \begin{array}{l} \text{Factor Employment Conditions} \\ \text{(for Price-Taking Firm} \\ \text{in Factor Markets)} \end{array}$$

These equations correspond to Equation (11.12) which applied when there was only a single variable factor. But there is one important complication in the multi-factor case: the Marginal Product mp_a, and therefore the Marginal Revenue

---

[16] *Mathematical Footnote*: First, $dq = (\partial q / \partial a)da + (\partial q / \partial b)db$. Since $C = h_a a + h_b b$ then $dC = h_a da + h_b db$. So:

$$MC \equiv \frac{dC}{dq} = \frac{h_a da + h_b db}{(\partial q / \partial a)da + (\partial q / \partial b)db}$$

Since $h_a / (\partial q / \partial a) = h_b / (\partial q / \partial b)$ from the Factor Balance Equation, it follows algebraically that:

$$MC = \frac{h_a}{\partial q / \partial a} = \frac{h_b}{\partial q / \partial b}$$

Product mrp_a, may depend upon the employment of the other factor B—and similarly, of course, mp_b and mrp_b may depend upon the amount of factor A.[17]

Two factors are said to be *complementary* if increased employment of one raises the Marginal Product of the other. Executives and secretaries, ships and sailors, land and fertilizer are examples of complementary pairs. If one factor has no effect at all upon the marginal productivity of the other, the two are said to be *independent*. Handcraftsmen and mass-production machines might be such a pair. It may be that the handcraftsmen work entirely apart from the machines so that there is no interaction one way or the other between them. If increased use of one factor actually *reduces* Marginal Product of the other, the two are *anticomplementary*.[18] Inputs that are close substitutes for one another tend to be anticomplementary. An increase in employment of A naturally reduces its *own* Marginal Product mp_a (in the economically relevant range where the Law of Diminishing Marginal Returns applies), since A is a perfect substitute for itself. If resource B is a close substitute for A, increased employment of A will also reduce mp_b. Examples might be different grades of raw cotton for a textile firm, or male waiters versus female waitresses for a restaurant.[19]

Figure 11.12 shows two complementary factors A and B. The crucial point is that the mp_a curves shift *upward* as the amount of factor B increases from b_0 to b_1 to b_2; similarly, the mp_b curves move higher as A rises from a_0 to a_1 to a_2.

11.B.4 □ Shifts in Factor Prices: Substitution and Scale Effects

We saw in Chapter 4 that a change in the price of a good has a *substitution effect* and an *income effect* upon the consumer's purchases. Similarly, a change in the price of a factor has a *substitution effect* and a *scale effect* upon factor employment. If its hire-price h_a falls, factor A will be substituted for B even at the same level of output; this is the pure substitution effect. But the reduction in h_a will very likely also induce the firm to change its scale of production; this is the scale effect.

The substitution effect is shown in Figure 11.13. Q° represents an initial position on the Scale Expansion Path SEP°, at a tangency of an isocost C° and an isoquant q°. A fall in h_a lowers (flattens) the absolute slope h_a/h_b of the isocost line. The tangency therefore moves from Q° to Q'. The new Scale Expansion Path

---

[17] *Mathematical Footnote*: If $q = F(a, b)$, the Marginal Products or partial derivatives $\partial q/\partial a$ and $\partial q/\partial b$ will in general both be functions of a and b. Geometrically, in Figure 11.7 we see that the slope along the Total Product curves tp_a in the a-direction ($\partial q/\partial a$) varies not only as a increases but also from one curve to the next as b increases. And similarly for the slope along the tp_b curves ($\partial q/\partial b$).

[18] *Mathematical Footnote*: The presence or absence of complementarity corresponds to the sign of the second cross-derivative of the production function. In the normal *complementary* case, $\partial(\partial q/\partial a)/\partial b \equiv \partial^2 q/\partial a\partial b$ is positive. *Independence* corresponds to a zero cross-derivative, and *anticomplementarity* to a negative cross-derivative.

[19] Anticomplementarity should be distinguished from what might be called *interference*, where the two factors actually hamper each other. Thus, in some cases, hiring more females might actually reduce output of male workers and vice versa. Anticomplementarity means that employing more A reduces the *Marginal* Product of B; with interference, employing more A reduces the *Total* Product of factor B. A firm would employ only one of two interfering factors, to the exclusion of the other. But simultaneous employment of anticomplementary factors is not at all absurd.

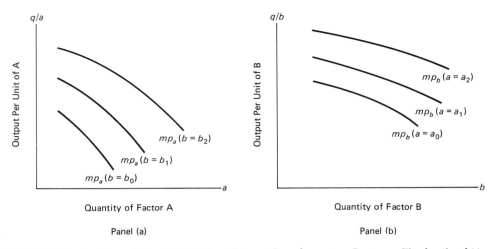

FIGURE 11.12 Families of Marginal Product Curves: Complementary Factors. The family of Marginal Product curves mp_a in Panel (a) is derived from the corresponding family of Total Product curves tp_a in Panel (a) of Figure 11.8. The mp_b curves in Panel (b) correspond similarly to the tp_b curves in Panel (b) of Figure 11.8. Only the ranges where the curves have negative slope (where the Marginal Product of each factor is a decreasing function of its own quantity) are illustrated here. The curves also shift upward as the quantity of the *other* factor increases (the Marginal Product of each factor is an increasing function of the quantity of the other input). This illustrates the normal case of complementarity.

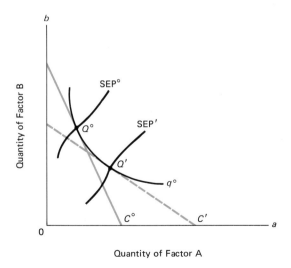

FIGURE 11.13 Factor Substitution Effect. At initial hire-prices h_a° and h_b° a Scale Expansion Path (SEP°) connects all points of tangency between isocosts C and isoquants q. $C°$ and $q°$ are such a pair. If h_a falls from h_a° to h_a', the new isocosts have flatter slope, like C'. The changed price ratio h_a'/h_b' determines a new Scale Expansion Path SEP'. From an initial position $Q°$, the *factor substitution effect* is the increased employment of A due to moving to a new tangency at Q' along the original isoquant $q°$.

SEP' will therefore be displaced to the right, as indicated. The firm will tend to shift employment *toward the relatively cheapened factor A*.

EXAMPLE 11.4
Factor Prices and Ocean Shipping

Newly constructed ships used by Japanese, continental European, and British shippers during the years 1952 to 1955 were examined by W. Y. Oi to compare the relative factor proportions employed. In ocean shipping the important factors of production may be divided into: (1) "capital" (lease cost of vessel, or annualized construction expenses, plus ship maintenance), (2) fuel, and (3) labor (wages plus subsistence at sea). In the period studied, fuel prices were very similar for all shippers. So the essential element was the ratio of labor cost versus capital cost. Labor costs were relatively cheapest for the Japanese shippers and most expensive for the continental Europeans, with the British in between.

One consequence of relatively high labor cost (or, equivalently, relatively low capital cost) is the employment of ships with a high designed speed. Faster ships are costlier to construct and maintain, but permit a saving of labor time per voyage. The table indicates that, as anticipated, the Japanese chose ships with lowest and the continental Europeans with highest designed speed.

Median Design Speed (knots)

	Small Ships (3000–9000 dwt)	Large Ships (Over 9000 dwt)
Japanese shippers	11.46	13.81
British shippers	14.00	14.04
European shippers	14.86	14.93

Source: W. Y. Oi, "The Cost of Ocean Shipping," in A. R. Ferguson et al., eds., *The Economic Value of the United States Merchant Marine* (Evanston, Ill.: The Transportation Center at Northwestern University, 1961), p. 160.

The scale effect is somewhat trickier. In Figure 11.14, as h_a falls from h_a^o to h_a', the isocost rotates outward from C^o to C''. The new tangency will necessarily be on a higher output isoquant q''. Thus, *at any given cost* it will be optimal for the firm to produce more output after a cheapening of a factor.

Figures 11.13 and 11.14 together show that if *output* is held constant after hire-price h_a falls, then cost will be less—while if *cost* is held constant, then output will be greater. So it seems likely that a fall in factor price would lead to an expansion of the optimum scale of output. But this does not *necessarily* follow. It is true that cheapening of any factor will always lower the Total Cost curve. But optimal output is determined by the relation between *Marginal* Cost and *Marginal* Revenue ($MC = MR$)—that is, between the *slopes* of the Total Cost and Total Revenue curves. Panel (a) in Figure 11.15 shows a normal situation in which the lowering of the Total Cost curve from TC^o to TC' does lead to an expansion of optimal output from q^o to q'. Panel (b) shows the more surprising case in which the lower-

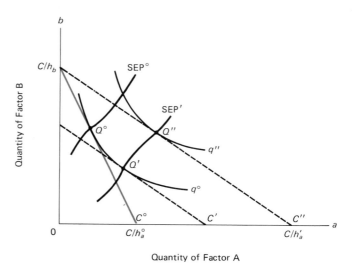

FIGURE 11.14 Cheapening of Factor A. As in the preceding diagram, $Q°$ is an initial factor combination and Q' a new combination achieved in response to a fall in hire-price h_a. As between $Q°$ and Q', output q is held constant. This diagram shows also the new position Q'' reached if Cost C is held constant instead of output q. The points Q' and Q'' are both on the new Scale Expansion Path SEP'.

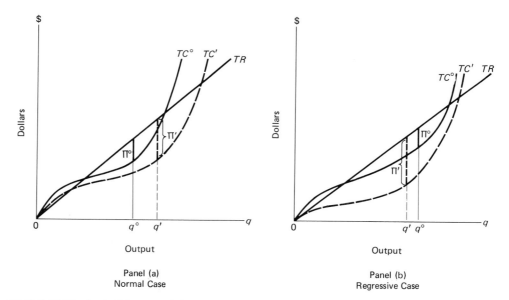

Panel (a)
Normal Case

Panel (b)
Regressive Case

FIGURE 11.15 Scale Effect. A fall in the hire-price h_a of any factor employed reduces Total Cost. So in both panels here the new TC' curve lies everywhere below the original $TC°$ curve. But profit $\Pi = TR - TC$ is greatest where Marginal Revenue (slope along the TR curve) equals Marginal Cost (slope along the TC curve). In the normal case shown in Panel (a), the TC' curve is not only lower than the $TC°$ curve at each output but also flatter—so Marginal Cost has also fallen everywhere. Then the new optimal output q' is greater than the previous $q°$. But in the "regressive" case of Panel (b), the TC' curve is lower but (over a portion of its range) *steeper* rather than flatter than $TC°$. In this range *Marginal Cost* is greater than before, and so the new optimal output q' is less than $q°$. But in either case, the new profit Π' is necessarily greater than the original profit $\Pi°$.

ing from $TC°$ to TC' is combined with a *steepening* of the slope (thus increasing the MC) in the relevant region, so that the new optimal output q' is less than $q°$.

In this latter case, A is called a "regressive" factor. Think of A as a factor particularly specialized to and useful for small-scale production, for example skilled craftsmen. If the price of skilled craftsmen falls, it may pay a firm to shift away from large-scale mass production toward small-scale craft methods of production, earning more profit with smaller output.

> CONCLUSION: A change in factor price leads to a substitution effect and a scale effect upon factor employment and firm output. The substitution effect is *always* in the normal direction: more of the now cheapened factor will be used. The scale effect of a fall in factor price is normally also to increase output, and of a rise in factor price to decrease output. But in the case of a "regressive" factor, the scale effect is reversed; cheapening of a factor *may* lead to smaller output.

11.B.5 ☐ The Firm's Demand for Factor Services

In the single-variable-factor situation, the firm's demand curve for the factor was given by the downward-sloping part of its Marginal Revenue Product curve *mrp*. However, with more than one factor, matters are more complicated.

To derive the firm's demand curve for factor A, suppose that at point G in Figure 11.16 the Factor Employment Conditions in Equations (11.20) are all met. At the initial hire prices $h_a°$ and $h_b°$, the firm hires $a°$ units of A and $b°$ units of factor B. Now let the hire-price of A fall from $h_a°$ to h_a'. If the quantity of the other factor B remained unchanged, the diagram indicates that the firm would want to employ $\hat{a}$ units of factor A—since that is where $mrp_a(b = b°) = h_a'$. But suppose factors A and B are complementary. If so, the increase from $a°$ to $\hat{a}$ is not the full adjustment. Increased use of factor A will increase the Marginal Product of factor B, so mrp_b shifts up. This leads to increased use of factor B, which makes factor A more productive, which shifts mrp_a up, and so on. This "reverberation" process must have a limit, however. There must be some increased employment of *both* factors that restores the equalities (11.20). The restored equalities can be expressed more explicitly as:

(11.20')
$$\begin{cases} mrp_a(b = b') = h_a' \\ mrp_b(a = a') = h_b° \end{cases}$$

Note that the hire-price of B is still at its original level; only the price of factor A has changed.

The upshot is that in Figure 11.16 the demand curve d_a goes through points G and K, not through G and L. So the firm's demand curve for factor A, when A and B are complementary, is flatter than the mrp_a curves.

If the factors are *independent* rather than *complementary* in production, the interaction effect disappears. A change in the hire-price of factor A will not affect the marginal productivity of the other factor B. The initial adjustment is the full

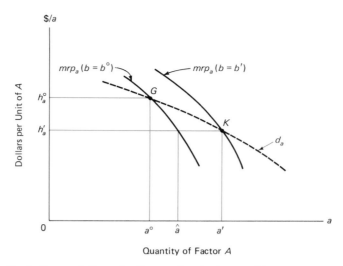

$/a

Dollars per Unit of A

Quantity of Factor A

FIGURE 11.16 Firm's Demand Curve for Factor A. At the initial hire-price h_a the Factor Employment Conditions (11.20) have been met by employments $a = a°$ and $b = b°$. Thus $mrp_a (b = b°)$ equals $h_a°$ at G—providing one point along the firm's demand curve for factor A. If the hire-price of A falls to h_a', increased employment of A in the amount $\hat{a}$ would be indicated by a movement along $mrp_a (b = b°)$. But this movement throws the employment condition for factor B out of equality, if there is any complementarity (or anticomplementarity) between A and B. Restoring the equality for factor B will then (regardless of whether the interaction is complementary or anticomplementary) raise the Marginal Product of factor A. The Factor Employment Condition can only be re-established at a point like K, where h_a' is set equal to $mrp_a (b = b')$—with b' representing the adjusted amount of the *other* factor. The firm's demand curve d_a for factor A is therefore flatter than the general slope of the mrp_a curves, wherever there is a complementary (or anticomplementary) interaction between the factors.

adjustment. The reason is that, in the case of productive *independence* between factors, each factor's family of *mrp* curves coalesces into a single *mrp* curve that is not affected by the employment of the other factor.

What about "anticomplementary" factors? You might think that if d_a is *flatter* than the mrp_a curves in the complementary case and is *the same* as the (unique) mrp_a curve in the case of independence, d_a would have to be steeper than the mrp_a curves in the anticomplementary case. *This is incorrect!* In the anticomplementary as in the normal complementary case, the firm's demand curve for factor is *flatter* than the *mrp* curves, as illustrated in Figure 11.16. [*Challenge to the student*: Verify this. In Figure 11.16, after the initial adjustment from $a°$ to $\hat{a}$, in the anticomplementary case do the mrp_b curves shift up or down? What is the direction of the effect upon the employment of B? Does that secondary effect shift the mrp_a curves up or down?]

CONCLUSION: Given complementarity or anticomplementarity between factors, the demand curve for any factor is flatter (more elastic) than the Marginal Revenue Product curves. One implication is that employment of a variable factor tends to be more sensitive to price changes in the *long run*, when the amounts of the "fixed" factors can be varied.

Another important result follows directly from this analysis: *factor demand curves always have negative slope.* That is, there can be no such thing as a "Giffen factor." A lower hire-price h_a cannot lead to smaller employment of A, since mp_a is negatively sloped and any interaction with factor B makes d_a flatter rather than steeper. **

11.C
INDUSTRY DEMAND FOR FACTORS

We will now proceed from the *firm's* demand to the *industry's* demand for a factor of production, beginning with the case of a single variable factor.

First, consider a *monopolized* industry (i.e., an industry composed of a single seller in the product market). Evidently, the demand of a monopolized industry for a factor of production will be identical to the demand of the monopolist firm itself, as shown in Figure 11.4.

Next, let us consider the case where the industry consists of a large number of *competitive* producers in the product market. The two panels of Figure 11.17 show a typical firm and then the competitive industry as a whole. Suppose an initial equilibrium exists at factor price h_a^o and product price P^o. The firm's demand curve is shown in Panel (a) as the curve labeled $d_a(P = P^o)$. Along the $d_a(P = P^o)$ curve, a^o is the firm's employment of factor A. For the industry as a whole, we can sum these firm demand curves horizontally so as to obtain the curve labeled $\Sigma d_a(P = P^o)$. At the initial factor price h_a^o, this horizontal summation curve shows industry employment $A^o = \Sigma a^o$ of the factor (at point K).

There is a complication, however. Suppose factor price falls to h_a'. In Panel (a) the firm will first move along the initial demand curve, $d_a(P = P^o)$, to employment level $\hat{a}$ of factor A. The corresponding industrywide movement in Panel (b) would be to the aggregate employment level $\hat{A}$ (point N). But this is not the full solution. As the firms in the industry increase their employment of factor A, the industry will normally produce increased aggregate output Q. Product price P will then fall, say to a new equilibrium P'. And since $vmp_a \equiv P(mp_a)$, each firm will then observe a downward shift of its vmp_a curve. So its d_a curve will fall.

As the individual firm's demand curve d_a shifts down to the dashed line in Panel (a), for the industry as a whole the horizontal sum Σd_a also shifts down to the dashed line in Panel (b). At the hire-price h_a', the firm will end up employing a' units while the industry hires A' units at point L. Note that the true demand D_a through points K and L is *steeper* (less elastic) than the simple horizontal sum of the firms' demand curves.

Exercise 11.7: With production function $q = 2\sqrt{a}$ and product price $P = 60$, the price-taking firm's demand equation for factor A was found in a previous exercise to be $h_a = 60/\sqrt{a}$. Suppose the industry consists of 1000 identical such firms, and that the consumers' demand curve for product Q is given by the equation $P = 90 - Q/1000$. (a) What is the equation corresponding to the curve labeled $\Sigma d_a(P = P^o)$ in Figure 11.17? (b) What is the industry demand equation D_a for factor A? (c) If $h_a^o = 4$ initially, compare the effect on the firm and the industry if the hire-price falls to $h_a' = 3$.

** End of marked section.

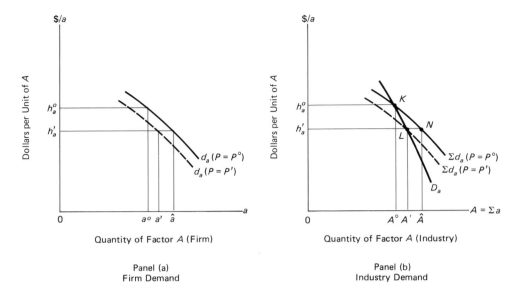

$/a

Dollars per Unit of A

h_a^o

h_a'

$d_a (P = P^o)$
$d_a (P = P')$

0   a^o a' $\hat{a}$ a

Quantity of Factor A (Firm)

Panel (a)
Firm Demand

$/a

Dollars per Unit of A

h_a^o

h_a'

K

N

L

$\Sigma d_a (P = P^o)$
$\Sigma d_a (P = P')$

D_a

0   A^o A' $\hat{A}$ $A = \Sigma a$

Quantity of Factor A (Industry)

Panel (b)
Industry Demand

FIGURE 11.17 **Demand for Factor: Competitive Firm and Industry, Product-Price Effect.** Panel (a) pictures a firm's demand for factor A; Panel (b) pictures industry demand. At an initial hire-price h_a^o and product price P^o, position K in Panel (b) represents a point on the industry demand curve for factor A. The associated firm demand curve is $d_a (P = P^o)$ in Panel (a). In Panel (b) the solid curve $\Sigma d_a (P = P^o)$ is the horizontal summation of these firm demand curves. When factor price falls to h_a', the firm aims to expand production from a^o to $\hat{a}$—the corresponding industrywide summations in Panel (b) being A^o and $\hat{A}$. But as firms expand employment of A, industrywide output Q also tends to rise, driving down product price to some level P'. Thus the firm's demand curve will fall to a position like the (dashed) curve $d_a (P = P')$ in Panel (a); the dashed summation curve in Panel (b) will move similarly. The new point on the industry factor demand curve in Panel (b) will be L. Thus, the product-product-price effect tends to make the industry demand curve for a factor more inelastic.

Answer: (a) The individual firm's factor demand equation, when $P = P^o = 60$, can be rewritten as $a = 3600/h_a^2$. For 1000 identical firms, $A \equiv 1000a = 3,600,000/h_a^2$. (b) We now want to take into account the effect of changes in h_a upon changes in P. Since $Q \equiv 1000q$, the consumers' demand curve can be written $P = 90 - q$. And we know from an earlier exercise that $mp_a = 1/\sqrt{a}$. Since each price-taking firm sets $vmp_a \equiv P(mp_a) = h_a$, we have $(90 - q)(1/\sqrt{a}) = h_a$. But $q = 2\sqrt{a}$, and so $(90 - 2\sqrt{a})(1/\sqrt{a}) = 90/\sqrt{a} - 2 = h_a$. Then, since $A \equiv 1000a$, the industry's demand equation can be written $A = 8,100,000/(h_a + 2)^2$. (c) Using the firm's demand curve, desired employment would rise from $a^o = 225$ to $\hat{a} = 400$. But as industry hiring expands beyond $A^o = 225,000$, product price P falls. In fact, at the new equilibrium employment is only $A = 324,000$ and not 400,000. (This can be confirmed with the industry demand equation.) Product price falls from $P^o = 60$ to $P' = 54$.

We must also consider entry and exit of firms. If factor A becomes cheaper, for example, profits rise and new firms will enter. This will naturally cause the sum of the firms' demand curves Σd_a to *rise*, which tends to make the true demand D_a *flatter*. This works against the product-price effect, so we cannot be sure whether the true demand D_a will be steeper or flatter than the sum of firms' demands. If the product-price effect is large (because of inelastic consumer demand) then the true demand D_a will be steeper. But if the entry-exit effect is large, the true demand D_a will be flatter.

> CONCLUSION: Industry demand for a factor tends to be steeper (less elastic) than the horizontal sum of firms' demand curves when consumer demand for output has normal negative slope. (This is the product-price effect.) On the other hand, if firms can easily enter or leave the industry this tends to make the industry demand for the factor flatter or more elastic (entry-exit effect).

Finally, what if there are other variable factors? As employment of A expands in response to a fall in its hire-price h_a, in the normal complementarity case the industry will be attempting also to increase use of other factors $B, C, \ldots$. But the consequence on the industry level will be that the hire-prices $h_b, h_c, \ldots$ will tend to *rise*; therefore employment of these cooperating factors *will not increase as much* as would otherwise have occurred. And so the demand for factor A will not benefit as much from complementarity as the picture in Figure 11.16 might suggest. In the case of anticomplementary factors, their employment *will not decrease as much*. We leave it for the student to work out the implications of these interactions.

11.D
MONOPSONY IN THE FACTOR MARKET

Just as a monopolist is a sole seller in a market, a *monopsonist* is a sole *buyer*. If everyone in a small town works for a single coal mine, then the mine has monopsony power in the local labor market. A price-taking employer of a factor faces a horizontal supply curve, meaning that its own hiring decisions are such a small element in the market that hire-price will be unaffected. But the monopsonist is the *whole* demand side of its market, so the factor supply curve it faces is upward-sloping.

The curve labeled $s_a \equiv afc_a$ in Figure 11.18 shows the supply of factor A to a monopsonist. At any employment level a, the Average Factor Cost afc (i.e., the wage or hire-price h_a per unit of A employed) is given by the height of the supply curve. Marginal Factor Cost mfc_a, as shown in the diagram, rises *faster* than afc_a. The reason is that mfc_a consists of two elements: the hire-price paid to the "extra" unit *plus* the additional payments to the previous units:

(11.21)
$$mfc_a \equiv \frac{\Delta C_a}{\Delta a} \equiv h_a + a\frac{\Delta h_a}{\Delta a}$$

Turning now to the monopsonist's employment decision, the optimal quantity to hire, a^*, is found where $mfc = mrp$ (point M in the diagram). Here the marginal expense of hiring one more unit is equal to the marginal benefit due to the extra revenue

(11.22) $mfc_a = mrp_a$ Factor Employment Condition (Monopsonist)

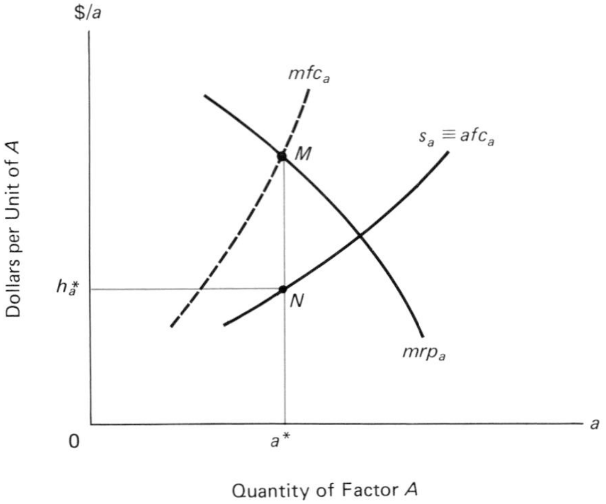

FIGURE 11.18 Monopsony in the Factor Market.
The rising supply curve of A to the firm, s_a, is also a curve of Average Factor Cost afc_a. The curve of Marginal Factor Cost mfc_a will then lie above afc_a, as shown here. The optimum factor employment for the firm is a^*, where the mfc_a and mrp_a curves intersect (point M). The associated hire-price h_a^* is the price along the s_a curve at this level of employment.

The hire-price h_a^* is, of course, the height of afc at $a = a^*$. (Note that the hire-price is *not* the height of point M, but of point N in the diagram.)

Exercise 11.8: Suppose the firm of Exercise 11.4, with production function $q = 2\sqrt{a}$, not only has monopoly power in its product market (faces demand curve $P = 90 - q$) but also has monopsony power in the factor market. Specifically, let the supply curve of factor A to the firm be $h_a = 1 + a/75$. What is the profit-maximizing solution for employment of input and production of output?

Answer: The firm will set $mrp_a \equiv MR\,(mp_a) = mfc_a$. Marginal Revenue is $MR = 90 - 2q$, and Marginal Product here is $mp_a = 1/\sqrt{a}$. With a linear factor supply curve, it can be verified that the curve of Marginal Factor cost is also linear and rises twice as fast. Thus, $mfc_a = 1 + 2a/75$. The condition $mrp_a = mfc_a$ can then be expressed either in terms of the variable q or the variable a. Working for convenience in terms of q, the equation becomes $(90 - 2q)(2/q) = 1 + (q^2/2)/75$, which reduces to $q^3 + 750q = 27,000$. The solution is $q^* = 21.9$, which implies $a^* = 120.2$.

EXAMPLE 11.5
Monopsony in Professional Baseball

The leading (and perhaps the only important) example of labor-market monopsony exists in the realm of professional sports. Here a legal quirk, perhaps based upon the idea that sports are play (a pastime) rather than a business, has permitted employers to form buyers' cartels. The most important cartel instrument is the "reserve clause." While there are exceptions, the reserve clause basically makes the player the exclusive property of the team that first signs him up, or to which he is traded thereafter. Should a player refuse to accept the wage offer of the team whose property he is, he cannot play for any other team in the cartel.

Gerald W. Scully investigated the effect of the reserve clause in major-league baseball. He anticipated that the buyers' cartel would cause a divergence between Marginal Revenue Product *mrp* and wage (as in Figure 11.18).

But first, differences in player *quality* had to be allowed for. Using 1968 and 1969 data, Scully estimated the "gross" *mrp* in terms of the player's effect on gate receipts and broadcast revenues. Deduction of related expenses, and in particular player development costs, led to estimates of "net" *mrp* for players of different qualities. Since substantial player development costs, on the order of $300,000, are incurred before it is known how successful the athlete will be, net *mrp* may turn out to be negative. On the average, however, in a competitive situation wages should be equal to net *mrp*. If the actual structure is one of monopsony, on the other hand, wages on the average should fall short of net *mrp*.

The table shows some of Scully's results. Net *mrp* and average salary are compared for batters and pitchers falling into different quality groups. While for "mediocre" players salary is above net *mrp*—and indeed, the latter is actually negative—for "average" and "star" players, net *mrp* far exceeds salary. Thus, on balance, there is considerable evidence of monopsony power.

Quality versus Pay of Baseball Players

	Quality Group	Net mrp	Salary
Hitters	Mediocre	$−30,000	$17,200
	Average	128,300	29,100
	Star	319,000	52,100
Pitchers	Mediocre	−10,600	15,700
	Average	159,600	33,000
	Star	405,300	66,800

Source: G. W. Scully, "Pay and Performance in Major League Baseball," *American Economic Review*, v. 64 (Dec. 1974), p. 928.

COMMENT: Contrary to common opinion among fans and sports writers, star players are not "overpaid." In fact, they receive far less than their economic worth. Since the time of Scully's study, the reserve clause in professional sports has been substantially weakened. And in consequence, stars' salaries have tended to rise.

In a later study, Paul M. Sommers and Noel Quinton[a] examined the earnings of "free agents"—players who are free to play for whichever club offers the best salary. They found the earnings of free agents to be much more in line with Marginal Revenue Product. Free-agent hitters had an average *mrp* of $521,923, while teams paid them an average of $827,393 in salaries, benefits, and development costs. Free-agent pitchers had an average *mrp* of $259,658, while teams paid them an average of $257,600.

[a] Paul M. Sommers and Noel Quinton, "Pay and Performance in Major League Baseball: The Case of the First Family of Free Agents," *Journal of Human Resources*, v. 17 (Summer 1982).

Table 11.1 summarizes the Factor Employment Conditions (best amount of input to hire) and Optimal Output Conditions (best amount of output to sell) for the different market structures we have discussed. Note that the conditions

$MC = MR$ and $mfc = mrp$ *always* apply. When the firm is a price-taker in the product market or the factor market (or both), these conditions still remain valid—but then *additional* equalities also hold, as summarized in the table.

TABLE 11.1

Factor Employment Condition and Optimal Output Condition, Summary

Factor Market Structure	Product Market Structure	
	Monopolist	Price-taker
Monopsonistt	$\left\{ \begin{array}{l} mfc = mrp \\ MC = MR \end{array} \right.$	$\left\{ \begin{array}{l} mfc = mrp \equiv vmp \\ MC = MR \equiv P \end{array} \right.$
Price-taker	$\left\{ \begin{array}{l} h \equiv mfc = mrp \\ MC = MR \end{array} \right.$	$\left\{ \begin{array}{l} h \equiv mfc = mrp \equiv vmp \\ MC = MR \equiv P \end{array} \right.$

11.E
AN APPLICATION: MINIMUM-WAGE LAWS

There are two possible models for explaining the effects of minimum-wage laws: the *competitive-market model* versus the *monopsony-market model*.

The competitive model is illustrated in Figure 11.19. The commodity is a certain grade or class of labor L, whose hire-price is the wage rate w. The competitive equilibrium wage is w_c and employment L_c. Now suppose a legal minimum wage $w°$ is imposed, at a level higher than w_c. At wage $w°$ the labor offered on the market is L_s but the labor demanded is only L_d. So the *unemployment gap* at the legal wage is the quantity BC or $L_s - L_d$. However, the *disemployment effect* actually

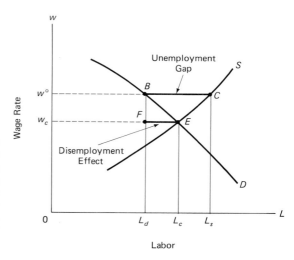

FIGURE 11.19 Minimum Wage: Competitive Model. The competitive equilibrium point E is associated with wage w_c and employment L_c. If a wage floor or minimum wage were imposed at the level $w°$, employment would fall to L_d. The quantity FE is the "disemployment effect." At the higher wage there would be L_s units of labor seeking employment, so the perceived "unemployment gap" would be the larger quantity BC.

due to the wage floor is the somewhat lesser amount FE or $L_c - L_d$. When a minimum wage is imposed the competitive-market model would clearly predict *disemployment* and an even larger degree of *unemployment*—provided only that the minimum wage is "effective,"—that is, is set higher than the pre-existing market equilibrium wage.

The monopsony model has rather different implications, as shown in Figure 11.20. Employment is initially L_m (at the intersection of the *mrp* and *mfc* curves); the wage $w_m < mrp$ is determined along the labor supply curve S. With the introduction of an effective minimum-wage law, *the market supply curve is replaced by a horizontal line at the level of the imposed minimum wage* (in the range where the market supply curve S lies below the level of the minimum wage). That is, the monopsonist employer is *forced to be a price-taker* at the minimum wage, wherever the market supply conditions would otherwise have permitted establishing a monopsony hire-price lower than the legally imposed floor.

Three classes of possibilities are illustrated in Figure 11.20. First, suppose the minimum wage is only a little higher than w_m, for example w' in the diagram. Then the *effective* supply curve to the firm is horizontal at the level w' until the S curve is reached at point N. In this range the Marginal Factor Cost *mfc* also equals w'. If the firm could actually hire as many units as desired at wage w', it would employ the quantity associated with point G, where $w' = mrp$. But this is not possible. Beyond point N, the effective supply curve of labor to the firm rejoins the original S curve; the laborers are not willing to supply more than L' units at wage w'. It follows also that, beyond employment L', the effective Marginal Factor Cost leaps upward discontinuously to rejoin the original *mfc* curve (at point U). Since the *mrp* curve in the diagram passes through this vertical discontinuity of the *mfc* curve, the firm will find it optimal to employ L' workers at wage w'. Note that, relative to L_m, the minimum-wage law here has *increased* employment! Nor is there any perceived unemployment at the legally imposed wage.

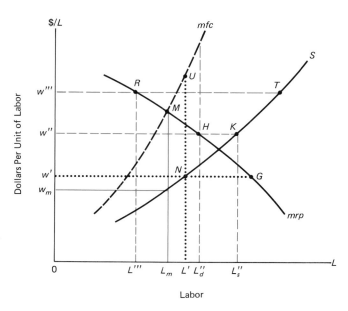

FIGURE 11.20 Minimum Wage: Monopsony Model. Under monopsony, the optimality condition $mfc = mrp$ determines the wage w_m at employment L_m. If a minimum wage were imposed at the relatively low wage w', the optimality condition is satisfied at employment L'— both wage and employment would rise slightly. At an intermediate minimum wage w'', employment would be L_d''. Here there is a considerable increase in both wage and employment; nevertheless, a perceived "unemployment gap" HK arises, since at wage w'' the offered labor supply is L_s''. At a sufficiently high minimum wage like w''', employment falls to L'''.

Now consider a somewhat higher minimum wage, w''. At this wage the firm would again be forced to be a price-taker, and would not want to employ more than L_d'' units (at point H), using the condition $w'' = mrp$. This employment is also greater than the L_m of the unregulated monopsony solution; no *disemployment* takes place. However, at wage w'' some *unemployment* will be perceived. At the w'' wage the offered labor supply would be L_s'', which is more than the firm wants to hire. The resulting unemployment gap is indicated by the distance NK in the diagram.

Finally, w''' represents a still higher minimum wage, higher than the level at which the *mrp* and *mfc* curves intersect. Here the effective employment would be reduced to L'''. Thus, a minimum wage as high as w''' would lead to the same qualitative implications as in the competitive-market model. With this high wage there would be some *disemployment* as compared with L_m, and a larger *unemployment* gap represented by the distance RT in the diagram.

CONCLUSION: The competitive-market model implies that both disemployment (less L employed) and unemployment (a supply-demand gap) would result from an effective minimum wage. The monopsony-market model has three possible outcomes: (1) If the minimum wage is set at a relatively low level, then employment *increases* and there is no unemployment. (2) At an intermediate minimum wage, employment increases but there will also be some unemployment. (3) At a relatively high minimum wage, as in the competitive model, there is both disemployment and unemployment.

It is important to remember that there is a spectrum of labor skill and quality. Some workers will already be earning more than the minimum wage and others less. So we would expect minimum-wage laws to have quite different impacts upon high-wage and low-wage workers.

Using the *competitive* model, low-skilled (low-wage) workers would be affected as in Figure 11.19. Their wage rates would rise, but some of them would lose their jobs. For higher-skilled workers, in contrast, the equilibrium wage level is likely to be already above the minimum wage—so no direct impact is to be expected. If the *monopsony* model of Figure 11.20 were valid, on the other hand, then: (1) For very low-skilled workers the imposed minimum wage would be effectively at a high level, like w'' in Figure 11.20, so higher wages but lesser employment would be expected. (2) For medium-skilled workers, the wage might be between w' and w'', so *both* wage rate and employment might increase. (3) For quite high-skilled workers, the imposed minimum wage would be relatively low, even lower than w' in Figure 11.20—so there will be no direct effect on wages or employment.

Which of these models is the correct picture? That is an empirical question that has been investigated by a number of economists.

EXAMPLE 11.6
Minimum-Wage Legislation

Minimum-wage laws in the United States, in contrast with those of most other advanced nations, specify fixed dollar wage rates that are uniform over the entire country. There are no differentials on the basis of age, experience, or geography. In contrast, most European countries have youth differentials—in Great Britain, for example, the youth minimum is only about 30 percent of the adult minimum. In Canada, minimum-wage schedules are set by the provinces rather than by the central government, which automatically allows for differentials between geographical regions. The absence of any differentials in the United States leads us to expect that the brunt of any unemployment effects of minimum-wage laws will be suffered by low-wage regions like the South and by low-wage age groups such as youthful workers.

The effects upon youth have been examined by a number of researchers. A study by Y. Brozen[a] found that successive increases in the legal minimum wage were indeed reflected by rises in the teenage unemployment rate. But as productivity and inflation progressed over time, the equilibrium wage for teenagers tended to "catch up" with the legally fixed minimum so as to erode the disemployment effect, until the next round of minimum-wage legislation began the cycle over again.

For the period 1954 to 1968, a statistical regression analysis by T. G. Moore allowed not only for the *level* of the minimum-wage but also for *coverage* of the labor force (since, over time, not only level but coverage has tended to increase). The table shows the elasticities of the unemployment rate for various age-sex groups in response to changes in minimum-wage coverage and level.

Effect of Minimum Wage upon Younger Age-Group Unemployment (Elasticities)

UNEMPLOYMENT RATE OF:	DETERMINING VARIABLES	
	Employed Workers Covered by Minimum Wage (%)	Minimum Wage as Proportion of Hourly Earnings
Nonwhites, 16–19	0.2549	1.75927
Whites, 16–19	0.0777	0.58461
Males, 16–19	0.080	0.61649
Females, 16–19	0.171	0.73988
Males, 20–24	0.063	0.05346

Source: T. G. Moore, "The Effect of Minimum Wages on Teenage Unemployment Rates," *Journal of Political Economy,* v. 79 (July/Aug. 1971), p. 901.

The data in the table may be interpreted as follows, using the first row as an example. The unemployment rate of nonwhites aged 16 to 19: (1) increased 0.2549 percent for each percent rise in the *coverage* of the minimum-wage law, and (2) increased 1.75927 percent for each percent increase in the *ratio* of the legal minimum-wage to the average hourly earnings of production workers in private nonagricultural employment. Note that when it comes to unemployment, minimum-wage laws bear more heavily upon young nonwhites than whites, and upon young females more than young males. In contrast, males aged 20 to 24, above the teenage category, were *not* substantially affected by the minimum-wage legislation.

Using a somewhat different methodology, Mikhail S. Bernstam and Peter L. Swan studied white and black teenagers over the period 1960 to 1980. They obtained employment elasticities, for changes in minimum-wage *coverage*, of

−0.258 for whites and −2.139 for nonwhites. That is, a 1 percent increase in coverage would decrease black teenage employment by over 2 percent but would decrease white teenage employment by only about one-fourth of a percent. The corresponding figures for minimum-wage *levels* were −0.991 for blacks and −0.132 for whites. Once again, the much heavier impact upon nonwhites is evident. As an interesting point, Bernstam and Swan also found a strong association between the minimum-wage laws and the explosive growth of illegitimate births among teenage girls.

> COMMENT: All these studies provide solid confirmation for the predictions of the competitive model of Figure 11.19. The monopsony model does not seem to be supported by the historical evidence.

[a] Y. Brozen, "The Effect of Statutory Minimum Wage Increases on Teen-Age Unemployment," *Journal of Law and Economics*, v. 12 (Apr. 1969).
[b] Mikhail S. Bernstam and Peter L. Swan, "The State as the Marriage Partner of Last Resort: New Findings on Minimum Wage, Youth Joblessness, Welfare, and Single Motherhood in the United States, 1960–1980," Hoover Institution Working Papers in Economics E-86-82 (Oct. 1986).

Regardless of economic impact, minimum-wage laws have been politically popular. To get some idea why, we might look upon who is affected and how. First are the supposed "beneficiaries"—low-wage workers previously receiving less than the minimum wage (largely teenagers and minorities). While many of them will remain employed and may receive a substantial wage increase, a good proportion are likely to end up unemployed. So for them the effect is mixed. The strongest political pressure for higher minimum wages comes not from these "beneficiaries" but from organized labor, in particular the AFL-CIO. This may seem puzzling; unionized employees will not get any direct benefit, since union wages are far higher than the legislated minimum. But a higher minimum wage raises the cost to employers of hiring unskilled workers, thus tending to increase *relative* demand for the skilled workers represented by the AFL-CIO.

☐ SUMMARY OF CHAPTER 11

This chapter deals with the demand for factors of production. A key theme is that the optimal *output* decision and the optimal *input* decision are logically interconnected rather than independent choices.

The profit-maximizing Factor Employment Conditions for the firm depend upon *market structure*—both in the product market (whether the firm is a price-taker or else has monopoly power with regard to the output commodity) and in the factor market (whether the firm is a price-taker or else has "monopsony" power with regard to the input commodity).

The Factor Employment Condition for any variable factor A, in most general form, is:

$$mfc_a = mrp_a$$

That is, the firm operates where the cost of hiring one more unit (mfc_a) is equal to the revenue it generates (mrp_a). If the firm is a *product-market* price-taker, then vmp_a (Value of the Marginal Product) can be substituted for mrp_a on the right-hand side of the Factor Employment Condition. If the firm is a *factor-market* price-taker, then the hire-price h_a can be substituted for mfc_a on the left-hand side of the Factor Employment Condition.

If the firm is a price-taker in the factor market, its demand curve for a single factor A is simply the downward-sloping branch of the mrp_a curve. Since $mrp_a \equiv MR(mp_a)$, we can see that factor demand depends both upon the marginal physical productivity of the factor (mp_a) and upon the value to the firm of the additional output produced (MR).

If there are two variable factors A and B, the Factor Employment Conditions (for a factor-price-taking firm) are:

$$\begin{cases} h_a = mrp_a \\ h_b = mrp_b \end{cases}$$

Factors are called *complementary* if an increase in employment of either raises the Marginal Product of the other, and *anticomplementary* if the reverse holds. Complementarity is the normal case. (If there is no interdependence, the factors are called *independent* in production.) Both complementarity and anticomplementarity make the firm's demand curve for either factor more elastic.

As factor prices shift, there will be a *substitution effect* and a *scale effect* upon factor employment. When the hire-price falls the substitution effect, considered alone, dictates increased employment of the relatively cheapened factor and decreased employment of the other. The scale effect (change in firm output) will normally increase employment of the cheapened factor A further. (But a "regressive" case is possible, in which cheapening of a factor leads to a reduction in the optimal output.)

The competitive *industry's* demand for a factor is based on the summation of the member firms' demands. But there are several complications. As the hire-price h_a falls, the industry will employ more A and thus normally also expand output Q. The effect will be to drive down the product price P, and therefore to reduce somewhat the degree of industry response to changes in h_a (i.e., to make the industry demand for A more inelastic). But a reduction in h_a will also make the industry more profitable and thus induce *entry*. The entry-exit effect cuts in the opposite direction and tends to make the industry demand for a factor more elastic.

Summing up: Demand for a factor A tends to be *greater*: (1) where the employers are product-market competitors rather than monopolists, and are factor-market price-takers rather than monopsonists; (2) where the physical Marginal Product mp_a is high; and (3) where the additional output produced by employing A is highly valued by consumers. Demand for A tends to be *more elastic*: (1) the more elastic is the consumers' demand for the output; (2) the less powerfully the Law of Diminishing Returns operates as employment of A increases; (3) the greater the normal productive interdependence (complementarity) between A and other factors; and (4) the greater the exit-entry effect as the hire-price h_a changes.

☐ QUESTIONS FOR CHAPTER 11

MAINLY FOR REVIEW

R1. Distinguish the *productivity* and the *revenue* considerations entering into a firm's demand for a factor.

*R2. Does the curve of Marginal Revenue Product for factor A, mrp_a, necessarily lie below (to the left of) the curve of Value of the Marginal Product, vmp_a? Explain. Which is the firm's demand curve for factor A?

R3. Why is $mrp_a = h_a$ the Factor Employment Condition for a price-taking firm in the *factor* market? What if the firm is not a price-taker in the *product* market? Is this condition sufficient, or are there other subsidiary conditions that must be met?

*R4. Is it ever rational to employ so much of a factor as to be in the region of diminishing marginal returns? In the region of diminishing average returns? In the region of diminishing total returns?

*R5. With two factors A and B, explain why the conditions $mrp_a = h_a$ and $mrp_b = h_b$ lead not only to the choice of optimal factor proportions but also to the optimal *scale* of output.

*R6. With two factors of production, is the slope of the output isoquant equal (in absolute value) to the ratio of the Marginal Products? Explain. Interpret the absolute slope of the *isocost* line as a ratio.

R7. Explain why, if two factors are complementary, the firm's demand curve for either is flatter than the *mrp* curves. What if the factors are anticomplementary?

*R8. Is the factor demand curve of a competitive industry necessarily less elastic than the summation of the demand curves of the separate firms?

*R9. True or false (explain in each case)? The economywide demand curve for factor A will be more elastic:
   a. The more elastic is consumer demand for products that use factor A.
   b. The weaker is the operation of the Law of Diminishing Returns as employment of A increases.
   c. The more elastic is the *supply* of factors complementary to A.

R10. In the competitive minimum-wage model of Figure 11.21, why is the "unemployment gap" bigger than the "disemployment effect"?

R11. Show how, upon imposition of a minimum-wage law, the monopsony model might predict *increased* employment. Given an initial dispersion of wage rates (high-skilled, mid-skilled, and low-skilled workers) under this model, which groups would tend to find employment decreasing and which increasing? Compare the predictions with the competitive model.

FOR FURTHER THOUGHT AND DISCUSSION

*T1. Are there examples in this text providing empirical support for the Laws of Diminishing Marginal and Average Returns? Would you expect to find any exceptions?

*T2. Can a demand curve for factor A be derived if the employer is a *monopsonist*? That is, is there a relation that shows the quantity employed as a function of price? Why or why not?

T3. With regard to Table 11.1, the monopolist-monopsonist Factor Employment Con-

---

* The answers to starred questions appear at the end of the book.

dition $mfc_a = mrp_a$ is said to be the "most general." Show how this condition also covers the case of a firm that is a price-taker in both product and factor markets.

*T4. Why might a firm at a given moment hire positive amounts of two factors that are anticomplementary?

T5. Would you expect, typically, that combinations of different classes of labor (like skilled versus unskilled) are more or less likely to be complementary—in comparison with combinations of labor and machines?

T6. Assuming that labor organizations were interested only in the selfish gains of their members, would you expect them to oppose immigration?

*T7. Historically, wages in the United States have been high relative to wages elsewhere. Does the chapter shed light on this phenomenon? Explain.

*T8. Would you expect technological progress to raise wage rates, on the average?

T9. A minimum-wage law raises firms' *relative* demand for skilled labor versus unskilled. Would it tend to raise the *absolute* demand for skilled labor, if skilled and unskilled are complementary? If they are anticomplementary? How does your answer bear upon the attitudes of trade unions toward minimum-wage laws?

12

CORE CHAPTER

RESOURCE SUPPLY AND FACTOR-MARKET EQUILIBRIUM

This chapter completes our trip around the circuit of economic activity (see Figure 1.1). We have looked at the demand and supply of consumption goods (the *product market*) in Chapters 3 through 10. Chapter 11 analyzed the demands for resources to be used in production. This chapter examines the supply of resources, and then brings supply and demand together to study equilibrium in the *factor market*.

12.A
THE OPTIMUM OF THE RESOURCE-OWNER

In the analysis of consumption and demand in Chapter 4, the individual was supposed to be already in possession of a given income I out of which he or she could purchase desired consumption goods. But, of course, this income does not come out of thin air. *Income consists of the earnings from resources (factors) owned.* The consumer has income only because he or she is also a resource-owner.

As resource-owners, individuals must decide how much to supply on the market, and how much to retain for nonmarket or *reservation* uses. Think of labor as the owned resource. Then the decision problem is to choose *between labor income and "leisure."* The word "leisure" perhaps suggests a mere lazing away of time. But the term as used here may include productive activities as well, so long as these are outside the market. An enormously important example is homemaking, an activity which involves productive services that would be extremely costly to buy on the market.

Figure 12.1 shows an individual's indifference curves between *income I* and *leisure R* (i.e., reservation uses of time). The arrows indicating preference directions show that income and leisure are both "goods" rather than "bads." Before any exchange takes place, the individual at endowment position E has $\bar{R}$ units of leisure (24 hours per day, let us say) and $\bar{I}$ units (dollars) of non-labor income (from property earnings, perhaps). The diagram is bounded both on the right and on the left. The bound on the right at $\bar{R}$ says that, no matter what, the individual cannot retain more than 24 hours of leisure per day; the bound on the left at zero says that the individual cannot sell more than 24 hours of labor.

The opportunity set is the shaded area lying below the budget line EK. Starting from E, as an hour of labor is sold (as an hour of leisure is sacrificed) an hourly wage h_L is received, where h_L is the "hire-price" of labor. If the individual

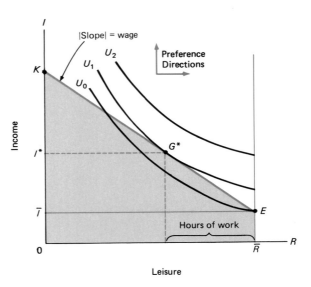

FIGURE 12.1 Optimum of the Resource-Owner. The resource-owner's preferences, as indicated by indifference curves $U_0, U_1, U_2, \ldots$, show that income I and reservation uses (or "leisure") R are both goods. At endowment position E the person has initial income $\bar{I}$ and $\bar{R}$ of leisure. The slope of the budget line EK indicates the hire-price or wage at which the individual can obtain income by sacrificing leisure. The tangency point G^* is the resource-owner's optimum position.

is a price-taker with respect to the wage rate, the budget line has constant slope $\Delta I / \Delta R = -h_L$.[1] The wage rate h_L can be regarded either as the price to the employer of an hour of *labor* or the price to the worker of an hour of *leisure*. The individual's *resource-employment optimum* (optimal choice of income versus leisure) is at the tangency position G^* in Figure 12.1. (The logic is just the same as in choosing the consumer's optimum in Chapter 4.)

The equation of the budget line is:

(12.1) $$h_L R + I = h_L \bar{R} + \bar{I}$$

This equation tells us that the value of the individual's endowment, shown on the right-hand side as non-labor income $\bar{I}$ plus the market value $h_L \bar{R}$ of endowed time, must equal his or her achieved income I plus the market value $h_L R$ of the leisure "purchased" (by not working). Alternatively, this same relation can be formulated in terms of *labor or working hours* L rather than leisure hours R, where by definition $L \equiv \bar{R} - R$. Then (12.1) can be rewritten:

(12.1') $$\bar{I} + h_L L = I$$

In this form, the budget equation says that the person's achieved income I is composed of endowed or property income $\bar{I}$ plus labor earnings $h_L L$.

At the optimum point G^* two conditions must hold:

1. The resource-owner must be at the boundary of his opportunity set. (He does not throw away either income or leisure.)
2. The indifference curve must have the same slope as the budget line. (His marginal

---

[1] More explicitly, the slope of the budget line might be expressed as $-h_L/P_I$, where P_I is the "price" of a unit of income. But P_I is by definition unity, since income is measured in units of *numéraire* (in this case, dollars).

willingness to trade leisure for income just equals the wage that the market offers for doing so.)

The first condition says that the equation of the budget line, in the form either of (12.1) or (12.1′), must hold. Turning to the second condition, the absolute value of the slope of the budget line is h_L. The slope of the indifference curve is called the *Marginal Rate of Substitution in Resource Supply* (MRS_R). This represents the number of units of income I (i.e., the number of dollars) the individual is willing to give up per unit increase of leisure R. Since, as we have seen, the slope of the budget line is $-h_L$, the second condition is:

(12.2)
$$MRS_R = h_L$$

MRS_R can also be interpreted as the ratio of the *Marginal Utilities* of leisure and income—$MRS_R \equiv MU_R/MU_I$. So (12.2) can equivalently be written:[2]

(12.2′)
$$\frac{MU_R}{MU_I} = h_L$$

The "convex" curvature of the indifference curves of Figure 12.1 is required if we are to explain the fact that individuals typically diversify between income and leisure. (People normally work somewhere between 0 and 24 hours per day.) Of course, an individual who is very well endowed with property income (has very large $\bar{I}$) might choose not to work at all. In terms of the geometry, such a "corner solution" would be preferred if the indifference curve U_0 in Figure 12.1 were steeper than the budget line EK even at the endowment position E.[3]

---

[2] *Mathematical Footnote*: Using the method of Lagrangian multipliers, the optimization problem of the resource-owner can be expressed as:

$$\underset{(I,R,\lambda)}{\text{Max}}\ K = U(I,R) + \lambda(h_I R + I - h_L \bar{R} - \bar{I})$$

Then:

$$\frac{\partial K}{\partial I} = \frac{\partial U}{\partial I} + \lambda = 0$$

$$\frac{\partial K}{\partial R} = \frac{\partial U}{\partial R} + \lambda h_L = 0$$

$$\frac{\partial K}{\partial \lambda} = h_L R + I - h_L \bar{R} - \bar{I} = 0$$

Eliminating λ in the first two equations:

$$\frac{\partial U/\partial R}{\partial U/\partial I} = h_L$$

This is the form of (12.2′). And (12.2) follows immediately since:

$$MRS_R \equiv -dI/dR \equiv \frac{\partial U/\partial R}{\partial U/\partial I}$$

[3] The analytical condition for a corner solution is that $MRS_R > h_L$ even at $R = \bar{R}$.

Exercise 12.1 An individual is endowed with $\bar{R} = 24$ hours of leisure per day and $\bar{I} = 120$ units of income (dollars) per day. His Marginal Rate of Substitution in Resource Supply is $MRS_R = I/R$. The wage facing him is $h_L = 10$. How many hours of labor will he supply, and what will be his income from labor?

Answer: The budget constraint of Equation (12.1) becomes $10R + I = 10(24) + 120 = 360$. Using (12.2), he will set $MRS_R = I/R = h_L = 10$. Putting the equations together, the solution is $R^* = 18$, $I^* = 180$. Thus, he works 6 hours per day and earns \$60 per day from labor.

Let us now consider what happens when: (1) endowed (non-labor) income $\bar{I}$ varies, and (2) the hire-price (wage) h_L changes.

The effect of rising income is shown in Figure 12.2, where the budget line moves up successively from $E^\circ K^\circ$ to $E'K'$ to $E''K''$. Both income I and leisure R are, it is reasonable to assume, "normal" (or "superior") goods. That is, an upward shift of the budget line due to growth of endowed non-labor income $\bar{I}$ would lead the individual to choose more income I *and* more leisure R. The result is a positively sloped *Income Expansion Path* (IEP).

Figure 12.3 shows the effect of an increase in h_L, the wage rate or "price of leisure." As the wage rate rises, the budget line gets steeper, rotating around the endowment position E. The *Price Expansion Path* (PEP) goes through all the tangency-optimum positions along these steepening budget lines EK°, EK', EK'', ... For relatively low wage rates the negative slope of PEP indicates that more labor L will be offered (i.e., less leisure R "purchased") as the wage rises. But for high wage rates, it is quite possible for PEP to become positively sloped. In Figure 12.3, above point H' a higher wage will lead the individual to work *less*.

This possibly surprising situation is due to the interaction of the *income effect* and the *substitution effect* of the price (wage) change. We saw in Chapter 4 that for the substitution effect alone (i.e., when real income is held constant), a *rise* in price must lead to a *fall* in quantity purchased. In this case, an increase in the wage rate

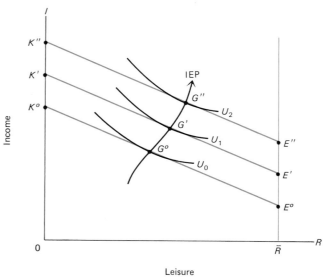

FIGURE 12.2 Income Expansion Path. As endowed income $\bar{I}$ rises, with the hire-price (wage) held constant, the budget line shifts upward parallel to itself. If I and R are both normal (superior) goods, the successive resource-employment optimum positions $G^\circ, G', G'', \ldots$ show that more income and more leisure will be chosen. Thus, the Income Expansion Path (IEP) has positive slope.

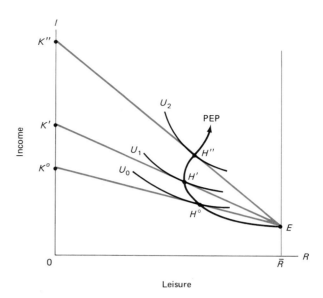

FIGURE 12.3 **Price Expansion Path.** As the wage or hire-price h_L increases, the budget line rotates clockwise around E. In an initial range where the wage rate is still low, increases in h_L will lead to choice of more income but less leisure (that is, more labor will be offered). Thus, the Price Expansion Path (PEP) has negative slope. A range *may* be reached where further increases in h_L lead to less labor being offered—the PEP curve may "bend backward" for sufficiently high h_L.

h_L means a rise in the price of leisure and so less leisure will be "purchased." A smaller amount of leisure means that labor supplied must be larger. So the *substitution effect* says that the higher the wage h_L, the greater the hours worked L.

But as usual there is an income effect as well as a substitution effect. Since the individual is a *seller of labor*, an increase in the wage rate makes him richer. And since leisure is a normal good, enrichment would lead to *greater* "purchases" of leisure. Thus, for resource supply the income and substitution effects of a price (wage) change normally act in opposite directions. (This contrasts with the analysis of consumption demand in Chapter 4, where, for a "normal" superior good, the substitution effect and the income effect of a price change are *reinforcing*.)

Not only does the income effect act in opposition to the substitution effect in the labor-supply decision, but the *magnitude* of the income effect is relatively large. The reason is the contrast between "diversification in consumption" and "specialization in production." Since the consumer generally buys a wide variety of products, a rise in the price of any single commodity is not likely to impoverish him or her substantially. But in terms of factor supply, there is one single price that will be *very* important for the resource-owner—namely, the wage of the particular type of labor service in which he or she specializes. Changes in this wage will typically have a big impact upon the individual's real income.

Nevertheless, *the substitution effect is always more powerful than the income effect at very low wage rates.* This may be seen as follows. Since the indifference-curve slope is negative at the endowment position E, there is some wage rate so low that the individual would offer zero hours of labor. For wage rates only slightly above this, any "enrichment" must be very small. The enrichment due to a wage increase is on the order of $L(\Delta h_L)$, where Δh_L is the wage increment and L is the hours worked. When L is close to zero, the person cannot be *substantially* enriched by a wage-rate change. It is only in the upper regions of the PEP curve that enough hours are worked to make the enrichment $L(\Delta h_L)$ substantial enough to possibly overcome the substitution effect. It follows from this discussion that the PEP curve of Figure 12.2 *must*, starting from the endowment point E, initially move in a northwest direction. Beyond a certain point, it *may* curve back toward the northeast.

CONCLUSION: The income and substitution effects of a change in hire-price h_L normally work in opposite directions. The substitution effect must dominate (more employment will be chosen as h_L rises) at low hire-prices; the income effect may dominate, however, for sufficiently high h_L.

EXAMPLE 12.1
Retirement Decisions

In recent years the labor-force participation of the elderly has declined markedly. Of white males aged 65 and over, 46.5 percent participated in the labor force in 1948 but only 22.5 percent in 1974. For nonwhite males the decline was from 50.3 percent to 21.7 percent.[a] To explain these changes, a study by Michael J. Boskin[b] examined the retirement decisions of white married males who were aged 61 to 65 in 1968.

The statistical evidence for the period 1968 to 1972 indicated that, other things equal, an increase of $1000 in annual income from assets (equivalent to an upward shift of the endowment point E in Figure 12.2) *increased* the probability of retirement by 15 percent. An increase of $1000 in net earnings (equivalent to a clockwise rotation of the budget line in Figure 12.3) *reduced* the probability of retirement by about 60 percent.

Boskin was particularly concerned to investigate the effect of Social Security benefits upon these retirement decisions. He found that a $1000 increase in these benefits more than doubled the probability of retirement. Since increased Social Security benefits act like increased income from assets to shift the endowment point E upward as in Figure 12.2, it seemed puzzling that the Social Security effect was so large. There are a number of possible explanations, some of the more important of which are connected with the fact that *receiving Social Security payments limits the income that an individual is legally permitted to receive from working*. During the period in question, any income from employment earned by Social Security recipients fell into four ranges: (1) there was a certain exempt level that the recipient could retain without penalty; (2) above the exemption, a certain range where earned income was in effect taxed 50 percent (by a corresponding reduction in Social Security benefits); (3) above the 50 percent bracket, another bracket where earned income was taxed 100 percent; (4) above this bracket, a final range where income earned could again be fully retained (since no Social Security benefits remain to be reduced as earnings increase). The key point is that, for many people, an increase in Social Security

[a] From *Manpower Report of the President, 1975* (Washington, D.C.: U.S. Government Printing Office).

[b] Michael J. Boskin, "Social Security and Retirement Decisions," *Economic Inquiry*, v. 15 (Jan. 1977).

benefits would be largely taxed away *unless* they chose to retire (or, at any rate, chose to work considerably less than before). Since eligibility for increased Social Security benefits depended heavily upon the individual's not working, increases in benefits had a powerful tendency to promote retirement.

12.B
AN APPLICATION: THE "NEGATIVE INCOME TAX" PROPOSAL

Programs to help the poor tend to have one problem in common: they reduce the incentive to work. The Negative Income Tax (NIT) is a proposal intended to minimize this problem.

Figure 12.4 is an illustration of a simplified welfare system in which the government guarantees a minimum income of, say, $6000 per year. If an individual's earnings are below this, government welfare payments make up the difference. Notice that this means government benefits are lost, dollar for dollar, if the individual has any earnings up to $6000.

In the absence of a welfare system the individual's optimum in the diagram would be the tangency point G along the budget line EK. He is earning, say, $7000 per year and retaining 115 days of leisure per year (working $365 - 115 = 250$ days). But if an income of $6000 is guaranteed by welfare, the budget line becomes the "kinked" line MLK. Given the shape of this person's indifference curves, the optimum is now at M, where he does not work at all. By not working he is sacrificing $1000 of income, but the increased leisure is worth it in terms of his preferences.

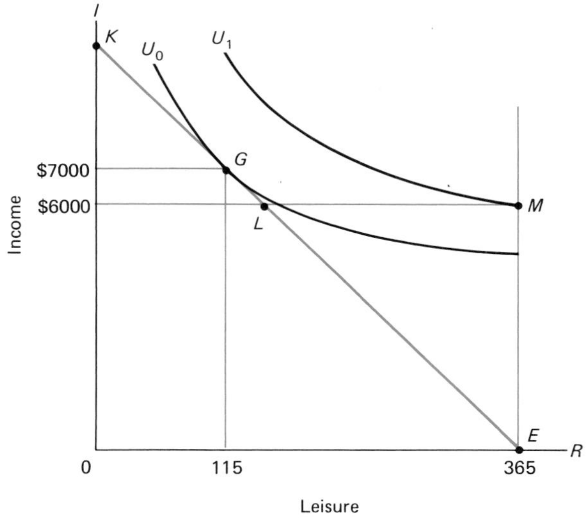

FIGURE 12.4 **Employment versus Welfare.** In the absence of a welfare-relief system the individual's optimum is at G on indifference curve U_0, where he earns $7,000 and works $365 - 115 = 250$ days per year. If the welfare guarantee is $6,000, on condition that the person not work, the effective constraint is the kinked line MLK. Along this budget line the optimum is the no-work position M on indifference curve U_1.

As an alternative to the welfare system, the Negative Income Tax would still guarantee the individual a minimum income of, say, $6000 per year, but with a difference: the recipient can now keep a fraction—perhaps half—of whatever he or she earns from working. For example, a worker who earns $3000 would receive the $6000 minimum plus half of $3000, or a total of $7500. Earnings of $12,000 are the "breakeven" level—at $12,000 the worker does equally well with or without the NIT. At still higher earnings, the worker would no longer receive any income assistance.

Figure 12.5 compares the NIT with a conventional welfare system. As before, with no government assistance the budget line would be the line *EK*, with an optimum at *G*. Under conventional welfare the budget line becomes *MLK* as before, with an optimum at *M* (not working). Under the NIT the budget line becomes *MFN*. There is no "kink" here, since a single proportionate tax is assumed to apply to all income earned. As the indifference curves are drawn, the optimum under the NIT is at *H*. The recipient works less than with no government assistance at all, but works more than under a conventional welfare system.

But the NIT has at least two flaws. (1) Since the breakeven level before receiving government assistance has increased (doubled in our example), a *much larger number* of workers will now choose to receive at least some "unearned" benefits from government. (And so fewer unsubsidized workers are left to pay the taxes that are needed to support the program.) (2) Furthermore, in contrast with what is shown in Figure 12.5, many recipients can end up working *fewer* hours

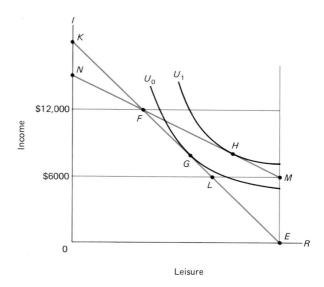

FIGURE 12.5 Negative Income Tax and Employment, I. In the illustration here, under the NIT the guaranteed income is $6000 and the breakeven level is $12,000. The individual's effective constraint is *MFN*. Along this budget line the optimum is at *H*. Whereas under simple welfare with relief level $6000 the individual would not work at all (point *M* is preferred to point *G*), here he chooses to work some hours (point *H* is preferred to *M*). But under NIT he still works less than at the no-welfare optimum point *G*.

rather than more. Both of these flaws are illustrated in Figure 12.6. Here the worker would *not* accept simple welfare, since his working optimum at *G* is on a higher indifference curve than the unemployment position *M*. Offered the NIT budget line *MFN*, however, the new optimum *H* means that he accepts a subsidized status and reduces his hours of work.

Which effect, the favorable or the unfavorable, is likely to be stronger? Unfortunately, experiments have produced rather unfavorable results.

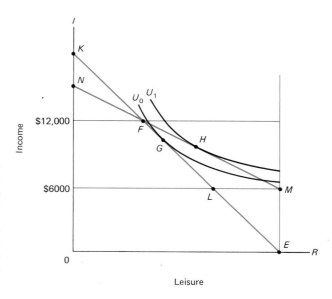

FIGURE 12.6 Negative Income Tax and Employment, II. While this diagram looks very similar to the preceding, the results are entirely different. Owing to a change in the shape of his indifference curves, the individual prefers working (at point *G*) to the no-work welfare solution (at point *M*). So the availability of welfare relief would not reduce his hours of work at all. But under the NIT his optimum position is *H*, where he works less than at *G*.

EXAMPLE 12.3
Negative Income Tax Experiments

The Federal Office of Economic Opportunity initiated an extensive experiment in 1967 aimed at estimating the effect of the Negative Income Tax (NIT) upon work incentives. Families in four cities in New Jersey and Pennsylvania were assigned to one of eight experimental NIT programs or to a control group.

A study by John F. Cogan[a] found, among those families choosing to participate, a rather substantial work-disincentive effect: an average reduction of 5 to 7 labor-hours per week. The reduced level of employment under the NIT was also associated with a heavy increase in required government payments. Thus, this experiment suggests that the possible favorable effects of NIT upon employment incentives and taxpayer burdens (as in Figure 12.5) may be outweighed by the negative possibilities (Figure 12.6).

Another series of experiments, in Seattle and Denver, was analyzed by Robert Spiegelman and K. E. Yaeger.[b] Once again the results showed significant work disincentives. The NIT caused, depending upon the specifics of the program, annual hours of work to fall by 6 to 11 percent for husbands, 23 to 32 percent for wives, and 0 to 15 percent for single female heads of families.

[a] John F. Cogan, *Negative Income Taxation and Labor Supply: New Evidence from the New Jersey–Pennsylvania Experiment*, RAND Corporation, R-2155-HEW (Feb. 1978).

[b] Robert G. Spiegelman and K. E. Yaeger, "Overview of NIT Studies," *Journal of Human Resources*, v. 15 (Fall 1980).

12.C
RESOURCE SUPPLY TO THE MARKET, AND FACTOR-MARKET EQUILIBRIUM

The data from the Price Expansion Path PEP of Figure 12.3 could be plotted in a separate diagram on R, h_L axes as the individual's "demand curve for leisure." It is more usual, however, to present the data on L, h_L axes as the individual's *supply curve for labor.*

Figure 12.7 shows such an individual supply curve s_L. The hire-prices h_L°, h_L', and h_L'' in Figure 12.7 correspond respectively to the slopes of the budget lines EK°, EK', and EK'' in Figure 12.3. The lower range in which the PEP of the earlier diagram is curving northwest corresponds to the range of hire-prices where the supply curve s_L has normal positive slope—where an increased wage elicits increased labor-hours. Above this range, however, the PEP *may* (as shown in Figure 12.3) begin to curve back to the northeast. That is, higher wages above some critical wage h_L' may *reduce* the amount of labor supplied. If so, in this range the labor supply curve is said to be "backward-bending."

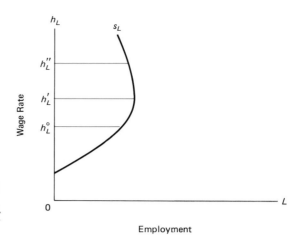

FIGURE 12.7 Backward-Bending Supply Curve of Labor. The supply curve of labor shown here, s_L, has normal positive slope for wage rates up to h_L' but "bends backward" above that wage.

EXAMPLE 12.4
The Supply of Nursing Services

A study by Charles Link and Russell Settle[a] examined the individual labor supply decisions of married professional nurses. Using 1970 Census data they found that the labor supply curve bent backwards, with the bend occurring (depending upon race, age, and other factors) at after-tax wage rates between $2.20 and $3.00 in current dollars of that date. Furthermore, most individuals were actually in the backward-bending range—that is, the average going wage for each group was above or just about at the bending-backward point. Another powerful influence upon nurses' labor supply decisions was spouse's income. Among white registered nurses, for example, a $1 increase in husband's wage caused a reduction of from 140 to 252 hours of annual nursing services supplied.

These facts pose a severe policy problem for medical-service planners. Programs such as Medicare and Medicaid have greatly increased the demand for nurses, tending to drive up wage rates. But, the data indicate, at higher wage rates there will be *fewer* hours supplied from nurses currently employed. What helps remedy the situation, however, is that higher wages in nursing will tend to attract newcomers into the nursing profession.

[a] Charles Link and Russell Settle, "Wage Incentives and Married Professional Nurses: A Case of Backward-Bending Supply?" *Economic Inquiry*, v. 19 (Jan. 1981).

Figure 12.8 shows the overall market supply of labor S_L, obtained by horizontally summing all the separate individuals' supply curves. Even if many of the *individual* supply curves are backward-bending as in Figure 12.7 just above, the *market* supply curve may not be. At higher wages the existing workers in any industry may offer fewer hours, but new workers will be attracted from other in-

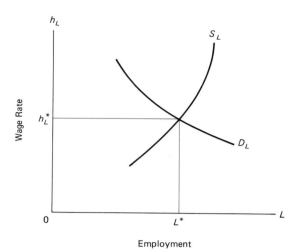

FIGURE 12.8 Equilibrium in the Factor Market.
The intersection of the aggregate demand curve for labor D_L and the aggregate supply curve of labor S_L determines the equilibrium wage rate h_L^* and the level of market employment L^*.

dustries or from leisure (from nonmarket employments). In fact, the supply of a particular type of labor to a single industry will almost never be backward-bending. Imagine, for example, that the wages of supermarket cashiers rise. Existing cashiers may now choose to work fewer hours, but very likely a flood of new applicants will be attracted from other jobs.

EXAMPLE 12.5
Braceros and the Supply of "Stoop Labor"

From 1953 to 1964 the supply of agricultural workers in the United States was supplemented by foreign contract workers from Mexico, known as "braceros." There was strong domestic political opposition to the bracero program, but employers contended that it would not be possible to find American workers willing to do the "stoop labor" in the fields, even at higher wages. In effect, the employers were arguing, the supply curve of American "stoop labor" was vertical or even backward-bending.

Despite these arguments the bracero program was in fact terminated in 1965. As it turned out, growers found it possible to attract American labor—though at a much higher wage. A study by Donald E. Wise[a] indicated that, for California winter melons, abolition of the bracero program led to a 67 percent increase in the wage rate, a 262 percent increase in employment of American workers (but a 22 percent reduction in *total* employment, since braceros were no longer used), and a 23 percent reduction of output.

[a] Donald E. Wise, "The Effect of the Bracero on Agricultural Production in California," *Economic Inquiry*, v. 12 (Dec. 1974).

Competitive equilibrium in the factor market is of course determined by the intersection of the supply and demand curves, as shown in Figure 12.8. Changes in equilibrium, as always, come about as a result of shifts in supply or in demand, or both.

Forces that may alter *factor demands* can involve:

1. *Technological change*: Technical progress tends to shift Marginal Product (*mp*) upward, and hence to raise the curve of $mrp \equiv MR(mp)$ that determines firms' demand for factors.[4]

2. *Demand for final products*: Similarly, an increase in the demand for a product, leading to a rise in its price and therefore in the Marginal Revenue received by firms in that industry, will increase the demand for any factor used in producing that commodity.

3. *Supply of cooperating or competing factors*: The demand for any one factor will be affected by changes in the availability of other factors that can complement it or substitute for it in production. In particular, an increase in the *supply* of one factor will raise the *demand* for factors that are complementary to it.

The forces that shift *factor supply* functions may involve:

1. *Wealth*: Higher wealth increases resource-owners' ability to retain or "purchase" *reservation uses*, thus reducing the supply offered on the market.

2. *Social trends and legislation*: In some societies women have been excluded from all but domestic activity. In other communities there have been severe restrictions upon the market uses of land or other resources. Changes in these customs or laws may therefore affect the market availability of factors.

3. *Investment and accumulation*: In recent centuries in the Western world, stocks of produced resources ("capital goods") have accumulated enormously over time. Each generation has left its successor better endowed with these manufactured resources. (This topic will be considered further in the next chapter.)

4. *Demography*: The aggregate size of the human population and its age-sex composition will obviously affect the supply of labor available to the market.

[4] This is the normal situation. But consider "labor-saving" inventions. These raise average productivity, but *may* reduce the demand for labor. The explanation is that demand for a factor depends upon *Marginal* Product. An invention can raise a factor's Average Product *ap* while reducing its Marginal Product *mp* (at least over a certain range).

EXAMPLE 12.6
The Black Death[a]

The Black Death (1348 to 1350) is generally believed to have wiped out between a quarter and a third of the population of Western Europe. Later recurrences of plague in 1360 to 1361, 1369, and 1374 may each have killed perhaps 5 percent of the populations remaining. The consequent drastic reduction in labor supply had an immediate effect on wages. "The increase due to the plague is 32 percent for the threshing of wheat, 38 percent for barley, 111 percent for oats in the eastern counties. In the middle counties the percentages of rise are 40, 69, 111; in the south, 33, 38, 75; in the west, 26, 41, 44; in the north, 32, 43, and 100."[b]

[a] Discussion based upon J. Hirshleifer, *Disaster and Recovery: The Black Death in Western Europe*, RAND Corporation, Memorandum RM-4700-TAB (Feb. 1966).

[b] H. Robbins, "A Comparison of the Effects of the Black Death on the Economic Organization of France and England," *Journal of Political Economy*, v. 36 (Aug. 1928), p. 463.

The English government responded to this shock with what we would now call a "wage freeze," eventually formalized as the Statute of Laborers (1351). This decree not only froze wages but forbade idleness and required reasonable prices for necessities. Another ordinance in the same year prohibited emigration. But all these regulations failed. The increased scarcity of labor dictated a rise in wages and in per-capita incomes of the laboring classes. When this occurred, members of the upper classes complained about upstarts and nobodies rising to positions of rank and honor, about the need to recontract or entirely remit feudal dues, and even about the clothing worn by social inferiors. (A Statute of Dress of 1363 forbade the lower classes to imitate upper-class attire.)

COMMENT: The feudal system was about as far removed from the economists' competitive model as can be imagined. Feudal economic relationships are in principle dictated solely by custom and status. Nevertheless, competitive forces could not be denied. The system could not withstand the pressure of such a drastic and sudden change in factor availabilities as represented by the Black Death; hence the complaints about flight of labor, vagrancy, "wasting," and the like, and calls upon the government to cancel the market concessions gained by the laborers. An attempt in the reign of Richard II to reverse the clock and enforce the old feudal status relationships led to the Peasants' Revolt of 1381, which came within a hair of overturning the monarchy. Among the peasants' demands were the abolition of serfdom, of feudal dues and services, of governmental monopolies, and of restrictions on buying and selling. In short, the peasants wanted *laissez faire* so that marketplace revisions of economic status could proceed in their favor without government interference.

12.D
MONOPOLIES AND CARTELS IN FACTOR SUPPLY

"Monopsony" on the *demand* side of factor markets was studied in the preceding chapter. Monopoly on the *supply* side of the factor market is the subject here.

Since every firm's product is in some respects unique, every firm has *some* degree of monopoly power in the product market. Similarly for resources: every resource has some degree of uniqueness and therefore every resource-owner has *some* monopoly power in the factor market. But since there almost always are close substitutes for any person's owned resources, an individual monopoly over factor supply is significant only in very unusual cases. (Motion picture stars and athletic champions are examples.) On the other hand, *cartels* of resource-suppliers (e.g., trade unions) are very common.

12.D.1 □ Optimum of the Monopolist Resource-Owner

The optimizing decision for the resource-monopolist is a simple one in the special case where he or she has no reservation uses for the factor. Then the monopolist will merely seek to maximize "Total Revenue" or, we shall say, *Total Factor Income (TFI)*. TFI is equal to the factor earnings $h_L L$ from the owner's given endowment $\bar{R}$ of resources. This maximization *may* dictate holding some units of the resource off the market, not for reservation uses (since, by assumption, there are none) but simply in the interests of obtaining a higher price through monopoly power. Figure 12.9 illustrates such a situation, in terms of a "total" function in the upper panel, and "average-marginal" functions in the lower. The monopolist's income-maximizing employment L^* occurs at the maximum of the *TFI* curve in the upper panel; the lower panel shows, equivalently, how L^* is determined at the point where *Marginal Factor Income MFI* $\equiv \Delta I / \Delta L$ falls to zero. The wage set by the factor-monopolist will be h_L^*, the height of the factor demand curve D_L at $L = L^*$; this wage equals the slope of the dotted line in the upper panel. Since $h_L \equiv TFI/L$, the factor demand curve can be identified with the factor-monopolist's *Average Factor Income* function (*AFI*).

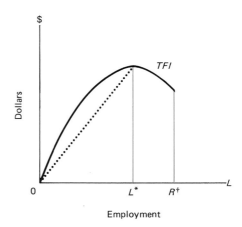

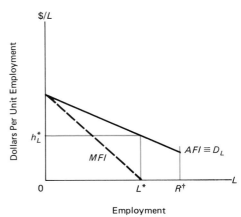

FIGURE 12.9 Factor Monopoly: No Reservation Uses. In the upper panel the curve of Total Factor Income *TFI* represents total earnings of a monopolist seller. In the lower panel the corresponding curve of Average Factor Income *AFI* is also the market demand curve D_L for the factor. The dashed line is the Marginal Factor Income *MFI*. At employment L^*, *TFI* is at its peak, while *MFI* is zero. L^* will be the amount of the resource offered on the market.

What if the curve of Total Factor Income *TFI* is rising throughout the relevant range where $L \le \bar{R}$? (That is, if the factor demand curve is *elastic* throughout.) In that case *MFI* remains greater than zero at $L \equiv \bar{R}$, where all of the resource available is employed. Then the resource-monopolist will *not* find it advantageous to hold any units off the market.

Exercise 12.2: An individual is a monopolist of a resource A, for which he has no reservation uses. (a) If the demand equation is $h_A = 120 - A$, how many units will he hold off the market if his endowment is $R_A = 100$? (b) If the endowment is $R_A = 50$?

Answer: (a) The hire-price h_A is also the Average Factor Income *AFI*. Since $AFI = 120 - A$ is a straight-line equation, Marginal Factor Income is $MFI = 120 - 2A$. Setting $MFI = 0$, we have $A* = 60$. The monopolist will therefore hold $100 - 60 = 40$ units off the market. (b) If he is endowed only with 50 units of A, then *MFI* remains positive even when he sells all 50 units, so he will not hold any off the market.

But if there are *reservation uses*, the monopolist would have to balance them against factor earnings in the market. In Figure 12.10, the shaded opportunity set is bounded by a concave curve rather than a straight line. This concave "budget curve" represents the fact that the wage h_L is *not* constant, but rather is a decreasing function of employment $L \equiv \bar{R} - R$. The monopolist's optimum position is of course at the indifference-curve tangency $G*$; the reservation quantity is $R*$, and the corresponding employment quantity is $L* = \bar{R} - R*$.

This solution is translated to a price-quantity diagram in Figure 12.11. The Marginal Factor Income $MFI \equiv \Delta I/\Delta L$ for any employment level L is the absolute slope $-\Delta I/\Delta R$ (since $\Delta L \equiv -\Delta R$) of the concave budget curve in Figure 12.10. This is the "Marginal Revenue" in income units of sacrificing an hour of leisure. What corresponds to "Marginal Cost" for the factor-monopolist is the *marginal value of reservation uses*, which is nothing but the Marginal Rate of Substitution MRS_R as analyzed in Section 12.A. The rising curve MRS_R in Figure 12.11 shows

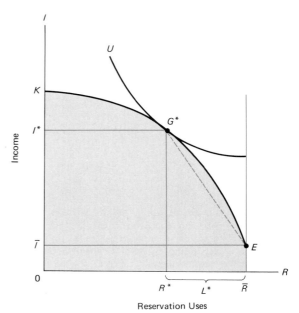

FIGURE 12.10 Factor Monopolist with Reservation Uses, I. On R, I axes a factor monopolist will have a "budget curve" *EK* bounding the shaded market opportunity set. If he has reservation uses for the resource, the optimum is at $G*$, the tangency of *EK* with the highest attainable indifference curve *U*. Retained reservation uses are $R*$; offered employment is $L* = \bar{R} - R*$. The slope of the dashed line $EG*$ represents the market wage for the offered level of employment. *EK* can also be regarded as a Total Factor Income (*TFI*) curve as *L* increases to the left.

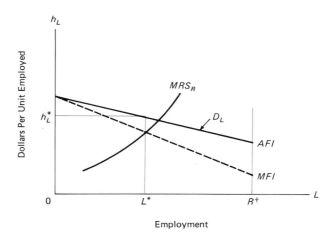

FIGURE 12.11 **Factor Monopolist with Reservation Uses.** The curves of Average Factor Income *AFI* (the demand curve D_L for the factor) and of Marginal Factor Income *MFI* are derived from the budget curve *EK* of the previous diagram. The curve MRS_R, showing the Marginal Rate of Substitution in Resource Supply, represents the Marginal Cost is terms of the individual's foregone value of reservation uses (leisure). The intersection of *MFI* and MRS_R determines the factor monopolist's optimum level of employment *L**, with h_L^* the associated price charged to employers.

increasing "Marginal Cost" of accepting income in place of leisure. So the tangency at G^* in Figure 12.10 (equality of the budget-curve slope and indifference-curve slope) corresponds to the intersection of *MFI* and MRS_R in Figure 12.11. The monopoly optimum wage h_L^* in Figure 12.11 similarly corresponds to the absolute slope of the dashed line EG^* in Figure 12.10.

Exercise 12.3: An individual is endowed with $\overline{R} = 24$ hours of leisure and $\overline{I} = 40$ units of income (dollars). His Marginal Rate of Substitution between income *I* and reservation uses *R* is $MRS_R = I/R$. He is the monopolist of a special type of labor for which the demand is $w = 50 - 4L$, where w is the wage rate and $L \equiv 24 - R$. How much labor should he offer? At what wage? What is the attained income *I*?

Answer: He will want to set MRS_R equal to Marginal Factor Income *MFI*. Average Factor Income *AFI* is $w = 50 - 4L$, and so $MFI = 50 - 8L$. The equation to solve is $50 - 8L = I/(24 - L)$. The achieved income is $I = 40 + wL = 40 + (50 - 4L)L$. After substituting, a quadratic equation is obtained with two solutions: $L = 5$ and $L = 19.33$. The latter violates economic logic since it implies $MFI < 0$, so $L = 5$ is the correct result. When 5 hours of labor are put on the market, the wage is $w = 30$. The attained income is $I = 40 + 5(30) = 190$.

CONCLUSION: The monopolist supplier of a resource, like the monopolist supplier of a product, will set Marginal Revenue equal to Marginal Cost. In the factor market, Marginal Revenue corresponds to Marginal Factor Income *MFI*. Marginal Cost corresponds to MRS_R, the owner's Marginal Rate of Substitution between income and reservation uses of the resource. If there are no reservation uses, MRS_R will be everywhere zero. Even so, the monopolist factor-supplier may still hold some units of the factor off the market, if *MFI* falls to zero before the marketed quantity exhausts the owned supply.

12.D.2 ☐ Resource Cartels

Trade unions are a labor cartel. Workers who have no individual monopoly power band together as a group to raise wages by restricting the supply of labor. Workers gain higher wages at the expense of employers and consumers, but suffer some loss of employment.

As explained in Chapter 8, cartels have a major weakness: "chiseling" by their members. Once the union has raised wages, each member has an incentive to accept less than the standard pay—or, at least, to work harder or longer than before. If a union is to survive, it needs a way to prevent chiseling. One method is social ostracism or even violence. Another way is to secure pro-union legislation.

Under the National Labor Relations Act in the United States, an election is normally held to choose a "collective bargaining agent." Any union that wins a majority of the votes cast becomes the exclusive bargaining agent for *all* workers in the collective-bargaining unit. ("No union" is also one of the options.) When a collective-bargaining agent has been officially certified, individual bargaining is prohibited, so that chiseling is effectively made illegal. No single worker can get additional hours of work by accepting a lesser hourly wage, nor can any outsider come in by offering to work for less.

EXAMPLE 12.7
Union Wage Gains

Do unions raise wages? If so, by how much? Surveying several studies by economists, C. J. Parsley[a] found that wage gains varied widely by occupation. A sample is shown in the table below.

Union Wage Premium (%)

Industrial	15–20
Construction	40–50
Teaching	12–14
Firemen	15

The major weakness of evidence such as this is failure to adjust for differences in the quality of workers. For example, union wage premiums in construction may be high, in part at least, because union members are better trained or more experienced than nonunion workers.

One way to adjust for differences in worker quality is to look at the wages of the same worker as a union and nonunion member. This approach was taken by Wesley Mellow.[b] Using Current Population Survey data from the years 1974 to 1975 and 1977 to 1978, he was able to identify those workers who either joined or quit a union during the sample period. Then, adjusting for changes in education and experience, he found that on average workers' wage rates rose by 7.5 percent upon joining a union and fell by 7 percent upon leaving. Another very important question is the extent to which unionized workers may have suffered some loss of employment as a result of the higher wage received. This question was not directly examined in the study. However, the "wage" measure used was average weekly earnings. This measure already allows for reduced hours of work within the week, but not for any reduction in weeks worked.

[a] C. J. Parsley, "Labor Union Effects on Wage Gains: A Survey of Recent Literature," *Journal of Economic Literature*, v. 18 (Mar. 1980), p. 1.

[b] Wesley Mellow, "Unionism and Wages: A Longitudinal Analysis," *Review of Economics and Statistics*, v. 63 (1981), p. 43.

Trade unions are by no means the only resource cartels. Professional associations, such as the American Medical Association (see Example 12.11, "Returns to Medical Education") are frequently charged with cartel-like behavior. In general, loosely organized resource-supply cartels find it easier to achieve their ends by *restricting entry to the trade*. While price-chiseling may be hidden and difficult to control, entry is relatively visible. A sufficiently tight lid on supply, through control of entry, will inevitably force the market price up even if individual behavior remains competitive. In a supply-demand equilibrium like that of Figure 12.8, entry control might be able to shift the supply curve S_L so far to the left as to achieve a monopoly-like outcome.

EXAMPLE 12.8
Maximum-Hours Laws for Women

A number of states have laws that limit the working hours of adult women. A study by Elisabeth M. Landes[a] noted that in 1900 only eleven states had such legislation, but by 1920 this had increased to forty states and the District of Columbia.

Landes found that, on average, women worked about eight hours less in states with maximum-hours laws. But the effect was primarily upon immigrant women, who had typically been working longer hours. There were also quite significant effects upon *employment*. The employment of foreign-born women fell by as much as 30 percent in the most restrictive states, while employment of native women was largely unaffected. Landes also found that the greater the manufacturing employment of foreign-born women in a state in 1900, the earlier that state tended to enact maximum-hours law for women.

This evidence suggests that state maximum-hours laws tended to exclude immigrants from employment, thus increasing the demand for native American workers. The political logic of this is that native American women workers were more influential than the immigrants from a voting point of view. Native women were more numerous, and more likely to be voters themselves or to have male family members eligible to vote. (In most states the suffrage had not yet been extended to women even by 1920, but the economic interests of wives and daughters would have influenced the votes of male family members.)

[a] Elisabeth M. Landes, "The Effect of State Maximum-Hours Laws on the Employment of Women in 1920," *Journal of Political Economy*, v. 88 (1980).

One notable exception to tight control over occupational entry is the legal profession. A very large increase in the capacity of law schools and in their throughput of students into the profession has occurred in the United States recently, without apparent objection from established lawyers. This exception is, however, understandable and in a sense "proves the rule." Each additional barber or doctor or accountant competes with his or her fellows and takes away business. But the legal process is such that each additional practitioner, by adding to the number of lawsuits, presentments, hearings, trials, pleadings, appeals, writs, demurrers, briefs, rebuttals, rejoinders, and so on, makes *more* business for his or her colleagues.[5] Of course, cartels may be effective over nonlabor resources as well, as the following example indicates.

EXAMPLE 12.9
Tobacco Allotments

Under the market order[a] regulating the supply of tobacco, only those specific acres of farmland that carry "allotments" may be used to grow tobacco. Anyone may become a tobacco grower, but he or she must buy or rent some "allotted" acres. Thus, the government-sponsored cartel works on behalf of owners of the resource of "allotted" land, not on behalf of growers as such. One study has estimated the *premium* paid by growers, for land with an allotment (over equivalent land without allotment), as between $962 and $2500 per acre (for land suitable for growing flue-cured tobacco in North Carolina and Virginia counties in the period 1954 to 1957).[b] A later study[c] estimated that by 1962 the premium had risen to $3281 per acre in eastern North Carolina.

[a] See also Example 8.5, "Agricultural Marketing Orders."
[b] F. H. Maier, J. L. Hedrick, and W. L. Givson, Jr., "The Sale Value of Flue-Cured Tobacco Allotments," Agricultural Experiment Station, Virginia Polytechnic Institute, Technical Bulletin No. 148 (Apr. 1960), p. 40.
[c] James A. Seagraves, "Capitalized Value of Tobacco Allotments and the Rate of Return to Allotment Owners," *American Journal of Agricultural Economics*, v. 51 (May 1969).

12.E
THE "FUNCTIONAL" DISTRIBUTION OF INCOME

12.E.1 ☐ The Problem of Classification

Factors of production have traditionally been classified under the headings of *labor, land,* and *capital*. These were thought to correspond to three categories of "functional" factor returns, namely: *wages* to labor, *rent* to land, and *interest* to capital. In the emerging period of economic thought, most particularly in England in the late eighteenth and early nineteenth centuries, these factor groupings corresponded to major social classes of the time. Land was mainly owned by the aristocracy, capital (material assets other than land) was owned by the rising bourgeoisie, while the working classes could be regarded as owning their labor power. Even sociologically speaking, this classification was not very applicable to societies (like

---

[5] Old folk saying: "When will a lawyer be poor? When he's the only lawyer in town."

America) lacking a feudally based aristocracy. In any case, the claim that these three factors are "functionally" distinct in economic terms is not analytically valid.

LAND VERSUS CAPITAL: *Land* is traditionally defined as the "natural and inexhaustible productive powers of the soil"—that is, its native fertility, topographical features, and geographical location. *Capital*, in contrast with land, is thought of as "produced means of production." But the distinction collapses once it is realized that the actual powers of the soil are as much a human creation as any building or machine. Human effort went into the discovery of the vast new lands of America, and, for that matter, into the draining of marshes and clearing of wasteland in the Old World. Nor can the fertility of land be maintained except by continuing human effort and sacrifice. Most important of all, the original *source* of any productive power is only of historical, not of economic or functional, significance.

It is sometimes claimed that a useful distinction between land and capital can be made in terms of supply curves. Supposedly, the supply of land is absolutely fixed by Nature (a vertical supply curve) while the supply of any manufactured resource is responsive to price (a positively sloping curve). But the supply of land is not fixed. More land *will* be provided when the price is right (if necessary, reclaimed from the ocean), while existing land will be permitted to erode away if the reward for maintaining it is insufficient. Furthermore, even if the amount of physical land were fixed, as long as there are any reservation uses the supply of land *to the market* will respond to price.[6]

LABOR VERSUS CAPITAL: Nor is it possible in the last analysis to distinguish between *labor power* (the source of human services) and capital. In modern society a worker does not sell raw labor power, but rather his or her trained and educated capacity to apply effort. Training is part of the worker's capital ("human capital"), just as a tool he or she owns is a part of capital. There is no functional difference between the worker's sacrificing time and effort in order to acquire training (to improve labor skills) on the one hand, or to purchase a set of tools (to acquire material capital) on the other.

---

[6] The supply curve of land to *all* uses (including reservation uses) will indeed be a vertical line independent of price. But this is true for any resource, including labor. (If "leisure" is counted as a use of labor, the supply of labor is necessarily the entire amount in existence.) Meaningful supply curves always refer to quantities offered for *market* use, excluding reservation uses.

EXAMPLE 12.10
Income Sources of the Wealthy in Britain

A study by Peter H. Lindert has revealed a remarkable change during the past century in the sources of income received by wealthy people in Great Britain. The table here compares the income sources of the upper 10 percent of the population for the years 1867 versus 1972–73. At the earlier date, profits and interest on investments were by far the major component, labor earnings a distant second, with land rents still substantial. By the later date land rents had shrunk into insignificance. And labor earnings had become over-whelmingly the most important source of income for the wealthy, followed by a relatively small share of investment income in the form of profits and interest.

Sources of Income in Britain (Top 10% of Population)

	England and Wales 1867 (%)	United Kingdom 1972–73 (%)
Land rents	13	1
Interest, etc.	69	15
Labor earnings	18	84
TOTAL	100	100

Source: Adapted from Peter H. Lindert, "Unequal English Wealth Since 1670," *Journal of Political Economy*, v. 94 (Dec. 1986), p. 1155.

While the change in income shares is most striking for the wealthy, the same holds true over the population at large. Lindert estimated the overall shares of national income attributable specifically to human skills rose from around 15 percent in 1867 to 52 percent in the years 1972 to 1973.

COMMENT: The main explanation, it appears, is that the vast accu-mulation of durable material capital over the past century has re-duced its scarcity value and therefore the rate of earnings of that type of resource. Labor, in contrast, has become relatively scarce. Furthermore, the complexity of modern society has made skills (hu-man capital) increasingly costly to acquire (long years of training and education are required), and these costs must be paid for by markedly higher earnings.

Of course, even if different types of factors are not really functionally dis-tinct, there can still be important differences among them. Suppose, for example, that you are a resource-owner concerned with the threat of confiscation. Then the "portability" of alternative ways of holding your resource wealth might be very important for you. Land is evidently the least portable form of capital asset, one that is hard to pick up and walk away with. Manufactured capital goods can range from quite immovable buildings to easily transportable light tools. Most portable of all is human capital, which anyone can carry around without much extra cost. So people who fear confiscation might be expected to hold their wealth largely in the form of portable resources, especially human capital.

12.E.2 □ An Application: Investment in Human Capital

Figure 12.12 shows an individual who adds to his "human capital" by invest-ing in education or training. Suppose that with no education he would locate at

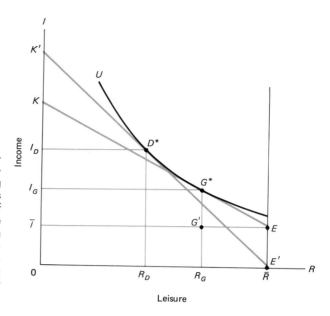

FIGURE 12.12 Returns to Education. The individual here is just indifferent as to an investment in education. With endowment at E, along the initial budget line EK the optimal position is G^* on indifference curve U. Incurring a cost of education, represented by the vertical distance EE', raises his market wage so that he has a new steeper budget line $E'L'$. The new tangency optimum D^* along $E'K'$ lies to the northwest of G^*, showing that the individual making the educational investment will thereafter choose less leisure.

G^* along the budget line EK. Non-wage income is $\bar{I}$. Education will have two effects: first, non-wage income will be reduced because of tuition and foregone earnings. Assume this shifts the endowment from E down to E'. Second, his wage will be higher because of his education. Thus the new budget line $E'K'$ is steeper. Now suppose that his new optimum D^* is on the same indifference curve as G^*. In other words, he is just on the borderline as to obtaining the education or not. At the new optimum D^*, income I_D is higher than before but leisure R_D is less. Note the possibly surprising result: becoming educated means you should rationally work harder ever after! [*Question for the student*: The analysis above considers an individual who is indifferent (just on the borderline) between receiving the training or not. But most people who obtain an education do so with the expectation of being definitely better off. Would such a person be more likely, or less likely, to work longer hours afterward than someone who was just on the borderline?]

EXAMPLE 12.11
Returns to Medical Education

The professional medical associations, in particular the AMA, have been accused of functioning as entry-restricting cartels. Evidence has been brought forward showing that, *in terms of income achieved*, there seems to be an "excess" return to investment in medical education. That is, medical education seems to be exceptionally profitable, suggesting that there may be a cartel at work effectively limiting entry. C. M. Lindsay has contended, however, that a comparison solely in terms of income achieved fails to allow properly for the fact that, after making human-capital investments such as medical training, individuals will typically be enjoying *less leisure* than before.

In the table the "unadjusted" MD returns represent the seeming excess value of medical education ($24,376) in comparison with ordinary college education. This amount is the net additional income achieved, deducting the cost of medical training, but *without* any offset for additional working hours of MDs. There are two ways of allowing for the extra hours worked by MDs: adjusting college-graduate hours worked *up*, or adjusting MD hours worked *down*. (The true comparison must lie between the results of these two alternative adjustments.)

Reportedly, MDs worked 62 hours per week on the average. For the sake of comparison, alternative assumptions of a 40- and a 45-hour average workweek were used for college graduates. If college graduates are working 45 hours per week, the table shows an excess net return to medical education somewhere between the two estimates of $10,830 and $1,950. On the 40-hour assumption, however, the two adjustments average out very close to zero. So if college graduates generally are working close to 40 hours per week, there is no evidence of an excess return to medical education—once the MDs' loss of leisure is properly taken into account.

Excess Returns to Medical Education

	40-Hour Week	45-Hour Week
Unadjusted MD excess returns	$24,376	$24,376
Adjusted by raising college graduate hours (to 62)	4,660	10,830
Adjusted by lowering MD hours	−4,580	1,950

Source: C. M. Lindsay, "Real Returns to Medical Education," *Journal of Human Resources*, v. 8 (Summer 1973), p. 338. An interest rate of 10 percent was used to represent the "normal" return from which the "excess" was calculated. (The original source shows the computation in terms of interest rates of both 5 percent and 10 percent).

COMMENT: The 62-hour figure for MDs, being self-reported, may be suspect. Doctors (like other people) are apt to report themselves working harder than they really are. If doctors do not in fact work as many as 62 hours per week, the evidence here would tend to support the hypothesis of an excess (cartel-like) return to medical education.

*12.E.3 □ Another Application: Land Rent and Urban Location

We now will go somewhat further afield, to address a rather different kind of problem: land rent as related to urban location.

For simplicity, think of a linear city as pictured in Figure 12.13. Everyone works in the Central Business District (CBD). Consider a household deciding

*Marked sections, beginning with a single asterisk and ending with a double asterisk, may contain somewhat more difficult or advanced material and can be omitted without appreciable loss of continuity.

FIGURE 12.13 A Linear City. Everyone is employed in the Central Business District (*CBD*). Individuals reside at various distances (*d*) in either direction from the *CBD*.

where to live—that is, choosing the optimal distance $d*$ from the CBD at which to reside. Figure 12.14 illustrates the elements in the decision. First there is the curve V representing the desirability or utility value of closer-in versus farther-out locations. For simplicity, V is taken as constant here (a horizontal line in the diagram), though more generally it might be either a rising or a falling function of distance d. Against the value must be weighed the commuting costs, represented by the rising TCC (Total Commuting Cost) curve in the diagram. The *vertical difference* between these curves serves to define the "bid-rent" *br*. The bid-rent represents the *maximum* that the household would be willing to pay for any given location:

$$br = V - TCC$$

We now have to bring in the market opportunities. Specifically here, the *market land rent*, as a function of distance d, is represented by the bold dashed curve LR. As shown in the diagram, the household can advantageously locate anywhere between L_1 and L_2, the range of distances from the CBD in which its *br* curve lies above the LR curve (its willingness to pay exceeds the market land rent). But of course the best location, $d*$, is where the vertical difference $br - LR$ is greatest. At this point the household's marginal loss of locational desirability (reduction in willingness to pay) from increased distance d just equals its marginal saving in reduced land rent.

From the point of view of the household the market land rent curve LR is given. But for the community as a whole the LR curve represents an equilibrium

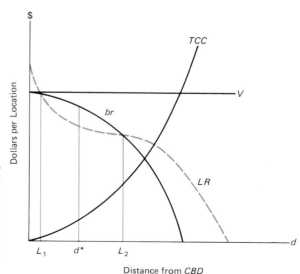

FIGURE 12.14 Optimal Residential Location. The value *V* to individuals of different locations is assumed to be independent of distance *d*. A person's bid-rent curve *br* is the vertical difference between *V* and his or her Total Commuting Cost (TCC). The housing market opportunities take the form of a Land Rent curve *LR*. The individual's optimal location, *d**, is where the vertical difference between the *br* and *LR* curves is greatest.

that results from the locational decisions of all of the households in the city (together with the decisions of the various firms and agencies competing with households for urban space). The equilibrium land rent will normally be a declining function of distance, for several reasons. First, because were it not for a rent differential all households would be trying to locate nearer to the CBD,[7] which would be impossible. A second reason is geometry. Adopting the more reasonable assumption that the city is circular rather than linear, the area available increases as the square of the distance from the CBD. So close-in locations are not only in greater demand but in lesser supply. Third, the most urgent of the *nonresidential* demands for space are for locations close to the CBD. The city might not even exist except for some important industry or activity, like a harbor or a government headquarters, which forms the heart of the CBD.

Let us now explore more closely how the market land-rent curve *LR* is derived. In Figure 12.14 we saw the bid-rent curve *br* for a particular household. More generally every household, firm, or other agency demanding space will have its own bid-rent curve. If any such entity is to remain in the city, it will have to be the high bidder for space *somewhere*.[8] In Figure 12.15 we see bid-rent curves for three such bidders. As the number of bidders grows very large, the *upper bound* or "envelope" of their various br_i curves becomes an essentially continuous curve. This is the equilibrium market land-rent curve *LR* for the city as a whole. [*Query:* Under what circumstances would we expect to observe a steep *LR* curve? A flat *LR* curve?] **

**End of marked section.

[7] This would not necessarily be the case if we diverged from our simplifying assumption that the value V of location is independent of distance. For people who value the purer air or other amenities of the outskirts, V could be a rising function of d. This effect might be sufficiently strong, for some households, to overcome the commuting-cost disadvantage of locations farther out.

[8] In Figure 12.14 it was assumed that each household located at a single best *point*. More generally, we would want to allow households or other agencies to locate over distance *intervals* (or areas, if we were to consider more than one space dimension). However, this would require a more complicated analysis than can be pursued here.

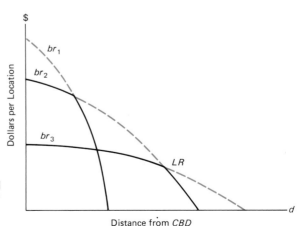

FIGURE 12.15 Bid Rents and Market Land Rent. The market land-rent (*LR*) curve is the outer envelope of the individuals' separate bid-rent (*br_i*) curves.

12.F
CAPITAL VERSUS INCOME: THE RATE OF INTEREST

For some purposes it is essential to distinguish between *sources* of productive services and the *productive services* themselves. The human being is the source of labor services, but the labor service is the "man-hour" (or other unit representing the employment of a worker over some defined period of time). Similarly, land is a source of productive services, but the service itself is measured in units of acre-years. And again, it is necessary to distinguish buildings and machines (both sources) from the services of building and machines.

Sources and their services may both be traded in markets. There is a price for an acre of land, and a price for a year's use of an acre of land (the latter being the hire-price or rental). There is a price for a building, and a rental for use of the building over some period of time. Labor is a special case. The *sources* of labor services (the human beings themselves) may not be sold, though labor still can be hired for a periodic wage (the hire-price per man-hour). The "factor prices" discussed in this and previous chapters have been the *hire or rental prices of the productive services*—not the prices of the resources themselves.

The sources of factor services constitute an individual's or a nation's "capital." Land is capital, machines and buildings are capital, and the human being's training, strength, and skill are his or her human capital.

EXAMPLE 12.12
Capital in the Slave-Owning South

The following table, based on a study by Louis Rose, summarizes the value of various categories of property (capital) in the fifteen states where slaves were emancipated by President Lincoln's proclamation. Slave values varied greatly with age and other characteristics; the mean was $933. Emancipation constituted an enormous loss to the slave-owners but this was of course balanced by a corresponding gain to the slaves (in the form of the transferred ownership of their own persons).

Wealth Data, 15 Southern States, 1860 (millions of dollars)

Value of real estate and personal property	$8644
Value of land in farms	2550
Value of implements and machinery in use	104
Value of livestock	515
Value of slaves emancipated	3685

Source: L. Rose, "Capital Losses of Southern Slaveholders Due to Emancipation," *Western Economic Journal*, v. 3 (Fall 1964), pp. 43, 49.

COMMENT: A complete tabulation should also include the labor-power value of the free population. Counting both slave and free labor power, it seems likely that the value of the "human capital" of the 1860 South exceeded all other capital combined. Very likely this remains true today for all modern Western economies. Even though material capital has grown more rapidly than the human population since 1860 (a greater quantity of machines and other productive tools are now available per worker), owing to factor complementarity there has been an enormous increase in the *value* of a labor-hour in comparison with a machine-hour.

There are two senses of the word "capital." *Real-capital* refers to the sources themselves—land, buildings, labor power, etc. *Capital-value* refers to the market values of the sources, measured in dollars. Similarly, *real income* refers to a flow of goods, but when the word "income" is used alone it is usually understood to mean a flow of dollars. The Marginal Product of an acre of land represents real income (bushels of wheat per year), while the Value of the Marginal Product represents money income (dollars per year).

If a resource is tradable, there will be a market-determined ratio between the *annual value of the service* and the *value of the source*—that is, the ratio of income to capital-value. This ratio is the *rate of interest* earned from ownership of the resource. Suppose an acre of land is valued at $1000 and generates real income (has a Marginal Product) of 50 bushels of wheat per year. If the price of wheat is $2 per bushel, the income (Value of the Marginal Product) is $100 per year. Then the rate of interest r earned upon the investment in land is $100/$1000, or 10 percent per year. More generally, for any asset:

$$(12.3) \qquad \text{Rate of interest earned} \quad r \equiv \frac{\text{Annual income}}{\text{Value of asset}}$$

Of course, if the asset *depreciates* in value during the year this should be counted against income. For some asset A, let P_A represent its market value, let ΔP_A be the change in ths value (appreciation or depreciation) during the year, and z_A be the "cash flow" it generates during the year. Then we can rewrite Equation (12.3) as:

$$(12.3') \qquad r_A \equiv \frac{z_A + \Delta P_A}{P_A}$$

There is a fundamental relation between income and capital-value:

PROPOSITION: The proportionate yield (the rate of interest earned) on all assets tends to come to equality.

If asset A has a higher-than-normal yield, people will want to buy it, and its price P_A will be bid up. Obviously, as P_A rises in Equation (12.3'), the yield r_A will fall. This process will only stop when the yield on asset A is equal to the yield on other equivalent assets.

An important implication is that assets whose values are expected to *depreciate* during a given time period should yield large cash flows z; assets whose values are expected to *appreciate* may be attractive despite small cash flows. A land speculator may pay a steep price for a city lot, even though intending to hold it vacant for a year or more. Here there would be no positive cash flow at all, and indeed very likely a substantial negative cash flow due to taxes. But the speculator expects the value of the site to appreciate enough to make the investment worthwhile.

Exercise 12.4: In an economy where the interest rate r is 5 percent, suppose there are three assets: acres of land (A), for which the annual cash flow is $z_A = 50$ and neither appreciation nor depreciation is anticipated; barrels of maturing wine (B), for which the cash flow is $z_B = -30$ (there are no receipts, only storage expenses) but which are expected to appreciate 8% in value over the year; and machines (M), yielding a cash flow $z_M = 100$ but expected to depreciate 5% in value over the year. Find the asset prices P_A, P_B, and P_M.

Answer: In each case we will use the equation $r = (z + \Delta P)/P$. For asset A, appreciation is $\Delta P = 0$ and so the equation has the simple form $0.05 = 50/P$, the solution being $P_A = 1000$. For asset B, the expected appreciation is $\Delta P = 0.08P$. Thus the equation becomes $0.05 = (-30 + 0.08P)/P$, so that $P_B = 1000$ also. For asset M, $\Delta P = -5\%$ and so the equation is $0.05 = (50 - 0.05P)/P$. Once again the solution is $P_M = 1000$. All three assets have the same value; the numbers are such that for asset B anticipated appreciation exactly offsets a negative cash flow, while for asset M a positive cash flow exactly offsets depreciation.

Since rent is the hire-price of land, *annual rent* on land will (in equilibrium) be equal to *the interest yield on the price or capital-value* of the land. In a slave economy, annual wages as the hire-price of labor would tend to equal the interest yield on the capital-value of the slave. And even in a free economy, the additional income due to investment in training would, allowing for loss of leisure, tend to equal the interest yield on the cost of acquiring that training (see the example "Returns to Medical Education"). For any factor A, then, in equilibrium:

(12.4)
$$h_A = rP_A$$

> CONCLUSION: Interest is not the return to a particular factor called "capital." Rather, in equilibrium the income returned to any factor will be equal to the interest yield on the price or *capital-value* of the resource. Or put another way: The interest rate is, for any factor, the ratio between the hire-price of the factor and the market value of the *source* of the factor services.

Since elements of material capital can be freely traded in the economy, there is no special reason to expect different types of material resources to yield higher returns than others do (after allowing for appreciation or depreciation as discussed above). But human capital, being tied to its owner, is not freely marketable. So we might possibly anticipate some demographic differences in the returns from human capital investments.

EXAMPLE 12.13
Human Capital and Religion

A number of different studies have shown that Jews in Western nations tend to have significantly higher average per-capita earnings than non-Jews. To some extent this may be a statistical accident. For example, Jews live predominantly in major urban cities where high earnings are offset by a high cost of living. Also, Jews tend to have small families, which means they can devote less time to nonmarket employments such as parental care. Jews also notably invest more in education on average. Consequently, their higher earnings are in large part just the returns to the larger amounts of human capital they have chosen to accumulate.

The question remains, do Jews typically achieve a higher *rate of return* on human capital investments? Two conflicting theories have been proposed. According to the first theory, for genetic or cultural reasons Jews have a greater capacity to put education and training to productive use. This theory predicts, therefore, that Jews would invest more in human capital and would also achieve a *higher* rate of return on these investments. The second theory is that Jews have traditionally emphasized investment in human capital only because that form of wealth has proved historically to be less easily confiscated. According to this theory, Jews will invest more in education and training, but, owing to the law of diminishing returns, they should receive on average a *lower* rate of return on these investments.

A study by Nigel Tomes using data from the 1971 Canadian census seemed to provide a clear answer to this question. With regard to schooling, the table indicates that Jews achieved a markedly *higher* rate of return despite having invested more years in education. He also found that Jews also benefited more from job experience. Thus, the higher observed earnings of Jews seem to be a combination of two elements: investing more in human capital and a higher rate of return on that form of investment.

	Jews	Protestants	Catholics	Other/None
Av. years of education	9.055	8.297	7.246	7.704
Av. rate of return (%)	5.77	4.24	3.69	3.23

Source: Nigel Tomes, "Religion and the Rate of Return on Human Capital: The Evidence from Canada," *Canadian Journal of Economics*, v. 116 (Feb. 1983).

12.G
ECONOMIC RENT AND PRODUCER SURPLUS

What is sometimes called "economic rent" is a rather special concept used by economists. It must be distinguished from the usual sense of rent as the hire-price of a piece of land or a building. Economic rent is the "excess" return to a factor, meaning the difference between what a factor is paid and what its owner would have been barely willing to accept. Economic rent is therefore very similar to the concept of Producer Surplus introduced in Chapter 7. The only difference is that Producer Surplus refers to a seller's gain from trade *in the product market*, while economic rent measures the seller's gain from trade *in the factor market*.

Economic rent is shown in Figure 12.16 as the *area above the supply curve and below the price*. (Note how similar this is to the picture of Producer Surplus in Figure 7.7, the difference being that the horizontal axis here is scaled in units of factor A rather than units of output Q.) Economic rent exists because the sellers receive h_a^* for all A^* units sold, even though they would have been willing to sell all but the last unit at a lower hire-price—down to h_a^o for the first unit sold.

Economic rent is a slippery category, which must be used with care. Its mag-

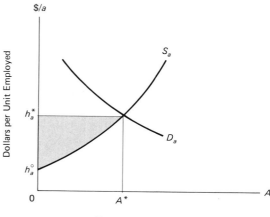

FIGURE 12.16 **Economic Rent.** Economic rent is the area lying above the factor supply curve S_a but below the market equilibrium hire-price h_a^*.

Employment of Factor A

nitude depends upon the range of alternatives considered. First of all, notice that the size of economic rent in Figure 12.16 is closely related to the shape of the supply curve S_a. The steeper is S_a, the greater the fraction of the factor return that falls into the category of economic rent. (In the limit, if S_a were vertical at $A = A^*$, the entire payment $h_a A^*$ would be economic rent.) The slope of the supply curve to a narrowly defined activity, like being a cashier, is likely to be quite flat. This means that the economic rent—the "excess" return of being a cashier rather than one's next best job as, say, a typist or salesperson—will be small. But someone who is getting only a small economic rent *as a cashier* may be receiving a large economic rent as against the alternative of not working at all (leisure). His or her supply curve to employment in general may be quite steep, even when the supply curve to a single narrowly defined occupation is very flat.

The presence of economic rent, and the problems associated with the slipperiness of that concept, have important implications for taxation. The famous "single-tax" proposal by Henry George[9] was based upon the idea that, since land is in fixed supply (its supply curve is supposedly vertical), practically all of land rent can be taxed away without affecting the amount of land made available for productive use. In short, Henry George thought that all land rent was economic rent. But this is not the case: (1) As we have seen, land is not literally in fixed supply. A very heavy tax on land rent would not only discourage reclaiming new land from the ocean, but would rule out the investments needed to prevent erosion and waterlogging on existing land. (2) Even if land were in physically fixed supply, its supply *to the market* is not fixed. With a sufficiently high tax on market rent, landowners would retain their land in reservation uses—they would keep large residential estates, or would engage in home farming. (3) A very high tax on land would make it less important for the owner to seek out the *best* use of his land, since he will be able to keep little of its earnings in the highest-paying use.

In general, the flaws in the single-tax proposal all involve a confusion of "rent" as payment to land with true "economic rent" as an excess that can be taxed away without affecting the amount or use of land.

[9] Henry George, 1839–1897, American economist and reformer.

EXAMPLE 12.14 *
Economic Rent and the Military Draft

Until recently a sizable number of U.S. military personnel were conscripted. In 1967 Walter Oi[a] analyzed the losses of economic rents that would be suffered, given a continuation of conscription, by suppliers of labor services to the armed forces. For a desired intake of 472,000 recruits annually, it was estimated that the yearly recruitment at the then-current starting wage of $2500 per year would be composed of 263,000 "true" volunteers, 153,700 "reluctant" volunteers (individuals induced to volunteer only to gain some advantages over being drafted), and 55,300 draftees.

The draft viewed as a "tax" affects these groups differently. The true volunteers are those already willing to serve at the $2500 military wage. But if military salaries were raised enough to eliminate any need for reluctant volunteers or draftees, the true volunteers would also receive more pay. Under the most favorable assumption as to the elasticity of voluntary supply to the armed forces, Oi estimated that to attract the required numbers the annual wage would have to be $5900. (Under what he regarded as a more realistic assumption, the wage would have to be $7450.) The loss of this benefit (the economic rent that a true volunteer would have received if the wage were $5900) is therefore at least $3400 per true volunteer per year.

The reluctant volunteers, it is reasonable to assume, had better market opportunities than the true volunteers. As a result of enlistment at the $2500 rather than $5900 wage, they were estimated to lose on average $918 per year from foregoing these market opportunities, leaving $2482 as their average loss in economic rent (where $918 + $2482 = $3400). For the draftees, individuals who had to be compelled to serve, market opportunities were presumably better still. Oi estimated the $3400 loss to them as divided between $3165 per year in foregone market opportunities and only $235 per year in economic rent. (These estimates for reluctant volunteers and draftees are minimal figures, which would be appropriate only if individuals drafted or induced to volunteer were those with the poorest alternative nonmilitary employments.)

[a] W. Y. Oi, "The Economic Cost of the Draft," *American Economic Review*, v. 57 (May 1967), pp. 39–62.

12.H
CAPITAL, INTERTEMPORAL CHOICE, AND THE CIRCULAR FLOW

We have now studied individuals' choices as *consumers* and as *resource-owners*. But there remains a third dimension of choice: *between consumption and increased resource-ownership*. Each person not only has to decide how to consume income and how to employ resources owned but also whether and to what extent to refrain from consuming now (to save) so as to acquire more resources for the future. When individuals save, they can physically produce new resources for themselves (as when Robinson Crusoe gives up some current consumption in order to weave a net so as to catch more fish in the future). Or, more usually in a modern economy, people save by purchasing claims or titles to resources (for example, when they buy stocks or bonds). When savers buy bonds or shares, other individuals or firms can obtain the funds needed to manufacture new resources like buildings or machines. *Saving* is the process of refraining from consumption; the process of actually building new real-capital is called *investment*.

Since saving provides increased income for the future, today's consumption-versus-saving decision can also be interpreted as a choice between *present* consumption and *future* consumption. The topic of intertemporal choice will be the subject of Chapter 14.

The familiar picture in Figure 1.1 of the circular flow of economic activity can now be made more realistic by separating consumption and saving (see Figure 12.17). Imagine there are two types of firms: those producing *consumption goods* and those producing real-capital or *investment goods* (buildings, land, machines, etc.). In the upper portion of the diagram (the product market), individuals purchase the two types of goods by consumption expenditures and savings expenditures, respectively. In the lower part of the diagram (the factor market), individu-

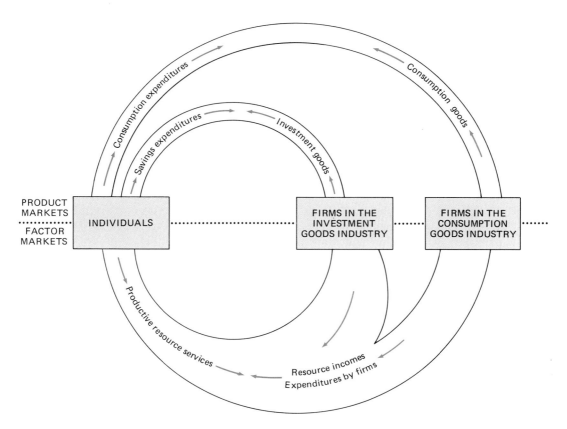

FIGURE 12.17 The Circular Flow: Consumption and Investment

als supply factor services to the employing firms. When someone decides to save rather than to consume he increases his stock of owned resources so that, in the future, he will be able to supply a larger quantity of productive services and thereby earn more income.[10]

□ SUMMARY OF CHAPTER 12

In the product markets, individuals are demanders of goods; in the factor markets they are suppliers of resource services. The payments people receive for factor services become their incomes available for spending on consumer goods.

The owner of any resource A must decide between offering it on the market to obtain income I or else retaining it for "leisure" or reservation uses R_a. At the resource-owner's optimum, his or her Marginal Rate of Substitution in Resource Supply MRS_R (the marginal value of the reservation uses) will be equal to the factor hire-price h_a. As endowed income (income from other sources) changes, an Income Expansion Path IEP will be traced out. Assuming that R_a and I are both normal goods, the IEP will have positive slope—showing that as income rises more reservation uses will be chosen (less of the factor will be supplied to the market). As hire-price h_a varies, a Price Expansion Path PEP will be traced out. In decisions concerning factor supply, the income and substitution effects normally work in opposite directions. At very low hire-prices (in the neighborhood of the all-leisure corner solution) the substitution effect must dominate, so that the PEP has normal negative slope. But for sufficiently high h_a the income effect may dominate; the PEP may "bend backward."

Corresponding to the possible backward-bending range of the PEP would be a backward-bending range of the factor supply curve (where *less* is offered as the hire-price rises). However, even if the overall supply curve *to the entire market* (as against the alternative of leisure) bends backward, the supply of resource *to any limited sector or particular activity* is almost certain to have the standard positive slope—since there are so many other alternative factor uses to draw supply from as h_a rises.

Market equilibrium for any factor A, under competition, is found where the supply and demand curves cross. Factor demand tends to rise with technological progress, with higher consumer demand for final products, and with increased supply of cooperating factors. On the supply side, greater wealth increases overall factor availability, but at the same time tends to decrease the fraction provided to the market—since suppliers can afford to "purchase" more reservation uses of their resources.

A monopolist of a factor faces a "budget curve" instead of a budget line in choosing between income and leisure. In deciding how much of the resource to offer on the market, the factor-monopolist would balance Marginal Factor Income MFI against the Marginal Cost of providing the factor. This Marginal Cost would be the individual's Marginal Rate of Substitution in Resource Supply, MRS_R. In the absence of reservation uses, the factor-monopolist's MRS_R would be

---

[10] The implicit assumption underlying the diagram is that all resources are *owned* by individuals and *rented* to firms for productive employment. In actuality firms themselves may legally own as well as hire resources. But resource-ownership on the part of firms can be regarded merely as a convenient fiction, since ultimately all firms are themselves owned by individuals.

zero and so he or she would simply maximize Total Factor Income *TFI* (would set $MFI = 0$).

Trade unions and other forms of resource cartels are attempts by smaller suppliers to act as a collective monopolist. As in the case of product-market cartels, there are strong incentives to "chisel"—which, for the most part, can be effectively countered only by government support of the cartel.

A traditional classification divides factors of production into the categories of *land* (resources provided by Nature), *capital* (resources provided by human sacrifice and forethought), and *labor* (the human resource itself). This classification is not logically defensible: elements provided by Nature and elements provided by human effort enter into all three of the usual categories.

A more valid distinction is that between *productive services* (such as a man-hour of labor or an acre-year of land) and the *sources* of these services. These sources, whether in the form of land or machines or human beings, are the "real-capital" of the economy. For any resource A, the relation between the price P_A of the source and the hire-price h_A of its services involves the *interest rate r*: to wit, $h_A = rP_A$. Put another way, r is the ratio between the annual net income of any asset (adjusted for depreciation or appreciation) and the value of the asset itself.

Economic rent is the excess of what a resource-seller is paid over what he or she would have been barely willing to accept for supplying a resource to the market. What was called Producer Surplus in Chapter 7 is essentially the same as economic rent. Economic rent is smaller the narrower the range of uses considered. So, even if the owner's economic rent as against the alternative of nonmarket uses or leisure is large, the economic rent received in the best (as against the second-best) market use may be quite small.

The individual's decisions *as a consumer* concern what goods to buy. *As a resource-owner*, the choice is among alternative employments of the owned factors. A third decision problem is between consuming versus saving or investing so as to acquire more resources. This last is in effect a choice between present consumption and future consumption.

☐ QUESTIONS FOR CHAPTER 12

MAINLY FOR REVIEW

R1. "Leisure" is a reservation use of labor. What other resources are likely to have significant nonmarket or reservation uses yielding utility to their owners?

R2. Explain, in terms of income and substitution effects, how a "backward-bending" supply curve of a resource service can come about.

*R3. If leisure were an inferior good, would a backward-bending supply curve of labor be possible?

*R4. Why *must* the substitution effect dominate the income effect at very low wage rates?

*R5. Is the supply curve of a resource to a particular employment likely to be more or less elastic than the supply to all market uses? Why?

R6. In what way does the market opportunity set of a factor-monopolist differ from that of a competitive supplier of factor services? How will the optimum of the resource-owner be affected?

*R7. Physicians commonly work unusually long hours, and are often praised for their dedication to healing the sick and alleviating human suffering. Show why, even if physicians are not exceptionally tenderhearted, they would still be likely to work long hours.

R8. Explain the traditional "functional" classification of factors of production.

*R9. How can land and labor power be thought of as capital?

*R10. What is the relationship between the hire-price of a factor and the purchase price of that factor?

R11. What causes the rate of return on all material assets to tend toward equality?

*R12. What is economic rent? What is its relation to Producer Surplus?

FOR FURTHER THOUGHT AND DISCUSSION

*T1. The term "leisure" really stands for reservation or nonmarket uses of one's labor. What would be the effect upon women's demand for "leisure" of: (a) a decline in the birth rate; (b) improved household technology (as with the introduction of washing machines, vacuum cleaners, etc.); (c) a fall in the price of prepared foods? In each case, what would be the effect on men's supply of labor?

T2. What would be the effect upon the budget line and the resource-owner's optimum of a *progressive* income tax on labor earnings? Of a time-and-a-half rule for overtime work?

T3. Diagram a situation in which a resource-owner chooses a "corner solution" so as to devote all of his or her resource to reservation uses. Does this necessarily imply that income I must be a "bad" or a "neuter" commodity at the solution point? Diagram a situation in which the resource-owner's optimum is such that no reservation uses R are retained. Does this imply that R must be a "bad" or a "neuter" commodity at the solution point? Explain.

*T4. With the advent of the women's liberation movement, there is reason to believe that women's preferences may be changing so as to make reservation uses of their time less attractive than before, in comparison with market employment. What effect would such a change have upon the supply curve of female labor? Upon the relative market wages of male and female workers?

*T5. In modern times, real wealth and real wage rates have steadily increased throughout the Western world. But average working hours in market employment have steadily fallen. Would the pure "income effect" (due to rising per-capita wealth) tend to lead to reduced market employment? Would the pure "substitution effect" (due to the relative price shift represented by the rising wage rate) tend to have this effect? Comment upon the relative importance of the two in light of the evidence.

*T6. Historians generally believe that slave labor is less productive than free labor. Analyze this contention.

T7. There have been proposals that wage rates ought to be based upon "comparable worth" rather than upon supply and demand. A number of states and other political jurisdictions have already accepted this principle for determining salaries of public employees. In fact, there is now a flourishing business of "comparable-worth consultants" who provide formulas as to how salaries should be computed in accordance with the knowledge and skill required, the complexity of the task, physical demands of the job, etc. But these various formulas differ drastically from one another. Is there any way of objectively determining "comparable worth" apart from supply and demand? What consequences would you anticipate if a wage set in accordance with "comparable worth" diverged from that indicated by supply and demand?

T8. According to the "single-tax" movement, a land tax would not affect the productive uses of land—since the supply of land is fixed. Is this valid? Distinguish between the consequences of (a) a tax on *market uses* of land, versus (b) a tax on *ownership* of land.

*T9. In the case of labor, distinguish between the consequences of (a) a tax upon labor earnings (market uses of labor), versus (b) a tax upon labor capacity (that is, a tax calculated upon the individual's *ability to earn*, whether he or she works or not).

*T10. What *supply-side* considerations help explain the relatively high wages received by U.S. workers?

T11. Over a century ago Karl Marx, in what is known as the "immiserization hypothesis," predicted that workers' wages and incomes in the advanced industrial countries would tend to fall—thus bringing on a socialist revolution. This prediction has failed. Some defenders of Marx have argued that the reason why immiserization did not occur is that in the meantime capitalism has adopted "socialistic" reforms. Among these might perhaps be classed minimum-wage laws, the forty-hour week, welfare relief for the unemployed, and laws encouraging trade unions and collective bargaining. What effects would you expect each of these reforms to have upon wage rates? Upon workers' incomes?

*T12. Wage rates are high in New York City, compared to the rest of the United States. But so is the cost of living. Would you conclude that typical New York workers really are, or are not, more productive than workers elsewhere?

T13. In terms of urban location, would *high* commuting costs tend to make for a steep market land-rent curve? Would *sharply increasing* commuting costs (high *marginal* cost of traveling greater distance) tend to do so?

* The answers to starred questions appear at the end of the book.

13
CORE CHAPTER

EXCHANGE, TRANSACTION COSTS, AND MONEY

The Fundamental Theorem of Exchange—that voluntary trade benefits both buyer and seller—was introduced in Chapter 7. We also saw there how Consumer Surplus and Producer Surplus measure, respectively, the buyers' and sellers' gains from exchange. Errors of economic reasoning (for example, the most commonly encountered arguments for protective tariffs) often rest upon failure to appreciate the obvious truth that voluntary trade must benefit both sides.

There are, however, debatable aspects of this theorem. (1) Suppose trickery has taken place: a purchaser has paid good money for a beachfront lot that turns out to be a mile out to sea. (Here there was no actual *agreement*, no meeting of minds.) (2) Momentary desires may not represent an individual's true considered preferences. Esau sold his birthright to Jacob for a mess of pottage, and regretted the transaction afterward. (3) Still more seriously, do individuals always benefit from having even their fully considered preferences satisfied? What about a person who chooses to consume narcotics? That a person's desires do not necessarily lead to where his or her true benefit lies has been a theme of moralists through the ages.

While these philosophical questions cannot be studied here, we see that there are possible qualifications to the Fundamental Theorem. Nevertheless, it remains the case that each trader who engages in exchange *believes* that he or she will gain, even though an outside observer may not think so.

There are two distinct elements in the mutual gain from trade. The first element is the *improved allocation of consumption goods* among individuals. Suppose there are two persons, let us call them John and Karl, both endowed with equal quantities of tea and coffee. If John prefers tea and Karl prefers coffee, the potential gain from trade will be obvious. Nor are differences of taste necessary. Suppose John and Karl have the same preferences as to bread and butter, but John initially has all the bread and Karl all the butter. Again, trade can obviously benefit both.

The second source of mutual gain is that trade makes it possible for the parties to arrive at a *better arrangement of production*. If John is superior at baking bread and Karl at churning butter, the possibility of later trading permits each to specialize in producing what he is better at.

CONCLUSION: Voluntary exchange is mutually beneficial because individuals can: (1) trade existing goods so that each achieves a preferred bundle, and (2) specialize in production so as to increase the social totals of goods available.

In this chapter we will be probing more deeply into the familiar supply-demand equilibrium of markets. We will also face the fact that exchange is not a costless process, and that *transaction costs* place a limit upon the achievable benefits from trade. The role of *money* in minimizing such costs of transacting will be the last topic of the chapter.

13.A
PURE-EXCHANGE EQUILIBRIUM: THE EDGEWORTH BOX

This section takes up the first category of benefits mentioned above: that exchange permits individuals to redistribute existing goods in accord with individual preferences. (Each party can get more of whichever good he or she needs more or likes better.)

For concreteness, consider international trade. The United States has traditionally exported wheat to Britain in exchange for manufactured goods such as clothing and textiles. The situations of typical citizens of the two countries are pictured in Figure 13.1. Notice that for A, the American, the starting-point or "endowment" position (E^a) is toward the northwest (near the y-axis, where y stands for amounts of wheat). For B, the Briton, the endowment (E^b) is toward the southeast x-axis, where x stands for amounts of manufactured goods). Given that A and B both have normal diversified preferences, there is a potential gain from exchange.

The exchange process can be analyzed using the "Edgeworth box" of Figure 13.2. The box is constructed by rotating the picture of one of the individuals in the previous diagram. Specifically here, B's preference map has been rotated and superimposed upon A's in such a way as *to make the endowment positions coincide* (at point E). A's preference directions remain north and east (up and to the right), but B's are now south and west (down and to the left).

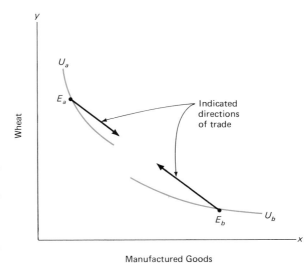

FIGURE 13.1 **Differing Endowments and Potential Trade.** At E_a the typical American is relatively heavily endowed with wheat (Y). At E_b the typical Briton is relatively heavily endowed with manufactured goods (X). Given normal diversified preferences as indicated by their respective indifference curves U_a and U_b, they can both benefit by trade.

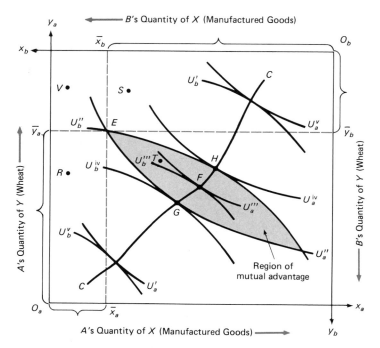

FIGURE 13.2 Edgeworth Box. *A*'s consumption of *X* and *Y* is measured by distances east and north of the origin O_a. For *B* the axes are inverted: his consumption of *X* is measured by distance west of the origin O_b, and his consumption of *Y* by distance south of O_b. *A*'s preferences are represented by the indifference curves $U'_a, U''_a, \ldots$ with utility increasing moving northeast, *B*'s by the curves $U'_b, U''_b, \ldots$ with utility rising moving southwest. The overall width of the box corresponds to the fixed social total $\overline{X}$, and the overall height to the fixed social total $\overline{Y}$. Any point in the diagram represents an allocation of these social totals between the two parties. Starting at the endowment position *E*, the allocations preferred by both individuals to *E* (that are on higher U_a and on higher U_b indifference curves) are shown by the shaded Region of Mutual Advantage.

The size of the Edgeworth box is determined by the total quantities of wheat *Y* and manufactures *X* available. The American A is endowed with $\overline{y}_a$ units of *Y*, and the Briton B has $\overline{y}_b$ units, so the height of the box is $\overline{Y} = \overline{y}_a + \overline{y}_b$. Similarly, the width of the box is determined by the amount of *X* available: $\overline{X} = \overline{x}_a + \overline{x}_b$.

At the endowment point *E*, A is on his indifference curve U''_a and B is on his U''_b. If A sells B some wheat in exchange for manufactures, the two parties can move southeast in the diagram to some point like *T* where each would be on a higher indifference curve. So they should be willing to trade from the endowment position *E* to point *T*. They would *not* both be willing to trade to points like *R*, *S*, or *V*, however. [The reader should verify that moving from *E* to point *R* makes A worse off, that moving to point *S* makes B worse off, and that moving to point *V* makes both parties worse off.]

The shaded lens-shaped area in the diagram is the *region of mutual advantage*. It consists of all points like *T* that are preferred to the endowment position *E* by *both* traders. Thus, both would be willing to make any trade moving them from *E* to some point in the region of mutual advantage.

Suppose the traders have reached a point like F, which is within the region of mutual advantage and where, in addition, their indifference curves are tangent to one another. Now A and B are no longer able to engage in mutually advantageous exchange: moving in any direction from point F must make at least one of them worse off. Connecting all the points like F that represent mutual tangencies of the indifference curves in the Edgeworth box traces out what is known as the Contract Curve CC. There will be some region of mutual advantage starting from any point in the Edgeworth box, *except* for points along CC.

EXAMPLE 13.1
Economic Exchange and the American Civil War

Before the Civil War the northern and southern states had engaged in a mutually advantageous economic exchange. The South produced a vast surplus of cotton which was sold in the North, the proceeds being used to purchase manufactured products. Less than 10 percent of the total prewar (1860) national value of manufactures had been produced in the seceded states.[a]

With the onset of the war, direct North–South trade was interrupted. The interruption hit the Confederacy much harder than the Union. While cotton prices in the North jumped, this was an inconvenience rather than a catastrophe. But the Union blockade largely prevented the South from exporting cotton or importing manufactured products. (The small blockade-running traffic was largely used for the import of luxury goods. "When Captain Hobart Pasha of the *Venus* asked a southern woman in England what was most needed in the Confederacy, she unhesitatingly replied, 'Corsets.'")[b] The South was brought to economic and military collapse by inability to acquire essential manufactured civilian products and implements of war, while huge stocks of unsalable cotton piled up uselessly.

Confederate trade policy was seriously misguided. Export of the huge cotton crops of 1861 and 1862 would have been possible, since the Union blockade did not really become effective until later years. The Confederate government discouraged this export. They reasoned that, since "Cotton is king," withholding the crop would force northern and foreign industrial interests to support the secession. Relying on their opponents' loss of the advantage of trade, the South's leaders failed to realize how much more vulnerable their own largely one-crop economy was to the interruption of mutually advantageous exchange.

An even more striking error was the policy of the Confederate government that banned trade through the lines with the North, partly on moralistic grounds, partly again to withhold "King Cotton." This was illogical for several reasons, one of which was that most of the cotton run through the blockade to Cuba or Bermuda was transshipped to the North anyway. But more important, a strict ban on trade through the lines was, for the Union, a logical complement to the sea blockade that was strangling the southern economy. In contrast, it

[a] Albert D. Kirwan, ed., *The Confederacy* (New York: Meridian Books, 1959), p. 63.
[b] Clement Eaton, *A History of the Southern Confederacy* (New York: Macmillan, 1954), p. 144.

was almost as much in the interest of the South to break this overland blockade as to evade the sea blockade. The cotton and tobacco that could have been sent North would, to a minor degree, have helped the northern war economy. But the Confederacy, its economy collapsing because of inability to dispose of its surpluses for imports of all kinds, was more desperately in need of northern manufactures. (Actually, a substantial amount of illegal trade did pass through the lines, despite the attempts of officials on both sides to stop the practice.) Curiously, even today historians commonly take a moralistic attitude on this question. They fail to appreciate the fundamental asymmetry that made maintenance of the land blockade a wise policy for the Union, but an unwise one for the Confederacy.[c]

[c] This discussion is based on J. Hirshleifer, *Disaster and Recovery: A Historical Survey*, RAND Corporation, Memorandum RM-3079-PR (Apr. 1963), Section IV.

Figure 13.2 showed that voluntary trade leads both parties from the endowment position E to some point within the region of mutual advantage. On the assumption that both traders are *price-takers* (neither has any monopoly or monopsony power), and that each is a typical representative of one side of the wheat/manufactures market, Figure 13.3 indicates how the equilibrium price ratio and the actual solution point are determined.

We know from Chapter 4 that the absolute slope of the budget line corresponds to the price ratio—in this case, to the ratio P_x/P_y. Suppose hypothetically that prices are such as to determine a slope as shown by the dashed line KL through E. This line is then the budget line for individuals A and B both. (But recall that the two of them are looking at the budget line from different directions. KL bounds A's opportunity set toward the northeast, while the same line bounds B's opportunity set toward the southwest.)

With KL as budget line in Figure 13.3, individual A would want to proceed to a consumptive optimum indicated by the position Q_a. Similarly, B would want to move to his optimum along KL at Q_b. But these two points do not coincide! This means that the quantity of X that A wishes to purchase, offering Y in exchange in accordance with the price ratio represented by the slope of KL, is *not* equal to the quantity that B is prepared to supply at that price ratio. The situation is not one of competitive equilibrium. Since good X is too cheap relative to Y, the buyer A is seeking to take more of X than the seller B is willing to offer.

An equilibrium price ratio for competitive trading is represented by the steeper line $K'L'$, corresponding to a higher price ratio P'_x/P'_y. At this price ratio both parties are led to *coinciding* preferred positions $Q_a^* = Q_b^*$. This means that the amount of commodity X offered by B exactly equals the amount willingly purchased by A. (Correspondingly, of course, the quantity of Y offered by individual A in payment must also exactly balance the amount required by individual B.)

PROPOSITION: In the Edgeworth box, the competitive equilibrium allocation of the two commodities (1) lies in the region of mutual advantage, and (2) represents a mutual tangency of both traders' indifference curves with each other and with a common budget line.

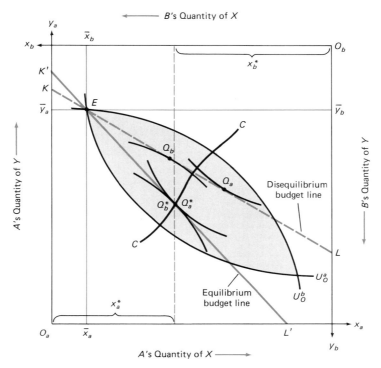

A's Quantity of X ⟶

FIGURE 13.3 Budget Lines and Competitive Equilibrium. Any price ratio P_x/P_y determines the slope of a corresponding budget line through the endowment position E. Each such budget line is a northeast boundary of the opportunity set for A and a southwest boundary for B. The dashed budget line KL does not correspond to a competitive market equilibrium for these two traders, since along KL there is a divergence between A's optimum Q_a and B's optimum Q_b. $K'L'$ does correspond to an equilibrium price ratio, since the optimum positions Q_a^* and Q_b^* coincide. The equilibrium must occur at a mutual tangency of the indifference curves. The Contract Curve CC shows all such possible equilibrium positions.

Expressing these conditions mathematically, the following equations must hold for the individual traders:

(13.1)
$$P_x x_a + P_y y_a = P_x \overline{x}_a + P_y \overline{y}_a \quad \text{and} \quad P_x x_b + P_y y_b = P_x \overline{y}_b + P_y \overline{y}_b$$
$$MRS_C^a = P_x/P_y = MRS_C^b$$

And as regards the market as a whole, equilibrium requires that the sum of the individuals' demands must equal the social totals available, for each commodity. This condition corresponds to the equations:

(13.2)
$$\begin{cases} x_a + x_b = \overline{X} = \overline{x}_a + \overline{x}_b \\ x_a + y_b = \overline{Y} = \overline{y}_a + \overline{y}_b \end{cases}$$

Exercise 13.1: Suppose A's Marginal Rate of Substitution in Consumption is $MRS_C^a = y_a/x_a$, and for B, similarly, $MRS_C^b = y_b/x_b$. Let the endowments be $(\overline{x}_a, \overline{y}_a) = (10, 100)$ and

$(\overline{x}_b, \overline{y}_b) = (50, 20)$. Verify that if Y is the *numéraire* (so that $P_y \equiv 1$), the competitive equilibrium price is $P_x^* = 2$.

Answer: First finding A's consumptive optimum at $P_x = 2$, the equations that must be satisfied are:

$$2x_a + y_a = 2(10) + 100 \quad \text{and} \quad y_a/x_a = 2$$

So A's consumptive optimum solution is $(x_a^*, y_a^*) = (30, 60)$. For B the corresponding equations are $2x_b + y_b = 2(50) + 20$ and $y_b/x_b = 2$, leading to the same numerical solution: $(x_b^*, y_b^*) = (30, 60)$. Now we need only verify that the social totals are met:

$$x_a + x_b \equiv \overline{X} \equiv \overline{x}_a + \overline{x}_b = 60$$
$$y_a + y_b \equiv \overline{Y} \equiv \overline{y}_a + \overline{y}_b = 120$$

13.B
SUPPLY AND DEMAND IN PURE EXCHANGE

The Edgeworth box is a useful tool for visualizing the properties of equilibrium *once it is reached*. To describe *how* it is reached we naturally think in terms of supply and demand.

The Price Expansion Path PEP in Panel (a) of Figure 13.4 looks very much like the PEP of Chapter 4, except for one feature. In Chapter 4 the endowment point E was always on the vertical (Y) axis. So we were assuming that the individual was not endowed with any X at all. In Figure 13.4 here, the endowment points are in the interior, meaning that each individual starts out instead with positive amounts of both X and Y. This change has an important result. In Chapter 4 the individual endowed only with commodity Y could never be a supplier of X. But here A's endowment point E lies toward but not quite at the vertical axis; he has a large endowment of Y, but also some positive endowment of X. (Thus, America produces lots of wheat, but also some manufactures.) We would therefore expect A *usually* to be a supplier of Y and a demander of X, but not necessarily *always*. There is some price ratio P_x/P_y so high (some budget line K^oL^o so steep) that he will want to stand pat with his endowment combination and not make any purchases or sales at all. This is called the "sustaining" price ratio. And for even higher price ratios (even steeper budget lines through E_a), A would actually be a net supplier of X to the market—that is, his optimum would lie northwest of E_a. Similarly for individual B, Panel (b) reveals that he will usually be a supplier of X (demander of Y), but at a sufficiently low price ratio P_x/P_y his market behavior would reverse.

The data in the PEP curves of Figure 13.4 can be used to generate supply and demand curves. This can be done in two different ways, which we must be careful not to confuse. The first runs in terms of the whole or "full" quantities demanded or supplied, the second runs in terms of the net or "transaction" quantities.

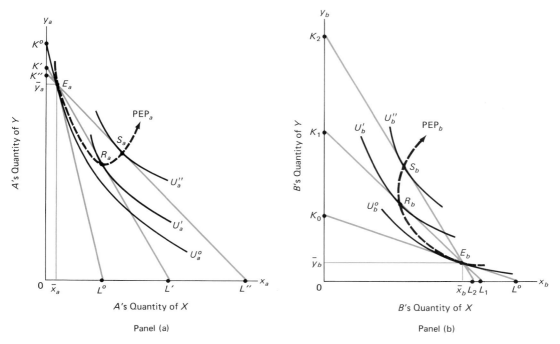

Panel (a)

Panel (b)

FIGURE 13.4 Price Expansion Paths. As the price ratio changes, the budget lines through the endowment positions E_a for A in Panel (a) and E_b for B in Panel (b) tilt. For price ratios leading to points on PEP_a east of E_a, individual A will be a net demander of X; at the "sustaining" price ratio (budget line $K^\circ L^\circ$) leading to a tangency of E_a itself he will stand pat and not trade; for still higher price ratios he will be a supplier of X (indicated by the range of PEP_a to the west of E_a). A corresponding analysis holds for individual B in the other panel.

Definitions

1. An individual's *full demand* for any commodity X (at price P_x) is the total quantity of X consumed. It is equal to the endowed quantity already in his or her possession plus the quantity bought in the market.

2. An individual's *transaction demand* for X is the quantity bought in the market. It is equal to full demand less the individual's endowed quantity of X.

3. An individual's *full supply* of X is his or her endowed quantity.

4. An individual's *transaction supply* of X is the quantity sold on the market. It is equal to the endowed quantity less the amount retained for consumption.

On the demand side, the "full" quantity demanded of good X *includes* the endowed quantity $\bar{x}$—this is the demand concept relevant for purposes of consumption. The "transaction" demand quantity *excludes* the quantity endowed (the quantity self-supplied) and thus represents the demand concept relevant for purposes of market trading. On the supply side the "full" quantity is simply the fixed endowment amount, while the "transaction" quantity is that portion of the endowment offered to the market. Think of the "full" quantities as those demanded from or supplied *to the economy*, while the "transaction" quantities are the (normally smaller) amounts demanded from or supplied *to the market*.

The relation between transaction demand and full demands, for any individual i, is given by:

(13.3) $x_i^t \equiv x_i - \overline{x}_i$ Transaction Demands and Full Demands

As for the transaction and full *supplies*, these are simply the negative of the above (since positive supply is negative demand and vice versa).

In Panel (a) of Figure 13.4, A's *full* demand for X at any point along the PEP_a curve is simply the x-coordinate of that position. His transaction demand is this horizontal distance *less* the endowed amount $\overline{x}_a$. It follows that at his *sustaining* price ratio, A's full demand for X equals $\overline{x}_a$ while his transaction demand for X is zero.

The transaction demand x_i^t in Equation (13.3) can be either positive or negative. Negative transaction demand is, of course, positive transaction supply. But full demand and full supply quantities are necessarily non-negative; neither consumption nor endowment can ever be less than zero.

The distinction between full and transaction magnitudes is important in a number of applications, among them taxation. A tax on *consumption* is levied upon the full demands; a tax on *purchases* falls only upon the transaction demands. Put another way, endowed quantities that are self-consumed escape a "transaction tax" on purchases, but do not escape a tax on consumption. (A tariff is a transaction tax that burdens international trading but not domestic trading—the latter representing quantities that are "self-supplied" from the viewpoint of the nation as a whole.) As transaction taxes become higher, individuals will find it increasingly attractive to self-supply their wants rather than deal in the market. It seems very likely that the growth of the "do-it-yourself" movement is in large part a response to the increasing burden of transaction taxes.

As the price ratio P_x/P_y (or simply P_x, if Y is the *numéraire* so that $P_y \equiv 1$) varies, Figure 13.5 shows how the supply and demand curves of any individual i

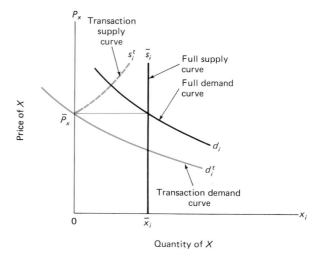

FIGURE 13.5 Full and Transaction Supply and Demand Curves (Pure Exchange). The individual's *full demand curve* d_i shows, at any price P_x, his or her desired consumption quantity. The *full supply curve* $\overline{s}_i$ represents the fixed endowment quantity. The *transaction demand curve* d_i^t shows, at any price P_x, the amount demanded from the market (horizontal difference between d_i and $\overline{s}_i$). In the range where transaction demand d_i^t is negative, it is usually more convenient to speak of a positive *transaction supply curve* s_i^t. Transaction demand and transaction supply are exactly zero at the sustaining price $\overline{P}_x$.

for commodity X are traced out. The "full demand curve" d_i corresponds to the desired consumption quantity x_i, the "full supply curve" is the fixed endowed quantity $\bar{x}_i$, and the "transaction demand curve" d_i^t is the difference between the two—x_i^t. Note that above the "sustaining price" P_x it is more convenient to visualize a positive "transaction supply" (the dashed curve) rather than a negative "transaction demand." [Justifying the shapes of these curves is left as an exercise for the reader.]

Figure 13.6 brings supply and demand together in two different instructive ways: in terms of the transaction magnitudes in Panel (a) and in terms of the full magnitudes in Panel (b). The picture here sums up the supplies and demands of our two "typical" individuals A and B, but more generally there would of course ordinarily be many traders involved. Panel (a) represents the supply and demand *to the market*, and Panel (b) the supply and demand *to the economy*. Notice that the equilibrium price P_x^* can be regarded as determined in either panel. [*Challenge to the reader:* Verify the correspondence between the two panels.]

CONCLUSION: Competitive supply-demand equilibrium can be expressed in two ways. The intersection of the aggregate *transaction* supply curve and the aggregate *transaction* demand curve shows the quantity actually traded in markets. The intersection of the aggregate *full* supply curve and the aggregate *full* demand curve shows the entire economywide consumption, which must equal the aggregate economy-

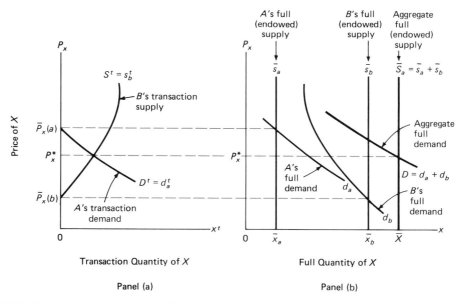

FIGURE 13.6 **Supply-Demand Equilibrium.** Panel (a) shows a demand-supply equilibrium for commodity X in terms of the *transaction* quantities; Panel (b) pictures the same equilibrium in terms of the *full* quantities. The equilibrium in Panel (a) is at the intersection of A's *transaction demand curve* d_a^t and B's *transaction supply curve* s_b^t. In Panel (b) the aggregate *full supply curve* $\bar{S}$ to the economy as a whole is the sum of $\bar{s}_a$ and $\bar{s}_b$. The aggregate *full demand curve* D is similarly the sum of d_a and d_b. The S and D curves in Panel (b) must intersect at the same equilibrium price P_x^* as at the intersection of S^t and D^t.

wide supply availability of the commodity. Both pictures determine the same equilibrium price.

We should, of course, be thinking of the market process as involving not just two commodities X and Y but rather all goods simultaneously. The result is a *general* equilibrium of prices and quantities. However, the underlying principles— that individuals optimize, and that in equilibrium demand and supply balance in the market—are in no way different from the principles illustrated in the simplified two-good world.

Exercise 13.2: Using the data of Exercise 13.1, find: (a) the "full" supply and demand curves for each individual and for the society, and (b) the corresponding "transaction" supply and demand curves. Verify the solution $P_x^* = 2$ in each case.

Answer: (a) A's budget equation is $P_x x_a + y_a = 10P_x + 100$ and his Substitution Equivalence Equation is $y_a/x_a = P_x$. Eliminating y_a, his "full" demand equation is $x_a = 5 + 50/P_x$. For B the conditions are $P_x x_b + y_b = 50P_x + 20$ and $y_b/x_b = P_x$, leading to his "full" demand equation $x_b = 25 + 10/P_x$. The aggregate full demand equation is then $X_d = x_a + x_b = 30 + 60/P_x$. The "full" supplies are simply $\bar{x}_a = 10$ and $\bar{x}_b = 50$, so that in aggregate $X_s = 60$. Setting $X_s = X_d$, the solution is indeed $P_x^* = 2$. (b) A's "transaction" demand is $x_a - \bar{x}_a \equiv x_a^t = -5 + 50/P_x$. B's is $x_b - \bar{x}_b \equiv x_b^t = -25 + 10/P_x$. In the neighborhood of equilibrium A is a net demander of good X and B is a net supplier. So the aggregate transaction demand is $X_d^t = x_a^t = -5 + 50/P_x$. For the aggregate transaction supply we can take the negative of B's transaction demand: $X_s^t = -x_b^t = 25 - 10/P_x$. Setting $X_d^t = X_s^t$, the solution once again is $P_x^* = 2$.

13.C
EXCHANGE AND PRODUCTION

So far in this chapter we have considered trade in a world without production, a world of "pure exchange." Under pure exchange people can modify their endowments *only* through market trading. But in the actual world individuals can also change endowments by *production*, by transacting (so to speak) with Nature. At the other extreme, Robinson Crusoe could deal only with Nature: he could produce and consume, but could not trade. What we really want to analyze is a world where transactions both with Nature (production) and with other persons (exchange) can take place.

In Figure 13.7 the shaded region shows the *productive opportunity set*—all the possible baskets of commodities X and Y that a person might have the capacity to produce. The northeast boundary QQ of the productive opportunity set is called the *transformation locus* or *Production-Possibility Curve* (PPC). Its "concave" shape reflects diminishing returns. Suppose an individual or a nation tried to specialize in the production of wheat—that is, tried to produce a combination well toward the Y-axis along QQ. As specialization is pushed further and further, each increment of Y requires a greater and greater sacrifice of manufactures X—*increasing opportunity costs* are encountered.

For a Robinson Crusoe possessing *only* productive opportunities, the optimum as shown in Figure 13.7 is R^*, the tangency of his transformation locus QQ with his highest attainable indifference curve U^0. Since Crusoe cannot engage in

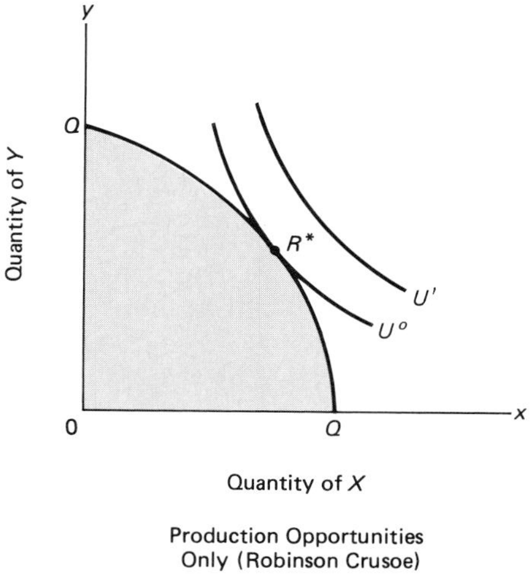

FIGURE 13.7 **Productive and Consumptive Optimum: Robinson Crusoe.** The shaded region shows a productive opportunity set QQ subject to diminishing returns as the individual specializes in production of either X or Y. Since an isolated Robinson Crusoe must produce what he consumes, the best attainable position is the tangency of QQ with indifference curve U° at point R^*.

Quantity of X

Production Opportunities
Only (Robinson Crusoe)

trade, R^* is both his consumptive optimum and productive optimum. The tangency condition can be expressed as the equation

(13.4) $$MRS_C = MRS_T \qquad \text{Robinson Crusoe Optimum}$$

Here MRS_C, the Marginal Rate of Substitution in Consumption, corresponds, as in Chapter 4, to the absolute indifference-curve slope $|\Delta y/\Delta x|$. The new symbol MRS_T stands for the *Marginal Rate of Substitution in Productive Transformation*; more briefly, the *Marginal Rate of Transformation*. MRS_T is the absolute slope $|\Delta y/\Delta x|$ of the Production-Possibility Curve, the additional amount of Y that can be produced per unit sacrifice of X. Note how the opposing curvatures guarantee that there will be a unique tangency R^*.[1]

> CONCLUSION: Robinson Crusoe, who can produce but cannot trade, has a productive-consumptive optimum at the point where his Marginal Rate of Substitution in Consumption MRS_C equals his Marginal Rate of Transformation MRS_T along the boundary of his productive opportunity set.

Robinson Crusoe situations may seem fanciful, but this is not necessarily so. We might, for example, sometimes want to consider a nation as a whole as a kind of Robinson Crusoe. There have been historical instances of nations isolated from

---

[1] *Mathematical Footnote:* In terms of derivatives, the condition can be expressed as:

$$\left.\frac{dy}{dx}\right|_U = \left.\frac{dy}{dx}\right|_Q$$

In addition, the individual must be on his Production-Possibility Curve, so that the equation $Q(x,y) = 0$ is satisfied.

trade—sometimes owing to geography, sometimes to deliberate choice. A famous instance is Japan, which had closed itself to trade for over two centuries before Commodore M. C. Perry's visit in 1854.

EXAMPLE 13.2
Animal Robinson Crusoes

Trade is a human invention. Since they do not engage in exchange with one another, nonhuman animals make all their economic decisions under Robinson Crusoe conditions. An example of such a decision is the problem of "optimal diet breadth."[a]

Think of X and Y as two sources of food for a predator—for example, two prey species. Because of diminishing returns the productive opportunity set typically has a shape like the shaded region in the diagram. The more the predator concentrates upon consuming prey species X, the scarcer and harder to capture X becomes relative to the availability of Y (increasing Marginal Rate of Transformation MRS_T toward the x-axis). The predator also has "preferences" as represented by the indifference curves in the diagram. Each such curve represents a set of equally acceptable diets. The convexity of the indifference curves reflects the fact that diversity in consumption helps provide the many metabolic inputs required by living organisms. The greater the consumption of food source X, the harder it becomes for the animal to achieve nutritional needs by additional consumption of X as compared to the nutritional benefit of a unit of Y (decreasing Marginal Rate of Substitution in Consumption MRS_C toward the x-axis).

The optimal position for the animal is of course at the "Robinson Crusoe" tangency point $R*$, which will ordinarily represent an interior (mixed-diet) solution.

[a] The discussion here is based on D. J. Rapport, "An Optimization Model of Food Selection," *The American Naturalist*, v. 105 (Nov.-Dec. 1971) and M. L. Cody, "Optimization in Ecology," *Science*, v. 183 (Mar. 22, 1974).

Now let us go beyond the isolated individual to consider a world with both production and trade. We can imagine that Robinson Crusoe has been discovered but chooses to remain on his island while trading with the rest of the world. His market opportunities are shown in Figure 13.8 by the budget line MM, which has slope $-P_x/P_y$ and is just tangent to his transformation locus QQ. The market now permits Robinson to *separate his productive and consumptive decisions*. Specifically, in Figure 13.8 he can now produce at $Q*$ and consume at $C*$. Think of this as a two-step procedure. First, a person moves along QQ to a *productive optimum* $Q*$, where the Production-Possibility Curve is tangent to a highest attainable budget line[2] MM. Second, by exchanging X for Y he or she can move southeast from $Q*$, along

[2] We could construct other budget lines, all with slope $-P_x/P_y$, in the diagram. Those lying parallel to MM but below it are attainable by the individual, should he choose a production point other than $Q*$, but are all obviously inferior to MM. Budget lines above MM would be superior, but are not attainable.

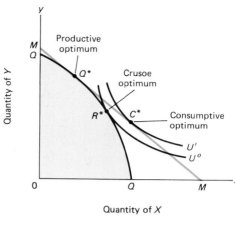

FIGURE 13.8 **Productive and Consumptive Optimum with Exchange Opportunities.** If a market exists, the individual can exchange X for Y at the market price ratio P_x/P_y, as well as engage in production. His productive optimum is at the tangency Q^*, which places him on the highest attainable budget line MM. Along this budget line, the final consumptive optimum C^* on indifference curve U' is preferred to the Crusoe optimum R^* on indifference curve $U°$.

MM to a *consumptive optimum* at C^*. A comparison of C^* with the Robinson Crusoe solution R^* shows the advantage gained from trade.

The *productive optimum* position Q^* in Figure 13.8 is described by the equation:

(13.5) $$MRS_T = \frac{P_x}{P_y}$$ Productive Optimum Condition

That is, at the productive optimum the absolute slopes of the Production-Possibility Curve (MRS_T) and of the budget line (P_x/P_y) must be equal. The familiar *consumptive optimum* condition, achieved by movement along MM to C^*, is:

(13.6) $$\frac{P_x}{P_y} = MRS_C$$ Consumptive Optimum Condition

Notice that (13.5) and (13.6) together imply $MRS_T = MRS_C$. So Equation (13.4) holds in a world of exchange as well as for an isolated Robinson Crusoe. But for Crusoe the slopes MRS_C and MRS_T are equated *at a single point* R^* along QQ, whereas someone engaged in trade can generally do even better—by being able to set $MRS_T = P_x/P_y$ at the productive optimum Q^* and $P_x/P_y = MRS_C$ at the consumptive optimum C^* which need not be along QQ.

Exercise 13.3: Robinson Crusoe's Production-Possibility Curve (PPC) is expressed by the equation $f^2/2 + g = 150$, where f is the amount of fish and g the amount of grain he can obtain, depending upon the way he divides his time and effort. (Think of g as plotted on the vertical axis, f as on the horizontal axis.) Robinson's Marginal Rate of Substitution in Consumption (absolute indifference-curve slope) is $MRS_C = g/f$. (a) Find Robinson's production-consumption optimum R^*. (b) If Robinson is discovered by a world market in which $P_f = 5$, where grain is the *numéraire* so that $P_g \equiv 1$, determine his productive optimum Q^* and consumptive optimum C^*. (c) Verify that he prefers C^* to R^*.

Answer: (a) Robinson's Marginal Rate of Transformation MRS_T is the absolute slope along his Production-Possibility Curve. By calculus it can be found that $MRS_T = f$. (This can be approximately verified by tabulating $\Delta g/\Delta f$ along the PPC.) Setting $MRS_T = MRS_C$, the condition becomes $f = g/f$, or $g = f^2$. Substituting in the PPC equation, the R^* solution is $f = 10$, $g = 100$. (b) Robinson finds Q^* by setting $MRS_T = P_f = 5$ in his PPC equation. Thus, $f = 5$, $g = 137.5$ is his productive optimum. To find his consumptive optimum, we use the budget condition and Substitution Equivalence Equation. That is: $5f + g = 5(5) + 137.5$ and $g/f = 5$. The C^* solution is therefore $f = 16.25$, $g = 81.25$. (c) He has it in his power to buy the R^* combination and even have something left over—yet chooses not to do so.

Figure 13.9 translates the information pictured in Figure 13.8 into supply and demand curves. Once again it will be useful to distinguish "full" versus "transaction" supply and demand concepts.

Figure 13.9 is similar to Figure 13.5, with one important difference. In pure exchange the individual's full supply of X to the economy was simply his fixed endowed quantity $\bar{x}_i$ (the vertical line $\bar{s}_i$ in Figure 13.5). But in a world of production and exchange, an individual's fully supply of X will vary with price. As P_x rises (with P_y held constant), the market line MM in Figure 13.8 gets steeper. The tangency of MM with the transformation locus QQ at Q^* therefore shifts toward the southeast. This shift means that an increased quantity of X is produced. So the individual's full supply curve s_i^q for commodity X is a rising function of price P_x. The full demand curve d_i of Figure 13.9 similarly represents, for any price P_x, the x-coordinate of the individual's consumptive optimum C^* in Figure 13.8.

What about *transaction* demand and supply? Just as in the last section, the individual's transaction demand d_i^t is his net demand in the market (difference between his full demand and full supply) and transaction supply s_i^t is his net supply

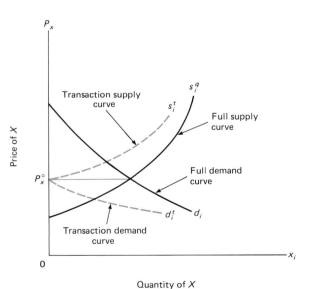

FIGURE 13.9 **Individual Demand and Supply, with Production.** As P_x rises, individual i produces an increased quantity of X, so his full supply curve s_i^q has positive slope. His full demand curve d_i normally has negative slope. His transaction supply and demand for X are exactly zero at his "autarky price" P_x^o, the price at which the full demand curve and the full supply curve intersect. Above this price his full supply exceeds full demand, so there will be positive *transaction supply* s_i^t—increasing as P_x rises. Below this price his full demand exceeds full supply, so there will be positive *transaction demand* d_i^t—increasing as P_x falls.

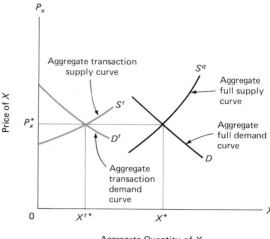

FIGURE 13.10 **Equilibrium of Supply and Demand.** The aggregate full supply curve S^q and full demand curve D represent horizontal summations of the corresponding individual curves of the preceding diagram, and similarly for the aggregate transaction supply and transaction demand curves S^t and D^t. The equilibrium price P_x^* is determined by the intersection of either pair of curves. At the equilibrium the aggregate full quantity produced and consumed is X^* while the aggregate transaction quantity traded among individuals is X^{t*}. (The difference is the aggregate quantity self-supplied by individuals for their own consumption.)

to the market (difference between full supply and full demand). At what is known as the "autarky price"[3] the net amount demanded or supplied is zero.

Figure 13.9 applies for a single trader. Equilibrium in the market as a whole is the result of balancing *aggregate* supply and *aggregate* demand. Figure 13.10 shows the solutions for both X^*, the full social total of X produced and consumed, and X^{t*}, the transaction amount of X exchanged in the market. The difference between X^* and X^{t*} represents the equilibrium total of X that individuals produce for their own personal consumption. Note that the transaction supply and demand curves S^t and D^t intersect at the same price as the full supply and demand curves S^q and D.

The model of pure exchange illustrated one of the advantages of trade: redistributing existing goods to their highest-valued uses. The model of production and exchange demonstrates the second advantage as well: enlarging the social totals of goods through *productive specialization*.

In Figure 13.11 the two panels show Production-Possibility Curves QQ for a typical American A and typical Briton B. As we have been assuming, A is best at producing wheat Y while B is best at producing manufactures X. Without trade they could only achieve their respective "Robinson Crusoe" solutions R_a^* and R_b^*. Since each of them desires to consume both commodities, in isolation each would have to devote efforts to producing a good which he is not very well equipped to produce.

The opening of trade makes available budget lines MM (of slope $-P_x/P_y$) to both parties. A takes advantage of the market by shifting his productive solution northwest along QQ to Q_a^*—that is, he now *specializes in producing Y*. And this does not in any way require a corresponding loss of "diversity in consumption," for he will be selling off the excess. Correspondingly, of course, B specializes in the production of X, and sells the excess to A. Thus the market exchange process induces each person (as if led by an "Invisible Hand") to serve the interests of the other.

---

[3] The autarky price P_x^o is analogous to the "sustaining price" $\bar{P}_x$ of pure exchange; each represents the price at which the individual does not participate in trade.

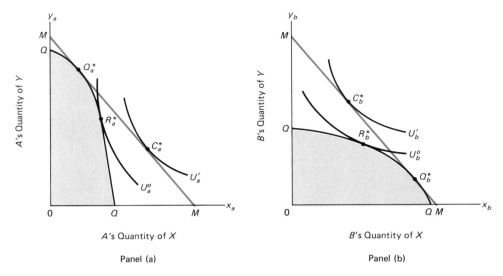

Panel (a)

A's Quantity of X

Panel (b)

B's Quantity of X

FIGURE 13.11 **Productive Specialization.** In the absence of exchange, each individual would go to an optimum productive-consumptive combination at his "Robinson Crusoe" solution R^*. The opening of trade permits each to specialize in producing the commodity favored by his transformation opportunities. A's productive solution Q_a^* involves heavier production of Y, while B's involves heavier production of X. By trading with one another, each can move along a market line MM to achieve a superior consumption basket C^*.

Trade allows individuals and nations to reach higher levels of preference. Furthermore, owing to specialization in production the social totals of the traded goods increase. For these reasons, economists have usually favored free trade among nations.

EXAMPLE 13.3
International Specialization

Individuals tend to specialize in production but to diversify in consumption. We work at just one job, or a very few, but consume hundreds of different products. Should we expect the same thing of countries? To some extent, surely yes. But the degree of productive specialization should be less for *larger* countries, which tend to have more highly varied resources and thus are less dependent upon international trade to secure diversity in consumption.

A study by M. Michaely compared the extent of specialization in the exports and imports of 44 countries, in terms of 1954 (or, in some cases, 1953 or 1952) data. The table shows, for a number of countries, indexes of specialization in exports and in imports. The measure of specialization employed was the "Gini coefficient," which in this case has a possible range of from 8.2 to 100.0.[a] The countries in the table are ranked in decreasing order of export (productive) specialization. As can be seen, the highly specialized group at the top tend to be small countries, while the group at the bottom tend to be large countries. No particular pattern is evident in the specialization index of imports, a result consistent with the principle of diversity in consumption.

Indexes of Specialization of International Trade

Country	Exports	Imports
Egypt	84.2	18.6
Colombia	84.0	23.9
Gold Coast	83.5	21.4
Iceland	80.3	19.1
Finland	38.1	19.2
Mexico	35.0	26.8
Libya	34.1	18.9
Spain	33.9	24.5
Italy	20.5	20.7
U.K.	19.2	16.1
U.S.	18.8	20.5
France	18.0	20.4

Source: Michael Michaely, "Concentration of Exports and Imports: An International Comparison," *Economic Journal,* v. 68 (Dec. 1958), p. 725.

[a] The Gini coefficient for exports is defined as $100 \sqrt{\Sigma_{i=1}^{N} (x_i/X^2)}$. Here x_i is a nation's annual value of exports of a particular good i, and X is its total annual value of exports. The goods were classified into $N = 150$ categories. If a country exported only a single good, the specialization index would be 100.0. If it exported all 150 goods in equal amounts, the result would be an index of 8.2. The measure of import specialization is similarly defined and has the same range.

13.D
IMPERFECT MARKETS: COSTS OF EXCHANGE

In previous chapters we have sometimes departed from the assumption of *perfect competition* (price-taking behavior on both sides of the market)—for example, in the chapters on monopoly and oligopoly. But one assumption has been maintained up to now: *perfect markets.* A market is said to be perfect (even if not competitive) if at any moment of time there is a single price, known to all participants, at which transactions may be executed without further fee or penalty. Elaborating a bit, there are three main characteristics of perfect markets:

1. *Perfect communication:* The market must be integrated, not segmented by limitations of information. Real-world markets have informational imperfections, as we can see by the efforts made to overcome them: classified newspaper advertising, specialized "middlemen" (such as real-estate brokers), and organized exchanges (such as the New York Stock Exchange).

2. *Instantaneous equilibrium:* A perfect market would instantly reach the correct market-clearing price. But no such ideal can be achieved in the real world. A farmer bringing vegetables to a city market may by cleverness or chance realize a sale at terms higher than the (unknown) true equilibrium price. Or, unluckily, the farmer may ac-

cept a price lower than he should have held out for. Thus, in real-world markets there is some "trading at false prices." (One of the functions of *speculation* is to minimize fluctuations of price that lead to false trading, since speculators buy when they perceive that the price is accidentally too low and sell when price is accidentally too high.)

3. *Costless transactions:* Markets that are perfect would also be costless. In the real world, market middlemen such as wholesalers and retailers, brokers, dealers, and jobbers—although they improve the perfection of the market—obviously must be paid for their services. Transaction taxes, in which *government* collects "middleman" payments (possibly reflecting actual services to taxpayers, but possibly not), also may make exchange costly.

EXAMPLE 13.4
Experiments in Perfect and Imperfect Markets

An interesting series of economic experiments on the functioning of markets has been conducted by Vernon L. Smith.[a] One question studied was the following: given that real-world situations can never fully meet the theoretical conditions of "perfect markets," how far can the conditions diverge from "perfection" and still achieve the same essential results? For example, if traders are not in perfect communication, or if "trading at false prices" may occur, to what extent is it the case that equilibrium is nevertheless attained quite quickly and at a price-quantity outcome close to the theoretical ideal?

In one experiment each participant was provided with information only as to demand price (the maximum he or she should be willing to bid if buying) or supply price (the minimum he or she should be willing to accept if selling). Thus the subjects did not know the *aggregate* supply and demand functions and so could not calculate the "true" equilibrium price.

Under the experimental conditions any buyer (or seller) could make an offer at any time, which, if accepted by another trader, became a binding contract. The process was public, so that the terms of any deals consummated became known to as-yet-uncommitted traders. A trading "week" consisted of five trading "days" (periods) within which supply and demand conditions remained unchanged. A typical experimental series went as follows. In the first week the supply and demand conditions implied a theoretical equilibrium price of 465; after the end of the third day practically all transactions took place exactly at the correct price of 465. At the beginning of the second week demand and supply conditions were shifted to make the equilibrium price 285; the participants were now more experienced, and trading settled down to the correct price by the end of the second day. For the third week a new set of supply-demand conditions made the equilibrium price 735; convergence to the new equilibrium

[a] V. L. Smith, "An Experimental Study of Competitive Market Behavior," *Journal of Political Economy*, v. 70 (Apr. 1962); "Effects of Market Organization on Competitive Equilibrium," *Quarterly Journal of Economics*, v. 78 (May 1964); "Experimental Auction Markets and the Walrasian Hypothesis," *Journal of Political Economy*, v. 73 (Aug. 1965).

was so rapid that virtually all trades were made at the equilibrium price, almost from the very beginning.

The model of perfect markets therefore turned out to provide an excellent prediction of actual transaction prices in this experiment. Furthermore, the *quantities* exchanged were also very close to the theoretical ideal. In short, substantially all the potential advantages of trade (in the form of Consumer Surplus and Producer Surplus) were in fact achieved despite the experimental departure from ideal conditions.

Results such as these suggest that the economist's perfect-markets model is "robust," in the sense of having a high degree of predictive reliability even though the exact conditions for its validity are not fully met. A very similar situation in physics is the model of a "perfect gas" that leads to the prediction known as Boyle's Law. No actual gas can meet the requirements of a "perfect gas," and yet Boyle's Law is a very reliable predictive equation in physics.

In the discussion that follows, markets will generally be assumed perfect *except* for transaction costs. This amounts to assuming that middlemen function so effectively as to totally eliminate other types of market imperfection—such as limited communication and false trading at nonequilibrium prices. But of course these efficient middleman services must be paid for. Costs of exchange have, we shall see, important consequences for the scope of trading and for the degree of specialization in production and consumption.

EXAMPLE 13.5
Cost of Trading on the New York Stock Exchange

An organized exchange like the New York Stock Exchange goes a considerable way toward the ideal of a perfect market. Since the exchange guarantees the quality of merchandise delivered and the payment arrangements, the buyer can forego personal inspection of the merchandise and the seller need not be concerned with the credit standing or the character of the buyer. In dealing on the New York Stock Exchange, the buyer does not have to worry about whether the stock certificates acquired are counterfeit and the seller need not fear that the buyer may be making payment with a bad check.

However, there are costs of trading on the New York Stock Exchange. These fall into two main categories: (1) commission charges, and (2) bid-ask price spread. The *commission charges* are the explicit fees paid to brokers. These charges are quoted separately from the amounts paid or received for the securities themselves. The *bid-ask spread* is a less obvious portion of the cost of transacting. At any instant of time the market price to a seller of a stock like General Motors, the "bid price," is less than the "ask price" that a buyer of GM stock would have to pay. The difference goes mainly to the Exchange's "specialist" in General Motors stock (see Example 8.1) who plays the role of making a continuous market in that security. Specialists, like retail or wholesale merchants, must on the average buy for less (the bid price) than they sell for (the ask price) if they are to remain in business. (The customer's *broker*, in contrast with the specialist, is normally a pure intermediary who does not buy or sell for his or her own account.)

A study by Harold Demsetz[a] indicated that in 1965 the bid-ask spread on the New York Stock Exchange comprised about 40 percent and explicit commission charges about 60 percent of total transaction cost, on the average. The two together amounted to about 1.3 percent of the value of the securities exchanged. The study also found that the bid-ask spread is normally much lower for frequently traded than for infrequently traded securities. This is reasonable if we regard the Exchange's specialist as a merchant who must hold an "inventory" of securities in order always to stand ready to sell. On average the specialist's funds must be tied up longer holding a "slow-moving" commodity like an infrequently traded stock. Commission charges were also lower in percentage terms for bigger transactions, which is easily understandable in terms of the savings in communications and recording costs.

[a] H. Demsetz, "The Cost of Transacting," *Quarterly Journal of Economics*, v. 82 (Feb. 1968).

Large proportions of national resources appear to be devoted to the process of exchange. In 1982 around 22 percent of U.S. nonagricultural employment fell into the occupational category Wholesale and Retail Trade. And many workers classified under other headings—for example, Transportation and Communication; Finance, Insurance, and Real Estate; and Services—might also be regarded as engaged in facilitating exchange. This suggests that middlemen are an enormous drain upon the nation's resources.

Such an initial impression is misleading. A crucial distinction must be made between two logically distinct classes of interpersonal "transactions." The *trading* of goods and services—that is, the social process of market exchange—is one thing. The sheer physical *turnover* of commodities from one person to another is a separate matter. Any economy that integrates the activities of a great number of individuals so as to take advantage of productive specialization and the division of labor, whether it be an economy of saints, of monks, of slaves, of ants, or of utility-maximizers under free markets, would still involve turnover of commodities. *Activities and costs due to the necessary fact of turnover must not be attributed to market trading*.

Consider an extreme "command economy" in which all economic decisions are made by a central authority. The economy might be a slave society in which everyone works for the benefit of a single master. Or it might be a socialist dictatorship which aims (let us say) to achieve popular well-being. Specialization in production could still be achieved, but by command rather than by an "invisible hand." Farmers would be ordered to grow crops and turn them over to railroads; railroads ordered to ship them to cities, and turn them over to warehouses; warehouses ordered to store them, and turn them over to retail outlets, and so forth. Every transfer of control of goods would involve costs: handling, shipping, storing, record-keeping, and so forth.

The costs associated with the physical turnovers that would persist even in a totally dictated economy fall logically under the economic category of *production* costs rather than exchange costs. This accounts for essentially all transportation services. "Adding" transportation to a good so as to physically bring it to a consumer is in principle the same as "adding" baking services to dough so as to make it into bread. The consequence is that *the costs of market exchange as a process are not nearly so great as might have first been thought.* Many of the persons classified under Wholesale and Retail Trade, for example, are really engaged in the physical warehousing of goods that would still have to take place even in a total command economy with no market process at all.

What then are the *costs of exchange* proper? These are the costs, in a non-command or "free" economy, that stem specifically from the market process. For voluntary transactions to take place, offers must be communicated and alternatives compared. Contracts must be negotiated, and their execution verified. Fraud or other nonperformance must be guarded against. All these activities involve costs.[4] All the expenses of an institution like the New York Stock Exchange, for example, fall under one or more of these headings. (Without private ownership there would no need for a Stock Exchange, since there would be no corporate shares.)

[4] There might also be severe communication and enforcement problems in any actual attempt to construct a functioning *command* economy. And in fact such "costs of command"—the resource wastage in attempting to enforce an economic dictatorship—would almost surely far exceed the costs of market exchange.

EXAMPLE 13.6
Farmer, Consumer, Middleman

"Consumerists" contend that food prices are too high, while farmers complain that the prices they receive are too low. It is natural for both groups to blame the middleman. And, in fact, payments to middlemen have over the years been accounting for an increasing share of consumer expenditure on food.

But of course middlemen are providing services: processing, transporting, packaging, distributing, and so forth. Over time the amounts of middleman services incorporated into food products have been increasing. We have been choosing to consume food that has traveled further, been processed more elaborately, and is distributed in more complex ways than in earlier times.

One explanation of this phenomenon is that middleman services are a relatively superior or "luxury" commodity compared to the raw farm products. If so, the *income elasticity of demand* for off-farm food services is greater than for farm products alone. Confirming this, one study has indicated an overall income elasticity of demand of 0.705 for food products—but when this figure is divided between the farm and off-farm components, the income elasticity is only 0.279 for the farm component but 1.322 for the off-farm element.[a] So the increasing share of the middleman in food sales is largely a result of rising consumer incomes, which have permitted an increase in the purchases of middleman services as a relatively superior good.

[a] E. W. Bunkers and W. W. Cochrane, "On the Income Elasticity of Food Services," *Review of Economics and Statistics*, v. 30 (May 1957), p. 217.

Costs of exchange may depend upon: (1) the volume of goods traded; (2) the frequency of trades; (3) the number of parties involved in a transaction; and (4) the number of distinct commodities per transaction. In the next sections we will be dealing only with two-party, two-commodity trades, ruling out the third and fourth elements above. (Some comments upon costs of multi-party and multi-commodity trading will be made later on.) For simplicity, let us look first at costs that depend only on volume ("proportional" transaction costs), and then at costs that depend only on the frequency of trading ("lump-sum" transaction costs).

13.D.1 □ Proportional Transaction Costs

From a trader's point of view, transaction costs are like *taxes* on exchange (as discussed in Chapter 2). If a tax of G per unit were levied upon purchases of a commodity X, then the *gross price* P_x^+ paid by buyers would necessarily be $G greater than the *net price* P_x^- received by sellers. In Figure 13.12, the shaded area would represent the tax collections.

We can apply the same diagram to analyze proportional transaction costs. The *price gap* $G \equiv P_x^+ - P_x^-$ would be the fee per unit charged by middlemen—for example, the "bid–ask spread" in the New York Stock Exchange. The shaded area would represent the aggregate amounts received by middlemen for their services. Note that a proportional transaction charge, like a per-unit tax, reduces the amount of exchange that would otherwise have taken place.

Figure 13.13 shows how proportional transaction costs affect a typical trader. In a world of *costless* exchange an individual could, starting from an endowment point E, trade to any position along the solid market line KL. The market opportunity set would be the entire triangle OKL. The slope of the market line is $-P_x/P_y$, or simply $-P_x$ if as usual, we interpret Y as a *numéraire* (representing "all other goods") with price $P_y \equiv 1$. The dashed line-segments show the impact of

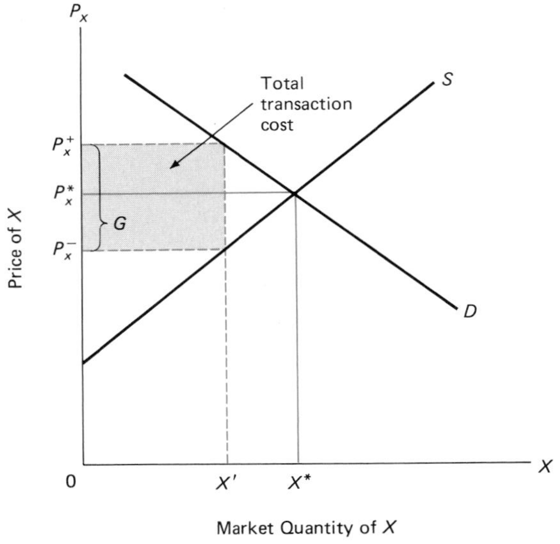

FIGURE 13.12 Proportional Transaction Costs. Here there is a proportional transaction charge, in the amount of G per unit of commodity X exchanged. In equilibrium, there must be a price gap of this amount between the price paid by demanders (P_x^+) and the price received by suppliers (P_x^-). The quantity exchanged is X', and the shaded area represents the aggregate transaction costs paid by traders.

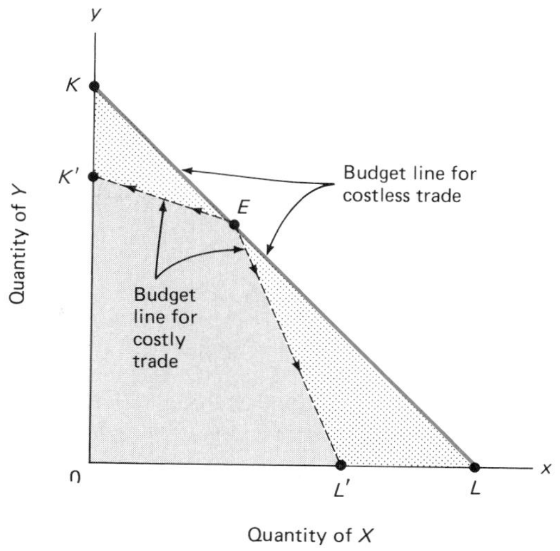

FIGURE 13.13 **Individual Trading Opportunity: Cost-less versus Costly Exchange.** If an individual has initial endowment *E*, under costless exchange his or her market opportunity set consists of the entire triangle *OKL*. But if there is a proportional transaction charge, the person would face a flatter budget line as seller of *X* (line-segment *EK′*) and steeper budget line as buyer of *X* (line-segment *EL′*). The market opportunity set is therefore reduced to the shaded area.

a proportional trading charge. Trying to buy X by moving *southeast* from E (note the direction of the arrows), the slope along line-segment EL' is steeper than along EL because P_x^+ is greater than P_x. And trying to sell X by moving *northwest* along EK', the trader receives only the lower price P_x^- reflected in the flat slope of EK'. Transaction costs therefore shrink the opportunity set, from the triangle OKL to the quadrilateral $OK'EL'$.

Transaction costs reduce the gains from trade. They hinder the process of redistributing consumption goods in accordance with people's desires, and decrease specialization in production. In the limiting case, transaction costs may lead individuals to forego trade entirely—to choose *autarky*.

Whether or not autarky solutions will be preferred under costly exchange depends upon the buying and selling prices P_x^+ and P_x^- and of course also upon productive opportunities and preferences. For the Production Possibility curve QQ in Figure 13.14, the two dotted areas show the enlargement of the overall opportunity set due to the possibility of trading (even though a transaction charge is being levied). Consider the dotted area at the upper left. A is the point where QQ has the same slope as (is tangent to) the dashed market line-segment whose flatter slope represents the lower selling price P_x^-. Hence, in attempting to move northwest (acquire Y by giving up X), beyond point A the individual does better along AK' (selling X for Y in the market) than along QQ (converting X into Y via productive transformation). A corresponding argument applies, of course, for the dotted area at the lower right, which is bounded by the steeper line-segment BL' whose slope represents the higher buying price P_x^+.

Now if the preference map is as shown in Figure 13.14, where the Crusoe tangency R^* *falls between* points A and B, autarky is preferred. The high buying price P_x^+ and the low selling price P_x^- *straddle* the common value of $MRS_C = MRS_T$ at the autarky point. On the other hand, if R^* falls outside the range AB along QQ, the individual will engage in trade. Specifically, suppose the R^* tangency falls northwest of A along QQ as in Figure 13.15. In this range the individual can do better (can reach a higher indifference curve) by trading along the market line-segment AK' than along QQ. The *productive* optimum Q^* would then be at the

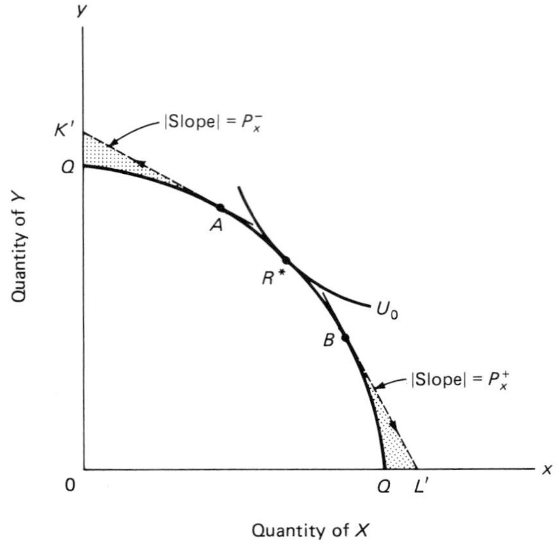

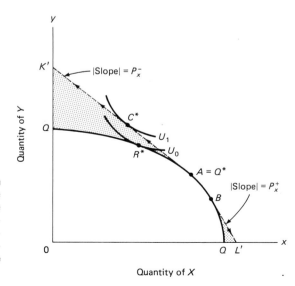

FIGURE 13.14 Opportunity Set with Transaction Costs: Autarky Solution. The gross price P_x^+ determines the slope of the line-segment BL' tangent to the Production-Possibility Curve QQ at point B, thus adding the lower-right dotted area, the individual's overall opportunity set. Similarly, the net price $P_{\bar{x}}$ determines the slope of the line-segment AK' tangent to QQ at point A, which adds the upper-left dotted area to the overall opportunities. Here the autarky solution R^* remains preferred, since R^* lies between A and B.

point A and the person would sell X for Y to attain a *consumptive* optimum C^* along AK'.

An individual will be a net seller of X (will specialize in production of X), despite the existence of a price gap G, when *the net price P_x^- exceeds* the common value of $MRS_C = MRS_T$ at the autarky point. A corresponding argument will apply to the opposite case of specialization in production of Y: this will occur only if the *gross price P_x^+ is less than* the common value of $MRS_C = MRS_T$ at R^*.

The individual and overall market supply-demand pictures are represented in Figure 13.16. In Panel (a) the individual's autarky price is P_x^o. (This represents the absolute slope of the tangency at the Crusoe solution R^* of the previous dia-

FIGURE 13.15 Opportunity Set with Transaction Costs: Non-Autarky Solution. Here R^* does not lie between the tangency points A and B on QQ. The productive optimum Q^* is at point A. The consumptive optimum C^* lies to the northwest along AK', indicating that the individual sells some of the produced X (at the low selling price $P_{\bar{x}}$) to obtain more of Y.

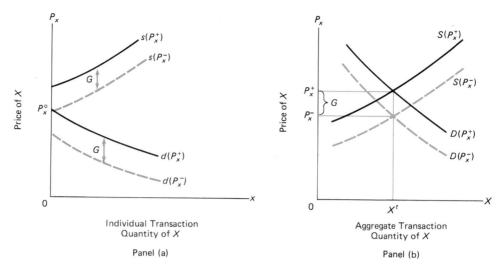

FIGURE 13.16 Supply and Demand: Proportional Exchange Cost. In Panel (a), for a given individual the inner pair of curves represent his transaction supply as a function of the *net* selling price P_x^- (where this exceeds the autarky price P_x^o) and his transaction demand as a function of the *gross* buying price P_x^+ (where this is less than the autarky price). The upper solid curve shows supply as related to the gross price, and the lower dashed curve shows demand as related to the net price. Panel (b) pictures the marketwide aggregates of these four curves. The equilibrium transaction quantity X^t is found at the intersection of either the two (solid) curves defined in terms of the gross prices or the two (dashed) curves defined in terms of the net prices; the equilibrium gross and net prices are determined accordingly.

grams). If the *net* market price P_x^- exceeds P_x^o the individual will be a supplier as shown by the dashed curve labeled $s(P_x^-)$. Similarly, this person will be a net demander only if the *gross* price P_x^+ is lower than P_x^o as shown by the solid curve labeled $d(P_x^+)$. Thus, it is the *inner pair* of curves in Panel (a) that picture the individual's market behavior. It is convenient, however, also to show the (solid) supply curve in terms of the gross price, $s(P_x^+)$, and the (dashed) demand curve in terms of the net price, $d(P_x^-)$. Each of these differs from its partner by the constant vertical distance G—the price gap.

Summing over all the individuals, we have the corresponding pairs of aggregate market supply and demand curves shown in Panel (b). Now we can see why it was convenient to draw the curves in terms of both gross and net prices. The solution that determines the gross or buying price P_x^+ will be at the intersection of $S(P_x^+)$ and $D(P_x^+)$, the two solid curves. This intersection will be at the same market quantity X^t as the intersection of the two dashed curves $S(P_x^-)$ and $D(P_x^-)$ that determines the net or selling price P_x^-. The two prices differ by the fixed gap G that represents the fee charged by middlemen.

What would happen if the bid-ask spread, the size of the gap G, were to increase? In Panel (a) of Figure 13.16 the *inner pair* of curves would remain unchanged, since they directly represent individual behavior in terms of the relevant (gross or net) prices. But the outer pair of curves would be pushed further outward as G rises. Since the equilibrium solution determined in Panel (b) necessarily involves an intersection with one or the other of the outer curves, *higher transaction costs reduce the volume of transactions.*

CONCLUSION: Proportional transaction costs create a gap between buying price and selling price. The higher the transaction charge, the more likely individuals are to choose autarky solutions, and the smaller will be the aggregate volume of market trading.

EXAMPLE 13.7
Urban-Farm Food Cost Differentials

In the absence of transaction costs there would be no reason for a specialist in the *production* of commodity X to be a particularly heavy consumer of X. The tailor would not have an unusually ample wardrobe, the candlestick maker would still use electric lights in his home, and the Detroit assembly-line worker would have no special inducement to drive a car rather than use public transit. It follows that where we *do* observe a producer heavily consuming his or her own product, transaction costs are likely to be an important factor.

Urban and farm consumption expenditures for 1960 to 1961 were studied by F. Y. Lee and K. E. Phillips. As can be seen in the table, farmers spend relatively more on "Food prepared at home," urban-dwellers relatively more on "Food prepared away from home." There seems little reason to doubt that transaction costs impose a greater degree of autarky upon farmers, making it more advantageous for them to consume home-prepared food.

On the other hand, costs of *exchange* are not the sole explanation of the divergence visible in the table. Costs of turnover also play a role: for example, the cost of transporting food from farm to factory and then back to farm might dictate that farmers consume more home-prepared food even under a command economy. It is also possible that farmers simply have a greater comparative preference for home-prepared food. Perhaps more important, in the period studied farm families on the average were poorer than urban families. Since "Food prepared away from home" is a relatively superior good (income elasticity greater than unity), the income difference may also provide a partial explanation.

Food Expenditures as Percentage of Total Consumption

| | NORTHEAST | | WEST | |
EXPENDITURE	Urban	Farm	Urban	Farm
Food prepared at home	21.0	31.0	18.9	27.5
Food prepared away from home	4.8	3.0	4.9	2.9

Source: F. Y. Lee and K. E. Phillips, "Differences in Consumption Patterns of Farm and Non-farm Households in the United States," *American Journal of Agricultural Economics*, v. 53 (Nov. 1971), p. 575.

Certain types of markets seem to disappear as a country gets wealthier: for example, the market for used containers or for cigarettes by the unit (rather than by the pack). The market for used clothes is one that has largely vanished in the United States. It has become cheaper to throw used clothes away rather than pay for the middleman services required to make such a market function.

*13.D.2 ☐ Lump-Sum Transaction Costs

Proportional transaction costs help us understand certain facts about the exchange process—to wit, the normal gap between buying and selling prices. But one crucial aspect of exchange remains to be explained: why we observe *inventories* (stocks of goods) held for purposes of trading. The reason is that people do not trade continuously; we go to market on specific occasions. Between trips to the market a consumer has to hold inventories, and sellers have to hold them while awaiting the irregular visits of purchasers.

If costs of exchange take the form only of a fixed lump-sum *fee per transaction*, the consumer will seek to minimize his or her frequency of trades (trips to the market). But the less frequent the transactions, the larger the average inventories that need to be held. The cost of holding inventories must therefore be balanced against the cost of frequent trading.

Suppose the lump-sum charge is a fixed amount F for each trade. Think of it as an "entry fee." The individual trader's problem is to choose an *optimal trading interval I*. Figure 13.17 shows a possible inventory history for an individual with constant production and consumption flows of a commodity X, who trades at a regular time-interval of I. There is a self-supplied productive flow at the rate x^q. At discrete intervals I, $2I$, $3I$, etc., the individual purchases each time a quantity k of commodity X. This makes it possible to maintain a level consumption flow of $x^c = x^q + (x^k/I)$ continuously. For example, if $x^q = 10$ units per day, k is 140 units, and $I = 7$ days, a consumption rate of $10 + (140/7) = 30$ units per day can be maintained.

To be a buyer of X, this person must of course be a seller of some other commodity Y; a similar diagram, showing regular accumulation rather than de-

---

*Marked sections, beginning with a single asterisk and ending with a double asterisk, may contain somewhat more difficult or advanced material and can be omitted without appreciable loss of continuity.

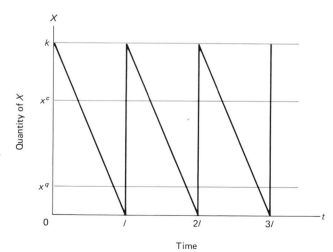

FIGURE 13.17   **Inventory History for an Individual.** The individual has a self-supplied continuous production flow x^q while maintaining a continuous consumption flow x^c, the difference being made up by discrete market purchases at time-intervals I. At each multiple of I, inventory falls to zero and a new stock quantity k is purchased.

crease of inventory between trades, would picture the person's inventory history for commodity Y.

Now let us consider the individual's decision whether or not to trade at all. Figure 13.18 shows a situation where not trading, or autarky, is preferred. In this diagram the "Robinson Crusoe solution" R^*, at the tangency of the Production-Possibility Curve QQ and the indifference curve U_1, is the person's best position attainable. With lump-sum transaction costs there are two disadvantages of trading. The first is *inventory holding costs*. In the diagram these have the effect of shrinking the Production-Possibility Curve from the solid QQ curve to the dashed $\hat{Q}\hat{Q}$ curve. The reason is that resources devoted to maintaining inventories cannot be applied to production. The second disadvantage is, of course, the *lump-sum trading charges* themselves—the explicit fee F paid at each transaction. In the diagram, the average fee incurred per unit of time is represented by the vertical distance $\hat{Q}^* - N^*$. This distance is equal to F/I, paid out in units of Y. The key point is that the individual in this model must, if he or she engages in exchange, trade along the market line NN parallel to but below the market line MM. The line NN represents the *effective* trading opportunities, the combinations of X and Y achievable in the market after paying the average lump-sum charges F/I.

Autarky is of course not inevitable. Smaller costs of holding inventories would decrease the gap between QQ and $\hat{Q}\hat{Q}$; smaller transaction charges would decrease the gap between MM and NN. As these costs fall, the trading solution (the tangency C^* with the highest indifference curve attained along the market line NN) becomes more attractive in comparison with the autarky solution R^*. For the trading solution to be superior, C^* would of course have to lie on a higher indifference curve than R^*.

The outcome as to autarky or trading will also depend upon the market price P_x. Returning to Figure 13.18, as P_x falls MM and NN both become flatter. The tangency of NN with $\hat{Q}\hat{Q}$ (the point $\hat{Q}^*$) will rotate along $\hat{Q}\hat{Q}$ to the northwest,

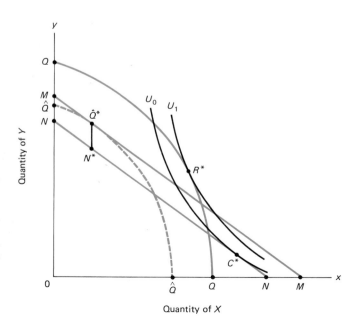

FIGURE 13.18 Autarky and Lump-Sum Transaction Costs. The autarky solution is at R^* on the (solid) Production-Possibility Curve QQ. To engage in trading, inventories must be held, reducing the effective production possibilities to the (dashed) $\hat{Q}\hat{Q}$. Also, to enter the market at time intervals I a lump-sum transaction charge F must be paid each time, so per unit of time a cost of F/I is incurred. If F/I is represented by the vertical distance $\hat{Q}^*N^*$, the individual's trading occurs along the market line NN. In this diagram the autarky solution R^* (on indifference curve U_1) is preferred to the best position C^* (on U_0) that can be attained through trading.

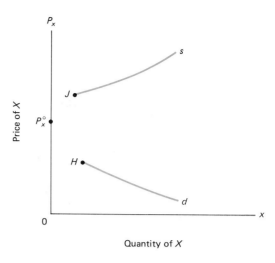

FIGURE 13.19 **Individual Net Supply and Demand: Lump-Sum Transaction Cost.** If there is a lump-sum cost per transaction, the market price must diverge from the autarky price P_x^0 by a certain discrete amount before the individual will enter the market as a supplier or a demander. If the price divergence is just great enough, the individual will offer or demand a minimal discrete quantity—represented by the point J where the supply curve begins and the point H where the demand curve begins.

enlarging the trading opportunity set to the right of the tangency. Eventually, a price may be reached at which the trading optimum C^* along NN will be preferred to R^*—the individual will enter the market as a net demander of X. Similarly, at a sufficiently high price P_x the person may enter the market as a net supplier of X.

Translating this information into a supply-demand diagram leads to Figure 13.19. If the only transaction cost is a lump-sum fee, there is no divergence between the buying price and selling price; middlemen are reimbursed by lump-sum transaction payments F, not by a price gap G. As before, for each individual there is an autarky price P_x^0 represented by the common slope $MRS_C = MRS_T$ at the Crusoe solution R^*. There will now be a *range* of prices around the autarky price for which it will not pay him or her to engage in exchange. But as the market price increasingly diverges from P_x^0, trade becomes more attractive: it will pay to incur the average trading fee F/I and the inventory costs associated with market exchanges.

Another interesting feature of Figure 13.19 is that the supply and demand curves start at points J and H rather than at the vertical axis. The price P_x must be sufficiently above or below the autarky price P_x^0 before it pays to enter the market—and when trade does begin to pay, there will also be a minimum positive quantity traded. [Verification of this point is left as a challenge to the reader.]

The individual transaction supply and demand curves can as usual be aggregated into market-wide supply and demand curves. For lump-sum transaction costs, as for proportional transaction costs, there is a serious possibility that the market-wide curves will not intersect. If so, the market disappears; there is no price at which any buyer-seller pair of traders are willing to incur the transaction charges and associated inventory costs of market dealings in preference to autarky solutions.

CONCLUSION: Lump-sum transaction costs do not create a price gap. But they dictate that exchanges take place at discrete intervals, so that inventories must be held. Heavy transaction charges and the resulting high inventory costs make individual autarky solutions more likely, reduce the aggregate volume of market trade, and may even eliminate the market. [**]

13.E
THE ROLE OF MONEY

Money is a device that reduces the cost of market trading. But recall that the cost of market trading must be distinguished from the cost of physical turnovers—which are, as we have seen, really costs of production that are unavoidable in any economy with specialization and a division of labor. When producers and consumers are geographically dispersed, for example, shipping costs would have to be incurred even in a perfectly functioning command economy. Money can do nothing to reduce shipping costs. And similarly, when production and consumption cannot be perfectly synchronized, commodity inventories will be required along the manufacturer-wholesaler-retailer-consumer chain. Again, money cannot eliminate this category of expense.

Money reduces the costs of bargaining and negotiating by serving as *medium of exchange* and *temporary store of value*. These functions can be best visualized if we consider three hypothetical social regimes in logical succession: (1) a pure command economy, with no trading whatsoever but only dictated physical commodity turnovers; (2) a barter economy, with trading but without any monetary commodity; and (3) a money economy.

Money as medium of exchange:

Suppose an economy has N individuals and N goods, where everyone specializes in producing just one of the commodities. But each person would still like to consume positive quantities of all N goods. Thus, there is specialization in production but diversity in consumption—the normal situation.

Under a pure command regime, imagine that the dictator is perfectly efficient and benevolent. In such an economy there is no "waste" due to *costs of trading* since there is no bidding, negotiating, or contracting. Even so, the *costs of turnover* such as transportation expense may make some of the $N(N - 1)$ possible commodity movements uneconomic. Suppose oranges are produced in California, and lobsters in Maine. Lobsters might be so expensive to ship that, from the viewpoint of overall economic efficiency, the dictator correctly decides that Californians would have to do without them. But oranges are not so costly to ship, let us suppose, and so the dictator correctly commands that California oranges be sent to Maine.

Now suppose a revolution displaces the dictator, substituting a regime of barter trade. In this regime, we will imagine, *only two-party trade is feasible.* (Multiparty barter trades are exceedingly costly to negotiate and enforce and are therefore relatively rare.) Then, and this is the crucial point, instead of the $N(N - 1)$ possible *one-directional commodity movements* that were available to the dictator in a command economy, under bilateral barter only $N(N - 1)/2$ possible *two-way chan-*

[**]End of marked section.

nels of exchange are possible. If shipment of Maine lobsters to California is econom- ically unfeasible owing to the high transportation costs, then the two-way channel is blocked. The California oranges cannot go to Maine either, even though it is not so costly to transport oranges, because the lobstermen cannot compensate the orange growers. As compared with an ideal command economy (perfectly efficient and benevolent dictator), there is not only wastage of resources due to the necessity of negotiating trades but also an inferior allocation of production and consumption due to a higher degree of autarky.

We can now see the function of money as a *medium of exchange*. The com- modity serving as money can be one of the original N goods or else an artificial new commodity like paper currency. In either case, the effect is *to make multilateral trading indirectly possible*.

Suppose, to begin with, that one of the N initial commodities is chosen as medium of exchange. In the prisoner-of-war situation of Chapter 4, *cigarettes* served this function. But in keeping with modern economic history, let us assume that the medium of exchange is *gold*. Then other commodities are no longer traded for one another, but only for gold. This drastically reduces the number of different types of transactions.

In the barter economy the number of possible two-way trading channels is $N(N - 1)/2$. For five goods (four ordinary consumption goods A, B, C, D plus gold G), Figure 13.20 pictures the 5(4)/2 or *ten* trading channels required. But if all other commodities are traded only for gold, *four* channels or markets will suffice. In general, a money (gold) economy would need only $N - 1$ types of transactions. As compared with barter, the costs of finding partners and of negoti- ating, recording, and enforcing trades will be reduced.

But this direct saving from having a medium of exchange is less important than the *indirect* gain due to the effect upon the degree of productive specializa- tion made possible. Consider the lobster-orange example once again. In a mone- tary economy the Maine lobsters still cannot go to California. The transportation

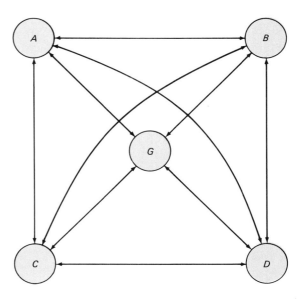

FIGURE 13.20 Trading Channels: Five Goods. With five commodities, under two-way barter ex- change there would have to be *ten* channels of trade or markets. If commodity G is instead the sole medium of exchange, only *four* markets would be needed.

costs are too high, and money cannot change that fact. But the California oranges can now go to Maine! The Maine lobstermen can pay for oranges in *gold*, which they obtain by selling lobsters to other, non-Californian customers. Thus, gold makes possible triangular or still more complex exchanges without requiring anything beyond bilateral trading.

One element of cost is likely to be greater in a gold economy than in a barter economy: there will be increased handling and shipping of *gold*. Clearing arrangements, one aspect of banking, arise to reduce these costs. Also, gold can be replaced by an artificial commodity such as paper money, for which the shipping and handling costs are less. Modern economies tend to move toward a nonphysical, purely abstract medium of exchange, *banking deposits*, to minimize these handling and shipping costs.

Money as temporary store of value:

The other important role of money is as *temporary store of value* ("abode of purchasing power"). Inventories of money help bridge time intervals between receipts and payments. By carrying an inventory of money, a baker selling bread today can buy meat tomorrow.

To grasp the significance of this, let us think again of the hypothetical pure command economy. Even there, inventories of goods are required for productive purposes. But if a revolution takes place overthrowing the dictator in favor of a regime of bilateral voluntary barter exchange, additional *trading inventories* have to come into existence. Suppose three individuals 1, 2, and 3 are the sole specialized producers of commodities A, B, and C, respectively. Imagine that the desired pattern of trade is triangular: commodity A is to flow from person 1 to 2, commodity B from 2 to 3, and commodity C from 3 to 1. If multilateral trading is ruled out, we have here the famous "double coincidence" problem of barter. Consider individual 2, who wants commodity A from individual 1 but produces nothing that individual 1 wants from him. Although 2 can provide commodity B to individual 3, the latter produces nothing that 2 desires.

This dilemma is resolved by having some or all individuals hold a trading inventory of the third commodity—that is, of the one they neither produce nor consume. People accept "trade goods" in exchange for commodities they produce, in order to have something available to exchange for commodities they do wish to consume.

Rather than hold inventories of many different types of trade goods, it is obviously efficient for everyone to accept in exchange some single "store of value" commodity. It should be a commodity that is both cheap to produce and cheap to store, and preferably one that is not eroded (as were cigarettes in the P.O.W. example) by consumption. Again, there will be a natural tendency to move toward a purely abstract money commodity like banking deposits, which are almost costless to produce and to store and are not needed for consumption.

CONCLUSION: The invention of money reduces the costs of market trading, not the costs of physical turnovers which would be required in any economic system employing a division of labor. When one commodity becomes the sole *medium of exchange*, fewer types of transactions are required. A medium of exchange makes possible triangular or even more complex trade patterns that would be impossible under barter. Where inventories of goods must be carried for trading purposes, this is done most economically by everyone agreeing upon a single monetary commodity which then serves also as *temporary store of value*.

EXAMPLE 13.8
Barter in the East Indies

An interesting network of exchanges among primitive peoples in the East Indies (see Figure 13.21) was analyzed by the anthropologist M. Sahlins.[a] A puzzling problem was described by Sahlins. The Busama, who serve as middlemen between the Tami Islanders and certain southern villages, allegedly acquire bowls worth 10 to 12 shillings from Tami Island which they then carry to the south and exchange one-for-one against pots worth only 8 shillings!

The explanation offered was that, while pots and bowls are desired throughout the region, the Busama are producers of taro which is wanted only by the southern villagers. The latter can only pay in pots. Because these are in excess of the Busama's own requirements, the Busama carry the excess pots to Tami and exchange them against bowls as the only product there available. The quantity of bowls thus acquired being again in excess of the Busama's own needs, some are carried back down to the southern villages to be traded along with taro once again for pots.

> COMMENT: It is clearly not rational for the Busama to carry bowls from Tami—where they are, according to the report, *more* highly valued than pots (10 to 12 shillings against 8)—to southern villages where bowls are relatively *less* highly valued (one against one). Indeed, the logic of the situation strongly suggests that the relative values have been misreported. Surely the pots are relatively less highly valued where they are plentiful, at their origin in the south, and the bowls relatively less highly valued at their origin on Tami Island. Only if this is the case does the two-way shipping traffic of the Busama become understandable. The Busama must accept pots from the southern villagers, their only customers for taro, but nothing forces the Busama to carry bowls from north to south at a loss.
>
> Another point to note is that since this is a situation of barter exchange, the cited shilling values may lack any real meaning. Since shillings are not actually employed as a medium of exchange, price quotations may be reported that do not reflect the actual terms at which trades are taking place. Thus, a pot may be "worth" 8 shillings somewhere, but not necessarily on Tami Island if shillings are not actually exchanged for pots there.

[a] Marshall Sahlins, *Stone Age Economics* (Chicago: Aldine, 1972), Chap. 6.

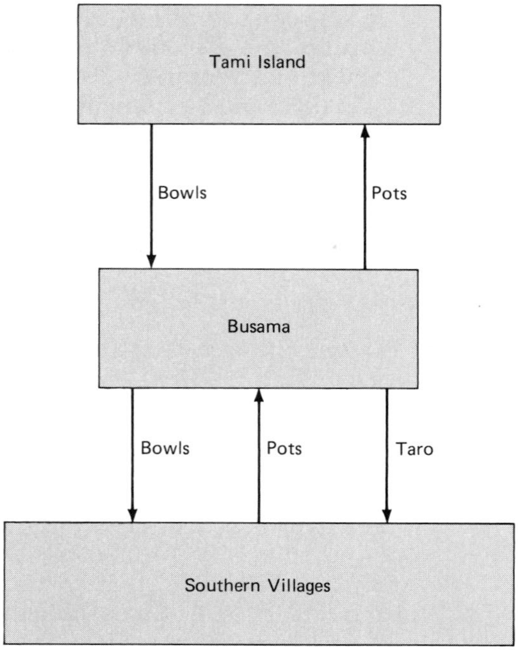

FIGURE 13.21 A Pattern of Barter Trade. The Busama are producers of taro, which is desired only in certain southern villages. While these villagers also desire bowls from Tami Island in the north, they can pay only in pots. The Busama carry the southerners' pots, in excess of their own needs, to Tami Island to exchange for bowls which will ultimately be carried back to the southern villages. For this trade to be possible, bowls must be relatively more highly valued in comparison to pots in the southern villages, and pots relatively more heavily valued at Tami Island in the north.

□ SUMMARY OF CHAPTER 13

This chapter examines the process of exchange and the benefits of trade. Transaction costs and the role of money are analyzed.

Benefits of exchange fall into two main categories: *reallocation of existing stocks* of goods to the consumers who value them the most, and *increased quantities* of goods made possible by specialization in production.

The first benefit stands out most clearly in a world of pure exchange, where the society has fixed stocks of all commodities. In a simplified world of two goods X and Y, the Edgeworth box shows how two parties can both achieve greater satisfaction by trading into the "region of mutual advantage." At competitive equilibrium in pure exchange, each trader will exchange X for Y (or vice versa) until his or her Marginal Rate of Substitution in Consumption MRS_C becomes equal to the market price ratio P_x/P_y. This corresponds to achieving a point on the "Contract Curve" in the Edgeworth box.

In a world of production and exchange, the individual's *productive optimum* Q^* will in general be distinct from his or her *consumptive optimum* C^*. At Q^* the condition satisfied is $MRS_T = P_x/P_y$, where MRS_T is the person's Marginal Rate of Substitution in Productive Transformation (or Marginal Rate of Transformation); at C^* the condition is $MRS_C = P_x/P_y$ as before. The availability of trade leads to specialization in which each trader concentrates on the activity at which he or she is most productive. The increased output of goods due to this greater division of labor is the second benefit of trade.

Full demand (the desired consumption quantity at any given price) and *full supply* (the total amount endowed or produced at that price) must be distinguished from *transaction demand* and *transaction supply*. The *full* quantities are the amounts supplied to or demanded from the economy; the *transaction* quantities are the amounts traded in markets. The two magnitudes differ by the quantity of goods that individuals self-supply for their own consumption.

Perfect markets involve perfect communication between buyers and sellers, instantaneous equilibrium with a single price at which all trading takes place, and absence of transaction costs. Actual markets can only approximate these ideal conditions. The function of "middlemen" is to overcome market imperfections, but this cannot be done costlessly since the middlemen must themselves be compensated. The costs of *trading*, properly speaking, are the costs of operating a market system. Not all "middleman" services represent costs of trading. Services like transportation, warehousing of goods, and retail distribution would persist even in a total command economy.

Costs of trading are, among other things, a function of the amount of goods exchanged and of the frequency of trading. Two polar cases were analyzed: transaction costs that are proportional to the quantity of goods changing hands, or that are incurred as a fixed lump sum each time a transaction takes place. Both types of transaction costs diminish the extent of specialization in production, and make autarky solutions more likely.

Money is a device that reduces the cost of trading. The presence of money as a *medium of exchange* reduces the number of different types of two-way exchanges (in comparison with barter). This lowers the costs of collecting information, keeping records, and shipping goods to settle transactions. Even more important, it opens up triangular or even more complex patterns of trade that would be blocked under two-way barter. As a *store of value*, money economizes on the trading inventories that would have to be carried under barter. By facilitating exchange, the institution of money makes possible a better distribution of consumption goods together with increased specialization in production.

☐ QUESTIONS FOR CHAPTER 13

Mainly For Review

R1. Explain how the possibility of trade can lead to *consumptive* benefits (improved allocations of given social totals of goods among the different individuals) and to *productive* benefits (larger social totals of desired goods). How is the consumptive improvement illustrated in the Edgeworth box? Can the productive improvement be illustrated in the Edgeworth box?

*R2. If two persons have identical preferences (indifference-curve maps), does it follow that they cannot trade to mutual advantage? What if they have identical preferences *and* identical endowments in a world of pure exchange? In a world of production, what if they have identical preferences and identical productive opportunities?

*The answers to starred questions appear at the end of the book.

*R3. We normally observe a strong tendency toward specialization in production but diversification (nonspecialization) in consumption. What shapes of the individuals' Production-Possibility Curves and preference maps lead to this pattern of behavior? Could this pattern be achieved in the absence of trade?

R4. What is meant by an individual's "sustaining price" for a particular good? What happens at higher prices? At lower prices? How does the "sustaining price" differ from the "autarky price"?

R5. What condition must hold for each individual at competitive equilibrium in a world of *pure exchange*? What additional condition characterizes the market as a whole?

*R6. What are the productive and consumptive conditions that must hold for each individual in a world of *production and exchange*? What additional conditions characterize the market as a whole?

*R7. If market equilibrium takes place at the intersection of the aggregate *transaction* demand and *transaction* supply curves, how can the intersection of the *full* demand and *full* supply curves also determine the equilibrium?

R8. "For every individual, the s_i^t and d_i^t curves must intersect along the vertical axis, as in Figure 13.9. It is therefore quite impossible for the aggregate S^t and D^t curves to intersect in the interior, as in Figure 13.10." True or false? Explain.

R9. What are perfect markets? What is perfect competition?

*R10. Can autarky occur in costless exchange? Why is autarky more likely, the higher are transaction costs? Do you think that the increasing burdens of payroll taxes (income tax, Social Security tax) and sales taxes in recent decades have anything to do with the "do-it-yourself" trend observed in such areas of activity as furniture construction and repair, car maintenance, dressmaking, etc.?

R11. Some markets are illegal (markets for babies, for narcotic drugs, for government favors, and so on). Law enforcement that is short of being *totally* effective can be regarded as imposing a transaction cost upon participants. In terms of this chapter's analysis, what effects would you anticipate from increased law-enforcement effort against the narcotic traffic? Would the volume of transactions be affected? What about the gross price paid by buyers in comparison with the net price received by sellers?

R12. Illustrate how sufficiently heavy *proportional* transaction costs might make a market nonviable. Do the same for *lump-sum* transaction costs.

*R13. Since the existence of markets necessarily involves some burden of transaction costs, wouldn't a command economy dispensing with markets always be more efficient? Explain.

R14. Distinguish between turnover costs and exchange costs. How would you class transportation of goods between producer and consumer? What about the costs of negotiating a contract? Enforcing a contract?

For Further Thought and Discussion

T1. From Omar Khayyám:

> I often wonder what the Vintners buy
> One half so precious as the Goods they sell.

Omar seems to be suggesting that vintners ought not engage in exchange, since wine is more precious than anything else. Where is the fallacy in his reasoning?

*T2. Compare the likely effects of taxes levied upon *consumption*, upon *production*, and upon *exchange* of a commodity.

*T3. Suppose Robinson Crusoe is superior to Friday in producing *either* of the two goods, fish and bananas, available on their island. For example, it may take Robinson one hour to catch a fish and two hours to pick a bunch of bananas, while it takes Friday four hours to do either. Show that they still can engage in mutually beneficial exchange. (In international trade this is called the "principle of comparative advantage.")

*T4. Imagine an initial Edgeworth-box competitive equilibrium, starting from an endowment position where individual i has all of commodity G (grain) and individual j has all of commodity Y (numéraire). Suppose i's endowment of grain doubles, everything else remaining unchanged. Can we be sure that i is better off at the new competitive equilibrium? That j is better off? That at least one of them is better off? [*Hint:* Are wheat farmers necessarily better off if the crop is large? What about consumers of wheat?]

T5. Give examples of markets that have existed historically, but do not now exist. Can you explain their disappearance?

T6. According to economist K. E. Boulding, a tariff can be regarded as a "negative railroad." Whereas a railroad connects trading communities, a tariff separates them. Is the analogy valid?

*T7. In the text it was stated that, in a world of two commodities X and Y, trade would normally lead to greater quantities produced of both goods. Is this *necessarily* the case? Might there possibly be, say, greater production of X but reduced production of Y? Explain. [*Hint:* Consider the case where only trader i has productive opportunities, while j has a fixed endowment.]

*T8. Flowers provide bees with nectar, while bees facilitate the pollination of flowers. Is this exchange?

T9. Fresh fruits are cheaper at farm roadstands than in city markets. Does the price difference reflect turnover costs or exchange costs, or are there elements of each?

T10. Give examples of exchange costs that are reduced by the existence of money as a *medium of exchange*. Of money as a *store of value*.

*T11. If *rationing* is introduced, money is no longer fully effective as a medium of exchange. What types of additional exchange costs emerge in a world where ration coupons and cash are *both* required in order to effectuate a transaction?

*T12. According to elementary textbooks, a commodity selected to serve as money should be portable, divisible, storable, generally recognizable, and homogeneous. In terms of the discussion in this chapter, why are these desirable qualities? Can you think of other desirable qualities? [*Hint:* Think of cigarettes serving as money in a prisoner-of-war camp.]

14

SUPPLEMENTARY CHAPTER

THE ECONOMICS OF TIME: SAVING, INVESTMENT, AND INTEREST

Up to now we have studied two main types of individual decisions: (1) how to spend current income (what consumption goods to purchase) and (2) how to earn current income (what amounts of resource services to offer on the market). In this chapter a third type of decision is examined: how to strike a balance between consuming today versus arranging, through saving or investment, to consume more in the future.

What is meant by "saving" and "investment"? *Saving* is simply refraining from current consumption. *Investment*, in contrast, refers to the actual creation of new sources of productive services like buildings or machines. For an isolated Robinson Crusoe, saving must match investment. When Robinson takes time off from catching fish by hand in order to weave a fishing net, it is his own saving (giving up some fish today) that makes it possible for him to invest (create the fishing net). In an exchange economy, however, those who save and those who invest do not have to be the same people. The person who puts money in the bank is not generally the one who creates a new resource by constructing a house. Through the process of borrowing and lending, the market puts the savings of some individuals to work financing the investment activities of others.

Why would you save or invest, rather than consume today? Only so you, or your heirs, can consume more in the future. Someone who builds a house is arranging for future shelter; a farmer who plants a tree is intending to pick future fruit; a business that incurs costs to maintain its machinery is providing for future earnings.

Section 14.A analyzes these choices between present and future. We will see how the *interest rate* serves as a kind of price in relation to time. Section 14.B takes up an important practical topic: the criteria used by business firms and by government agencies in making their investment decisions. The role of risk is examined in Section 14.C, and the distinction between real interest and monetary interest is introduced in Section 14.D. The concluding section reviews the underlying forces that explain why interest rates are high in some countries, low in others—or have been high in some eras, while low in other historical periods.

14.A
CONSUMPTION AND PRODUCTION OVER TIME

For simplicity, assume there is only a single desired consumption good C (corn). The objects of choice here are *dated* quantities of C symbolized as C_0 (this year's corn), C_1 (corn one year from now), C_2 (corn two years from now), etc. To begin with, let us consider elementary two-period choices: between consuming corn this year or next year. (Notice that the analysis is in real units: the choice is between present and future *corn* rather than present and future *dollars*.)

14.A.1 ☐ Borrowing-Lending Equilibrium

The key to understanding consumption decisions over time (the choice between C_0 and C_1) is to notice that the underlying logic is exactly the same as in choosing between ordinary commodities X and Y within a single period of time. Figure 14.1 looks almost exactly like the "optimum of the consumer" diagrams in Chapter 4. Once again there are indifference curves U', U'' U''', . . . and a budget line KL. The optimum of the consumer will again be at a tangency point C^*—here representing a best "consumption basket" in the form of c_0^* of current corn and c_1^* of future corn.

The intertemporal endowment position E shows the individual's starting-point in the form of initial entitlements to current consumption $(\bar{c}_0)$ and to anticipated future consumption $(\bar{c}_1)$.[1] When the individual trades northwest along the budget line KL from endowment position E, he or she is said to be "lending"—giving up current corn C_0 in exchange for future corn C_1. Should the person move southeast, obtaining more C_0 at the expense of C_1, he or she is said to be "borrowing." The individual pictured in Figure 14.1 is lending $\bar{c}_0 - c_0^*$ of current corn, with an anticipated repayment next year of $c_1^* - \bar{c}_1$. Had the endowment position E been further to the northwest along the budget line, the individual would have been a borrower. Such a person, with an endowment mainly in the form of future income, is like the "heir with great expectations" in Charles Dickens' novel. He is poor today but has rich prospects for the future.

---

[1] *Uncertainty* is ruled out here, so anticipations as to the future are sure to be realized.

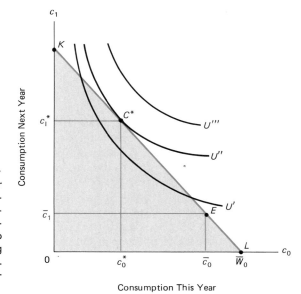

FIGURE 14.1 Intertemporal Consumptive Optimum. The decision between consumption this year C_0 and consumption next year C_1 involves the preference map (indifference curves U', U'', U'''), endowment position (E), and budget line (KL). The optimum position is C^*. The individual here chooses to lend the amount $\bar{c}_0 - c_0^*$ of current claims, receiving in repayment the amount $c_1^* - \bar{c}_1$ of future claims. $\overline{W}_0$ is the endowed wealth measured in units of current claims C_0.

What is the rate of exchange at which the market will permit borrowing or lending—that is, trading current corn against future corn? This rate corresponds geometrically to the slope of the budget line. Let the price of C_0 be symbolized as P_0 and the price of C_1 be P_1. Then the ratio at which the two claims can be exchanged, $\Delta c_1/\Delta c_0$, equals $-P_0/P_1$. (The minus sign is needed since, as usual, Δc_1 and Δc_0 have opposite signs—one must be given up to obtain more of the other.) We will be assuming that current claims C_0 serve as the *numéraire* or basis of pricing, so that $P_0 \equiv 1$.

The *interest rate* r is a special kind of price. Specifically, the annual rate of interest r is defined as the *premium* on the relative value of a unit of current consumption in comparison with one-year-in-the-future consumption—the extra worth of corn today over corn next year. Looking at it the other way, the price P_1 of future corn is such that $1 + r$ units of future corn have the same value today as a single unit of current corn:

(14.1)
$$P_1(1 + r) \equiv P_0 \equiv 1$$

Or, we can use either of the following logically equivalent formulas:

(14.1′)
$$\frac{P_1}{P_0} \equiv \frac{1}{1 + r}$$

(14.1″)
$$r \equiv \frac{P_0}{P_1} - 1$$

Consequently, the slope $-P_0/P_1$ of the budget line in Figure 14.1 can also be written as $-(1 + r)$.

Exercise 14.1: (a) If the interest rate is $r = 10\%$, what is the implied price P_1 of a one-year future claim to corn? (b) What if $r = 100\%$? (c) If future claims become almost valueless (P_1 approaches zero), what would happen to r? (d) Are negative interest rates ($r < 0$) meaningful?

Answer: (a) Using Equation (14.1′), if $r = 0.1$ then $P_1 = P_1/P_0 \equiv 1/(1 + r) = 1/1.1 = 0.9091$. (b) If $r = 1.0$ then $P_1 = 1/2 = 0.5$. (c) As P_1 approaches zero, r goes to infinity. (d) Yes, $r < 0$ means only that $P_1 > P_0$—that a future claim is worth *more* than a present claim. This is not at all impossible. For example, it might come about if people anticipated great scarcities in the future.

In Chapter 4 it was the individual's *income* I that constrained his or her choices. But the budget equation $P_x x + P_y y = I$ that was used in Chapter 4 failed to allow for the fact that people often spend less than their current income (they may save) or more than their income (they may borrow). We are now in a position to correct this flaw. It is not *income* I that limits a person's consumption choices over time but rather his or her endowed *wealth* $\overline{W}_0$.

> DEFINITION: Endowed wealth $\overline{W}_0$ is the value of an individual's endowment of present and future claims.
> In terms of the prices P_0 and P_1, endowed wealth is:

(14.2)
$$\overline{W}_0 \equiv P_0 \overline{c}_0 + P_1 \overline{c}_1$$

And in the alternative "interest" notation, since $P_0 \equiv 1$ and $P_1 \equiv 1/(1 + r)$, endowed wealth becomes:

(14.2′)
$$\overline{W}_0 \equiv \overline{c}_0 + \frac{\overline{c}_1}{1 + r}$$

Assuming $P_0 \equiv 1$, endowed wealth is the horizontal intercept of the budget line KL. (The subscript 0 is attached to the symbol for wealth because wealth signifies a *present* market value, the worth *today* of a person's present and future income claims.)

The equation for the budget line KL of Figure 14.1 can similarly be expressed in two ways:

(14.3)
$$P_0 c_0 + P_1 c_1 = \overline{W}_0$$

(14.3′)[2]
$$c_0 + \frac{c_1}{1 + r} = \overline{W}_0$$

What about the equilibrium in the market as a whole? This is derived in exactly the same way as the familiar market equilibrium involving commodities X and Y. By imagining different prices P_1 (or interest rates r) determining different budget lines through the endowment position, a Price Expansion Path is obtained for each individual. As in Chapter 13, these can then be translated into "full" or "transaction" supply and demand curves—first for the separate individuals, and then for the market as a whole. The final result is pictured in Figure 14.2, where lending corresponds to transaction supply and borrowing corresponds to transac-

[2] *Mathematical Footnote*: Notice the difference between Equations (14.2) and (14.3), or between (14.2′) and (14.3′). Equations (14.2) and (14.2′) *define* endowed wealth in terms of the endowed current and future income elements $\overline{c}_0$ and $\overline{c}_1$—which are given constants. But c_0 and c_1 in Equations (14.3) or (14.3′) are *variables*, representing the current and future consumption amounts achievable out of a given endowed wealth.

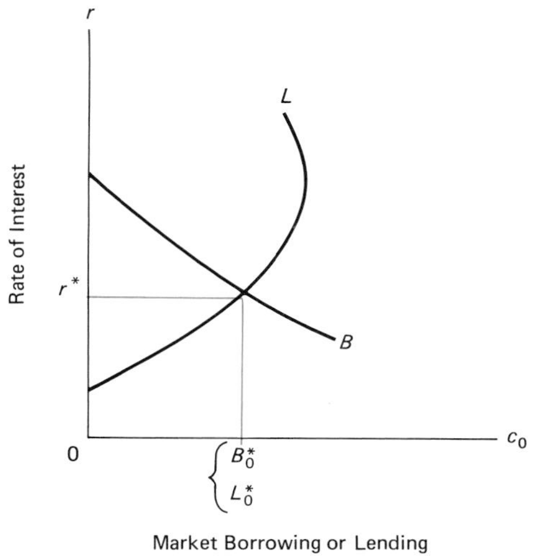

FIGURE 14.2 Borrowing-Lending Equilibrium. The L curve shows the aggregate supply of current claims offered for lending at each interest rate r. The B curve shows the aggregate demand for borrowing at each r. The intersection determines the equilibrium amount borrowed and lent, and the equilibrium interest rate r^*.

tion demand. On the vertical axis of the borrowing-lending diagram we can put the interest rate r. The L curve is the *market supply of lending*, the sum of the "transaction quantities" of current claims C_0 that the various individuals are willing to offer on the loan market at each interest rate r. The B curve represents the *market demand for borrowing*, the aggregate amount of C_0 that all the individuals together will be willing to demand on the loan market at any r. The supply-demand intersection determines the equilibrium amounts of borrowing and lending $B_0^* = L_0^*$ and the equilibrium rate of interest r^*.

Exercise 14.2: Suppose John's Marginal Rate of Substitution (between C_0 and C_1) is given by $MRS_C^j = c_1^j/c_0^j$ and Karl's by $MRS_C^k = c_1^k/c_0^k$. Let the corresponding intertemporal endowments be $(\bar{c}_0^j, \bar{c}_1^j) = (10, 100)$ and $(\bar{c}_0^k, \bar{c}_1^k) = (50, 20)$. (a) Find John's demand for borrowing b_0 and Karl's supply of lending l_0. (b) If the two represent the supply and demand sides of a competitive market, find the market equilibrium in terms of both the price ratio and the interest rate.

Answer: (a) To find John's consumption optimum, the usual equations are $c_1^j/c_0^j = 1/P_1$ ($\equiv P_0/P_1$) and $c_0^j + P_1 c_1^j = 10 + 100P_1$. Eliminating c_1^j we have: $c_0^j = 5 + 50P_1$, or $c_0^j = 5 + 50/(1 + r)$. This equation represents John's "full" demand curve for current corn (inclusive of his own consumption). His demand for borrowing is a "transaction" demand curve, so we must subtract his endowed quantity of current corn: $b_0^j = c_0^j - \bar{c}_0^j = -5 + 50/(1 + r)$. A similar analysis for Karl leads to $c_0^k = 25 + 10/(1 + r)$, implying $l_0^k = \bar{c}_0^k - c_0^k = 25 - 10/(1 + r)$. (b) The equilibrium is at $r = 100\%$, or $P_1/P_0 = 1/2$. Here John borrows $b_0^j = 20$ units of C_0, equal to the amount l_0^k that Karl is willing to lend.

14.A.2 ☐ Saving-Investment Equilibrium

In the pure borrowing-lending equilibrium just discussed, the lenders were saving (refraining from consumption) but their saving was exactly counterbalanced by *dis-saving* on the part of the borrowers. No *investment* was taking place. Investment, which is the construction of new real-capital like machines or buildings, is a kind of production. Consequently, the analysis of the saving-investment equilibrium will closely parallel the discussion of "Exchange and Production" in Chapter 13. In equilibrium, the net positive total of individuals' savings and dissavings exactly balances ("finances") the actual investment in the economy.

Figure 14.3 shows a Robinson Crusoe isolated from all trade. His endowment combination E can be written in consumption units as $(\bar{c}_0, \bar{c}_1)$ or in production units as $(\bar{q}_0, \bar{q}_1)$, these being always the same for him. The productive transformation opportunities are indicated by his Production-Possibility Curve QQ. The optimum position for Robinson is the tangency point R^* in the diagram. Of course, Robinson must produce exactly what he consumes: $R^* = (c_0^*, c_1^*) = (q_0^*, q_1^*)$.

Robinson's *saving* (refraining from consumption) is the horizontal distance $\bar{c}_0 - c_0^*$. But here no lending occurs, since there is no one to lend to. Rather, Robinson's saving is used solely for physical *investment* (for example, planting seed corn): $\bar{c}_0 - c_0^* = \bar{q}_0 - q_0^*$. The yield in terms of future corn is shown in the diagram by the vertical distance $q_1^* - \bar{q}_1 = c_1^* - \bar{c}_1$. For an isolated Robinson Crusoe, therefore, plantings of seed (investing) exactly equal nonconsumption of current

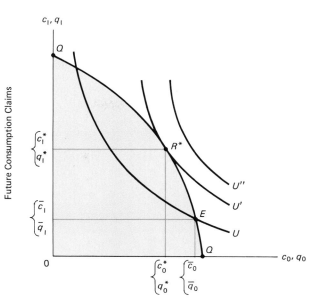

FIGURE 14.3 Intertemporal Productive-Consumptive Optimum: Robinson Crusoe. Robinson Crusoe has no intertemporal *exchange* (borrowing-lending) opportunities, but can engage in *productive* transformations between consumption this year and consumption next year. QQ is the Production-Possibility Curve through his endowment position E. The Crusoe optimum is at R^*, where QQ is tangent to the highest attainable indifference curve. This is an "autarky" solution: the amounts produced (q_0^*, q_1^*) equal, respectively, the amounts consumed (c_0^*, c_1^*).

corn (saving). Similarly for an isolated *country*: in the absence of foreign trade, a country's saving must equal its own investment.

Once borrowing and lending are possible, an individual's saving no longer has to equal his or her own investment. Figure 14.4 pictures an individual with *both* productive opportunities and market opportunities. The productive opportunities are represented, as before, by the Production-Possibility Curve QQ. The market opportunities are shown by budget lines of slope $-P_0/P_1 \equiv -(1 + r)$ through attainable points on QQ. Each budget line represents a certain level of wealth according to the equation:

$$(14.4) \qquad W_0 \equiv q_0 + \frac{q_1}{1 + r}$$

One such line, MM, shows possible trades from the endowment position E—the associated wealth being $\overline{W}_0$ as before. But the individual here can do better by producing at Q^*, where he reaches the *highest* attainable budget line NN. NN therefore represents the maximum attainable level of wealth, W_0^*:

$$(14.5) \qquad W_0^* \equiv q_0^* + \frac{q_1^*}{1 + r}$$

Having maximized his or her wealth, the person can *then* engage in market exchange along NN, attaining a consumptive optimum at C^*. (Note that C^* is on a higher indifference curve than R^*.) For someone able to borrow or lend as well as invest, therefore, the effective *constraint* on consumption is not the Production-

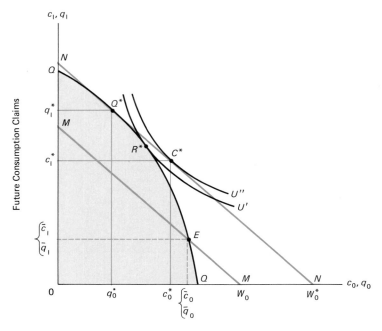

FIGURE 14.4 **Intertemporal Productive-Consumptive Optimum with Exchange.** The individual here has intertemporal productive opportunities (shown by the Production-Possibility Curve QQ) as well as exchange opportunities indicated by budget lines like MM and NN of slope $-P_0/P_1 \equiv -(1+r)$. The productive optimum Q^* involves investment in the amount $\bar{q}_0 - q_0^*$. The consumptive optimum C^* indicates that only the amount $\bar{c}_0 - c_0^*$ is provided by this individual's own saving; the remainder of the investment is financed by borrowing in the market.

Possibility Curve QQ but the budget line NN. The budget-line equation, in terms of the consumption quantities as variables, is:[3]

$$(14.6) \qquad c_0 + \frac{c_1}{1+r} = W_0^*$$

The individual pictured in Figure 14.4 is investing (planting seed corn) in an amount equal to the horizontal distance $\bar{q}_0 - q_0^*$. But his *saving* is only the horizontal distance $\bar{c}_0 - c_0^*$. It follows that some other members of the society must be saving enough to help "finance" his investment by providing the remainder of the needed seed corn.

Market equilibrium is shown in Figure 14.5 in two ways: (1) as a balance between the overall "supply of saving" S and "demand for investment" I, and (2) as a balance between the overall "supply of lending" L and "demand for borrowing" B. (Recall the diagram in the preceding chapter that showed equilibrium solutions

---

[3] *Mathematical Footnote:* As in the preceding footnote, note the difference between Equations (14.5) and (14.6). (14.5) is an identity in which the maximized wealth W_0^* is *defined*. (14.6) is a conditional equation, in which W_0^* is a constant that constrains the consumption quantities c_0 and c_1.

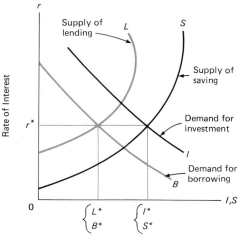

FIGURE 14.5 **Intertemporal Equilibrium with Productive Investment.** When productive investment can take place, the equilibrium interest rate r^* simultaneously balances: (1) the aggregate *supply of saving S* with the aggregate *demand for investment I*, and (2) the aggregate *supply of lending L* with the aggregate *demand for borrowing B*. The difference between the two magnitudes, at any interest rate r, is accounted for by the amount of investment self-financed out of investors' own savings.

in terms of "full" supply and demand versus "transaction" supply and demand.) The difference between the "full" magnitude of saving-investment versus the "transaction" amount of borrowing-lending is accounted for by the amount of investment that is *self-financed* through investors' own savings.

CONCLUSION: In the absence of productive investment opportunities, at any given interest rate r each individual will engage in borrowing or lending so as to achieve a preferred intertemporal pattern of consumption. At the equilibrium interest rate r^* the overall market supply of lending balances the overall market demand for borrowing. In an economy with investment opportunities, each individual will choose the scale of investment that maximizes his or her wealth—while also borrowing or lending as required to achieved a preferred time-pattern of consumption. Then the equilibrium interest r^* balances the aggregate supply of saving with the aggregate demand for investment, and *also* balances the aggregate supply of lending with the aggregate demand for borrowing.

EXAMPLE 14.1
Growth versus Investment—International Comparisons

For nations as for individuals, some save and invest more than others. We would expect nations with higher rates of investment to display more rapid growth over time. The table below indicates that this tends to be the case, where growth is measured in terms of annual changes in Gross Domestic Product (GDP).

Growth, Investment, and Saving (1973–1984)

	Growth Rate of GDP (% p.a.)	Investment Rate (%)	Saving Rate (%)
FIVE HIGHEST GROWTH RATES			
Egypt	8.5	25	12
Yemen Arab Rep.	8.1	21	−22
Cameroon	7.1	26	33
Syrian Arab Rep.	7.0	24	12
Indonesia	6.8	21	20
FIVE LOWEST GROWTH RATES			
Zambia	0.4	14	15
El Salvador	−0.3	12	4
Ghana	− 0.9	6	5
Zaire	−1.0	NA	NA
Uganda	−1.3	8	6

Source: Selected from The World Bank, *The World Development Report* (1986).

COMMENT: To interpret these data, it is important to keep in mind the distinction between saving and investment. A high *saving* rate by residents of a country would lead to increases in wealth, but not necessarily to increases in GDP—if, for example, the saving is invested abroad. Conversely, a country can maintain high *investment* despite low saving if funds flow in from abroad. Yemen clearly falls into this category; it had a very high investment rate despite a large negative saving rate. (Saudi Arabia provided large financial assistance to Yemen during this period.) Overall, however, there is some correlation between investment rates and savings rates, since it is generally easier and safer for people to invest their savings at home rather than abroad. The countries with very low saving and investment rates here were almost all subject to great political disturbances during this period, while those with extraordinarily high rates tended to be beneficiaries of the oil boom.

The distinction between saving and investment also plays a central role in the example that follows.

EXAMPLE 14.2
Social Security, Saving, and National Income

Before the Social Security program came into effect in the United States, individuals generally provided for their retirement by saving out of income earned in their productive working years. These savings entered the financial markets and helped provide funds for the economy-wide real investments that increased the real-capital of the nation.

The Social Security program reduced peoples' need to provide for their old age through financial instruments like insurance or bank accounts. Also, Social

Security taxes on earnings in their working years left people with less income available for saving. So aggregate *private* saving would be expected to decline as a result of the Social Security program. On the other hand, the federal government was receiving huge inflows of Social Security contributions. Had the government adopted a policy of "funding" these contributions, the cash inflows would have been used to accumulate a financial reserve in the form of stocks, bonds, real estate, and so on. (Indeed, this is precisely what insurance companies do with premiums paid in under their private "social security" programs for individuals who purchase retirement annuities.) Then the collective saving of the Social Security Administration would have balanced the reduction in private savings.

However, a political decision was made *not* to fund Social Security. No reserves were accumulated. Instead, Social Security tax revenues were used to support the current expenses of government. Some economists have contended that, in consequence, there has been a severe adverse effect upon aggregate saving in the economy (and therefore also upon aggregate real investment). Martin Feldstein[a] estimated that the Social Security program reduced overall private saving by 38 percent—without, as just explained, providing any compensating increase in collective or government saving. The lower scale of saving and investment over the years has substantially reduced the nation's stock of real-capital. And since real-capital contributes to production (raises the Average Product of labor and other resources), total and per-capita national income have also been affected. Feldstein estimated that, by 1972, the Social Security program had led to a startling reduction in GNP—between 11 and 15 percent.

These calculations and estimates have been subjected to criticism by other economists. One objection raised was that Feldstein had assumed all private saving was for retirement purposes, whereas in actuality many people save in order to pass on bequests to heirs. Taking account of this and other criticisms, Michael R. Darby[b] has produced revised estimates. He concluded that Social Security was responsible for a decrease of between 5 and 20 percent in the capital stock, and between 2 and 7 percent in national income. These results tend to confirm Feldstein's contention about the way in which the Social Security program affects saving and national income, but the calculated effects are numerically smaller than Feldstein's original estimates.

[a] Martin Feldstein, "Social Security, Induced Retirement, and Aggregate Capital Accumulation," *Journal of Political Economy*, v. 82 (Sept./Oct. 1974).

[b] Michael R. Darby, *The Effects of Social Security on Income and Capital Stock* (Washington, D.C.: American Enterprise Institute for Public Policy Research, 1979), esp. p. 79.

14.B
INVESTMENT DECISIONS
AND THE PRESENT-VALUE RULE

The economics of time is not a matter of concern only for theorists. It has very practical implications in the world of affairs. Decision-makers in government and business continually face such choices as what investment projects to adopt;

how to finance the set of chosen projects; and over what time frame to pay out the benefits. We can now begin to analyze certain of these investment decision problems.

14.B.1 □ The Separation Theorem

An essential feature of Figure 14.4 is that *the productive optimum position is entirely independent of the individual's preferences.* The location of Q^* depends only on the shape of the Production-Possibility curve QQ and on the slope of the market lines, and not at all on the indifference curves. But this *Separation Theorem* applies only if there are perfect and costless markets (see Chapter 13) for borrowing and lending. What if such transactions were costly, so that (for example) an individual could only borrow at a rate of interest higher than the rate at which he or she could lend? The amount to be invested, the choice of Q^* on the Production-Possibility curve, would then depend in part upon preferences—that is, upon the person's willingness to self-finance (to save). Take the extreme case of an isolated Robinson Crusoe, where costs of transacting are infinite (there are no market opportunities at all). For Robinson Crusoe the productive and consumptive decisions must be identical; *all* his physical investment must be self-financed, and so his time-preferences will surely affect his scale of investment.

If the conditions underlying the Separation Theorem are approximately applicable, important practical results follow. Suppose an individual who owns a firm delegates productive decisions to an agent or manager. *The manager would not have to know anything about the time-preferences of the owner.* If the manager simply aims to maximize the firm's attained wealth, this assures that the owner is made as well off as possible.

Even more important, a manager could work simultaneously for a number of *different* owners with different time-preferences. These owners can thus combine their wealth in a corporation (see Chapter 6). A manager maximizing the wealth of the corporation also maximizes the wealth of the owners, regardless of their time-preferences. So the amounts and types of investments undertaken (the Q^* decision) will be the same whether the owners are seeking to consume more in the present ("heirs with great expectations") or are more oriented toward the future.[4]

14.B.2 □ The Present-Value Rule

Suppose a "project," that is, an investment opportunity, is under consideration for adoption. What is the appropriate *investment decision rule* for choosing between good projects and bad ones?

A project always generates a sequence of dated income flows or payments. Let z_0 be the payment in the current period, z_1 next period, etc. If z_0 is negative and z_1 is positive, present income is being sacrificed for future income and we have an *investment* project. If z_0 were positive and z_1 negative, it would be a *disinvestment* project.

---

[4] When the Separation Theorem is *inapplicable*, there is said to be a "clientele effect" in the decisions of the firm. We would expect investors with different tastes to combine in different types of firms, each of which would cater to the particular time-preferences of its owners.

The *Present Value* V_0 of a two-period project is defined as:

(14.7)
$$V_0 \equiv z_0 + \frac{z_1}{1 + r}$$

Comparison with the definition of wealth in Equation (14.4) shows that Present Value can be regarded as the *wealth increment* achieved by adopting the project. If the Separation Theorem is applicable, all productive decisions should be aimed at wealth-maximization: more wealth is always desirable. These considerations lead to two rules:

> PRESENT-VALUE RULE 1: Adopt any project for which Present Value V_0 is positive; reject any project for which Present Value V_0 is negative. (Note that this rule has the same form for investment or disinvestment projects.)

There are complications where projects are *interdependent*. Adoption of one project might change the z_0, z_1 payoffs of another. For example, sowing seed corn might make it more worthwhile to dig an irrigation canal. The obvious implication is to adopt that *set* of projects whose combined payment stream has maximum Present Value. We shall not go through all the possibilities here, but rather state the rule that applies when projects or combinations of projects are *mutually exclusive*.[5]

> PRESENT-VALUE RULE 2: If two projects (or combinations of projects) are mutually exclusive, adopt the one with higher Present Value V_0.

For example, a landowner might be considering whether to put a gas station on his lot or an office building. Since these projects are mutually exclusive, he should pick the one with the higher Present Value.

Exercise 14.3: (a) For a certain project the anticipated cash flows are $z_0 = -100$, $z_1 = 125$. Is this an investment or a disinvestment? What is its Present Value V_0 when the interest rate r is 10%? At $r = 20\%$? At $r = 30\%$? What is the highest rate of interest at which the project should be adopted? (b) The table shows alternative payments sequences for two interdependent projects M and N. The columns headed "Alone" show the payments associated with either if adopted separately; the other columns show the payments to each when both are adopted. If the interest rate r were 20% and you were required to adopt no more than one project, which (if any) should be adopted? If you could adopt both together, would you want to do so?

PROJECT	ALONE		WITH THE OTHER PROJECT	
	z_0	z_1	z_0	z_1
M	−100	125	−95	110
N	−50	90	−60	95

[5] Any list of alternative projects, interdependent or not, can be grouped into mutually exclusive combinations. Thus, three projects A, B, C can be sorted into the eight mutually exclusive combinations $0, A, B, C, AB, AC, BC$, and ABC (where 0 represents adopting *no* project at all).

Answer: (a) This is an investment project. When $r = 10\%$, $V_0 = -100 + 125/(1 + 0.1) = 13.64$. When $r = 20\%$, $V_0 = 4.167$. When $r = 30\%$, $V_0 = -3.85$. To find the highest rate of interest at which the project should be adopted, solve for r in $V_0 = 0 = -100 + 125/(1 + r)$. The answer is $r = 25\%$. The project should be adopted for any r *below* 25%. (b) The easiest way to do this is to compare Present Values of the three mutually exclusive investment alternatives M, N, and MN—in comparison with the do-nothing alternative 0. At 20%, $V_0(M) = -100 + 125/1.2 = 4.17$ and $V_0(N) = -50 + 90/1.2 = 25$. For the combination MN the combined payments are $z_0 = -155$ and $z_1 = 205$, so that $V_0(MN) = -155 + 205/1.2 = 15.83$. The best option is to adopt N alone, even if you could adopt both.

14.B.3 ☐ Multi-Period Analysis

Until now we have considered only two periods: "now" (date 0) and "one year from now" (date 1). But the same general principles apply for any number of periods. Instead of choosing between only two dates, individuals more generally will be planning their consumption choices over all dates from "now" to some future horizon T. We can analyze these decisions by generalizing the concept of Present Value to a multi-period form. The prices of consumption claims at different dates can be written as $P_0, P_1, \ldots, P_T$.[6] As usual let us set $P_0 \equiv 1$, so that current income claims continue to serve as *numéraire*.

In translating from *prices* to *interest rates*, there are two useful formulations. First, consider the successive one-year price ratios P_1/P_0, P_2/P_1, $\ldots$, P_T/P_{T-1}. These can be used to define the one-year "short-term" interest rates $r_1, r_2, \ldots, r_T$ on the left side of the Table of Interest-Rate Equivalents below. Here r_1 is the interest rate for transactions between date 0 and date 1, while r_2 is the rate between date 1 and date 2, etc.

Alternatively, consider the ratios P_1/P_0, P_2/P_0, $\ldots$, P_T/P_0—defined so that P_0 appears in all the denominators. These can be used, as on the right side of the table, to define the "long-term" interest rates $R_1, R_2, \ldots, R_T$. These are the interest rates governing transactions between date 0 and any future date up to T.

Table of Interest–Rate Equivalents

Short-Term Interest Rates	Long–Term Interest Rates
$\dfrac{P_1}{P_0} = \dfrac{1}{1 + r_1}$	$\dfrac{P_1}{P_0} = \dfrac{1}{1 + R_1}$
$\dfrac{P_2}{P_1} = \dfrac{1}{1 + r_2}$	$\dfrac{P_2}{P_0} = \dfrac{1}{(1 + R_2)^2}$
$\cdots\cdots\cdots\cdots\cdots\cdots\cdots$	$\cdots\cdots\cdots\cdots\cdots\cdots\cdots$
$\dfrac{P_T}{P_{T-1}} = \dfrac{1}{1 + r_T}$	$\dfrac{P_T}{P_0} = \dfrac{1}{(1 + R_T)^T}$

The Present Value of a stream of payments from date 0 to date T can be expressed either in terms of the long-term or the short-term interest rates:

---

[6] While the claims represent rights to income at different dates, the prices are those quoted in the trading that takes place now. P_1 is the price *today* of a claim to income payable one year in the future, P_2 is the price *today* of a claim payable two years in the future, etc.

$$(14.8) \qquad V_0 \equiv z_0 + \frac{z_1}{1 + R_1} + \frac{z_2}{(1 + R_2)^2} + \ldots + \frac{z_T}{(1 + R_T)^T}$$

$$(14.9) \qquad V_0 \equiv z_0 + \frac{z_1}{1 + r_1} + \frac{z_2}{(1 + r_2)(1 + r_1)}$$

$$+ \ldots + \frac{z_T}{(1 + r_T) \ldots (1 + r_2)(1 + r_1)}$$

For some purposes the first formulation is the more convenient; for other purposes, the second. There is no logical difference between them, since the long-term rate R_t is an average of the short-term rates $r_1, r_2, \ldots, r_t$ between now and date t.

While the "term structure" of the r_t or R_t interest rates is sometimes important, in most practical applications it is assumed that the currently applicable rate will maintain itself into the future. Of course, if the r_t are all equal to some common value r then all the R_t will also be equal to r, in which case the two formulas (14.8) and (14.9) both reduce to:

$$(14.10) \qquad V_0 \equiv z_0 + \frac{z_1}{1 + r} + \frac{z_2}{(1 + r)^2} + \ldots + \frac{z_T}{(1 + r)^T}$$

Let us construct a special case of Equation (14.10), making the following assumptions. First, assume that the "economic horizon" T is infinite. Second, suppose that returns on the project begin at date 1. And third, assume that the future receipts $z_1, z_2, \ldots$ are constant forever and equal to z. Then (14.10) becomes:[7]

$$(14.10') \qquad V_0 \equiv \frac{z}{r} \qquad \text{or} \qquad r \equiv \frac{z}{V_0}$$

For example, if $r = .10$, the Present Value of \$10 per year forever is $V_0 = 10/.10 = \$100$. Put another way, if you put \$100 in the bank at 10% interest, it would yield \$10 per year forever.

This formulation shows the relation between the annual income from some asset (z) and the current market value of the asset itself (V_0). We can now see a dif-

[7] *Mathematical Footnote*: The derivation proceeds from (14.10), under the special assumptions above, as follows:

$$V_0 = z \left[\frac{1}{1 + r} + \frac{1}{(1 + r)^2} + \ldots \right]$$

Let $1/(1 + r)$ be denoted k. Then:

$$V_0 = z(1 + k + k^2 + \ldots) - z = \frac{z}{1 - k} - z$$

But

$$1 - k = 1 - \frac{1}{1 + r} = \frac{r}{1 + r}$$

So

$$V_0 = z\left(\frac{1 + r}{r}\right) - z = \frac{z}{r}$$

ferent aspect of the interest rate r. Previously we defined it as a time-premium, the extra market value of earlier over later consumption income. But Equation (14.10′) shows that the interest rate is also the ratio between income flow and the value of the source of income. This justifies the discussion in Chapter 12 that described the interest rate as the ratio between the hire-price of a factor and the value of the factor itself.

Exercise 14.4: (a) If the one-period (short-term) interest rate is $r_1 = 10\%$ and the two-period (long-term) interest rate is $R_2 = 20\%$, what is the implied "forward" short-term rate r_2? Assuming $P_0 \equiv 1$ as usual, what are the implied prices P_1 and P_2 for one-year-future and two-year-future claims, respectively? (b) Suppose that a three-period project has the cash-flow sequence $-1, 2, 1$. Assuming the interest rate r is constant over time, over what range of r is this a good project? What if the cash-flow sequence is $-1, 5, -6$?

Answer: (a) Since $P_2/P_0 = (P_2/P_1)(P_1/P_0)$, from the Table of Interest-Rate Equivalents we can see that $(1 + R_2)^2 = (1 + r_2)(1 + r_1)$, or numerically here $(1.2)^2 = 1.1(1 + r_2)$. The solution for the forward short-term rate is $r_2 = 30.9\%$. The implied prices for the future claims are $P_1 = 1/(1 + r_1) = 0.91$ and $P_2 = 1/(1 + R_2)^2 = 0.69$. (b) We want to find the range of r for which $V_0 > 0$. With the first cash-flow sequence the inequality becomes: $-1 + 2/(1 + r) + 1/(1 + r)^2 > 0$. Solving the quadratic, the root is $r = 141.4\%$. Thus the Present Value is positive for any interest rate $r < 141.4\%$. (The quadratic has another root, $r = -141.4\%$, but interest rates less than -100% are impossible.) For the second cash-flow sequence it turns out that V_0 is negative for all allowable interest rates below 100%, becomes positive in the range between $r = 100\%$ and $r = 200\%$, but then turns negative again for still higher r.

EXAMPLE 14.3
Education and Earnings

A study by A. Razin and J. D. Campbell[a] calculated Present Values of lifetime earnings for holders of bachelor's degrees in various fields. National Science Foundation 1968 data on yearly incomes of scientific manpower were used. The authors assumed that earnings begin in the fifth year after admission to college, and terminate in the forty-fourth year, so that Equation (14.10) was applied in the special form:

$$V_0 = \frac{z_5}{(1 + r)^5} + \frac{z_6}{(1 + r)^6} + \ldots + \frac{z_{44}}{(1 + r)^{44}}$$

Calculating in terms of an interest rate $r = 3\%$, the following table indicates some of the results obtained. (The relatively favorable position of the economics degree is consistent with the salary standing of economics instructors reported in Example 1.2.)

[a] Assaf Razin and James D. Campbell, "Internal Allocation of University Resources," *Western Economic Journal*, v. 10 (Sept. 1972), esp. p. 315.

Present Values of Earnings for Bachelor's Degrees	
Mathematics	$342,068
Economics	339,482
Computer sciences	306,733
Political science	300,000
Physics	282,758
Psychology	262,127
Agriculture science	225,118
Biological science	215,691
Sociology	213,590

These numbers do not represent the *net* or overall Present Value of going to college and receiving the degree. Only the benefits, the earnings received by holders of the degree, have been shown. The cost side of the picture, which would allow for college-related outlays (tuition, living expenses, books, etc.) and also for earnings foregone during the four college years, has not been taken into account.

There is still another difficulty: we cannot assume that the higher earnings of educated individuals are due to their education alone. People who go to college may earn more because they are smart to begin with, or come from more affluent families, etc. To eliminate such sources of bias J. R. Behrman, R. A. Pollak, and P. Taubman[b] compared the earnings of *identical twins* with different amounts of schooling. They found that the following formula best fitted the observations:

$$\log\left(\frac{E_1}{E_2}\right) = 0.28 \log\left(\frac{S_1}{S_2}\right) + 0.014$$

Here E_1 and E_2 represent the annual earnings of the two twins, and S_1 and S_2 represent their years of schooling.

With this equation we can estimate that if an individual has a twelfth-grade education and earns $18,400 per year (these were typical figures in 1980), then his twin with four years of college will earn $20,225 per year—an improvement of $1825 or only 9.9 percent. Assuming a forty-year working life and an interest rate of 3 percent, the Present Value of additional earnings attributable to attending four years of college is $42,176. Note how much smaller this figure is than those in the Razin-Campbell study, and recall that neither study makes any allowance for *costs* of attending college.

Does this mean that college is a bad investment? Not necessarily. Presumably, individuals are deriving some benefits from college apart from improvement in future earnings. Among the possibilities are intellectual enrichment, new friends, potential marriage partners, and fun and games.

[b] Jere R. Behrman, Robert A. Pollak, and Paul Taubman, "Parental Preferences and Provision for Progeny," *Journal of Political Economy*, v. 90 (Feb. 1982).

AN APPLICATION: THE ECONOMICS
OF EXHAUSTIBLE RESOURCES

A resource like petroleum exists in finite quantity on the globe. The economic problem is how to divide up and extract this quantity over earlier and later dates. Associated with the *time-path of extraction* there will also be a *time-path of prices* for the resource.

In order to simplify matters and concentrate attention solely upon the timing problem, let us assume (unrealistically) that there are no extraction costs at all: the oil gushes out freely until it is all finally exhausted. The question to be examined is whether there will be any difference between the extraction and price paths for a competitive versus a monopolized industry.

Let us start with the competitive case. Assume that the demands each year are independent of what happens in other years, and furthermore remain the same from year to year. The annual demands are pictured as the (solid) straight-line curve $D^0 = D^1 = D^2 = \ldots$ in Figure 14.6. Note the choke-price P^+, which will play an important role in the analysis. The extraction quantity at any date t is q_t and the price at that date is P^t. The latter symbol is understood to mean the current price (that is, the date-t price) of oil at date t.[8]

---

*Marked sections, beginning with a single asterisk and ending with a double asterisk, may contain somewhat more difficult or advanced material and can be omitted without appreciable loss of continuity.

[8] The superscript notation is used here because P^1, for example, has quite a different meaning from P_1 as used earlier in the chapter. P_1 is the *price today* of income (corn) to be received at date 1. But P^1 here means the *price at date 1* of oil at date 1. Similarly, P_0 was defined above as the price today of corn today, and was ordinarily set equal to unity as the *numéraire* or basis of pricing. But P^0 here means the price today of oil today (which would not ordinarily be equal to unity but would vary depending upon the current scarcity of oil compared to other goods).

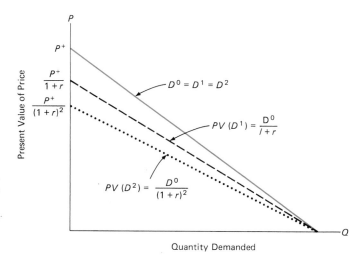

FIGURE 14.6 **Current and Discounted Demand Curves.** The demand for oil is assumed to be the same each year ($D^0 = D^1 = D^2$). But in terms of present values, $PV(D^1)$ is lower than D^0 (divided vertically by the factor $1 + r$), and $PV(D^2)$ is lower by the factor $(1 + r)^2$.

Any price P^1 to be received for next year's oil is equivalent in present-value worth to the amount $P^0 = P^1/(1 + r)$ received for this year's oil. Generalizing, the industry will be in competitive intertemporal equilibrium if:

(14.11)
$$P^0 = \frac{P^1}{1 + r} = \frac{P^2}{(1 + r)^2} = \cdots$$

In Figure 14.6 notice also the dashed $PV(D^1)$ and the dotted $PV(D^2)$ curves. As this symbolism suggests, the heights of these curves represent the present-value or *discounted* equivalents of the actual demand curves for dates 1 and 2. Specifically, if the interest rate were 20%, then for each quantity the height along $PV(D^1)$ would be found by dividing the height along the original or undiscounted demand curve by the factor $1 + r = 1.2$. And similarly, the height along $PV(D^2)$ is found by dividing through by the factor $(1 + r)^2 = 1.44$.

To progress further, suppose for the moment that we need consider only two time-periods: date 0 and date 1. (It might be, for example, that the demand is only expected to persist for two time-periods.) The width along the horizontal axis in the upper panel of Figure 14.7 represents the available fixed stock Q,

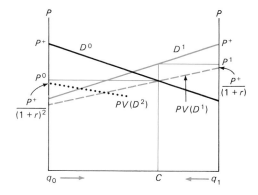

Competitive Industry

FIGURE 14.7 Extraction and Prices over Two or Three Dates. Here extraction is assumed costless. With only two dates, for a competitive industry (upper panel) the extraction amounts q_0 and q_1 are determined by the intersection of the current-date demand curve D^0 and the present value of the future-date demand curve $PV(D^1)$. Then $q_0 > q_1$ and so $P^0 < P^1$. In the situation illustrated, the competitive industry would not reserve any of the product for a third date (time 2). For the monopolized industry in the lower panel, the extractions would be determined by the intersection of the current-date Marginal Revenue MR^0 and $PV(MR^1)$. The monopolist extracts somewhat less in the current period, and in fact would reserve some of the resource for a third date (time 2).

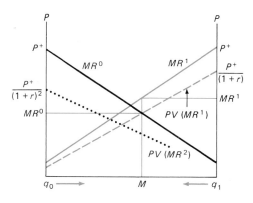

Monopolistic Industry

which is to be distributed between q_0 (extraction at date 0) and q_1 (extraction at date 1). As can be seen, the directions of the D^1 and $PV(D^1)$ curves have been reversed in the diagram. The advantage of this construction is that it shows immediately that condition (14.11) is met *at the intersection of the D^0 and $PV(D^1)$ curves.* The competitive equilibrium is at point C along the horizontal axis, which shows the extraction quantities q_0 and q_1 for the two dates. Notice that $q_0 > q_1$, which must necessarily hold if the interest rate r is positive. The price P^0 is of course read directly from the D^0 curve. As for P^1, this must be read from the D^1 curve rather than the $PV(D^1)$ curve. The geometry shows also that $P^1 > P^0$, which of course follows directly from the equilibrium condition (14.11) if $r > 0$. Summarizing: for a resource in fixed supply a competitive industry will have a *declining extraction path* and a *rising price path*.

Let us now ask, if the demand were expected to persist at least into a third time-period (date 2), would a competitive industry "conserve" any of the resource for that date? In the upper panel of Figure 14.7, note the (dotted) $PV(D^2)$ curve drawn in the normal direction from the vertical axis. The discounted choke price for date 2, which is equal to $P^+/(1 + r)^2$, is the intercept of this curve on the vertical axis—which, in this case, lies *below* the intersection of the D^0 and $PV(D^1)$ curves. This means that even the very first (most highly desired) unit left over for date 2 is not worth as much, in present-value terms, as the marginal unit at dates 0 and 1. Consequently, in this case all of the resource would be extracted in the first two time-periods. But had the discounted choke price been *higher* than the equilibrium values of $P^0 = P^1/(1 + r)$, some of the resource would instead have been conserved for extraction at date 2. (And similarly of course for even later dates.) Notice that the lower the interest rate r, the greater will be the amounts retained for future dates.

What if the industry were monopolized? Without going through the logic in detail, it will be evident that the condition corresponding to (14.11) will be:

(14.12)
$$MR^0 = \frac{MR^1}{1 + r} = \frac{MR^2}{(1 + r)^2} = \dots$$

That is, the monopolist will want to set the discounted *Marginal Revenues* equal at each date, rather than the discounted *prices*.

In the lower panel of Figure 14.7, MR^0 is the Marginal Revenue curve associated with the same D^0 demand curve of the previous diagram. (To reduce clutter, the demand curves are omitted from the lower panel.) And similarly $PV(MR^1)$ and $PV(MR^2)$ show the *discounted* Marginal Revenue curves for dates 1 and 2. Here the intersection of the MR^0 and $PV(MR^1)$ curves (above point M on the horizontal axis) shows the amounts q_0 and q_1 that a monopolist would extract in a two-period situation. Will anything be left over for date 2? That depends upon whether or not the discounted date-2 choke price $P^+/(1 + r)^2$ is greater than the *Marginal Revenues* $MR^0 = PV(MR^1)$ at the intersection above point M. In the diagram here, the monopolist would in fact conserve some of the resource for date 2 even though the competitive industry did not.

Exercise 14.5: The annual demand curve for an exhaustible resource is given by $P^t = 100 - q_t$ (for any date t). The total stock of the resource is $Q = 56$, and the interest rate is $r = 25\%$. (a) Find the extraction path and the price path for a competitive industry if there are only two time-periods (dates 0 and 1). If there is also date 2 to be considered, would any of the resource be conserved for that date? (b) Same questions, for a monopolized industry.

Answer: (a) The equilibrium condition $P^0 = P^1/(1 + r)$ here implies $100 - q_0 = 80 - .8q_1$. Also, $q_0 + q_1 = 56$. Solving the simultaneous equations, the solution is the extraction path $q_0 = 36$, $q_1 = 20$. The implied price path is $P^0 = 64$, $P^1 = 80$. If some of the resource is to be held for a third date, the discounted choke price $P^+/(1 + r)^2$ would have to exceed $P^0 = P^1/(1 + r) = 64$. But here the discounted choke price is $100/(1.25)^2 = 64$ exactly, so nothing would be conserved for date 2. (b) Under monopoly the condition $MR^0 = MR^1/(1 + r)$ implies $100 - 2q_0 = 80 - 1.6q_1$. And as before, $q_0 + q_1 = 56$. The solution for the extraction path is $q_0 = 30.4$, $q_1 = 25.6$ and for the price path is $P^0 = 69.6$, $P^1 = 74.4$. (The monopoly price path starts higher but ends up lower than the competitive price path.) The monopolist would conserve some of the resource for date 2 if the discounted choke price $100/(1 + r)^2 = 64$ exceeds $MR^0 = 100 - 2q_0 = 39.2$. This condition is indeed met, so the monopolist would distribute the resource over at least the three dates 0, 1, and 2. (This would of course change the previous numerical results that applied when there were only two dates.)

Figure 14.8 illustrates extraction paths and price paths for a competitive versus a monopolistic industry, where time is now assumed to run continuously over many periods. Notice that, as suggested by the analysis above:

1. The monopolized industry will *extract less at early dates* and *more at later dates* than a competitive industry. The monopolist is "more conservationist"!

2. It follows that the *prices* for a monopolized industry will be *initially higher* but become *eventually lower* at later dates. Specifically, the competitive price path must be rising at

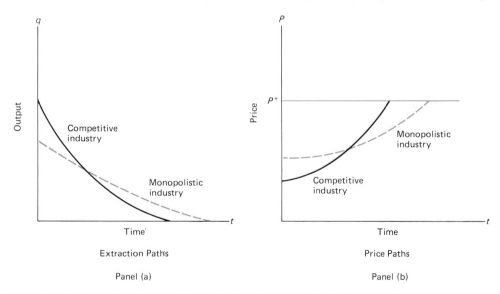

FIGURE 14.8 Extraction Paths and Price Paths. A competitive industry tends to extract more at early dates and less at later dates in comparison with a monopolist. The corresponding price paths are lower at first for a competitive industry, but ultimately higher.

a compound-interest rate, as indicated by condition (14.11). For monopoly, it is the Marginal Revenues that rise at compound interest, which implies that the prices will be growing somewhat more slowly. Of course, both price paths must eventually approach the same choke price P^+.[9] **

14.D
SOURCES OF VARIATION IN INTEREST RATES

When practical decision-makers in business or government evaluate projects by calculating Present Value, they almost always find that the numerical interest rate employed has a surprisingly big effect. This is especially true when the annual payments z_t extend over many years into the future. So determining the correct rate of interest to use for purposes of discounting is a very important issue.

[9] The assumption that there is a finite choke price plays an important role here. It assures, at least for sufficiently high prices, that demand becomes more elastic as price rises. (As would be true, for example, everywhere along a straight-line demand curve.) Without this assumption the conclusion in the text about price paths would not necessarily follow. In the case of a constant-elasticity demand curve, for example, Marginal Revenue will always be a constant fraction of price (see Equation (8.5)). Then the monopolist's price will be rising over time just as rapidly as the competitive price.

** End of marked section.

EXAMPLE 14.4
Present Values for the Feather River Project

The Feather River Project is an enormous undertaking of the State of California to bring water from the northern part of the state to delivery points in the central and southern portions. The table here shows the results of an independent assessment (made prior to construction) of the prospective costs and receipts of the project and of the net balance of the two, all calculated in terms of Present Values. Three alternative routes then under consideration were evaluated. The present-value calculation considered two alternative interest rates, 2.7 percent and 5 percent.

Present Values of the Feather River Project (Millions of dollars)

Interest Rate	Costs	Receipts	Net Present Value	Net Present Value, Adjusted*
2.7%				
Route 1	$1241	$1079	$−162	$−97
Route 8A	1123	1012	−111	−46
Route 10A	1029	919	−110	−46
5%				
Route 1	1035	515	−520	−502
Route 8A	860	445	−415	−397
Route 10A	799	409	−391	−372

Source: J. C. DeHaven and J. Hirshleifer, "Feather River Water for Southern California," *Land Economics*, v. 33 (Aug. 1957), p. 201. (Some technical footnotes omitted.)

Adjustment credits an allowance for flood-control benefit and salvage value.

While all the net Present Values were negative, the higher 5 percent interest rate was associated with relatively lower figures for both costs and receipts. Since the cost sequence is a series of positive payments at each date, and the receipts sequence also a series of positive elements, the larger the r the smaller is the discounted sum for each, as may be seen from Equation (14.10). But the table shows that a higher r has a greater effect upon receipts than upon costs. The reason is that receipts are typically received *later*, so that a rise in the discount factor $1 + r$ operates more powerfully upon them owing to greater compounding over time. In fact, it is a reliable rule *the higher the r, the less attractive the project*.

> COMMENT: The Feather River Project was adopted, despite the showing of negative net Present Value. Thus, the investment decision rule of this chapter was violated. Indeed, the route selected was the one with the *most unfavorable* receipts-cost balance. (Possible explanations are touched upon when the politcal process is analyzed in Chapter 16.)

The next example also illustrates the powerful effect of interest rates upon Present Values.

EXAMPLE 14.5
Professors and Publications

Professors devote a considerable portion of their time to research. The output of successful research usually takes the form of articles published in scholarly journals. Published articles lead to professional recognition and so tend to raise the lifetime earnings of their authors.

H. P. Tuckman and J. Leahey[a] studied the worth to economics professors of having articles published. Their results indicate that a *first* article by an assistant professor is associated with an increase of $12,340 in Present Value of lifetime earnings, calculated at an interest rate of 5 percent. At a higher 10 percent interest rate, the future earnings gains are discounted more heavily, however, leading to a lower estimate of $7074.

The Present Values of lifetime income increments due to articles published by associate and full professors were generally lower than for assistant professors, the main explanation being the fact that the higher-rank professors are nearer retirement. Another interesting point observed was the operation of the Law of Diminishing Returns. At the lower $r = 5\%$, the Present Value of a marginal article published by an assistant professor steadily declined from $12,340 for the first article, to $4310 for the fifth article, down to only $1544 for the thirtieth published article.

[a] Howard P. Tuckman and Jack Leahey, "How Much Is an Article Worth?" *Journal of Political Economy*, v. 83 (Oct. 1975).

An interest rate of $r = 3$ percent was used in one of the studies reported above; a second employed two alternative rates, 2.7 percent and 5 percent; and the third used 5 percent and 10 percent. Can all these be correct? How do we determine the correct rate to use?

Interest rates may vary for a number of reasons. First, they change historically, so that decisions involving Present Values calculated in 1950 or 1960 were subject to a different r than were 1970 or 1980 decisions. And even at a specific moment of time, there is a "term structure" of interest rates—different rates for near versus future income claims. On May 2, 1986, for example, U.S. Treasury issues (bonds and notes) of different maturities were selling at prices representing different net interest yields to purchasers. Issues maturing in the nearer future (1986 and 1987) were typically yielding from 6.3 to 6.4 percent; issues maturing in the medium future (1990) were yielding about 7.2 percent; while distant future maturities (beyond 2000) were yielding around 7.8 percent.

The major reason for the variety of interest rates at a moment of time, however, is the element of *risk*. Even if maturity and all other elements are the same, bonds of foreign governments or of private corporations are generally considered riskier than U.S. Treasury issues—and so can only be sold at prices generating a higher risk-compensating interest yield to their holders. For similar reasons a potential borrower will find that a bank may require a higher rate for an unsecured loan than for a loan secured by a mortgage or other collateral.

Two different aspects of risk should be distinguished:

1. *Default risk*: Suppose a bank makes a one-year $1000 loan to an individual at an interest rate of 10 percent, and imagine that the bank has 99 percent confidence in the borrower's performance but believes there is a 1 percent chance of a complete default on both principal and interest. Then the "expected" or average interest yield for the bank is not 10 percent but only 8.9 percent.[10] It is the 8.9 percent that approximates the "true" interest rate; 10 percent is the "nominal" interest rate, the difference being an adjustment or premium for default risk.

2. *Variability risk*: Some financial instruments, like common stocks, do not carry any explicit promise of payments. The returns to the investor come in the form of dividends that may vary considerably up or down from the average; this is variability risk. In general, people dislike variability risk. As between two securities with the same average yield, the typical investor will prefer the one more nearly approaching a fully certain yield. It follows that securities whose returns are highly uncertain will sell at prices yielding their holders greater average earnings—the difference being needed to adjust for the greater variability risk.

[10] The bank anticipates receiving $1100 at the end of the year if all goes well (99 percent probability), but otherwise receiving nothing. Its "expected" or average net interest return is $0.99(\$1100) + 0.01(\$0) - \$1000$, or $89, which is a yield of 8.9 percent on the $1000 principal amount.

EXAMPLE 14.6
Term and Risk Premiums

Roger G. Ibbotson and Rex A. Sinquefield examined the actual yields obtained during the period 1926 to 1981 by investors holding different classes of financial instruments. In the table, a difference between the average yield on long-term government bonds versus short-term U.S. Treasury bills would represent a *term premium* offered investors. Over the period studied this difference, as can be seen, was nil. On the other hand, the excess of experienced yield on common stocks over government bonds indicates that during this period those investors willing to incur *variability risk* received a substantial premium for doing so.

Experienced Average Yields, 1926–1981 (%)

	Arithmetic Mean	Geometric Mean
U.S. Treasury bills	3.1	3.0
Long-term government bonds	3.1	3.0
Common stocks	11.4	9.1

Source: Roger G. Ibbotson and Rex A. Sinquefield, *Stocks, Bonds, Bills and Inflation: The Past and the Future* (Charlottesville, Va.: Financial Analysts Research Foundation, 1982), esp. p. 71.

The difference between the results calculated in terms of the arithmetic mean versus the geometric mean of the annual experienced yields is also of significance. The arithmetic mean answers the question, on average what yield can be expected in *any given year* on this type of investment? The geometric mean answers the question, what *average long-term compounded yield* can be expected on this type of investment?

The problem of choosing an interest rate for calculating Present Value may arise in either *normative* or *positive* analysis (as discussed in Chapter 1). From the *positive* point of view we may ask: "What interest rates are decision-makers actually using in their investment decisions?" From a *normative* point of view we could be asking: "What interest rate should a decision-maker employ in accepting or rejecting an investment project?"

Example 14.3 on the Present Value of a bachelor's degree represented positive analysis; the *r* used was an estimate of how heavily college students were discounting anticipated future earnings in deciding whether or not to earn a college degree. Example 14.5 on the worth of a published article, and Example 14.6 on the realized rates of return observed in the financial markets, also represent positive analyses. Example 14.3, in contrast, represents *normative* analysis. The economists there were concerned with the question: "Should the Feather River Project have been built by the State of California?" What is the appropriate rate to use for such a normative analysis? In general, the correct rate (the one that would lead to the correct decision in terms of maximizing California citizens' wealth) would be the rate used by the market in evaluating investments of comparable risk.

EXAMPLE 14.7
On Appreciating Art

The return received from holding a durable asset may take a number of forms, including: (1) productive yield, as from agricultural land, (2) consumptive utility, as from a home, or (3) anticipated appreciation of market value ("capital gain"). The prospect of value appreciation may be critically important for deciding whether or not to invest.

By examining auction prices from 1946 to 1968, J. P. Stein[a] estimated the appreciation gain from ownership of paintings. He found that over this period the return averaged 10.5 percent per annum, as compared to 14.3 percent for dividends plus appreciation on corporate stocks. Even after adjusting for risk and certain other special circumstances, Stein found the financial return on paintings to be about 1.6 percentage points less than comparable stock returns. The explanation, presumably, is that investors were willing to sacrifice some financial return because of the consumptive utility gained from owning works of art.

[a] John P. Stein, "The Monetary Appreciation of Paintings," *Journal of Political Economy*, v. 85 (Oct. 1977).

14.E
REAL INTEREST AND MONEY INTEREST: ALLOWING FOR INFLATION

So far in this chapter we have been analyzing the *real* rate of interest. Following the usual practice in microeconomics we have looked behind the "veil of money." But in practice people almost always deal in terms of *money* rates of interest. Suppose a bank advertises that it pays 8%. That means if you make a money deposit of $100 you can withdraw $108 of money at the end of the year (plus a little more, if interest is compounded more frequently than once a year). The main reason why the real interest rate and the money interest rate often diverge is the prospect of *inflation or deflation*—which represent changes in the relative values of money versus real goods.

The *real* interest rate is the premium on claims to current versus future real goods (corn)—or, we can say, the extra amount of future corn that must be offered in the market in exchange for current corn. Let us write this as:

$$(14.13) \qquad 1 + r \equiv -\frac{\Delta c_1}{\Delta c_0}$$

(As usual, we need a minus sign to allow for the fact that market exchange involves getting more of one item and less of the other.) Correspondingly, the *money* interest rate, which we will symbolize as r', is the premium on claims to current money versus future money. Thus, r' is the extra amount of future money that must be returned in exchange for current money:

$$(14.14) \qquad 1 + r' \equiv -\frac{\Delta m_1}{\Delta m_0}$$

We need to introduce the relation between money and real goods. This is the *price level*: the amount of money required to purchase real goods. The *current* and *future* price levels are:

$$(14.15) \qquad P_0^m \equiv -\frac{\Delta m_0}{\Delta c_0} \qquad \text{and} \qquad P_1^m \equiv -\frac{\Delta m_1}{\Delta c_1}$$

Let us now write out the identity:

$$\frac{\Delta m_1}{\Delta m_0} \equiv \frac{\Delta m_1}{\Delta c_1} \frac{\Delta c_1}{\Delta c_0} \frac{\Delta c_0}{\Delta m_0}$$

Making the indicated substitutions from the preceding equations we have:

$$(14.16) \qquad 1 + r' = \frac{P_1^m}{P_0^m} (1 + r)$$

We can also define a, the anticipated rate of price inflation, as the rate of increase in the price level:

$$(14.17) \qquad 1 + a \equiv \frac{P_1^m}{P_0^m}$$

It follows immediately that:

$$(14.18) \qquad 1 + r' \equiv (1 + a)(1 + r)$$

Or, simplifying:

$$(14.18a) \qquad r' \equiv r + a + ar.$$

Accordingly, the money rate of interest equals the real rate of interest plus the anticipated rate of price inflation, plus the cross-product of the latter two. When r and a remain in their usual range of percentage points, the cross-product term can to a good approximation be ignored. With *compound* interest, the shorter the period of compounding the more correct it is to omit the cross-product. For continuously compounded interest, the cross-product drops out entirely and we have exactly:

$$(14.19) \qquad r' \equiv r + a$$

It is in this simple form that the relation between real and money interest is usually expressed.[11]

[11] *Mathematical Footnote*: If i is an annually compounded interest rate, a dollar will grow in value to $1 + i$ dollars at the end of one year. With quarterly compounding, the terminal value will be $(1 + i/4)^4$. Generalizing, with any compounding frequency of f per year, terminal value will be $(1 + i/f)^f$. For continuous compounding, we let f approach infinity. Then $\lim_{f \to \infty}(1 + i/f)^f \equiv \lim_{h \to \infty}[(1 + 1/h)^h]^i$ where $h \equiv f/i$. But the limit within the brackets is e, the base of the natural logarithms. The terminal

PROPOSITION: The money rate of interest equals the real rate of interest plus the anticipated rate of price inflation.

EXAMPLE 14.8
Real and Money Rates of Interest

William E. Gibson[a] examined the effects of inflationary expectations upon the rates of interest paid on U.S. Treasury securities in the period 1962 to 1970. In all such studies the practical problem is to evaluate "inflationary anticipations," which are not directly visible. The measure used by Gibson was derived from a semiannual survey of economists conducted by Joseph Livingston, a nationally syndicated financial columnist.

Using this measure of anticipated inflation a, and the recorded interest rates as the measure of the money rate r', Gibson statistically estimated an equation in the form:

$$r' = H + Ka$$

Here H and K were the parameters of the line of best fit to the observed data. On the assumption that the *real* rate of interest r was constant over this period, comparison with Equation (14.19) shows that the fitted parameter H is an estimate of the real rate r. Also, the fitted parameter K should be simply equal to unity.

The statistical evidence varied somewhat according to the type of security considered. But the estimated H suggests a *real* rate of interest between 2% and 3% (considerably lower than the money interest rates in this inflationary period, of course). And the K estimates were not far from unity (for example, 0.9300 for three-month Treasury bills, 0.8959 for three-year to five-year Treasury notes).

One interesting point is that the K estimates were closer to unity in the later than in the earlier portion of the period. The suggestion is that the general public was gradually learning to adjust to the prospect of continuing inflation.

[a] William E. Gibson, "Interest Rates and Inflationary Expectations: New Evidence," *American Economic Review*, v. 62 (Dec. 1972).

Equation (14.19) has important implications for macroeconomic policy. If people expect inflation to be high, Equation (14.19) says that the money interest rate r' will be high. What normally causes inflation is expansion of the money

---

value of a dollar continuously compounded at interest rate i, at the end of a year, is then e^i. The terminal value of Z dollars at the end of T years is Ze^{iT}.

Expressed in terms of continuously compounded rates, Equation (14.18) becomes:

$$e^{r'} = e^r e^a$$

Taking logarithms, $r' = r + a$ follows directly.

supply. On the other hand, expansion of the money supply may tend to *lower* money interest rates in the short run. Suppose the government unexpectedly pays some of its bills with newly printed money. People will then find themselves with *current* cash balances m_0 that are larger than expected. If people do not anticipate correspondingly larger *future* cash balances m_1, they should be willing to trade larger amounts Δm_0 in exchange for Δm_1. Then the money interest rate r' in equation (14.14) must fall. On the other hand, if the government is engaging in a *continuing* pattern of money expansion, an increase in m_0 may lead people to anticipate that future money balances m_1 will be even larger. Thus a *one-time* expansion of the money supply lowers the money rate r', but a *continuing* monetary expansion may generate inflationary expectations that raise r'.

The main lesson to be learned from this discussion is that high monetary or "nominal" rates of interest do not necessarily imply high real yields to investors. In fact, taking inflation into account the experience of investors over the past half-century has been unimpressive.

EXAMPLE 14.9
Nominal and Real Yields, 1926–1981

The first column of the table below, repeated from Example 14.6, shows the arithmetic mean of the *nominal* annual returns from holding various types of securities over the 55-year period 1926 to 1981. The second column shows the inflation-adjusted or *real* average annual returns. As can be seen, the real return has been practically zero on both short-term and long-term government issues. Only common stocks show a positive real return. Thus, while there has been some reward for bearing variability risk over this period, savers and investors have on average received little or no premium in future real income for current sacrifices of consumption.

Nominal and Real Yields, 1926–1981 (arithmetic means)

	Nominal Yield (%)	Real Yield (%)
U.S. Treasury bills	3.1	0.1
Long-term government bonds	3.1	0.3
Common stocks	11.4	8.3

Source: Roger G. Ibbotson and Rex A. Sinquefield, *Stocks, Bonds, Bills and Inflation: The Past and the Future* (Charlottesville, Va.: Financial Analysts Research Foundation, 1982), esp. p. 71.

Furthermore, the returns from holding Treasury or corporate securities are taxable to investors. The real *tax-adjusted* returns, while varying across individuals depending upon tax brackets, will all be smaller than those shown above. As a final twist of the screw, in the United States (and many other nations as well) the income tax is levied not on the real but on the nominal return. This has a most damaging effect. Consider an individual who purchases a common stock for $100, receives $12 in dividends (this is a better-than-average 12 percent nominal yield) and finds his stock still priced at $100 at the end of the year. Suppose the rate of inflation is 10 percent, and his marginal tax rate is 33.33 percent. He will pay $4 in tax, which knocks down his 12 percent pre-tax yield to 8 percent after-tax yield. But, with 10 percent inflation, the real end-of-the-year value of his common stock is not $100 but $100/1.1 = $91 (approximately). So the depreciation of the real value of his security has exceeded his real after-tax dividend return; his true real yield has been negative. U.S. investors have generally incurred negative real after-tax yields over the past half-century—even for securities like common stocks. We should not be surprised, therefore, to learn that the amount of saving in relation to income in the United States has become, in the opinion of many observers, disturbingly low.

14.F
DETERMINANTS OF INTEREST RATES

Why are interest rates high in some countries and low in others, high in some historical periods and low in others? In line with the analysis here, the determinants of *real* interest rates may be classified under the headings of: (1) time-preference (impatience), (2) time-endowment, and (3) time-productivity. Given these determinants of *real* interest, the money interest rate is accounted for by incorporating the anticipations of price-level inflation as shown by Equation (14.19).

1. Time-preference: The more impatient people are, the more they prefer *current* as against *future* consumption. Impatience or high time-preference leads to steep indifference curves in Figure 14.1, and so to high real interest rates. Low time-preference is associated with personal characteristics such as farsightedness, strong family ties, willingness to defer enjoyment, and the like. The latter years of the Roman Empire were characterized by a decline in such "puritanical" attitudes, and interest rates were accordingly high. A similar shift in values appears to be taking place in the Western world today, which might help explain the recent tendency of real interest rates to rise.

2. Time-endowment: As we have seen, an "heir with great expectations," whose personal income-endowment lies mainly in the future, tends to be a borrower. If an entire society were expecting future income to be much greater than current income, the interest rate would correspondingly tend to be high. A notable example is a community struck by a disaster. A catastrophe usually damages goods relatively close to consumption more drastically than it injures the basic productive powers of the economy. A drought or a hurricane, for example, may destroy growing crops while leaving long-term productive fundamentals such as fertility of the land unimpaired. Since present or near-future incomes are affected more seriously, interest rates tend to rise.

3. Time-productivity: Higher time-productivity of investment would be represented by a steeper Production-Possibility Curve *QQ* in Figure 14.4. If this pattern is typical of a community, investment will be high and interest rates will be high. Thus interest rates have tended to be high in newer and more productive communities—for example, higher in America than in England, and higher in California than in Massachusetts. Also, technological change works somewhat like new settlement of territory in making available improved opportunities for investment. Thus, interest rates tend to be higher in technologically progressive than in more static countries and eras.

Finally, a very important consideration is the *degree of isolation* of a community. There may be a very special situation as to time-preferences, time-endowments, or time-productivity in a small local area. Nevertheless, unless that region is isolated from commerce, the interest rates there cannot diverge too far from the more normal rates in the outside world. With integrated financial markets there will be a flow of investments and loans (in the form of money and real claims) from the low-interest area to the high-interest area. The differences historically observed between interest rates in England and America, or between Massachusetts and California, have therefore been much smaller than would have been the case had the communities in question been isolated from one another.

EXAMPLE 14.10
Interest and the Gold Rush[a]

Gold was discovered in California in 1848, and the gold rush was on. The gold miners (and most other Californians as well) typically thought of themselves as having little current endowed income, but as prospectively very rich. Thus, they were like "heirs with great expectations," who are inclined to be borrowers.

However, until the completion of the first transcontinental railroad in 1869, California was largely isolated from the rest of the world. Californians for the most part could only borrow from one another. Consequently, the interest rate during the period of the gold rush was generally very high, 24 percent per annum being a typical figure. This was far higher than interest rates in the East. After completion of the transcontinental railroad, it became much more feasible to bring in resources from the East, and the interest rate in California dropped to around 6 percent.

[a] See Irving Fisher, *The Theory of Interest* (New York: Macmillan, 1930; reprinted [Fairfield, N.J.: Augustus M. Kelley] 1955), Chap. 18.

☐ SUMMARY OF CHAPTER 14

Saving is consuming less than income; *investing* is a productive operation that transforms potential current income into future income. Individuals' decisions as to present versus future consumption interact in the market to determine the price ratio between current and future claims, P_0/P_1. This ratio is also defined as $1 + r$, where r is the real rate of interest.

In a world of pure exchange, where investment opportunities are absent, each individual would choose an optimum time-pattern of consumption subject to a fixed wealth constraint. Saving by some people (lending) would necessarily be balanced by the dis-saving of others (borrowing). The intersection of the aggregate supply curve of lending and the aggregate demand curve for borrowing determine the equilibrium interest rate and the amount of borrowing and lending. Where there are real investment opportunities, however, individuals would choose a wealth-maximizing *productive optimum* solution (determining their level of investment) together with a utility-maximizing *consumptive optimum* solution (determining their level of saving). In the market as a whole, the intersection of the aggregate supply curve of saving and the aggregate demand curve for investment would determine the equilibrium rate of interest and the amount of saving and investment. At this interest rate, aggregate borrowing would also equal aggregate lending.

If markets for intertemporal claims are perfect, the Separation Theorem holds. Since production decisions can be aimed solely at maximizing wealth, independently of preferences as to future versus later consumption, owners can more easily delegate this task to an agent or manager. This feature facilitates the formation of firms. If managers maximize the wealth of the firm, they will also be maximizing wealth for all the owners individually.

A project or set of projects that is wealth-increasing has a positive Present Value V_0. In the simple two-period case, with cash flows z_0 and z_1, Present Value is defined as:

$$V_0 \equiv z_0 + \frac{z_1}{1 + r}$$

Any project with positive Present Value should be adopted; any project with negative Present Value should be rejected. The equation defining Present Value can be generalized to the multi-period case, making use of the anticipated stream of payments $z_0, z_1, \ldots, z_T$ and the sequence of either the short-term interest rates $r_1, \ldots, r_T$ or the long-term rates $R_1, R_2, \ldots, R_T$. If the interest rate is expected to be constant at the level r over time, the generalization takes the simple form:

$$V_0 \equiv z_0 + \frac{z_1}{1 + r} + \ldots + \frac{z_T}{(1 + r)^T}$$

An important issue is the selection of an appropriate interest rate r for the Present-Value calculation. The major problem is to allow properly for risk. Securities promising fixed payments (e.g., bonds) are subject to *default risk*; securities with uncertain returns varying around some expected average level (e.g., stocks) are subject to *variability risk*. For any type of investment there will be an appropriate risk-premium element in the interest rate used for calculating Present Value.

The *real* interest rate r is the extra market value of current real goods over future real goods. The *money* interest rate r' is the extra market value of current money over future money. The relation between the real interest rate and the money interest rate depends on the anticipated rate of price-level inflation, a:

$$r' = r + a$$

The explanation is that someone who borrows money, in order to repay in money, must offer the lender an additional return to cover the expected fall in the real value of the monetary commodity.

The determinants of the real interest rate r in a community include individuals' patterns of *time-preference* (more urgent desires for current goods raise interest rates), *time-endowment* (anticipations of higher future income raise interest rates), and *time-productivity* (better investment opportunities raise interest rates). The monetary rate r' will diverge from the real interest rate by the amount of *anticipated inflation*.

☐ QUESTIONS FOR CHAPTER 14

Mainly for Review

R1. Explain the analogy between the intertemporal optimum of the consumer (choice between current consumption C_0 and future consumption C_1) and the optimum of the consumer at a moment of time (choice between consumption of commodity X and commodity Y).

*R2. Which is correct?
   a. The annual rate of interest is the ratio P_0/P_1, the price of a current consumption claim divided by the price of a consumption claim dated one year in the future.
   b. The annual rate of interest is the *premium* on the value of current relative to one-year future claims, as given by the expression $P_0/P_1 - 1$.
   Explain.

R3. What is *wealth*? How is it related to current and future *incomes*?

*R4. In a pure-exchange situation, at market equilibrium the total of borrowing equals the total of lending. What can be said about saving and investment?

*R5. In a productive situation, at market equilibrium the total of saving equals the total of investment. What can be said about borrowing and lending?

R6. What is the Separation Theorem? What is its importance? What would tend to happen if it were not applicable?

*R7. What is the Present-Value Rule? Will this rule always lead decision-makers to correct choices of projects when the Separation Theorem holds? What if the Separation Theorem does not hold?

R8. Explain the relation between the rate of interest r as defined in the equation $r = P_0/P_1 - 1$ and as defined in the equation $r = z/V_0$.

R9. What is the *money* rate of interest, and how is it related to the *real* rate of interest?

For Further Thought and Discussion

T1. In a two-period preference diagram, illustrate plausible endowment positions in the following cases. Indicate whether the person is likely to be a borrower or a lender.
   a. A young man with an elderly, wealthy, loving uncle in Australia.
   b. A farmer whose crop has been destroyed by hurricane.
   c. A sugar-*beet* farmer who has just learned that this year's sugar-*cane* crop has been destroyed by hurricane.
   d. A 35-year-old star baseball player.

*T2 "Saving need not equal investment for any single individual, but the two must be equal for the market as a whole." Is this necessarily true in equilibrium? Would it be true in a disequilibrium situation, as might result from a floor or ceiling upon interest rates?

*T3. In a newly settled country, resources are likely to have great potential but are as yet undeveloped. Would you expect the real interest rate to be high or low? Comparing situations in which the new country is or is not in close contact with the rest of the world, in which situation will the interest rate be higher? In which will more investment take place? Explain.

*The answers to starred questions appear at the end of the book.

*T4. One country is "stagnant" (i.e., little investment and little economic growth are taking place) because productive opportunities yielding a good return on investment are lacking. Another "stagnant" country has excellent investment opportunities, but little investment is occurring because the citizens' time-preferences are very high. Which country would tend to have a high, and which a low, real interest rate? Explain.

T5. Money interest rates throughout the world have generally been higher since World War II than they were in the prewar period. Indicate which of the following might provide part of the explanation, and analyze:
   a. Higher rates of time-preference (changes in tastes).
   b. Higher rates of time-productivity (changes in investment opportunities).
   c. Lower ratios of current to anticipated future incomes (increased relative scarcity of current endowments).
   d. Higher rates of inflation (changes in anticipations as to monetary policies of governments).

*T6. Are negative rates of interest impossible? Is there a limit upon how negative the interest rate can be?

T7. "Annual income twenty pounds, annual expenditure nineteen nineteen six, result happiness. Annual income twenty pounds, annual expenditure twenty pounds ought and six, result misery"—Mr. Micawber in Dickens' *David Copperfield*. Is this sound economics? Analyze.

*T8. In the April 1972 issue of *Consumer Reports*, a publication of the well-known consumer advice organization Consumers Union, the question was raised whether a homebuyer might advantageously finance purchase of appliances by an addition to his or her home mortgage. The alternatives considered were: (1) purchase of appliances through a retail store for $675, financed by a two-year contract at 15 percent interest; and (2) purchase of the same appliances for $450 through the homebuilder, financed by a mortgage add-on 27-year contract at 7.75 percent interest. The CR article contended that the first option was superior. The justification offered was that, for the two-year 15 percent contract, the total of interest-plus-principal payments would add up to only $785—whereas, for the 27-year mortgage add-on contract at 7.75 percent, the total payments would eventually sum to $1075. Analyze.

*T9. During World War II it was necessary to decide how much of the budgeted military expenditures were to be financed by taxation and how much by government borrowing. Some economists argued that financing the war by borrowing would be "shifting the burden to future generations." Is this correct? How would you go about determining how much of the cost of the war was borne by the current generation versus future generations?

*T10. A television news commentator reports: "The stock market was higher in today's trading. Economists said the reason was that interest rates fell yesterday." Does the explanation make sense? Explain.

*T11. In exploiting an exhaustible resource, a monopoly tends to be more "conservationist" than a competitive industry—that is, it tends to stretch out the supply over a longer period of time. Does this mean that, at least with regard to decisions over time, monopoly may be more efficient than pure competition?

15

SUPPLEMENTARY CHAPTER

WELFARE ECONOMICS: THE THEORY OF ECONOMIC POLICY

In this book the main emphasis has been upon economics as a *positive* science. The intent has been to analyze how the market economy works—without regard to whether the outcomes may or may not be socially desirable. But the discipline of economics was originally called "political economy," reflecting the concern of early economic thinkers with *normative* issues of public policy. This raises the question: How are we to decide whether a proposed intervention or reform is a good idea or not? In other words, what are the theoretical justifications for economic policies that a government might adopt? This area of study, known as "welfare economics," is the subject of the present chapter.

The first section of the chapter considers the *goals* of the policy. Section 15.B reviews Adam Smith's "Theorem of the Invisible Hand," a proposition which seems to imply that the unregulated *laissez-faire* economy has certain very desirable qualities, so that intervention or reform may make things worse rather than better. A discussion of the real or alleged failures of the Invisible Hand then follows.

15.A
GOALS OF ECONOMIC POLICY

Economists have tended to emphasize two of the many possible goals of policy: (1) efficiency, and (2) distributive equity. Roughly speaking, these two criteria represent the *size* of the economic pie and the *distribution* of slices among the possible claimants.

15.A.1 ☐ Efficiency versus Equity

To begin with, suppose an individual's well-being depends only on his or her income I. For two persons John and Karl the alternative social allocations of income might be represented on I^j, I^k axes as in Figure 15.1. The shaded area shows the set of income combinations available.

The curve II' that bounds the social opportunity set, the Social Opportunity Frontier, might have any of a variety of shapes. As drawn, it is concave to the origin, suggesting that total social income $I^T \equiv I^j + I^k$ is larger toward the middle of II' rather than at the corners. In other words, the economy is not a

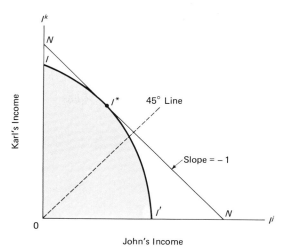

FIGURE 15.1 **Social Allocations of Income.** The shaded region is the social opportunity set, showing the attainable combinations of income for John (I^j) and Karl (I^k); its boundary is the Social Opportunity Frontier II'. Total social income is maximized at I^*, where II' is just tangent to a line of slope -1 (line NN).

"constant-sum game." If Karl produces more, John will not lose the entire amount that Karl gains.

Let us now consider *efficiency* as a goal of social policy. It might seem natural to define efficiency as achieving the largest *sum* of income I^T. Geometrically, this maximum is reached at I^* in Figure 15.1. I^* is the point where II' touches the dashed line NN, the highest attainable line of slope -1 in the diagram. But this is not the way the economist defines efficiency. For, treating I^* as some kind of social maximum involves a hidden assumption—that it would be acceptable to deprive John of one dollar if Karl thereby gets two dollars, or to deprive Karl of a smaller amount if John can thereby get a larger amount. Instead, the economist uses a somewhat weaker concept of efficiency. Any particular income distribution I^j, I^k is called *efficient* if it corresponds to a point on the Social Opportunity Frontier II' rather than in the interior of the shaded region.[1]

But income, even if measured in real rather than money units, isn't always a reliable indicator of well-being. The effort or risk required to generate the income, and the value of the reservation uses of resources (leisure) that have to be sacrificed, should also be taken into account. In addition, other important sources of satisfaction—such as personal liberty and human companionship—do not enter at all into measured income. Yet any or all of these might be affected by government policies.

We can get around this problem by using the familiar concept of *utility*. Figure 15.2 shows the social opportunity set in terms of the individuals' achievable utilities U^j and U^k. Utility, we saw in Chapter 3, is regarded as only an *ordinal* magnitude. A person is assumed to be able to distinguish a more preferred from a less preferred outcome, but there is no basis for measuring the utility difference between them. Also, utility cannot be compared between individuals. For both

---

[1] It might be asked, why not have the parties go initially to I^* and then *redistribute* the maximized total income I^T along NN on any basis agreed between them? Moving along NN, a point could always be found that is superior for both parties (yields higher income for each) as compared with any point along II' away from I^*. But such redistribution is not possible, by the definition of II' as the Social Opportunity Frontier. (If it were possible, the line NN would *be* the frontier.)

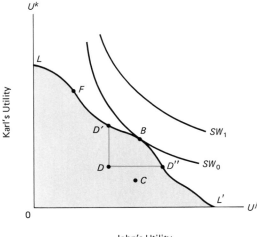

FIGURE 15.2 **Social Allocations of Utility.** Since utility has no unique cardinal scaling, in utility units only the *ordinal* properties of the Social Opportunity Frontier *LL'* are relevant—that John cannot be made better off without making Karl worse off, and vice versa. So all we know about *LL'* is that it has negative slope. SW_0 and SW_1 are hypothetical indifference contours of social well-being or "welfare," whose magnitude would be maximized at point *B*. But if comparisons can be made only in terms of the Pareto criterion, no such contours exist. All that can be said is that distributions to the northeast of any point like *D* (those in the region *DD' BD"*) are preferred to *D*. The Social Opportunity Frontier *LL'* is the set of Pareto-efficient distributions; Pareto comparisons cannot be made between points on *LL'*.

these reasons the Social Opportunity Frontier in terms of utilities (*LL'* in Figure 15.2) has no meaningful shape apart from the ordinal property represented by its negative slope. This negative slope tells us only that one party cannot be made better off without making the other worse off.

> *DEFINITION:* One allocation of goods in an economy is said to be "Pareto-preferred,"[2] in comparison with another, if in the first arrangement all parties concerned are *at least* as well off and one or more of the parties is actually better off.

Consider the allocation *D* in the interior of the social opportunity set of Figure 15.2. Comparing *D'* with *D*, Karl is better off and John is no worse off, so *D'* is Pareto-preferred to *D*. At *D"* John is better off and Karl is no worse off, so *D"* is also Pareto-preferred to *D*. And for any point *between D'* and *D"* along the boundary *LL'*, *both* parties are better off so that any such point is Pareto-preferred to *D*.

Generalizing this reasoning, for any point like *D* in the interior of the social opportunity set there will be points on the frontier *LL'* that are Pareto-preferred to it. But comparing any two allocations along the boundary *LL'* itself, any utility gain to one party will cause a utility loss to the other. Hence, no point on the frontier is Pareto-preferred to any other.

---

[2] Vilfredo Pareto (1848–1923), Italian economist and sociologist (mentioned also in Chapter 3).

The set of boundary points, the Social Opportunity Frontier, is called the set of *Pareto-optimal* allocations. Any of these points can be said to "maximize the size of the economic pie," in the sense that there is no allocation Pareto-preferred to it. *In utility terms, the efficient set of income allocations is the Pareto-optimal set.*

What about the goal of distributive equity? Here we lack any principle as compelling as Pareto-optimality.[3] *Equality* as a goal receives a great deal of support, but "equality of utilities" is meaningless. In practice, therefore, many people argue for equality of incomes. A related question is whether the initial distribution, the *status quo*, ought to have any special standing. (If it does, that will conflict with the aim of egalitarian redistribution.) In fact, our laws do generally provide that property cannot be taken from one person and given to another without a specific reason. But from an abstract point of view, there is perhaps no sound justification for this presumption in favor of the *status quo*.

One tradition in welfare economics "solves" the social optimality problem by imagining a special kind of interpersonal utility measure summarized in a so-called *social welfare function*. In Figure 15.2 we might lay down indifference contours of social utility or "welfare" (SW_0 and SW_1 in the diagram) and declare that the social optimum occurs at point B where the boundary LL' touches the highest attainable welfare-indifference contour. The only difficulty is that people will not agree on the shape of such a social welfare function—most people would be inclined to weight their own well-being more heavily than others would allow them to.

15.A.2 ☐ Utilitarianism

Turning to somewhat deeper issues, not everyone will agree with the "utilitarian" philosophy underlying welfare economics.[4] The main contentions of utilitarianism are that: (1) social policies, rules, and institutions are to be judged solely in terms of their *consequences*; and (2) the only relevant consequences are *individuals' gratifications* (pleasures and pains).

The first assertion represents a kind of social pragmatism. For utilitarians all social practices or institutions (e.g., monarchy or voting or the market or capital punishment or the family or the nation) are merely means or instruments. They should not be adopted or rejected because they agree or disagree with the word of the Bible, or with natural law, or with the dictates of ethical principles, or with historical tradition or timeless custom. Instead, the only criterion is: Does this arrangement give rise to desirable social outcomes? Where others might say, "The ends do not justify the means," the utilitarian replies, "What can justify means except the ends attained?"

The second assertion represents radical individualism. Policies may or may not serve the purposes of God, may or may not advance science and learning, may or may not promote the survival of the race or the nation or the gene pool; none of this is relevant for the utilitarian. What counts is whether or not the results satisfy individual desires. President John F. Kennedy once declared, "Ask not what your country can do for you, ask what you can do for your country!" To

---

[3] There are even objections to Pareto-optimality, as will be seen in the section following.

[4] The terms "utility" and "utilitarianism" were both popularized by Jeremy Bentham.

which a utilitarian might reply, "Why have a country except for what it can do for you?"

A somewhat separate question turns on the issue of *hedonism*. In calculating a person's well-being, should we count only sensate satisfactions like a warm house or a full belly? What about "higher wants," for example, the desire to do one's duty or to help others? Utilitarians would probably count benevolent desires as well as hedonistic ones, to the extent that they are actually present—as measured, for example, by individuals' willingness to sacrifice sensate gratifications for higher goals. Unfortunately, in the world as we know it there are also "lower wants," for example, malevolent urges to punish or dominate others. What legitimate weight to attach to such wants remains a problem for utilitarians.

Upon departing from utilitarian premises, *both* efficiency and equity as goals lose much of their force. Nonutilitarians might make any of the following arguments:

1. Social policy should be directed not at giving individuals what they *want*, but what they *ought to have*. As the great moralists and our sacred texts have told us, as observation of others and candid self-examination reveal, and as history demonstrates, most of what people want most of the time they would be better off not getting. Efficiency is a goal for raising pigs, not for the social life of a community of people. Even the "equity" goal means little more than fair division among pigs at the trough.

2. Even admitting that an efficient and equitable distribution of satisfactions of individual wants might to some extent be a legitimate aim, it is absurd to assert that this is the only social goal. Liberty, justice, order, community—all express goals of policy that transcend the satisfaction of individual wants.

3. Apart from *outcomes* is the question of *means*. An allocation of goods and services, however imperfect, that is arrived at in a spirit of voluntary cooperation under law might be better than a perfectly ideal allocation established by dictatorial decree or political trickery.

4. What individuals desire is largely a result of their social conditioning. Much more important than the *want-satisfaction* process is the *want-creation* process. The main goal of policy should not be to give people what they want but to get people to desire the proper things.

No resolution of these difficult philosophical questions can be provided here. Utilitarianism can be criticized from many different points of view: dictatorial or democratic, radical or conservative, ethical or cynical. But recall that economics is the science of the *instrumental*, of the choice of proper means for *given* ends. Economics helps us indicate policies that aim at achieving people's ends, whether or not these ends are in accord with utilitarian philosophy.

15.A.3 □ An Application: Efficient versus "Envy-Free" Allocations

The concept of efficiency can be visualized in terms of the Edgeworth box of Figure 15.3. The shaded area, the lens-shaped "region of mutual advantage," is the set of allocations of the two commodities X and Y that are *Pareto-preferred* to the endowment position E. We saw in Chapter 13 that the Contract Curve CC through all the mutual tangencies of the indifference curves is the set of points

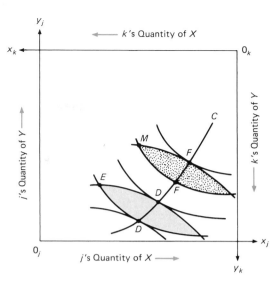

FIGURE 15.3 **Pareto-preferred and Pareto-optimal Allocations.** Given an initial allocation of income *E*, the points in the shaded lens-shaped area are all *Pareto-preferred* to *E*. The Contract Curve *CC* represents the set of *Pareto-optimal* income allocations. Only points within the range *DD* along the Contract Curve are both Pareto-optimal and Pareto-preferred to *E*. At *M*, the midpoint of the diagram, the individuals are materially equal, in the sense of consuming identical amounts of both goods. But, in general, *M* will be neither Pareto-optimal nor Pareto-preferred to *E*.

for which no region of mutual advantage exists. The contract curve *CC* therefore corresponds to the set of *Pareto-optimal* (or *efficient*) allocations.

Notice that there are allocations Pareto-preferred to *E* (points in the region of mutual advantage) that are not Pareto-optimal (not on the Contract Curve). Correspondingly, there are some Pareto-optimal points along *CC* that are not Pareto-preferred to *E* (that are not within the region of mutual advantage). Only allocations falling in the range *DD*, the bounded portion of the Contract Curve within the region of mutual advantage, are *both* Pareto-optimal and Pareto-preferred to *E*. (Recall that, as seen in Chapter 13, the competitive equilibrium outcome falls on the Contract Curve within the region of mutual advantage, and so is indeed both Pareto-optimal and Pareto-preferred in comparison with the endowment position.)

In the Edgeworth box, being in the region of mutual advantage (Pareto-preference) is a distributive criterion that amounts to requiring *unanimous approval* for any change. But what of other possible distributive criteria, in particular *equality*? In the Edgeworth box there would be material equality at the midpoint *M*, where each party receives exactly the same amount of each commodity. But since in general people's tastes differ, material equality would not be very appealing to the parties involved. In fact, since *M* will not ordinarily lie on the Contract Curve *CC*, if the individuals were initially placed at *M* they would voluntarily trade away from it—to some "unequal" point lying in the region of mutual advantage (the dotted area in Figure 15.3).

A somewhat subtler interpretation of equality has recently been introduced by economists under the heading of "envy-free" allocations. The idea is that two individuals are effectively equal if neither is "envious"—that is, if neither would prefer to *change places* with the other.

"Changing places" in the Edgeworth box means moving from any given point to its diagonally opposite counterpart. In Figure 15.4, *G* and *G'* are diagonally opposite each other, meaning that they lie at equal distances in opposite directions from the midpoint *M*. Similarly, the southeast and northwest corners of

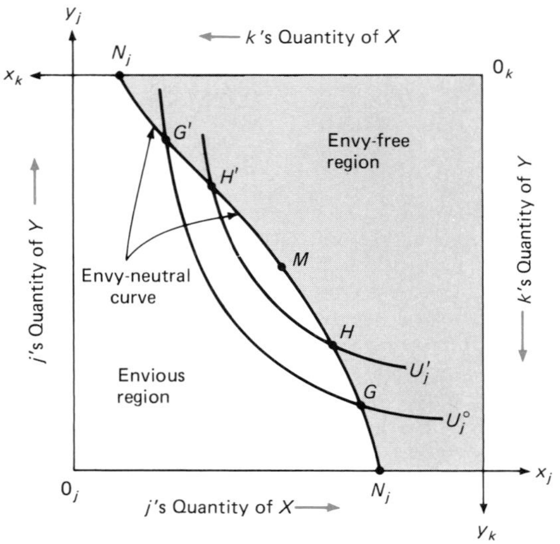

FIGURE 15.4 Envy-Neutral and Envy-Free Allocations. G and G' are diagonally opposite points that lie on one of John's indifference curves. Therefore, John would be just indifferent as to "changing places" with Karl from G to G', or vice versa. So G and G' are *envy-neutral* for John, as are the points H and H'. Connecting all such points generates John's envy-neutral curve $N_j N_j$. John's *envy-free* region, the set of points that he prefers to their "changing places" counterparts, lies northeast of $N_j N_j$. His *envious* region is the set of points southwest of $N_j N_j$.

the box are diagonally opposite one another, as are the southwest and northeast corners.

Let us look now for the set of points that are *envy-neutral* for one of the parties—say, for John. This means that John is indifferent between the given position and its "changing-places" (diagonally opposite) counterpart. In Figure 15.4 the points G and G' are such a pair, both lying on John's indifference curve U_j^o. Similarly, H and H' are envy-neutral points for John, both lying on his indifference curve U_j'. In fact, all of John's envy-neutral points must fall on a curve like $N_j N_j$ that has a generally northwest-southeast slope through the midpoint M. (The midpoint lies on the curve because it is its own "diagonally opposite" image.) [*Query*: It is obvious that any two indifferent points must lie southeast–northwest of each other, owing to the shape of the indifference curves. But why do all the envy-neutral points lie on a *single* southeast–northwest curve? *Hint*: If G and G' are diagonally opposite points that are indifferent, can a point lying directly south of G be indifferent to its diagonally opposite counterpart lying directly north of G'?]

Since the curve $N_j N_j$ in Figure 15.4 connects all of John's envy-neutral points, the shaded region to the northeast of the curve shows all the points that he actually *prefers* over their "changing-places" counterparts. This shaded area (inclusive of the $N_j N_j$ curve) therefore represents the set of John's "envy-free" allocations. A corresponding envy-neutral curve $N_k N_k$ can also be constructed for the other party Karl, where of course Karl's envy-free region would lie *southwest* of his envy-neutral curve. $N_j N_j$ and $N_k N_k$ are both plotted in Figure 15.5, where they serve to define the dotted region as the set of *mutually envy-free* allocations. The two envy-neutral curves must intersect at the midpoint M. While the curves *may* intersect more than once, for simplicity a single intersection is assumed here. On this assumption, the dotted region lies entirely on one side of the midpoint (and, of course, it includes the midpoint itself). Notice also that the Contract Curve CC lies on the same side of the midpoint. [*Query*: Why is this the case? *Hint*: If the

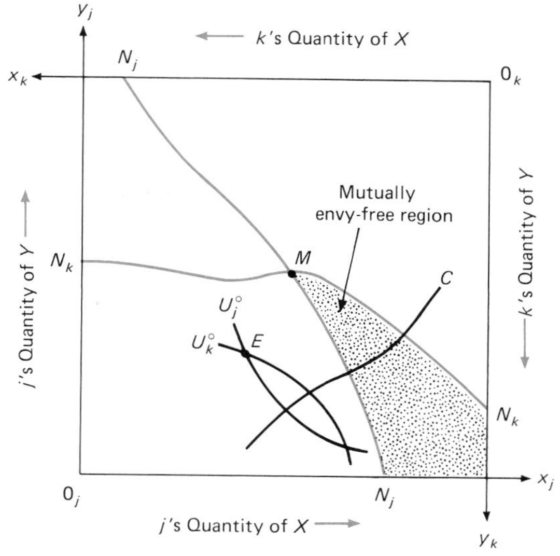

FIGURE 15.5 **Mutually Envy-Free Allocations.**
Since John's envy-free region lies northeast of $N_j N_j$
and Karl's envy-free region lies southwest of $N_k N_k$,
the *mutually* envy-free region is the shaded area.
The Contract Curve CC passes through this region,
so there will always be allocations that are both
efficient and mutually envy-free. But such points are
not necessarily Pareto-preferred to the initial endowment position E.

parties are at a mutual indifference-curve tangency along CC, could they ever *both*
prefer to change places?]

We see therefore that it is always possible to find allocations that are Pareto-
optimal (that lie along the Contract Curve) and are also mutually envy-free (that
fall in the dotted region of Figure 15.5). Thus the efficiency condition can be met
plus envy-freeness as a condition of "distributive equity." However, there is no
point in the envy-free region that is Pareto-preferred to an endowment position
like E in Figure 15.5. So while it is possible to find allocations that are both Pareto-
optimal and envy-free, or allocations that are both Pareto-optimal and Pareto-
preferred, there may be no allocations meeting *all three* conditions.

15.B
THE THEOREM OF THE INVISIBLE HAND

Adam Smith asserted that the invisible hand of self-interest "frequently"
leads men to promote the interests of others. Economists in modern times have
refined this idea into a more precise theorem that can be worded as follows: *Given
a number of ideal conditions, optimizing behavior on the part of individuals and firms under pure competition leads to an efficient (Pareto-optimal) social outcome.* In this section
we shall go through the meaning of this "Theorem of the Invisible Hand." But
note that the theorem relates solely to the social goal of *efficiency* and says nothing
about distributive *equity*. Economic efficiency requires the following:

1. *Efficient Production*: In producing goods X and Y, on the margin it should not be possible for one producer to be able to convert Y into X at a different rate from another
   producer. That is, the Marginal Rates of Transformation MRS_T between goods X and
   Y must be equal for all producers. Suppose this were not the case. Producer A can

transform, say, one unit of Y into one additional unit of X, while B can change one unit of Y into two additional units of X. Clearly, A should cut back his activities and B should expand his, until the Law of Diminishing Returns makes the rates at which the two producers can transform Y into X equal. So the efficiency condition is:

$$(15.1) \qquad\qquad MRS_T^A = MRS_T^B$$

If the amount of commodity Y foregone is interpreted as the *cost* of producing X, we can write this condition as:

$$(15.1') \qquad\qquad MC_x^A = MC_x^B$$

That is, for efficiency in production each producer should be operating at the same Marginal Cost MC.

2. *Efficient consumption*: Whatever goods are produced should be distributed so that, on the margin, no one person will be more willing to sacrifice Y for X than any other individual. (Because, if there were any such difference, they could mutually gain by trade.) This means that the Marginal Rates of Substitution in Consumption, MRS_C, must be equal for all consumers:

$$(15.2) \qquad\qquad MRS_C^A = MRS_C^B$$

We could also interpret MRS_C as the individual's "demand price" or Marginal Value MV for commodity X, in terms of the amount of Y he or she would be willing to offer. Then Equation (15.2) can be rewritten as:

$$(15.2') \qquad\qquad MV_x^A = MV_x^B$$

That is, for efficiency in consumption each individual's Marginal Value for the good must be the same.

3. *Efficient balance between production and consumption*: The rate at which producers can convert Y into X should be equal to the rate at which consumers are willing to substitute Y for X in their consumption. In other words:

$$(15.3) \qquad\qquad MRS_T = MRS_C$$

This condition should hold for all producers and consumers. Interpreting MRS_T as Marginal Cost of producing X, and MRS_C as the Marginal Value, we can also write:

$$(15.3') \qquad\qquad MC_x = MV_x$$

Let us now turn to the role of market price. Think in terms of commodity Y as *numéraire* so that $P_y \equiv 1$. Then the different producers do not *directly* aim at equating their Marginal Rates of Transformation as in Equation (15.1). Rather, each sets his MRS_T (which corresponds to the Marginal Cost of producing X) equal to P_x/P_y or simply P_x. And similarly, the different consumers do not *directly* aim at equating their Marginal Rates of Substitution in Consumption as in Equation (15.2). Rather, each sets MRS_C (his indifference-curve slope) equal to P_x/P_y or P_x (the budget-line slope). Thus the market price P_x serves to bring about the conditions of efficiency by "mediating" all the individuals' productive and consumptive decisions. We can express this compactly in the equations:

$$MRS_T = P_x/P_y = MRS_C$$

Or:

(15.4')

$$MC_x = P_x = MV_x$$

These equations hold over all goods and all individuals.[5] We can portray them pictorially in the form:

(15.4")

$$\frac{MRS_T^A}{MRS_C^A} = P_x/P_y = \frac{MRS_T^B}{MRS_C^B} \quad or \quad \frac{MC^A}{MV^A} = P_x = \frac{MC^B}{MV^B}$$

> CONCLUSION: In a free-market economy, the forces of supply and demand will bring about a set of equilibrium prices that lead individuals to meet the conditions of efficient production, efficient consumption, and efficient balance of production and consumption.

[5] This conclusion is subject to certain technical qualifications as discussed in previous chapters, such as the absence of corner solutions, second-order conditions, etc.

EXAMPLE 15.1
Marginal Excess Burden of Taxation

Taxes impose a "wedge" between buying prices and selling prices, and thus prevent the efficiency conditions (the equalities involving the various Marginal Rates of Substitution) from being satisfied. Each additional dollar of taxes is therefore associated with an efficiency loss.

Charles L. Ballard, John B. Shoven, and John Whalley estimated this "marginal excess burden" (MEB) of taxation to be generally in the range of 17 to 56 cents per dollar. This means that a government project would have to produce marginal benefits of $1.17 to $1.56 per dollar expended, depending upon the tax considered, for that project not to represent an efficiency loss.

In the table here, notice that the MEB for sales taxes overall is $.39, but for taxes other than those on alcohol, tobacco, and gasoline it is only $.12. It follows that the taxes on these three specific goods must involve extremely high

MARGINAL EXCESS BURDENS OF SPECIFIED TAX CATEGORIES*

Tax	MEB ($)
Capital taxes	.46
Sales taxes	.39
Sales taxes (other than alcohol, tobacco, and gasoline)	.12
Income taxes	.31
All Taxes	.33

*Assuming elasticities of 0.4 and 0.15 for saving and labor supply, respectively.

Source: Adapted from Charles L. Ballard, John B. Shoven, and John Whalley, "General Equilibrium Computations of the Marginal Welfare Costs of Taxes in the United States," American Economic Review, v. 75 (Mar. 1985), p. 136.

marginal excess burdens. [*Query*: These three goods are taxed at exceptionally high rates. Would you expect a very heavy percentage tax on some particular good to have a larger MEB, *for the last dollar collected*, than a dollar collected from a small percentage tax? Why?]

In developing these efficiency conditions we have looked only at individuals, and not at firms. Also, the conditions were formulated only in terms of final goods or *products*, and decisions involving the offer and use of *resource services* do not explicitly appear. It is possible to state additional conditions of efficiency to cover these aspects of economic activity as well, but the fundamental principles would remain the same. Since firms are ultimately owned by individuals, firms' decisions implicitly reflect individuals' decisions. And instead of thinking in terms of individuals offering resource services, we can think of them as demanding the consumption "goods" represented by reservation uses of those services. With these interpretations, the three conditions of efficiency shown above are sufficient.

15.C
WHAT CAN GO WRONG? ALMOST EVERYTHING!

The trouble is, the Theorem of the Invisible Hand is too good to be true. Even apart from taxation and other government interventions, there are many ways in which things can go wrong.

15.C.1 □ Monopoly

First of all, consider *monopoly*. Firms might be monopolist sellers of products or monopsonist employers of resources; individuals might be monopolist sellers of resources or monopsonist buyers of products. And it is not necessarily monopoly or monopsony in the strict sense that may lead to failure of the theorem. Any non-price-taking behavior, whether due to cartels, oligopoly, or to any of the market-structure situations analyzed in Chapters 8 through 10, implies violation of the efficiency conditions of the preceding section.

Where monopoly exists, the Invisible Hand does not operate ideally. The profit-maximizing monopoly firm is motivated to set $MC = MR$ rather than $MC = P$ as required by Equation (15.4). So the monopolist produces too little output. Similarly, a monopsonistic employer would hire too few inputs, and a monopolistic resource-supplier would offer too little of the resource on the factor market.

CONCLUSION: Under both monopoly and monopsony there is "too little" market exchange. And in consequence, there will also be "too little" productive specialization and "too little" market employment of factors.

Monopoly and monopsony deprive society of some of the mutual benefits of trade. The violation of the efficiency conditions tells us that, if monopoly could somehow be abolished, the gain would be great enough to permit compensating the monopolist while still leaving something over for the rest of society.

15.C.2 □ Disequilibrium

Another difficulty is *market disequilibrium*. Section 15.B demonstrated the mediating role of prices in achieving the efficiency conditions. But what if the currently quoted price is not the right one for clearing a market? It is true that there will then surely be corrective forces at work tending to restore equilibrium, as explained in Chapter 2. But in the real world the chances are that prices will hardly ever be exactly at their equilibrium values.

Since prices will sometimes be too high and at other times too low, it might be thought that the effects of disequilibrium would more or less cancel out. That, however, is not the case. Prices that are either too high or too low both *reduce* quantities exchanged in markets. Like monopoly, disequilibrium wipes out some of the potential gains from trade.

Figure 15.6 pictures a market with normally sloping supply and demand curves. The price P' is too high to equate supply and demand. At that price the effective quantity exchanged Q' is the *lesser* of the supply and demand quantities, in this case, the demand quantity. It is true that at the high price P' there are unsatisfied sellers, but they cannot find customers. ("It takes two to tango.") The price P'', on the other hand, is too low to clear the market, but again here it is the *lesser* (offered) quantity Q'' that governs; there are now unsatisfied buyers, but they cannot find willing suppliers. While price is in the one case above and in the other case below the equilibrium P^*, in both situations the quantity exchanged is *less* than the equilibrium Q^*.

CONCLUSION: Disequilibrium, like monopoly, leads to non-Pareto-optimal outcomes owing to the reduced volume of trade.

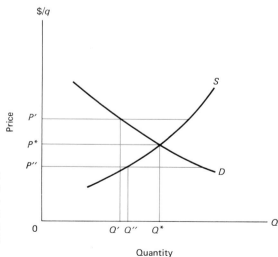

FIGURE 15.6 **Disequilibrium.** Equilibrium price is P^* and quantity exchanged is Q^*. If the price were at the high disequilibrium level P', the quantity exchanged would be Q'; at the low disequilibrium price P'' the quantity would be Q''. Whether price is above or below equilibrium, the quantity exchanged is always *less* than the equilibrium amount.

15.C.3 □ Externalities and Coase's Theorem

"Externalities" are said to arise if some people's actions affect other persons—when these others are not consulted to give their consent, nor compensated in the event of loss or damage. But this definition is too broad for present purposes. Everyone is affected to some extent by actions of people all over the globe that can raise or lower the prices of commodities he or she consumes or produces. We here rule out those merely "pecuniary" externalities that affect others only through movements in market prices. Rather, we will be concerned with the so-called "direct" externalities—those which occur when one person's actions have a technological impact and not a merely pecuniary effect upon the consumption or production possibilities available to others.

Consider *pollution*. An upstream use of water may degrade downstream water quality. For example, chemical pollution may reduce potability, or heat pollution may make the stream less effective for industrial cooling. *Congestion* is a kind of pollution. Each additional driver crowds the highways for other drivers; each additional broadcasting station impairs reception of other stations' signals; each additional well drilled reduces water levels in neighbors' wells.

But a direct externality may also conceivably be beneficial. An upstream user's activities might actually improve the quality of river water. What might be called a "beneficial congestion" externality can also occur—for example, in drainage of marshy soils. Each farmer's attempt to drain his own land lowers water levels and therefore improves the productivity of neighboring land.

A harmful externality is pictured in Figure 15.7. We can suppose that a competitive (price-taking) firm maximizes profit by setting perceived Marginal Cost MC equal to price P_x at output x^*. But as the firm's production x increases, it imposes costs on other firms—due, say, to pollution. The true social Marginal Cost MC at any output x is then the vertical sum $MC + ME$, where ME may be called the Marginal Externality. The output x^{**} at which true social MC equals price P_x, the efficient output, is evidently less than x^*. [*Query*: What happens in the case of a beneficial externality?]

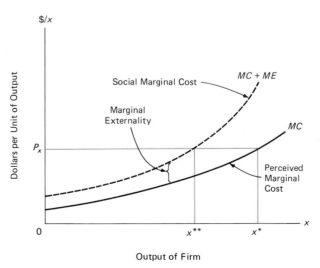

FIGURE 15.7 Harmful Externality. The competitive firm is motivated to produce output x^* where perceived Marginal Cost MC equals price P_x. But the true social Marginal Cost is the vertical summation $MC + ME$ (dashed curve), where ME is the Marginal Externality. So, when a harmful externality exists, the efficient output is $x^{**} < x^*$.

472

EXAMPLE 15.2
Health Costs of Nuclear Power Versus Coal Power

A great deal of concern has been expressed about the health consequences of nuclear power. In judging these, a comparison with the health consequences of electricity generation from alternative sources (predominantly from coal) is highly relevant.

L. B. Lave and L. C. Freeburg[a] analyzed coal versus nuclear power, taking into account the entire fuel cycle from exploration through extraction, transportation, refining, generation, and recovery. So far as occupational health effects (effects upon workers in the industry) were concerned, the mining phase was the main consideration. For nuclear the costs of mine accidents and chronic diseases were estimated at around 2.4 cents per 1000 kilowatt-hours of energy produced—but at around 32 cents per 1000 kWh, more than thirteen times as great, for coal. (*Note:* If these *occupational* health hazards are known to workers and reflected in higher wages, the associated costs would not be *externalities*—they would be paid for and thus taken into account by producers. On the other hand, to the extent that occupational health costs are borne by others, as in the case of the government program to help coal-miners suffering from black lung disease, an externality is being imposed upon the rest of the community.)

A much more uncertain part of the analysis examined health effects upon the outside public. These definitely are externalities. Several elements had to be left out of the comparison for lack of generally agreed-upon data, including the risk of nuclear accidents, the chance of terrorist hijacking of nuclear materials, and the long-term environmental effects of coal- and nuclear-waste disposal. Setting these aside, the public-health costs are mainly the result of chronic low-intensity radiation exposure in the case of nuclear, and pollution of air and water by combustion waste products in the case of coal. For nuclear the estimated public-health costs were within the range of 0.0003 to 0.03 cents per 1000 kWh; note that even the upper limit is small relative to the already small occupational health costs. For coal, on the other hand, the estimated range for public health costs was 10 cents to $5.00 per 1000 kWh—more than 3000 times as great as nuclear at the upper limit, and 16,000 times as great as nuclear at the lower limit! These results suggest, therefore, that some of the concern about the health hazards of nuclear power might better be redirected toward the very significant health externalities associated with coal power.

> COMMENT: As often occurs in analysis of practical decision problems, the unknown or "unquantifiable" elements might be very large here. The accident record at nuclear plants has on the whole been excellent, and accidental nuclear detonation is considered close to impossible. But, as the 1979 Three Mile Island incident in Pennsylvania indicated, the *potential* consequences should a major accident occur are truly enormous. While no identifiable health injury ensued from Three Mile Island, the 1986 Chernobyl incident in the Soviet Union caused around 30 direct fatalities (plus much higher esti-

mated long-run deaths due to increased rates of cancer). It is more difficult still to estimate the likelihood or the consequences of a terrorist group's acquiring enough fissionable material to fabricate atomic weapons. So although nuclear power has an enormous advantage with regard to calculable health costs and externalities, it would be foolhardy not to attach weight to these less quantifiable hazards.

ª Lester B. Lave and Linnea C. Freeburg, "Health Effects of Electricity Generation from Coal, Oil and Nuclear Fuels," *Nuclear Safety*, v. 14 (Sept./Oct. 1973).

CONCLUSION: Direct externalities, beneficial or harmful, lead the Invisible Hand astray. In the interests of efficiency, an agent generating a harmful externality ought to reduce output short of the profit-maximizing level. If the externality is beneficial, output should be expanded beyond the profit-maximizing amount.

Where technological externalities exist, there are three traditional public-policy approaches to the problem of achieving efficient production.

1. *Tax-subsidy adjustments*: If harmful externalities were taxed, producing firms would be motivated to reduce the harm imposed on others. An ideal corrective tax would be equal to the Marginal Externality. Then the private Marginal Cost plus the tax penalty would equal the total true social Marginal Cost of production. For a beneficial externality, a corrective *subsidy* would be called for to induce an ideal (greater) level of the externality-generating activity.

2. *Unitization*: If upstream and downstream uses of river water, for example, were merged or "unitized" under the control of a single economic agent, what was previously an externality would be *internalized*. The single integrated water-using enterprise would now carry on the polluting activity at a socially efficient level—that is, it would pollute only so long as the marginal upstream gain exceeded the marginal downstream loss. Or, consider oilfield operations. The externality here is a congestion effect: pumping at any well reduces the output of other wells in the same field (by drawing away the oil, and by reducing gas pressure). The result is inefficient overdrilling and overpumping. The owner of each well is motivated to pump faster than he otherwise would, to capture oil under others' land and to prevent others from capturing the oil under his land. And the owner of land is similarly induced to drill more wells, and to locate them inefficiently along the boundaries of his tract. With unitization, sole ownerships of individual wells would be exchanged for pro-rata shares in the overall operation of the oilfield. This eliminates the motivation to overpump or to overdrill.

3. *Property reassignment*: The fundamental source of the externality problem is defective property rights. If property rights were perfectly defined and enforced, externalities would not occur. In the river-water example, the downstream user might ideally be assigned a property right to receive water of some specified quality. An upstream user who degrades the quality below this level would be liable for the damages suffered, and so could not impose harm on others without penalty. But whatever the initial assignment, it is essential that property rights remain exchangeable. If the downstream user was initially entitled to absolutely pure water, for example, in the

interests of efficiency the upstream producer should nevertheless be permitted to purchase the other's consent to degrade the river to some agreed degree.[6]

This last concept has been generalized into what is known as *Coase's Theorem*,[7] which can be stated as follows:

COASE'S THEOREM: Regardless of the specific initial assignment of property rights, in market equilibrium the final outcome will be efficient—provided that the initial legal assignment is well defined and that transactions involving exchange rights are costless.

The thrust of Coase's Theorem is that the Invisible Hand is much more effective than our above discussion about externalities may at first suggest. There are natural market forces always at work tending to bring the "external" effects into the calculations of the responsible parties. Suppose a firm has the legal right to pollute the air. The victims of the pollution could then pay the firm *not* to do so. Or perhaps the people in the area have a legal right to clean air. The firm could then pay them a fee in return for their permission to pollute. (In the case of a beneficial externality, of course, the argument applies in reverse.) So long as the legal rights are well-defined and marketable, the Invisible Hand will tend to lead the parties to an efficient outcome—that is, to a result that exhausts all possibilities for further mutual gain.

---

[6] Where the valuable resource takes the form of a "common pool," as in the case of fish in the ocean, or underground water or petroleum, it has been proposed to establish a new kind of property right—marketable entitlements to uncaught fish, or to unpumped water or oil. Overexploitation would be discouraged by the fact that anyone extracting a unit of the resource must also purchase an entitlement to do so. The market price of these titles would reflect investors' estimates of the market value of the resource in *future* uses. See Vernon L. Smith, "Water Deeds: A Proposed Solution to the Water Valuation Problem," *Arizona Review*, v. 26 (Jan. 1977).

[7] R. H. Coase, "The Problem of Social Cost," *Journal of Law and Economics*, v. 3 (Oct. 1960).

EXAMPLE 15.3
The Apples and the Bees

One of the classical illustrations used in economists' discussions of externalities has been a tale of the apples and the bees. The apple-grower's orchard provides the beneficial externality of nectar for his neighbor's bees, a contribution to the production of honey for which the orchardist receives no reward. And the bees in return pollinate the apple blossoms, a valuable service provided without charge. These interacting externalities were assumed to represent a clear case of inadequate guidance by the Invisible Hand. Government action was supposed to be necessary to induce the orchardist to optimally cooperate with the beekeeper—that is, to grow *more* nectar-yielding apple blossoms than the orchardist's self-interested calculation would dictate. And similarly, it was supposed, something had to be done to induce the beekeeper to provide *more* pollination benefits to his apple-growing neighbor.

Upon looking into beekeeping in the state of Washington, however, Steven

N. S. Cheung found the Invisible Hand alive and well. In actual fact, beekeepers and orchardists are quite aware of the beneficial externalities. In consequence, active market dealings govern the placement of beehives. The financial arrangements depend upon the relative values of the two interacting "external" benefits: the honey yield to the beekeeper as against the pollination services gained by the grower. The table here illustrates that where honey yield is great, the beekeeper ordinarily pays an "apiary rent" to buy the right to place his hive on the grower's land. Where the honey yield is small, the grower pays pollination fees for the privilege of having hives placed on his land. (Washington bees are even exported to California to help pollinate the early-season almond crop.) Evidently, market processes are at work to bring "externalities" into private economic calculations.

Honey Yields and Pricing Arrangements, Washington 1970–1971

Season	Crop	Surplus Honey (lb/hive)	Pollination Fees ($)	Apiary Rent/ Hive($)
Early spring	Almond (Calif.)	0	5–8	—
	Cherry	0	6–8	—
Late spring (major pollination season)	Apples and soft fruits	0	9–10	—
	Blueberry (with maple)	40	5	—
	Cabbage	15	8	—
	Cherry	0	9–10	—
	Cranberry	5	9	—
Summer and early fall (major honey season)	Alfalfa	60	—	.13–.60
	Alfalfa (with pollination)	25–35	3–5	—
	Fireweed	60	—	.25–.63
	Mint	70–75	—	.15–.65
	Pasture	60	—	.15–.65
	Red clover	60	—	.65
	Red clover (with pollination)	0–35	3–6	—
	Sweet clover	60	—	.20–.25

Source: Steven N. S. Cheung, "The Fable of the Bees: An Economic Investigation," *Journal of Law and Economics*, v. 16 (Apr. 1973), p. 23.

So far so good. But Coase's Theorem seems to prove too much. Consider the case of simple monopoly, which (by the standard analysis) leads to an inefficient outcome—underproduction of the monopolized good. But wherever there is inefficiency there must be an opportunity to engage in mutually advantageous trade. So, according to Coase's Theorem, the Invisible Hand should lead the monopolist and his customers to get together in some efficient arrangement; the monopolist can be made at least as well off as before, while the customers will do better. Monopoly should disappear, along with externalities!

The problem with the application of Coase's Theorem to "solve" the problem of monopoly or the problem of externalities is that negotiations are costly. Where large numbers of people are involved, it may be impossible to reach agreement. *Unitization*, for example, as an efficient solution of the externality problem in oilfields should, according to Coase's Theorem, tend to come about simply in response to the Invisible Hand. But in practice it has been necessary to pass special legislation whereby holdout minority tract-owners in an oilfield are compelled to comply. It is the "free rider" problem that makes unanimity almost impossible. If the majority agree to cease overpumping their wells, it pays to be a member of the noncomplying minority.[8]

If the numbers involved are small, on the other hand, the problem becomes one of *strategic behavior* (as discussed in Chapter 10). When a small number of bargainers face one another, the mere possibility of a mutually advantageous agreement does not guarantee that such an agreement will be reached.

[8] The motivation is essentially the same as that of the "chiselers" in a cartel situation. But, it should be noted, absolutely unanimous cooperation is not strictly necessary for a workable degree of agreement in either the unitization or cartel contexts.

EXAMPLE 15.4
An Experimental Test of Coase's Theorem

E. Hoffman and M. L. Spitzer conducted a series of experiments to examine the conditions under which two-person or three-person groups could arrive at mutually beneficial outcomes.

In the two-person studies, one subject was chosen at random to be the "controller"—who had the right to impose an externality upon the other party. The controller had a choice of two options: option *A* might, say, yield him $10 and the other person $2; option *B* might yield him $4 and the other party $10. Thus option *B* is socially more efficient, but in the absence of trade it is in the controller's private interest to choose option *A*. However, the second party was allowed to negotiate and possibly offer the controller a sufficient inducement to shift the choice from *A* to *B*.

One question examined was whether or not a *continuing relationship* between the parties might help achieve cooperation. In the experiment a continuing relationship lasted for two successive periods, neither party knowing during the first session who would become controller in the second session. So someone behaving in a noncooperative way during the first session might be subject to reprisal by his or her partner in the second. The second question examined was whether cooperation was more likely when the parties had *full information* about each other's payoffs.

The results for the two-person experiments showed surprising success in achieving group efficiency. While a continuing relationship and full information did lead to some improvement, efficiency was almost always attained even lacking their aid.

In the three-person interactions, the experimenters introduced the complication of "joint controllers," who had to agree whether or not to accept any offer made by the third party. This factor was expected to reduce the likelihood of efficient outcomes. Overall, however, in the three-person experiments efficiency was again achieved in the great majority of cases. Even in the most difficult condition, joint controllership with limited information, efficiency was achieved in 9 of 15 cases.

Achievement of Efficient Outcomes in Two-Party and Three-Party Interactions

	Cases in Which Efficiency Achieved	Cases in Which Efficiency Not Achieved
TWO-PARTY INTERACTIONS		
Full information		
Continuing relationship	12	0
No continuing relationship	11	1
Limited information		
Continuing relationship	8	0
No continuing relationship	11	1
THREE-PARTY INTERACTIONS (with continuing relationship)		
Full information		
Single controller	12	1
Joint controller	15	1
Limited information		
Single controller	19	2
Joint controller	9	6

Source: Extracted from Elizabeth Hoffman and Matthew L. Spitzer, "The Coase Theorem: Some Experimental Tests," *Journal of Law and Economics,* v. 25 (Apr. 1982), esp. p. 92.

COMMENT: These results suggest that the negotiations required to bring about efficiency may not be as difficult as suggested in the text discussion above.

From a policy point of view, Coase's Theorem indicates that *the unambiguous assignment of exchangeable property rights*, whatever the specific nature of the assignment may be, might be an important step in promoting efficiency.

15.D
PUBLIC GOODS

A commodity is called a "public good" if its consumption by any one person does not reduce the amount available for others. Or putting it another way, a good is "public" if providing the good for *anyone* makes it possible, without additional cost, to provide it for *everyone*. Public goods thus represent a particular type of beneficial externality.

The traditional example is the lighthouse. If one ship receives the benefit of the light signal, that in no way deprives others from doing so. Or in radio or television, a broadcast program is available to any and all persons equipped with suitable receivers.[9]

[9] Since there are *some* costs to users (stationing a lookout to watch for the lighthouse, buying a receiving set for the broadcasts), the goods mentioned are not absolutely "pure" public goods. Many goods lie in the intermediate range of the spectrum between wholly private and wholly public. A stage performance, for example, is "public" as among the members of a given audience. But the capacity of the theater sets a limit on the number who can be concurrently served, all others being excluded.

EXAMPLE 15.5
Water Law[a]

In the eastern states the law governing the use of flowing streams is based mainly upon the "riparian" doctrine; in the West, the "appropriation" doctrine dominates.

Under the riparian principle, every owner of land bordering a stream has an equal right to reasonable use of the flow. Property rights so defined are ambiguous and of limited exchangeability. What is "reasonable" will always be an arguable matter. Water-users are deterred from making costly investments for fear that a later judicial or administrative redetermination of "reasonable" uses may take away the water they counted on having. Nor can any user buy another's water right, since all are equally entitled to the flow.

In the relatively arid western states, the inefficient riparian doctrine was replaced by the appropriation principle: that "first in time is first in right." Subject to qualifications and conditions that vary from state to state, first users were given the right to appropriate specified quantities of flow, sometimes limited also as to time, place, or manner of diversion. Appropriated water was no longer tied to "riparian" uses but could be transferred away from the stream. The appropriation doctrine represented a considerable improvement from the point of view of *certainty* of rights. However, the *exchangeability* of rights has remained subject to erratic legal intervention.

In recent years there has been a tendency, even in the western states, for administrative agencies or courts to revert toward the "reasonable-use" philosophy. In consequence, ambiguity has been increasing rather than decreasing. The California Supreme Court, for example, ruled in 1983 that under the "doctrine of public trust" environmentalist groups could challenge diversions of water by the City of Los Angeles from the Mono Basin—despite the fact that the city had long ago purchased the rights to those waters, and had made extensive investments to develop them and to build aqueduct connections to the metropolis. Recent legislation has also tended to be increasingly hostile to market exchanges of water rights. Under the statutes of Colorado, for example, it is illegal to sell water originating in Colorado outside the state boundaries. Colorado legislators seem to think that their citizens are too naive to exact an appropriate price from wily out-of-staters.

[a] Discussion based upon J. Hirshleifer, J. C. DeHaven, and J. W. Milliman, *Water Supply: Economics, Technology, and Policy* (Chicago: University of Chicago Press, 1960), Chap. 9.

The difference between ordinary goods (that are used *exclusively*) and public goods (that can be used *concurrently* by many people) makes for a change in the efficiency conditions. For concreteness, think in terms of the simplest possible community—say, Robinson Crusoe and Friday on their island. Let bananas (B) be the ordinary private good, and wood (W) the public good. (Since Robinson and Friday share living quarters, they both benefit from having wood to burn for warmth.) The efficiency conditions of Equation (15.4), which apply for ordinary private goods, can be written here in the form: $MRS_T^r = MRS_T^f = MRS_C^r = MRS_C^f$ (where "r" stands for Robinson and "f" for Friday). That is, all the Marginal Rates of Substitution in Consumption must be equal for both individuals. But when one of the commodities is a public good, the conditions (where the *MRS* magnitudes are defined in terms of the amount of private good *B* given up) become instead:

(15.5)
$$MRS_T^r = MRS_T^f = MRS_C^r + MRS_C^f$$

Note that the right-hand side is a summation. For convenience of notation, let us once again interpret each person's MRS_T as his *Marginal Cost MC* of producing the public good *W* (in terms of the amount of *B* sacrificed) and his MRS_C as his corresponding "demand price" or Marginal Value *MV*. Then the equation becomes:

(15.5′)
$$MC^r = MC^f = MV^r + MV^f$$

> PROPOSITION: For a good that can be *concurrently* consumed, the efficiency conditions require that each producer's Marginal Cost be equal to the *sum* of the consumers' Marginal Values.

How these conditions may be met is pictured in Figure 15.8. Robinson's rising MC^r curve and falling MV^r (demand) curve are shown as solid, and Friday's corresponding MC^f and MV^f curves as dashed. The crucial point is that the overall or communitywide $\overline{MC}$ curve is the horizontal sum of the individuals' *MC* curves, while the overall demand or $\overline{MV}$ curve is the *vertical* sum of the individuals' *MV* curves.[10] The intersection of $\overline{MC}$ and $\overline{MV}$ determines the efficient total W^* of wood supplied and consumed. Of this quantity, Robinson should supply w_s^r and Friday w_s^f.

[10] In constructing the *MV* curves in the diagram, the "income effect" has been ruled out. Normally, Robinson's MV, his marginal willingness to pay for additional wood, should be larger the more wood has been provided by Friday—since any such provision enriches Robinson.

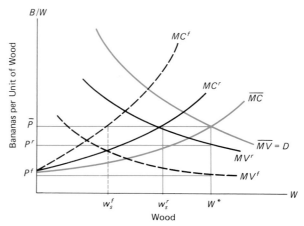

FIGURE 15.8 Efficient Provision of Public Good. Wood *W* (for warmth) is a public good for Robinson and Friday. The social Marginal Cost $\overline{MC}$ of providing the public good is the *horizontal* sum of the individual *MC* curves, while the social value $\overline{MV}$ is the *vertical* sum of the individual *MV* curves. The efficient output of the public good is W^*. Since each individual should produce to the point where his *MC* is equal to the social value $\overline{P}$ of the public good, Robinson should supply w_s^r and Friday w_s^f. If the value $\overline{P}$ is divided into amounts P^r and P^f to be paid by Robinson and Friday, respectively, each would demand the entire amount of the public good produced.

The diagram also shows the prices that must be set in order to clear the market. Notice that the price charged Robinson (P^r) must exceed the price charged Friday (P^f). For a public good the "price-mediating" conditions of Equation (15.4″), required to induce private parties to produce and consume the efficient amounts can be stated as:

$$(15.6) \qquad \begin{cases} MC^r = \overline{P} \\ MC^f = \overline{P} \end{cases} \quad \text{and} \quad \begin{cases} MV^r = P^r \\ MV^f = P^f \end{cases} \quad (\text{where} \quad \overline{P} = P^r + P^f)$$

Thus a set of prices does exist that would give correct "Invisible-Hand" signals to the separate individuals. We now have to consider whether a market process could generate these prices.

A necessary condition for a price system to work at all is *excludability* of non-payers. Sometimes this may be difficult to achieve. In our example, if Friday refused to pay he might still be able to enjoy the warmth from the wood supplied by Robinson. In the case of radio or television broadcasting there is a technological solution to the excludability problem: it is possible to scramble the transmission so that only those who pay can decode the message. (Notice that excludability is a question of law and technology and not of the publicness or privateness of the good. Ordinary private goods may also, in some cases, be non-excludable. For example, the laws of a certain community might say that nonpayers can enter a restaurant and eat on equal terms with those who pay!)

Assuming excludability, two features of Equations (15.6) are of interest: (1) Suppliers of the public good must receive a higher price ($\overline{P}$) than the individual demanders pay (P^r or P^f). (2) Since the prices paid by demanders (P^r and P^f) will generally not be equal to each other, "price discrimination" will be required. To some extent these conditions could be met by an intermediary firm or "middleman" between the primary producers and consumers. For example, a television station could buy independently produced programs at the price $\overline{P}$ and then sell them to viewers at prices P^r and P^f. And if the intermediary has monopoly power price discrimination among consumers might be possible (see Chapter 8). But if price discrimination is not possible, the aggregate MV curve will be lower than $\overline{MV}$ in the diagram, which would elicit less than the efficient supply of the public good.

> CONCLUSION: The efficiency conditions for provision of public goods require that each supplier's Marginal Cost be equal to the *sum* of all the demanders' Marginal Values. If exclusion of nonpayers is possible, a hypothetical system of prices does exist that would elicit the efficient total supply and would charge enough to demanders so as to clear the market. But this system of prices requires price discrimination, and so could not be achieved under competition. A competitive industry would tend to undersupply a public good because of inability to discriminate; a monopolist would tend to undersupply in order to exploit its monopoly power.

Exercise 15.1: Robinson's demand for wood (W) is given by $MV^r = 80 - 2W = P^r$ and Friday's by $MV^f = 30 - W = P^f$. The Marginal Cost functions are $MC^r = 2 + 4w^r$

and $MC^f = 2 + 6w^f$. (a) Find the set of prices that would lead to the efficient production and consumption quantities. (b) What would happen if discriminatory prices could not be charged?

Answer: (a) Adding the demand curves *vertically*, the aggregate $\overline{MV}$ curve is $110 - 3W = P^r + P^f = \overline{P}$. Summing the Marginal Cost curves *horizontally* leads to the aggregate $\overline{MC}$ curve which is $w^r + w^f \equiv W = 5/12(\overline{P} - 2)$. From these two equations we obtain $\overline{P} = 50$, $W = 20$. To clear the market, the respective prices charged the consumers are $P^r = 40$ and $P^f = 10$, which of course sum to $\overline{P} = 50$. The quantities produced will be $w_s^r = 12$ and $w_s^f = 8$, which correspondingly sum to $W = 20$. (b) In the absence of price discrimination the effective aggregate $\overline{MV}$ curve would be just twice the height of the lower (Friday's) demand curve, so that $\overline{MC} = 2MV^f = 60 - 2W = \overline{P}$. The equation for the aggregate Marginal Cost (the horizontal sum) is unchanged. Solving simultaneously leads now to the lower equilibrium price $\overline{P} = 33.64$ (approximately), P^r and P^f now being each half of this (16.82). At $\overline{P} = 33.64$ Robinson would produce about 7.91 units and Friday about 5.27, the total being $W = 13.18$. Charged the price $P^f = 16.82$, Friday would want to consume exactly the 13.18 units of W produced. Robinson would want to consume even more, but would of course be unable to do so. Evidently, less than the efficient quantity of the public good is produced in the absence of price discrimination.

According to some welfare theorists, the various difficulties in private supply of public goods dictate that they be "publicly" (i.e., governmentally) provided instead. Indeed, some have thought that the concept of public goods serves to define the proper scope of government: "Private goods" ought to be privately supplied, and "public goods" ought to be publicly supplied. But in fact we do observe private firms supplying public goods. Television broadcasting is the obvious example, but even lighthouse services have at times been privately provided. And on the other hand government agencies, while supplying public goods like national defense, are also in the business of producing a vast range of private goods. Among the many examples are electric power (TVA), irrigation water (the U.S. Bureau of Reclamation), insurance (Social Security), education (public schools), and of course postal services (the U.S. Postal Service).

The actual forces underlying government versus private provision, whether of public goods or of ordinary goods, will be considered further in the next chapter. That chapter will also cover a somewhat different approach to public goods—namely, provision in the absence of any market at all.

15.E
APPROPRIATIVE ACTIVITY OR "RENT-SEEKING"

Coase's Theorem asserts that market trading will always lead to an efficient outcome—provided, among other things, that property rights are "well defined." What does this condition mean, and what happens when property rights are not "well defined"?

Property rights can be said to be well defined if: (1) all resources are *appropriated* (belong legally to someone), and (2) legal rights to property are perfectly and costlessly *enforced*.

Consider the second condition. If property rights are not perfectly enforced, then it may become more profitable to steal rather than work. Even without violating the law, some people may be able to take others' property by instituting groundless lawsuits or by inducing legislators to change the law (or by inducing judges or bureaucrats to reinterpret the law) in their favor. The present owners are likely to respond with defensive measures: patrolling their property to prevent theft or invasion, hiring expensive lawyers to fight lawsuits, lobbying against new legislation, and so forth. All such proceedings, both offensive or defensive, come under the heading of *appropriative activity*—efforts to impose or to prevent involuntary changes in the ownership of property. (In the special context where individuals or firms compete to acquire legal privileges like licenses or franchises from government, we speak of "rent-seeking.") Appropriative efforts are not costless. They absorb resources that could have been devoted to production and exchange instead.

Turning back now to the first condition, if there are valuable resources that do not legally belong to anyone, we can expect to observe appropriative activity. A dramatic historical instance was the Oklahoma land rush of 1889. When the settlers raced to stake out former Indian territories, the resources devoted to "rushing" so as to gain possession ahead of others were an efficiency loss.[11] Some of the externality problems discussed earlier in this chapter are also associated with attempts to gain control of unappropriated resources: overpumping of oil is due to the fact that the petroleum is no one's property until brought to the surface. Settling new territories or pumping oil are productive actions in and of themselves; what is inefficient is the waste in "rushing" to act before others do.

The efficiency loss due to appropriative activity, it is important to emphasize, is not a consequence of the *existence* of property rights under law. It is a consequence of *imperfections* in their assignment or enforcement. A totally lawless society would not avoid appropriative activity; on the contrary, under anarchy the struggle to acquire and defend control over resources would become everyone's main occupation.

The race to acquire unowned resources has been called *preclusive competition*. Figure 15.9 illustrates both the efficient level of effort in the attempt to acquire such resources and the extent of inefficient "rushing" that can be anticipated.

For concreteness, think of a community of identical fishermen. If no property rights exist in fish until they are caught, there will be preclusive competition. The typical individual will determine his or her privately optimal amount of appropriative (fishing) effort, a, by balancing the cost and the benefit. The upward-sloping *moc* curve in the diagram is the individual's *Marginal Opportunity Cost* of resources devoted to appropriative effort. This cost is the sacrifice of alternative uses of the resources used up in "rushing." The benefits of appropriative activity are shown by the familiar *Value of the Average Product* (*vap*) and *Value of the Marginal Product* (*vmp*) curves.

The efficient level of appropriative activity is a^*, where Marginal Opportunity Cost (*moc*) equals Value of the Marginal Product (*vmp*). But the crucial point is that, in the absence of preassigned property rights, the individual would engage in a' of appropriative effort, to the point where *moc* equals the Value of the *Average* Product (*vap*). From his last unit of effort (last hour of fishing) he will do just as well as any other identical fisherman and thus can capture the *Average* Product f/a of hours devoted to fishing. This is greater than the additional catch due to his

---

[11] The famous Oklahoma "Sooners" were those who cheated by beating the starting gun.

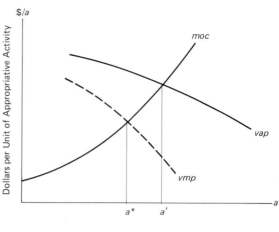

FIGURE 15.9 Appropriative Activity and Preclusive Competition. The efficient level of appropriative activity for any individual is a^*, where his Marginal Opportunity Cost *moc* equals his Value of the Marginal Product *vmp*. However, if the resource is unowned (like fish in the ocean), the individual will want to set his *moc* equal to the Value of the Average Product *vap* at activity level $a' > a^*$. Thus, preclusive competition leads to excessive appropriative effort.

last unit of effort, which is only his *Marginal* Product $\Delta f/\Delta a$. He can take home more than his true Marginal Product because his fishing effort will haul in not only "new" fish but also fish that would otherwise have been taken by other fishermen anyway.[12]

Exercise 15.2: An isolated village surrounded by wilderness contains a cultivated banana grove. Bananas (B) are the only consumption good. The grove produces bananas according to the production function $B_g = 12L_g - L_g^2$, where L_g is the number of villagers working in the grove. Bananas also grow in the wilderness, where the production function is $B_w = 2L_w$. The village has 12 identical workers, none of whom have any desire for leisure, and there are no other resources or products that need be considered. (a) As a benevolent dictator, how would you divide the 12 laborers between grove and wilderness to maximize banana output? (b) Compare the results if the grove were instead "unowned" property, so that any villager can enter and pick what he pleases. (c) What property rights could be assigned to achieve efficiency without a centralized dictatorship?

Answer: (a) Take bananas as the *numéraire* so that $P_B \equiv 1$. Then the Marginal Product is also the Value of the Marginal Product of labor in the grove. This can be found, by calculus or by plotting, to be $vmp_g = 12 - 2L_g$. The Marginal Opportunity Cost here is the constant return to labor in the wilderness, or $moc = 2$. The benevolent dictator would set $moc = vmp_g$, or $2 = 12 - 2L_g$. The result is the efficient assignment $L_g = 5$ and $L_w = 7$. The banana outputs will be $B_g = 35$ and $B_w = 14$, or a total of 49. (b) If the grove is unowned, each villager will go wherever his *Average* Product is greater. So, in equilibrium, $B_g/L_g = B_w/L_w$. When this holds there will be 10 workers in the grove and only 2 in the wilderness. The Total Product will be 24, which is the same as if the grove did not exist at all! (c) Each villager could be assigned one-twelfth of the grove as his own to work (or to rent out to others).

Preclusive competition is one type of appropriative activity; "rent-seeking" is another. The analysis is very similar. Let us suppose that in a certain community a

---

[12] What we have here is a kind of "congestion externality."

fixed number of taxicab licenses are periodically assigned to drivers through some bureaucratic process. Depending upon the detailed arrangements, drivers might compete for the licenses by demonstrating their skills and high character in a public hearing, by engaging accountants or economists to prepare written documented proposals, or even by making private under-the-table arrangements with whoever is in a position to select the winners. As before, each driver will engage in appropriative effort up to the point where his Marginal Opportunity Cost *moc* equals the Value of the Average Product *vap*.

Rent-seeking differs from the more general case of appropriative activity in that, by definition, there is no true social product at all from rent-seeking. Regardless of the resources expended in seeking taxicab licenses, there will be the same number of cabs on the streets. (However, if the selection process does find *better-quality* drivers, there could be some social gain.) Notice that if the taxicab licenses were simply auctioned to the highest bidders there would not be any waste of resources. The amounts paid to acquire a license would just be a distributive transfer between the drivers and the community treasury. (By the same token, if the licenses were auctioned to those willing to pay the highest bribes, there would again be no efficiency loss—only this time the distributive transfers would go to some public official personally rather than to the public treasury.)

EXAMPLE 15.6
Rent-Seeking in India

In nations whose economies are characterized by pervasive government controls, the overall fraction of national income dissipated by rent-seeking may be very large. In a recent study of the Indian economy, Sharif Mohammad and John Whalley classified rent-seeking activities under four major headings: those associated with import and export quotas and privileges, with capital market subsidies and controls, with price controls in product markets, and finally with labor markets. Overall, they estimated that rent-seeking losses amounted to the remarkable total of between 30 percent and 45 percent of India's GNP in 1980 and 1981—needless to say, a heavy burden for such an impoverished nation. Their conclusions are summarized in the table.

Cost of Rent-Seeking in India, 1980–1981

Category	Percentage of GNP
Import licenses and export incentives	3.8
Capital market controls	8.2–16.3
Product market controls	16.3–20.2
Labor market controls	2.9
Total	29.9–43.2

Source: Sharif Mohammad and John Whalley, "Rent Seeking in India: Its Costs and Policy Significance," *Kyklos*, v. 37 (1984).

An individual or firm awarded a license to import a good into India, for example, is in a position to buy the commodity at its low world price in international commerce and then resell it (perhaps after some processing) at its high domestic price in the protected Indian economy. Rather typically, Mohammad and Whalley found, this premium was on the order of 100 percent of the world price. Needless to say, import licenses are avidly sought. In the case of exports, firms struggle to obtain subsidies like tax exemptions and freight concessions that the government grants to approved exporters. Resources are wasted because, for example, to support a request to import raw materials, a firm might have installed excess productive capacity; to justify import of machinery it might have employed an excessive number of workers. In addition, there are the actual costs of hiring economists, accountants, lawyers, and so forth, for the paperwork and hearings involved in the review process.

Similar considerations are involved in the other important areas of rent-seeking. In capital markets there are licenses required for making major investments, and subsidized credit to approved categories of undertakings; in product markets there is access to price-controlled commodities that are rationed under a variety of schemes; and in labor markets there are the high-paid jobs in the government bureaucracy to be allocated. In this last category, rent-seeking may take the form of acquiring excessive credentials through overinvestment in education.

15.F
WELFARE ECONOMICS: CONCLUSION

Welfare economics has mainly been concerned with the problem of *efficiency*—that is, how to reach the Social Opportunity Frontier (as shown, for example, by the curve LL' in Figure 15.2). Any such allocation is efficient in the sense that there exists no other that is Pareto-preferred to it.

Achievement of efficiency is, however, neither necessary nor sufficient as a criterion of ideal social policy. The *distribution* of income as among individuals and social classes is another important criterion. Even granting the appropriateness of a certain tilt toward distributive *equality*, the question remains how far to go in sacrificing efficiency. And there are, of course, many other criteria with some claim to be considered: liberty to retain and to use lawfully acquired talents or property, community versus individualistic values, and other nonutilitarian considerations.

Nevertheless, economists' emphasis upon the efficiency criterion has probably played a useful social role. The political processes that determine social policy tend to ignore efficiency almost entirely. Whether the issue be the progressive income tax, the protection of some industries by tariffs, the penalization of others for "excessive" profits, combating monopoly, or choosing the proper scale of government, it has become a function of the economist to point out that there are efficiency implications to be considered. Alternative government policies affect the size of the aggregate "pie" of income, apart from the question of how the pie is to be sliced up.

An older generation of economists tended to think of economic policy as a shotgun with two barrels: (1) The first barrel was a tendency to favor free trade and *laissez faire*, owing to the efficiency advantages of a market economy guided by the Invisible Hand, as described in Section 15.B. (2) The second barrel was a countervailing tendency to favor government intervention and regulation, where needed, to remedy recognized imperfections and failures of the market economy, as described in Section 15.C. Neither barrel of the shotgun quite hits the target. Suppose the Invisible Hand did its work perfectly. Even so, the efficient allocations of goods and resources thereby achieved by the market economy might violate other desirable ends of public policy, such as distributive equity or preservation of community values. On the other hand, when it comes to remedying the flaws of the market system, we must guard against what has been called "the Nirvana fallacy": the presumption that government intervention will in actual practice improve matters. One must not forget that government decision systems have flaws of their own.

This last point indicates the need for an economic approach to political or governmental decision-making. Economists have indeed, though only very recently, turned to serious *positive* analysis of government—that is, to examining the economic consequences of what government *actually* does as opposed to what in some ideal sense it "ought" to do. This will be the topic of the following chapter.

□ SUMMARY OF CHAPTER 15

The study of the principles underlying correct public policy is called "welfare economics." While there are many possible goals of policy, economists' attention has traditionally been concentrated on only two: efficiency and distributive equity. Efficiency is increased by making any change that is Pareto-preferred—that is, that increases the utility of any person or persons without decreasing the utility of any other. An outcome is said to be efficient or Pareto-optimal when there are no other outcomes Pareto-preferred to it. (However, it is not true that an efficient outcome is Pareto-preferred to *every* outcome that is not efficient.) The goal of distributive equity is ordinarily interpreted as *equality*. But while equality may be definable in terms of objective incomes, there is no way to say when two individuals' utilities are equal. We can, however, determine when allocations of goods are *envy-free*, meaning that neither party would want to change places with the other. Both efficiency and equality as goals are based on utilitarian philosophy. Nonutilitarians have criticized such goals as being, among other things, excessively individualistic and excessively materialistic.

The Theorem of the Invisible Hand states that, under ideal conditions, a *laissez-faire* economy will achieve an efficient utilization of resources. As people respond to prices, efficiency will be attained among producers, among consumers, and in the exchange of goods between consumers and producers.

However, there are several grounds on which the Invisible Hand might fail in the actual world: (1) Monopolies of many types exist, all leading to inefficient outcomes if operated for private gain. (2) Disequilibrium prices do not give the correct signals to buyers and sellers. (3) If the existing structure of property rights allows some agents to impose direct externalities on others, incentives are distorted. Coase's Theorem asserts that property rights will be exchanged to eliminate inefficient externalities, but this holds only under ideal conditions: property rights must be well defined, and transactions costless.

Public goods represent a special type of externality: when a public good is provided for one person, there is no additional cost in providing it to others. If a public good is or can be made excludable in the market, it can be privately provided. There is a pattern of discriminatory prices that can achieve efficiency in the private production and use of *excludable* public goods, but in practice such goods are likely to be undersupplied in the market. If a public good is nonexcludable, on the other hand, it can scarcely be provided by the market at all. (But neither could a nonexcludable *private* good.) Finally, where property rights are not well defined, individuals will be motivated to undertake socially wasteful appropriative or "rent-seeking" activities aimed at changing control over resources (or at preventing such changes).

In view of the uncertainties of distributive equity (or its usual practical counterpart, income equality) as goals, economists have tended to concentrate upon achievement of efficiency. This has probably served a socially useful function. While one must treat with reserve the proposition that an actual *laissez-faire* economy would approximate an efficient outcome, it remains to be seen whether actual government interventions normally tend to correct any failure to do so.

☐ QUESTIONS FOR CHAPTER 15

MAINLY FOR REVIEW

R1. Explain and justify the normally "concave" shape of the Social Opportunity Frontier in income terms (Figure 15.1). What can be said about the shape of the Social Opportunity Frontier in utility terms (Figure 15.2)?

*R2. Show how a Social Opportunity Frontier in utility terms for two individuals may be derived from the *Contract Curve* in the Edgeworth-box diagram of Chapter 13.

*R3. What meaning, if any, can be given to the concept of a "social optimum"? How valid is efficiency or Pareto-optimality as a criterion of social optimality?

R4. What is the Theorem of the Invisible Hand?

R5. What are the conditions of efficiency reached under ideal conditions by the unregulated market process? Can the conditions be achieved, in principle, without use of the market?

R6. Why does disequilibrium of markets lead to inefficiency?

*R7. Explain why a firm that is a monopolist in the product market is said to hire "too little" of the factors it uses for production. Explain why a firm that is a monopsonist in the factor market is also said to hire "too little." Does it follow that too large a proportion of the community's resources are employed by competitive firms, or are retained for reservation uses by resource-owners, or both?

R8. What are public goods? What are externalities? Is a public good a special case of an externality?

R9. How would inability to exclude nonpayers affect the private supply of public goods? The private supply of private goods?

*R10. What is the efficiency condition for optimal provision of a public good? In the case of public goods why do we sum individual demand curves *vertically*, whereas for private goods the summation takes place *horizontally*?

*The answers to starred questions appear at the end of the book.

*R11. What limits the possibility of private supply of public goods? Will public provision mean that a more nearly optimal amount will be supplied?

R12. What is Coase's Theorem? Explain the relevance of each of the following conditions for the actual empirical applicability of the theorem: (a) well-defined property rights, and (b) low costs of negotiating and enforcing agreements.

R13. What is "appropriative activity"? What is "rent-seeking"? What is "preclusive competition"? What are the implications of such activities for economic efficiency?

FOR FURTHER THOUGHT AND DISCUSSION

*T1. Fragment of a conversation based upon Robert Browning's poem, "My Last Duchess":

> But my dear Dr. H., your own textbook proves that in terms of economic efficiency I was amply justified in taking the life of my last duchess. For, being of not inconsiderable means, I was willing to pay more for her death than she could have afforded to pay to prevent it.
>
> The Duke of Ferrara

In terms of economic efficiency, was the Duke justified in murdering his wife?

*T2. "An efficient allocation of resources maximizes the dollar value of national income." True or false? Explain.

T3. In the apples-bees example in the text, the externality is mutually beneficial. Provide an example of a reciprocal relation in which the mutually imposed externalities are harmful. Can there be a case in which in one direction the effect is beneficial but in the other direction harmful?

*T4. What sorts of real-world considerations may forestall the working of Coase's Theorem by making property rights ambiguous or uncertain? By raising the costs of negotiating and enforcing contracts?

T5. What are the major considerations bearing upon the likelihood or effectiveness of achieving efficiency through market versus nonmarket means?

*T6. "An ideal market would achieve a Pareto-efficient outcome, but only one that is Pareto-preferred to the endowment situation; an ideal dictatorship would not be so limited." True or false? Explain.

*T7. Steps have been taken in the United States to ban the commercial market in human blood. (One of the arguments given was that commercially provided blood is more likely to be infected with hepatitis than volunteered blood.) Can this ban be justified on efficiency grounds, or any other grounds?

*T8. One "market intervention" is the law against polygamy. Historically, many human societies have permitted polygyny (multiple wives) and some even polyandry (multiple husbands). It has been contended that the laws banning polygyny work to the *disadvantage* of women as suppliers of wife-services—just as a law forbidding more than one car per customer would be disadvantageous to suppliers of automobiles. Is this sound? Who are the main losers and main gainers from monogamy laws? Can the monogamy laws be defended in terms of efficiency? In terms of equality?

16
SUPPLEMENTARY CHAPTER

POLITICAL ECONOMY

In 1984 the expenditures of federal, state, and local government in the United States amounted to around 20 percent of GNP, counting only government purchases of goods and services. When transfer payments like social security and aid to the poor are included, the figure approaches 40 percent. In a number of other countries these proportions are even higher. So, to get an overall picture of how resources are organized and goods are produced in modern economies, not only the market sphere but also the political domain must be analyzed.

Market transactions are voluntary. One person contracts to sell, the other contracts to buy, under terms to which both of them consent. But politics is characterized by *involuntary* transactions. To pay for a service like a public road, a government will typically tax many people in the community who will be deriving no benefit whatever from the road, who may even be injured by it. What is far more drastic, governments define certain behaviors as crimes for which citizens may be punished by fines, imprisonment, or death. Or, a government may make war against its enemies, possibly drafting unwilling citizens as soldiers. Involuntary transactions like these are dictated ones. The essence of politics is who dictates to whom, who governs and who is governed.

Some philosophers contend that people always behave selfishly in the marketplace, but when it comes to politics they are more inclined to act in the public interest. This naive view is rejected here. Market decisions and political choices are made by the same people, with the same motives. And specifically, we will assume that people are about equally self-interested in both spheres. To explain observed differences between market behavior and political behavior we must look not to differences in motives but to differences in the rules of the game.

This chapter first analyzes a hypothetical "public-choice state." In such a state the government is a creation of citizen-consumers who have voluntarily banded together in order to provide themselves with certain goods and services—national defense or public roads, for example—that are more effectively secured through a collective-choice arrangement than through markets. The power to vote, like the power to purchase in markets, allows each individual to have some influence upon the final outcome. Just as the market system has its failures and inadequacies, the public-choice state will also necessarily be an imperfect mechanism for achieving individuals' desires. The chapter will analyze some of these imperfections. What is perhaps even more important, the public-choice state is a very idealized model of how government works. Such a model does not allow for violence and coercion, which are close to the heart of politics. Later in the chapter these issues will be taken up under the heading of "Political Conflict."

THE PUBLIC-CHOICE STATE
AND ITS IMPERFECTIONS

The public-choice state can best be grasped by thinking of *political parties* as akin to *business firms*. Business firms offer goods and services, at specified prices, to the consumers. Political parties offer packages of government policies, at certain costs in the form of taxes and other burdens, to the citizens. Firms try to make a profit by providing *consumers* with what they want. Politicians try to make a "profit" (which might, in some degree, represent satisfactions like power or glory apart from money) by providing *citizens* with what they want.

Ideal free enterprise in the economy corresponds to ideal democracy in the polity.[1] What forces businesspeople to satisfy the desires of consumers is the same as what pushes politicians to satisfy the desires of citizens—the pressure of *competition*. In the ideal market economy, perfect competition among firms drives profits to zero in long-run equilibrium (as discussed in Chapter 7). Then firms have no power to do anything other than what consumers want, since any firm that fails to satisfy consumers will be driven out of business by other firms. In the ideal polity, perfect competition among politicians similarly drives political "profit" to zero. Parties or candidates would have no power to do anything other than what citizens want, since failing to satisfy the citizens means being voted out of office. Thus, Adam Smith's Invisible Hand—the force that induces individuals, in their own self-interest, to satisfy the needs of others—operates to some degree in the political arena as well as in the market economy.

The preceding chapter analyzed certain imperfections of real-world market systems (monopoly, disequilibrium, externalities, and so on). But, viewed as ways whereby citizen-consumers attempt to achieve their desires, political mechanisms also have important shortcomings.

16.A.1 ☐ Political Competition

Just as ideal democracy in the polity corresponds to perfect competition in the market, political dictatorship corresponds to monopoly in the market. But political dictatorship has far more drastic consequences. Customers can often avoid doing business with a market monopolist who overcharges, but escaping an oppressive government may be impossible. Furthermore, the market monopolist wants only our money while the political dictator may want our very lives. Yet even the most absolute dictator still faces competition. Possible conquest from outside, or revolution from within, set limits on a dictator's power.

Democratic political systems are characterized by relatively free entry into the contest for political power. But there appear to be strong economies of scale in the political process. As a result, in democratic nations most commonly there are only two (or at any rate only a very few) effective political parties. So democratic political competition is closer to oligopoly (Chapter 10) than to perfect competition. Furthermore, rare exceptions apart, citizens do not vote directly on poli-

---

[1] See Gary S. Becker, "Competition and Democracy," *Journal of Law and Economics*, v. 1 (Oct. 1958).

cies. They vote only for delegates in the legislative, judicial, and executive branches of government; these delegates supposedly represent the citizens in making the actual policy decisions. But elections of delegates are relatively infrequent. Whereas consumers make and reconsider market choices every single day, citizens can choose or recall their political representatives only at election intervals measured in years. And some of the most important political decision-makers, such as U.S. Supreme Court justices, are only indirectly "elected" and once chosen are beyond effective recall.

The *limited options* available further erode the control that citizens have over their delegates. Many issues are "bundled" together in the election process. A voter may prefer the position of one candidate on one question, of a competing candidate on a second issue, and so forth. But the delegate elected will be representing (or misrepresenting) the voter in *all* decisions to be made during his or her term of office.

So even in a highly democratic system delegates may have a considerable degree of "power" (i.e., of leeway to violate the preferences of their constituents). The clearest evidence of this is the willingness of candidates and parties to expend enormous sums to win political office. U.S. Senate and House candidates were reported by the Federal Elections Commission to have spent about $314 million seeking congressional seats in the 1982 election. And this figure takes no account of the volunteer efforts of sympathizers and party workers, of free publicity from supporting newspapers and other media, of propaganda put out by unions and businesses hoping to win favors, and so on.

EXAMPLE 16.1
Shirking by Legislators

One way in which elected legislators may fail their constituents is to shirk their duties. A very obvious form of shirking is simply failing to show up and vote when issues come up for decision. Of course, the constituents may punish shirking legislators by not re-electing them to office. However, this control will be less effective for those legislators who are voluntarily retiring and so will not be running for re-election anyway.

John R. Lott, Jr., studied the voting participation rates of retiring and nonretiring members of the 95th U.S. Congress. Some of his results are shown in the table below. As can be seen, retiring members of Congress voted noticeably less often. This remained the case even when an adjustment was made for illness as a possible cause of retirement.

Lott also examined the question of whether post-elective political employment, for the legislator himself or his children, might provide a way in which

Voting Participation Rates (%)

	Those Retiring	Those Not Retiring
All congressmen	79.72	89.36
Congressmen not ill	84.57	89.64

Source: John R. Lott, Jr., "Attendance Rates, Political Shirking, and the Effect of Post-Elective Office Employment," Hoover Institution Working Papers in Economics E-86-80 (Oct. 1986), p. 16.

the party leaders could control shirking by retiring legislators. While the evidence was not conclusive, that factor did seem to have some effect. Also, as a possibly related point, those members of Congress who retired while still relatively young were less likely to shirk in their last session.

16.A.2 ☐ The Problem of Voting

It is the *vote* that represents the ultimate control that citizens have on their delegates. But the effectiveness of a single vote is tiny, so much so that the ordinary citizen is scarcely motivated to go to the polls at all. Even if the election of the preferred candidate were worth an enormous sum to the voter, it would be fantastically improbable that a single person's ballot would determine the outcome. Or if the citizen is not so interested in electing a particular candidate as in swelling the poll for an ideological position, again one vote more or less would scarcely ever be noticeable. And even if the voter has no selfish aims at all but intends to cast a purely public-spirited ballot, that single vote will no more measurably serve the *public* interest than it would the voter's own *selfish* interest.

If it were possible and legal for a candidate to *buy* votes, there would be no problem of motivating the voter. In fact, a surprisingly good case can be made for buying citizens' votes at election time. Payment for votes before election would compensate for the scarcely controllable power granted the delegates after their election.

There are other problems with voting. In the marketplace you "get what you pay for." In the political arena, it is all too easy to elect a candidate and not get the anticipated results. In view of the difficulties of finding and electing a candidate supporting the whole bundle of one's preferred policies, and of ensuring that he or she abides by the promises made, it simply is not worthwhile for the rational citizen to invest heavily in determining what *are* the best policies. Voting is cheap, but voting *intelligently* may be quite costly. And so, a subtler flaw of the political process is that citizens typically find it entirely rational to remain ill-informed on the issues.

If votes are not paid for, if the chance of affecting the outcome is negligible, and if the results remain unpredictable even if your candidate wins, why are so many votes actually cast in elections? Assuming citizens are rational, it can only be that the *costs of casting a ballot are low.* And indeed, at least for city-dwellers and when the weather is good, the cost is small. Voting may actually be fun; it provides sociability and a feeling of civic accomplishment to offset the small travel and time cost involved.

EXAMPLE 16.2
Determinants of Voter Turnout

If a citizen rationally considers whether to turn out and vote, his or her decision should depend in part upon (1) the importance of the election, and (2) the probability of affecting the outcome. Y. Barzel and E. Silberberg[a] investigated the impact of these determinants upon the proportion of citizens actually casting ballots in U.S. gubernatorial elections in the years 1962, 1964, 1966, and 1968 (122 elections).

The found, among other results, that:

1. *The larger the population, the smaller the percent of turnout.* This represents rational behavior, since the larger the population the smaller is the probability of a single person's vote determining the election. An *increase* of 1,000,000 in voting-age population of the state was associated with a 6 percent *decline* in the percent voting.

2. *The more one-sided the election, the smaller the turnout.* Again rational, since if voters had some inkling in advance of the one-sidedness they would place lower credence upon their own single ballot affecting the outcome. Statistically a 10 percent *increase* in the majority fraction was associated with a 7.7 percent *decline* in percentage voting.

3. *Coincidence of nongubernatorial with gubernatorial elections increased turnout.* Statistically, a presidential candidacy raised the fraction voting by 11.1 percent; a senatorial candidacy raised it by 5.5 percent. Obviously, it is more rational to vote if the election is more important.

COMMENT: It would have been of interest to see if the difficulty and cost of voting significantly affected turnout. One would anticipate a larger fraction voting the better the weather, the less the average distance to the polls, the more convenient the voting hours, and so on. As another point, it is also reasonable to expect a larger turnout on the part of those who expect to be able to cast *intelligent* ballots. (College graduates? Economics students?)

[a] Y. Barzel and E. Silberberg, "Is the Act of Voting Rational?" *Public Choice*, v. 16 (Fall 1973).

16.A.3 □ Majority and Minority

Democratic political systems operate mainly on the principle of *majority rule*. The necessity of making decisions through delegates poses a problem, since a delegate may not faithfully serve constituents' interests. But what if the constituents differ among themselves? Then, to be elected, delegates need only serve the majority interest; they must please only 50 percent-plus-one of those who turn out to vote.

This obviously puts the minority at a grave disadvantage. Their most vital interests may be at the mercy of the majority. If 75 percent of the voters prefer alternative 1 and 25 percent prefer alternative 2, the delegate's actions—for example, his or her votes on legislative issues—are unlikely to be divided in this proportion. Rather, the delegate will be motivated to act solely on behalf of the majority. In contrast, majority and minority preferences are normally *both* provided for, in due proportion, in the market. If 75 percent of consumers prefer chocolate and 25 percent prefer vanilla, chocolate and vanilla flavors will normally be provided in just about these proportions.

To help protect minority rights, a constitution may limit the types of laws a majority can pass. A very interesting phenomenon that also helps minorities is called "log-rolling." Suppose minority legislators feel very strongly on a particular issue A. Then to swing over votes on issue A, they may promise other legislators to support *their* positions on separate issues B, C, D, etc. In this way the *intensity* of minority preferences may help counterbalance the mere numbers of the majority.

Log-rolling brings market considerations into the political process. Delegates' votes on some issues are "bought" to be "paid for" later by votes on other issues. Log-rolling, though often regarded as an evil, reminds us of the *mutual advantage of trade*. Indeed, efficiency in the sense of a *Pareto-optimal* outcome—a result in which it is no longer possible to achieve any further gains to anyone without hurting others (see Chapter 15)—would be achieved if legislators' votes on issues could be openly purchased for money!

The underlying logic is this. An ideal system of "political exchange" would be one requiring *unanimous* consent for every government action. To achieve unanimity, those who suffer from the chosen action would have to be compensated by the purchase of their votes. This would guarantee that all political actions undertaken are actually Pareto-preferred over the initial situation (i.e., would constitute an improvement for some, and an injury for none). With a majority rather than a unanimity rule, it is true that compensation need not be paid to all those affected—only to a number sufficient to comprise a voting majority. Nevertheless, since *both* sides will be trying to buy votes, the winning side will be the one able to bid higher. Hence under a bought-vote system the more highly valued alternative would always be chosen. The result is Pareto-*optimal*, though not in general unanimously preferred (Pareto-*preferred*) over the status quo.

16.A.4 ☐ The Cycling Paradox and the Median-Voter Theorem

One problem with majority voting that has received a great deal of attention is called *the cycling paradox*. Suppose three voters a, b, c must select among three political candidates or policies X, Y, Z. Two alternative possible sets of voters' rankings are:

Voter	Preferences Subject to Cycling	Preferences Not Subject to Cycling
a	X, Y, Z	X, Y, Z
b	Y, Z, X	Y, Z, X
c	Z, X, Y	Z, Y, X

Using the first set of preferences, when X and Y are the alternatives, then X has a 2:1 majority. When Y and Z are the alternatives, then Y has a 2:1 majority. But when X and Z are the alternatives, then Z has a 2:1 majority! In the terminology of Chapter 3, majority-rule choices may violate the condition known as *transitivity*. [*Challenge to the reader*: Verify that with the second set of preferences cycling will not occur. Which alternative is sure to be chosen?]

Where cycling is possible, as with the first set of preferences, the voting sequence (the "agenda") can determine the final outcome. Suppose you are individual a, and as chairman of the meeting you have the power to determine the agenda. Then you should call first for a vote between Y and Z, the winner to be matched against X. Y would win the first vote, but would be defeated by your favored policy X in the second vote. Any other person as chairman could equally well manipulate the agenda in his or her own favor.

A question that has concerned analysts is: Under what circumstances will an *equilibrium* exist in a majority-voting system? To start with the simplest case, suppose there is only one issue to be voted on: say, the size of the government budget. In Figure 16.1, voters a through e are located at positions along a horizontal axis representing their ideal choices for the percent of GNP to be devoted to government. And, we will assume, in moving away from the ideal point in either direction each voter will always prefer an option closer to his or her ideal over one that is farther away. (Notice that this involves only *ranking* of preferences in a given direction. Distance along the line need not be a "cardinal" measure for *scaling* preferences.)

Any choice process, whether it be market dealings or voting, should ideally lead to an outcome that is Pareto-optimal (efficient). In this case the range from a to e along the horizontal axis is the set of Pareto-optimal choices. Starting from any point outside the range, there would be unanimous agreement in favor of moving to some point or points within. So the range $\overline{ae}$ is like the Contract Curve *CC* in the Edgeworth box of Figure 15.3. (It is not necessarily true, however, that *every* point within the range $\overline{ae}$ will be unanimously preferred over any point outside the range; as we saw in Figure 15.3, not every *Pareto-optimal* point is *Pareto-preferred* to a given starting position.) Of course, within the Pareto-optimal range $\overline{ae}$, any move in either direction must necessarily make at least one voter worse off.

Suppose points V, W, X, Y, Z represent the alternative proposals (percentages of GNP devoted to government) to be voted on. For there to be a unique equilibrium that is independent of the sequence in which the proposals are offered, some single option must be able to win a majority vote against each and every one of the others. Will there necessarily be such a winner in Figure 16.1? Notice that X will win a majority against V or W to its left while Y will win against Z to its right. So regardless of the agenda (so long as all the options are actually offered), the final winner must be either X or Y—the options lying just on either side of c, the ideal choice of the *median voter*. Whether X or Y turns out to be the winner will therefore depend solely upon which of the two is more preferred by the median voter. (The diagram does not show which of the two it will be.)[2]

___

[2] In the diagram, point Y is closer than point X to the median voter's ideal position c, but X and Y lie in different directions from c. Since distance is not a cardinal measure of utility here, distances in different directions cannot be compared.

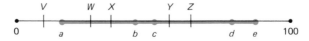

% of GNP Devoted to Government Budget

FIGURE 16.1 The Median-Voter Theorem: Single-Choice Dimension. Voters a through e are choosing, by majority rule, among proposals V through Z for size of government budget. The range $\overline{ae}$ is Pareto-optimal. Regardless of the agenda, the ultimate winner will be either X or Y (the proposals lying on either side of the median voter's preferred position c), depending upon which of the two the median voter prefers.

If we make the more general assumption that each and every possible budget from 0 to 100 percent is an option offered the voters, we obtain a more precise result: the final outcome will be exactly at the ideal position of the median voter. In either case the outcome will be in the Pareto-optimal region. Finally, since the median voter's choice will defeat each and every alternative proposal, there can be no cycling.

> *THE MEDIAN-VOTER THEOREM:* In majority-rule voting upon a single issue, if voters always prefer proposals that are nearer over those farther from their ideal positions in any given direction, a unique equilibrium will exist regardless of the agenda. (There will be no cycling.) Furthermore, the outcome must be in the Pareto-efficient region. If there is a continuum of options, the result will be exactly at the ideal position of the median voter. With a finite number of options, the outcome will be whichever of the two proposals on either side of the median position that is preferred by the median voter.

Why did we not have cycling here? The reason is the condition known as *single-peaked preferences*: that each voter always prefers an option nearer his or her ideal position. (It would violate single-peakedness if, for example, a voter for whom the ideal budget was 25 percent of GNP nevertheless prefers 60 percent to 50 percent.) Single-peakedness seems reasonable to assume here, though not necessarily so in all circumstances. Where it holds, we can safely conclude there will be no cycling.

EXAMPLE 16.3
The Median-Voter Theorem in Professional Football

Before 1982, professional football players in the United States negotiated their salaries individually with the team managements of the National Football League (NFL). After a long strike, the National Football League Players Association (NFLPA) succeeded in achieving a contract with the NFL that provided for a salary schedule placing considerable weight upon years of playing experience in the league. Since the NFLPA was a democratic organization operating upon the principle of majority rule, it might be expected that the interests of the median voters—in this case, players with the median number of years of experience—would tend to be favored by the NFLPA. A study by Michael D. White, which estimated the expected player gains on the basis of the new contract provisions, indicated that this did indeed occur. In the NFL, the median experience was four years of play. As the table shows, while all classes of players were estimated to gain over the life of the contract, those with four years of experience were on average the biggest gainers.

Predicted Gains over Life of Contract

Experience (yr)	Gain (%)
1	9.0
2	36.3
3	63.5

Experience (yr)	Gain (%)
4	107.4
5	88.1
6	85.4
7	82.7
8	80.0
9	77.3
10	74.6
11	71.9
12	69.2

Source: Adapted from Michael D. White, "Self-Interest Redistribution and the National Football League Players Association," *Economic Inquiry,* v. 24 (Oct. 1986), p. 677.

COMMENT: The data suggest that, moving away from the median experience in either direction, more senior players tended to do better in comparison with junior players. This is understandable in terms of political influence. Very junior players are much less likely to have gained the friends and knowhow needed for carrying a lot of weight in a political process.

Continuing to assume single-peaked preferences, now consider Figure 16.2. Here there are three voters a, b, c facing *two* issues (say, size of the government budget and number of immigrants to be admitted) that are bundled together for simultaneous choice.[3] For example, political candidates might run on platforms representing combined policy positions on the two issues. The *Pareto-optimal set* is the roughly triangular area connecting the three ideal points a, b, c. The ab boundary of the triangle goes through the mutual tangencies of the (approximately circular) indifference curves of individuals a and b, and similarly for the other boundaries of the triangle.[4]

Point X here represents any arbitrarily selected option within the efficient abc region. The different voters' indifference curves through any point like X necessarily intersect so as to determine three shaded petal-shaped areas. These areas represent policy options that can command a 2:1 majority vote over X. (For example, the petal at the upper left is the policy region that voters a and b both prefer to X.) Since such a petal diagram can be constructed for any point X, *cycling is inevitable* when every point in the diagram is a possible option. However, if there are only a finite number of alternatives, cycling is possible but not inevitable. For

[3] The discussion that follows is based upon Gordon Tullock, *Toward a Mathematics of Politics* (Ann Arbor: University of Michigan Press, 1967), Chaps. 2, 3.

[4] The indifference curves are only approximately circular, since we are not assuming that distance is a cardinal measure for *scaling* utility independent of direction. If distance were a cardinal measure, everyone's indifference curves would be exactly circular around the ideal point, and the Pareto-optimal region abc would be exactly triangular.

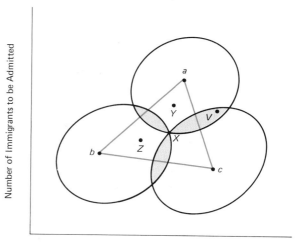

FIGURE 16.2 The Median-Voter Theorem: Two Choice Dimensions. There are three voters with respective ideal two-dimensional positions *a, b, c*. The approximately triangular region *abc* is the Pareto-optimal set, whose boundaries are the mutual-tangency points of the (roughly circular) indifference curves. For any point like *X* within *abc*, there are three petal-shaped areas. Each of these areas is a set of proposals that can command a 2:1 majority over *X*, so cycling is inevitable if all possible positions are in contention. Furthermore, the petal-shaped regions include points like *V* that are outside the Pareto-optimal set. But if *X, Y, Z* are the only alternatives offered the voters, *X* is a noncycling equilibrium.

example, if the only options were *X, Y, Z* as in the diagram, there is no cycling: *X* would defeat each of the others in majority voting and so be the winner regardless of the agenda. Finally, notice that even a non-Pareto-optimal point (like *V*) can sometimes command a majority over a Pareto-optimal point (like *X*). In short, the rather nice results obtained for single-issue majority voting seem to disappear when two or more issues are packaged together.

> *PROPOSITION:* Even with single-peaked preferences, when three voters face two issues and there is a continuum of options, cycling is inevitable. With a finite set of options, cycling is possible but need not always occur. In either case, outcomes outside the Pareto-optimal region may command a majority against efficient policies within the region.

Of the many possible ways of extending the analysis, one result is of particular interest: the Median-Voter Theorem does tend to hold, after all, even when issues are packaged together—*provided that the number of voters is very large.* In Figure 16.3 the rectangle represents a continuum of options in two dimensions. But now assume there are an infinite number of voters, and for simplicity let their ideal points be distributed uniformly over the entire rectangle. (Then the Pareto-optimal region is the entire rectangle, since no one position is *unanimously* preferred to any other.) Again for simplicity, suppose now that distance can serve as a "cardinal" scale for ranking options. These assumptions lead to an exceedingly strong and simple result: *Any option closer to the midpoint will defeat any farther away.* It follows that the median voter's ideal point, which is the midpoint, will win a majority over any other outcome whatsoever. The reason is clear from the diagram. The portion of the box to the southwest of the dashed line *KK* represents the fraction of the voters who will vote for *M* as against some alternative like *T*. Evidently, no matter where *T* lies away from *M*, a majority of the population will choose *M* over *T*.

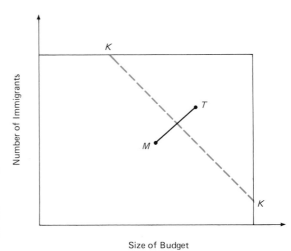

FIGURE 16.3 The Median-Voter Theorem: Two Choice Dimensions, Many Voters. There are an infinite number of voters, with ideal points distributed evenly over the rectangle of two-dimensional options. If distance is a "cardinal" scale of preference, any proposal closer to the midpoint M will defeat one like T that is farther away.

Size of Budget

16.A.5 □ An Application of the Median-Voter Theorem: Income Redistribution through Government

Modern governments engage in a great deal of income redistribution from the rich to the poor. According to U.S. data, for example, in 1976 the lowest 20 percent of families initially received only 0.3 percent of the national total of income, but after redistribution through taxes and transfers their share rose to 7.2 percent.[5]

The Median-Voter Theorem has certain implications for the redistribution process. Assume for simplicity that all redistribution takes place by taxing away a certain percent of the income of a population fraction at the top end, and giving it to a fraction at the low end. There will then be three population groups: the top fraction T who are taxed, the bottom fraction B who benefit, and a neutral middle fraction N who are neither taxed nor benefited. Assuming self-interested behavior, the median voter will want the beneficiary group B to include just 50 percent of the population: himself, and everyone below him on the income scale. So he will set $B = .5$. The question at issue remains, what division between the T and the N groups will the median voter prefer?

At first sight the problem may seem trivial. At any given tax rate (for example, if the redistributive tax takes away one-fifth of the income earned by the fraction T in the taxed group), surely the benefit to the median voter is greatest when *all* of the 50 percent of the people above him, rather than any smaller fraction, are taxed. However, this does not allow for the cost side of the process. Income redistribution requires taxation that will burden the economy in a number of ways tending to reduce the median voter's own income. For example, members of the taxed group are likely to shift toward retaining more of their resources for nontaxable reservation uses rather than for taxable market employment; the conse-

[5] Edgar K. Browning and Jacquelene M. Browning, *Public Finance and the Price System* (New York: Macmillan, 1979), pp. 203–205.

quent loss of some of the mutual gains from trade would tend to reduce the income of everyone including the median voter.

In Figure 16.4 the population is assumed to be ranked from the highest income at the left to the lowest at the right. The median voter's redistribution decision will be to select a fraction T (between 0 and .5) to be taxed. In the upper panel the solid curves picture the median voter's Total Benefit (TB_1), and Total Cost (TC) as functions of the fraction T. As the curves are drawn, the Total Benefit to the median voter remains considerably higher than the Total Cost even as the taxed fraction approaches 50 percent. However, the most advantageous choice for the median voter is where *Marginal* Benefit equals *Marginal* Cost. As shown in the lower panel, the optimal fraction, T_1, is well short of 50 percent.

This analysis has a possibly surprising implication. Suppose the income distribution had been somewhat less unequal to begin with. This would clearly reduce the *Total* Benefit of redistributive taxation to the median voter. So it might seem that lesser initial inequality would always tend to reduce the extent of redistributive taxation. But that is not the case here! While the new TB_2 curve (that

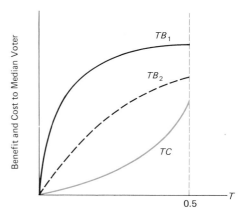

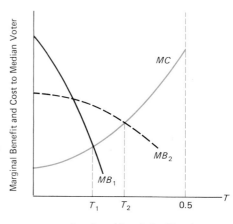

FIGURE 16.4 **Redistribution and the Median Voter.** The upper panel shows the Total Benefit (*TB*) and the Total Cost (*TC*) of redistributive taxation to the median voter, while the lower panel shows the corresponding Marginal Benefit (*MB*) and Marginal Cost (*MC*). In the initial situation, the intersection of MB_1 with MC leads the median voter to favor taxing the fraction $T_1 < .5$ of the population at the upper end of the income distribution. With greater initial equality of income, TB_2 is everywhere lower than TB_1, but over part of the range MB_2 *may* be higher than MB_1. If so, paradoxically, greater initial equality may lead to more redistributive taxation, as in this case where $T_2 > T_1$.

would apply for a lesser degree of initial income inequality) is indeed everywhere lower than TB_1, the *marginal* comparison is quite different. The dashed MB_2 curve is lower than MB_1 to begin with, but it has a generally flatter slope. The reason is that with lesser inequality, the taxable income serving as the source for redistribution does not fall off so sharply in moving from any given percentile to the next lower percentile of the population. Consequently, it may easily happen that MB_2 cuts through MB_1 so as to remain higher in the relevant range. When this is the case, as the initial distribution becomes less unequal the median voter will want to tax a *larger* rather than a smaller proportion of the population fraction above him on the income scale ($T_2 > T_1$).

EXAMPLE 16.4
Redistributive Taxation

In recent years increasing before-tax income equality and increasing redistributive taxation have gone hand in hand. This is surprising since, one's first impression would be, greater initial income equality ought to reduce the political pressures for redistributive taxation. However, our discussion of the Median-Voter Theorem showed that greater equality could conceivably lead to increased redistributive taxation. Taking an even stronger position, the economist Sam Peltzman has contended that greater initial equality would *generally* increase the political pressure in favor of egalitarian redistribution.

The data tabulated here illustrate some of the evidence brought to bear by Peltzman. In the first column countries are ranked by income equality (1 representing the most equal distribution); in the second column they are ranked by the percentage increase in government spending (assumed to be largely for redistributive purposes) between 1953–54 and 1973–74. While the correlation of the columns is not extremely strong either way, if anything there is a positive association between income equality and increasing redistribution.

COMMENT: The accuracy, comparability, and relevance of the data here may be subject to challenge. For example, different researchers have arrived at drastically different rankings of countries by income equality. And not all government expenditures are for redistribution, nor is *growth* of government the same as *size* of government. So the evidence as to the association of equality and redistribution is not fully convincing either way.

Countries Ranked by Income Equality and Growth of Government

Country	Income equality*	Growth of government†
Australia	1	8
Denmark	2	1
United Kingdom	3	7
Sweden	4	2
Germany	5.5	12
Norway	5.5	3
Canada	7	6
Belgium	8	5

Country	Income equality*	Growth of government†
United States	9	11
Austria	10	10
Netherlands	11	4
Finland	12	9
France	13	14
Japan	14	13

Source: Sam Peltzman, "The Growth of Government," *Journal of Law and Economics,* v. 23 (Oct. 1980).

*Peltzman, p. 261, column of Table 11 showing "Lydall" data.

†Peltzman, p. 260, computed from last column of Table 10.

16.B
VOLUNTARY PROVISION OF PUBLIC GOODS

The previous chapter showed that public goods like lighthouses, television broadcasts, or even community defense could in principle be supplied on the market. If this is to occur, however, suppliers must be able to exclude nonpayers. In the case of television, for example, broadcasts may be scrambled. But what if exclusion of nonpayers is impossible? Even so, to some extent public goods may be supplied by self-interested individuals on a strictly voluntary basis outside the market. The amount of the public good voluntarily offered would of course be less than if it were possible to exclude nonpayers, the reason being the free-rider problem. No one is eager to incur private costs in producing a public good; everyone is motivated to free-ride, to let others pick up the tab. Then, the question is, under what circumstances and to what extent will individuals be willing to supply any of the public good at all?

Two important propositions will be demonstrated here:

PROPOSITION 1: Wealthy individuals tend to provide *disproportionately* more of the public good.

PROPOSITION 2: As community size increases, provision of the public good will grow but much less than in proportion to population size.

Why would a self-interested individual ever voluntarily supply any of a public good without payment? Two factors are involved: (1) The individual wants to provide some for his *own* consumption. (2) As others supply him with "free" amounts of the public good he becomes in effect wealthier, which tends to make him want even more of the public good.

Let us return to Robinson Crusoe choosing between a private good B (bananas) and a public good W (wood) shared with Friday. In Figure 16.5, at Robinson's initial endowment position E° he has $\overline{b}$ of the private good and zero of the public good. His Production-Possibility Curve (PPC) is $E^\circ K^\circ$. Evidently, if he

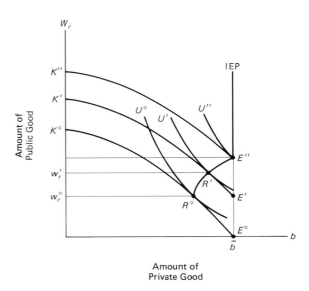

FIGURE 16.5 **Choice between Private Good and Public Good.** In Friday's absence Robinson's endowment position is $E°$, where he has zero of the public good W and the amount $\bar{b}$ of the private good B. His Production-Possibility Curve is $E°K°$, and his productive-consumptive optimum is $R°$. If Friday provides any W, Robinson's endowment position shifts upward by the same amount. As a function of Friday's provision, Robinson's optimum positions trace out an Income Expansion Path IEP. If B and W are both normal goods for him, Robinson's IEP curve will have a positive slope, becoming vertical when the limiting quantity $\bar{b}$ is reached.

were alone on the island the productive-consumptive solution would be $R°$, where he is providing himself with the amount $w_r°$ of W. For the sake of the argument, imagine that Friday produces (solely for *his* own consumption) an amount of W equal to the vertical distance between $E°$ and E'. Robinson is then richer by that amount; in effect, his endowment position in the diagram shifts upward from $E°$ to E'. Since Robinson's productive opportunities are unaffected, his PPC curve also shifts upward to become $E'K'$. The new optimum is R'. Since (as we normally assume) both B and W are superior goods for him, Robinson will end up *consuming* more of both.

However, and this is a crucial point, thanks to being able to free-ride on Friday's production, Robinson can now *consume more* of the public good while *producing less*. And in fact he will want to do exactly that. Being in effect richer owing to Friday's contribution, he will normally want to consume more of both B and W. But without reducing his own production of W he could not provide himself with any more of the private good B.

As we consider all possible amounts that Friday might supply, Robinson's optimum solutions trace out an Income Expansion Path (IEP) in the diagram. Eventually, when Friday is providing an amount of the public good equivalent to the distance $E'' - E°$, Robinson's IEP hits the barrier formed by the vertical line through $\bar{b}$. Beyond this point Friday is providing the public good so amply that Robinson would really like to trade in some of W in order to be able to consume even more of B—but of course that is impossible.

Using the data summarized by the Income Expansion Path, we can construct in Figure 16.6 Robinson's *Reaction Curve RC_r*, showing how he will adjust his produced quantity of the public good in response to whatever W Friday has provided. (Compare the duopolists' Reaction Curves in Chapter 10.) Note that RC_r is steeper than the dashed 135° line. This indicates that, as Friday increases his production of W by one unit, Robinson will cut back his own production but *by less than 1:1*. Friday would also have a Reaction Curve RC_f, which by similar reasoning will be flatter than the 135° line (owing to the reversal of the axes).

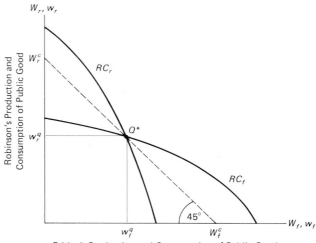

FIGURE 16.6 Cournot Solution for Supply of Public Good. Robinson's Reaction Curve RC_r shows the quantity of the public good W that he will produce for any given amount provided by Friday. Similarly, RC_f is Friday's Reaction Curve. The intersection Q^* shows the respective production quantities for the public good, w_r^q and w_f^q. The consumption quantities are the same for each, being the sum $W_r^c = W_f^c = w_r^q + w_f^q$—shown geometrically as the intercepts along the axes of the 135° line through Q^*.

Friday's Production and Consumption of Public Good

The *Cournot solution* (see Chapter 10) is point Q^* at the intersection of the two Reaction Curves. Here each person is satisfied with his own production decision, given the decision made by the other. The location of Q^* determines the respective production quantities w_r^q and w_f^q along the axes. What of the *consumption* quantities? Each individual is in a position to consume the *sum* $w_r^q + w_f^q$ of the amounts produced. These are found by the intercepts at the axes of the 135° line drawn through Q^*. These consumption magnitudes W_r^c and W_f^c are necessarily equal to each other, as well as to the sum of the produced quantities.

Let us now consider Proposition 1 above. As Robinson becomes wealthier he would have more resources and so a bigger $\bar{b}$ endowment in Figure 16.5. Then R° would shift northeast, so he would produce more of the public good just for his own use. But this would provide Friday with even more of a "free" gift of W, so Friday would produce less. In Figure 16.6 Robinson's Reaction Curve RC_r would shift upward, so Q^* would shift to the northwest. Thus a richer individual will end up providing *disproportionately* more of the public good.

EXAMPLE 16.5
The Economics of Alliance

An *alliance* between independent countries is generally undertaken in the interests of mutual defense. But defense is a kind of public good for a group of allied nations. If your ally destroys an enemy's bombers, that reduces the threat to your nation as well. So each ally is tempted to free-ride on the efforts of the others. However, the larger nations are not in a position to free-ride to nearly the same degree as the smaller ones.

A study of the North Atlantic Treaty Organization (NATO) defense expenditures in 1964 verified the differential expenditures of larger and smaller participants. The table compares the rankings of NATO nations as to size (measured by GNP) and as to proportion of budget devoted to defense expenditures. The larger and wealthier nations evidently contributed proportionately more. (The most conspicuous exception, Portugal, is explainable on other grounds. That nation, while tiny in GNP, supported a large defense budget because of its colonial commitments in Africa rather than its participation in NATO.)

NATO Statistics

	GNP, 1964		DEFENSE BUDGET AS PERCENTAGE OF GNP	
	$ Billion	Rank	Percent	Rank
United States	569.03	1	9.0	1
Germany	88.87	2	5.5	6
United Kingdom	79.46	3	7.0	3
France	73.40	4	6.7	4
Italy	43.63	5	4.1	10
Canada	38.14	6	4.4	8
Netherlands	15.00	7	4.9	7
Belgium	13.43	8	3.7	12
Denmark	7.73	9	3.3	13
Turkey	6.69	10	5.8	5
Norway	5.64	11	3.9	11
Greece	4.31	12	4.2	9
Portugal	2.88	13	7.7	2
Luxembourg	0.53	14	1.7	14

Source: M. Olson, Jr., and R. Zeckauser, "An Economic Theory of Alliances," *Review of Economics and Statistics*, v. 48 (Aug. 1966), p. 267.

Exercise 16.1: Suppose Robinson's preferences lead to an Income Expansion Path IEP (in the region before the vertical barrier is reached in Figure 16.5) given by the equation $W_r^c = 2b_r$. His Production-Possibility Curve equation is $W_r^c + b_r = \bar{b}_r + w_f^q$. (This equation would correspond to a straight-line PPC in Figure 16.5, and notice that it shifts upward as Friday's production w_f^q increases.) Friday is identical to Robinson except for a difference in endowments: $\bar{b}_r = 1800$ while $\bar{b}_f = 900$. Find: (a) the Reaction Curves, (b) the amounts of the public good produced by each, and (c) the consumptive solution.

Answer: (a) Substituting from Robinson's IEP into his PPC equation leads to: $W_r^c + 1/2(W_r^c) = 1800 + w_f^q$, or $W_r^c = 1200 + 2/3(w_f^q)$. But $W_r^c = w_r^q + w_f^q$, and so $w_r^q = 1200 - 1/3(w_f^q)$. This is the equation for Robinson's Reaction Curve. (Notice that Robinson cuts back his production of W by 1/3 of a unit for each additional unit provided by Friday.) Similarly, the RC_f equation is: $w_f^q = 600 - 1/3(w_r^q)$. (b) Solving the Reaction Curve equations simultaneously leads to the results $w_r^q = 1125$ and $w_f^q = 225$. (Thus, as contended in Proposition 1, Robinson is providing a disproportionately larger amount of the public good.) (c) The reader should verify that *both* Robinson and Friday consume 1350 of W and 675 of B.

Let us turn now to Proposition 2. An intuitive explanation is as follows. Suppose a third person, call her Saturday, joins Robinson and Friday. We can then think of Robinson's Reaction Curve RC_r in Figure 16.6 as representing his reaction to the *combined* production of Friday and Saturday scaled on the horizontal axis. This combined production would surely always be greater than Friday would have produced alone (since Friday will cut back by less than 1:1 in response to any additional units of the public good that are provided by Saturday). Consequently, the combined Friday + Saturday RC curve would represent a shift to the right in comparison with the previous RC_f curve in the diagram, so that the intersection point Q^* must move to the southeast. Thus, although *total* provision of the public good will increase with community size, as new members enter, each of the original citizens will somewhat scale back his or her own individual production.

A third proposition follows directly from the preceding analysis.

PROPOSITION 3: As community size increases, although production rises there will be *increasing underprovision* (shortfall of production of the public good in comparison with the Pareto-efficient amount).

The condition of efficiency for a community of two individuals, as derived in the previous chapter, can be written:

$$(16.1) \qquad MC_r = MC_f = MV_r + MV_f$$

That is, each individual should produce to the point where his or her Marginal Cost equals the *sum* of the marginal values. As the number of individuals forming the community grows, the summation on the right grows accordingly. Consequently, to achieve efficiency *each and every producer should be increasing his or her production* of the public good. But, we have just seen, each individual producer would in fact be cutting back production. Hence the shortfall increases, and indeed at an increasing rate, as community size grows.

Exercise 16.2: Starting with the community of the previous exercise, imagine that the new arrival, Saturday, has exactly the same preferences and endowment as Friday. Compare with the previous result.

Answer: All three individuals now have the same IEP curve $W_i^c = 2b_i$ as before. Their PPC curves now become:

$$\text{(Robinson)} \quad W_r^c + b_r = 1800 + w_f^q + w_s^q$$

$$\text{(Friday)} \quad W_f^c + b_f = 900 + w_r^q + w_s^q$$

$$\text{(Saturday)} \quad W_s^c + b_s = 900 + w_r^q + w_f^q$$

Substituting from the respective IEP equations:

$$W_r^c = 1200 + 2/3(w_f^q + w_s^q)$$

$$W_f^c = 600 + 2/3(w_r^q + w_s^q)$$

$$W_s^c = 600 + 2/3(w_r^q + w_f^q)$$

Since all three consumed quantities on the left of these equations must be equal to one another and to the *sum* of the three produced quantities, we obtain:

$$w_r^q = 1200 - 1/3(w_f^q + w_s^q)$$

$$w_f^q = 600 - 1/3(w_r^q + w_s^q)$$

$$w_s^q = 600 - 1/3(w_r^q + w_f^q)$$

These can be solved simultaneously to yield the produced amounts of the public good:

$$w_r^q = 1080, \qquad w_f^q = 180, \text{ and} \qquad w_s^q = 180$$

The total of W produced is 1440. This is only a little larger than the previous two-person total of 1350 units, since both Robinson and Friday now have cut back in response to Saturday's production. All three individuals now consume 1440 of W and 720 of B.

To some extent, therefore, public goods can be provided without either markets or government. NATO may be performing adequately, for example, without being a super-government capable of coercing its members. But, we have seen, there will be a very considerable shortfall from the ideal, increasingly so as community size grows. So, the larger the population, the stronger is the case for coercive government provision of the public good. That is, the government would provide the good and impose the corresponding tax burden upon the citizens. In a public-choice state, this provision and burden would in effect have been chosen by the citizens collectively through some arrangement like majority-rule voting.

The difference between the effectiveness of large and small groups in overcoming the free-rider problem, so as to achieve collective ends, has an important political implication. Members of a compact "special interest" (for example, businesspeople and workers in a particular industry) are few in number compared to the population at large. Nevertheless, they are often successful in achieving political favors like tariffs or subsidies at the expense of the general consuming public. The reason is that the effective influence of the individual citizen-voter upon government is, for the various reasons outlined in Section A of this chapter, extremely weak. Filling the vacuum are "pressure groups," which are subcollectives of individuals interested in pushing particular policies or points of view upon the delegated representatives of the voters. Special interests have two factors on their side in forming pressure groups. First, their motivation is stronger. Since their financial interest is concentrated (as in the case of a tariff affecting a single industry), they gain far more from appropriate political action than any comparably sized group of the general public stands to lose, even though the *entire* public may suffer in the aggregate a much greater loss. Second, being few in number, they are more likely to contribute to and achieve what is for them (but not for the general community) a public good—advantages for their own pressure group.

EXAMPLE 16.6
Regulated Electricity Rates

Electricity, as a "natural monopoly," is now governmentally regulated throughout the United States. The problem of collective action suggests that *large* consumers of electricity will have an advantage over the multitude of *small* consumers of electricity in forming a pressure group to influence the political agencies responsible for regulating rates.

This hypothesis was tested by George Stigler and Claire Friedland, making use of data from earlier years when there were still a considerable number of unregulated states. Since it can be presumed that *industrial* users of electricity are relatively large in scale (and small in number) in comparison with *residential* users, the ratio of the residential price to the industrial price is a measure of the extent that large users are favored over small. This ratio alone is not a satisfactory criterion, however, since there may well be differences in the cost of service that would warrant some degree of rate inequality between industrial and residential users. But there is no obvious reason *for the ratio to differ as between regulated and unregulated states.*

Average Ratio $\dfrac{\textit{Residential Price}}{\textit{Industrial Price}}$ for Electricity

	1917	1937
Regulated states	1.616	2.459
Unregulated states	1.445	2.047

Source: G. J. Stigler and C. Friedland, "What Can Regulators Regulate? The Case of Electricity," *Journal of Law and Economics*, v. 5 (Oct. 1962), p. 9.

The data in the table show that the ratio was indeed substantially higher for the regulated states, consistent with the hypothesis that regulation works to the comparative advantage of large consumers over small consumers.

A related point is that since production is generally a *specialized* activity and consumption an *unspecialized* one, government interventions have historically tended to favor producers over consumers.[6] Because we are all *both* producers and consumers, it might be thought that the effects cancel out. But the political measures that favor producers (for example, permitting formation of a cartel) tend to be anticompetitive. This leads to a loss of economic efficiency, apart from possibly objectionable effects upon wealth distribution.

Of course, the political strength of "special-interest" groups is only one side of the picture. It is easier for a small specialized group to organize and bring its weight to bear, but it remains a group small in number. Landlords can organize *against* rent controls more effectively than tenants *for* them, but a politician cannot ignore the fact that there are many more tenant votes than landlord votes.

16.C
BUREAUCRACY

The bureaucracy consists of government personnel not responsible for *making* policy decisions but for *implementing* them. Supposedly impartial and neutral, bureaucrats are not subject to election or recall at the hands of the voters. It fol-

[6] The political success of one important type of "pro-consumer" intervention, residential rent control, is connected with the fact that consumers *are* somewhat specialized when it comes to housing. The single rental transaction typically accounts for a large fraction of consumer budgets. This concentration makes it worthwhile to bear the cost of forming a pressure group aimed at getting the government rather than the market to set the level of rents.

lows that if bureaucrats really do determine the actual outcomes of decisions, then the ability of citizens to achieve their desires through the political mechanism (i.e., through their control over elected delegates) is even weaker than has previously been indicated. For all practical purposes, implementation *is* the actual decision. So the bureaucracy surely does have substantial power.

What are the interests of the bureaucracy? Apart from high wages for easy work, a critical aim is *security of tenure*. This not only keeps jobs safe, but provides valued clout: a bureaucrat who could be easily fired would have to tread warily in dealing with elected delegates or with outside pressure groups. In modern times, the government bureaucracy has achieved extraordinary job security through civil-service regulations that forbid demotion or dismissal except "for cause." While civil-service reform is in many respects preferable to the spoils system, it has nevertheless changed the balance of power within government in favor of the bureaucrats.

In any government agency, a natural aim of the officeholders is *agency growth*. All those involved generally benefit by building empires, by increasing the resources under their control. According to "Parkinson's Law,"[7] no matter how much the business of a governmental unit may fall off, the number of officials will still increase. Let the Royal Navy diminish in size, the Admiralty bureaucracy will grow. Let the colonies declare their independence, Her Majesty's Colonial Office in London will continue to expand. And in the United States the Department of Agriculture will go on swelling in budget and employment even while the number of farmers shrinks.

[7] C. Northcote Parkinson, *Parkinson's Law* (Boston: Houghton Mifflin, 1957).

EXAMPLE 16.7
Government Wages

An obvious way in which bureaucrats might employ their political power, if they have any, is to obtain higher pay for less work.

A study by Steven Benti[a] compared wages of U.S. federal government employees with those in the private sector. Census data from the 1982 Current Population Survey indicated that, in comparison with private employment, men earn about 33 percent more in the federal sector and women about 39 percent more. However, a substantial portion of this difference may be accounted for by variables such as the special skills and educational background required for federal jobs. On the other hand, federal employment also offers more favorable fringe benefits and employment conditions. Taking these factors into account, Benti concluded that the federal government could attract and retain a labor force of the existing size and quality at average wages of about 16 percent less for men and 42 percent less for women.

COMMENT: These data indicate, as common sense would already have suggested, that bureaucrats' strategic position in government does give them considerable influence over issues of importance to them, notably their own wages. The extra advantage of women in federal employment might be regarded as evidence that the federal

16.D
POLITICAL CONFLICT

In the hypothetical model of the public-choice state, government serves only as the instrument through which citizens make collective decisions. We have noticed certain imperfections of this process: elected delegates may not represent the desires of constituents, there is a problem of majority versus minority rights, and so on. But what is a much more drastic real-world "imperfection," rulers may not be serving the population at all. The goal of a government might be to fleece and rob its subjects, or perhaps to use them as slaves or cannon fodder. What might be called the *exploitation state* is at least as important historically as the public-choice state.

Let us now go to the opposite extreme and develop the idea that *conflict* rather than "public choice" is the essence of politics. Conflict arises in many contexts: among nations, between rulers and subjects within nations, between criminals and victims, and so forth. It is also useful sometimes to think of activities like lawsuits or industrial strikes and lockouts as instances of conflict, even though bodily violence may not be involved. Conflict may be said to occur when each party to an interaction is willing to incur costs in order to impose his will upon the opponent—rather than come to a compromise settlement. From one point of view, conflict is "an agreement to disagree." It is also in a way an educational process: each contender tries to convince the other that he is the one better able to take and to deliver punishment.

16.D.1   □ Elements of Conflict

Among the important sources of conflict are:

1. *Antipathy*: One party may be willing, from hatred or envy, to incur costs in seeking to injure the other. An example was Hitler's war against the Jews.
2. *Rivalry*: If resources are too scarce to meet the requirements of both parties, one or the other may try to improve his position through aggression. While antipathy leads to hot emotion-laden conflict, rivalry may be deadly yet quite cool. ("I got nothing against you, Wyatt Earp, but this town ain't big enough for the two of us.")
3. *Overconfidence*: The stronger the belief in one's own chances of winning the battle, the less the willingness to come to a compromise settlement.
4. *Nonenforceability of agreements*: Sometimes both parties might be happy to come to a compromise settlement. But, if there is no way to prevent violation of any agreement made, there is no point in compromise.

In Panel (a) of Figure 16.7 the curve II' (like the similar curve in Figure 15.1 of the preceding chapter) shows the Social Opportunity Frontier—the income combinations attainable by two decision-makers.[8] We may think of the two sides either as individuals or as groups: let us call them the Blues and the Grays. And "income" may stand for territory, power, or ability to purchase consumption goods.

Suppose the Blues believe that a conflict would leave them with an income of I_B^o. Let I_G^o be the corresponding outcome anticipated by the Grays. Then, evidently, the roughly triangular area MSS' represents a "region of mutual advantage" wherein both parties can gain by peaceful compromise—assuming that a compromise settlement would be enforceable. An *efficient* solution would of course lie somewhere in the range SS' along the opportunity frontier.

Panel (b) represents a contrasting situation where each party has become much more *confident* in the event of a clash. Here there is no region of mutual advantage, so no compromise settlement is possible. A battle is inevitable since *both* contenders expect to do better by fighting than by settling. (Of course, one or the other must be overoptimistic about its chances of winning the struggle, or quite possibly both are.)

After having experienced the test of battle, the parties will very likely learn the hard truth about their limited strength. This may not lead immediately to a peaceful settlement, however. While the loser will become more willing to compromise, the winner may become less willing. Another factor that more clearly leads to eventual settlement is exhaustion of resources. As both sides become

[8] The analysis here is based in part upon Donald Wittman, "How a War Ends," *Journal of Conflict Resolution*, v. 23 (Dec. 1979) and David Friedman, "Many, Few, One: Social Harmony and the Shrunken Choice Set," *American Economic Review*, v. 70 (Mar. 1980).

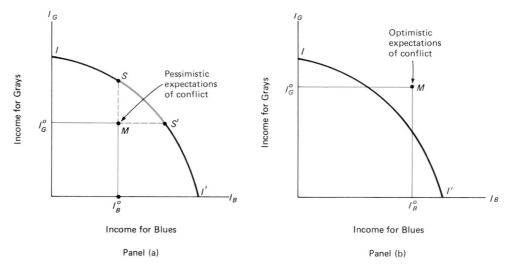

FIGURE 16.7 **Confidence and Conflict.**   In Panel (a) the Blues anticipate that in the event of conflict their benefit, *on average*, will be equivalent to an income of I_B^o. The Grays similarly anticipate I_G^o. There is a region of mutual advantage MSS' achievable by a compromise agreement; the efficient solutions lie along the range SS'. In Panel (b) there is no possibility of a compromise solution.

poorer, devoting resources to war will grow more and more painful, while there may be less and less left to gain from victory.

Figure 16.7 highlights the role of *confidence* as a source of conflict. Figure 16.8 illustrates the effect of *rivalry*. Panel (a) represents a strongly rivalrous situation; the shape of the II' curve shows that the interests of the two parties are sharply opposed. Here even relatively pessimistic anticipations I_B^o and I_G^o as to the outcome of a conflict may not lead to any compromise settlement. Panel (b) represents the opposite situation, where the two parties' interests are strongly complementary—each is highly useful to the other. Accordingly, even if each contender is quite optimistic about his chances in the event of conflict, a compromise settlement might still be preferred by both.

Finally, Figure 16.9 illustrates the role of antipathy (and its opposite, sympathy). In Panel (a) the two parties are antipathetic. For the Blues, Gray income I_G is a *bad* as indicated by the positively sloping indifference curve U_B^o through point M—and similarly for the Grays. The effect is to diminish the size of MSS', the region of mutual advantage, and make peaceful settlement less probable. In Panel (b) on the other hand, the parties are *sympathetic* to each other, making peaceful settlement more likely.

If agreements are not *enforceable*, parties who otherwise could profit from cooperation may not be able to reach a settlement. There are two main ways of getting people to live up to agreements. The first is through a neutral umpire. A judicial system to enforce private contracts is one of the main services that a government can provide. Second, some contracts may be *self-enforcing*. Two parties can so tie themselves to each other that it does not pay either to defect. Usually this happens when there is a profitable continuing relationship between them. If firm A has agreed to deliver materials to firm B, one reason for A not to cheat on quantity or quality—apart from the possibility of a lawsuit—may be the fear of permanently losing a valuable customer.

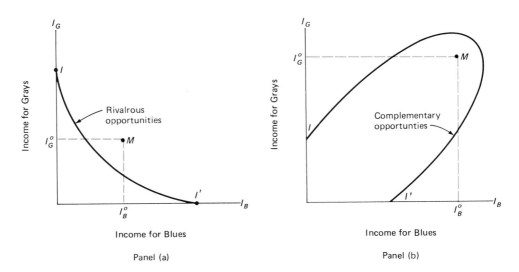

FIGURE 16.8 **Rivalry and Conflict.** In Panel (a) the two parties are strongly rivalrous, and a compromise settlement is unlikely. In Panel (b) their interests are highly complementary, making a compromise much easier to achieve.

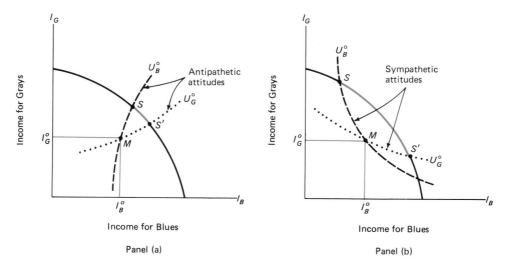

FIGURE 16.9 Antipathy and Conflict. In Panel (a) the parties are mutually antipathetic, which diminishes the region of mutual advantage *MSS'* and makes conflict more likely. In Panel (b) the parties are mutually sympathetic, making *MSS'* large and conflict therefore less likely.

Enforceability of agreements is a matter of degree. Even if a judicial system stands behind contracts, going to court is expensive and judges are not infallible. As for "self-enforcing" agreements, they will be adhered to only as long as violating them remains unprofitable. So anyone who has made a deal must always be looking over his shoulder at the possibility that the other side will not carry out its share of the bargain. Furthermore, if he himself is just on the edge of deciding to violate the agreement, fear that the other party may be about to do the same is likely to provide the decisive push.

The possible profitability of conflict raises very serious questions about the validity of Coase's Theorem (as discussed in the preceding chapter). That theorem says essentially that *all mutually advantageous agreements will be undertaken—* and, by implication, *adhered to.* We saw above that Coase's Theorem appeared to "prove too much" in suggesting that monopoly would not permanently exist, that individuals would voluntarily contract with one another so as to internalize all externalities, and so on. But what is much more drastic, the Coase Theorem is inconsistent with the persistence of war, crime, and politics! In fact, the Coase Theorem, along with Adam Smith's Invisible Hand, is valid only under very ideal conditions. Certain of these conditions were already mentioned in the preceding chapter: among them are well-defined property rights and absence of transaction costs. But more important, *individuals will be led by self-interest to serve others only to the extent that agreement appears, for each of them, to be more profitable than conflict.* Given the sources of conflict mentioned above—antipathy, rivalry, and overconfidence, plus the limited enforceability of compromise settlements—we can be quite sure that war, crime, and politics will be with us for a long time.

Economists have just barely begun to analyze conflict. We can expect future research to look into (1) the advantages of offensive versus defensive strategies, (2) the circumstances that sometimes keep conflict limited rather than total, (3) the "production function" that converts resource inputs into chances for victory, (4) the additional issues raised by three-sided or even more complex struggles, and (5) the extent to which political developments like the size of nations or the balance of influence among social classes are explainable by coercive strength. But enough has been said to indicate that the *economics of conflict* is just as important as the *economics of exchange and markets*.

EXAMPLE 16.8
Rationality and International Conflict

The political scientist Bruce Bueno de Mesquita explored the implications of assuming that international conflict was initiated only where doing so was rational. In effect, he asserted that each nation could be regarded as having a single utility function, which its leader maximized in making decisions about initiating conflict. Among the factors entering into this utility function, according to his analysis, were: (1) the relative strengths of the attacker and defender, (2) the significance to the attacker of changing the defender's policies by conflict or the threat thereof, and (3) the prospects and consequences of intervention by third parties.

Using data from 251 cases of conflict, Bueno de Mesquita classified them by degree of severity ranging from outright war to threats short of war. Within each category, the table indicates those which (on his calculations) yielded positive and negative utility to the initiators.

Expected Utility and Conflict Initiation

	Positive or Zero	Negative
Expected utility to initiator:		
Interstate wars	65	11
Interstate interventions	78	24
Interstate threats	50	23
Totals	193	58

Source: Calculated from Bruce Bueno de Mesquita, *The War Trap* (New Haven: Yale University Press, 1981), pp. 128–30.

Evidently, most of the time the initiator gained from conflict. Furthermore, the tendency toward positive expected utility increases with increased seriousness of the conflict (upper rows of the table). This is understandable, since a nation might well *threaten* to engage in conflict even at a disadvantage in utility terms, but it is less likely to actually go to war unless there is a gain from doing so.

COMMENT: The crucial problem here is how to measure a nation's utility from conflict. In terms of the elements to be counted on the positive side, Bueno de Mesquita emphasizes bringing about "policy changes" in the target country. This is sometimes, but perhaps not very often, the aim of war; direct conquest may be a more common aim. On the negative side, his categories omit the losses of life and treasure that most people would regard as the major costs of war.

*16.D.2 □ Conflict and Game Theory

As indicated in Chapter 10, various types of game payoff matrices can be used to distinguish the sometimes subtly different ways in which elements of co-operation and of conflict may be combined. Table 16.1 shows four such patterns where, as in Chapter 10, within each matrix the first number in each cell is the Row player's payoff and the second number is the Column player's.

TABLE 16.1

Payoff Matrices for Four Games

	LAND OR SEA	
	Land	Sea
Land	2, 1	1, 2
Sea	1, 2	2, 1

	PRISONERS' DILEMMA	
	Disarm	Arm
Disarm	3, 3	1, 4
Arm	4, 1	2, 2*

	HAWK-DOVE	
	Dove	Hawk
Dove	3, 3	2, 4*
Hawk	4, 2*	1, 1

	BATTLE OF THE SEXES	
	Patton	Montgomery
Patton	3, 2*	1, 1
Montgomery	1, 1	2, 3*

*Nash solution (see text).

The payoffs here are in rank-ordered form, meaning that for each player higher numbers represent *ordinally* preferred outcomes. (There may also be ties.) These ranking patterns are in fact what define the "families" of games known as Land or Sea, Prisoners' Dilemma, and so on. Any conclusions that can be drawn solely in terms of the ranked outcomes (i.e., in terms of an *ordinal* measure of benefit or utility to each player) will therefore apply to the entire corresponding "family" of games.

The Land or Sea matrix in the table corresponds to a duel for survival, a "this town ain't big enough for the two of us" situation. It is not, strictly speaking, a zero-sum game, since we cannot meaningfully sum up two parties' ordinal utilities. Nevertheless, this is the most rivalrous of the four cases.

In Prisoners' Dilemma the rivalry of interests is less total: there is more scope for mutual gain from agreement. An important example is an arms race between two powers, assuming that their preferences are as indicated in the table. Here the Disarm/Disarm strategy-pair (payoffs ranked 3 for each) is mutually preferred to Arm/Arm (payoffs ranked 2 for each). The parties should obviously agree on Disarm/Disarm, but if the agreement is not enforceable there are strong pressures leading them toward the Arm/Arm "trap."

*Marked sections, beginning with a single asterisk and ending with a double asterisk, may contain somewhat more difficult or advanced material and can be omitted without appreciable loss of continuity.

Hawk-Dove (sometimes called the game of "Chicken")[9] is another very important pattern of mixed conflict-cooperation incentives. The idea is that whichever party plays Hawk will win out over an opponent playing Dove—but Hawk-Hawk encounters will be extremely costly for both sides. This last point, the mutual desire to avoid the 1,1 payoffs at the lower-right cell, means that the Hawk-Dove pattern involves less intense rivalry than Prisoners' Dilemma (which in turn was less rivalrous then Land or Sea). Many kinds of *negotiation* situations correspond to Hawk-Dove: for example, negotiations aimed at avoiding industrial conflicts (strikes and lockouts) or legal conflicts (a court trial). Here the incentive for each side to be a tough bargainer (to play the Hawk strategy) is balanced by the fear that a mutually undesired conflict may ensue if both hang tough simultaneously.

The last matrix in the table—Battle of the Sexes[10]—represents the mildest rivalry of all. Here the two parties both desire to avoid the off-diagonal cells, the question at issue being which one is to reap the larger share of the mutual gain. This pattern commonly emerges in struggles within an alliance. One such instance occurred during World War II in the early Fall of 1944. After breaking out from the Normandy perimeter, American forces under General Patton were approaching the German border from eastern France while British troops in Belgium under Field Marshal Montgomery were nearing Germany from the north. The United States (the Column player) could have provided Patton with supplies for an attack in the south, while the British (the Row player) could have supplied Montgomery's attack in the north. Both agreed that it was better to concentrate the supplies and make only a single attack, but the Americans favored a drive by Patton while the British favored supplying Montgomery. In this case, the Allies eventually agreed on the attack by Montgomery.[11]

Game theory helps us describe different types of conflict situations, but can it tell us also what the *outcome* is likely to be? When will an efficient or conflict-minimizing result be achieved? Which party is likely to gain the advantage? The actual outcome will of course depend upon the "rules of the game" that apply. Two possible "rules of the game" are as follows: (1) *Sequential moves*: One party (say, Row) moves first, after which the Column player makes his or her choice in response.[12] (2) *Simultaneous moves*: Each player makes his or her decision in ignorance of the opponent's move (for example, a sealed-bid auction).

The solutions arrived at under rational play are summarized in Table 16.2. Under sequential-move rules, a discussion of one of the cases, Hawk-Dove, will suffice. Here the first mover (Row) will surely play Hawk (the lower row of the Hawk-Dove matrix in Table 16.1). Then the best that the second mover can do is to respond with Dove (the left-hand column). So the solution is the lower-left (*LL*) cell, with payoffs 4,2 that evidently favor the first mover. This outcome is also efficient, since no other is *unanimously* preferred to it.

---

[9] The traditional story has two teenagers racing their jalopies toward one another on a one-lane road. Whoever turns aside first is the chicken.

[10] The story here has a husband and wife going out for the evening. While they definitely want to be together, the wife prefers the opera while the husband prefers a boxing match.

[11] This turned out to be the wrong decision, which led to the disaster at Arnhem.

[12] The "entry-deterrence game" described in Chapter 10 was an example of a sequential-move situation.

TABLE 16.2
Equilibria For Four Different Payoff Matrices

	LAND OR SEA	PRISONERS' DILEMMA	HAWK-DOVE	BATTLE OF THE SEXES
Degree of Rivalry	Greatest	Large	Moderate	Small
Sequential-move game (Row moves first)				
Outcome (Payoff)	1, 2	2, 2	4, 2	3, 2
(Cells)	UR or LL	LR	LL	UL
Efficient?	Yes	No	Yes	Yes
Advantage to ?	Second-mover	Neither	First-mover	First-mover
Simultaneous-move game (symmetrical solutions with mixed strategies)				
Outcome (Payoff)	1.5, 1.5	2, 2	2.5, 2.5	1.67, 1.67
Probability mix	.5, .5	0, 1	.5, .5	.67, .33
Efficient?	Yes	No	No	No
Advantage to ?	Neither	Neither	Neither	Neither

Some points of interest about the various sequential-move solutions are:

1. Except for Prisoners' Dilemma, an efficient outcome is achieved in all cases. (But this is trivial under Land or Sea, where all four cells are efficient!)
2. For Land or Sea, the first mover (Row) does equally badly regardless of his or her choice.
3. The advantage lies with the second mover when the degree of rivalry is greatest (Land or Sea), tending to shift in favor of the first mover as the rivalry diminishes (Hawk-Dove and Battle of the Sexes).

Directing attention now to the *simultaneous-move* rules, the correct solution concept is not so easy to arrive at. What is best for Row to do may depend upon Column's move, but Column's best choice in turn may depend upon Row's move—so in general there is no strictly rational way of choosing. This impasse does not apply to Prisoners' Dilemma, however. Since Row in Prisoners' Dilemma does better choosing the less cooperative strategy *regardless* of the other's move, and similarly for Column, the inefficient outcome at the lower-right (*LR*) remains the solution for rational players.

In Chapter 10 the *Nash solution* was introduced and shown to be the game-theory equivalent of the "Cournot solution" in duopoly. Any strategy-pair such that neither party would want to unilaterally revise his or her choice is a Nash solution. The outcomes meeting this criterion are starred in Table 16.1. As can be seen, in Land or Sea none of the four cells is starred; in Prisoners' Dilemma only the single rational equilibrium is starred; in Hawk-Dove the two off-diagonal corners are starred; and in Battle of the Sexes, the two diagonal corners are starred. So it would appear that, in general, there are multiple Nash equilibria.

We can push matters further by making use of one additional consideration. In a simultaneous-move game both parties are in exactly the same situation. Consequently, it is reasonable to consider only those solutions that are entirely *symmet-*

rical—that is, where both players end up using the same strategies and receiving the same payoffs. To arrive at a symmetrical solution requires introducing another important game-theory concept: that of a *mixed strategy*. Take Land or Sea. Since under simultaneous play it is so difficult to choose, any player might instead toss a fair coin. If both players do this, the payoff to each will be 1.5 on average. The lower portion of Table 16.2 is constructed on the premise that mixed strategies are indeed used to obtain a symmetrical solution. (Except, of course, in Prisoners' Dilemma, where we do not need mixed strategies to find the single symmetrical Nash equilibrium.) In the Land or Sea game, with the numerical payoffs as shown a .5, .5 mixture is obviously best for each player. It turns out that, once again given the payoffs shown, .5, .5 is also best in Hawk-Dove.[13] But in Battle of the Sexes, each player should choose the strategy more favorable to himself or herself with 2/3 probability.[14]

Some points of interest concerning the simultaneous-move games are:

1. Since we have considered only symmetrical solutions, neither party ever gains any advantage over the other.

2. While efficient outcomes were achieved for the *sequential-move* game in the case of both Hawk-Dove and Battle of the Sexes, for the *simultaneous-move* game this is no longer the case. The reason is that, owing to the use of probability mixtures on both sides, there is now some positive chance of ending up at a mutually undesired outcome. Under Hawk-Dove, so as not to be exploited as a Dove each player has to be a tough Hawk negotiator a certain fraction of the time—and when both players are tough simultaneously, the 1,1 outcome will occur and so they both suffer. Under Battle of the Sexes, similarly, with mixed strategies there will be some positive probability that the players end up at one or the other of the two mutually undesired outcomes.

---

[13] Calculation of the optimal mixed strategy for Hawk-Dove proceeds as follows. When Column has chosen his best mixture, Row will be indifferent as between his two possible choices. For Row to be indifferent, Column must have chosen his p (probability of playing the first column) such that:

$$3p + 2(1 - p) = 4p + 1(1 - p)$$

The solution is $p = 1/2$. (*Note:* In making these calculations it has been assumed that the numbers in Table 16.1 are actual *cardinal* payoffs rather than only rankings. With the same rankings but different cardinal payoffs, the probability mix will change.) The payoff to Row can then be calculated from either of his strategies:

$$3(.5) + 2(.5) = 2.5$$

Of course, the payoff to Column will be the same.

[14] For the Battle of the Sexes matrix, Row will be indifferent if Column has chosen a p (probability of playing the first column) such that:

$$3p + 1(1 - p) = 1(p) + 2(1 - p)$$

The result is $p = 1/3$. Thus, Column will assign 2/3 weight to his second (right-hand) strategy. By a corresponding argument, Row will assign 2/3 weight to his first (upper) strategy. The payoff to Row can be calculated:

$$3(1/3) + 1(2/3) = 1.67$$

Again, the payoff to Column will be the same.

The theory of games is of course by no means limited to the rather elementary interactions so far examined. There are many important complications and extensions such as: (1) *repeated play*, where the parties do not engage in only a one-time interaction, as assumed here, but expect to be in contact with one another over a long period of time; (2) *conditional strategies*, where one or the other player can be in a position to make and execute threats or promises; (3) *multi-party games*, where not just two but three or more players are simultaneously contending with one another. Unfortunately, space does not permit exploring such topics in this text. **

GROWTH OF GOVERNMENT

Growth of government was discussed in Section 16.A, in connection with income redistribution. But there are many other important functions of government in modern economics, and it seems that almost all of these have been steadily growing in magnitude. Consider the defense function. As the technology of attack and destruction has improved so drastically (nuclear bombs, intercontinental missiles, etc.), the complexity and cost of defense have increased, and consequently the defense budget has increased as well. But suppose we entirely exclude the defense function of government. The scope and cost of government have risen enormously in the nondefense sector as well.

** End of marked section.

EXAMPLE 16.9
Growth of Government

Various stages in the expansion of the overall government sector in the United States are shown in the table.

Growth of Government in the United States

	TOTAL EXPENDITURES		NONDEFENSE EXPENDITURES	
DATE	$ Billions	Percentage of GNP	$ Billions	Percentage of GNP
1890	0.8	6.5	0.7	5.0
1902	1.5	7.3	1.2	5.8
1913	3.2	7.8	2.8	6.8
1922	9.3	12.6	7.9	10.7
1929	10.7	10.4	9.5	9.2
1940	17.6	17.6	15.5	15.5
1950	65.9	23.1	42.2	14.8
1960	151.3	29.9	102.4	20.2
1970	333.0	33.5	248.7	25.1
1980	958.7	36.4	809.2	30.7
1983	1350.9	40.9	1122.1	34.0

Source: Through 1980, R. A. Musgrave and P. B. Musgrave, *Public Finance in Theory and Practice* (New York: McGraw-Hill, 1973), p. 118. For later dates, calculated from The Tax Foundation, *Facts and Figures on Government Finance*, 23rd ed. (1986), Table A7.

As may be seen, government expenditures have more than kept up with the real growth of the economy and with the inflation of prices to constitute a steadily increasing fraction of GNP. While big jumps in expenditures have typically taken place in wartime, peacetime civilian expenditures have also grown steadily. In fact, in recent years the fraction of government expenditure accounted for by national defense has been shrinking; between 1960 and 1983 the defense share fell from around 32 to 17 percent.

Basically, there are two possible explanations for the expansion of government. The first gives primary weight to the *voluntarist* or public-choice aspect of political decision. In this view, government has grown in response to desires on the part of the community for those types of services that government can best provide. The second approach emphasizes, in contrast, *changes in the balance of political power* permitting certain organized groups on the political scene to increase their exploitation of others through expanded government.

Voluntaristic explanations might run in terms of some or all of the following points: (1) Public goods, in contrast with private goods, might have income elasticity greater than unity (see Chapter 5). In that case, as incomes have risen over time, citizen-voters have desired more of the public goods that government characteristically provides. (2) With increasing wealth and population, the limited geographical space we inhabit has become more and more crowded. In our daily lives we are therefore increasingly imposing *externalities* (see Chapter 15) upon one another—hence the need for more government control of activities that could have safely been left private in a less crowded society. (3) The technical efficiency of government may have grown relative to the private sector. Computers, for example, have made it possible to conduct enterprises efficiently on a much larger scale than previously. Government, as the largest-scale enterprise in society, may have gained in relative effectiveness.

Explanations that run in terms of exploitation and political power, on the other hand, might point to considerations like the following: (1) The government bureaucracy, as it grows in numbers, becomes an increasingly potent political force. Wars and defense crises that require gigantic budgetary expansions leave in their wake a mass of officeholders, with sufficient political clout to resist layoffs when the crises pass. (2) The *educated class* in the population (say, those with college degrees) has grown sharply. Educated persons are more inclined to achieve status and power through government rather than in business. Legislators, bureaucrats, and other important actors on the political scene are themselves members of the educated class and inclined to be responsive to its interests, especially as the educated are much more politically active than the population at large. (3) A related point is that the extraordinary and continuing advances in ability to communicate with large audiences—due to improvements in printing, the spread of literacy, and of course radio and television—have made it increasingly possible to weld large numbers of people into exploitative political movements and pressure groups.

The degree of truth in each of these points, and the comparative explanatory values of the public-choice versus exploitation approaches, remain unsettled problems in political economy.

Whereas market transactions are voluntary, the political sphere is characterized by coercive interactions. The individuals who comprise the government are able, with the ultimate backing of force, to dictate to the rest of us.

Two extreme models of government are the *public-choice state* and the *exploitation state*. The public-choice state is merely an instrument whereby citizen-consumers achieve their collective aims. The exploitation state, in contrast, is a government whose rulers are in conflict with their subjects, seeking only to extract resources from them.

In an ideally democratic public-choice state, competition for political leadership acts like competition in the marketplace. Just as competition for sales forces firms to satisfy consumers' desires, competition for office forces political parties to satisfy citizens' wishes.

Market competition has serious imperfections, but the imperfections of political competition are even more severe. Citizens vote only at relatively rare intervals; there are few political parties among which to choose (commonly, just two); and many issues are bundled together in the position of each candidate. Under majority rule, there is the very serious problem of adequate provision for minority desires. "Log-rolling" allows intense minority preferences on some issues to be exchanged for votes on other issues. In principle, log-rolling or even direct purchase of votes will lead to Pareto-optimal outcomes. Another source of imperfection is the fact that a voter has little motivation to incur the informational costs necessary to cast an intelligent ballot.

Majority rule also commonly leads to the paradox of *cycling*: proposal X may be favored by a majority over Y, Y over Z, but Z in turn over X. Where conditions rule out cycling, there is a strong tendency for the winning proposal to be the one favored by the *median voter*.

While public or collective goods can sometimes be provided through the market, as analyzed in Chapter 15, even in the absence of a market there may still be a certain amount of strictly voluntary provision. An entirely self-interested individual may be inclined to supply some of the public good, strictly for his or her own personal consumption. Since the good is thereby also made available to the rest of the community, there is a *free-rider problem*—each person is motivated to let the others bear the burden. Three propositions were shown to hold about voluntary private supply of public goods: (1) Wealthier individuals tend to provide disproportionately greater amounts. (2) Aggregate provision of the public good increases with community size, but in smaller proportion. (3) *Underprovision* of the public good, the shortfall of the aggregate amount voluntarily supplied in comparison with the Pareto-optimal quantity, grows rapidly as community size increases.

To overcome the free-rider problem, government may be called upon to provide public goods. Everyone might agree to a collective purchase when costs are to be shared via the tax system. But since it is costly to influence government policy, and the benefits are shared by many individuals, citizens face a similar free-rider problem in trying to get their way in a political system. Compact special interests have the advantage in forming pressure groups. This explains why democratic governments tend to favor producer interests at the expense of consumers.

The individuals comprising the government fall into a number of different categories, with differing motivations. One important category is the bureaucracy, the permanent (nonelected) personnel who actually implement political decisions. Bureaucrats are motivated to seek security of tenure in office, and to increase the size of their agencies.

Models of *conflict*, as between different states or between rulers and subjects, are only beginning to be studied by economists. Conflict is promoted by emotional antipathy, by rivalry for resources, by overconfidence in one's ability to deliver and bear up under punishment, and by lack of enforceability of agreements. Since in the real world all agreements are only imperfectly enforceable, Coase's Theorem (that all mutually advantageous bargains will be achieved) can be valid only to a limited extent. Hence we cannot expect the abolition of war, crime, and politics.

☐ QUESTIONS FOR CHAPTER 16

MAINLY FOR REVIEW

*R1. In market competition among firms, economic profit tends to be eliminated (the "zero-profit theorem" of Chapter 7). Does something analogous tend to occur in political competition between parties? Why or why not?

*R2. What are some of the major obstacles preventing the expression of the "will of the people" through the political system? How are these analogous to, and how different from, the difficulties of the market system?

R3. How may *delegation* of decision-making power to political representatives lead to decisions diverging from the desires of constituents? Considering the corporation as a kind of political system, what protections and escape hatches do stockholders have that may not be available to members of the polity?

R4. How do the goals and opportunities of bureaucrats differ from those of elected officials? How do they differ from those of managers of private firms?

*R5. Is a unanimous-consent rule, in which dissident votes must be purchased, an ideal political system—apart from transaction costs? Does the process of "log-rolling" provide some approximation of this result? What are some objections to log-rolling?

R6. What conditions are necessary for the validity of the Median-Voter Theorem? What types of elections are likely to meet these conditions?

R7. Show how emotional antipathy, rivalry for resources, and overconfidence all tend to promote conflict.

R8. In a situation where there would be a mutual gain from agreement, show how agreement might not be achieved in the absence of outside enforcement.

*R9. What are "self-enforcing agreements"? Give an example.

R10. Show how different types of conflict can be represented in game-theory terms. Which are more and which less likely to lead to cooperative solutions?

*R11. Under what circumstances does the "free-rider" problem emerge? How valid is the assertion that all government is fundamentally a response to the free-rider problem?

* The answers to starred questions appear at the end of the book.

R12. Why do "single-peaked" preferences rule out majority-vote cycling if there is only a single dimension of choice? What happens if there is more than one dimension?

*T1. Why is the "public-choice" approach to the problem of political behavior particularly amenable to economic analysis? What other approaches are there?

*T2. If votes could be bought for money, would *both* the rich and the poor be better off in accordance with the mutual advantage of trade? What is the objection to buying votes for money?

T3. Under what political mechanisms or situations do majorities tend to exploit minorities? Under what mechanisms or situations is it the other way around?

*T4. Which is more likely to gain legislative approval: a bill that would simply redistribute cash from the rich to the poor, or one to establish a bureaucracy to provide services to the poor? Explain.

T5. How are the administrative decisions of a commissioner with a limited period of office likely to differ from those of a lifetime civil servant?

*T6. Would the fidelity of the political system to citizen desires be improved by any or all of the following: more frequent elections; more numerous legislatures; elected rather than appointed judges; the spoils system rather than the merit system in the civil service? Comment.

*T7. Suppose there were a sudden unexpected increase in demand for a product now provided through the government sector. Would you expect any systematic differences in the price-quantity response as compared with a product provided through the private sector? What about the response to a decrease in demand? What about responses to increases or decreases in cost of production?

T8. Under a system that might be called "open corruption," government officials (including judges) could sell their decisions to the highest bidder. How bad would this be?

*T9. How is it that public goods can sometimes be provided voluntarily, with no market compensation at all? If a market were feasible would more of the public good be provided with or without a market? Explain.

*T10. What explains the steady growth of the government sector relative to the private sector in the past century? Why was there a relative decline in the government sector during the era of industrialization in Great Britain?

ANSWERS

CHAPTER 1

R1. (a) Economics is a set of models or theories whose implications provide testable propositions about the real world. These models must stand or fall on the accuracy of their predictions. It is this use of evidence to judge theories that is scientific.

   (b) Vegetables will be cheaper in season than out of season. People will seldom be observed throwing money away. Advertisers will claim that their products are better than competitors' products. To take a more extended example: sharply higher gasoline prices will tend to reduce auto travel generally, and also to lower average highway speeds (with a consequent reduction in accidents). It will also encourage sales of smaller cars, and thus lead Detroit to produce new models aiming at gas economy. In the longer run a trend to more compact cities will be observed. (Of course, all such predictions must be understood in an "other things equal" sense.)

   (c) Certainly, economic science cannot predict everything. We have little or no idea as to causes of changes in tastes or social attitudes (the Protestant ethic versus "Consciousness III"), or as to determinants of ideological movements like fascism or Marxism or Christianity, or as to social trends like growth of government. And even important issues of a more narrowly defined "economic" nature, such as causes of business fluctuations, remain unresolved.

R2. (a) Behavior may be defined as rational either in terms of *method* of decision (the choice is made by calculating the costs and benefits of alternative actions) or in terms of *results* (the action chosen turns out to be well-suited for achieving one's goals).

(b) In terms of *method*, a prospective wagerer at roulette might calculate the odds and observe the behavior of the wheel before choosing a number. It would be irrational to place a bet on the basis of a dream or heavenly vision. In terms of *results*, it's probably irrational to bet at all.

(c) Aggregated over many individuals, a limited degree of individual rationality will show up as a tendency toward rational behavior for the group as a whole. Even if the rational element is small, it operates in a consistent and predictable direction.

R7. (a) In a market economy, self-interested individuals will devote their resources to satisfying others by providing desired goods and services. What others are willing to pay enables the sellers to earn higher income and so better satisfy their own desires.

(b) (c) (d) No. If their own income is not increased by serving others, self-interested individuals will not do so.

R9. (a) "Real" flow are flows of goods or services (e.g., lamb chops, labor). "Financial" flows are flows of general purchasing power (money). Each flow represents one side of a class of transaction. Goods or services are traded for general purchasing power.

(b) In the "product market," firms trade the goods and services that they produce to consumers for dollars. In the "factor market," consumers in their capacity as resource-owners trade their factor services to firms for dollars. The dollars that consumers can pay for goods and services must match what they receive for providing factor services. Similarly, the dollars that firms pay for factor services are those which they receive for the goods and services they produce.

T1. (a) Yes, *other things equal*. (If other things were not equal, a state or nation with capital punishment might also be found to have a high murder rate—if, for example, it was the high frequency of murder that led to the imposition of the death penalty in that jurisdiction.)

(b) Yes. Increasing this tax exemption lowers the cost of having children and so should result (other things equal) in an increase in the birth rate.

T2. If insurance companies refused to recognize "mental illness" as an insurable category of sickness, and if the government did not finance treatment under Medicare, doctors would be less motivated to diagnose patients' psychological problems as "disease." This would surely lower the reported incidence of "mental illness." Making medical treatment more costly would also induce potential patients to confront their problems rather than accept the dependent status of being "sick." Note that these predicted effects do *not* depend upon whether Dr. Szasz's theory about mental illness is in fact correct.

T5. The principle of the Invisible Hand applies to *market* interactions, which are voluntary and mutual in nature. Since the kinds of interactions mentioned in this question (crime, etc.) are not voluntary market exchanges, self-serving behavior may not benefit others.

T6. Drivers, being safer than before, would probably take a little less care to avoid accidents. Thus, *pedestrian* deaths might rise, though *driver* deaths would not.

T7. Dr. Johnson probably had in mind the Invisible Hand. Charles Baudelaire probably had in mind his publisher's refusing to give him a bigger advance on his royalties.

CHAPTER 2

R1. (a) Optimization. (b) Equilibrium. (c) Equilibrium. (d) Optimization. (e) Equilibrium. (f) Optimization.

R3. The price of a good X is the amount of another good (usually money) that must be given up in order to acquire a unit of X. Consequently, price is a ratio of amounts, or a ratio of quantities (money/X).

R6. Yes. Shifting the supply curve up by $\$T$ leads to a solution at the intersection of the *gross* (of tax) supply curve with the original demand curve. Shifting the demand curve down by $\$T$ leads to a solution at the intersection of the *net* (of tax) demand curve with the original supply curve. As the only difference between gross and net supply or demand curves is a vertical displacement of $\$T$, the intersections take place at the same quantity. The intersection of the gross supply curve with the demand curve determines the gross price. The intersection of the net demand curve with the supply curve determines the net (of tax) price. But, of course, it is unnecessary to carry out both constructions; either suffices since the gross price and net price are related by $P^+ \equiv P^- + T$.

R7. (a) Both. (b) Raise price paid by consumers. (c), (d) Lower price received by sellers.

R9. (a) A meaningful price ceiling must be set *below* the equilibrium price, and a meaningful price floor must be set *above* the equilibrium price.
(b) Because trade is voluntary, it is the *smaller* of the desired transaction magnitudes (quantity supplied or quantity demanded) that determines the actual quantity traded. Price ceilings decrease the quantity that sellers are willing to offer. Price floors decrease the quantity that consumers wish to buy. Both decrease the actual quantity traded in the market.
(c) If a "meaningful" price floor, above the equilibrium level, is supported, sellers are able to complete some sales for which there are no demanders (apart from the supporting agency). Transactions then depend solely on the existence of supply at that price. If the floor price is above equilibrium, the quantity sold will increase. The supporting agency, however, will accumulate inventories.

R12. (a) May be true or false. (b) True. (c) False. (d) May be true or false. (e) True. (f) May be true or false.

T1. (a) The tax would have a *small* effect on quantity exchanged in the market, a *small* effect on the gross price paid by buyers, but a *large* effect on net price to sellers. (The result here is seen more clearly if the demand curve is shifted down, rather than the supply curve up.)
(b) The steep supply curve means that suppliers are willing to offer even a slightly larger quantity only at a much higher price. Since the tax reduces quantity sold by lowering the *net* demand, the net price received by sellers falls sharply. The gross price paid by consumers rises, but only slightly, since the market quantity declines just slightly.

T3. (a) Since it would be more costly to operate automobiles, the demand curve for cars would shift to the left, leading to a fall in their price.

(b) The prices of big, heavy cars ("gas-guzzlers") would fall more.

T4. (a) A change in economic data occurs, affecting demand or supply (or both). The new supply-demand equilibrium is attained with no transactions taking place at "wrong" prices. In effect, the new equilibrium is arrived at instantaneously.

(b) In the real world, these conditions are never precisely met. But in a market where traders are well informed, the model may be a close approximation of reality.

T6. (a) Wherever the Roman armies marched, the demand for foodstuffs increased because of the addition of military demands to civilian demands. This increase in demand resulted in an increase in equilibrium price.

(b) Diocletian's edict set a price ceiling below the (new) equilibrium price. As a result, there must have been unsatisfied buyers. It is likely that Diocletian's armies made up a large portion of these unsatisfied buyers. So either efforts to evade the edict were successful or Diocletian's armies went hungry, unless indeed they simply confiscated the food they wanted. (See Jacob Burckhardt, *The Age of Constantine the Great* [New York: Pantheon, 1949], Chap. 2.)

T7. At $Q = 0, 3, 6$ the Total Revenues are respectively $R = 0, 60, 72$. The upward variation from $Q = 3$ to $Q = 6$ provides an estimate of $(72 - 60)/3 = 4$ for the Marginal Revenue at $Q = 4\frac{1}{2}$. The downward variation from $Q = 3$ to $Q = 0$ provides an estimate of $(60 - 0)/3 = 20$ for the Marginal Revenue at $Q = 1\frac{1}{2}$. Interpolating, we obtain the approximation $MR = 12$ at $Q = 3$.

CHAPTER 3

R1. (a) Violates the Axiom of Comparison. (b) Expresses indifference, but does not violate the laws. (c) Indicates *inconsistency*, and thus also violates the Axiom of Comparison.

R4. Utility is simply an indicator of preference ranking. Of two bundles, the fact that one is preferred indicates that its utility is higher.

R6. Since ordinal utility indicates only direction of preference, only the *signs* and not the quantitative increments of utility can be determined as amount consumed rises.

R8. (a) Ordinal. (b) Cardinal. (c) Interpersonal comparability.

T1. No.

T3. Placement in a horse race, or a tennis ladder, or a job seniority list. An interesting scientific example is a measure commonly used for *hardness*, based on the relation "scratches." Thus, diamond is harder than glass, and glass is harder than chalk, but this measure does not indicate *how much* harder.

T5. Any shape that is symmetrical across the 45° line. This would indicate, for example, that I am indifferent between the combination "His Income is $2000 while My Income is $1000" and the combination "My Income is $2000 while His Income is $1000."

T6. The preference map would take the form of rays out of the origin. Along any single ray, representing a fixed *ratio* of "My Income" to "His Income," the individual would be equally happy. For such an individual the preference directions would be such that "My Income" is a good, while "His Income" is à bad.

CHAPTER 4

R3. (a) The budget line is the northeast boundary of an individual's market opportunity set. It is the locus of the achievable consumption bundles if the individual spends all of his income.
(b) The equation of the budget line is $I = P_x x + P_y y$.
(c) The slope of the budget line depends upon the relative prices of the goods X and Y. This slope will be $-P_x/P_y$.

R4. The optimum of the consumer is found geometrically as the point on the budget line touching the highest achievable indifference curve. If both goods are consumed, this will be an interior solution. If only one good is consumed (if the budget line touches the highest indifference curve at one axis), this will be a corner solution.

R6. (a) The Consumption Balance Equation is $MU_x/P_x = MU_y/P_y$. The Substitution Equivalence Equation is $MRS_C = MRS_E$ (or, slope of indifference curve = slope of budget line). The Consumption Balance Equation can be reduced to the Substitution Equivalence Equation, but not vice versa. This is because the CBE requires cardinal utility while the SEE requires only ordinal utility. (Cardinal utility implies ordinal utility, but not vice versa.)
(b) Both equations apply to interior solutions. At a corner solution an *inequality* will ordinarily hold, dictating spending all one's income on one of the commodities.

R10. (a) If the IEP has a positive slope, the Engel Curve for each good will have positive slope.
(b) The Engel Expenditure Curve for each good will have a positive slope, but this slope will not exceed unity (the slope of the 45° line).
(c) If X is an inferior good, the Engel Curve will have negative slope.

R13. If the Law of Demand holds, the PEP never curls back (toward the northwest).

R17. As long as a commodity X is a *good* (rather than a neuter or a bad), those receiving vouchers for purchase of X will consume at least the voucher equivalent. For those previously consuming less than this, the voucher will always increase consumption. For this reason, vouchers are particularly effective (relative to subsidies) in increasing consumption among persons who would otherwise have consumed little or none of a good.

T1. (a) An experiment could reveal the *maximum* amount of Y an individual might be willing to pay for a small increment of X. This would be an approximation of the MRS_C.
(b) No known experiment could reveal Marginal Utility.

T3. (a) In moving northwest, the PEP is entering regions of higher y but lower x. Since utility is increasing along the PEP, it must be that y is increasing fast enough to more than compensate for the decrease in x. But the amount of y it is possible to acquire is bounded by the horizontal line through the starting-point K. So this process can continue only over a limited range of the PEP—which must eventually turn northeast.
(b) This is impossible. Utility is increasing everywhere along the PEP, and the same starting-point cannot have both lower and higher utility.

T4. (a) An increase in P_x would tend to shift the IEP to the northwest.
(b) An increase in I would tend to displace the PEP toward the northeast (assuming X and Y are both normal superior goods).

T7. The pair of close substitutes is more likely to have a member that is an inferior good. The reason is that complements tend to be consumed together, while substitutes do not. Therefore, increased income is likely to result in increased consumption of both bread and butter (complements). But with increased income an individual is likely to consume less margarine, since he can now better afford the preferred (but more expensive) substitute—butter.

T8. Since usually only a limited fraction of income is spent on any single good X, the income effect (enrichment or impoverishment) due to a change in P_x will be relatively small.

T10. The market base price should *rise*, because increased quantities will be demanded. The effect will be to partially cancel the impact of the subsidy or voucher.

T12. (a) Coach travel is an inferior good here, since the purchased quantity of coach travel falls as income rises. Specifically, if income were to rise above $100, more first-class travel and less coach travel would be purchased.
  (b) If the traveler's budget is so small that he can complete the trip *only* by traveling entirely in coach, then he will do so. If the traveler's budget permits the trip to be completed by traveling entirely in first-class, then only first-class travel will be purchased.

T13. (a) Yes.
  (b) If the budget-line slope is exactly the same as the indifference-curve slope for the two perfect substitutes, then the individual does not care whether he consumes only one of the goods, or only the other good, or any mixture of the two.

T14. No, the two IEP curves cannot intersect. Assuming $P_y \equiv 1$ throughout, every point on the original $IEP°$ curve represents an indifference-curve tangency with a budget line of slope $-P_x°$. Every point on the new IEP' curve represents a tangency with a budget line of slope $-P_x'$. If the two IEP curves crossed, their point of intersection would have to be where an indifference curve is tangent to two budget lines of different slopes, which is impossible.

T15. Here $P_x = 120$ is the choke price for X; at that price, the quantity demanded falls to zero. For $P_x > 120$, the demand-curve equation given indicates a negative amount of X demanded, which we rule out as impossible. The correct demand equation, in the range where $P_x > 120$, is simply $x = 0$.

CHAPTER 5

R2. Such Engel Curves (of different steepness, but all being straight lines through the origin) depict the same *proportionate response* of changes in consumption to changes in income. For such curves, greater steepness shows not greater income elasticity but rather that x/I is higher—i.e., that the commodity is absolutely more important in the consumer's budget.

R5. (a) "Elastic demand" means that the absolute value of the price elasticity of demand exceeds one. "Inelastic demand" means that the absolute value of the price elasticity of demand is less than one.
  (b) For a linear demand curve, the elasticity at any point is the ratio of two slopes: the slope of a ray from the origin *to* that point on the curve, divided by the constant slope *along* the curve. For a nonlinear demand curve, the slope *along* the curve is interpreted as the slope of the tangent to the curve at that point.

R6. (a) Negative infinity. (b) Zero. (c) −1.

R9. Price elasticity is −1. Income elasticity is +1.

R10. Permitting the sale of coupons would benefit both the wealthy and the poor. The poor could sell coupons for dollars, shift their *income* constraint outward, and attain a more preferred position. The wealthy could buy coupons for dollars, shift their *ration* constraint upward, and also attain a more preferred position.

R12. This corresponds to the statement that the income index $\mathscr{E}$ is greater than the Laspeyres index of prices $\mathscr{L}_P$—which implies also that the Paasche index of quantities $\mathscr{P}_Q$ is greater than one. The statement is true.

T1. Assuming for simplicity just two goods X and Y, the equation that we want to prove can be written

$$\frac{P_x x}{I}\left(\frac{\Delta x}{\Delta I}\frac{I}{x}\right) + \frac{P_y y}{I}\left(\frac{\Delta y}{\Delta I}\frac{I}{y}\right) = 1$$

After cancellations:

$$\frac{P_x \Delta x + P_y \Delta y}{\Delta I} = 1$$

But since $I = P_x x + P_y y$, with P_x and P_y as constants, $\Delta I = P_x \Delta x + P_y \Delta y$. So the numerator and denominator of the fraction above are equal, proving that their ratio does indeed equal unity.

T2. (a) Since $PX = 100$, expenditure is constant at any price and elasticity is therefore unity. Since expenditure is constant, the share of the budget is also constant.

(b) It can be shown with calculus that the (inverse) slope of the demand curve dX/dP is $-200/P^3$. Multiply by P/X to obtain elasticity: $\eta = -200/(P^2 X)$. Since $P^2 X = 200$ (demand equation), this reduces to $-200/100 = -2$. Elasticity is constant, and each 1 percent fall in price increases quantity by 2 percent. Thus the budget share rises as price falls.

(c) Using the same method as in (b) above, slope is $-50/P^{1.5}$, and elasticity is $\eta = -50/(P^{.5} X)$. This reduces to $-50/100 = -1/2$. Here a 1 percent fall in price increases quantity by 0.5 percent, so budget share falls as price falls.

(d) "Importance" in the budget may change in either direction as price changes, even when elasticity is constant. In general, there is no necessary relation between importance and elasticity of demand.

T3. (a) At low incomes consumers are likely to be interested only in nutrition. High-quality and low-quality beef are good substitutes as far as nutrition is concerned. At high incomes other characteristics such as flavor become increasingly important to consumers. Here, low-quality beef is not a good substitute for high-quality beef. Higher indifference curves would therefore have greater curvature.

(b) Because high-quality beef is a luxury (it has a stronger positive income effect than low-quality beef), the price elasticity of demand for high-quality beef should be high relative to the price elasticity for low-quality beef.

T5. The secretary is mistaken. The prof would undoubtedly be *willing* to pay something more in total for three tickets than for two. But if the price is only $10, *he does not have to* pay more for three tickets than he would have paid for two at a price of $20 each. Looking at this another way, the $10 is the worth of a *third* ticket to the prof, not the worth of each of three tickets. (If the objection were valid, it would never make sense for a consumer to have an inelastic demand for a good.)

T6. This is indeed possible, though opinions may differ about how likely it is. Consumers seeking snob appeal gain utility from *exclusiveness*. At a high price, they are getting not only the commodity but also the exclusivity. The fact that the price is high guarantees that not many people can afford the commodity, and therefore makes "snob" consumers more willing to buy than at a low price. But if the exclusiveness were provided in some other way (as by the medieval Statute of Dress that made it illegal for the lower orders to wear upper-class clothes), presumably the Law of Demand would hold.

T7. This is very much like the previous question, but here the additional element gained by the consumer from the high-price product (or so he believes) is *quality*. There is of course nothing paradoxical if someone prefers high quality even at a high price over low quality at a low price. Again, if the quality were guaranteed in some other way than by high price (perhaps by a consumer organization's rating of the product), presumably the Law of Demand would hold—a high-quality product at a low price would be chosen over the *same* high-quality product at a high price.

T8. (a) The usual justification is that rationed commodities tend to be those that are "essential" to life or health. If ration allowances were exchangeable, rich people might end up with more than "their fair share" of these essential commodities. Note that this assumes that the poorer people who sell their allowances are foolish in giving up some "essentials" for nonessentials—or else possibly that poorer people have to be forced to remain in good working condition for the sake of the war effort, though they themselves might prefer otherwise!

(b) The adverse consequences include the loss of the gains from trade, plus the diversion of resources into black-market activities and the policing efforts required to minimize such activities.

T9. Consumption requires both income and time. A consumer will choose a most preferred position subject to both an income constraint and a time constraint. When relatively poor, the income constraint will tend to be binding. When relatively rich, the time constraint will tend to be binding. While "time-saving" devices in effect allow outward shifts of the time constraint, this has not occurred as rapidly as rising incomes have shifted out the income constraint. So the time constraint is increasingly the binding one upon individuals' consumption. Rich people simply do not have enough time to consume all the things they might enjoy and be able to pay for.

T13. (a) Shoppers have different tastes, and it is reasonable for each customer to shop at the market where his or her "typical basket" is cheaper. So Market A's prices are likely to be lower for the goods preferred by its own customers, and the same will be true for Market B.

(b) This is a question about index numbers of price. The proposition in the text about price comparisons *over time* can be adapted to comparisons *between markets*. Think of Market A as equivalent to the "base year" and Market B as the "given year." Also, think of the "index of money-income change" $\mathscr{E}$ as the ratio of Market B typical consumer expenditures to Market A typical consumer expenditures. (This would be a measure of the comparative overall grocery budgets of customers in the two markets.) Then customers in Market B are surely better off if $\mathscr{E}$ exceeds the Laspeyres price index $\mathscr{L}_P$. And customers in Market A are surely better off if the Paasche price index $\mathscr{P}_P$ exceeds $\mathscr{E}$. If neither of these conditions holds, then we cannot say that one market's prices are unquestionably lower: instead, each has lower prices for the goods desired by its own customers.

CHAPTER 6

R3. (a) Economic profit is the difference between revenues and economic costs—i.e., costs *inclusive* of implicit payments for self-supplied resources.

(b) Since owners receive profits, maximization of profit (owner wealth) is an appropriate goal for owners. Managers, if they are not also owners, have no claim on profits and so would be uninterested in maximizing profit. Managers might be interested in power, growth, stability, and a favorable corporate image as well as in larger salaries and more pleasant working conditions.

(c) Mechanisms tend to be developed by owners to impose their profit-maximizing goal upon managers. Lawsuits and proxy fights can punish managers who are not pursuing owners' goals. Similarly, profit-sharing and stock-option plans reward managers for pursuing owners' goals. These mechanisms are imperfect, though, so the likely result is that the firm will pursue some mixture of owner and manager goals.

R5. (a) Yes. At the vertical axis, AC is greater than or equal to MC, since AC allows for Fixed Costs while MC does not. As MC falls from its initial level along the vertical axis, it forces AC to be falling as well.

(b) No. By Proposition 2.2a, when AC is falling, MC lies below AC, but MC can be less than AC and still not be itself falling.

R7. A firm will make short-run adjustments to changes in economic conditions if such changes are viewed as temporary. A firm will make long-run adjustments to changes in economic conditions if such changes are viewed as permanent.

T1. Taking on additional traffic at a price lower than Average Cost would be financially advantageous if the price exceeds *Marginal* Cost. Even if AVC is only one-third of AC, Marginal Cost might not be low enough to warrant taking on the new traffic. (In fact, MC might even be above AC.)

T2. (a) If changing conditions are viewed as temporary, some factors may be held fixed in the face of a contraction of output to avoid the transaction costs incurred in selling the factors and then buying them back when conditions return to normal—or, for an expansion of output, to avoid the costs of buying factors and then selling them back. A similar result holds to the extent that the firm's operations involve *specializing* resources to the firm. Such specialized resources can only be sold at a low price to others, yet must be purchased at a high price. Then these resources may be held fixed during temporary changes in output.

(b) The factors that are held fixed are those which are highly specialized to the firm, or for which transaction costs are high.

T6. The short-run Marginal Cost is the additional cost of temporarily increasing output. Whether these costs are paid immediately (overtime wages, increased usage of power, etc.) or at a later time (deferred maintenance), they are all costs. The factory manager is confusing short-run costs with costs that must be *paid* immediately. They are not the same.

T8. (a) The Marginal Cost of providing service to more passengers when trains are running empty is quite low. Another passenger can be transported at very little additional cost. When trains are running full, however, the Marginal Cost of providing service is much higher. Additional trains must be run, or further unpleasant crowding imposed on passengers. Since Marginal Cost is very low in off-hours, the transit line should encourage off-hour business, not discourage it.

The management consultant is confusing Marginal Cost with Average Cost.

    (b) Commutation tickets will increase ridership at rush hours, but it is during these times that the trains are already running full. If the cost of running additional trains, or of imposing crowding on customers, is high then the transit line is likely to be worse off by selling commutation tickets. Discount tickets for *off-hour* riders, on the other hand, would likely increase revenues without a commensurate increase in cost. This type of discount would be a good idea.

CHAPTER 7

R1.   Yes. Steepness and elasticity of supply, *at a given point*, must be inversely related.

R2.   Whether the proposition (that doubling *all* inputs would always double output) is or is not true is arguable, but in any case it is not economically relevant. In the real world, it is never possible to double *all* relevant inputs.

R4.   Where there are no "external" effects, the industry supply curve will be less steep than the firm supply curve but will have the same elasticity (the *proportionate* response of output to price will be the same).

R6.   (a) In long-run equilibrium, the marginal firm is just on the borderline between staying in the industry and leaving. The value of its opportunities elsewhere practically equals what it can earn in this industry. Consequently, the economic profit of the marginal firm will be (only negligibly above) zero.

    (b) Infra-marginal firms have access to some special resources particularly suited to producing in this industry. Other firms will bid for the right to use these special resources. When the infra-marginal firm charges itself the *opportunity cost*—what it could get by offering the special resources to these other bidders—it is also left with zero economic profit.

T1.   True. A competitive firm will produce positive output only if Marginal Cost exceeds Average Variable Cost (in the short run) or Average Cost (in the long run). So *AVC* in the former case, or *AC* in the latter case, must be rising.

T4.   No. All firms may be earning zero economic profit, and yet some may be able to survive even if product price falls. These will be the "infra-marginal" firms (see Question R6).

T6.   (a) If all coupons were used initially, allowing resale would only redistribute coupons. Only if some coupons were initially unused would sale of coupons tend to raise the price of petroleum and elicit more supply.

    (b) Salability, though, would cause a redistribution of coupons to those consumers having the highest demand prices for gasoline—at least as high as the sum of the product price and the price paid for a coupon.

    (c) Without the sale of coupons, some buyers may receive little or no Consumer Surplus from their purchases of gasoline while others who would receive great Consumer Surplus may be unable to make purchases. Salability will allow those previously unable to make purchases to bid away the coupons from those currently receiving little Consumer Surplus from gasoline.

T7.   If the nonsalable ration coupons are all assigned to consumers who are unwilling to pay even the low ceiling price, then it might seem that all trading of the good will be entirely blocked because no one would want to buy at the ceiling price. But this is not correct, since, as a consequence of the reduced demand, the market price could fall below the ceiling price. In fact, unless all the nonsalable ration tickets went to individuals unwilling to pay even the *choke price for supply*, the new market equilibrium price would be below the ceiling price but above the choke price for supply, and so trade would take place. On the other hand, if the coupons were salable they would be resold to those who value them the most. Then there would be trading at the ceiling price.

T9. No. The output from existing wells is based, even in the short run, upon a calculation of the price received for oil versus the cost of pumping. The higher the price, the more it pays to pump. In the longer run, the more it will pay to extend the life of an existing well by heating, flooding, redrilling, etc.

T11. (a) By reversing the analysis pictured in Figure 7.9, it can be seen that Consumer Surplus will increase (rather than decrease) because of the lower price to consumers, and Producer Surplus will increase (rather than decrease) because of the higher price to sellers.

(b) No. A tax leads to inefficiency due to reduced exchange; a subsidy leads to inefficiency due to excessive exchange. Since the price received by sellers exceeds the price paid by consumers, there will be units produced and sold whose value to consumers does not cover the Marginal Cost of production. It may seem puzzling that Consumer Surplus and Producer Surplus both increase in this market and yet there is inefficiency. The explanation is that the subsidy here reduces Consumer Surplus and Producer Surplus elsewhere. Other industries must be taxed to finance the subsidy.

CHAPTER 8

R1. To maximize profit, a monopolist will set $MR = MC$. Since Marginal Cost is always positive, the monopolist will always produce where Marginal Revenue is positive. $MR > 0$ implies $|\eta| > 1$.

R3. In comparison with pure competition, monopoly results in a smaller rate of output. Because less is produced and traded, some of the gains from specialization and trade are lost—the sum of Consumer Surplus and Producer Surplus is smaller.

R5. Owners of monopolies may not be any more interested in nonprofit goals than owners of competitive firms, but reduced competitive pressure allows indulging such goals. As another matter, they may be less able to successfully impose the goal of profit maximization upon managers, since owners of monopolies cannot measure their managers' performances by looking at the performance of rival firms. Also, antitrust policy may act as a threat. (If profits are too large, perhaps an antitrust suit will be forthcoming.) Finally, many monopolies are regulated and so prevented from maximizing profits. For any of these reasons, monopolies may not pursue profits as vigorously as do competitive firms.

R7. In deriving the supply curve of the competitive industry, we assume that each separate firm will have set Marginal Cost equal to price. The height of the point on the supply curve therefore shows the Marginal Cost of each and every firm for that level of industry output. Consequently, that point on the supply curve also shows what the Marginal Cost would be if that industry were monopolized.

T1. Yes. An effective monopolist always operates in the range of elastic demand (see Question R1). But if demand is elastic, higher prices will have a big effect on quantity demanded.

T3. (a) At the simple monopoly optimum $MR = MC$, price exceeds Marginal Cost. A perfectly discriminating monopolist, on the other hand, will expand output until price *equals* Marginal Cost. A perfectly discriminating monopolist, then, might be expected to produce more than a simple monopolist. However, if the *income effect* is very strong, this conclusion may not hold. The discriminating monopolist extracts more income from consumers at each level of output, which tends to reduce demand for additional units.

(b) A market-segmentation monopolist will charge a price higher than the simple monopoly price to some market segments and so sell less in those segments, but will also charge a price lower than the simple monopoly price to the other segments and so sell more there. The total produced and sold by a market segmentation monopolist, then, may be more or less than that of a simple monopolist.

(c) While a multi-part pricing monopolist will charge a price higher than the simple monopoly price for small purchases, he will charge a price lower than the simple monopoly price for purchases beyond a certain size. Some customers will buy less because they purchase too little to receive the lower marginal price. Other customers will purchase enough to receive the lower marginal price and so will purchase more (in the absence of a strong income effect) than if faced with a single monopoly price. The multi-part pricing monopolist, therefore, also may or may not produce more than a simple monopolist.

T4. For a price-discriminating selling scheme to be effective, resale of the commodity must be difficult. Resale of services is more difficult than resale of manufactured goods.

T5. Many customers will lie about their age.

T6. (a) Yes. The markets are divided between customers who are and customers who are not willing to take the trouble of collecting and using coupons.

(b) There should be little or no "leakage," since those not using coupons (and so paying higher prices) are unwilling to take the time and trouble needed to shift to the lower-price market.

(c) Yes, the consumers with more elastic demands will find it more worthwhile to go to the trouble of using coupons.

T10. Yes. Consider theft, for example. The marginal yield to the "industry" as a whole is probably less than that perceived by the individual competitive thief. One thief may steal on Tuesday what another thief had in mind filching on Wednesday. Also, any increase in the scale of thievery tends to raise the intensity of defensive actions by potential victims, thereby reducing the returns to thieves in the aggregate. A monopolized theft industry would take all this into account and therefore engage in fewer (but more remunerative, on the average) crimes.

CHAPTER 9

R1. The greater the number of plants, the closer plants are on the average to customers, and so the smaller the transport losses incurred. This will lead to a larger aggregate demand for the product itself. Similarly, the greater the number of varieties, the more closely the available products match customer preferences, and so the smaller the satisfaction loss to consumers. Again this will lead to a larger aggregate demand.

R2. (a) While increased variety does raise the aggregate demand curve, it does so at a decreasing rate. Consequently, the *incremental* benefits to the monopoly firm from offering greater and greater variety are decreasing. On the other hand, the incremental cost of providing increased variety—in the text example, this is the fixed cost associated with each added plant—is ordinarily nondecreasing. There will be some point, then, where still greater variety raises cost more than it raises revenue.

(b) If individuals' desires are for very similar products, there will be little benefit to the firm if it offers increased variety. And if there are large economies of scale, increased variety can only be offered at high cost. These two considerations may be powerful enough to induce the monopolist to offer only a single variety.

R6. The monopolist is really interested in producing *services* (S) desired by consumers, where the service amount is $s \equiv qz$ (quantity of physical product times "quality" in terms of service provided by each unit of physical product). Normally, there will be increasing Marginal Cost of expanding s either by increasing quantity or by increasing quality. So, if a monopolist desires to produce a smaller service output s, he will normally cut back on both quantity and quality.

R7. (a) A monopolist would obviously not suppress an invention that lowered costs. Nor, if consumers are fully informed, would it pay to suppress an invention that raised quality at a given cost. (The only possible exception would be if the invention somehow destroyed the monopoly.)

(b) Consumers would not necessarily be better off. It is conceivable that adoption of a cost-reducing invention would lead the monopolist to produce a smaller amount than before, at a higher price. A similar result may come about for a quality-increasing invention.

T1. No, monopolistic competition emerges when consumers' tastes for different *varieties* provide each supplier with a degree of monopoly power over a "clientele" for its product. In contrast, if there is a single generally recognized *quality* attribute desired by all consumers, they will purchase from whichever firm offers this attribute at the lowest price. If there are many firms, each can survive only by offering the same price as the others, per unit of quality attribute. As price-taking suppliers of the single quality attribute, the firms are engaging in pure competition.

T5. The discussion of "Suppression of Inventions" showed that an invention lowering Total and Average Cost at every level of output *might* conceivably raise Marginal Cost in some ranges of output. If so, even for a competitive industry, a cost-reducing invention *might* reduce the quantity offered at some prices. (This could happen only over a limited range, and even so seems a rather unlikely possibility.) Since a quality-improving invention is logically equivalent to a cost-reducing invention (in terms of the cost of producing the attribute desired by consumers), a corresponding analysis applies: the invention *might* conceivably (though this seems improbable) be adverse to consumers' interests.

T6. Think of oranges as providing various amounts of a desired attribute, flavor. High-quality oranges contain more attribute than low-quality oranges. But it costs no more to ship a high-quality than a lower-quality orange. Then shipping costs *per unit of quality attribute* will be less if higher-quality oranges are shipped. Consequently, oranges shipped to distant locations tend to be of higher quality.

T7. The explanation seems to be that transportation itself (or the time that transport takes) degrades the quality of lobsters. If so, top-quality lobsters simply cannot be found except near the source. Oranges, in contrast, seem to retain their quality even when shipped long distances.

T8. This is similar to the situation with oranges. As a result of the tax, it becomes *relatively* cheaper than before to supply high-quality (high-mileage) gasoline. Some firms that previously found it more advantageous to produce a lower grade of gasoline are likely now to shift over to a better grade.

T10. The text considered only producers' *supply* of products at different quality levels and did not examine consumer *demands* for higher and lower quality. But it is reasonable to expect that a similar analysis would apply on the demand side. Consumers really desire the services S provided by consumption goods, and once again the amount of service is given by $s \equiv qz$, where q is physical quantity of the good, and z is the "quality" (service provided per unit of physical quantity). Then, if a kind of diminishing marginal returns applies to consumption as well as production, a poorer consumer would normally purchase a smaller quantity and a lower quality as well.

T11. Since there is some tradeoff between quantity and quality, the program that restricted only the *number of acres planted* motivated farmers to enlarge output at the expense of quality. So in this period American tobacco farmers specialized in high-yield but low-quality varieties. The reformed program had exactly the opposite effect. Since the restriction was only upon the *number of pounds produced*, it paid farmers to make each pound of tobacco a more valuable product. So American farmers shifted over to high-quality strains of tobacco. See J. A. Seagraves, "The Life Cycle of the Flue-Cured Tobacco Program," Dept. of Economics and Business, North Carolina State Univ., Working Paper No. 34 (Mar. 1983).

CHAPTER 10

R2. The "Prisoners' Dilemma" is a social interaction situation in which each participant is motivated to adopt a shortsightedly selfish strategy—with the result that all parties lose. The source of the difficulty is that an individual choosing a cooperative strategy has no way to induce or compel the others to do the same, so the unselfish player ends up worse off than the others. Evidently there is an unexploited mutual gain from exchange here, due to *inability to make binding agreements*.

R3. Monopolistic competition is a market structure in which each firm's product is differentiated from the others, but the relatively large number of firms rules out strategic behavior. In contrast, strategic behavior is the essence of oligopoly (competition among the few). Under oligopoly, products of the different firms may or may not be differentiated (the heterogeneous versus homogeneous cases).

R4. In the Nash solution of game theory, each party is doing the best he can *given* the strategies of the others. The Cournot solution for oligopoly similarly assumes that each firm adopts the best choice for its decision variable (price or quantity) *given* the choices made by the others.

R7. (a) If the demand curve is "kinked," the Marginal Revenue curve will have a vertical gap at the rate of output at which this kink exists. To maximize profit, the firm will set $MR = MC$. Assuming that MC initially cuts through the gap in MR, moderate changes in MC will still leave MC cutting through this gap in MR. As long as this is the case, the firm will not change its rate of output or price. Moderate shifts in the demand curve to the left or right may also leave MC cutting through the gap in MR—now at a greater or smaller rate of output. Again, price will tend to be rigid.

(b) One method of enforcing a collusive agreement is for "loyal" firms to match any price cut by a defecting firm, but to refrain from matching any price increase. This leads to each potential defector viewing its demand curve as kinked at the agreed level of prices.

T2. "Learning" on the part of the firms opens up many new possibilities and the final outcome is not easily predictable. Suppose first that at each output of the other firm, the "learned" duopolist produces more than the simple duopolist. If both firms "learn," the Reaction Curve of each will shift to the right relative to the Reaction Curves of simple duopolists. The consequence is that the outcome approaches the competitive solution—both firms are worse off than before! So they may "learn" by this to behave more cooperatively, holding back on output so as to approach the monopoly solution instead. But if one firm learns that the other is inclined to hold back, the first is tempted to "free-ride" and produce more. So the final result is unclear.

T3. Even though the monopolist might find it more profitable to share the market with any *single* new entrant, once he establishes that precedent many new competitors are likely to try to enter. So the monopolist would want to build a reputation for always being a ruthless price-cutter against new entrants. He can then point out to a potential new competitor that his threat is credible, since otherwise his reputation for toughness would be ruined and he would lose his monopoly position.

T4. Yes. The kink would have a more extreme form under homogeneous oligopoly. A firm that raised its price, while other firms were keeping their prices constant, would lose *all* its business—so above the kink the demand curve would be flat (perfectly elastic). A firm that lowered price would find that other firms follow, so its demand below the kink would be no more elastic than the overall industry demand.

T6. (a) Table 10.6 shows that the symmetrical Collusive solution is not generally better than the Threat solution for *both* parties. If the threat can be made effective without having to be enforced very often, the "predatory price-cutter" can do better than under collusion.

(b) Predatory price-cutting is more likely to emerge where one firm is much more powerful or aggressive than the other, so that the threat is highly credible.

CHAPTER 11

R2. (a) For a monopolist in the product market, Marginal Revenue is always less than product price. Consequently, for such a monopolist mrp_a will always lie below (to the left of) vmp_a. For a competitor in the product market, Marginal Revenue equals product price. For such a competitor, mrp_a will be identical to vmp_a. So only for a monopolist in the product market will the mrp_a lie to the left of vmp_a.

(b) Whether the firm is a monopolist or a competitor in the product market, mrp_a is the firm's demand curve for factor A (within the relevant range of the curve).

R4. (a) Since mrp_a must be declining for $mrp_a = h_a$ to be an optimum, for a competitor in the product market it will never be rational *not* to be in the region of diminishing *marginal* returns (mp_a declining). For a monopolist in the product market, MR is also declining, so it *may* be possible to achieve declining mrp_a even with rising mp_a.

(b) $mrp_a = h_a$ may hold in the region of diminishing marginal returns but rising *average* returns (where mp_a lies above ap_a). But then $h_a = mrp_a \equiv MR(mp_a) >$

$MR(ap_a)$. Then for a competitive firm, $h_a > P(q/a)$, or $h_a a > Pq$. This means that the expenditure on factor A alone exceeds Total Revenue! So a competitive firm would *always* operate in the region of diminishing average returns.

(c) $mrp_a = h_a$ could never hold in the region of diminishing *total* returns. Here mp_a is negative and so mrp_a must also be negative. Since factor hire-price h_a can never be negative, a profit-maximizing firm would never hire so much factor as to be in the region of diminishing total returns.

R5. The conditions $mrp_a = h_a$ and $mrp_b = h_b$ imply that $mp_a/h_a = mp_b/h_b$. This equation states that an extra dollar spent on either factor A or factor B will increase output by the same amount. Consequently, factor proportions are optimal. And $mrp_a/h_a = mrp_b/h_b = 1$ is also implied, which is equivalent to $MR/MC = 1$. Consequently, the scale of output is also optimal.

R6. (a) Yes. The slope of the output isoquant shows the rate at which factor B can be substituted for factor A while maintaining output. If one unit less of factor A is employed, the fall in output will be (approximately) mp_a. The number of units of factor B which must be hired to maintain output will be (approximately) mp_a/mp_b. The approximation approaches exactness for very small changes. So the absolute value of the slope at a point on the output isoquant is mp_a/mp_b.

(b) The absolute value of the slope along a cost isoquant is the rate at which factor B can be traded for factor A in the market—equal to h_a/h_b.

R8. No, because firms can enter or leave the industry. The entry-exit effect tends to make the industry's demand for a factor more elastic.

R9. (a) True. A drop in the hire-price of factor A will lead to an increase in the employment of factor A and so normally to an increase in output. If the demand curve for product is *inelastic*, this will induce a relatively large fall in product price. So the industry will respond to a fall in the hire-price with only a small increase in the employment of factor A (and a small increase in output). The demand curve for factor A will be steep and so tend to be inelastic.

(b) True. The weaker the operation of the Law of Diminishing Returns, the more gradual the decline in mp_a as more A is hired. When this decline is more gradual, firm demand curves for factor A and the resulting market demand curve will be relatively flat and so tend to be elastic.

(c) True. As the hire-price of factor A falls, more A will be hired and so the demand for complementary factors will increase. The more elastic the supply curves of factors complementary to factor A, the greater the increase in employent of these factors when the demand for them increases. The large increase in the quantity of complementary factors leads to a large upward shift in mrp_a and so to a relatively large increase in the quantity of factor A employed. Consequently, each firm's demand curve (and so the market demand curve) for factor A will be flatter and so tend to be more elastic, the more elastic the supply of complementary factors.

T1. (a) See Examples 11.1 through 11.3.

(b) This is a question of fact. The Laws of Diminishing Returns appear to be founded upon certain very general physical aspects of the world. Note, however, that economists admit a range of exceptions when they say only that Marginal or Average or Total returns *eventually* diminish as employment of one factor increases relative to others. It is possible that in a practical situation the "eventual" point may not be reached, so increasing returns apply in the relevant range.

T2. No. Here, the employer is not a price-taker. Consequently, there is no fixed relation between quantity employed and hire-price.

T4. Even if two factors are anticomplementary, it is quite possible that each has positive Marginal Product. For each factor it is its *mp* that enters into *mrp* ≡ *MR(mp)*, to be compared with its hire-price *h* in making the employment decision.

T7. This chapter examines aspects of the *demand* for labor. Supply considerations (to be studied in the next chapter) also have a bearing upon whether wages are high or low: Demand for labor has been high in the United States as a result mainly of the presence of large amounts of complementary factors. In the early years these took the form of rich natural resources (fertile land, mineral wealth, navigable rivers). In more recent years, accumulations of complementary manufactured resources (machines, roads) have contributed to the demand for labor. Other possible sources of high demand for labor in the United States include rapid technological progress (see next question), relatively strong competition in product markets (so that *mrp* does not diverge very much from *vmp* for labor), and comparative absence of firms with effective monopsony power in the labor markets.

T8. Technological progress by definition tends to raise the *Average* Product of labor. It will tend to raise wages if the *Marginal* Product of labor increases. While the effects on Average Product and Marginal Product are usually parallel, there are exceptions. A "labor-saving" invention may raise the productivity of the first few workers employed so much that the Marginal Product for larger numbers falls. There is another line of causation, however, associated with the general enrichment that technological progress brings about. With higher wealth, there will be more demand for products involving labor of all types. So wages will tend to rise as a result of "revenue" considerations (see Question R1) even if the "productivity" considerations are affected adversely.

CHAPTER 12

R3. No. The supply curve can bend backward only if the income effect opposes the substitution effect. If leisure is an inferior good, the enrichment due to a wage increase would lead to less consumption of leisure (more supply of labor), thus *reinforcing* the substitution effect of the wage increase.

R4. At very low wage rates, few hours are being worked. A wage increase, multiplied by only a small number of hours, will have only a small enrichment effect compared with the substitution effect.

R5. The supply curve to a particular employment is likely to be much more elastic. Different employments of labor are probably, from the worker's point of view, close substitutes in his or her preference function. Then a relatively small change in the wage differential between two employments will induce a relatively large shift in labor supply from the less attractive to the more attractive employment.

R7. At a high wage, a physician will tend to consume less leisure. Indeed, if the investment in medical training leaves the individual only as well off as before (on the same indifference curve), that person will surely work more, as shown in Figure 12.12. Here only the substitution effect of the wage increase is effective; the income effect is exactly canceled by the income loss due to the cost of training. If the individual ends up on a higher indifference curve as a result of the investment, however, then there will be a net income effect which *may* lead to working less.

R9. Each is a source of productive services, and thus is a portion of society's real capital.

R10. This relationship is $h_a = rP_A$. The hire-price of the factor is equal to the interest yield on the capital value or purchase price of the factor. This is an *equilibrium* relation. The purchase price of the factor will be bid up or down until the relation holds.

R12. Economic rent is that portion of payment to a factor in excess of the amount required to call it into employment. Economic rent is a measure of the resource-owner's (seller's) net gain from trade in the factor market. It is, then, analogous to Producer Surplus, which is a measure of the seller's net gain from trade in the product market.

T1. (a) A decline in the birth rate would reduce women's demand for "leisure"—that is, for nonmarket uses of time. As women earn more in the market, their husbands will seek less market employment.

(b) Here again, reduced time required for housework will reduce women's demand for "leisure" time. They will work more in the market and their husbands will work less.

(c) Same as (b) above.

T4. (a) Such a change in taste would lead to an outward shift of the market supply curve of female labor. More labor would be offered at each wage rate.

(b) If males and females make up at least partially distinguishable types of labor, the outward shift in the supply of female labor would lead to a *decrease* in the equilibrium wage rate for female workers relative to male workers.

T5. As long as leisure is a normal good, rising per-capita *wealth* in the form of non-labor income will lead to an increase in leisure and so to a decrease in the number of hours worked. Rising real *wages* embody both an income and a substitution effect. The pure substitution effect always implies a decrease in leisure and an increase in hours worked, but the income effect works in the opposite direction. Since hours worked have been steadily falling as real wages have risen, the pure substitution effect of rising real wages appears to have been overwhelmed by the sum of the two income effects: that due to rising per-capita wealth (property income), plus the income effect of rising real wages.

T6. Given the choice, a slave would prefer all leisure (working less than a free person would), while the master would choose no leisure, with the slave working more than a free person would. Thus, a master with strong control may be able to make his slave more productive than a free worker. However, it is costly to control a slave, so the master's control will not be absolute. The productivity of slave versus free labor is thus a question of circumstances. Where monitoring and negative incentives (punishments) are not too costly, slave labor may turn out to be very productive. But on the whole, the rewards (positive incentives) that free persons can achieve by working seem to have been more effective, especially where motivation and intelligent effort are needed for doing a good job.

T9. A tax on *earnings* would generate a substitution effect (work less) and also an income effect (work more or less, depending on whether leisure is a normal or inferior good). A tax on labor *capacity* would generate only an income effect, so the labor-reducing substitution effect is not present. A tax on labor capacity thus creates less of a work disincentive.

T10. If labor supply were more effectively cartelized in the United States, wages would tend to be higher. This seems unlikely, however. It may be that U.S. laborers are willing to work harder, which would tend to raise their wages. Probably most important, there is more educational and training investment ("human capital") bound up in typical U.S. workers, making them more productive.

T12. Wage rates are high in New York City mainly because in that area a very unusual combination of natural and manufactured resources (the harbor, buildings and streets, railroads and subways, etc.) raises workers' productivity. If these circumstances were not balanced by other considerations, workers would flow in from the rest of the country to take advantage of these high wages. As they do so, however, crowding of the New York area tends to raise the cost of living there until the net advantage of such movement disappears and the population stabilizes.

CHAPTER 13

R2. (a) It does not follow. Mutually beneficial trade can occur as long as their MRS_C's differ at their endowed positions (or at their Crusoe optimum positions, if production is possible).

(b) If individuals have identical preferences and identical endowments in a world of pure exchange, each individual's MRS_C will be the same and no mutually beneficial trade can occur.

(c) Similarly, if they have identical preferences and identical productive opportunities, each individual's MRS_C at the Crusoe optimum will be the same and no mutually beneficial trade can occur.

R3. (a) Asymmetrical Production-Possibility Curves will tend to lead to specialization in production. (Another possibility would be a range of increasing returns.) An individual who is relatively well-suited to producing one good will tend to specialize in production of that good. Symmetrical indifference curves tend to lead to diversification in consumption.

(b) No. In the absence of trade an individual's degrees of specialization in production and in consumption would have to be identical. Trade allows the simultaneous existence of productive specialization and consumptive diversification.

R6. In a world of production and exchange (assuming interior solutions), at the productive optimum, each individual must be producing at a point along his or her Production-Possibility Curve such that the MRS_T equals the ratio of market prices. Similarly, at the consumptive optimum, each individual's MRS_C must equal the ratio of market prices. Additionally, for each good, the sum over all individuals of the produced quantities must equal the sum of the consumed quantities.

R7. The intersection of the full demand and supply curves determines the point at which the total quantity desired for consumption just equals the total quantity available for consumption. The intersection of the transaction demand and supply curves determines the point at which the quantity desired in exchange equals the quantity offered for exchange. Since the two pairs of curves differ only by the *nontraded* amounts of the good (endowed and self-consumed quantities in pure exchange, or produced and self-consumed quantities in a world of production), the price that brings desired transaction quantities into equilibrium must also bring desired full quantities into equilibrium.

R10. (a) Yes, but only in a very special case. Autarky will occur in costless exchange if, for every individual, the ratio of market prices exactly equals the MRS_C and MRS_T at his or her Crusoe solution.

(b) Transaction costs create a spread between the gross and net price ratios. Any time an individual's MRS_C and MRS_T at the Crusoe solution fall inside this spread, the individual will choose an autarky solution (the Crusoe solution). The higher the transaction costs, the greater this spread and the more likely the autarky solution.

(c) Both payroll taxes and sales taxes can be viewed as transaction costs. Each type of tax creates a spread between the buyer's (gross) price and the seller's (net) price for goods and services traded in the market. But neither tax bears upon *self-supplied* goods and services. The increasing weight of payroll and sales taxes, by increasing the spread between buy and sell prices, raises the attractiveness and likelihood of self-supply (autarky) solutions as exemplified by the "do-it-yourself" trend.

R13. A command economy could avoid transaction costs by dispensing with markets, but it might incur larger enforcement costs than transaction costs saved. While market economies must use resources to integrate individual decisions, command economies must use resources to enforce central decisions. At least as important, the commanders would require an enormous input of information if the economy is to function rationally—information automatically provided by price signals in market economies. Most important of all, what the command economy will aim at is "efficiency" in carrying out the desires of the commanders, which may be quite different from the desires of consumers.

T2. A tax on *consumption* will reduce the incentive to acquire the taxed good either by production or by exchange. There will be less consumption and less production, whether for self-supply or for the market. A tax on *production* will have quite similar effects. A tax on *exchange*, in contrast, will tend to diminish production for the market but to increase production for self-supply. On balance, consumption of the good will also be less since some of the cost-reducing advantages of specialization will have been lost.

T3. For Robinson, a bunch of bananas has an "opportunity cost" of two fish, while for Friday, a bunch of bananas costs only one fish. Robinson has an *absolute* advantage in both activities, but Friday has a *comparative* advantage in picking bananas. Robinson could, for example, pick one less bunch of bananas and use the time to catch two fish. He could then sell one fish to Friday for one bunch of bananas and have the other fish left over to eat. In total, the community thus gains one fish from this specialization in production.

T4. Clearly, at least one of the two parties must be better off, since there is more of G and no less of Y available. But i (the seller of G) might end up worse off. If the demand for grain is inelastic, i will get less revenue in Y-units as he sells more G. More surprisingly, j (the buyer of G) might alternatively end up worse off—if Y is an inferior good for j. (Work this out!)

T7. If j has a fixed endowment, he cannot revise his production plans after the opening of trade with i. Individual j, on the other hand, will almost always revise his production plans so as to produce somewhat more X and less Y, or vice versa. Either way there will be less total production of one of the two commodities. Thus, we cannot say that trade *necessarily* leads to larger produced totals of all goods.

T8. A Martian observer, unfamiliar with the mental limitations of flowers and bees, might indeed fail to appreciate the difference as compared with human exchange. Perhaps we're kidding ourselves, but we like to think that our exchanges are the result of *choice*. Presumably, the behavior of the bees is governed entirely by blind instinct, while the flowers are even further from having any choice as to whether or not to offer their nectar to bees.

T11. Where both ration coupons and cash are required for trade, traders must maintain inventories of coupons as well as cash. In addition, traders must transport, authenticate, and physically transfer ration coupons as well as cash. If coupons can be bought and sold, there is also the cost of the coupon market. If coupons cannot be bought and sold, there are the costs of enforcing (and the costs of evading) the restrictions on the sale of coupons.

T12. All these qualities reduce the cost of using money as medium of exchange or as store of value. A somewhat less obvious but very important quality, illustrated by the prisoner-of-war example, is that the monetary commodity should not also be a consumption good. And, of course, the money should be cheap to produce.

CHAPTER 14

R2. (b) is correct. The ratio P_0/P_1 is the rate at which current consumption claims can be traded for one-year future consumption claims. If a current consumption claim is foregone, the market will pay back that claim plus interest next year. So $P_0/P_1 \equiv 1 + r$. Consequently, $r \equiv (P_0/P_1) - 1$. The annual rate of interest is the *premium* on the relative value of current over one-year future consumption claims.

R4. Investment must always equal zero in a world of pure exchange. So, at equilibrium, aggregate saving equals aggregate investment at zero.

R5. At equilibrium in a productive situation, aggregate saving equals aggregate investment. It is also true that aggregate borrowing equals aggregate lending, but the total of borrowing or lending will generally be less than the total of saving or investment.

R7. (a) The Present-Value Rule directs decision-makers to adopt any incremental project for which the Present Value is positive and to reject projects for which Present Value is negative.
    (b) As long as the Separation Theorem holds, productive optimization is equivalent to wealth maximization. Since the Present-Value Rule is a wealth-maximizing rule, decision-makers will then be led to the productive optimum.
    (c) If the Separation Theorem does not hold, however, wealth maximization and productive optimization are not identical. Here, not only wealth but its distribution over time becomes important, and so the Present-Value Rule will not necessarily lead to a productive optimum.

T2. At equilibrium it must be true that—even though saving need not equal investment for any individual—both actual and desired saving equal actual and desired investment in the aggregate. If this were not the case, the interest rate would adjust to bring about the equality. If a floor or ceiling were placed upon the interest rate, it will still be true that *actual* aggregate saving equals *actual* investment. Here, the smaller of desired aggregate saving and desired aggregate investment will determine the actual quantity of saving and investment. It will not be true, in general, that *desired* aggregate saving equals *desired* aggregate investment at the "frozen" market interest rate.

T3. (a) Because time-productivity will be relatively great in such a newly settled country, the real interest rate will tend to be high.
    (b) The more isolated such a country is, the higher its real interest rate will be.
    (c) Close contact with the rest of the world will lead to an inflow of resources which will increase total investment and decrease the real rate of interest in the new country.

T4.   If little investment is taking place because of low time-productivity, real interest rates will be low. If little investment is taking place because of high time-preference, interest rates will be high.

T6.   (a) Negative rates of interest are not impossible. As Equation (14.1) indicates, all that is required is that future claims exchange at a premium against current claims ($P_0 < P_1$). Negative interest rates are rarely observed, however. In most situations there are attractive investment opportunities which increase the investment demand for current funds, while time-preference (impatience) raises the consumptive demand for current funds. The combination assures that current funds will almost always exchange at a premium against future funds.

      (b) Yes. In Equation (14.1″), since P_0/P_1 cannot be less than zero, r cannot fall below -1. In terms of percentages, the interest rate cannot be less than -100%.

T8.   One does not find the present worth of a stream of payments by adding up the simple total of the interest-plus-principal installments over the years. This fails to allow for the fact that, due to the force of interest, a future payment is worth less today. In fact, at 7.75 percent a dollar payment deferred 27 years is worth today only about 13 cents. At 7.75 percent interest, the payments required by the two-year contract ($392.50 one year from now, and an equal amount two years from now) have a present worth of $702.34. But the 27 annual payments (of $39.81 each) of the other contract have a present worth of only $445.21! So the consumer advice provided was seriously off the mark. (Note that the quoted "price" of the appliances is irrelevant for these calculations; only the actual cash payments matter.)

T9.   When a government finances a war by borrowing, that does not "shift the burden to future generations" any more than financing a war by taxation. Borrowing and taxing are only intermediate processes. The extent to which the burden is shifted to future generations depends upon the degree to which the war reduces *consumption* or reduces *investment*. In the former case the burden falls on the current generation, since there is less to eat now; in the latter case more of the burden falls upon future generations, since there will be less to eat in the future. So what matters is the extent to which citizens cut back on consumption or on investment when they lend or pay taxes to government.

T10. The explanation does not make much sense. Stock prices, like all asset prices, are based upon Present Values of anticipated future earnings. In the simplified version of Equation (14.10′), we know that $V_0 = z/r$. If anticipated future earnings z are unchanged, any fall in interest rates r *necessarily* implies an increase in asset values V_0. So the fall in r is not the "reason" in the sense of causation, since one could equally well say that it was the rise in V_0 that caused the fall in r. On the other hand, the stock market might rise because of more optimistic anticipations about earnings z, and this could happen even with no change in the interest rate r.

T11. No, "conservation" is not necessarily economically efficient. For each resource there is an efficient pattern of use over time, not too fast and not too slow. Unless there are "externalities" (discussed in Chapter 15), competition leads to the most efficient pattern of resource use.

CHAPTER 15

R2.   The Contract Curve of the Edgeworth-box diagram shows all those allocations from which no mutually beneficial trade can occur. Consequently, the utilities of the two individuals at a point on the Contract Curve become the coordinates for a point on the utility Social Opportunity Frontier.

R3. (a) A "social optimum" can be defined only in terms of a social criterion. Given a social criterion, the "social optimum" is simply that allocation which best achieves the criterion. Currently, there seems to be no agreement as to a social criterion, and so the term "social optimum" lacks agreed meaning. For example, some people regard unlimited abortion as social progress, others see it as social calamity.

(b) Efficiency seems a valid goal, but there are many reasons why it should not be the only element in a social criterion. For one thing, considerations of equity may indicate some sacrifice of efficiency. Also, efficiency is based upon the satisfaction of individual wants as the measure of well-being. It might be argued that individuals are poor judges of what will actually benefit them, or that wants are not autonomous but really socially determined, or that supra-individualistic policy goals (liberty, justice, community) are also important.

R7. (a) The product-market monopolist and the factor-market monopsonist both violate the efficiency condition $vmp_a = h_a$. The product-market monopolist sets $h_a = mrp_a < vmp_a$. The factor-market monopsonist sets mrp_a (which may equal vmp_a) $= mfc_a > h_a$. That they both produce "too little" follows, since in either case $vmp_a > h_a$. This causes an efficiency loss because these firms could, by producing more, convert units of resource A into a larger product value than competitive firms satisfying the condition $vmp_a = h_a$.

(b) Yes, it follows that "too much" of resource A is used by competitive firms and that "too much" A is retained for reservation uses that could more efficiently be devoted to market employment.

R10. (a) This efficiency condition is $MC^i = \Sigma MV^i$—i.e., the Marginal Cost for each supplier i of providing the public good must equal the sum of all the consumers' Marginal Values for the public good.

(b) For a public good, since *every* consumer can receive the same unit, the vertical summation of individual demand curves for a public good shows the social marginal valuation. For a private good, only one consumer receives each unit—so the social marginal valuation of the private good is simply the marginal valuation of the consumer receiving the marginal unit. It is, however, incorrect to view the vertical summation of individual demand curves for a public good as a *demand curve* for the public good. This vertical summation does *not* indicate the quantity that would be purchased at any price; all it shows is the social marginal valuation of the public good.

R11. (a) The private supply of public goods is limited, first, by the difficulty and cost of exclusion. Nonpayers would have to be excluded for private provision to be feasible, and this may be impossible or quite costly. Where exclusion costs are sufficiently low, a private firm may provide a public good but will still not likely provide an efficient quantity. For efficient provision, firms would have to charge different prices to different individuals. Such price discrimination might be illegal or simply too costly.

(b) Public provision *may* result in a more nearly optimal quantity, but this depends upon the forces determining governmental decisions (to be studied in Chapter 16). Where exclusion is impossible or very costly, private provision is unlikely, and so public provision may be inevitable.

T1. The Duke did not read the text carefully enough. If the Duchess were initially endowed with a property right in her own life, a Pareto-preferred movement toward an efficient solution would have to be *mutually* beneficial. It seems unlikely that the Duke could have paid enough to have the Duchess agree to her own death. If the Duke initially possessed the right to take the Duchess's life, on the other hand, his argument would be valid on efficiency grounds. Even then, however, he was not necessarily "justified" in terms of moral criteria.

T2. Definitely false. First of all, conventional national income measures fail to allow for a whole variety of sources of utility and disutility: for example, homemakers' services are not counted, nor is the value of leisure, nor degradation of the environment as a negative element. But the statement would not be true even if there were a perfect national income measure. Monopolization of a good, for example, might raise the market value of national income while reducing efficiency.

T4. Property rights will be ill-defined when laws or court rulings are ambiguous and where legal precedents are conflicting or in a state of flux. Also, if it is costly to learn about one's rights, subjective uncertainty may persist even if the underlying legal theory is settled. The costs of transacting (negotiating and enforcing contracts) will tend to be high when multilateral contracting is required, or when individuals have incentives to behave strategically in order to capture more of the gains from an agreement. Some potential trades are hampered by the difficulty of describing the good or service in advance, or of measuring delivery performance thereafter. For example, contracts for labor service cannot generally guarantee in advance how devotedly the worker will perform, and this may even be hard to measure afterward. Another example is the used-car business, where prior determination of quality is notoriously difficult and where writing a level of agreed quality into the contract is almost impossible.

T6. True, since market reallocations of resources must be mutually beneficial. A dictator, in contrast, might achieve a Pareto-*efficient* outcome that was not Pareto-*preferred* to the original situation.

T7. Such a ban is certainly inefficient. The hepatitis problem is not a sufficient reason for banning the market in blood, since buyers are at liberty to use whatever method they deem appropriate in screening commercial donors. (As might have been anticipated, the prohibition of blood sales has caused dangerous blood "shortages.")

T8. (a) Yes, the analogy is sound. Laws banning polygyny reduce the demand for wife-services. Since only women can provide those services, the laws work to the disadvantage of women in general (For exceptions, see below.)

(b) Women in general lose, and especially those who would rather be one of the wives of a desirable husband than remain unmarried or be an only wife of a less desirable spouse. Those men who would have been willing and able to acquire multiple wives also lose. The gainers from monogamy laws include women who are exceptionally desirable wives, assuming they prefer to be the sole wife. If polygyny were legal, any such woman could still contract with her husband to be the sole wife but might have to pay a high price for that privilege. But the biggest gainers from the monogamy laws are undoubtedly those men who would not otherwise have been able to obtain wives.

(c) Monogamy laws cannot be defended in terms of efficiency.

(d) Monogamy laws tend to *increase equality among men*, since males who are less attractive husbands have better chances of acquiring wives. They probably *increase inequality among women*, however, since they improve the ability of more-desirable wives to monopolize the best husbands.

CHAPTER 16

R.1 Yes, while a political party in office might capture a "profit" by simply looting the taxpayers, or more subtly by carrying out ideological programs in opposition to voters' desires, its ability to do so is limited by the competition from other parties. Ideally, new parties would enter the politics "industry" until no such profit opportunity remained: the surviving parties would have to do exactly what the voters wanted. However, political competition is less effective than market competition (see the following question), and so political profit may not be driven to zero.

R2. The imperfections of the democratic political system as a mechanism for serving citizen desires are analogous to, but more severe than, the imperfections of the market. In the political system citizens almost never make choices directly on substantive issues; actual decisions are made by imperfectly controllable delegates. Second, citizens have only a very narrow range of choice even of delegates. They must select from a very limited number of candidates (i.e., political competition is highly imperfect) at widely separated election intervals, whereas in the market individuals select almost continuously from a vast menu of choices. Third, the political system may not be democratic, and even democratic majority rule is likely to override minority desires. Fourth, the cost of acquiring information is much higher for political choices.

R5. (a) Unanimous consent, involving the purchase of dissident votes, would permit only those decisions that improve the welfare of each and every voter. In terms of Pareto-efficiency, this would be an ideal political system.

(b) Log-rolling allows voters to trade votes on one issue for votes on another issue, and so would tend indeed to lead to Pareto-preferred outcomes—a series of decisions which together leave everyone better off. The objections to log-rolling are due primarily to the fact that *delegates*, not citizens, actually vote on policies. When the delegate is better off, that does not mean the constituents are necessarily better off.

R9. An agreement is "self-enforcing" when neither party to the agreement can gain by defecting. For example, a doctor and his or her patient might have invested significant effort in getting to know one another. In order to maintain the relationship, the patient may pay his or her bills and the doctor may provide good service even in the absence of legal enforcement.

R11. (a) A free-rider problem in the provision of goods will tend to arise whenever it is difficult to exclude nonpayers from the benefits of group action—as when public goods are provided even to those who do not contribute to defray the costs.

(b) Not very valid. While much of government activity appears to be concerned with the provision of public goods—defense, law, and redistribution all can be viewed as having public-good characteristics—governments are also heavily involved with the provision of private goods. And to the extent that the "exploitation" model is valid, government may not be interested in serving the citizens at all.

T1. The public-choice approach views politics as a kind of *exchange process*. Citizens shop for the type of government that provides them the highest utility. Political parties compete to become the government and so to capture the "profit" of being in power. Since utility maximization, exchange, and competition are all involved, this approach is particularly amenable to economic analysis. An alternative approach views politics as a *conflict process*, in which some individuals and groups are attempting to exploit others.

T2. Any voluntary trade is mutually beneficial. So if the poor traded votes to the rich for money, both would gain in comparison with the initial situation. Objections to this practice are probably based on objections to the fact that the rich have more money to begin with.

T4. Cash redistributions are not unknown. Social Security comes close to falling into this category, being a redistribution from the working age-group to the retired age-group. But politicians generally prefer to establish service programs to "help" the poor by health care, job training, education, etc. The advantages to legislators of being in on the ground floor when a bureaucracy is being established to staff a new service program (jobs to political supporters) is obvious.

T6. More frequent elections, more numerous legislatures, and elected judges would all give citizens the *potential* of more control over government officials. However, the more frequent are elections and the more numerous the legislatures, the less important is any single election and so the less informed will voters typically be. So it is not clear whether or not any of these proposals would actually improve the fidelity of the political system to citizen desires. Replacing the merit system in civil service by the spoils system would give citizens more control over bureaucrats. The spoils system would therefore make the governmental mechanism more accountable to citizen desires but might reduce the quality of personnel in government.

T7. When government is viewed in a public-choice framework, changes in demand or costs should have somewhat similar effects upon price and output for a governmentally provided good as for a privately provided good. The strength of the effects, however, will differ. Bureaucrats tend to have an interest in larger output and so in keeping prices low to users. With an increase in demand, therefore, government provision will tend to result in a greater increase in quantity and a smaller increase in price than in the case of private provision. For a decrease in demand, government provision will probably result in a smaller decrease in quantity and a larger fall in price than private provision. Analogous conclusions apply for changes in costs.

T9. (a) Since each individual is a member of the "public," he will want to provide some of the public good simply for his own consumption. Furthermore, when others do the same he will become effectively richer, making him want to consume more of the public good than before. So he will not cut back his own contribution 1:1 as others increase theirs.

(b) If a market were feasible (if it were possible to collect a price from consumers of the public good), the analysis of Chapter 15 applies: firms would enter to supply the public good. While fully efficient provision of the public good can occur only when different prices can be charged to different classes of users (price discrimination), nevertheless we can be confident that—if any supplying firms survive at all—there will be more of the public good provided than in the absence of a market. There will always be more supplied when the motivation to do so is not only to provide for one's own consumption but also to receive payment from others. Furthermore, the surviving firms in the market are likely to be the most efficient suppliers. So there will be more specialization in production of the public good.

T10. (a) Public-choice explanations look for reasons why voters would prefer larger government. For example, a high income elasticity of demand for government-provided goods coupled with rising incomes would generate increases in the demand for such goods. Nonvoluntarist explanations might look for shifts in *political power* toward those who prefer larger governments. For example, the enlargement of bureaucracy in wartime might so increase the relative political power of bureaucrats as to preclude a return to a smaller level of government thereafter.

(b) Here again, there are various explanations. A public-choice explanation might be that the new factory-provided goods became cheaper relative to government-provided goods, and so the private sector grew in response to consumer-citizen desires. A conflict-model explanation might be that the newly rich merchant class had become sufficiently powerful to throw off the burden of a government dominated by the old landed aristocracy.

INDEX OF NAMES

INDEX OF TOPICS

Circular flow of economic activity, 15–18, 160, 378–80
Civil War, American, 389–90
Coal (see Nuclear vs. coal power)
Coase's Theorem, 472, 475–77
Coffee, 132–33
Collusion (see Cartels; Oligopoly)
Command economy, 18, 406, 418
Commodities (see Goods; Product)
Commodity Credit Corporation, 40
Comparative statics, method of, 26–27
Comparison, Axiom of, 56
Competition, 167, 202–04, 222, 391–92, 403 (see also Firm, competitive; Price-taker; Industry; etc.)
  monopolistic (see Monopolistic competition)
  perfect, 403
  political, 493–95
Complementarity:
  in consumption, 89–92
  in production, 325, 329–31
Concavity (see Indifference curves)
Concentration and monopoly power, 298
Conflict, 517
Conscription, military, 378
Constraints (see under Opportunity set)
Consumer Surplus, 204–06 (see also Exchange, gains from)
Consumers Union, 458
Consumption, 15–18, 378–80
  diversity in, 67–69
  intertemporal (see under Intertemporal choice)
  locale, 263
  "new theory" of, 145
  opportunities, 78–82, 92–93, 100–01 (see also Opportunity set)
  optimum, 78–88
    corner vs. interior solution, 82–85, 87, 101, 110
    variation with income, 92–100
    variation with prices, 100–07
Consumption Balance Equation, 83–84
Contract curve, 389
Contracts, 161–63, 492
Controls, price (see Price, ceilings; Price, floors)
Convexity (see Indifference curves)
Corner solution (see under Consumption, optimum)
Corn production experiment, 318–19
Corn yields, 307
Corporation, 162
Cost, 47–49, 167–68, 173
  Average, 47–49, 173, 309
  economic (opportunity), 163–64
  fixed vs. variable, 47, 168, 172–75, 177–81, 308–09
  function derived from production function, 308–09
  of living, 151
  long-run vs. short-run, 177–81
  Marginal, 47–49, 170–72
  Marginal Common, 185–87
  Marginal Distribution, 246
  Marginal Manufacturing, 246
  Marginal Separable, 185–87
  sunk, 180
  Total, 47–49, 168, 173–75
  transaction (see Transaction costs)

Cotton spindles, 197
Cournot solution (see under Oligopoly)
Crime and criminals, 10–11
"Cycling" (of majorities), 497–501

Deadweight loss (see Efficiency, economic; Efficiency loss)
Delegation, political, 496
Demand:
  determinants of, 133–35, 333, 359
  elasticity (see Elasticity of demand)
  for factors (see Factors of production, demand for)
  Giffen case, 102–03, 107, 135–36
  Law of, 103–04
Demand and supply (see Supply and demand)
Demand curve (demand function), 25, 41–43, 102–03, 107
  constant-elasticity, 127–29
  constant-slope, 127–29
  factor (see under Factors of production, demand for)
  full, 393–95, 400–01
  income-compensated, 152–53
  individual, 102–07, 392–96, 400–02
  "kinked," 292–95
  market, 107–08
  and product assortment, 262–65
  shifts of, 26–33, 105–06
  transaction, 393–95, 400–01
Demand price, 205
Democracy, 493
Depreciation, asset-value, 374
Derivative (mathematical), 43
Diminishing marginal utility, 62–64, 82–83
Diminishing returns, 181–84, 305–07, 317–19
Discrimination, price (see Price, discrimination)
Diseconomies (see Economies and diseconomies)
Disemployment effect, 336
Disequilibrium, 471–72
"Dismal science," 2
Distilled spirits, demand for, 130–31
Division of labor (see Specialization, productive)
Division of output among plants, 175–76
Draft, military, 378
Dumping abroad, 240, 253
Duopoly, 286 (see also Oligopoly)

Economics as a science, 4
Economies and diseconomies (see also Externalities):
  internal vs. external, 199–202
  pecuniary vs. technological, 200–01
  of scale, 203–04
Economists, salaries of, 6, 440–41
Edgeworth box, 387–88
Education and earnings, 440–41
Efficiency, economic, 207, 460, 467–70
Efficiency loss (see Monopoly; Disequilibrium; Hindrances to trade; etc.)
Elasticity, 117, 123
  arc, 120, 124
  point, 124–25
Elasticity of demand:
  cross, 125–26